The Camp of God's Tears

The History of the Mound Builders

by
**Marilyn Lee
John R. Mayfield**

cf

A Collective Frequency® Production
Phoenix, Arizona

Copyright © 2011

The Camp of God's Tears
"The History of the Mound Builders"
2nd Edition

A Collective Frequency ® Production
Copyright © 2011 by Marilyn Lee.& John R. Mayfield

All rights reserved. No part of this book may be used or reproduced In any manner whatsoever without written permission except in the case of brief quotations embodied in critical articles and reviews.

This book is a work of fiction. Names, characters, businesses, organizations, places, events and incidents are the product of the author imaginations, insights and inspirations or are used fictitiously. Any resemblance to actual persons living or dead or actual events is entirely coincidental.

Paperback ISBN: 978-0692203019

Websites: http://TheCampOfGodsTears.com
http://Facebook.com/thecampofgodstears
http://SpeakingThroughYourHeart.com

While the author has made every effort to provide accurate internet addresses at the time of publication the author assumes no responsibility for errors, or for changes that occur after publication.

Further, the author does not have any control over and does not assume any responsibility for third-party websites or their content.

Book format and cover design by Barb Anderson
http://dmbookpro.com

Serpent Mound drawing by Nick Drakides

Unless otherwise noted: Illustrations by John R. Mayfield.

This book is dedicated
to healing humankind

The Oneness Principle:
We are One

The Oneness Prayer

I am whole.

I am also part of a larger whole,

Which is part of a larger whole,

Which is part of a larger Whole.

The Whole is in each part

And in each part of each part.

We are One

Falling Star realized that most everyone had chosen to empty the village to follow an ego driven idea without a sense of responsibility to remain in alignment. With that realization, torrents of tears flooded her broken heart.

Their choice to go was a fatal one.

With that choice, the very last of
The People was doomed.

With that choice, all of Heaven cried.

With that choice, it became
The Camp of God's Tears.

CONTENTS

Acknowledgements	x
Foreword	xi
Prologue	xiii
Chapter 1 Tom Perkins	1
Chapter 2 The Story	11
Chapter 3 The Village	13
Chapter 4 Gray Wolf and Water Dog	23
Chapter 5 Red Fox	35
Chapter 6 Hal's Mystery	49
Chapter 7 Red Fox Builds the Model	51
Chapter 8 The Prophecy of Serpent Mound	63
Chapter 9 Red Fox Begins His Journey	77
Chapter 10 Traders and Wolf Encounter	89
Chapter 11 After the Traders Left	109
Chapter 12 Hal Takes Action	123
Chapter 13 Red Fox at Seip	125
Chapter 14 Red Fox at Baum	141
Chapter 15 Red Fox at Mound City	159
Chapter 16 Red Fox at Chillicothe	175
Chapter 17 Red Fox at High Bank	185
Chapter 18 On the Road Again	197
Chapter 19 Red Fox at Newark	207
Chapter 20 On the Way Home	229
Chapter 21 Hal Seeks to Save His Friend	245
Chapter 22 Hal Is on His Way	247
Chapter 23 Homecoming	249

Chapter 24 The Day of the Summer Solstice	267
Chapter 25 After the Summer Solstice Ceremony	273
Chapter 26 White Eagle's Dreams	293
Chapter 27 The Sweetness of the People	303
Chapter 28 Council Meeting at the Village Near the Great Serpent	315
Chapter 29 The Dialogue	331
Chapter 30 Snow Flurries	349
Chapter 31 Gray Wolf is Called Upon	357
Chapter 32 The Walk Home	369
Chapter 33 Gray Wolf Joins the Council of Twelve Plus One	377
Chapter 34 Gray Wolf Consults The Knowing	391
Chapter 35 The Journey to the Northern Moonrise Ceremony	403
Chapter 36 Council Fire of the Elders	419
Chapter 37 The Way West	421
Chapter 38 The Gathering of Migrants	439
Chapter 39 Tom's Cabin	451
Chapter 40 Tom's Rescue	453
Chapter 41 The Vision	455
Chapter 42 The Reunion	465
Chapter 43 Flames Shot Skyward	483
Chapter 44 The Blessing	497
Chapter 45 Eye of the Hawk Over the Bitterroots	503
Chapter 46 A Promise	513
Chapter 47 Falling Star and Little Turtle	523
Chapter 48 Falling Star and Mark of the Bear	531
Chapter 49 Summer Camp and Winter Camp	541
Chapter 50 The Camp of God's Tears	561
Chapter 51 The Transition	591

Chapter 52 Not the End	621
Afterword	624
Appendix	667
Bibliography	700
About the Authors	732

ACKNOWLEDGEMENTS

I wish to express gratitude for those who have helped put this story together. I would like to honor Red Coat for giving us the start regarding the insight and initial information as we began the journey of writing the story of The People.

I also thank our reviewers who performed a most daunting task of reading the material before it was ready for publication. Specifically, Mary Rocha is one reviewer who was able to get through both major versions with her insightful comments. I also thank Karen, Taffy, Doug and Scott for their detailed and most helpful observations. Thanks go to Carole Suihkonen for her editing and to Barb Anderson for all her efforts in getting us to publication.

And finally, I should like to express gratitude to John Mayfield for his relentless efforts performing exhaustive research that provides grounding evidence showing the veracity of details of this culture. (Bibliography can be found in unabridged version of *The Camp of God's Tears*)

And, a special note of gratitude to all those in spirit who helped along the way.

I wish to recognize the Angel who approached me in London for giving me direction to write the abridged version of this book. Last but certainly not least, I acknowledge Minnifeathers for his supreme contribution to my efforts in cleaning up this version. Thank you

FOREWARD

    We invite you to go on a journey with us back through time and space to North America, specifically Ohio, to experience a civilization so advanced as to challenge all generally accepted beliefs about the Native Americans who lived there prior to the coming of the Europeans. The only information we have about this highly developed culture comes from physical evidence left behind.

    This book calls attention to the detail and data as found by archeologists, scientists, and other researchers, and illustrates this information from multi-disciplinary sources within the context of a fictional structure. *The Camp of God's Tears* tells the tragic tale of a magnificent civilization as it falls. We know it was magnificent by virtue of what it left behind. We know it fell, because it ended just as mysteriously as it had thrived.

    Exactly who these people were remains another mystery. American archeologists have dubbed them, variously, as the Mound Builders, the Adena Culture and the Hopewell Culture. However, these names refer to no recognized Native American Tribe.

    What the people of this civilization left behind speaks to their material culture and products of human manufacturing, their social culture and their ideological culture as demonstrated in their architecture and artifacts.

    In order to construct their massive earthworks, in correct astronomical alignment, extensive knowledge of mathematics, engineering, trigonometry, Euclidean geometry, *pi*, *phi*, mathematical calculations, and the Pythagorean Theorem was required. Further, they had knowledge of the Fibonacci mathematical series.

    Without question, the Native Americans who constructed the High Bank Works, the Newark Complex, Serpent Mound and many other earthworks possessed this knowledge, and more. This revelation should lead to a complete reversal of scientific thought and a growing recognition of the very advanced state of knowledge possessed by the Mound Builders. However, their accomplishments remain outside the common awareness.

    In the telling of *The Camp of God's Tears* we do not know what names they gave for the locations mentioned in our story. As a matter of convenience, we utilize the contemporary names for places common to them and common to us, such as Newark and Chillicothe, Ohio, or St. Louis, Missouri, for example.

    Regarding their spoken language, the actual language they spoke is presently unknown. Although, we believe their language was a precursor to present day Native American languages. Use of contemporary English language streamlines the telling of the story.

Perhaps someday we will discover more about the Mound Builders which will bring even a greater understanding to the times in which we now live. They lived for over 1,000 years in peace. Among their other mysteries, maybe we will discover their secret to developing a civilization with a lasting peace and prosperity. [1]

And so, let us take you on a journey to experience the Mound Builder culture through the lives of our characters, a saga spanning six generations, as their magnificent civilization comes to its mysterious ending.

---

[1] Please see *Afterword* for a more detailed discussion of this remarkable civilization.

PROLOGUE

Blackness.
Blackness and some stars.
Blackness and gradually more stars emerged onto the black universe.
Blackness and many stars shined and twinkled.

Spinning, spinning, over and over itself a gray asteroid tumbled in the tapestry of blackness and starlight. It's rough contour shifted as the shadows emphasize its pocked surface of craters and scars from eons of time as it neared the Sun. Traveling at great speed it entered the solar system from some distant star in the Milky Way.

Sun.
Sun and solar system.
Earth.
Earth beckoned.

Bypassing several planets that orbit the Sun, this star relic passed too close to the Earth's gravitational pull and Earth drew it in. As Earth's atmosphere embraced the star remnant, it exploded into a fiery ball. Speeding ever faster, this once-was star piece jetted toward Earth's surface in roaring flames.

Earth spun on its axis in its normal orbit as it progressed around the Sun.

Earth spun in its orbit.
North America.
Ohio River Valley.
Impact.
Fiery explosion.

Earth, star remnants, gases, carbon, smoke, steam, clouds, and fallout rose up in a wide, twisting column. Gaseous fumes, fallout, clouds climb up and up and up before spreading out and over in a circular design.

After the dust and ashes settle, the deep impact crater lay barren in its nearly five-mile wide mouth. The stark emptiness left by the *astrobleme* impact contrasted noticeably against the lush vegetation and fertile surroundings of the Ohio River Valley environment.

The Ohio River Valley continued celebrating its beauty throughout the ages despite the gaping wound left forever sterile by the fallen star-remnant.

The impact, the explosion, the wound never forgotten by Earth. The clouds rose up.

Mist engulfed the skies.

WHITE EAGLE

*What's coming is the possible destruction of
our People, our culture and our civilization.
We don't know what it is exactly and worst
we don't know when. We have lived in peace
for the last thousand years.*

*We have seen signs among
us that our peaceful way of living the
Oneness Principle is eroding. We must
find a way to save ourselves, the
People and our way of life, and indeed,
our very civilization.*

I

TOM PERKINS

Racing up the highway, Tom clutches the steering wheel of his new silver Lexus RX Hybrid SUV. Arm muscles bulge with tension. Hands grip the wheel as if forcing his hands into oneness with the wheel. With continued speed, Tom's eyes see only the road as he races toward some uncertain objective. Tom seeks a respite from his life. His face, taut with tension, but tanned from working outside with engineers on his last assignment, remains rigid straining against feeling his anguished soul and empty heart.

Tom Perkins, mid-forties with rich brown hair laced slightly at the temples with silver strands, loved being an architect. He had just completed a prestigious international assignment, one of his many national and international projects. As a major talent in his field, he partnered in a world class firm. While he needed a rest from the intensity with which he consistently worked, the real issue was feeling lonely and unfulfilled in his personal life.

With a history of failed relationships, and now a divorce in process, Tom could not let go of some imagined creature, beautiful and adoring with whom he would live together forever. He so longed to find her. Most of the women he had been with either competed with him or gave so much to him as to make him feel emasculated. None had fit his template. Maybe none would. He just had to keep looking.

Lost in thought he replays in his mind over and over his exit scene from earlier this morning. Low hanging mist begins to cloud his view of the road as he remembers . . .

It was a late October morning and Tom had just left his townhouse. Driving the one week old Lexus took the sting out of the phone call from Mary, his soon to be former wife. "It's just a house sale. Why is it such a big deal? She didn't like it when we bought it, and now it has become a sacred cow," he spoke into the wind rushing by his open window. The sip on the cinnamon latte did not answer his question as he drove into his marked parking space in the reserved area of the basement of Perkins and Watkins, Architects, a Seattle based firm.

Four years ago Perkins and Watkins had been selected in a worldwide competition by the Chinese government for an earth-friendly, combined residential community, hotel and commercial office complex. Struggling with massive environmental concerns, which had been spotlighted by publicity during the Olympic Games, China needed to demonstrate its commitment to aggressively addressing green technology.

Tom's design had won hands down. After all, incorporating green technology in his designs was the primary focus for his work. It was his belief that earth-friendly structures would lend to more harmonious styles of living and the sustainability of Mother Earth. He believed that the architectural design of buildings could produce a tone that encouraged more harmonious social interaction.

He remembered initially describing his plans to the committee of Chinese officials and building professionals. He faced them standing tall as he looked straight into their eyes. They surrounded the large oval conference table on which the fully landscaped scale model of his vision rested.

He spoke softly and with confidence, "Rather than following the usual high-rise or multi-building paradigms, I envision a novel structure that integrates into the shape of the land.

"The horizontal components of this multi-purpose complex, as you can see, virtually float on vertical pedestals above shaded open spaces, gardens and lagoons, allowing the land and sea breezes to pass freely. As you can see on this cutaway," he moves a portion of his model, "the elevators, stairs and utility pipes and conduits are all contained in the vertical pedestals."

He paused briefly to allow his audience members to peer into the model and continued, "I am also proposing several open air escalators into various portions of the lagoon and garden areas beneath the complex.

"The main arm of the building undulates with the shape of the nearby seashore. Additional projections for the building reach horizontally out towards the sea affording a consistent vision and sense of oneness with the land and ocean. My innovative plan provides space for the multi-faceted activities of the complex to evolve and change," he said as he shifted his weight then went on.

"Also integrated into the design are special composite windows which utilize photo gray technology addressing high solar radiation, and which also protect against the forces of the region's typhoons." Pointing to the roof, he said, "Cutting edge solar panel and wind generator technology invisibly gathers additional electrical power for the complex." Tom looked for any indication of interest then continued,

"The cylindrically shaped tubular wind turbines are the latest innovative technology."

He paused to breathe a moment then said, "They are bird friendly, noise, and vibration free, unaffected by wind shifts, self-regulating in high winds and require little maintenance. Yet they generate nearly 2kW's of power per unit." Pointing to the appropriate segment of his model to draw the attention of his audience to that particular detail, "Even though roof mounted, they will not interfere with the 'green roof' gardens and walkways where the residents may go to relax and enjoy the ocean views or the night sky." Tom pauses momentarily to turn slightly addressing each individual listener.

"Wastewater is recycled. All refuse generated by the businesses, conference center, hotel, and private residences is reduced by a high tech 30,000 degree plasma furnace into synthetic gas, mostly hydrogen, which will be used to generate electricity."

He paused again to let that message sink in. Then, "That's it in a nutshell," he said looking up with an expression on his face that asked for questions from the listeners. "Here are my documents specifying all the details with research as backup."

He picked up a small stack of documents, some in folders. "I will leave the model here.

"It is a very flexible design. This model merely reflects my interpretation of the information provided in the solicitation for bid and proposal documents that you issued for this project."

Continuing to sip his latte, the ride to the 24th floor of his own office building soothed his aggravation and brought him back to his immediate desire to get out of town.

As the elevator doors open he takes a last swig and deposits the cup in the paper recycle wastebasket. Noticing a stray aluminum can in the paper trash receptacle, he removes it to its proper place for recycling.

"Good morning, Mr. Perkins. Mr. Watkins is in *your* office. He needs to see you right away," announced Julie, the receptionist.

As he entered his office, Tom mumbled aloud, "not another snag in the project? Why can't the clients listen to what I have to say? After all, this is a new approach, and this eco-friendly building will make them proud, as well as serve humanity *and* the Earth."

"Do I see some ego creeping in here?" Hal asked chuckling.

"So, what is it this time, clients upset again?" Tom questioned obviously annoyed.

"Gee, I wish that was the issue, but no. Mary just called me and she's pretty upset." Hal said. "You know, buddy, we've been through thick and thin together since we were kids especially when it came to women. I'm here for you, pal. Over the last several years I got to know Mary and really hoped you two would make it.

"No, she wanted to vent about the offer price on the house from what is it now, the fifth bidder?"

"Seventh," Tom corrected. "You gotta be kidding me. Now she's going behind my back and trying to get you involved . . . This is getting simply too much for me!" Tom heaved a disheartened sigh while turning his face upward as if pleading with an invisible force.

"Look, Tom, I know you have these problems with women. You fall in love when you see someone who you just know will be your final true love . . . the one you were promised to be with forever. Each one of them in one way or another resembled the woman in your dream.

"I remember those times when I had my troubles and you were always there for me. I guess I just don't understand sometimes. You seem driven to disaster in your relationships with women.

"You're really a great guy, and our firm is at the top of cutting edge structural design. You are at the top of your game with a successful career . . . and you are a *mess*!" Hal emphasized with emotion.

His eyes locked on Tom and he said, "You're a world-class talent. You have great connections *and a great future* . . . everything a guy could want. So here you are . . . breaking off another relationship with a really super woman and after only five years," said Harold E. Watkins with his back to the wall. The wall displayed Tom's architect degrees and multiple certificates of achievement, and a plethora of national and international awards.

Hal watched his lifelong friend who was gazing north out the window of his newly remodeled office. Clearly, something was not right. Usually, he wore business casual, but today Tom sported faded blue jeans and a sweatshirt with cut off sleeves. Hal noticed Tom rubbing his birthmark, three parallel lines of some width, on his upper left arm, a nervous habit. His casual attire showed off his lean build.

"Yeah," Tom responded, "I know I'm a mess." He paused briefly after looking out the window. Then turning back to his friend, he said, "You know, all of these awards," he waved his arm in a sweeping motion indicating the back wall full of framed certificates, "don't really mean anything to me. In spite of my successes, I feel an inward pain and this emptiness inside.

"Maybe I've achieved wealth and recognition to accomplish something even more profound. Many men in my shoes would be proud. What I do feel is humble. I feel humbled by the notion that I still have something left to do . . . something that is still part of my destiny . . . I just can't quite get my hands on it . . . I've had this feeling since childhood, it's like a forgotten memory . . . that I need to finish something I still have left to do . . . and somehow . . . I just don't know . . . it all feels so vague . . . like a secret or a mystery still hidden from me in the shadows of my soul . . . it haunts me . . . it has something to do with a woman . . . the woman in my dream . . ." His voice trailed off as he turned again toward the window.

After another brief pause, he resumed his conversation.

"Hal, old buddy, I'm not here today. I can't place two thoughts together," confessed Tom, choking on emotion while shaking his head. "With spending long hours over the past months finishing the last redesign during construction on our building in Shenzhen, China, plus its geothermal heating and cooling systems, and now the posturing that Mary and her lawyer are coming up with at the last minute, I need to get away for some time alone to get my act back together," Tom admitted, head bowed in sadness, as he turned to pick up his blackberry and laptop.

"Tom, there is some very good news that just arrived," Hal announced invitingly, wanting to grasp his partner's attention. "You're gonna want to hear this."

"What?" demanded Tom with irritation, his mind still in some distant place.

"No. Really, you're *really* gonna wanna hear this." The former college line-backer shifted his weight, grabbed several papers from the desk and shook them gently several times in the air. "We just got the results on the tests on the geothermal wells for the heating and cooling system for the building. They substantiated your decision to extend the depth of each well beyond the original plans."

"Really?" Tom replied, eyebrows raised, with his spirit uplifted suddenly by the infusion of success.

Hal continued, "The test results show an increased energy saving. Over time, this will more than offset the additional expense and significantly reduce the overall carbon footprint of this building."

"Any word on the off-shore electrical generators?" Tom inquired, his focus shifting to the work conversation.

"Even better, buddy." Hal said glad to see that his friend's mood was changing.

Tom interrupted with cynicism, "Well, we had to dump the idea of the offshore wind turbine farms because of their '*visual pollution*'." He gestured, with two fingers of each hand, quotation marks in the air as he spoke.

"Tom," Hal said, "I know we went over that, and that is past history. You stuck your neck out with this new underwater design and the initial results are very good." Hal shook the papers again, held them in the air as he did so, "I'm telling you, the sea bed anchors have withstood the stress of a recent typhoon. *They held* . . . There's no visual pollution. They are all underwater."

Hal then slammed the documents down on the desk, clearly excited, with the success story he had shared.

"These units, in combination with the solar power and wind turbines components, means that we will sell power back to the grid and realize recoupment of costs in less than ten years." Hal spitted out before he paused to take a breath then broke out into a broad smile, standing back and folding his generous arms in front of him like a proud papa.

Coming around from behind the overstated desk, Hal stopped and leaned up against the front edge of the large piece of furniture, "You once again stuck your neck out and have been totally vindicated! You're a hero, ol' buddy, for Mother Earth and humanity. You have made this project so energy efficient and eco-friendly, I am certain we will hear nothing but praise from the Chinese . . . not to mention the world press.

"*This is ground breaking!*" Hal exclaimed in exuberance, droplets of spit shooting out of his mouth while swinging both arms out boldly to further emphasize the implication of the news. He leaned back a moment, wiped his mouth with the back of his hand, raised his eyebrows, tilted his head slightly to the right, spoke softly, "Once again your vision has been realized."

Tom stood there another moment in silence. He took a breath and remained looking at his trusted friend and business partner. Another moment passed. Tom's shoulders hunched down slightly from holding them straight and square while he listened to the results of his work. His right arm moved across his body as if to rub away a phantom pain in the birthmark prominent on his upper left arm.

Coming out of the outward conversation with Hal and shifting into an internal dialogue, Tom finally spoke in a soft voice, "Hal, that's great, really." He cast his eyes downward, and then he looked up. "But I am heading to you know where. If you need me, text me or send an email. If you would handle these final details, I'd appreciate it." Shaking his head, he added, "I simply cannot deal with anything more right now." Turning away from Hal and slowly heading to the door, he said sadly, "Take care, and I will see you in a week or so."

Quickly Hal moved from the front edge of the desk to approach his friend and draped his arm across Tom's shoulder, "You got it, buddy . . . been there. Drive safe and give me a call when you get to the cabin. We had some really great times there and many more to come. Hang in there. This too shall pass."

After several hours on the road, Tom's cell phone rings interrupting his reverie of the morning's events as he continues to speed up the highway.

"Hi Hal," Tom answers.

"Just a welfare check to see if you really are doing this. You are coming up as a blip on my radar screen. Had to see how you are," Hal says.

"Yeah, I'm OK. I was actually expecting your call. I've been seeing a Red Hawk floating overhead riding the thermals for several minutes. I'm not too far from the cabin."

"Once you get settled, gimme a call."

"Hal, I'm going to need several days to shut down and work through this. I just can't get the notion that I still have something left to do out of my mind . . . something that is still part of my destiny . . . . I just can't figure it out. I think it might have something to do with a woman."

"Tom, I hope you are right. I hope you find who or what you are looking for."

"Hal, I'm losing the signal. Gotta go."

Heading into the mountains, Tom's Lexus is the only car on the road. The empty roadway glistens from a late afternoon shower accenting the broken remnants of lingering mist. To lift his spirits, he reaches for his favorite CDs. After flipping through several, his free hand connects with one that warms at his touch. He slides the CD in without looking at it.

As it plays, his mind drifts carried by the lyrics. His heart feels the words, "I know you're out there somewhere." Softly he whispers to himself, "I know I'll find you somewhere, and somehow you will return to me." His emotions feel haunted by a long forgotten promise that once inspired his heart.

As the mist slowly lifts, the late autumn afternoon sun filters through the large cloud formations tinted in shades of pinks, oranges, crimson and deep reds. The twilight space between day and night makes its presence felt in the concert of colors and shapes.

A sudden clap of thunder dissolves his daydream.

Tom slams on the brakes and skids sideways on the wet roadway, the car twisting and turning before sliding to a stop on the graveled shoulder.

Overcome with tingling sensations from head to toe, he steps slowly out of his car to witness the clouds moving, transforming into a woman's face silhouetted against the brilliant sunset. Stunned, he focuses his attention on the beauty of her face as it emerges. Her warmth embraces him as she reaches for him with her eyes. Transfixed by a sudden calmness, hypnotized by this vision, all tension and emotional stress disappear. For a moment, his anguished soul feels soothed as his heart leaps. He stands alone in the roadway as another song played.

The first time I saw you
The first time I saw you smile
The first time you spoke my name
Girl, I haven't been the same.
I find it hard to understand how
you came to me that day.
But with all the time between us now
I'd never change a day.
But I find it hard to understand
Why it took so long to find you
'Cuz it seems like I've known you for all time.
I am certain I have known you,
known you for all time.
Was it in another time?
Was it in another life?
Was it something you left behind
to remind me of you?

Mesmerized by her face, tears fill his eyes. As he leans against the car, Tom questions the experience as too strange to be real . . . *who is she . . . I feel I should know her* . . . and then in a moment of recognition, he whispered to the wind . . . "I can't believe this is happening."

With his expression of doubt, the vision evaporates like it never occurred.

Opening the driver's door, he pauses. With his right hand perched on the roof, left hand on the top of the doorframe, his body slumps with despair as a deep sigh painfully releases from his soul.

At Tom's mountain cabin, with a week's growth on his face, he reaches for his cordless phone dialing his best friend, "Hi Hal, just checking in. It's been pretty quiet these last few days. I've been sleeping day and night. The weather has been great. It rained earlier, and we've got some low clouds and it's misty. I'm lovin' it. Now I'm starting to feel more like myself again."

"Glad to hear it. That's exactly what you needed. I sure was worried about you."

"Hey, I didn't realize how screwed up I was. Let me tell ya' I had somethin' happen. It was just off the wall. I can't make it out. I don't know what it means. I don't even know if it really happened." Tom wanders from room to room, phone at his ear, glancing out windows acting like he is looking for someone.

"Well, what happened?"

"On my drive up here just about sunset, I saw the most incredible sunset I'd seen in years. I had to pull off the road. I got out of the car. There she was."

"What? What are you talking about? Who did you see?"

"I saw her face in the clouds."

"You mean, Mary?"

"No! I don't know her name, but I *know* her. I was tingling, like a wave of warm electricity washed over me. She . . . she . . . looked like the woman in my dream."

" . . . Uh . . . Are you sure you're OK?"

"I don't know. Because, as soon as I said 'this can't be happening', her face disappeared."

Hal pauses. Collecting his thoughts, he says, "In my mind's eye I think I am visualizing what you experienced. You and I have been close friends for nearly all our lives. Think about all the times we've been there for each other, maybe even in other lifetimes. What the hell do you think the vision means?"

Tom responds, "I don't know what it means. But I was playing the CD you burned for me when this all happened. So, what are you getting about all of this?"

"Here we go again, pal," Hal sighs. "The 'mean woman blues conversation.' We've had too many of these conversations lately. It sounds like you are doing okay now. Anything else I can take care of for you?"

"Yeah, just don't tell Mary where I am."

Tom peeks out another window. Some movement catches his eye.

"Hey, Hal, I've gotta go. I need to check out someone out in the back yard." Tom hangs up. A sense of urgency comes over him.

Moving quickly, he slides open the glass door to the back patio and steps outside, rubbing his birthmark as he does so.

As he looks across the patio toward the forest, he sees emerging from the mists of time an image of a Native American woman. She is wearing a long white buckskin dress. The dress is ceremoniously decorated with brilliantly colored porcupine quills and beads, fringed at the hem. Her boots match the dress. Around her neck rests a necklace with shells, grizzly bear teeth inlaid with pearls and ornaments. The centerpiece of the necklace is an abalone shell, blessed with an intriguing and simple design of metal inlaid into the pearlescent interior of the shell.

Fascinated, he cannot take his eyes off her. Her face is the same as the one he saw in the clouds.

Tom begins to move toward her. He is taken by her.

She moves toward him.

He becomes totally captivated.

As they draw close to arm's length, she reaches toward him with her right hand and he reached with his left. As their fingers are just about to touch . . . the mists embrace them.

2

THE STORY

(*Circa* 4th Century AD, North America)

Grandfather Gray Wolf, the last remaining of the elder shaman, lying on his worn buffalo robe bed, continued his telling of the Story of The People to his granddaughter, and about his life and what was told to him by Red Fox, White Eagle, and others.

3

THE VILLAGE

Clouds.
Clouds and mist.
Mists dispersing.
Ohio River Valley.
Newark Earthworks and High Bank Earthworks and the wide white road between them.
Serpent Mound.
Serpent Mound, villages and hamlets of homes tucked away among the forested hills.
Hamlets of homes dot the landscape for miles and miles laced by hardwood forests, green rolling hills, cultivated lands, and streamlets meandering down and around headed for the Ohio River.
Hamlets of homes.
Cozy homes, each made of branches woven between double rows of posts placed in parallel rows in a large oval, comprised the landscape of the village. The double row walls created a space for insulation of sand mixed with gravel. Both inside and outside walls were covered with an adobe-like mud. Dome roofs were sealed with woven watertight reed mats, covered with thatching. Mica windows reflected the early morning sun as they allowed the sun's rays to bring in the light. The doorway area of each home was covered with a canopy to allow for protection from the weather as the large baking ovens and cooking area were situated outside the living space.

Sun rising in the east on a late winter morning.

Early in the morning, I, Gray Wolf, remember my father, Black Bear, rising from slumbering next to my mother, Raven's Wing. He always arose first. He put on his heavy woven shirt, woven warm leggings that tie at the waist and his shoes, made from fur-lined woven fibers and leather, before stepping outside to greet the morning sun rising in the east. His morning greeting consisted of a prayer of gratitude to Father Sun for returning each day in the eastern sky, gratitude to Mother

Earth for the bountiful life we experience, and gratitude to Great Spirit for life itself in all its forms.

Everyday my father, as did most men and women, rises early to pray for the day, giving grace and thanksgiving for our bounty. Most others perform the same ritual. All of us know what we are given of the plants and animals come from Spirit, so that we can live in complete abundance of prosperity. Great Spirit is our Creator coming to us to sustain us through Mother Earth. Then my father usually ends his prayer with an offering of tobacco as a tangible form of thanksgiving.

Our village stirs early.

Only a few birds contribute their songs in greeting the sunrise on these cold, late winter days. Occasionally a dog barks. As my father steps back inside, he reaches for my mother's comb. Kneeling down next to the raised platform bed where she is still lying, gently he kisses her forehead and caresses the left side of her head. She smiles up at him as he begins to comb her long black hair. After enjoying the precious moments between them, my mother gets up, dons her warm winter tunic, dyed a dark red pulling it over her light shirt. She pulls up her winter leggings. As the sun continues to rise in the east, shafts of light pour in through our mica windows.

Our house warms as my mother adds fuel to the embers in our hearth in the corner. She soon produces a warm tea and porridge of cooked grains seasoned with herbs touched with a drop of maple syrup. Mother hands me a cup of rose hip tea as I sit up. Despite my comfortable bed softened with a quilts filled with mosses and goose down, I don't stay in bed late.

I hear other villagers stirring and wonder if my friends are up and about. I too put on a warm winter tunic, dyed a deep green, pulling it over my shirt, pull on my shoes, then tie my hair back with a twine. Anxious to see my friends before we each go to our respective trades, I walk past the bowl mother set for me at the table. As I move to step outside, my mother grabs my shirtsleeve at the elbow with a look on her face that means "take care of home's needs before you go." She then hands me a large basket woven so tightly as to hold water. I grab the basket handle and take off.

"Hey, Gray Wolf."

I hear my name called out by a familiar voice.

"You heading to the pond?" Water Dog easily strides the distance across the yard with his long legs.

"Yeah, you wanna come?"

"Sure" he says, "I see more Elders and Grandmothers coming into our village I've not seen in a long time. This council meeting seems pretty important. I wonder what's up." Dipping the water basket in a pond, created by damming rocks in the stream that rushes by it, provides easy access for filling baskets. I kick away some of the ice on the edge so as not to slip.

Water Dog accompanies me back to my house helping carry the water basket by holding on to the other handle. I look around for Red Fox and don't see him anywhere. He must have already left.

As I glance around still hoping to see my friend, I observe other men stepping out of their homes to give thanks for the day, sifting corn meal or other grains or tobacco on to the ground as part of the early morning ceremony. Not everyone performs the sacred ritual in the same way. It's a ceremony of recognition and gratitude, the essence of which comes from the heart. The form is a matter of personal preference.

We see my mother begin to start a fire in her oven under the canopy outside. I had helped my father build this large oven for my mother. My mouth begins to water just thinking of some of the tasty cakes my mother makes, especially when she puts maple syrup on them.

That thought reminds me that I am now hungry. Water Dog and I set the basket down where my mother points to on the ground. She looks at us. "Why don't both of you have some porridge before you go off for the day?" she offers.

Water Dog rubs his stomach, tilting his head to one side and back again, half grins, "I had something earlier. I suppose I could have another bowl now. Thanks."

Large in stature, Water Dog bends down to fit in under the canopy covering the work area just outside our home as he accepts my mother's offering. Water Dog is taller than me. He is almost eight feet tall with a large frame. I stand just over six feet tall.

Before we grab our spoons, we each bow our heads and say a prayer of reverence for this day of life and in gratitude for the food provided by Mother Earth. After we eat, both of us wash out our bowls and spoons and lay them on the shelf near where my mother is stirring up a batter for cakes to bake later.

Water Dog and I jostle each other as we begin our trek, running then stopping, playing as we head for our destinations. A gaggle of geese scatter, honking and squawking, as we plow through them on our way.

We have a ways to go before we get there. We go past the pipe makers setting up their tools to begin carving. We hear the subtle sounds of the flint knappers sorting out rocks for that day's work, and see the reed weavers' houses displaying brightly painted wall mats. The vibrant colors reflect the vibrancy of our village and The People. The interior of our homes display these beautiful wall mats. Some boast of colorful designs, while others document family history.

Brushing my shoulder with his, Water Dog causes me to turn in another direction. He looks at me grinning. Together we saunter toward another collection of houses clustered together. Bluebird Near the Lily appears busy puttering just outside her family's home scattering grain for our village's turkey flock. She notices us, and stands putting her hands on her hips of her petite frame with a big grin on her face. She waves gently, not at me. Her eyes set on Water Dog. Water Dog kicks the dirt, puts up a hand in passing, his eyes not leaving her delicate form as we move on.

Back on track toward our respective destinations, we see groups of people shouldering their trowels and rakes for work in the fields to prepare the ground for the spring planting.

Aromas, of sweet cakes, stews, seasoned venison roasting, hardwoods burning into coals in the outside ovens, drift across our path. The air is thick with savory scents, arousing our senses.

From somewhere we could hear the soothing notes of a pan flute player greeting the day with a fun little melody.

Voices carry across the little valley as villagers begin their day. We hear the gleeful sounds of children playing happily outside. We hear neighbors chatting with each other. None of the voices or sounds is distinct, muffled into a concert of comfort, reassurance, and harmony.

As we near the next group of houses, I feel quiet as I begin to tune in to the tasks that await me. Water Dog turns off and waves as he saunters in no particular hurry toward the pottery house. He is learning to make pots and other clay works, but prefers to walk the hills. He says he looks for game. I think he simply enjoys walking the Ohio landscape, hills garnished with trees of various kinds and other shrubs. I don't expect him to continue making pots for too much longer.

When I stop to watch him go, I can't help but notice several people I have never seen in our village before. They are dressed in highly colored robes, keenly decorated with pearls and other colored beads and copper ear spools, standing near the entrance to the long Council House. By their appearance clearly they are here to see White Eagle, obviously dignitaries from other settlements. Their faces appear tense and I notice few words are exchanged between them.

The Elder Grandmother, White Eagle, dressed in ceremonial garb, steps up from behind them, greets them with a solemn voice, a slight bow, and leads them into the Council house.

"Oh there you are, Gray Wolf," says Singing Hawk, our teacher. Despite her diminutive size, wizened face and graying hair, she remains sharp of mind with much ancient knowledge to share. She touches my left shoulder to get my attention. "Shining Bird is already here and has started on a new project. You might be interested to see what she's doing."

Pulling myself away from trying to envision what the Council of Elders might be meeting about, I move my shoulders to shake off a ghostly feeling. As I step into to the house of sacred objects, I see Shining Bird look up at me and smile, beckoning me to come near. On the table in front of her sit large lumps of copper just brought in by the traders from up north. Shining Bird's long artistic hands move away from the copper to caress my arm. She peers up into my face from her workbench searching for the meaning of my faraway look. We do not speak. As our eyes meet, words become unnecessary between us. A moment passes. I turn to Singing Hawk in response to her suggestion about proportions in a set of equations we had talked about earlier. These equations were in one of the birch bark scrolls I had been studying.

I notice several other students, one or two younger than I, and several older. They are learning to read and write the language passed down by the Ancient Ones. The birch bark scrolls preserve this information. Not all children choose to study with Singing Hawk. Each of us follows our own direction in expressing who we are, contributing to the community in a myriad of ways according to the talents and skills of each. Heads bent over birch bark scrolls, inscribed stones, and disks, they barely notice my arrival.

A keeper of the Ancient Knowledge and of sacred objects, Singing Hawk guides our awareness and education. Most of what we study is inscribed on the scrolls.

The many lines in her face did not distract from the light emitting from her glistening eyes, alive with life and love of her students as she shared her vast knowledge of the Universe and Mother Earth. Her gray hair peppered with a few black strands was pulled back held in a bun by a silver hair comb. Her mind served us questions with a quickness that often startled me.

She keeps caches of deer hides and birch bark scrolls marked with the ancient shapes, of circles, squares, triangles, designs with right angles, animal outlines, measuring devices and more. It is these ancient formulas and shapes that our ancestors used to build the astronomical observatories, other sacred places, and which our shamanic architects, astronomers, and engineers used in our lands today.

The breeze moving through Singing Hawk's house softly touches my cheek as I lift my head after several hours of concentration on a scroll. So intense was my focus, I didn't notice the day passing. The angle of the light coming through the windows informed me it was the middle of the afternoon. I looked around for Shining Bird. Her usual bench was vacant. Her table was cleared. Voices drifted in from outside. I got up and moved in the direction of the voices, stepping outside.

"Hello, mother. What's up?"

My mother is chatting with Singing Hawk and Shining Bird. "I am bringing Singing Hawk a basket of acorn flour and several cakes I baked this morning. Have one. I'm sure you could use a bite right about now."

Suddenly my stomach echoes my mother's comments. So I reach for one, bow my head in gratitude and say my prayer for the food given to me, then take a lavish bite. After a second bite, my gaze lands on the Council house down the way. My mother hands a clay pot of venison stew prepared with savory herbs and goose fat to Singing Hawk. Singing Hawk bows her head to my mother and gratefully accepts the gift. My mother smiles and nods back, glancing at me. I'm distracted as I notice dignitaries slowly leaving the Council House in ones and twos. At first they stand around looking in all directions to find their bearings, and then stroll off in different directions.

The Council House had been constructed a long time ago. No one could remember when it was built. It was similar to the individual homes only much larger.

The Council House was the largest building in the area of the Great Serpent. Often it was the location where the Elders, Grandmothers, and others would meet to discuss current events, social issues, and other matters needing conversation.

Inside the Council House in our village hang many tapestries of woven reeds, and cloth displaying artistic designs, colorful geometric shapes, meaningful codes, and pictorial and written histories of The People. Sacred objects also hang from the rafters. Large mica windows provided sunlight in the day and moonlight at night. The Council House is furnished with cots and benches. Sitting was made more comfortable with quilts and pillows filled with mosses and goose down feathers.

The People knew no government. Written rules and laws did not exist as they are not needed. The People require none as we live according to our internal dictates that for the most part align with our connections with Mother Earth and Great Spirit, our Creator.

Grandmothers carry the wisdom passing it down to the following generations. By virtue of their age, experience, and specifically remaining in tune with the Feminine, the life-giving Source, the Grandmothers are most honored. Elders, both men and women, are those who most strongly express spiritual connections with Great Spirit, as well as with Mother Earth.

Consistently, the Elders demonstrate wisdom, insight, as well as compassion. Occasionally, a young man or woman is included in councils of the Elders as their particular insights or views tend to be revealing and spiritually driven. Nearly all the shaman are counted as Elders.

Not all the Elders, Grandmothers and Grandfathers live in the nearby settlements. They live where they live, throughout the entire Ohio Valley and beyond, especially north to the Great Lakes and to the east toward the Atlantic Ocean.

So when White Eagle sent out messengers to the surrounding hamlets, villages, and places far way for a meeting, many came, or came when they could get there. Few would want to refuse such an invitation. Seldom were such meetings held. It had to be important. The primary meetings were held at times of high ceremony, such as the Solstices and Equinoxes and about every nine years for the northernmost moonrise, or the southernmost moonrise.

Regular ceremonies, such as for Sister Moon and Father Sun, are universal events because they are predicable. These events follow the normal rhythm of Mother Earth's cycles. For these it is much easier to make travel plans and food preparation with good timing when the events were scheduled.

This council is an unforeseen meeting. Change scents the air.

Early the next morning the Elders once again assembled in the Council House.

"Thank you, all, for coming," White Eagle begins as she nods to each Elder and Grandmother in attendance.

All wore ceremonial finery of beautifully dyed clothing, woven on fine looms, blushing with freshwater pearls, beads, feathers, elk and grizzly bear teeth. Some wore beautifully colored woven dresses over leather leggings or heavy woven fabric equally elegant to the decorated clothes. Many wore pearl necklaces, copper ear spools, and other such jewelry.

White Eagle, the most prominent shaman and Elder among The People, wore her treasured necklace which dropped in the center with an oval abalone shell, fashioned in the shape of the sacred turtle. The necklace itself was comprised of a variety of rare shells, rare stones, iron meteor pieces, silver spheres and bear teeth inset with freshwater pearls. The center presented a most spectacular design.

Inside the abalone shell had been carved a simple yet powerful design inlaid with silver and copper. The design was that of a ring of silver. Inside the silver circle perfectly proportioned breathed two copper triangles. These perfect triangles, each side equal in length, were positioned as inversions of each other, lying over one another creating a six-pointed star. Each point of the star touched the ring of silver. It reflected sunlight, moonlight, and firelight and created in everyone who was in its presence a sense of awe. Of all the amulets among The People, this one was the most powerful . . . the most honored . . . the most respected . . . the most beautiful and . . . the most sacred.

Grandmother White Eagle said the symbol inside her amulet had been honored among The People for thousands of years. It was a powerful symbol of the Ancient Ones of our Ancient Ones.

"We have all smoked the ceremonial pipe" she resumes. "The smoke lifts our prayers to Heaven.

> *"We all acknowledge the Great Spirit, our Creator, as the Sacred Force in the Universe. The Universe, created by Great Spirit, is the Great Spirit manifested in the physical world. All of Heaven and Mother Earth birthed from Great Spirit. The Will of the Creator is as above, so below. Just as Great Spirit provides nurturing of our souls, so does our Mother Earth provide us with bounty for meeting our human needs. We live in Oneness with each other. As we help each other, we help ourselves. Should we by some act bring harm to another, we harm ourselves. As we remain in tune and aligned with Great Spirit and Mother Earth, we know our way is guided, our path protected. All comes from the Creator, all Life. Everything that is, is part of Great Spirit."*

White Eagle pauses for a moment, looks everyone in the eye before continuing. "We live in the Fourth World. We are the Children of the Law of One. Maintaining a sense of oneness requires awareness of our connectedness to each other and to our Creator and Mother Earth. We are connected to All That Is through the frequencies of vibration that comprise the Universe. Our feelings drive our thoughts, words and actions which manifest into the world around us. What we experience results from that which we manifest."

Murmurings rumble among the council members.

"You are reminding us of what we already know and are aware of daily. The People live according to these truths and have for hundreds of generations since the beginning of the Fourth World, when Our People migrated across the great water in the west in ancient times. Please tell us you did not call us here for this," says one sounding irritated.

"It has come to my attention that certain imbalances in the energy of The People have been occurring from time to time . . . enough to bring me concern," responds White Eagle. "We are entrained to Mother Earth, so we stay in constant communication at a subliminal level. We behave as all life forms are related. Yet I have heard of a growing number of instances in which individuals have exhibited unwise behavior or behaved in ways to move themselves and others out of balance with All That Is.

"Before I sent out the call for this meeting I purified myself in the three day sweat lodge ceremony. I took only water and ate only bits of fruits and nuts. I spent this time in total focus of being aligned with Great Spirit and Mother Earth. Many troubling signs were shown to me. I prayed for guidance and for the wisdom of how to return the harmony and balance to The People. Mother Earth showed me, where in places far from here, men hunted and killed for sport and pride, not for need of food."

The audience gasps.

"Great Spirit showed me an incident that involved a young woman picking berries and several young men approached her, forced her and took her to their village." Murmurs come from those listening. "In my vision quest, I was shown a group of hunters pushing and shoving a young man, one of their village, much smaller and more frail than they. They put bruises on his body, kicked him when he was down, and left him bleeding on the ground."

Silence grips the air.

"This behavior is out of balance with the Universe, with all of Life. It is not known by our People. After our People migrated here from the west, we were joined by a different people from the east, from the great water. Mother Earth and Great Spirit communed with us. During the thousands of years we have lived here, sometimes parts of our People warred against other parts of The People.

"Eventually, we all came to live in harmony with each other. The people from the east brought with them Ancient Knowledge about the Universe that we did not have, how to observe the stars, how to build in ways we had not known, so we could honor Sister Moon and Father Sun in ceremony. We became one People. Together we lived in harmony with All That Is, communing individually in private, as well as together at the Ceremonial sites. We lived in balance with nature and each other. Great Spirit and Mother Earth have blessed us with over a thousand years of peace and harmony."

Heads nod in affirmation.

"My question to you is, what have you witnessed?"

Silence.

"What have you heard if anything that might confirm or repudiate this sense of out-of-balance behaviors? Do you know of similar incidents?"

After a strong silence, shuffling of feet, scratching here and there, starring at each other, staring at the floor, eventually discussion emerged from the resistance to speak to the question. This conversation ensued slowly yet steadily, painfully, for hours. When there was nothing left to say that day, each left, in ones and twos.

4

GRAY WOLF AND WATER DOG

Early one spring morning as the rays of the sun crept into the eastern sky, Water Dog and I were already on our way across the rolling hills to a more forested area of the Ohio Valley. We had prepared for our trek the night before, packing biscuits, dried fish and smoked meat for a day's adventure. It was a day away from the routine.

For weeks before he and I talked about taking a day to walk the land. I had sensed Water Dog's unhappiness and frustration for some time now. Getting away from the village for a while seemed like a good idea. It would give Water Dog an opportunity to put some space between himself and whatever it was that was bothering him. He went alone many times. This time he invited me to join him. I didn't like seeing his moodiness when he was down and that seemed like it was becoming more constant.

"So I guess you know where you are going?" I ask as we leap across a stream and trudge up a hill.

"Yeah, I pretty much know the area. I've been wandering around this part of the land for a long time now. One day I will travel across the big river to the west and go north." His eyes gaze wistfully into the westward distance as he spoke once again of his dreams. As he imagined his journey the tension leaves his face and a smile breaks out. I return the smile, glad to see my friend lighten up.

"Haven't seen Red Fox around too much lately. What's he up to these days? I sure miss his company," Water Dog changes the topic as we walk through a stand of trees. The three of us, Water Dog, Red Fox, and I, as best of friends, worked in the fields together when it was our turn. Many winter afternoons we spent happy times knutting together, talking and laughing. I don't know why it seemed like fun to us. The stone workers in our village designed these clever tools made from two pieces of flat rock. One stone had two rows of carved out depressions which matched the sizes of the acorns and other nuts we gathered. We would place the nuts in the hollowed out depressions. Then using the other flat rock, we would firmly crack the shells. Both Water Dog and Red Fox were much more skilled than I was at exerting the right pressure to crack the shell just so as to preserve the nutmeat without smashing it. At first my mother always supervised this as she collected the meat to prepare flour for foods later. Now we all were more skilled, and she did not need to spend as much time sifting out shell fragments.

We played together as small children, and generally spent time at each other's homes, learning from each other's parents and grandparents. Water Dog lived with his sister Floating Lily and his mother, Blooming Rose, who collected and sorted the pearls gathered by our community from the mussels we would feast on. She passed them on to other communities, like Seip, that specialized in weaving and making beautiful clothing for The People. Many of the articles of clothing included the attachment of pearls. Pearls were also made into fine jewelry.

Water Dog's father had walked on into Spirit.

Red Fox's mother, Laughing Willow, sewed clothes for many of us. She even made dresses from the fine fabrics available from the weavers in outlying villages or fabrics the traders brought to our village. Her best gift was decorating dresses and shirts with beads, elk and bear teeth, plus exotic feathers and sea shells we got from the traders who brought in such things from places farther away.

"Oh, yeah, Red Fox has been so busy doing his thing." I said. "You know he goes out and studies bird nests of all sorts. He even climbed to the top a tree to check out an eagle's nest. That eagle wasn't too happy with him I can tell you that," I added laughing. "He is studying architecture. I see him hanging out at Singing Hawk's sometimes. He brings in old bird nests, all different kinds, and studies how they were put together."

Water Dog shakes his head as he listens. "I guess it takes all kinds to contribute to the community."

"You're right." I said, "I'm not sure what my contribution is just yet. I'm not real good at making things. I'm not a true artisan. I don't paint or weave mats or fabric. I can help in the fields and help with other tasks as needed, so I'm not entirely without contributions. I spend so much time learning at Singing Hawk's. Sometimes I just sit in awe of what I have learned. I enjoy what I do and what I am learning. It's just I'm not sure where I will go with it. I feel so fulfilled doing what I am doing. I guess I won't worry about it right now. Maybe it will just happen, and then I will know."

The trees thin out and we stop to take in the view. We stand at the edge of a meadowed clearing where we can see undulating hilltops forested with stands of trees. We take in the beauty of the lush countryside. Water Dog heaves a heavy sigh, looks down at me from his grand height, raises his eyebrows, and breathes in again.

"That part you said about feeling fulfilled," he begins, "I don't think I can take one more day of making pots. I'm good at it. It just doesn't do it for me, if you know what I mean."

I lean up against a tree and just look at him waiting to hear more. He continues, "When I was little, I used to help my grandmother make her pots. She makes all kinds of pottery for the community. She taught me so much. She told me I was a natural at it after I had made a few myself. But now, after working at it for the past couple years, I can see it's not for me. The problem is I'm not sure what to do." Finally he's talking about what has been bothering him.

"So what do you want to do?" I ask.

Shrugging his shoulders, he leans his bulky weight against another tree and begins kicking the dirt with one foot, lost in thought.

"I want to marry Bluebird Near the Lily!" he exclaims with some determination.

That reply wasn't what I was expecting. I had known for some time that he wasn't happy making clay pots. This revelation adds another layer to my concern for my friend.

"You are going to have to help me out here," I say. "Let me see, looks like we have two separate issues, making pots or not, and marrying Bluebird Near the Lily. As I see it, the question becomes, how do we manage the clay pot issue and negotiate a marriage . . ." I take a deep breath. "Does she want to marry you?" I pause momentarily to let that question sink in before I go on, "What do the grandmothers say about all of this? How do your families feel?" He stops kicking the ground, stands limply, shoulders sagging.

"No one knows," he says sadly, head tilted to the left. "She is stuck taking care of her little brothers and sisters at home. As you know, her mother died in childbirth with her last brother. She's so fragile, I'm afraid that she works too hard for how delicate she is . . . Oh yes, I love her and she knows it. She can't leave right now and I can't move in, because her house is too small."

"All right then." I say. "We need to think about some options."

Water Dog puts his hand on my shoulder. "Wait," he exclaims softly changing the topic again, "I thought I saw some movement over there." He points, squinting his eyes trying to see something undetectable in the distance.

Instinctively, I turn toward the direction he is pointing. Elbows at my side, forearms and hands outstretched, I feel the energy of several deer heading in our direction. In the consciousness of One, I join with the deer, my energy, and their energy.

Mentally, I ask one buck if he would be willing to come forward and allow us to take him for food for Bluebird's family. The deer agrees and comes toward us gingerly stepping along, head and long neck bobbing up and down, weaving side to side, seeking the source of the call, knowing his transition to the next dimension is about to take place.

Seeing the buck moving deliberately toward us, Water Dog gracefully and just as deliberately reaches for his quiver and bow. Inadvertently, he jostles his quiver of arrows, searching for a specific one. The brittle sound of wood clacking together startles the buck. He stops in his tracks, ears standing straight up, poised in alarm.

I renew the connectedness with the deer's energy and my energy.

Snap! Whizzzz. Plunk.

I see the energy of the arrow swiftly free brother deer's spirit.

As I regain focus of the here and now, I see Water Dog standing with an empty bow. I turn my head to the meadow in front of us and gasp. The buck lies at peace with Water Dog's arrow lodged in his heart.

As the other deer scatter back into the forest, we pause and give thanks to the Creator and to the spirit of brother deer for the blessing of food and provisions that will be made from his body. Nothing goes to waste. Reverently we step toward the animal that provided food and supplies for The People.

Water Dog prepares for our honoring of brother deer. He removes his leather pouch containing corn meal and a piece of cloth. We turn the grand buck's body so he is facing east.

Like a hulk standing over the slain deer, Water Dog reaches his arms to the sky. At first he looks upward, then down at the ground with eyes closed, all the while saying a prayer to the spirit of brother deer and Mother Earth. He sifts the cornmeal between his fingers, letting it fall to the ground. I join him in his silent prayer of gratitude and recognition of the moment.

Taking his small cloth, he tenderly covers the lifeless eyes of the deer before he begins the field dressing. Water Dog finds his knife, bends over and begins to gut the animal.

I reach for the arrow shaft sticking out of the deer. With a little difficulty, I tug on it several times having to give it a twist before it releases from the carcass. Finally, I pull the arrow free, hold it up to look at it. It magnetizes my attention. For a moment, I find myself lost in focusing on the arrowhead, marveling at its beauty and precision.

Water Dog begins to slit the belly pulling out the guts and other internal organs.

"Hey, you gonna help here?" he asks.

"Oh, sure," I answer mechanically, my mind still on the arrowhead. I bend over and give an assist as Water Dog pulls out steaming organs from the body cavity.

He severs the liver and lifts it up like a trophy piece he admires. I take a step or two back. Water Dog can see that I am not overwhelmed at the huge liver presented to me. So he puts it down on the grass to slice off several pieces. After bowing his head in brief prayer of thanks, he hands a small piece to me, and the other he bites into voraciously. I bow my head also in prayer then take it, blood dripping down my hand, and begin to consume the prized organ of an animal that offered his life to grant the sustaining of life for members of The People.

It was not a sacrifice. To sacrifice means to make sacred. Since all of life is sacred, it is already sacred, and nothing more can be done to increase it sacredness. The event was an expression of the continuity of the Life Force that lives in everything, the continuity of energy. This cannot be destroyed, but can change form from particle to wave and back again as the eyewitness changes focus. The purpose of the killing was not to enhance ego, but to provide sustenance to a family struggling in a land of plenty.

Bluebird's family was not impoverished, because they lived among the People. The People prospered in everything they intended. Mother Earth provided crops of grains and vegetables, varieties of fish and other delicacies from the streams, like fresh water mussels, along with ducks, geese, turkey and deer in abundance. Many traders stopping by from far reaches of the world brought wondrous trade goods. Members of our little settlement gave food and supplies to Bluebird's family to ensure all needs were met. Yet for some reason with so many children and only one parent, and no grandmothers living there, life seemed a little stretched for them. So the grand buck, dropped by Water Dog's single arrow, graciously participated in the wealth of our oneness.

The strength of Water Dog amazed few people. He hoisted the carcass over his shoulder with the valued organs stuffed back inside and began walking home. He had already begun planning who to give the hide to for the making of shoes for Bluebird's siblings.

"Lone Tree is the best tanner and shoe maker I know. I will ask him if he will take this hide and work his magic. Children grow so fast, they will be needing new shoes for the fall. They all are okay for now, and then summer will be here. So I think he should make them a little bigger than what they would need right now."

"You talk like you are their father or uncle or something, Water Dog," I say with a smile. I could tell his heart was taken, and he was already behaving like he was part of that family.

"Yeah," he responds, "I feel the need to contribute to them. Yet at the same time, I wish to take her away from them. When we marry, I can't move in there. Too many people. It would not be comfortable. Besides, I'm too big for that house. Taking care of her brothers and sisters, her father, and then taking care of me as well, that's too much to ask of her. She is so frail as it is. No, we would have to move into our own house."

Along the hike back to the village, my mind would not let the image of Water Dog's arrowhead alone. The image kept turning over and over in my mind. Finally, I ask, "Where did you get this arrowhead? Did your father or grandfather give it to you? Did you get it from a local trader? It's really quite a specimen."

My friend yanks his mouth from side to side, up and down, rolls his eyes up and around, acting as though he really did not want to divulge his secret source of spectacular arrowheads. Finally he says simply, "I made it."

"What?" I exclaim. "You made it? *You made it*?" Water Dog hangs a sheepish expression on his face as I get excited. "What do you mean, you made it? Do you have any idea what a work of art this is?" He shakes his head side to side in limited agility with the deer hanging across his shoulders. "Well," I continue in my excitement, "How did you learn to make arrowheads? You never said you spent time with the flint knappers. I am totally taken by surprise here."

"It was several weeks ago when my grandmother sent me up to get more ground mollusks at Falcon's Crest's home. I usually visit with him and his family, bring him a pot or two whenever I make that walk up there. On my way back this last trip, I stopped by where the flint knappers usually sit and work with the flint. For some reason I was drawn to stop and visit with Barking Frog and Blue Larkspur while they worked.

"I asked them what they were working on as I felt drawn to the rock itself. 'Ceremonial pieces mainly,' Blue Larkspur told me. Surrounding them on the ground were various pieces of flint."

We continue our hike and Water Dog is not even breathing hard as he carries the deer on his shoulders like it wasn't even there. "I spotted a nice piece of flint with a beautiful mixture of red, blue, green, yellow and white colors in it that had been thrown aside. Next thing I knew it was in my hand. I remember turning it over and over in my hands, feeling it, feeling its energy. In my mind's eye I kept seeing the arrowhead. The arrowhead appeared in my mind exactly as you see it today. My hands warmed at its touch."

I have never heard Water Dog say so much all at once since I've known him. I felt reluctant to interrupt with a question. So he continued on, "I hurried home, gave the ground mollusks to my grandmother, and found a quiet place outside to sit. Somehow I found a piece of deer antler in my hand. What I found incredible was. . . as I worked the flint, I kept seeing the finished piece in my mind aglow in a radiance that felt like it was alive. My hands kept working. What I experienced was a connection of oneness with my mental image, my body, arms and hands, and the piece of rock. Before I knew it, the arrowhead appeared in my hand." Water Dog stopped talking, stopped walking. He just stood there as if in a trance.

Now I do interrupt him.

"Do you know what you've done?" I ask him not expecting an answer. "You've found your gift!" He blinks in response to my question. "You're not a pottery maker. You're a flint knapper!" I sputter in the passion of my realization. "C'mon. Let's get back as soon as we can. I want to talk to Rising Wolf right away."

We pick up our pace. As we approach the edge of our settlement where several houses crowd the edge of the forest, across the open area near the Council House, we both spotted several dignitaries. They are probably Elders and other shaman visiting from other settlements. Several looked familiar, but the rest we didn't recognize.

"Looks like we have visitors again," observes Water Dog with a wrinkle in his brow. "I'm telling you, something must be up." I agree with a nod.

"I'm taking this deer to get it butchered. I want to give the back strap of this grand animal to the Elders," says Water Dog.

By this time it is about mid-afternoon. I didn't stay to help skin the carcass. Water Dog had plenty of help for that. In fact he had a variety of volunteers to assist with the organs and butchering. I feel the need to go home. Feeling inadequate or unskilled, or just not attached to the nature of this task, I wait around a while before fading into the background.

Nearing the cluster of homes where I live, I stroll in to see my mother's new oven producing heat and offering delicious aromas I associate with my mother. I find her busy cooking or baking or something with food preparations. She glances up at me still involved in her tasks, "I'm glad you are home. Maybe you could lend me a hand here. Would you get me more wood, then another basket of water?" I turn on my heel and head for the wood supply stacked up several dozen or more yards away. When I return, I look at her puzzled by the special care and emotional involvement with which she is performing what seems to me to be ordinary.

"More Elders and Grandmothers showed up than last time," she says wiping her forehead with her forearm. "This is for them. They have traveled such a long way to meet with White Eagle. I wish I could get my hands on some fresh meat right now," she sighs.

Just as I turn around thinking of the deer Water Dog brought in, his little sister, Floating Lily shows up with the back strap Water Dog mentioned. "From your mouth to Heaven's ears," I pronounce with a broad smile.

"Good thing," she retorts with a smile, "I was about to send you out for some fish."

I'm itching to take Water Dog to see Rising Wolf, the most accomplished in flint in the entire Ohio Valley. He is also an Elder, a shaman, and partner to White Eagle.

I return to Water Dog's house. He is not there. Thinking back to our previous conversation in the day, I now know to look for him at Bluebird Near the Lily's home. As I passed Lone Tree's place, I could see the deer had been dispatched quickly and efficiently, although some helpers were still in process of finishing up.

Winding my way around through the settlement, I finally see Bluebird Near the Lily's house. Of course Water Dog is there. I see him leaning against the outside of a little wall of rocks. His vibrant rusty colored hair combined with his gigantic size contrasts sharply against her tiny frame laced by her black flowing tresses. She too leans against the rock wall, but from the inside. Her beautiful black hair floats up in strands as the cool spring breeze picks up. Talking softly or not talking with words, their hands touch briefly at first, almost repelled by the magnetism between them.

Electricity fills the air.

Bluebird sets her left hand down on top of the wall, then Water Dog gently covers her hand with his. I can't help but notice the contrast in size between the two lovers. He looks like a giant compared to her petite frame. His eight foot build towers over her. Despite her delicacy of stature, her eyes envelop him in a total embrace. In my mind's eye, I see him swimming in her love for him. As he ever so gracefully leans down to put his face close to hers maybe to kiss or brush cheeks, the atmosphere becomes rarified sanctifying the world with their love.

So taken with the beauty of the scene before me, I trip over my own feet, not really watching where I am going. "Oh, oooff, uff," I emit as I try to recover from my clumsiness. The ripple effect disturbs the energy field around them, causing the two lovers to look up as I approach. Their faces devoid of emotion looking at me, I see that I have caused them to return to the present, suddenly and without notice.

"I'm sorry I intruded. Hello, Bluebird Near the Lily. Water Dog," I say awkwardly.

Later in the day, Rising Wolf finds himself where he usually sits, outside his house set quite a ways away from the rest of the settled area. He is the oldest of the Elders, and has been a shaman since anyone can remember, and always involved in flint. He and White Eagle live there together. Their children and grandchildren live elsewhere.

His long white hair trails down his back allowing the spring breezes to gently lift sections of it in a graceful motion behind him. He sits there on a bench outside working a flint piece. The sounds of our voices carry up through the trees that block the view down to the village.

"You're late," he announces to us as we arrive. "I was expecting you long before this. What took you so long?" He challenges with an air of mystery, eyes open wide and eyebrows raised in question.

I shouldn't have been taken aback but I was, and so was Water Dog. Water Dog tried to speak in reply, but was stopped by Rising Wolf's gesturing for silence with a slight wave of his hand.

"So you've come to learn about flint, have you?"

Water Dog nods in silent response. Rising Wolf says, "There's a lot to know, boy. I've set aside some pieces for you to begin with." We both look around and see large and small pieces of various shapes, sizes, and colors. Rising Wolf turns to me and says, "You're not here for flint, are you, Gray Wolf? If not, then why are you still here?"

I offer the arrow I had been carrying that had been used to kill the deer. "Rising Wolf, I want to show you what Water Dog has made," I stammer showing it to Rising Wolf.

Rising Wolf replies with a stern tone of voice but eyes twinkling, "I see. I have known for some time that Water Dog would eventually be coming to see me. Now I see that he needed his friend to get him to come here."

Turning away from me and toward Water Dog, Rising Wolf begins his lecture on flint, putting pieces of it into Water Dog's hands to get the feel of each one. Feeling suddenly ignored, I turn to go, looking back at them after a few steps. I could see Water Dog's countenance lift, his attention totally focused on what he was learning. I smile and shrug, and then continue my way down the little hill.

More Elders and Grandmothers had shown up for the next Council meeting than for the previous meeting. White Eagle's eyes glisten as they arrive, giving a respective half-bow to each as they re-entered into the Council House after a break. Light flows into the House through the windows providing light as the visitors find their seating again. Some sit on the long soft benches, while others find comfort on the clay floor made cozy by the luxurious buffalo robes, and feathered-stuffed pillows.

White Eagle begins the pipe ceremony. After everyone participates, she offers her prayer, "We have all smoked the ceremonial pipe. The smoke carries our prayer to Heaven. We all acknowledge the Creator, Great Spirit, as the Sacred Force in the Universe. The Universe, created by Great Spirit . . . ." she continues her prayer as before. Then she goes on to remind them, "As we discussed earlier, we have a concern as to our People moving into out-of-balance with Mother Earth, Heaven, and each other. " Does anyone have more to share at this point?"

Uncomfortable silence breaks when two or three shaman from neighboring settlements indicate they wish to speak. Discussions go on for hours. At one point Floating Lily brings a water jug and a ladle. She offers water to drink as the conference continues. Her strawberry hair reflects brilliantly the flames of the warming fire adding an eerie dimension to the room as she moves among the Elders with the refreshment.

"If we have finished our stories, the next thing we must look at is the question, 'what do we do about it?' We have all agreed that there are a growing number of instances of disharmony occurring among our People," White Eagle says.

"We need to make this known. Even though we have heard the stories shared here today, The People at large remain relatively unaware," offers one grandmother.

"Yes, but how to make The People aware, that seems to be the question," says another. Heads nod in assent.

"Perhaps a ceremony of some kind?" asks another.

"Yeah, but if we have a ceremony about disharmony, won't that put the thought energy into manifesting more disharmony?" challenges another voice. "I don't think we want to turn attention to the disharmony. We want to focus on being in balance, not out-of-balance."

"How about a renewal ceremony about being in balance, and staying in balance with All That Is?" suggests one Elder.

Another Elder speaks up, "A renewal ceremony is a good thing. It endorses the message and encourages participation on a larger scale. However, I feel a ceremony is not enough. Just a ceremony, in my opinion, is not adequate to create the outcome we are after. A ceremony imprints the message into the minds and hearts of The People. Becoming out of balance is serious, critical, in fact, to our way of life, our very being. Something more is needed."

"How about getting The People involved before our actual ceremony?"

"Maybe the young adults or older children talking about it ahead of time?"

"That sounds good. How do we do that?"

". . . and what about the ceremony? What's that going to be?"

"The Summer Solstice is coming up in a few months. Why don't we tie that ceremony in with what we are talking about right now? After all ceremony is when The People come together to celebrate and remember to remember our relationships with all of creation."

Grandmothers and Elders nod in agreement around the room.

A Grandmother in the back suggests, "It seems like what we are needing is to create conversation about The People, our history, and what we acknowledge to be true, and remember to remember the meaning of our ways in this the Fourth World. If we involve the younger people that might be the way to encourage the conversation. They would talk about it among themselves, with their parents, grandparents, and the smaller children."

"That's exactly what we should do. How to create the conversation in the first place seems to be the issue," observes another.

Murmurs of agreement ripple through the group.

White Eagle holds up her hand and nods, "Yes, and let's not forget that the Summer Solstice ceremony is held at many ceremonial sites, not just at the Serpent Mound. If we combine the Solstice ceremony with perhaps the reason and purpose behind the Serpent Mound, itself, and create a conversation about it ahead of time, that might do it."

Then an Elder spoke who had not spoken earlier, "We could perhaps have someone create a model of the Serpent reflecting its exact proportions, then take it around to different villages, telling its story. That would stimulate conversation, and reinforce what it represents. Maybe we are not so out of balance that this effort will restore the harmony of the People."

"I don't see how that's going to work," says another Elder. "The Serpent is about a prophecy, one that does not necessarily portend a good result."

Still another chimes in, "Yes, that is true. Yet, the prophecy of the Serpent shows us to be mindful, giving us the opportunity to change the direction of the Fourth World."

A grandmother adds, "It's about choice and free-will, remember. We can stand by and let things go from bad to worse, or we can do something about it. Besides, the prophecy is not a prediction, but a warning, so that we can take action. I say we send out invitations in our respective communities to find someone who would be willing to make a model of the Serpent. That person can travel around to tell the story. This way we can, through these conversations, remind The People of who we are . . . and the need to remain in balance in the Oneness."

"Someone from each of our different regions can organize this kind of project and select the appropriate young person to go to each village and get the conversation going."

"Yeah, that might work . . ."

"This will take some organization to do, but we can get started once we return to our homes."

". . . Oh, I see. We will combine the story of the Great Serpent, its prophecy, with our prayers at the Summer Solstice ceremony. Discussions about it ahead of time will reinforce our awareness. I like this idea. I think it should work."

Louder sounds of approval, nods, pervade the group.

"Is this what we agree to do?" White Eagle asks all those assembled.

The council members quiet to a hush and focus all eyes on White Eagle.

"And so it is," she exclaims. Then she adds, "In light of this, I believe the ceremony at the Serpent Mound, and at all the other ceremonial sites, should be enhanced more than the usual. It should be a most colorful and memorable ceremony, so as to impress into our minds the potency of what the Serpent represents to us."

Agreement occurs.

By the time the meeting breaks up, nearly the entire day has gone by. As the Elders and Grandmothers begin to step out of the Council House, they begin to feel hunger after wrestling with the future of their People.

Aromas of delicious foods cooking float across the community area and arouse their hunger even more. They turn to face the source, wondering. The same little girl who brought them water comes running over to them with a smile. Floating Lily signals them to follow her to another house where a sumptuous feast has been prepared for them.

5

RED FOX

Red Fox showed up at Singing Hawk's house just after sunrise. He was anxious to begin building the model he had volunteered to do. He could hardly wait to get his hands on the materials to begin. Word had gone out to all the surrounding villages that White Eagle needed someone to build a model of the Serpent in preparation for the Summer Solstice. Red Fox could hardly believe his ears.

"What luck, Gray Wolf!" he had said to me after he found he was selected for this honor.

I replied, "It's not luck at all. You have been studying how to build stuff for a long time now. You have acquired much knowledge, and also others recognize your talent and dedication. It's not luck at all, my good friend. Nevertheless, as much as you know or think you know, you have so much more to learn. The Serpent Mound is layered with mystery. I think this will not be as easy as you expect."

Singing Hawk did not invite Red Fox in that day, or the next day. Red Fox was getting anxious to start building right away. For three days, she took no students into her house. Shining Bird, Red Fox, and I spent an afternoon together after waiting all morning for Singing Hawk to open her door to us.

The three of us stopped by my house on our way to the pond. My mother gave each of us a bowl of stew and some nut cakes. Bowing our heads in gratitude for the bounty from Mother Earth, each saying our own prayers, we ate in silence, washed up the bowls and spoons before leaving for the pond.

The pond was a soothing place to sit and contemplate, with the sounds of the creek running by, birds offering their songs among the trees rustling in the wind. Sounds of Mother Earth, yet stillness, prevailed. When we arrived, we walked around it and moved up near the top of the hill overlooking the pond to sit with our faces toward the sun. A breeze softly touched our cheeks as we made ourselves comfortable.

After many long moments, Shining Bird asks Red Fox, "What do you know about the Serpent Mound?"

By now he is remembering my past remark about the Serpent representing more than what meets the eye. He shifts his position on the ground from one of being moderately uncomfortable to one of even more discomfort. His personal discomfort is not from anything physical. He moves his legs and shifts his weight from one side to the other, all the while staring off into the sky appearing to look for the answer written in the clouds somewhere. Failing an answer, Red Fox pretends to be lost in thought, ignoring Shining Bird's question.

"So tell me, Red Fox, what *do* you know about the Serpent Mound? And are you prepared to learn whatever it is you need to learn to accomplish this task?" she says with a hint in her voice suggesting he had much to learn.

"What do you mean, Shining Bird?" he says to stall and save face in this gentle confrontation that he was not enjoying. Then as if lightning struck him, he volleys back to her, "Shining Bird, what is it that you think you know that you think I don't know?"

I roll my eyes and look away, not wanting to interfere in the energy field building around my two friends.

Shining Bird closes her eyes and takes in a deep breath calling upon her secret cache of love for the Great Oneness, and her desire to help her friend. As she speaks, translucence begins to emanate from her already beautiful face. I get comfortable anticipating the story she was about to reveal. Shining Bird begins.

"In the time of long ago, before there were villages in our valley, a star fell from the sky and caused a great cloud of smoke and unearthly destruction when it landed on Mother Earth's skin. Mother Earth was not able to heal this great circle of destruction. It was an ugly scar on the beautiful land. Eons went by, and the scar remained. Nothing would grow in the scar. Animals stayed away and the birds did not fly over it. Even when the rain fell, it would not gather as water in the bottom of this wound. Mother Earth was very sad, as she was not able to heal this herself.

"Very long ago, our great ancestors emerged onto this, the Fourth World. The Creator appeared to them and gave them wisdom. They were to separate into four groups and begin separate migrations to the four points of the directions, the East, the South, the West, and the North. Once they successfully completed these migrations, they would find the place where they would live and carry out their solemn oath to preserve the ancient teaching and preserve balance in the Fourth World. It was up to them to remain in balance.

"While on their migration from the East, our great ancestors came to the lands of our village. They found this large wound on the surface of Mother Earth. The Elders asked her what caused this to come about.

Mother Earth said, 'A star fell from the sky and wounded my body long before man and woman walked upon me. I have not been able to heal this wound.'

"Our Elders asked if they could help her. Mother Earth was pleased by their offer. She described the soils, plants and rocks that would heal the ancient and weathered astrobleme-star wound. The People gathered these things and sealed the wound. This task took several generations of The People.

"When they were finished, The People asked Mother Earth if they had performed the task correctly. 'You have done well, my Children, and I am grateful.' They asked, 'Is there anything else we can do? We have seen visions that we are to remain here until we receive a sign that it is time to resume our migration.' Mother Earth said, 'your visions are true and because of your efforts on my behalf, I have blessed these lands for you to live, prosper, and raise your families. I give you clear waters, bountiful lands, harvests, animals, fish and fowl that will sustain you and spirits that will watch over you. All I ask of you is that you continue to follow the ways of The Great Spirit, honor me as part of you, and protect these ways so that you do not feel separate from Great Spirit or from me. I will give you sacred places to build structures which will foretell the movements of Father Sun, Sister Moon and other travelers in the Heavens.'

"The People told Mother Earth that they would honor their promises. Mother Earth said, 'I have been watching you on your journeys and the way you are living in this, the Fourth World. As your hearts have remained pure, I will also give you knowledge of what may come. This will guide your way and the generations of your children who choose to travel on the path of Oneness. Promise me that you will properly use and preserve this knowledge. If you do, The People will be protected come what may.'

"Mother Earth continued, 'You must complete one more task. You must create a Great Serpent on these lands. The Serpent has great intelligence, and it is a protector of The People when its powers are used properly. If its powers are used for destructive purposes, great harm will result. It will be a reminder of the Prophecy I will give to you if you are faithful to your promise.

"Because it lives deep in the ground and moves without legs across my skin, you must use earth and rock to create the Serpent in strict accordance to my instructions."

"The Serpent will remind you of me and how you healed a wound that I could not. It will remind those who follow that we all come from the Great Oneness and the importance of remembering this. It will remind you and following generations of the importance of living in oneness with each other and me."

"So what you get to do," concludes Shining Bird with an instructional tone and attempting to be inviting, "is to recreate this monument, precisely as directed by Mother Earth, only on a smaller scale." Pausing to let her story sink in, she smiles and looks Red Fox straight in the eye, to lend him support for his task of monumental significance.

Red Fox gulps and looks away.

Silence.

The soft breeze lightly kisses his face as he continues to look down, not wishing to make eye contact . . . not wishing to punctuate the essay of feeling that was washing over him as it wrote its meaning into his awareness.

Long moments of awkward silence pass. Red Fox unceremoniously gets up, brushes off the leaves and debris sticking to his clothes, and then walks back to the village, needing to be alone for a while.

After Red Fox had walked off out of sight, I look over at Shining Bird. I am sitting to her left, knees up with feet flat on the ground, arms resting on my knees. My gaze rests on her face still emitting the translucent light from being in touch with Great Spirit and her story telling. I see the pupils of her eyes are dilated and her face begins to flush. The breeze picks up again, gently sweeping between us as if solidifying the bond that had been growing. A lock of her long dark hair lifts and dances with the moving air. I am suddenly taken by an energy of desire for her. My heart pounds. My manhood swells. I look into her face to see if an invitation exists there.

She leans into me, head turned slightly sideways, but her eyes lock on mine. I reach for her hand and feel her return the pressure. With that, I am feeling internal pressure. Unwilling to pause the direction in this new field of energy we are engaging in, I roll my body over next to her. With my right index finger I softly draw a line of affection down her left cheek. She sucks in her breath. Swimming in each other's eyes, I let my hand gently fall down her left arm from shoulder to wrist. She moans ever so faintly.

With a single finger, I caress an inside ankle in small circles. She sucks her breath in again. All in one movement, I drag my hand up her shin, pausing at her knee only momentarily, and continue drifting a loving touch up her left thigh. She moans again, slightly louder than before. I pause momentarily to take in the pleasure of the moment.

Then I begin again letting my hand slowly drift up the inside of her thigh to be rewarded by another soft groan from my beloved. Again, I pause and begin again at her ankle, and again slowly moving up her leg as she sucks in her breath. Her body now begins to clutch seized by an electric shock from the pleasure growing between us. Her body involuntarily convulses in a slow rhythm, aching for release of the sexual tension rising in her. The heat growing and pulsing between my legs screams as I delay its expression. I prefer pleasuring my partner until just the right moment of excitement in her.

Still, I drift lazy circles with my hand on her chest, lightly touching both breasts, gently teasing each nipple protruding through her clothes, then her abdomen and lower. Her body seizes up as she lets out a groan then sucks her breath back in again.

At that she falls back to the ground in a heap. I stop to breathe myself and allow my eyes to feast on the glowing beauty of my partner. When I see her move again, I begin again taking even longer to move up and down her body with my hand locking into an energetic groove designed to delight her body. Just before her body begins to clutch again, she lifts herself up on her elbows.

Shining Bird smiles into my eyes and opens her arms as she reclines again. We each make adjustments to our clothing to accommodate the fulfillment of our desires. My excitement increases as I roll on top of her, putting my weight on my knees and a forearm. I bury my face in her fragrant neck using one knee to move her legs apart for better ease in my approach.

Our bodies join in celebration of life. Much to my relief, we celebrated again and again until the sun's rays slanted through the trees that witnessed the joining of bodies and the joining of souls. We passed the rest of the afternoon honoring ourselves and each other, enjoying being in each other's presence.

Leaving the hill, I held her hand. Her face glowed with an angelic look and a smile.

The rest of the afternoon Red Fox spent his time in solitude. He remembered the sequence of events leading up to his selection for this assignment. He recalled how ambitious he felt when he first got word of the call for a young person to build a model of the Serpent. At the time the very thought aroused all his senses so much that he could barely contain himself. After he knew he was selected, his chest puffed out and his head swelled. His emotions crashed after hearing the story from Shining Bird that day. His ego deflated by an impending sense of responsibility. He choked on it and felt unable to speak. He asked himself the meaning of his feelings.

Red Fox could not fathom why his feelings were in such turmoil, or why he felt sick to his stomach. Then his insides cramped, and he doubled over when he was trying to quietly reflect. Why did he feel unnerved? Why did he sense he would be engaged in something more than just building a model that looked like a snake? He realized that this was something that he did not comprehend. A snake. No big deal. If he could put bird's nests back together, what could possibly be so difficult about modeling a body of a snake? Can't be *that* hard.

He had thought he knew so much. He felt so grand to be the chosen one to create something no one else either could do or wanted to do.

After hours of reflection and self-talk, Red Fox spoke to his Grandmother, Blue Lightning, about it. He put his hand on her arm as if to frame his intent, his eyes glued to her eyes. He wanted to know. When he asked her, she stood silent for an eternity. All he could hear was the thumping of his heart. All he could feel physically was his pulse throbbing. All he attended to was the great mystery swimming around in his head.

"What are the meanings of my feelings, Grandmother?" he asked again.

At last, Blue Lightning said, "Your feelings are a source of information. It is good that you acknowledge them and pay attention to them. It is good that you seek what they are telling you." He nodded his head in acceptance of what she said with his brows still furrowed. The question mark remained on his face.

She took his arm in both of her aged, wrinkled hands. "What I see in you is a talented young man. You are fifteen summers old and have spent much time pursuing what your heart desires. This is a good thing. What your heart desires is to build, to create, to manifest what you see in your mind's eye. You have spent much time studying these things as you found them in nature, the nests of birds, for example.

"When you were selected, the sense of acknowledgement, the sense of praise and prestige, the sense of being honored for your talent went to your head. Your ego began running you. It ran what you said, how you said it, and how you acted. You were seen knocking on Singing Hawk's door and waiting there for hours, looking in her windows, stomping your feet, and behaving like you were owed something. What a sense of disappointment it was for the community to see you behave like this.

"What you don't know is that you were selected for your heart and soul, then for your talent. Many were considered. You were the one selected. It is your heart and soul that they saw in you, combined with your intellect and talent that makes you so valuable in this effort."

Still holding his arm in her two hands, they moved to sit down. He sensed she had a lot more to say.

Red Fox looked up at her as she continued, "When you come from your heart, you sense the right thing to do. Your heart guides you to make the right choices for yourself, and for yourself among others as you interact with others. Great Spirit speaks to you through your heart. When your heart is open, you can hear, you can feel Great Spirit move through you. Your heart, your soul, and then your mind connect easily when this happens, and you always do the right thing, even if it doesn't seem like it at the time. What is thought and felt is acted out in behaviors. The body is part of this scenario. Your body is the medium, as it were, to experience . . . to experience your emotions and the result of your thoughts and words.

"Tell me, Red Fox," she asked, "what did you feel when you first learned you were chosen?"

He looked to the ceiling of his house for an answer, stuck out his tongue for an instant, licked his lips, and then pursed them before responding. His eyes opened wide as he spoke using an arm to point to an imagined eagle flying overhead, "I felt like an eagle soaring above everyone. I was better than anyone. I was chosen. I felt special." His Grandmother nodded.

This is something she already knew.

With her eyes half closed, a brilliant light shined through them.

"I know," she said after a pause. "You acted like you were above everyone else, like you were somehow better than the rest of us."

He hung his head, eyes dropped down, and he said. "It's true. That's what I felt."

Grandmother continued, "Then what happened?"

He tilted his head to his left and looked up to the right working to remember.

Angrily, he said, "Singing Hawk wouldn't let anyone in for several days. I couldn't believe it. Here I am chosen to do this work, and she shut me out. I'm supposed to work with her to make the model, and she wouldn't even let me in. So I went to the pond with Gray Wolf and Shining Bird today."

Grandmother nodded again and said, "Singing Hawk has spent the last three days in a sweat lodge. She's cleansing herself and seeking inspiration for the work she knows she must do with you. She has a responsibility to share ancient knowledge with you. She has been preparing herself for giving you what only few know, fewer comprehend . . . and even fewer can apply."

"Oh," is all he could say in reply.

"Continue," his Grandmother prompted.

Red Fox finishes his story, "So, I'm a mess. My friends seem sympathetic, and talking with them just upset me more. Shining Bird tells me the story of how the Serpent Mound was created and why. She hinted that there's much for me to learn. It's not just sculpting a snake in clay. I now realize that I must make an exact replica, with all of its nuances of meaning, and that much significance is embedded in it.

"I felt like I took a huge blow to the chest, then one to the gut when Shining Bird spoke to me. I spent hours suffering an internal struggle that caused me to throw up. I was in so much pain. That's when I knew I had to see you and talk with you about the meaning of it all."

Grandmother squinched up her mouth and wrinkled her nose, closed her eyes, seeking a response to her grandson's situation. Finally when she lifted her head and opened her eyes, she said, "When you felt high like a soaring eagle, you were feeling you were better, more elevated, than the rest of us. That feeling comes from your ego telling you that. When you listen to ego, like you did, you fragment yourself from the rest of us, and from Great Spirit. When you feel separate from others, your ego talks you into feeling special, because you are somehow better than everyone else, for whatever reason. As you separate yourself from others through your sense of feeling better than others, you separate yourself from Great Spirit also. This sense of separation is destructive.

"So, when you stomped around after banging on Singing Hawk's door and windows, did that improve the state of things? Did that behavior get you what you wanted? In all of that, did you stop to think that Singing Hawk might have had a reason for shutting down?" asks Grandmother.

She peered at her grandson, and then said, "Having a sense of separation from others drives ethics. When carried to an extreme, it becomes acceptable to ignore, punish, hurt or even kill others with impunity, without repercussion. Having a sense that we are separate from each other justifies this conduct as being appropriate. It comes simply because others don't fit *our* idea of what is right, or *we* don't approve of them.

"In truth, we all come from the Great Oneness. Our Creator is Great Spirit. We, each of us, are offspring of Great Spirit, an individualized spirit of The Great Oneness. That makes us all part of the One."

Red Fox's stomach started to settle down, and his body begins to relax. The energy of what his Grandmother told him began to heal his self-inflicted emotional wounds.

Grandmother paused a moment and then said, "The People acknowledge the importance of experiencing the consciousness of being at-one with our Creator. You've heard of the word 'at-one-ment'?" she asked him rhetorically, as she continued, "It means in the state of being at one with . . . Great Spirit. So, neither you, nor I, nor anyone can be 'better' or 'higher' than anyone else."

Red Fox began to stretch his body out a little more, giving a sign he was relaxing and moving through the emotional turmoil. He took a breath, leaned forward, indicating his willingness to hear more of what she had to say. He felt her words are healing his pain.

"Now, remember, my precious little one," Grandmother said lovingly, encouraged by Red Fox's physical response to her words. "Remember, that an ethic is not a rule to tell us what to do all the time. An ethic is not concerned with outcome. It is not value driven. An ethic drives behavior according to what you feel is right. Therefore, the question becomes, 'What is the right thing to do in this instance?'"

"Yes, Grandmother, how do I know what is the right thing to do?" Red Fox interrupted.

Grandmother paused, tilted her head slightly, bit her lip, and then said, "Before you can ask 'what is the right thing to do in any instance?' you must first ask the questions, 'what is my responsibility and what is my power to influence?' These two things go hand in hand.

"Power and responsibility must equal each other. A equals A. Remember, you have power over which you have responsibility. And the opposite is also true. You are responsible for that over which you have power. If you exercise power over that which is not your responsibility, then you become out of balance and behaviors become dysfunctional. If you do not have the power over which you are held responsible, you also become out of balance.

"You must always ask, 'what is my responsibility and do I have the power to influence the outcome?' Only after you have answered these two questions, can you then ask, 'What is the right thing to do, in each instance?'

"So, to answer your question of how do you know what the right thing to do is, your heart tells you. The right thing will be what is appropriate in each situation. Your heart will tell you. You must always listen to your heart. Allow it to be open, so that you can feel or hear Great Spirit speaking to you. You can trust the still, small voice speaking to you when you listen to your heart. It's about trust. It's about trusting the Great Oneness, trusting the voice of Spirit. That voice is the Great Spirit." Grandmother finally released her grip on his arm and gently held on to it with one hand and stroked it with the other as they sat in the middle of the house.

Red Fox then asked, "Yes, and how do I do this? How do I know? How do I make that happen?"

Grandmother sat back, stretched a little, and breathed in deeply before responding, "Your mind is a powerful tool. Never underestimate its power as a resource. You'll be using it in a way you have never imagined as you study the information that Singing Hawk has for you. As powerful as your mind can be, it still must serve your heart.

"Whenever you are uncertain as to what you should do, always bring your mind into your heart. Think through your heart. As you bring your head into your heart, you can start talking to the spirit within you. You will know in a way you can't explain in any other terms, that Great Spirit is speaking to you, guiding you to make the choices appropriate at the time.

"But . . . a problem sometimes comes up, something of which you must be aware so that you don't get taken in again," she cautioned him. "You were obviously taken in by this when you were at Singing Hawk's house. You thought you were better than others. That thought comes from your intellect, your mind, which often gives rise to the expression of ego. Your ego influenced you into thinking that you had the power to control others, to make them do what you want, because you want it.

"You had no real power in this situation, because you had no responsibility to make happen what you wanted to have happen. You behaved as if your power was thwarted. What you didn't take into account was that your only responsibility was to show up, to let Singing Hawk know that you were a willing participant in the process. That's all. As it was her responsibility to accept you as a student in this matter, she had the power to let you in, or not. You were not separate from the equation. Yet, your ego directed you to behave like you were the center, rather than a participant, in the process.

"When your ego runs you, your free will chooses behaviors that show you feel superior to others, and therefore separate from others. This feeling superior to others, and fragmented from them, can become a habit. When that happens, your intellect persuades you into thinking that it is, and should be, the source to which you listen.

"The intellect can be very powerful. One of the lessons you are learning is increasing your level of awareness. When you are not aware, you can easily get taken in by it. Then you assume that the intellect is always reliable. The intellect, especially when it is very powerful in a person, is useful for problem solving, useful in applying mathematics and analyzing issues. However, it is not the source for determining the answer to doing the right thing." As Grandmother finished speaking she now tilted her head and turned to look Red Fox in the eye to confirm that he comprehended.

Grandmother Blue Lightning continued, "So when people get taken in by the intellect, they start to think that what comes from the combination of the intellect, the ego, and then free will, is 'the heart.' Yes, it is a trinity, a trinity of separation, not the Trinity of Great Spirit. Many people do not realize that it is a false heart, so to speak. Now everyone has the heart in their soul that is the doorway or passage through which Great Spirit speaks to you. It's just that some people close that off and do not listen to it. We sometimes refer to them as those having two-hearts. Two-hearted people come from a way of seeing the world that is different from our way of seeing. Their worldview is one of separation."

"Oh," Red Fox lifted his voice in question, "I see. So, when I behaved like I did at Singing Hawk's house, The People saw me as a person acting as separate from them, and thought I was a person of two-hearts?"

Grandmother nodded, squinched her mouth again, and said with a tear in one eye, "Yes. They also hoped it would be temporary. Just because you act like that once, doesn't mean you are a two-hearted person. Sometimes we are provided an opportunity to experience the negative side of our being, so we can better appreciate the positive side."

"Grandmother," Red Fox asked after a brief pause, "tell me about the Trinity of Great Sprit, since it is different from the trinity of separation."

In response, Grandmother closed her eyes for a moment, opened them and looked at her grandson and said, "The Trinity of Great Spirit is another way to understand our oneness. The Great Oneness created everything in all of the Heavens and beyond even what we can know. And The Great Oneness *is* all of this creation as well, because It created all of this from within Itself.

"Many trinities exist within all Creation.

"We sometimes call It our Creator. Often we personalize our relationship to this vast and complex Oneness by calling It 'Great Spirit.' The particular Trinity of Great Spirit that we are talking about right now is a three-part relationship between the soul, the heart, and the body. We have already discussed that Great Spirit speaks to us through our hearts.

"Our souls are made of the same substance as Great Spirit. Our soul is our connection to Great Spirit. The heart is the direct line of communication between our soul and Great Spirit. That's why it is so important to keep our hearts open and to listen to our hearts."

"What about the body? How does that relate?" asked Red Fox.

"Good question," she said, "the body is the expression of all of this in the physical world. The body is the vehicle used to express all of this as we interact with each other and Mother Earth. Our souls are the same substance as Great Spirit. When we as a spirit operate a physical body, we are spiritual beings having a physical experience. As a result the body becomes part of the trinity, the Trinity of Great Spirit. It is three in one.

Red Fox heaved a great sigh of relief. "Grandmother, I feel so much better. Thank you for helping me see some things I did not know before."

He stopped for a moment and reflected. He stood up and stretched his body as he contemplated a question, not knowing exactly how to formulate it. Finally he said, "So help me to understand something more, if you would, please, Grandmother." Grandmother Blue Lightning still sitting looked up at her grandson, smiled with a radiance waiting for his question.

"So . . . if Great Spirit is the Power and Source of everything in the world, including giving life energy to Mother Earth, and to us, then why does the trinity of separation exist? Why doesn't Great Spirit just automatically *make* us do the right thing? Why do we have to search our heart for the right thing to do and then act it out in behaviors?"

The radiance coming from Grandmother's face increased. She felt rewarded that her grandson had heard her and was thinking about what she had told him.

Grandmother thought a moment and then said, "Great Spirit gave us free will for a reason. Great Spirit will never overrule the expression of free will. You use your free will all day long. While you make choices all day long, it's the choices that involve how you behave to others that matter. When you make them using only your intellect, your ego or both, and not your heart, you reinforce your sense of separation . . . separation from others, and often separation from yourself.

"When you make destructive choices, Great Spirit will not interfere with your free will. These kinds of choices will cause much destruction in your life, destruction of relationships, destruction of chances to improve your situation, destruction in many things. As this occurs, you can feel pain, emotional pain, physical pain, and even bad health. This causes deep suffering. At any point along the way, you can still use your free will to change, to make different choices . . . and that's the point. Creator gave us free will so we can *freely* choose Great Spirit as our Guide." Grandmother heaved a sigh after saying this.

Then she said, "We each have been given special talents and gifts by the Creator. We have the choice to use these to benefit ourselves. You have a gift that you are now being called upon to use. This opportunity gives you the power to meet your responsibility. It is your responsibility to express it and develop it to benefit yourself . . . and the community.

"Now go," she ordered Red Fox. "You must go and reflect on these things. Go now and wait for Singing Hawk to welcome you to her storehouse of Ancient Knowledge. If you have more questions, come back and we will talk again."

"The curves of the Serpent are *sine waves*," whispered Shining Bird covertly to Red Fox as he looked at a sketch of the Great Serpent. Then she added, "Each curve represents a different frequency, though." She quickly moved away from her friend when she saw Singing Hawk return.

Red Fox watched Singing Hawk carrying in bundles of birch bark scrolls. He would soon know what had been etched onto them.

"Sine waves?" questioned Red Fox under his breath, anxious to learn everything he could. He felt more than overwhelmed by his task as his stomach turned over in both trepidation and eagerness to begin the project.

Earlier that morning, Red Fox remembered Singing Hawk beckoning him into the teaching room, "Red Fox, come in. I've been expecting you. I've heard what you discovered in examining bird's nests and how you explained that to one of our Elders as a new way to make better homes in our village. That tells me that you have some very special gifts. Equally important is your willingness to travel from village to village telling the story of the Great Serpent.

"I heard that many were unwilling to assume this task, because it required the making of a very exact model of the Serpent. With your skills, I'm pleased that you're participating."

"I've been asked to get you started and give you the tools, supplies and the knowledge that you'll need to accomplish this task. You must do this completely by yourself. This will be part of your training. It will develop your talents. Now tell me what you know of the Great Serpent."

As he retold the story, Singing Hawk nodded and asked, "Red Fox, do you have any questions?"

Red Fox answered, "I have been studying the Great Serpent. How it lies on the plateau, its shape and how it curves upon the land. I've seen how the end of the plateau on which it rests even looks like a Serpent's head. I've been in the small cave that represents the underworld.

"From the time I was a small child, my parents took me to the Summer Solstice ceremony each year. I watched Father Sun set in exact alignment with the Serpent's head. My parents have also taken me to the Equinox sunrises and the Winter Solstice sunrise ceremonies that are marked by two of the curves of the Serpent's body.

"I am quite concerned about my ability to accurately make a scale model of this symbol and honor the great knowledge of our ancestors and their promises to Mother Earth. I've never attempted anything like

7

RED FOX BUILDS THE MODEL

Red Fox's task was to build a six-foot scale model of the Great Serpent Mound, which was over a quarter of a mile long. Red Fox was completely focused on the drawings of the Serpent on the scrolls as he sat on a stool at a worktable in the teaching room at Singing Hawk's.

The drawings depicted how his ancestors had designed it to follow the contours of the land on which it rested. He was waiting for Singing Hawk to return, so she could confirm the accuracy of his work so far. One question he had was his accuracy of his interpretation of the design equations. He kept going over his mathematical formulas, checking and double-checking his work.

So absorbed in his work was he that he had not noticed Singing Hawk standing in the doorway. His intellect had become so engaged with problem solving that awareness of everything outside of that mental zone he had created faded away.

A soft breeze carrying the scent of fresh nut cakes pulled him back to reality. As he turned his head, he saw Singing Hawk smiling down at him.

"How's it going?" she asked.

Her student looked up at her, opened his eyes wide, with a half-smile and half-grimace, and shrugged his shoulders.

"You've been at it for hours. Perhaps you need a break and something to eat. Floating Lily stopped by with some treats from Raven's Wing, and I have brewed a pot of tea," Singing Hawk said as she set the refreshments down on the worktable.

"Singing Hawk, I was not aware that you had come back," Red Fox said as he smiled in greeting. "I have a lot of questions." Then he said knitting his eyebrows as he spoke, "I want to make sure that I am on the right path here in my calculations. I'm sure glad I paid attention when I was learning math, because this trigonometry stuff is really making me stretch." They both giggled at his remark.

He continued, "I have this large rough draft. I've only gotten as far as the first curve." He paused as he pointed to the work he had accomplished so far. He looked up at her to ensure he had her attention.

Then he looked back down at his equations and added, "And . . . I'm not sure I've correctly done the scale model calculations. As you see, I've quite a few separate drawings in progress." He paused again to shuffle through several drawings. She bent over and looked at what he was showing her. Red Fox finished, "And, when I felt I had a section properly worked out, I transferred it to the big one, here, that I will use to mold the actual clay model." He pointed to the sketches on the worktable and then to the large tanned buckskin lying on the floor.

Singing Hawk took her time to review the work he had done so far, raising her eyebrows up and down, pursing and unpursing her lips all the while. "Well, it's certainly a good start," she said finally. Then, she added thoughtfully with a nod, "I see you understand the equations. And I see that you are using the various copper measuring devices and drafting tools properly."

Pausing again to review with head tilted to one side and back again before speaking, she said, "I like the way you decided to break down this large task into sections. It's more efficient that way, rather than attempting to tackle the whole thing at once."

She lifted her eyes up and looked off into the distance momentarily before speaking again. Then she whispered with a smile, "Indeed, that is the way that our Ancient Ones planned out each of the very large ceremonial earthworks. Sometimes they placed evenly spaced dirt markers on the ground to form an outline before constructing the earthen walls.

"For the Great Serpent, they traced out the shape of its body by using clay mixed with ashes along its entire length. They engineered our other grand earthworks in much the same way that you're approaching this task, section by section, once the master plan had been devised. According to everything I know about our ancestors, they always kept in mind the larger picture, continually verifying the correctness of each section in relation to the next and in relation to the overall design." Her face shone as she spoke, and her eyes glistened with a faraway light.

Silence.

Red Fox by this time succumbed to the tempting cakes, filled with morsels of meat in a savory gravy, and tea begging for attention. As he ate, Singing Hawk reached for a few more scrolls not yet unfolded, and then began again.

"As you know, the land on which the Great Serpent lies is not level," she said with a nod to him, ignoring the bite he had just stuffed into his mouth. "If you recall from walking around the Serpent, the land also undulates and drops down from the tail to the head of the Serpent."

He acknowledged her comment with several nods with his mouth full of cake.

She continued, "Their design took this into account, of course. The Serpent flows with the shape of the land. In spots where erosion might occur, they first placed beds of gravel before constructing the body. This would allow the rainfall and snowmelt to percolate through the body of the Serpent to reduce the amount of erosion. You might not know this, but they used special clays, sands and earth to insure that the Serpent would remain for a very long time.

"In other words, they built it to last. They intended it to speak to future generations of The People and to those who would follow," Singing Hawk said with a sigh that sounded like it came from far away.

After Red Fox had finished eating, he felt his body refreshed and his mind renewed to again tackle his task at hand. Seeing that her student appeared ready to continue, she began again.

"Let's see how you're doing. I want to look at it a little more closely. Perhaps I can give you some suggestions and observations." With a finger pointing to a space somewhere and nowhere, she reminded him, "Remember, that although the Serpent is over a quarter of a mile in length, it is still based on our standard long measure of 1053 feet. Each of its sections is a lesser multiple of this standard measure." Singing Hawk then unrolled several more birch bark scrolls.

After stretching them out so they both could see them, she pointed to one drawing.

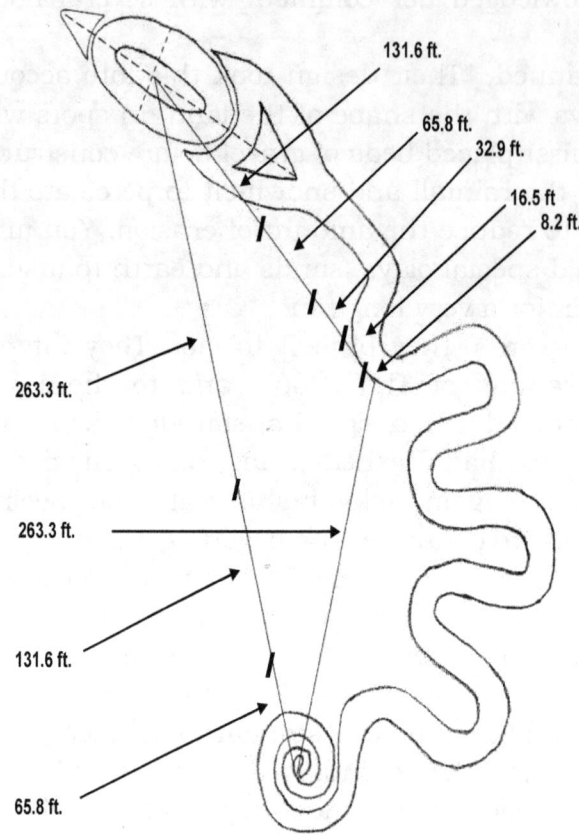

Redrawn and adapted from Romain 2000: 241 Fig. A.5

"As you can see, here, for example, the distance from the center of the oval, to the tip of the tail, is made up of sections of proportioned measurements."

Red Fox cocked his head to the side for a moment as he thought about what she had just said. Then he asked, "Well, can I just ask this?" She stepped back a moment as if to grant permission for the question. He looked up at her as he asked, "Can't I just draw a straight line from the center of the oval to the tip of the tail without marking the individual measurements that make up the total?"

"Actually, . . . no," his teacher responded softly with eyes down and with a tone of voice indicating no challenges would be tolerated. Red Fox shifted in his seat uncomfortable at her answer. She went on to explain, ignoring his discomfort. "That's a good question, though. The thing you must know is the individual measurements here are used as bench marks or reference points for other points on the body of the Serpent." She pointed to them on the drawing as she spoke. "This is where these other drafting and measuring tools come into play." As she spoke, she selected several of the copper devices to show him.

"Let me show you," she offered as she moved several pieces onto the scroll they were both looking at. "By placing them on these sub-measurement points, you can see how this helps in orienting the undulation curves and other alignments of the body. In effect, you can triangulate a detailed latticework of lines which enables you to construct an overriding matrix of arcs and angles from each of the waypoints to keep all the various sections in a harmonious relationship. As you can see, this can become rather complicated unless you proceed, as you have done, step by step, section by section."

Red Fox wiggled in his seat, obviously excited about what he was learning. Singing Hawk stood close to the worktable alongside Red Fox. She pointed to another portion of the same scroll. As she did so, Red Fox's mouth dropped open. The pupils of his eyes dilated at what he was seeing as if his eyes could not capture enough.

"The notations on this scroll show how the standard long measure of 1053 is divided by two, thus creating ever decreasing proportionate lengths.

"So, you can see how using these lesser multiples makes it easier to apply your equations in creating your master drawing on the buckskin hide," she added with nods of her head and then turned to look at him to see that he comprehended. He turned to look at her in response, his mouth still slightly open as he processed the information.

"Let's look at these drawings on these other scrolls," she said. "You see how these various reference points demonstrate the geometric relationships with all the other various points on the body of the Serpent?" She bent slightly to look at him. He nodded again in response. "This will assist you in lining everything up, making the arcs for the curves, and most importantly, keeping all the parts in their proper relationship to one another," Singing Hawk said placing her hand on his shoulder.

After allowing sufficient time for this information to sink in, Singing Hawk sighed before saying, "Now, we've discussed the alignments in the body of the Serpent in relationship to Father Sun and Sister Moon. These alignments were determined by our Ancient Ones. These alignments were based upon their observations of the travels of Father Sun and Sister Moon made from the plateau on which the Great Serpent lays."

Red Fox shifted in his seat again to sit more erect to better absorb everything she was telling him.

As she pointed again to the drawings before them, she said, "As you can see from this drawing, if you draw a straight line from the center of the tail to the tip of the triangle in the Serpent's head, it will point directly to the North Star." At this remark, Red Fox turned his head toward her quickly as if to verify what he had just heard.

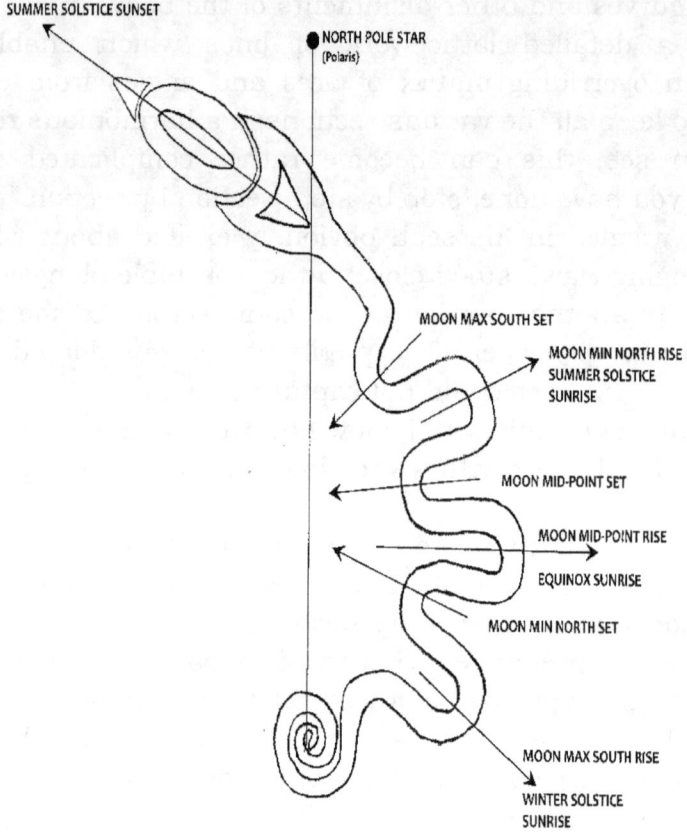

Redrawn and modified from Romain 2000, Fig. A.10; Hamilton 2001, Fig. 3

Singing Hawk heard the unasked question and answered, "Yes, indeed." He raised his eyebrows in acknowledgement. After a slight pause, his instructor went on.

"From this baseline then, the shapes of the curves were designed to mark Sister Moon's waypoints along her journey through the heavens."

"I am not sure I completely understand this." Red Fox said as he rubbed his head.

"Think of it this way," Singing Hawk responded. "As you know, Father Sun at the Summer Solstice has his most northern sunrise and sunset. Now, the Winter Solstice marks his southernmost rise and set. He does this every year then returns back again. This comprises one year of our time.

"Sister Moon, being part of our cosmic family, has a similar cycle every month along the horizon as she revolves between a northerly and southerly extreme.

"However, what we are talking about here is a very slow lunar cycle of her rising and setting points on the horizons over a period of about 18.6 years, nearly a generation of time. It takes her this amount of time to go from her northernmost point of rising on the horizon to her southernmost point and then back to the north to complete the full cycle.

"As you will learn at the Newark earthworks, the circle and octagon observatory marks the northernmost moonrise. Here at the Great Serpent earthwork, we mark Sister Moon's maximum southern rise," Singing Hawk said while watching for a sign that Red Fox comprehended this information.

"I see. It is like a pendulum swinging back and forth. And so it would be about 9.3 years for Sister Moon to move from the northernmost to the southernmost moonrise. And the mid-point rise and set would mark the halfway point in her cycle. Is that right?" asked Red Fox.

"Yes, that's correct," Singing Hawk said with a smile, pleased that he understood.

"I realize that you may already know this, and I will continue just to make sure. As shown on this scroll, these same curves mark the Summer Solstice, Equinox and Winter Solstice sunrises. I know that you have witnessed many times the Summer Solstice sunset. It is shown by this line from the tip of the triangle in the Serpent's head through the center of the oval on through the triangle in front of the oval," Singing Hawk said.

"You know this, because we celebrate the Summer Solstice here at the Great Serpent." He nodded. She continued, "We witness the sun setting in perfect alignment with the Serpent's head. As Father Sun goes down, the final rays shine through our mica structure that we place on the front triangle for just this occasion."

"But what does that have to do with the math I am working on here?" he asked.

Singing Hawk patted the air with her right hand then replied, "It has to do with everything. The thing is, in this ceremony, The People honor Father Sun setting at the horizon to the west on the Solstice day, the day that he stops his travels in one direction and shifts direction to begin traveling back again to the south in a rhythmic cycle. We acknowledge a year's passing from one Summer Solstice to the next. It's part of the cosmic rhythm of life that we celebrate as a renewal of all of life." Red Fox shifted position as he listened intently.

"As you also know from participating in the ceremony," she went on uninterrupted, "The People celebrate the entire night and await Father Sun's reappearance on the eastern horizon as part of the renewal of life as we know it. And we give prayers of gratitude for it especially on that occasion.

"Renewal of life as celebrated by this particular ceremony is a recognition that Mother Earth remains in balance. Our ceremonies are about giving gratitude for the harmony of the cosmic rhythms. Should a disruption occur, Mother Earth could fall out of balance. She could shift in such a way that we would see Father Sun rising in the west.

"Should that occur, life as we know would become challenging. This is why the Great Serpent's head points to the west on the evening of the Summer Solstice. It's a warning and a reminder that we want to stay in balance with each other and with Mother Earth . . . and most of all, help keep Mother Earth in balance."

Red Fox rubbed his chin contemplating what he had just heard and then said, "What I didn't realize until just now is the fact that the moonrise points correspond to the Solstice and Equinox sunrises. This is amazing."

Singing Hawk said, "Our Ancient Ones calculated the cosmic cycles, so that the Serpent, as well as our other earthworks, point to these alignments in the heavens. This is the reason we require such mathematical and geometric accuracy. As a people, we have grown to rely on this accuracy for our traditions. Should these alignments shift, we will know."

Red Fox turned more of his body toward his teacher, looked down, then up again and said, "I am beginning to see this." Singing Hawk turned her body slightly toward him as he continued to comment. "Grandmother Blue Lightning told me about how our earthworks are aligned to events occurring in the Heavens. While I did not completely understand what she was telling me at the time, it's becoming clearer now that I have actually used the math and studied these scrolls.

"My Grandmother Whistling Wind told me how our system of measurement is used in all of our earthworks.

"Yes," Shining Hawk said, "symmetry and geometric compatibility dominated the intellectual processes of the Ancient Ones when constructing our monuments. Part of their agenda was to reflect back on to the Earth plane what they knew of the cosmos."

Red Fox interrupted, "as above, so below."

"Exactly," she confirmed then added thoughtfully, "Although . . . that's not the only way to demonstrate this principle."

He smiled at her acknowledgement and turned back to the worktable. Singing Hawk paused thoughtfully, looked down then directly at him. She touched his shoulder to get his attention for what she needed to say next.

"Now, there are additional cosmic alignments that you need to know about that occur at the same time as the Summer Solstice."

"Really? There's more?" he asked.

She nodded emphatically.

"How should I put this?" she asked out loud. "Let me see." She paused briefly to formulate her thoughts then spoke, "Newark and High Bank are major ceremonial sites. They are our ceremonial doorways to the spirit world and the Great Mystery beyond our five senses. You will be visiting these sites on your journey. You will see the White Road of Sister Moon.

"This road connects both of these ceremonial sites. You will get to walk on it while on your journey, so you might want to make a mental note of it as you study these scrolls. This road is about sixty miles long and provides, not only a direct connection between these two locations, but something more . . . something more cosmic."

With this remark, Red Fox's attention was suddenly alerted to what she was about to reveal. His eyes widened in anticipation.

"Yes, Red Fox, something more," she repeated with eyebrows raised. "The People celebrate the Summer Solstice at other places besides the Great Serpent. However, at the time of the Summer Solstice, those walking on the White Road of Sister Moon can look up to the heavens and see the Milky Way directly overhead."

"What?" he asked.

"Yes, Red Fox," she clarified, "the Milky Way is a gathering of stars. It also is the passageway for souls traveling to and from the spirit world. The White Road of Sister Moon was built in alignment precisely parallel to the Milky Way at the specific time of the Summer Solstice."

Red Fox scratched his head again and put up a hand to signal he needed to ask a question. She looked down and paused her lecture.

Red Fox saw the opening and asked, "So, if I understand this correctly, our Ancient Ones knew of the Milky Way configuration with the timing of the Summer Solstice? Are you saying, they built Newark and High Bank at their exact positions based in part on this alignment?"

"Yes," she replied, "they are observatories to cosmic events. However, what I want to emphasize is that at this particular time, and I mean at the Summer Solstice, a spectacular configuration occurs.

"Imagine the night sky lighting up with the Milky Way. See it in your mind's eye as a white pathway in the sky. Then in your mind's eye, draw a line from the eastern horizon at the point of the Solstice sunrise to the point of the Solstice sunset. Being a perpendicular line to the Milky Way, it divides the heavens into four equal quadrants, which represent the four directions. Then see the White Road of Sister Moon

THE CAMP OF GOD'S TEARS

directly below the Milky Way in a perfect relationship, as in 'as above, so below'."

Then Red Fox gulped hard. While sitting there listening, Red Fox felt a wave of warm energy course through his body as the threads of different colors and textures woven in the warp and woof of this gigantic cosmic tapestry fell into place in his mind's eye.

He said, "If I understand this correctly, there is a balanced relationship of the Milky Way Summer Solstice alignment with the White Road of Sister Moon. It includes heaven, stars, Father Sun, Sister Moon, Mother Earth, the souls of our ancestors, the souls of those yet to be born, all coming together at one time and one place. It is a point in time when everything that is moving around the cosmos including Earth, come into a celestial alignment of perfect balance. It evidences renewal of the cycles of life, both in Heaven and Earth.

"This is what we celebrate," he said happily. "It's the celestial alignment in this configuration. If any one of these elements should fall out of balance, one with another, then life as we know it would come to an end."

At this last comment, Singing Hawk smiled broadly and tousled his hair with affection, then acknowledged with a nod, "Well done, my son. Your Grandmothers Blue Lightning and Whistling Wind taught you well. The three of us studied together."

After several weeks had passed, one late afternoon after all other students of Singing Hawk had left for the day, Shining Bird and I strolled into the large teaching room. Finding no one there, we moved on into the smaller teaching room in the back. We found Red Fox sitting on his stool bent over the table completely unaware of our presence.

Finally, Shining Bird disturbs the silence as she says, "So, that's what Red Fox looks like. It's been so long since I've seen him, I almost forgot what he looked like."

Red Fox looks up. Shining Bird grins so big that Red Fox cannot help but grin back.

Red Fox clumsily shifts off his stool. "I've been sitting there like that for so many hours, I think my body thought it should freeze in that position," he says as he greets us. "I'm sure glad to see you both. I'm learning so much. Sometimes I think my head might explode with all the detailed information. Then applying it to a physical model, well, all I can say is 'wow!'

"I can't tell you how happy I've been studying and learning and working," Red Fox says as he jerked his body in rhythm to his impromptu speech.

I reach toward my friend, grab his arm, squeeze and say, "We're so proud of you, and happy you are happy." Shining Bird nods in confirmation. I say, "We just needed to see you and give you support for what you're doing."

"So . . . when will it be done?" asks Shining Bird curiously.

"Well," he looks into both our faces as a light shines from his and answers, "after I finish here, building the model, that is, Singing Hawk must of course approve it. That comes after she has checked and doubled checked every measurement to ensure accuracy in its proportions and layout."

"Then will it be done?" Shining Bird asks again.

"All of that happens before it goes to the oven. I have to make it large enough to take into account shrinkage when it is fired," Red Fox says.

"Then will it be done?" she presses again.

"Well, no, not exactly," came the answer. "Then, naturally, Singing Hawk must again check it for accuracy after it is fired.

"Naturally," Shining Bird echoes. "Then will it be done?"

"Aaahh, no, not exactly," came the answer. "We have to make sure we have a steady frame on which to carry it. I'll be taking it to as many villages as possible. So we need to devise a way to do that."

"Then will it be done?" Shining Bird repeats.

Red Fox grimaces at the trial his friend is putting him through. Finally, he responds with frustration, "I really don't know. However long it takes, I guess. When all this is accomplished, I'll take it to my house so White Eagle can look at it."

"In other words," I interject, "it isn't done until White Eagle gives her approval, is that right?"

The three of us look at each other and grin.

"C'mon," I say, "let's get out of here. This conversation is getting entirely too serious. The three of us need to spend a little time together. We've some catching up to do. I'll bet my mother has something we could eat. Maybe, we could round up Water Dog, and maybe even Bluebird. We haven't been all together in a while. The five of us need to take some time together."

8

THE PROPHECY OF SERPENT MOUND

Whispering Rock, Red Fox's father, is impressed with the clay model of the Serpent that his son had made. He tells his son while nodding his head in affirmation, "You've done well and learned much." This makes my friend very happy. He will be using it in telling the Story of the Serpent throughout his journey to many villages, all in preparation for the Summer Solstice Ceremony. He still does not fully understand all of the mysteries of the Serpent. These mysteries are layered, one over the other.

Red Fox is excited about White Eagle coming to his home. She will review the model. She will question him about his knowledge to make certain that he understands the Serpent's significance to The People.

Red Fox was thinking about all that had happened since he began this project. Days before her visit he rehearsed his presentation with me. We were best friends, and I wanted him to do well. Because I studied much of the Ancient teachings, it made it easy for me to coach my friend. It was clear to me that Red Fox was gifted in designing, creating and building. I was impressed with his ability to craft the model of the Great Serpent.

The day arrived for White Eagle's visit.

"Red Fox, White Eagle is on her way and she will soon be here," announces Whispering Rock. At the signal of his father's words, Red Fox turns about and runs down the way to my house.

He knows I want to be with him when White Eagle arrives, and I know he needs me there for moral support. In anticipation, I wear my red ceremonial tunic, decorated with shells, feathers, and pearls for this occasion.

Just as he comes running up to my door, I stand up and step to the doorway ready to join him. Waving to my parents sitting on their bed talking leisurely, my mother gives me a nod that says she is proud of me. My father smiles the look of encouragement. As I turn to leave, I look to my Grandmother Shining Moon sitting on the other side of the room near the hearth. Her eyes glisten as she nods and waves in support.

Red Fox looks like he could jump out of his skin, and halts just before he gets to our door, surprised that I was already dressed and ready to go.

"Are you ready?" Red Fox asks nervously. I just look at him like he could not see the obvious.

"I feel so honored by the opportunity to speak with White Eagle. I just wish I wasn't so nervous," Red Fox says.

I say to my friend, "You're just scared that she might not like your work or ask you something you don't know. Don't worry, I know your model is accurate, and I will be there for you just in case. Singing Hawk is proud of you and your work. I have no doubt that White Eagle will be pleased too."

Red Fox expresses doubt on his face, "I don't know. I guess I am a little intimidated by the highest Elder and Grandmother visiting me, checking me out. You have to admit that's an honor." I nod in agreement.

When we arrive at his house, Red Fox kneels down and pulls out the model and its frame from beneath his bed. Together we lift it up to place it on the center table, bathed in sunlight filtering through the windows.

Laughing Willow, Red Fox's mother, had prepared a special tea and sweet cakes. His two Grandmothers, Blue Lightning and Whistling Wind, sat anxiously awaiting to hear Red Fox.

White Eagle was greeted in accordance to our ways as she entered. While he had been very nervous, a profound calmness came over Red Fox. He greeted her. When their eyes met and she held his hand, he felt warmness and love.

White Eagle went over to the table and examined the clay model with her sharp eyes.

No one breathed.

Anticipation froze the air.

After what seemed like an eternity, she smiled and said, "You have done well, my son." His heart almost jumped out of his chest.

White Eagle offered a prayer.

"Red Fox, you may now begin. Tell me the Story of how the Serpent Mound came to be," directs White Eagle.

As he begins to tell the Story, White Eagle sits down, as do his parents and Grandmothers. Red Fox stands as he speaks. I stand in the background so as not be noticed.

"Very good, Red Fox, you have learned well," says White Eagle after he had finished. "Now, tell me about the meaning of the shapes of the Serpent beginning with the tail."

Red Fox continues, "Before Mother Earth existed and before there was light, the universe was dark.

"The coils of the Serpent's tail represent the Great Mystery before Great Spirit began the creation of our universe, Mother Earth, Man, Woman and all the creatures.

"The spiraling action of the coil represents the Breath of Creation, which also brought light to this universe and our galaxy, the Milky Way.

"Great Spirit's Breath continues to expand and create, expand and create.

"As you can see, the Serpent's tail spirals around a small mound of dirt. This mound of dirt represents the Polar Star that does not move in our night sky. It guides us on our journeys. This mound of dirt also represents Mother Earth's spine that runs through her center. The Sacred Twins, who sit at the North and South Poles of her spine, send the vibrations of Mother Earth's heartbeat, through her spine and throughout all that lives in and on Mother Earth. One twin sits at the North Pole and the other at the South Pole. They are the guardians of the balance of Mother Earth, so that she spins to provide our days and nights. It also represents our own spines though which the vibrations of Mother Earth and Great Spirit give us life and knowledge."

White Eagle now asks him to discuss the first curve of the Serpent's body.

Red Fox responds, "The tail begins to uncoil and rises to make the first curve. This rise represents the beginning of the First World and the creation of Man, Woman and the first creatures.

"In the First World, Man, Woman, plants and all creatures were connected in the One. They could speak to one another and were not aware of any distinctions or separations between them. The animals and plants agreed to provide The People with what was needed to live. They lived in harmony with all that Mother Earth and Great Spirit had provided, and took only what they needed."

White Eagle asks, "How will this be shown in the Ceremony?"

Red Fox breathes in a moment then replies, "In the beginning of the Ceremony, you will see a man and a woman, who have been concealed by camouflage, rise up from the ground and start to walk around the coils. They will be joined by other dancers, symbolizing animals and plants of the First World. All will be dancing around each other as a way of showing they lived in harmony and balance. This world had its own frequency as shown by the shape of the first curve."

"The First World lasted a very long time and rose to great heights as shown by the height of the first curve." Red Fox's voice slightly increases in volume and animation while speaking clearly. He feels he is speaking a powerful truth.

He continues, "As time went on, disharmony and the sense of separation arose. The Serpent's body curving downward represents the growing disharmony. In the dramatization, the dancers will begin fighting as a result of feeling that they are separate from each other. This sense of separation causes the loss of harmony and balance in their hearts."

Red Fox looks around, lowers his head and raises his eyes to White Eagle, "You will notice that some of the dancers will have two red hearts painted on their chests. These will appear on some of the dancers as the Ceremony continues. These are the two-hearted people who have abandoned and rejected the ways of our ancestors. It is all part of the end of the First World."

"How did the First World end, Red Fox?" White Eagle asks.

"The First World came to an end here at the bottom of the first curve. It was destroyed by fire. In the Ceremony, its destruction by fire will be symbolized when wood placed around the first curve is set ablaze. Some of the dancers will act as if they are on fire and fall down pretending to be dead.

"Then an Elder appears. The dancers who represent The People will gather together with this Elder, standing apart from those with two hearts who are dying."

Taking in another big breath, Red Fox continues, "Only those few of The People who continued to follow the ways of Great Spirit were spared. Great Spirit asked the Ant People to shelter them in Mother Earth's womb while the great fires, volcanoes and earthquakes destroyed The First World. Several actors dressed like the Ant People join The Elder and dancers. The Ant People lead these dancers to the path that goes down the cliff toward the creek and to the cave opening. The cave represents the World of the Ant People, and the Womb of Mother Earth. They will remain there while the Ceremony continues."

"The Ant People had plenty of extra rooms and much stored food. As time went on their food supplies began to dwindle. Rather than depriving The People of the food they needed to survive, the Ant People kept tightening their belts. That is why Ants have such narrow waists today."

"Very good, Red Fox. Now tell me about the Second World and how its story will be told in the Ceremony," White Eagle gently says.

"The time came when Great Spirit decided to create the Second World. It would not be as easy to live upon because of damage created by the separations that destroyed the First World. When The People emerged from the World of the Ant People, Great Spirit spoke to them and told them that this world would not be as beautiful as the First World. Yet, if The People followed the Ways of Oneness, they would prosper. In this World the animals stayed away from The People and would not speak to them.

"Great Spirit will again appear and bring the dancers up from the cave for their emergence into the Second World. New dancers join them. Some will be dressed as animals, and when The People try to talk to them, the animals will run away. As before, all The People will appear to live in harmony and friendship.

"The People did spread far across the lands of the Second World. They built large villages, made things with their hands and stored food like the Ant People had taught them. As time passed, however, some began to trade and barter their goods and possessions with one another. While everything The People really needed was available, some wanted more and more of things they did not really need. They forgot to honor Mother Earth and Great Spirit. They began to sing praises for all things that they possessed. Little by little they moved away from the Ways of Oneness. They began to quarrel and fight among each other, and wars broke out between villages.

"As you see, the second curve rises to the top. Once again, disharmony and the sense of separation grew. The undulation of the Second World begins to curve downward, again, signaling spiritual decline.

"Many of The People continued to follow the Ways of Great Spirit. They were rejected by those others who saw no reason to follow the Ways of Oneness. The People continued to honor Mother Earth and Great Spirit and had to do so only in their hearts or risk attacks from those who scorned them.

"As before, fights and disagreements occur between the dancers. Some will appear to be worshipping material goods. Objects will be stolen or broken. This represents the return of disharmony. Note the shape of the second curve. Its frequency is different from the first.

"Great Spirit decided that the Second World must be destroyed and commanded the Sacred Twins to leave Mother Earth's spine at the North and the South Poles. With no one to control her rotations, Mother Earth lost balance, spun out of control and rolled over twice. She became covered with thick ice as she tumbled around in space. All that had been created by Man and Woman was destroyed. The Second World came to an end here at the bottom of the second curve."

Red Fox pauses and looks around to ensure he is still connecting with his listeners and continues. "In the Ceremony you will see this symbolized when the baskets of the white ash from our fires, representing ice, is spread over the Second World. Many of the dancers will shiver and fall down like they are freezing to death.

"Great Spirit once again asked the Ant People to protect The People, the true believers, in their underground homes, safe within the Womb of Mother Earth. Another Elder appears with the Ant People, who will once again take The People down to the cave.

"The People learned many more things from the Ant People. The People learned how to help the Ant People grow food underground. It was not tasty but did prevent hunger. The Ant People taught them how to organize themselves, so through organized efforts, they could accomplish more. This became very important. All of the old rooms were now filled. The People needed new places to live. The Ant People taught them how to move dirt efficiently and in great quantities. The People repaid the Ant People for their hospitality by building great living chambers, passageways and places to grow more food underground, so that the Ant People would continue to prosper. They all lived together in harmony for a very long time."

"Red Fox, please tell me about the creation of the Third World and how this will be shown in the Ceremony," White Eagle says as she shifts positions.

"Great Spirit decided it was time to begin the creation of the Third World and asked the Sacred Twins to return to their places at the Poles of Mother Earth. Mother Earth slowly righted herself and began rotating again.

"Now the Serpent's body again begins to rise creating the third curve. The ice melts and the world begins to warm. Great Spirit causes mountains to rise, rivers to flow, plants to grow, and creates the seas and lakes. Once again Mother Earth manifests life. The animals, birds, fish and all other creatures that made up the Third World appear. The Third World is now ready for the re-emergence of The People.

"Great Spirit spoke to the Ant People, 'You have once again served Me and my Children well. It is time for The People to emerge into the Third World.'

"As The People emerged from underground, Great Spirit greeted them and said, "this is the Third World. Your Remembers have told you about the two prior worlds. I have saved The People each time, because they were the only ones who continued to honor Me and Mother Earth. You have lived in harmony with all that I have created and with Mother Earth. Go forth and prosper, and remember your promises and honor the Ancient Wisdom of those who have gone before."

"Great Spirit will once again appear as the dancers are led from the cave and gather around the third curve of the Serpent. Once again they will be joined by a larger group of dancers. Things will appear to be going well and in harmony."

Red Fox puts his hand to his throat parched from his storytelling. Laughing Willow gets up, reaches for the large water ladle. She gently dips it in the water jug, then moves toward her son, handing him a drink. After accepting the refreshment, he looks at her gratefully then continues.

"In the First World, The People had lived simply with the animals. In the Second World, they had developed handicrafts, built homes and villages. As time went on in the Third World, The People spread even farther across the lands and greatly multiplied. They created big countries with many large cities. They created devices that crossed the land, crossed the great waters and devices made of metals that flew in the air. These devices were very fast and carried very powerful weapons that could destroy large cities. Great energy powered the civilizations that populated the Third World. As before, many lost the ways of old, failed to keep the ancient promises and became totally occupied with their earthly desires and pleasures. Soon thereafter, the great devices and the powerful energy they had created were used improperly. This was because of greed, lust, vengeance, hatred and the other frailties that demonstrate people feeling separate from each other and from their Source. Great wars killed millions, destroyed many cities and laid waste to Mother Earth.

"As before, those of The People who kept the Ways of Oneness suffered greatly from the ways of the two-hearted. Their lives had become very challenging. They prayed for guidance from Great Spirit and for protection as the threats to them were greater than ever before.

"Great Spirit appeared to the Elders in visions and told them to expect destruction of the Third World by a great flood that would cover the surface of Mother Earth. The instructions informed The People to cut down the huge bamboo-like plants that were hollow inside. They were told to gather together food, made from white corn meal and a supply of water. The two-hearted people saw this and, at first, just laughed at them. But as time went on, The People were threatened, and some of their houses were set on fire. When this occurred, Great Spirit once again spoke to the Elders in visions. The People were told to seal themselves inside the bamboo vessels that they had made when they hear a great sound that had never been heard before.

"In the Ceremony these events will be re-created by the dancers. There will be many models of our village homes that will be placed around the third curve of the Serpent. Dancers dressed as fierce warriors will have the flying devices in their hands that will rain fire down on the symbolic villages and set them ablaze. Others will fight with other groups of dancers causing symbolic death. The chaos will become frightening.

"An Elder will appear with bundles of reeds and lead the dancers representing The People down to the stream.

"Suddenly, Great Spirit caused the waters to flood all the lands with a great thunderous sound. Heavy rains fell and very strong winds raised the waters into destructive waves. The waters were so deep that even the great mountains were covered. All was destroyed.

"At this point the Serpent's third curve will be covered with deer hides painted with blue symbols representing the flood. The two-hearted dancers will be drenched with water by dancers dressed like clouds. They will act like they are swimming, then drowning and falling down pretending to be dead."

"Very good, Red Fox," White Eagle says, after taking a sip of her delicious tea. "Now tell me about how The People came to the Fourth World in which we are now living."

Red Fox looks at the Serpent and back to White Eagle, and then says, "Soon The People were floating on the flood waters and a powerful rain was falling. The waves kept moving them around with great force. One day the waves stopped. The water had become calm and the rain ceased. Although much time had passed, the food and water that they had lived on was always replenished by the Great Mystery. They had survived.

"One day their bamboo vessels came to rest against something. Carefully, The People opened the tops of the giant reeds and found that they had landed on a small piece of rocky land complctely surrounded by water.

"The Elders asked Great Spirit what was to become of them, because there was nothing but rock. The People were too many to live in this place. Great Spirit to them in dreams, saying, 'Use the giant bamboo vessels that you have been living in to construct rafts. You will now go on a long journey across the water on your rafts to find your place of emergence into the lands of the Fourth World. While you may encounter many new lands, look into your hearts, and you will be guided to the land that I have prepared for you. And remember, your journey of the heart will have just begun, as the Fourth World is one of duality.'

"Great Spirit said to The People, 'I have given you free will. You will get to choose which of many paths you will follow. You will get to choose the way in which you use the powers that I give you. The Fourth World is not as beautiful or as easy to live upon as the prior worlds. The ways in which you choose to exercise your free will is the determining factor as to whether The People will live in Oneness, or whether, in time, will manifest a sense of being separate from Oneness. The duality of the Fourth World will be a challenge to you. *Your future and the future of Mother Earth will depend on your choices'.*"

Standing in the shadows of the light, I remain motionless. I am so pleased with Red Fox's rendition of this Story. I smile to myself as he continues.

Red Fox goes on, "Great Spirit says to them, 'Remember always that guiding spirits will be there to help you, if you call upon them properly. Use your powers for the good of all concerned. Remember what I have told you and the ways of those who went before.'

"At this point in the ceremony, The People dancers, who have been waiting near the stream, will emerge with woven rafts. They will bring these rafts back to the top of the cliff and draw near with an Elder into the presence of Great Spirit. They will all be talking to the Elder and listening to Great Spirit, while standing on a mound of rocks that was prepared for the Ceremony.

"Other dancers will join the first group, and they will all begin paddling their rafts to and fro searching for their proper place of emergence into the Fourth World.

"After many adventures and long travels on their rafts The People found the place of beginning," Red Fox says and pauses a moment.

"At this point the dancers will gather at the beginning of the fourth curve. Great Spirit divides them, as our legends tell us, into four groups to represent the four colors of The People, brown, red, yellow and white.

"The dancers will now be dressed in garments representing the four colors of humankind. Great Spirit gives each group tablets upon which are inscribed sacred information and instructions for each group.

"As we are now living in the Fourth World, the shape of the fourth curve, and its frequency, is not yet fully determined. This is why the last curve is only partially formed," Red Fox concludes with sadness in his voice.

Silence.

Nodding in affirmation, White Eagle finally comments, "You have learned well the teachings of our ancestors. Now tell me about the Sacred Fire that will be lit at the end of the Ceremony."

"Now, at this point in the ceremony," Red Fox answers, "Father Sun will be slipping below the great waters to the west and entering the Land of Darkness. The last rays of Father Sun will illuminate the mica capstone that rests on the earthen triangle that is positioned in front of the oval.

"The three sided capstone is made of a mosaic of sheets of mica held together in wood and copper frames. Two sides are right triangles connected on their longest side and joined in the rear with an isosceles triangle. The isosceles triangle has been shaped as a convex lens.

"As light from the setting sun flows through the capstone, the rays intensify and illuminate the leading edge of the oval, signaling the time to light the Sacred Fire in the center of the oval. The fire will burn all night.

"Father Sun may choose not to return on his journey to the south or to start a new day. All night long we will be sending heart-felt prayers of acknowledgement and requests to Father Sun to stay on his path and to rise the next morning in the east. The celebration of dancing and music making will continue all night. We will greet Father Sun when he rises in the east in the morning." Red Fox finishes and sits down next to his parents.

White Eagle remains silent for some time after he finished.

Red Fox's mind races over all that he had said. He asks himself, "Did I leave anything out? Did I forget something important?" Sweat forms on his brow. He does not want to embarrass his parents.

White Eagle gets up and goes over to the table.

I could see that she is examining the four curves of the Serpent's body. Then she seems to focus on the Serpent's head, the oval and the two triangles. I could see Red Fox wrinkle his forehead slightly as if worried that he left something out.

"Red Fox and Gray Wolf," White Eagle says, "come over here to the table. I have some questions for you. Do you see how the shapes of the curves change from the First to the Fourth World?"

"Yes," we both answer simultaneously.

Now Red Fox is really nervous. He keeps flexing his hands while holding his arms stiffly at his sides. His eyes dart to me and back again to White Eagle.

Pointing to each of the curves of the Serpent, White Eagle asks, "Do either of you know what these differences represent?" Red Fox freezes, feeling he might have left something out.

I want to speak, and begin fidgeting and taking short breaths. I had something to say and did not want to intrude upon the moment.

A smile came to White Eagle's face and she says, "Gray Wolf, I think you have something you want to tell me."

"White Eagle, Red Fox may not know about what you are asking. I only recently learned of other stories from Singing Hawk."

"Yes, I know, Gray Wolf. I chatted with her this morning, and she spoke very highly of your skills and connection to Spirit. Tell me what you know," White Eagle says in a gentle, encouraging manner.

"The frequency vibrations, or sine waves, were very high at the time of the First World. At that time, Heaven was on Earth and the oval that we now see in the Serpent's mouth was then a circle. The Circle of Life, within which The People lived, was protected by the powers of the

Serpent. Also within this circle was the six pointed Star of Heaven on Earth, *as above so below.*

"And as Red Fox said, each world was destroyed. When the next world was created, it was more difficult to live in. Each world began with its own distinct vibrational frequency. However, as each world developed, its collective frequency varied depending on the attunement of humankind with the Great Oneness.

"For The People, this meant they had to work harder to keep their vibrational connections strong with Mother Earth and Great Spirit. More and more distractions occurred and more and more temptations presented themselves as civilization progressed in each World. This is why the shape of each curve is different from each other."

"I'm impressed, Gray Wolf," says White Eagle. "Now tell me why the Star of Heaven on Earth is not now in the oval."

Surprised by the unexpected question, I pause for a moment, swallow noticeably and breathe in as deep a breath as I could. Just last week Singing Hawk and Shining Bird had started making Star of Heaven on Earth pieces, fashioned from copper for those wanting them for the upcoming Solstice Ceremony. During the process of making them, Singing Hawk revealed the sacred meaning of the Star.

"White Eagle, as I understand this, we are now living in the Fourth World. You see that the fourth curve is not fully formed. It merely begins to rise to become the neck of the Serpent. Our legends from the ancients tell us that the Fourth World will become more advanced than the Third World. Many nations will rise, and the population of humankind will exceed that of all the prior three worlds. Intellect acquired through genetic evolution spurs the creation of devices and energies that we cannot even imagine.

"The Serpent represents the history and possible future of humankind on Earth. The Serpent is neutral in the events of humankind. Given free will, humankind can make choices.

"The Serpent's mouth holds the Circle of Life within which The People live.

"When free will is used destructively, this will result in great harm, harm to humankind and to Mother Earth. Those who misuse this power fail to honor the promises of our ancestors given in the Ancient of Days.

"Failure to honor Mother Earth, to damage her, harm her, rape her, and throw her systems out of balance, could bring damage to Mother Earth far worse than has ever happened before. The wounds inflicted upon Mother Earth by those living in the Fourth World could become so great that she might not be able to heal herself.

"The oval in the Serpent's mouth was once the Circle of Life. Within the Circle of Life was the Star of Heaven on Earth. What was once the

Circle of Life has now become an oval as the Serpent's mouth has begun to close, warning us against the misuse of power by humankind in the Fourth World.

"Our legends tell us, if the power and domination of those with two-hearts become too great, the mouth of the Serpent may close and destroy The People. Mother Earth's wounds would be so great, there will be no place for The People to be protected as they were when the three prior worlds came to an end.

"This is also shown by what has happened to the Star of Heaven on Earth. This foretells what may come to pass if humankind fails to honor Great Spirit and Mother Earth."

I pause to reflect a moment, contemplating as to whether I should go on. Then I say, "It is important to note that in the Ancient of Days, our ancestors knew this in their very core and did not have to speak it. The Star represents the Oneness and the promise that our ancestors made to Great Spirit not to separate from the consciousness of Oneness when they entered each of the Four Worlds.

"The Star of Heaven and Earth is comprised of two triangles placed in such a way as to represent a six-pointed star. One represents Earth, the one that points toward Heaven. The other triangle represents Heaven and points toward Earth. Each triangle represents a trinity.

"Now the triangle that represents Earth has moved in front of the oval. The triangle that represents Heaven, has been devoured by the Serpent. Neither are inside the Circle of Life.

"The two parts of the Star, the two triangles that were once one, are now torn apart and no longer represent *as above so below.*

"The Trinity of Heaven, heart, soul and free will, is below and the Trinity of Earth, the ego-mind, body and free will, appears above.

"This shows that during the Fourth World, that which is Celestial and of Great Spirit, the sense of oneness with each other and Mother Earth, is rejected.

"The Trinity of Earth is above the oval. In this position it represents the results of a breakdown in the sense of oneness with each other, Great Spirit, and Mother Earth. It appears that the priority of the Fourth World may become one of worship of the base elements of humankind, that which reinforces and promotes the ego and the sense of separateness from each other and from the Great Oneness.

"If this should come to be, this pressure or energy is so powerful that, not only the Fourth World, but The People, and quite possibly Mother Earth, may be destroyed. The only thing that can save the Fourth World is a very powerful *spiritual resurgence* of energy from The People for The People to help humankind address the absolute need to raise its collective frequency of its consciousness, awareness and sense of connectedness. This can be accomplished through collective will or collective intention.

"Only by returning to the Ways of Oneness and the sense that all humankind is connected to each other and to Mother Earth can the Fourth World be saved. This includes the need to serve Mother Earth, so she may begin to heal from all the damage done to her. Otherwise, Mother Earth may have to purge herself of all of humankind, so that she may survive, if indeed she can survive. She is a living entity. Only in this way would the oval transform itself back into the Circle of Life and hold the Star of Heaven and Earth in its center as shown by the sacred necklace that you are wearing, White Eagle."

Silence.

Shuffling sounds boom across the silence.

Silence.

White Eagle blinks.

White Eagle moves her mouth trying to form her words. She can't take her eyes off me. After even more awkward silence, she speaks with a waver in her voice as her emotions fight to express, "You have just given the Prophecy of the Serpent, Gray Wolf. You are already a shaman. You and I will speak of this more at a later time, Gray Wolf."

Now Red Fox knew things that he had not known before. He was proud we were friends. He felt that I needed to be present and now Red Fox knew why.

It was late afternoon the next day, Red Fox found me sitting on the hill above the pond.

"There you are," Red Fox exclaims. "Your Grandmother, Shining Moon, said she thought you'd be here."

I look up and find it hard to focus on the present and smile in greeting and say, "I've been thinking about what we experienced yesterday. It's been turning over and over in my mind."

"That's why I want to see you," Red Fox says. "I just need to talk about it." He pauses as both of us turn to look off into the clouds momentarily. Then he asks, "Tell me again about collective frequency."

I put down the stick I am toying with, turn my head to look at my friend, and say, "Collective frequency. Where do we start? Each of us vibrates at a specific frequency. When we are together, our frequencies become combined into a field. When several of us come together, this field becomes a collective frequency."

Red Fox furrows his eyebrows as he is works to comprehend.

I see this and say, "Our frequencies combine in this field to become one frequency, whether we are aware of it or not."

Red Fox then asks, "So, you are saying, it just happens?"

I respond, "Well, yes, it happens, but it works this way on purpose."

"We can't change our frequency? Is that what you are saying?" Red Fox asks.

"Actually. . . no," I say. "We can change our individual frequencies with the thoughts and intents of the heart."

Red Fox opens his eyes wide and says, "I get it. The collective frequency can then be changed to help Mother Earth and humankind as we will it or intend it together."

Smiling, I pat my friend on the back and say, "Yes, indeed . . . And that is why you, and the others, are traveling throughout the regions of The People . . . so you can remind everyone of the importance of the Prophecy of the Serpent. It's about helping them remember to remember. Our collective frequency occurs and changes with our thoughts as we focus our attention."

The two of us continue talking as we walk back to our village.

9

RED FOX BEGINS HIS JOURNEY

With the blessings of Singing Hawk, Shining Bird and I, Red Fox completed his project. The model was finished. White Eagle was obviously impressed with it. He had learned how to apply the mathematical formulas handed down from the Ancient of Days. He had learned more about our Ancient Ones and the history of The People. More importantly, he had been endowed with a new understanding of the Ancient Knowledge, the knowledge that guides our way in this, the Fourth World.

I fondly remember one incident with Red Fox while I was getting water for my mother.

"Hey there," a familiar voice calls to me. My friend, Red Fox, jumps and leaps as he moves in my direction almost breathless. "I just can't tell you how excited I am learning more about the Serpent and what is signifies. Singing Hawk has been spending a lot of time with me showing me how to measure, calculate formulas, about *phi* and more. I just can't tell you everything I'm learning. This is such a great experience!" he says to me.

"*Phi*?" I repeat.

"Yes, *phi*," Red Fox says, "It's the golden ratio found in nature that is useful in building and was used to construct the Great Serpent."

Filling the water basket, I look at him inquisitively.

Red Fox continues, "Okay. It's the ratio found in all of nature."

I shake my head in confusion. Before I can respond, Red Fox is off towards Singing Hawk's.

Whistling Wind, Red Fox's Grandmother, told him about the knowledge he was gaining, "This is a very positive indication that you have found your path. I am pleased with your spiritual growth and development, Red Fox." She added, "You are becoming a shamanic architect, and never forget that you know only so much. I have received a vision that your journey to the villages will open your eyes to even more."

Her words kept running through his mind as he prepared for the journey ahead of him. Red Fox tried to imagine traveling to many

THE CAMP OF GOD'S TEARS

villages and being far from home for several months. His uncle, Running Bear and one of our village elders, Morning Star, would be going with him.

Because the model of the Serpent was just over six feet long, a basket weaver had woven a special mat to cradle the model for the travois that Whispering Rock, his father, made. The travois would be pulled by one of our village's best portage dog teams. The dogs were strong and friendly and certainly up to the task that awaited them.

Laughing Willow, Red Fox's mother, had been very busy over the past several weeks, organizing supplies for her son's trip. She asked Lone Tree for smoked fish and other meats, Raven's Wing for cakes and other foods to get the group ready for this adventure. Laughing Willow knew they would be re-supplied by the villages they visited.

His mother even sewed him a new cape with a hood for protection against any spring storms that might come up.

It is just after dinner and Red Fox is outside washing the wooden dinner plates and bowls.

"Hey, Red Fox," I call out.

Turning, he looks up in our direction to see Shining Bird and me and approach.

"Tomorrow's the big day. Are you ready?" I ask smiling broadly, arm in arm with Shining Bird.

"Thanks for stopping by, Gray Wolf. I went by your house earlier today. Your mother told me that both of you had volunteered to help repair the fishing nets down by the river. I stopped by Water Dog's house, and Floating Lily said he was so anxious to get to Flint Ridge to continue his work with Rising Wolf that he took off yesterday without hardly a word to anyone."

"Yes, he is really excited about what he's doing now," I say.

Red Fox says, "His excitement cannot possibly equal what I am feeling right now." Red Fox's eyes open to a broad vision of an imaginary landscape he is about to step into.

I continue, "I envy you, and sometimes wish I could go with you. My mind races with all the places you will be. The villages at Seip, Baum, and its furnaces on top of Spruce Hill, all of the villages around the burial grounds near Chillicothe, the High Bank observatory . . . ." Each of us momentarily escapes into an imagined place along Red Fox's upcoming journey, vicariously experiencing some novel and indescribable event.

Returning to reality, I say as if the pause never occurred, "Then you will journey on the White Road of Sister Moon to Newark and the villages along it. I've not seen the White Road, but have heard of it."

Shining Bird chirps into the conversation, "What I would be anxious to see is the incredible Newark observatory complex and its Great Circle. I can only imagine the experience of visiting that place. I would love to see the vernal rise of the Pleiades, Orion and Sirius at the Great Circle. What a sight that must be!"

"Gray Wolf," asks Red Fox, "I think Flint Ridge will be close enough to Newark for me to see Water Dog and Rising Wolf, don't you think?"

"Indeed, you probably will," I respond. "Toward the end of your journey, you might visit Tremper. If you do, I have a request. They have pipe workshops there. Could you pick up a new pipe for my father before returning home? I just know he would love to have something unusual."

We remain standing outside his house for what seemed like endless moments, standing on a precipice of a rite of passage for our childhood friend.

Shining Bird reaches up to Red Fox with both arms offering him a supportive hug. He leans down to accept her embrace, choking on emotion as they release each other. Unable to hold back any longer, I seize my friend with both arms, tears run down my face. I feel both envy and support.

Shining Bird and I join hands as we walk away. She looks back at Red Fox watching us leave. We wouldn't see our friend again until the Summer Solstice and the Great Serpent ceremony.

After watching his friends reluctantly leave, Red Fox turned to go in to see his parents waiting for him. They talked by the fire until late as Red Fox continued packing and making sure that all his traveling packs were ready to go.

Lying in bed that night, Red Fox remembered what the Elders and Grandmothers had said to him about his journey. His thoughts swirled with all that lies before him.

He found it hard to go to sleep that night. The next thing he knew his mother was waking him. After breakfast he went outside to get some more firewood for her.

"Red Fox, are you ready? We need to get on our way. Father Sun waits for no one." Red Fox turned to see his uncle, Running Bear, Morning Star and the dog team with the travois in tow.

"Yes, good morning Running Bear and Morning Star. I am ready." Red Fox stepped inside the house. "Good bye mother, father, and Grandmothers. See you in about three months or so, maybe longer." Red Fox paused to take in a deep breath as he looked at his family. "My adventure begins," Red Fox said with a big smile swinging his pack up to his shoulders.

And so it began.

The crispness of the early morning welcomed them into the forested lands.

Their journey began towards the west along Brush Creek. As they left the valley, the travelers stopped to look back down to their village, their home. Gazing back at them was the Great Serpent. It lay high on the plateau with no trees surrounding it. Our villagers kept the entire plateau clear of trees and brush in all directions.

The travelers had many miles to go until they reached the first village. Every so often the group would stop to check the travois, rest and readjust to find just the right union between their bodies and their packs.

"Really gives you an appreciation for all that the traders deal with on their travels doesn't it?" Running Bear asks.

"Yes," says Red Fox, "while we are only going a couple of hundred miles, traders travel thousands of miles loaded down with all the goods and treasures, never really getting rid of everything. They trade what they have and replace it with an equal amount as they go from place to place."

"It's an honored profession among all the peoples. The goods they provide to all the settlements they visit are always appreciated. Because of the service they provide, not to mention news of other peoples, they receive safe passage in all the lands they travel," Morning Star added.

Soon they went. White billowing clouds decorated the blue sky. Faint fragrances of spring filled the air. The creek glistened in the morning sun as it melted remnants of snow tucked away in the forest. Occasionally, resident birds made their presence known.

Even though they had walked for hours, they felt little time had passed when they reached a clearing in the path. New vistas of rolling forested hills appeared and a cool breeze greeted their faces. While they rested a moment without talking, the silence was broken by the cries of a bald eagle overhead.

"He's soaring over the eagle effigy mound that I had visited with my father once," said Red Fox.

"Yes. It's not far from the Great Serpent," Running Bear added. "It's all contained within the great crater."

They resumed the trek tingling with the energy rush from the eagle experience. It was about eight miles to the large village where they would spend their first night.

They had four dogs. Two pulled the travois while the other two followed along. Every so often they would switch the teams so none would become too tired.

At midday, the travelers stopped by a shaded pool of water to eat something. The dogs wolfed down the nut cakes mixed with smoked meats and then jumped into the pool of water. Tongues and tails wagged as they came running back to where the trio sat. The dogs proceeded to shower them as they shook the water from their fur. Laughing at the joy of the moment the men hugged their dogs, gathered everything up and got back on the trail.

Time passed swiftly and the village appeared around a bend. The village was about one mile south of the summit of Fort Hill.

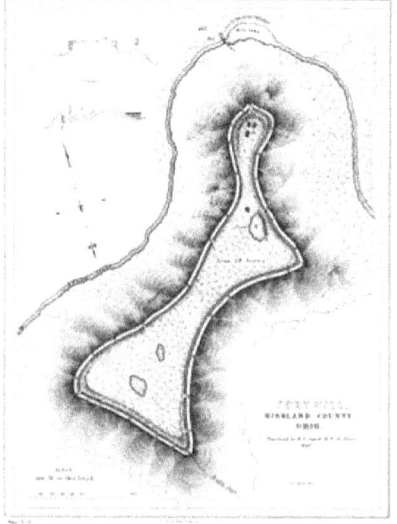

Diagram of Fort Hill, Squier and Davis 1848

As they approached the village they were greeted by village dogs, children and Elk Horn, a village Elder.

"Welcome, Morning Star, Running Bear and Red Fox. You must be weary from your journey. We have prepared a place for you in our village lodge and dinner is cooking. We have been expecting you," Elk Horn said with a welcoming smile, his arms extended in a gesture of greeting.

"We thank you, Elk Horn. We are looking forward to sharing stories tonight around a warm fire," said Running Bear feeling the evening chill. "We appreciate your hospitality. I have not seen you for some time. I imagine your grandchildren have grown quite a bit since then," Running Bear added, handing a leather pouch of tobacco to Elk Horn.

The village lodge was quite comfortable. A pot of tea sat steaming by the fireplace. Next to it was a plate of dried fruit and several nut cakes. Refreshed, the travelers went to Elk Horn's home and ate and ate, laughed and caught up on events. After dinner a large group gathered in the village center by a big fire anxious to hear what Red Fox had to say.

He told the Story of the Serpent and the upcoming ceremony. The Fort Hill villagers sat in rapt attention, hanging on to every word. While many older villagers already knew the story, many younger ones were only vaguely aware of it.

Red Fox told the Serpent Story with great enthusiasm. To have this Story re-told with the visual model of the Great Serpent added a heightened sense of reality to what needed to be remembered.

Red Fox positively glowed with passion as he recited the Story pointing to the different parts of the Serpent as appropriate. As Red Fox concluded, he looked at his listeners, his face invited questions or comments.

No one stirred. His audience sat frozen silently processing the meaning of the Story. After a long silence laced by the night chill, the villagers quietly left for their respective homes.

"You did well last night, Red Fox," said Morning Star with a nod.

"I was a little nervous at first. This is the first time I had ever spoken to so many people," Red Fox replied wistfully with eyebrows raised. He added thoughtfully as he replayed the event in his mind, "That soon was replaced with confidence in my information, and I saw how many were really listening." Not dwelling on the previous night's event and its outcome each turned to face the trail ahead.

At about midday, they saw the trail open to an expanse of lands not treed by the hardwoods usual to the Ohio area. They crossed a creek and headed to the next village and arrived just before sunset.

As before, The People warmly greeted them, taking them to one of their homes for the evening meal. Before joining them, Morning Star looked after the dogs. Then the trio followed their host to a place where the villagers were gathering. As Red Fox arrived with the model, they made way for him to move to a spot where all could see him and the model. At the conclusion, Red Fox again looked up to see if there were any questions.

One villager stood up, half bending forward, and asked, "So, you're saying that we are in the Fourth World?" Red Fox nodded in affirmation, surprised by the question.

"Then, if we are in the Fourth World, when will we know what is going to happen to the Fourth World?" the villager asked, then added, "What do we need to do to keep the Fourth World going?"

Murmurs rippled across the sitting audience like a wave across a pool.

Red Fox felt challenged by the question. He thought he had already covered this point. Still standing, he shifted his weight while looking at the man, ever so humble in his question. Yet the question loomed large in Red Fox's mind as if it was a threat to his credibility.

Breathing in deeply, Red Fox closed his eyes, lowered his head, taking a pause from the moment. Slowly he lifted his head and opened his eyes to focus on something unseen by anyone else. After another long moment, he replied, "Time is an illusion. We cannot know the future, because the future does not exist in the present. We can only know the present." The questioner resumed his seat.

"The future is a result of personal choices made by each of us in our exercise of free will, individually and collectively. Working together, we can help each other with our personal choices. Plus, we can support each other and ourselves by maintaining an awareness of the Oneness. So to answer your first question, I cannot offer 'the when' anything will happen.

"To answer your second question, we don't know if destruction of the Fourth World will happen, because The Prophecy is about what 'may' come. That '*maybe*' is dependent upon us and our choices, how we treat each other, both individually and collectively. It's really not about time at all, but rather about vibrational frequency. The keener our awareness of the Great Oneness, and the consistency with which we live in harmony, not just with each other, but with Mother Earth as well, the higher the frequency humankind will achieve and maintain.

"It's about the *collective frequency* of humankind.

"In the prophecy, the Fourth World becomes threatened with extinction when the collective frequency of humankind lowers, as shown by the curve here," Red Fox pointed to the curve closest to the Serpent's head.

Red Fox breathed in deeply and out slowly. His eyes then focused on the audience, and he said, "It's a choice. *Our* choice. It's our choice to follow the ways of Great Spirit, honoring Mother Earth and *each other*. We do this through the use of our heart energy to guide the exercise of our free will."

Silence.

The audience remained sitting in silence contemplating what they had just heard. Then individuals slowly rose to quietly return to their homes.

After everyone had left, Morning Star reached for Red Fox, patted his arm gently and gave him a look that meant, "good job." They slept well and were off the next morning.

The third night brought them to a village that was built near Paint Creek. Paint Creek also flowed by the Seip and Baum villages, on its winding way toward the Scioto River.

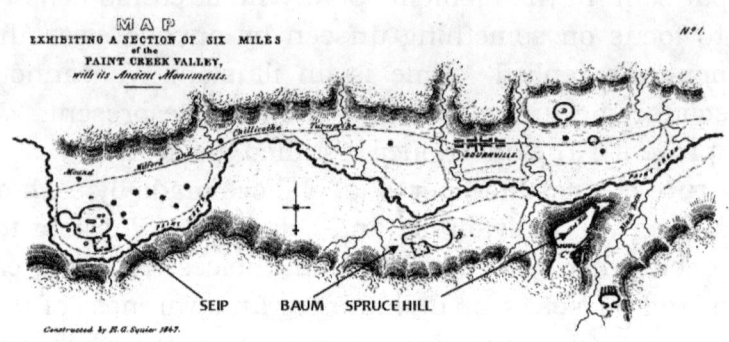

Diagram of Paint Creek Valley Earthworks Squier and Davis 1848

Once again they enjoyed the hospitality, food, and the telling of many stories. After an uneventful, but successful presentation, Red Fox felt his confidence growing.

The travelers got an early start the next morning. Although it had rained during the night, they found the trail not too muddy to travel. The land was alive with fragrances from the rain. Some of the higher hills were shrouded in clouds, and a mystical feeling hugged the land. Upon setting out they were greeted by a beautiful sky collage of colored clouds, some high in the sky and others closer to Mother Earth. The air felt cool and moist as they made good progress.

"We should arrive at Seip by mid-afternoon," said Running Bear. "I can see you are excited, Red Fox. It shows on your face." Morning Star turned and scrutinized Red Fox's face at that comment, and nodded in agreement.

Running Bear asked Red Fox, "This is the first time you've been to Seip, I think, is that right?"

Red Fox replied, "Yes. I am anxious to see the textile, pearl and mica artisans at work. I can hardly wait."

Then Morning Star said, "While each village has their own weavers and artisans of various types, Seip is known for its exquisite fabrics, pearl and shell ornaments and mica works. This is one of our centers for the production of artworks of exquisite beauty." Then he added, "Just seeing how each is made is impressive."

The group journeyed on, each lost in their own thoughts.

After a while, Running Bear broke the silence to talk about the area they would be visiting. "Seip and Baum lie in a broad and fertile valley along Paint Creek where many crops are raised. It's really something. Baum village is very large. It's the center for organizing the vast farming in this area. Morning Star, have you seen the many storage chambers they constructed in the ground to store food?"

Morning Star shook his head affirmatively, "Yes, indeed. If a village or villages meet hard times during a winter or summer, dried meats and fruits, corn, nutmeats, wild rice, seed flour, and other foods are made available so that no one goes hungry. This is also where much of the food comes from to feed the large gatherings for our ceremonies."

"Well, what I really want to see," interrupted Red Fox, "is the copper and iron smelting furnaces at Spruce Hill."

As they followed the Paint Creek they could see forested hills in front of them. Up ahead a large herd of deer watered at the creek. Once the deer saw the travelers, especially the dogs, they faded slowly back into the forest.

At the spot where the travelers agreed to cross the creek, they unhitched the travois and carried it across the water. The travelers unpacked bundles and built a fire for a meal. Fresh fish was on the menu. Morning Star had speared several nice fish.

After eating, Running Bear felt in a story-telling mood. "Red Fox, I have visited the Seip Earthworks a number of times," he said, as he leaned back. "The earthen wall outlines a large combined circle and square, a smaller circle, and a large square. This wall, over 10,000 feet in length, forms an enclosure of over 120 acres."

"Wow, I can't wait to see what it looks like," Red Fox said. "Can you tell me more about it?"

Breathing in slowly, Running Bear, paused and said, "The square represents Heaven. The circle represents Earth. The largest structure, part square, part circle, represents Heaven on Earth united."

Red Fox nodded in acknowledgement as they then gathered up to leave.

Up ahead they saw smoke from cooking and warming fires in the village. Many people strolled out to greet them. It was then that Red Fox saw the earthen walls of Seip.

He was amazed at all the time and effort that must have been required for The People to construct this expansive enclosure

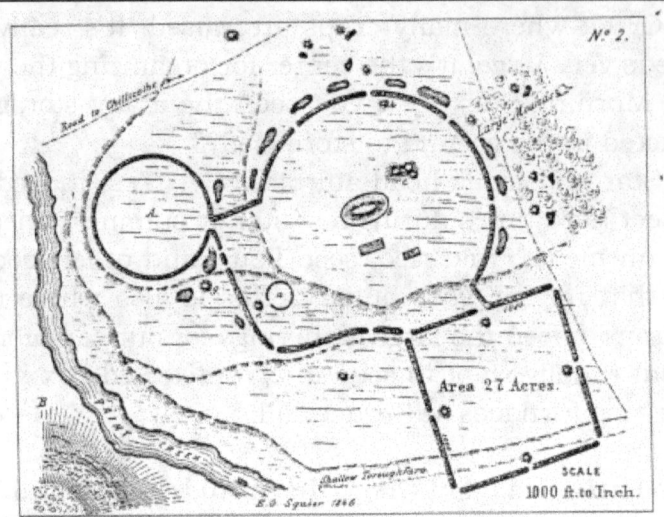
Diagram of Seip Earthworks Squier and Davis 1848

    Citizens of the Seip settlement graciously guided the visitors to a guest lodge. The travelers took off their packs, secured the travois found a place for the dogs. Afterwards, Red Fox wandered over to the Council House.

    Red Fox was the first to enter the cool interior of the oversized Council House. As he waited for his companions to join him, he began looking at it with the eye of a builder. Red Fox took in the construction and was most impressed with its dimensions. It was the largest building he had ever seen. Running Bear and Morning Star slipped in behind him noiselessly. Sunlight filtered in between the shadowed areas through the many mica windows. As his eyes adjusted to the darkened room, he felt a presence before he saw a giant shadow moving toward him in the filtered light.

    A voice boomed from the shadowed presence as it moved toward them, "Welcome all. We have been expecting you. I am Soaring Red Hawk, one of the Elders of Seip."

    Red Fox stepped back in awkward surprise, tripping over Morning Star's feet. Caught by Running Bear, Red Fox looked embarrassed as he scuffled to gain his standing composure. Soaring Red Hawk was taller than Waterdog's father had been and had the same red hair.

    "Red Fox," Soaring Red Hawk said laughing, "I guess you are not familiar with people of my stature?"

    "No, no," Red Fox stammered shaking his head slightly. "My friend, Waterdog is, and his father was also quite tall, and so are several other of our villagers. I apologize."

    "No need for apology. Many visiting our village for the first time have the same reaction when they first see me. I have much to tell you. First refresh yourselves. We have prepared some refreshments for all of you and your dogs," Soaring Red Hawk said, smiling broadly, opening his massive arms in a generous motion of an imagined embrace.

"I have so many questions," Red Fox finally found his voice. "I've heard amazing things about this village, Soaring Red Hawk. I've heard that you have many skilled artisans and that Seip is also a place for burial ceremonies."

"I will introduce you to those who work in our various workshops. I have also made arrangements for your presentation on the Great Serpent here in this lodge tomorrow night. We've been looking forward to your visit. Many of the villagers in this valley will be making the journey for the Solstice Setting of Father Sun at the Great Serpent," Soaring Red Hawk said.

Having finished refreshments the size of a meal, out of habit Red Fox began to gather up the wooden plates and bowls. He looked up and around and was just about to ask where he could take them to wash them.

"Red Fox, you are our honored guest, these will be taken care of. And thank you for offering to clear the table." Soaring Red Hawk placed a large hand on Red Fox's shoulder. "Now, where would you like to begin your tour?"

Red Fox, did not know what to say.

The giant continued, "Now, perhaps you would like to see the very elegant ceremonial dress our weavers are preparing for the next major ceremony at High Bank," said Soaring Red Hawk rising from the table.

Red Fox thought to himself, *"Who am I to argue with an Elder? Besides I have studied birds weaving their nests."* Then he replied, "Of course, I would love to."

And off they went.

10

TRADERS AND WOLF ENCOUNTER

Lyrical notes from several pan flutes drift up through the hollows, floating over the hills to the delighted ears of The People living in the village near the Serpent. The melodious sounds announce their arrival and sets up anticipation in the minds of the villagers before the traders actually appear. As the traders reach the edge of the village, the sounds of bells, attached to their packs, accentuate the melodies.

"They're here! They're here!" cries a youngster from across the way. "The traders are here! And they have more bells, lots of them."

People venture out of their homes smiling in expectation. Gleeful sounds emanate from those gathering to see the traders.

Traders brought in goods from faraway places and some places not so far away. Tradable items and interesting artifacts were not the only things of value traders brought to The People, such as news of other peoples and places. They traveled routes established for centuries by previous traders. They had become part of the cultural landscape among the differing communities. Welcomed guests they were. Happy, expectant faces began gathering around as the traders entered the village.

These particular traders had journeyed up from the south of the continent from deep below Mexico, then up and around the Gulf of Mexico, then up the Mississippi River. They ate off the land as they traveled from village to village, and were always glad to accept the generous hospitality of the people with whom they visited and traded. While they carried their wares in large packs on their backs, sometimes they had dogs to help carry the load. This group was larger than most.

Evidently, a small band of young men from deep within Mexico accompanied this trader. In exchange for joining the expedition along known paths up the continent, these young men helped carry some of the goods. They also provided another service. One of the apprentice traders had taken a nasty fall, breaking his leg. They pulled him on a makeshift travois constructed from deer hides and poles.

THE CAMP OF GOD'S TEARS

Once in the village, the band of traders put down their loads to stretch without the weight of the packs. Not stepping in any direction, they continue standing there, taking in the sights and sounds of The People, and the aromas of food wafting across the open area. Gently, they set down the injured trader.

The curious villagers part allowing Laughing Willow, and several other women to greet the visitors. They exchange pleasantries. Several Grandmothers, Whispering Moon, Shining Moon, Blue Lightning among them, stand off at a distance looking over the group of assorted young men who appear as something other than traders. Feeling wary of them, the Grandmothers do not approach, even though they are curious as to what interesting goods might be available but hidden in the packs.

The Grandmothers knew the trader, Turning Rabbit, from many previous visits to their village. The others with Turning Rabbit gave off a strange sense different from the trader energy. The Grandmothers could not quite determine what it was that made them feel uneasy.

As was their usual custom after the greetings, Laughing Willow and the other women lead the band to a small clearing away from the common area of the village to show them where they could set up their camp.

Some of the children, both older and younger, cannot resist watching the visitors as they unpack and move their belongings from the center of the settlement to the guest camp. Eyes widen when they see something very strange to them . . . highly colored birds in cages. The use of cages is unknown to the People. All wildlife sharing the land with them roam freely.

The birds present a wonder to them, as they had never seen such colors on a bird. They were used to seeing brightly colored hummingbirds, bluebirds, yellow tanagers, and the wild ducks colored distinctly between the species. These birds were full bodied in brilliant yellows, reds, greens, and blues. The parrots squawk occasionally as they are toted about.

Floating Lily, Water Dog's little sister, could be seen running around and around the group, almost getting in the trader's way as they move their belongings. As is her habit when visitors arrive, she bolts over to Raven's Wing's house, where Raven's Wing is already setting up an offering of small cakes made of nutmeats with wild rice for the traders.

"There's ten of them," she informs Raven's Wing. ". . . and one of them is sick. They brought him in on a travois."

Raven's Wing replies, "These nut cakes will hold them over until evening when the rest of the meal is put together. Why don't you see if any of the hunters have brought Lone Tree any fresh meat.

"Oh, and ask if he knows of anyone heading for the stream to catch some fish. Maybe they can bring back a few more."

After her conversation with Raven's Wing, Floating Lily heads over to Lone Tree's to check for a fresh meat supply. Returning to Raven's Wing with a large portion of hindquarters from a deer, Floating Lily hands it over in exchange for a basket of the cakes intended for the trader and company.

Arriving at the trader's encampment with her basket of cakes, Floating Lily finds herself entranced by some of the goods already unpacked, yards of dyed fabrics, abalone shells, several conch shells, a variety of flutes, and of course, the caged parrots.

"Raven's Wing sent these over for you. She said they should hold you until evening," she smiles up at Turning Rabbit as he welcomes her with that broad smile of his. Turning Rabbit remembers Floating Lily, but only as a much smaller version of herself from his last trip to this village.

"Floating Lily, my, have you grown," he says, while admiring her striking strawberry hair. "You've grown at least a foot or more since I saw you last. How old are you now, about thirteen?"

Floating Lily, nonplussed by his comment returns, "No, I'm ten."

As he takes the basket, he says, "Please tell Raven's Wing, 'thank you' for us. Also please mention to her that I have some of the herbs she likes to season with that she asked for the last time I was here . . . . Oh, and by the way, you might also say that I have several new ones for her to experiment with. I got them from very far away and liked how they flavor some of the foods I've eaten. I imagine she might have some fun with them until she figures out which foods they would go best with."

"Sure," Floating Lily says as she glances over toward where the parrots are arranged. "I'll be back toward evening when the meal is ready."

Turning Rabbit steps back, still smiling at her, watching her fascination with the caged birds. "We aren't going anywhere."

He turns to see how the bundles and packs are being arranged under the three-sided shelter so familiar to him for the several decades he has been trading in this part of the world. Then he remembers one more thing to tell Floating Lily. As he turns back to speak to her, he is not surprised to see she had already vanished.

Wondering where the sick man was as he obviously was no longer with the traders, Floating Lily finds her way over to the Healing House. As she nears, she smells incense. It is part of the healing environment that blends with the scent of the cedar planks lining the interior of the House.

She spots the travois lying on its side propped up against the wall of the building. Not wanting to disturb the focus of those inside, she silently steals up to the door, then peaks her head in. Two women and an elderly, white-haired man are attending the stranger who is lying on a bed in the center of the room. His bandages stripped off, his leg lies bare with the festering wound exposed. Fine needles made from thorns, porcupine quills and others of silver have been inserted at certain points in his leg and foot by Whispering Moon as she administers a poultice to the leg, wearied with infection.

The other woman, Thunder Cloud, sits beside the stranger in deep meditation listening to his body while holding his arm with both her hands.

The white-haired man, Speaks With Plants, attends the fire while preparing a tea for the sick man. As he fans the smoke heavy with scent using a hawk's wing to disperse it throughout the room, he notices Floating Lily's hand grasping the doorframe. Only part of her face appears with one eye staring inside.

Looking down at Whispering Moon, Speaks With Plants exhales with force, causing Whispering Moon to look up at him. All in one movement, she turns to see Floating Lily and gives one nod to her, lowering her head while keeping her eyes in contact with the young girl. Immediately, Floating Lily jerks as if shot with an electrical shock, turns and races down the way to Raven's Wing house.

"Where's Shining Moon?" Floating Lily demands impetuously, as she suddenly appears at Raven's Wing's outdoor kitchen. Shining Moon steps into the doorway dressed in her ceremonial garb. It is adorned with grizzly bear teeth, elk teeth, bones of eagles and hawks, colored beads and stones, enhanced with necklaces of shells, pearls and abalone, and various kinds of feathers. Her beaded purse, obviously full of items by how it bulged in places, hangs by leather cords from her arm.

"Here I am," she barks at Floating Lily, stepping past Raven's Wing. "We might need you later," she looks at Raven's Wing, "to make a soup. I'll know better when I return."

Late that afternoon I, Gray Wolf, was making my way back to our village having gathered some herbs and medicinal plants for Shining Moon, my Grandmother. She had told me stories about the plants that I was gathering and how over the ages we had learned the healing powers of these gifts from Mother Earth. This information was passed down from generation to generation to those who were able to communicate with the plants.

Disease was uncommon in our village. But when something did arise they would come to my Grandmother. Many times she would just ask questions and "see" with her spirit vision just the right teas, herbs, or which plants to prepare for the specific individual. Other times she would place her hands on the person and ask Spirit for guidance on what was needed to effect a healing.

Once in a while, she would be guided to a new combination of plants to treat a specific illness or injury. This time she was guided to yet another plant that she had used only once before to treat an infection in Guiding Crow's foot that had been injured while he was harvesting wild rice last fall in a wetland area not far from our village. Today she needed that same plant.

I had spent much time with my Grandmother walking in the woods, valleys, hills, and streams searching for the herbs and plants that she had learned about from her mother. I so much enjoyed our journeys and learning how to speak with the plants and feel their energy.

She also told me other stories about our medicinal plants and how this knowledge of their healing uses came to be. She taught me how to listen to the spirit of these medicinal plants and how they would show me the ways to use their medicine for healing.

"Gray Wolf," she said, "this is the realm where humans meet the sacred in these special plants. You must always remember that all human and animal life is dependent on the members of the plant family, from the smallest herbs to the largest trees. They are all important to us for food, shelter, clothing, and medicine. Many of our ceremonies honor and seek to renew our personal and community covenants with them. They are manifestations from our Creator given to us and the animals to sustain our existence on Mother Earth. Because all plants are rooted in Mother Earth she feels the pull each time a plant is removed from the soil. This is why we always give a proper prayer and offering when we harvest a plant regardless of how we intend to use it.

"This is especially true when we harvest the plants we use for medicine or for ceremony. If we do not properly ask the plant for permission, the medicine will not be as effective or the ceremony will not be as successful. We give our offerings and prayers so that Mother Earth recognizes that we comprehend our relationship to her and that we appreciate that she is giving us a part of her body. In so doing we are honoring and renewing our relationship with her, the spirits of all plants and the interdependent relationships of all life in the lands where we live."

Shining Moon was respected near and far for her healing gifts. Many times messengers from distant villages would come with questions from other healers who were perplexed by an illness in their village. Grandmother would go into meditation. She told me she could see the person who was ill and see inside their body to the area where the problem existed. She would then ask Spirit for guidance on what was needed to bring the person back into balance and remove the disease.

She explained to me that the word disease was really two words, *dis* and *ease*, meaning that a disharmony had settled in the body. Through the use of the proper plants, herbs, and prayer, the body could be returned to the *ease* of balance.

All of this was going through my mind as I walked. I remembered the times I had traveled with my Grandmother in the bountiful lands surrounding our village. Now she was not able to travel very far from the village to gather the medicines that she used. I felt acknowledged that she chose me to help her gather what she needed to heal others.

"Gray Wolf," she said with a loving smile on her face, her eyes sparkling with confidence, "you are developing your gifts as a healer. The healing gifts that have blessed our family for generations have been passed down to you." I felt honored. While I was not yet an accomplished healer, I was on the path.

Now I was assisting her. With her guidance I was now beginning to see the person's illness and getting visions of what plants and herbs were just right for treatment. A person would come into our home. She would ask me what I saw and ask for my suggestions on what was needed to treat the ailment or injury. Sometimes I did not get the correct solution, and we would talk after the person left. On occasion, although I had selected the proper plants or herbs, I did not understand that, in some instances, the plant or herb had to be harvested at a precise time in its growth or development for a specific treatment.

Suddenly a sound enters my ears that shook me out of my thoughts. At first I do not recognize what it is or where it is coming from. I stop in my tracks and open myself to the Oneness. I hear it again. It's coming from up ahead in a clump of bushes and boulders. The low whimpering sound comes from an injured animal.

I close my eyes and extend my arms, palms out with my elbows close to my waist. A vision appears in my mind. All that is between me and the sound disappears, and I saw a gray wolf lying on the ground having concealed himself in a place of relative safety. His left rear leg is injured. It is swollen and infected.

I join my thoughts and energy with his. At first he rejects my presence. He is old, suffering, in great pain and afraid of humans. I can feel his fear. He tries to get up to flee, but his leg is unable to support his weight and he collapses. He accepts the fact that it is his time to return to Spirit at the hands of a human. His mind relaxes and becomes quiet. Now I am able to speak to him but without words.

"Brother Wolf, I honor you. I am Gray Wolf. When I was born my Grandmother, Shining Moon, received a vision of a large gray wolf on a hilltop. He had been asked by Spirit to witness my birth. That is how I became known as Gray Wolf."

Silence.

Whimpering sounds.

Silence.

Then without words he speaks to me, "Gray Wolf, that was my father. He told me of your birth and that you were chosen to have a gray wolf as your spirit guide and that you would become a shaman, a healer, and a guide for your people. I am now old, and I injured my leg running after game. I know that it is now my time to join my ancestors. I cannot walk and I am in great pain. Thank you for acknowledging my situation and allowing me the peace to transition into Spirit."

"Brother Wolf, I am indebted to your father for the gift of my name. I ask for your permission to approach you and examine your wound. Your father told you that I was on the path to becoming a healer. I have been gathering plants and herbs for my Grandmother to treat a man who has an infected leg. I have seen the energy of your injury. I have enough medicine for both you and the man. If you will allow me, I believe that I can cure your infection. It is not yet your time."

Silence.

Out of nowhere a sweet scented breeze envelopes us. Birds begin to sing and a shaft of light from between the clouds focuses on where he lay.

Silence.

"Gray Wolf, I have seen your heart and know that it is pure and that you are of good intention. Yet, I am very afraid of the scent of man. I do not want to hurt you, but the emotion of fear, my vulnerability, and my pain may overtake me and cause you great harm."

I deepen my meditation and ask Spirit to calm the fears of Brother Wolf. A gentle calmness of Oneness enters both our minds. We are all related, all connected, in the Great Oneness. I sense that his fear is gone.

I approach slowly, staying in the energy of our connection. As I carefully part the bushes, I see Brother Wolf hidden in a small opening at the base of a cluster of large boulders. Our eyes meet. His teeth bare for an instant and then his jaw relaxes. I can see that he is in much pain and has accepted that I am here to help him. We maintain eye contact. Now our souls touch. He accepts my touch and licks my arm. Warm waves of love and Oneness envelope us. We are now one.

I examine his left leg. Yes, the infection has advanced into a serious stage. He relaxes. My intention of healing and calming his fears has taken hold.

"Brother Wolf," I say without words, "I will be able to help you with the medicines I have with me. I will need to clean your wound with water from the clay canteen that I am carrying. Then I will need to prepare a poultice from these plants and herbs. I see that you are weak and need food and water. You have been here for several days and your body needs nourishment. Please accept the offerings of my dried fish, smoked meat, cakes, and water."

Brother Wolf drinks water from my cupped hands and eats some of the dried fish, and a bite of the meat and cakes that I had left from my travels of this day.

Taking two nearby stones, I grind the plants and herbs and mix them with water into a paste. I cleanse his wound with water and then apply the poultice all over the infected area. A sigh issues from within his jaws.

"Gray Wolf, what you placed on my infection has greatly reduced the pain already. Thank you for the food and water. I need to rest now. Go on your way as they are waiting for your return. I am grateful to Spirit that you happened on to me today. Go in peace. I will be returning to Mother Earth before Father Sun returns."

"Brother Wolf, I am hoping that will not happen. I will return early when Father Sun rises. I will bring more water, food, and medicine for you. Before I leave today I will build a shelter of branches and limbs to protect you from scavengers. You need your rest. Remain connected with me in spirit. I will pray for you tonight. Your journey is not over."

Silence.

The breeze returns.

A bluebird lands near us with a sweet song.

"You see, Brother Wolf. You will survive with my help."

"Gray Wolf, you have been so very kind to me. This is as it was in the First World. Return in the morning if you wish. If I have not returned to Spirit, there is much to share between us. If I do pass during the night, I will visit you in a dream."

And so it is.

I gather my possessions and stroke his head, ears, and neck. I feel the energy of love of the Oneness between us. Slowly I withdraw until our eyes were no longer in contact. Quietly, I gather branches to build a shelter of protection around where Brother Wolf lies. He is going to sleep in the protection of Spirit. Our minds now are disengaged and he is at peace.

Deep in thought, I walk home. The events of that afternoon kept turning over and over in my mind. I need to talk with Grandmother to help process what I had just experienced.

Sounds of raucous enjoyment issued from the Big House. Often traders were invited as guests in ones or twos by individual families for meals. However, this time the strangers with Turning Rabbit did not receive any such personal invitations.

Satiated from the tasty foods prepared by Raven's Wing and several other village women, the band of young men gradually relaxed amid those villagers who were either willing or eager to talk with people from another place. The evening proved to be delightfully entertaining as all regaled in tales of bravery, astonishment, and humor.

Located quite a distance from the Big House, the Healing House entertained a different scenario. Shining Moon and her brother, Speaks With Plants, consulted quietly. Thunder Cloud had completed her meditation connecting with the stranger's body.

"The leg must be reset," Thunder Cloud grimly announced.

Silence.

The fevered trader, face flushed with beads of sweat, slowly rolled his languid eyes around and up at his caretakers. Breathing shallowly, he tried to speak, but could only utter unintelligible sounds.

"First, however," said Shining Moon, "we take care of the infection. Turning Rabbit did a good job applying his herbs and ointments to prevent gangrene, but the fever must be addressed before we reset the leg."

Everyone breathed again and nodded. Their patient lapsed into a sleep as the tension of the group relaxed slightly. Speaks With Plants turned and began assessing his assortment of herbs. He selected several to make a tea for the man to drink when he returned to consciousness. Shining Moon began to prepare, from her herb pouches and bags, yet another poultice to apply directly to the infected area.

Very late in the night Shining Moon leaves the Healing House trudging slowing home. On her way she notices several of the strange men accompanying Turning Rabbit back to their camp on the other side of the village. At that moment Turning Rabbit looks up and sees Shining Moon. He turns briefly to his companions, mutters something to them, and walks up the rolling hill in her direction. Shining Moon keeps on walking minding her own business. When Turning Rabbit reaches Shining Moon, she stops and looks up at him.

"Good evening, Grandmother," Turning Rabbit addresses her respectfully. "I am wondering about my friend, Warm Stone. How is he?"

"He is still alive, thanks to your efforts. He would have died had you not prevented gangrene. You did well in taking care of him." Turning Rabbit almost smiles at the praise, yet remains concerned for his friend.

"However," she continues, "the infection is causing a serious fever. Speaks With Plants, Whispering Moon, Thunder Cloud and I are preparing the appropriate treatments for him."

"Oh," Turning Rabbit says, "I am glad we were able to get him here in time. I did what I could for him. My stomach has been tied in knots worrying about his condition. I really didn't want to take him with me, but he insisted on learning about being a trader. He comes from very far away toward the Great Water to the west and very far south. I envisioned him becoming a great trader. Even so, he was inexperienced at traveling the great distances that I do. The country changes so much between where he is from and here. He just didn't realize how dangerous some of the country can be. I don't think he imagined how much country stretches between settlements. Although, I did notice a growing number of them while coming up the Mississippi River."

Grandmother Shining Moon nods in acknowledgement and says, "How long do you plan on staying with us, Turning Rabbit?"

"I hadn't planned on staying more than a few days, a week at most. It depends on how much trading we accomplish. Why do you ask, Grandmother?" he asks.

"Your friend, Warm Stone, will need to be staying with us for a lot longer than that," she says with a nod of her head, raising her eyebrows, like she was serving him a sentence. Turning Rabbit pales at the news and steps back.

She continues, "We will be resetting his leg after we get his fever down. Even though you did well in treating the infection, his bone did not set properly. It is important for him to be able to walk, is it not? If we let his leg bone mend as it is now, he will never walk as he should. His life as a trader, walking great distances, will end right here. He would be a cripple, unable to walk much . . . if at all. That is not the path he and Spirit and Mother Earth agreed to when he contracted for this life.

"You had best not plan on taking him with you when you leave. You can pick him up on your way back after you make your rounds up toward Flint Ridge and further into Canada. I suspect it will be a while at least before he will be ready to walk with you across the country again as a trader."

With that news, Turning Rabbit slumps his shoulders and lowers his eyes. "Thank you, Grandmother," he finally says. "I'll be by in a couple days to see how he is doing." With that, Turning Rabbit sadly turns and slowly walks back down the hill heading toward his camp.

"Hello son," says Black Bear, my father, as I enter our home. "We expected you home before now." The smells of the roasted venison and fresh cakes make me realize I am hungry. Even though they had finished eating, I serve up myself the luscious food my dear mother had prepared. Bowing my head in gratitude for what I was about to receive, I say a prayer in my heart to the Creator and Mother Earth. I eat almost twice as much as usual, slice after slice of venison, many corn cakes and wild rice until my mother says to me.

"Gray Wolf, exactly what happened today?"

"Mother, Grandmother and I need to talk tomorrow, and then I can tell you and father what I learned and did today," I respond enigmatically. My mother and father look at me then at each other and say nothing. I clean up and wash out the bowls and then head straight to bed. My mind is still racing over the events of the day and sleep does not come easy. I toss and turn.

Finally, I get up to sit outside for a bit, putting on a tunic jacket, and I grab a blanket to warm me against the spring night. I sit there awhile, focusing my attention on the moonrise.

Crunch. Crunch. Crunch.

I hear footsteps.

"Grandmother?" I whisper with a smile. Tired as she is, she does not go into the house. Instead she sits down next to me, resting her hand on my leg, looks into my face and nods.

"I can see that you have had an adventure that has changed your life, little one," she says.

I tell her of my experience with Brother Wolf.

"Gray Wolf, you have experienced the Oneness. This is a very spiritual experience that only some of our people have in their lifetimes. You have done well, and Brother Wolf is grateful for your kindness and healing. I will give you additional medicines for him before you return to him in the morning. For the time being, speak to no one else about this experience. Great Spirit has touched you today, and you need to reflect on all that has happened. We will speak more of this tomorrow after you return from seeing Brother Wolf."

She pauses and looks into my eyes and says, "Gray Wolf, you are tired. Many times the energy that we use to heal drains our reserves. You connected with Brother Wolf. You overcame his fear of humans, and you were shown what you needed to do." With a big smile on her face she holds my hand and says, "My dearest grandson, you have had quite a day today."

With that, we both rise and enter the house together. Grandmother sits on her bed for a moment, pulls up her red blanket with one black stripe at each end, reaches for her buffalo hide, and falls into a slumber. I crawl into my bed pulling up my blankets around my neck. Sister Moon rises higher, and her light comes through my mica window with a soothing and gentle touch, and I drift off.

I dreamed I was soaring over our village and valley like an eagle. The next thing I knew I was sitting by Brother Wolf near a flowing stream. Its waters made a quiet, heavenly musical sound. Brother Wolf was aglow in the moonlight. He was sitting upright. His left rear leg was completely healed. I was startled by how young he now looked. We could now speak to each other in words. I was stunned at first. Then I realized what he had said to me before we parted.

"Gray Wolf, I have passed into Spirit. I will be with you now along with your other spirit guides for your lifetime. The kindness you showed me, the healing of my pain, our joining of spirits allowed me to transition without disturbance, in peace and joy. My physical body is where you left it. What I am about to tell you is very important. You may be a little uncomfortable with what you must do, but this is from Spirit. All of this will become clear to you as you grow older.

"You must harvest my body yourself. Bury all my organs in the place where you found me. Cover them with dirt and place the burial herbs and plants on top of the earthen mound when you have finished.

"Then say a prayer for me to the Creator and Mother Earth. Take the rest of my body into your village and have my entire hide tanned. Ask that you be allowed to keep my upper and lower jaws with the teeth intact. The upper jaw is for you, a sacred object for your medicine bundle . . . a direct connection to your gray wolf spirit guides of which you have several, including me. Call upon us when you need to. As for the lower jaw, also keep this in your medicine bundle. When the time comes, you will be shown what to do with it. This is powerful medicine given to you by Spirit."

I said, "I will have the hide tanned by Lone Tree, the best tanner in our village."

"Gray Wolf, you will become a great shaman for your people. You will go on a great journey in this lifetime. You will be an important spiritual guide and healer for The People. As you grow older, the use of my hide and jaws will be revealed to you. Now I must leave you and go to my ancestors."

Suddenly, I awake.

My entire body is tingling in the warmth of the Oneness. Sister Moon had gone to rest and the first light of Father Sun brings a new direction to my life.

Upon awaking, my thoughts crowd all around themselves about Brother Wolf and my dream. I jump up still clothed from the night before and begin gathering foods and some of my healing herbs for the gray wolf. I did not want to believe my dream had been real, stark and clear as it was. As I quietly bustle about, I glance over to my sleeping grandmother. I would share my dream with her when I returned.

As I go out the door, I see my mother busy preparing more food. "Just a minute," she warns as she grabs my sleeve. Looking at me with her beautiful face, she catches my eye then looks down at the water baskets. Dutifully I set down my satchel and pick up the handles of one basket and head down to the pond.

After delivering the water to my mother, I find myself suddenly hungry again. As I look around for something to eat, I see that my angel mother has already prepared a bowl for me and some left over corn cakes to add to my traveling food. I look at her with a grateful smile, bow my head and give thanks before I eat.

As I prepare to leave, I poke my head in to see if my Grandmother is up. Her bed is empty. The red blanket, her favorite, is spread neatly over her bed. This blanket is one that was given to her by a trader when she was a young girl, because she had healed a wound he had suffered.

The herbs I left for her were gone and different herbs were on my bed and I added to my satchel. I guessed she was about her healing work.

My journey back to Brother Wolf took longer than I supposed. Searching around for him, I half expected him to at least whine at me to signal where he was. Stumbling around the rocks and bushes among the trees, I spot the branches I had layered over him. Before I can walk over to that place, my dream suddenly returned to me along with everything Brother Wolf had said.

Tears found their way down my face as I removed the shelter I built to protect him. Accepting the validity of my dream, I looked down at the beautiful creature lying there and marveled at his serenity and grace. A prayer uttered itself in my heart as I stood there struck by a sense of awe of this creature's power, wisdom, and connectedness. His death blessed me with a sense of who I am.

While the words of a prayer passed my lips, I used my flint knife and elk shoulder blade shovel to follow the instructions of Brother Wolf. My task completed, I placed the burial herbs and plants on the earthen mound. I was overcome with emotion and sat listening to the forest.

Almost in a trance I made my way back down to the village carrying the carcass of my friend.

As I approach the village, I see Lone Tree standing out in front of his house as if waiting for me, hands on his hips.

"What do you have there, Gray Wolf?" he smiles good-naturedly. I shake my head as I put the carcass of the beautiful creature down on his table outside.

"It's a gift from Spirit," I say softly.

Lone Tree says, "I know you didn't kill him. What happened?"

Rendering the story again moves me emotionally. I tell him the instructions I received in the dream. I lower my voice so as not to be overheard.

Lone Tree notices and comprehends the privacy of the issue, shaking his head in agreement. "I understand. I'll take care of it." He pauses as I turn to leave, then adds, "Say, does your mom have cakes leftover?"

As I back away, I say, "I'll see what's there."

Shortly thereafter, Floating Lily shows up at Lone Tree's with a basket of delicious stew, sweet cakes, and other delicacies.

Two days later Turning Rabbit showed up at the Healing House fearing the worst as he contemplated the deadly fever of his young comrade. Anxiety and his sense of responsibility ate away at his stomach and drained his face of all color, anticipating the leg bone being broken again and then reset. No, he was not looking forward to facing his friend, Warm Stone. At least the shaman healers gave him credit for preventing gangrene and the possibility of Warm Stone losing a leg.

As he entered the Healing House, he was greeted by a warm smile, "I am so glad to see you, Turning Rabbit." Turning Rabbit took a step back in surprise. The warm greeting was indeed extended by none other than his road companion, Warm Stone.

"Thank you so much for getting me here," Warm Stone continued. "I don't know where I was or how I got here but I got to tell you, I'm feeling pretty good. I just can't go anywhere right now, but . . . ," he said glancing at his bandaged leg. He lowered his voice then and looked at each of the three healers in the eye as he finished, "they helped me get through something I'd rather not describe. I really thought I was gone. They just kept placing poultices on my leg, giving me teas, sticking needles in me, and chanting all night long. Suddenly at dawn, my fever broke and I came back hungry."

Watching his grinning friend, Turning Rabbit was speechless from shock and found he could not get words out. Words he had formulated to be of comfort were no longer needed. He was surprised by this turn of events.

The shaman healers busied themselves with preparations for the leg reset. They melted some fat in a small cooking pot and added medicinal herbs and other ingredients to the mixture.

Turning Rabbit finally found his voice, "I am so glad you are doing well. I must say, this is not what I had expected. Wow! What can I say? This is wonderful news. So what now?" he asked the air, his question was not addressed to anyone in particular.

Thunder Cloud answered the seemingly rhetorical question, "Grandmother Shining Moon will be here soon, then we will break his leg and reset it. If we don't, he may never walk again, at least very far at any one time."

Turning Rabbit gulped, "Maybe I'd better leave, then. I really don't think I should be here. I might interfere."

Warm Stone suddenly grabbed Turning Rabbit's arm tight, squeezed, and then pleaded, "Oh, why don't you stay? I think I'd like a friend here with me." Looking around at the healers, then added not wanting to offend the very people who had helped him recover from his intense life-threatening fever, ". . . Oh, I mean, someone I know, someone I've known for a while." Speaks With Plants, Thunder Cloud, and Whispering Moon all smiled and nodded in understanding of his fear.

Awkward silence.

Finally, Whispering Moon assured Warm Stone that it certainly was all right that Turning Rabbit stay.

Nobody assured Turning Rabbit of anything. His sense of responsibility kept him from leaving. Yet his fear of pain and seeing his friend in pain made him want to leave, and leave in a hurry. Feeling trapped between the conflicting feelings, he couldn't pull his hand out of Warm Stone's grip.

Just then Grandmother Shining Moon entered from outside with leather bags bumping each other as they swung from her arms. Turning Rabbit sighed and shrugged in surrender to the moment.

Shining Moon remained focused on something far away, something not seen by those present. As she went about her business, she did not acknowledge Turning Rabbit. Turning Rabbit remained sitting on a stool next to Warm Stone.

Turning Rabbit saw Speaks With Plants smudging the room with a mixture made from herbs. The smoke carried an uplifting scent.

Turning Rabbit felt stunned into silence as he looked at his friend on the bed in the middle of the room.

As Turning Rabbit continued to hold Warm Stone's hand, the four shamanic healers began to chant, low at first, then a little louder. Grandmother Shining Moon positioned herself on the other side of Warm Stone, holding his hand in hers. Warm Stone could feel the soft pads staged between the deep lines of her hands and then he breathed deeply, letting go of any lingering fears. Her touch reassured him.

She looked deeply into Warm Stone's eyes, and said, "You'll be all right. We're going to reset your leg. It hasn't healed properly. You need to walk properly to become more of who you already are." Her tone was soft, firm, and vibrated at a level uncommon in everyday speech. Warm Stone felt her words more clearly than he heard them.

"You should feel no pain. We will break the bone where it was broken before. Then we will position your leg in such a way as to promote proper mending."

Turning Rabbit sobered into stone cold silence.

"Warm Stone, do you have any questions before we begin?" she asked her patient. Warm Stone swallowed hard and nodded his head side to side, while gripping Turning Rabbit's hand even tighter.

Chanting, rhythmic and steady, could be heard from the Healing House. Speaks With Plants held the large abalone shell, fanning the smudge scent over each individual. Chanting continued. Grandmother Shining Moon pulled out an array of needles on a cloth. Gently removing the bandages and poultices from the night's application, she exposed the wounded leg.

Chanting.
Needles inserted.
Chanting.
Smudge.
Chanting.
Needles inserted.
Smudge.
Chanting.
Needles inserted.

Grandmother Shining Moon lifted her eyes to Heaven, and then before anyone could really see, she lifted her right hand over the leg so her baby finger is closest to the leg and her thumb points to Heaven, and gave one downward chopping motion.

Snap.

The hand chop to the leg broke the bone simply and evenly. Warm Stone exhaled with gusto and fell limply back into the soft pillows he was laying on, eyelids dropped. He felt no pain.

Whispering Moon produced a thick piece of rawhide that had been soaking in warm water that made it soft and pliable. Together, she and Speaks With Plants generously lined the rawhide with the medicinal herb and fat mixture. While they were performing this task, Thunder Cloud continued to chant and smudge. Watching the needles in Warm Stone's leg for an indication as to when they could be removed, Shining Moon finally pulled them out. After she tended to the wound, she signaled for the treated rawhide to be wrapped around the patient's leg and tied.

"Now, what we are doing," explained Shining Moon, "is wrapping your leg in this thick rawhide, shaping it to your leg and securing it with rawhide strips. As it dries, it will tighten and firmly hold your leg in proper alignment, so the bone will heal correctly."

Shining Moon chanted as she inserted other needles in other parts of Warm Stone's exposed flesh including the bottom of his feet. At the end of this ceremony, Warm Stone lapsed into a deep sleep with a slight smile on his face, releasing his grasp of Turning Rabbit's hand.

Leaving the Healing House in a state of shock, Turning Rabbit felt an acute awareness from this experience. Experiencing the painless healing of his friend left him hypersensitive to the environment. The birds were singing louder. The breezes touched his face like they were alive with hands and fingers caressing him gently. The trees hummed softly, swaying rhythmically. All moved in tune with a sense that everything is connected and Oneness abounds.

Suddenly Turning Rabbit was confronted by an out of balance scene. One of his traveling companions, the one with the scarred face, was posturing near a house, arms gesturing while talking. He appeared like he was trying to win an argument with one of the Grandmothers. Grandmother Blue Lightning stood in front of him without moving.

She calmly did not move, did not back up, and continued to stand boring holes into his energy field with powerful eyes, unaffected by his gyrations and loud sounds.

"What's going on here?" Turning Rabbit inquired with a tone that meant 'this conflict is over.' Before the Mayan native could finish drawing in a breath to answer, Turning Rabbit shot a meaningful glance to Grandmother Blue Lightning, then grabbed the young man by the arm and marched him across the village to their camp.

Several hours later, Turning Rabbit began to pack up in readiness to move on to another hamlet on his circular journey to the north and northeast. His traveling companions appeared anxious. Already they've created disturbances when mingling among the villagers. Some of the young men stayed too long, lounging near the Council House, staring lustfully at the young women, causing some discomfort among them. Occasionally, these outsiders broke out into fights between themselves over nothing that the villagers could detect. Welcomed by the villagers as they were, they brought with them a vibration that was strange and out of order with the ways of The People.

"They call themselves, 'The People'." Turning Rabbit began as he started packing.

"The People?" one asked. "What do they mean, 'The People'? Aren't we people too?" another inquired stiffly.

"They see themselves as part of all Creation, living in a sense of total connectedness with Mother Earth and the Creator. They call themselves Children of the Law of One. To them it means they live embraced by Spirit, the Great Oneness," Turning Rabbit explained to his band of young companions.

"You've traveled with me great distances, near the great water where the sun sets. You said you wanted to see the country and see new peoples from the equator to the great north and the other great water from which the sun rises." They nodded and all looked at each other then turned their gaze back to Turning Rabbit. "As I have told you earlier, we will be seeing and visiting with people different from what you are used to, different from what you know, different from what you assume to be true."

"Right. Back home," another young man passionately said, "men rule. Our chiefs and leaders are men, not women. Women are for serving and having babies. The men here are not chiefs, and do not have power over anyone!"

Turning Rabbit nodded in agreement and said, "Yes, that is true. This culture is matriarchal. The elderly women are all referred to as Grandmother. Grandmothers carry the wisdom, insight, and memories from generations and generations back. Women are seen as the givers of life to family groups. They do not exclude men from this power base. They see men as necessary partners in the whole of everything. One cannot thrive without the other. *Balance and harmony rule.*"

Several listeners rolled their eyes and shifted their weight indicating this perspective made them feel uncomfortable. It conflicted with how they have experienced life. One spoke up again with a challenge, "We don't even know who's in charge around here. At home, we all know who is in charge, who answers to whom up a chain of command to the top chief of the entire kingdom."

Turning Rabbit stopped organizing his merchandise for a moment to think about this last observation. Then he said thoughtfully, "Yes, and if a man wants to gain more power, he must wrestle power away from another in some way. Men must compete for power or prestige. A patriarchal society fosters competition and aggression to gain personal power over others. The more people a man can command, the greater his power and influence, and the greater he can increase his personal wealth. Every man is separate from every other man.

"Yet, here, The People, this people, do not see themselves as separate from each other. Their matriarchal style of governing does not recognize personal power in the way that you do.

"The only power they recognize is the power found within. There is no power over others, only power with others. No one is in charge since they all belong to the One. They are entrained with Mother Earth, and each other. Everyone is connected to everyone and everything in the Great Oneness. So they have no need to rule over anyone.

"They share everything, so a sense of wealth does not exist here. What happens to one, happens to all. This matriarchal society fosters cooperation among everyone. No one goes hungry. No one goes without help regardless of the need. No one is considered separate. A sense of being separate from anyone or anything, including animals, Mother Earth, the stars, does not exist for them."

Turning Rabbit looked for feedback from the group of young tanned bodies, smaller by comparison to the average build of members of The People. Their faces revealed conflict with the ideas he just put forth. He observed that this information was not comprehensible to them.

Wanting to continue criticizing The People whom they found to be strange, one of the band asked, "What about their houses? They are made of sticks and poles with mud covered walls and thatched roofs. They don't even have any temples."

Another picked up, "Yeah, they have no temples and nothing is made of stone like our temples. All they have are these houses and no temples."

Shaking his head, Turning Rabbit said, "They do not need temples built of stone or of any other building material. They honor the Creator within each person. Their houses serve them for living and gathering. Besides they don't have that kind of stone around here anyway."

Scratching his nose, shifting his weight as he leaned on a pack, one of them asked, "So, are there more of these kinds of people around here?"

"Yes," Turning Rabbit affirmed, "they extend all the way north as far as I go and east as far as the great water."

As he spoke, he noticed that shoulders drooped, mouths turned sideways and back, eyes looked up then down. He continued, "There are thousands of them scattered all over in villages, hamlets, settlements of various sizes.

They've lived here for thousands of years. They recite stories about the Ancient of Days, and acknowledge that they have lived a thousand years of peace here."

"Those Grandmothers give me the willies," one grimaced. Then the others voiced agreement. "They just look at you and you feel helpless and overpowered. I don't think I want to hang around where they are." The others nodded agreement.

"As I told you before, I will tell you again. If you travel with me, you will honor the ways of the people we visit. You don't have to agree with anything they do or say. You simply must accept them and not behave in any way that will disrupt their sense of things. Clearly, your presence here has created a disturbance that upsets them. It's time we go," Turning Rabbit finished.

II

AFTER THE TRADERS LEFT

Several days after the traders left with their goods, The People felt relieved at their exit. Traders had always been welcomed. Yet, this last visit left them feeling a little out of balance. Balance and harmony had always prevailed. When it did not, then efforts were made to rebalance the energy.

Grandmother Whistling Wind led the large group of Grandmothers, Elders, and shaman who lived within the scope of our village in a ceremony at moonrise one evening. Many villagers attended and participated on the perimeters of a circle, layering another concentric circle of people in the ceremonial dance.

Drums beat rhythmically, matching the beat of their hearts. The People danced around and around one way, then back around the other way, each tapping their feet to the beat of the drums. The large center fire burned brightly, pungent with incense permeating the ceremony. Voices hypnotically chanted and complemented the steady beat of the drums. Prayers were sung up to heaven. Whistling Wind raised her arms to heaven and called out an ancient prayer, one used many times in the past to clear the energy field of The People. This time it addressed clearing the foreign energies introduced by those strangers accompanying the known trader.

A few weeks later, Bluebird Near the Lily wanders over to the Healing House to get her tea she takes for her menstrual cramps. As she enters the house, Warm Stone braces up against a wall staring out one of the mica windows. He boasts crutches for support. When Bluebird Near the Lily walks in, not noticing Warm Stone, she looks for Speaks With Plants. Warm Stone cannot take his eyes off her petite shape and long waves of black hair.

Speaks With Plants turns from the back of the room and looking up at her, says, "Bluebird Near the Lily, I was expecting you. I have your teas ready for you. Have you met Warm Stone?"

Startled that she had not noticed him earlier she says, "Oh, I'm sorry. I didn't see you there." As she apologizes, Warm Stone smiles his most impressive smile, assessing this treasure. Warm Stone nods his head in acceptance of her comment, then adds, "I was trying to blend into the wall. Not a problem." He smiles again.

She looks at him with her big dark eyes, smiles and says, "You did a great job at that. I must go. Nice to have met you," she smiles as she slips out the door with her package of tea.

"So . . . who was that?" Warm Stone asks of Speaks With Plants with interest.

"Hmmm," Speaks With Plants responds, "I think you are barking up the wrong tree there. Don't forget you are a stranger here. You are welcome here. You are welcome to all the medicinal help, all the food and care you require. You're not of The People, yet we take you in, save your life and your leg with no other thought than to help you complete yourself. So, you do want to honor the ways of The People who take you in. Bluebird Near the Lily is indeed a beautiful woman. No doubt about that. However, according to my sources, she has already set her eyes on someone, someone you would not want to challenge."

Warm Stone turns down the corners of his mouth as he listens to Speaks With Plants and looks down. Then he says hopefully lifting his eyebrows, "I know I have some healing to do. Maybe I could interest her and she might change her mind."

"Nice try there, young man. You're a trader. She couldn't follow you on your journeys. As beautiful as she is, her stamina is not what it should be. Just as her frame is petite and delicate, so is her constitution," Speaks With Plants says knitting his eyebrows, showing deep concern for a favorite patient. "Besides," he continues, "Bluebird Near the Lily belongs here with The People. She is not equipped to travel the trade routes with you, exposing herself to the elements and hardships that you routinely encounter. It would be too rigorous for her.

"No, she is better off here with her own support group and family. Your ways are not her ways, and her ways are not your ways," Speaks With Plants says as he raises his eyebrows, and shakes his head.

Warm Stone's head droops as he takes this in and then says, "I have always wanted to be a trader, to see the world. Now I see that I must look at this predicament. An apprentice trader stuck in a village that is bound to the Earth, not physically moving around to all the different and intriguing places available on several continents, my heart tugs at the conflict. I must say the thought did cross my mind about staying in such an Earth-bound community. My heart's desire, though, is to travel from ocean to ocean, arctic to the equator and past." Warm Stone shakes his head as he hobbles outside to sit in the sun.

Warm Stone speaks out loud to himself, "I sense my leg is healing nicely between the teas I drink and the incense laden air that I sleep in here at the Healing House, and the food, umm. Yes, the community I have landed in by sheer chance proved indeed to be one of the best possible to one in my position . . . I am realizing I am missing something though, something important. I will have to think about that," Warm Stone finishes under his breath.

After a while of enjoying the warming sun of a cool spring afternoon, Warm Stone sees two tall figures heading his way. He sits up a bit more erect with his bound leg stretched out before him. As the two forms emerge from the shadows, he sees Floating Lily and me, Gray Wolf. Warm Stone greets us with a smile.

"I'm glad to see you both. Floating Lily, I am especially glad to see you, because I suspect you are bringing more food. I guess I am definitely on the mend as just sitting here gives me an appetite."

"I'm glad to hear that, Warm Stone," says Floating Lily as she moves past him going inside with her bundle.

Warm Stone turns to look up at me and says, "I think I remember you. Haven't you been in and out during this past week or so?"

"Yes," I reply, "I'm Gray Wolf. I've been bringing healing herbs to the Healing House. Some are for you, and others are just supplies. You do look like you are recovering nicely," I conclude with a smile. Then I add, "Excuse me while I drop these off." I wave a carefully wrapped bundle as I tilt my head toward the House.

Warm Stone could hear conversation going on inside, and could not quite make out what was said. Looking expectantly at the place where the two of us vanished from his sight to enter the Healing House, he waits patiently for someone to come out. After a few more minutes, Floating Lily and I step out with dishes of food. "We decided to join you for a meal. You said you were hungry, and we wouldn't mind a bite or two. It's so nice outside today, we thought we could all eat out here," I say.

I hand a dish of stew still steaming and a utensil to Warm Stone. I see to it that Floating Lily has hers as well. While Warm Stone begins eating hungrily from his large bowl, both Floating Lily and I bow our heads in prayer and then sprinkle a pinch of cornmeal on the ground. Only then do we begin eating from smaller bowls. Warm Stone continues to eat heartily and at the same time watches us closely. When he has finished his bowl of stew, I hand him another bowl with wilted goosefoot leaves and biscuits to try.

Floating Lily and I finish our stew and take a taste of the spinach-like vegetable and split a biscuit. ". . . and what do we have for a finish?" I ask with a flourish and a smile when I see that all the food has been consumed.

Warm Stone tilts his head inquiring silently. I answer my own question, "My mother makes the best sweet cakes ever." Warm Stone smiles in anticipation. "Here you go," I say as I hand one to each and keep one for myself.

After we finish eating we appreciate the warmth of the sun. However, the gentle breeze begins to blow a little harder. Occasionally, large cloud formations move to block the sun creating a cooling feeling.

"Speaks With Plants asked me to speak to you about exercising. He says that you need to get up and about some. Sitting around here all day no longer is appropriate for your complete healing. You must start to walk a little," I inform Warm Stone.

Warm Stone gulps, blinks and then shrugs his shoulders in submission. "I must have faith in what he says. He certainly has done an excellent job taking care of me," Warm Stone says as he looks at me. "I still feel a little wobbly though."

"C'mon. Floating Lily and I can take you up to her house. I heard Water Dog is back and I want to see him," I say, ". . . that is after she and I wash up the dishes and put everything back." Then I stop for a moment, and say, "And before we do that I believe I need to get water for Speaks With Plants. I'll be right back." I gather up the dishes and take them inside, grab a water basket and head out to get the water.

"Floating Lily, you are so beautiful. I don't believe I have ever seen such rich red wavy hair. Everyone from where I come from all have black straight hair. Yours is the color of fire, reds, pinks, and gold," Warm Stone says as he relishes a few moments alone with a woman.

"You are kind to say so, Warm Stone," she responds with embarrassment. "I was born with this color hair. All my family has red or goldish red hair of one shade or another, all except my mother. She has brown hair, although then she's not as tall as the rest of us either. My brother's hair is more of a rusty color."

Warm Stone enjoying the rapport asks with a smile, ". . . and who is your brother? I'm not sure I have met him."

"Oh, he's been away. His name is Water Dog. He's becoming a flint knapper and must travel up to Flint Ridge and around. Rising Wolf, his mentor, takes him all over to dig for just the right flint. I guess it's hard work, and, well, my brother is so big, I don't think anything is hard for him."

"Is he as tall as you are?" Warm Stone asked raising his eyebrows over his twinkling eyes, "I don't believe I've ever encountered a woman quite as tall and striking as you."

"Warm Stone," Floating Lily stands up abruptly, puts her hands on her hips, bends forward slightly as if to scold him, "I'm not yet a woman. I've not begun my menses. I am ten years old. I think I'll go see what is holding up Gray Wolf." She disappears into the Healing House leaving her words trailing in the air.

The weight of her words pushes Warm Stone back like he had been shoved. Paling at the thought of children being as tall, or taller than most of the adults he knew, shocked him speechless. His thoughts tumbled over themselves as he remembers the words Speaks With Plants had spoken to him earlier. After sitting there a while reflecting on that last conversation, his curiosity is piqued. *These are an interesting people.*

With the chores done Floating Lily and I rejoin Warm Stone outside. Warm Stone looks up at Floating Lily and says, "I'm anxious to see this Water Dog brother of yours out of curiosity."

I hand Warm Stone a new pair of crutches fashioned by Waving Branches, a wood worker over in the next village.

"It's time we go. We'll each walk beside you. That'll give you reassurance," I say softly.

With Floating Lily on one side of him and me on the other, we walk slowly down the hill.

We stop every now and then when Warm Stone needs to pause.

"I'm not sure we should've set such a distant goal for you. Yet you do need to get moving about to bring strength back. When we get there, you can rest," I say.

When we finally get there, the day has darkened by large thunderclouds accompanied by the wind blowing in gusts. Blooming Rose, Floating Lily's mother sees us making our way slowly toward her house. Noticing the weather change, she comes outside to welcome us and invites us in. Her house is taller and larger than most of the others in our village.

"Blooming Rose, it is nice to see you again. I came to see if Water Dog was around and brought with me my new friend, Warm Stone," I say. "Warm Stone is the trader who was hurt."

"Hello, Gray Wolf. Oh, please sit down, Warm Stone," Blooming Rose says. "I'm glad to meet you. I hope your health is returning. You know, you had the best team of healers working on you," she adds with a warm smile. After a pause she asks looking at me, "Well, maybe I should fix us some tea or broth?"

"Thank you," I say gratefully, "we just ate, so maybe some refreshing tea after that walk. I'm sure Warm Stone felt it was a long walk. He held up pretty good. It was his first long walk since my Grandmother put that parfleche around it to hold the bone in place so it mends properly."

Warm Stone, grateful to find himself sitting propped on a comfortable bed with pillows behind him and his leg up on the bed, remains silent.

While her mother was busy making the tea, Floating Lily steps outside to spend a few moments alone.

I ask Blooming Rose, "Is Water Dog back yet? I was looking to catch up with him while he's here."

"Oh, yes," she says with a nod, "I expect him any time now. He just went over to Bluebird Near the Lily's to let her know he was home again. Honestly, I'll be glad when he can stick around for a while so he can settle down with Bluebird."

At that remark, Warm Stone's attention focuses in on the conversation. He had been looking around at the interior of the stick houses. They appeared tightly constructed of small trees or branches woven together. Even though the outside was simple and dull with the walls covered by a mud/clay compound, the inside proudly displays tapestries of woven reeds and heavy fabric either dyed or painted with brilliant colors. The inside walls were smooth and looked almost like pottery.

Windows neatly frame the mica slabs that allow for sunlight to brighten up the large room during the day. Interesting oil lamps hang on the walls. A shiny copper mirror is placed behind a small clay bowl holding a wick. The lamp is surrounded by a crescent-shaped mica piece that frames the unique lighting system.

In the center of the ceiling is a partially raised roof that allows smoke to escape upwards. The thatching of the roof is tightly bound, and lies over a very finely woven mat to prevent wet weather from penetrating. And, we are soon to experience just how waterproof this construction was.

Suddenly a clap of thunder split the sky, sharp and crackling.

At the sharp crack, Warm Stone jumps. Blooming Rose looks over at him to check on his condition. She had put the water on for tea and is preparing the cups for serving. "Looks like we might be in for a storm," she observes.

I stand in the doorway looking skyward to measure the intensity of the storm, "Yes, indeed, looks like we'll be in for it." As I continue to stand there, I see someone coming. Almost running up the hill is a man carrying a large bag. As he comes toward the house, the wind takes exception to him being there and buffets him about. Nearby trees rock in rhythm, branches waving in a symphonic movement with the gusts of wind blowing across the landscape. The sky darkens more as the black clouds boil around the valley.

Warm Stone graciously accepts the warm tea in the finely made pottery teacup offered by Blooming Rose. "Thank you," he says bowing his head in gratitude.

"We'll soon have one more who might appreciate a cup of your nourishing tea, Blooming Rose," I say, just as the stranger tramps up to the door, out of breath.

Blooming Rose looks up at the stranger and smiles, "Oh, so nice to see you again, Little Otter. Come in, come in. Sit down and have a cup of tea with us."

He gives a half smile, and plops himself down on a cushioned bench, setting his bag on the floor. "Thanks for the tea, Blooming Rose," he says as all eyes in the room land on him. "Looks like I might need to stay a little while, at least until the storm subsides," Little Otter says sheepishly.

"Not to worry," Blooming Rose reassures, "I've got room for you here."

Blooming Rose continues, "I've sorted out all the pearls by size. I hope you brought plenty of bags for each of the different sizes."

Warm Stone stops sipping his tea as his ears perk up. "Pearls?" he asks sitting up straighter.

Flash. Lightning crackles.

Crack, thunders the sky.

"Yes," Blooming Rose explains to Warm Stone, "I'm the pearl collector for our village. As our People collect them from the fresh water mussels, they bring them to me.

"Our streams and our rivers provide us with much in the way of food, especially mussels. We enjoy eating them, and appreciate them as a major source of meat and nutrients. We harvest them from time to time and often we find pearls in them. All the pearls collected in this area are brought to me. I sort them into sizes, and sometimes by color. Then I give them to the runners, like Little Otter, who collect them from each village. Runners give them to the pearl workers, who then treat them and drill them for either jewelry or to be sewn on to clothing."

The runner from Seip, Little Otter, leans back, takes a deep breath, obviously relaxing from his experience out in the blowing wind, nods in agreement. As Blooming Rose speaks, she pulls out baskets from under the benches and beds, full of pearls iridescent in what light is left of the day.

Warm Stone's eyes widen as his gaze falls on the baskets of pearls. "You mean you don't trade for them?" he asks.

Blooming Rose absent-mindedly responds, "No, why would I? I have everything I need. People from Baum and Seip bring us food and other items, such as fabrics, clothes, jewelry and more."

THE CAMP OF GOD'S TEARS

Warm Stone raises his eyebrows at this, trying to understand.

Flash, then the sky crackles with a sharp cutting boom as the sky continues to thunder. Rain begins to fall, lightly at first, then pounding in large droplets, hitting the neatly tied thatched roof and running off nicely in rivulets onto the ground.

During the conversation, Floating Lily slips back into the house unnoticed.

With the day darkening, Floating Lily moves almost invisibly around the room lighting each of the wall lamps fueled with nut oil. She then finishes her tea and sits back and wraps herself up in a comfortable blanket, relaxing to the rhythm of the rain, losing interest in the conversation. The rain obviously has a relaxing effect on the circle of friends sipping tea in the large and cozy home. The small fire used for heating the water for tea warms the home nicely.

Each of us settle into the tenor of the late afternoon as it glides into evening with the black storm clouds roiling about, lightning and thunder having their say, and we feel an enjoyable degree of comfort with each other.

Slosh, slosh, slosh. Stamp. Stamp.

Warm Stone looks up alarmingly at the door after the approaching sounds end.

The door swings open.

The harsh wind grabs the door and slams it against the outside of the house, banging it several times, rattling the hinges and intruding on the quiet serenity inside the home.

Warm Stone's eyes as big as saucers already from taking in the huge quantity of pearls, enlarge even more as he focuses on Water Dog standing in the doorway, bigger than life. Warm Stone has never set eyes on anyone as large and tall as Water Dog. *No wonder the height of the house and the doorway is so large.*

Dripping with water from the rain, Water Dog kicks off his wet shoes. He removes his outer garments and hangs them up outside under the protective canopy to keep the wetness outside. Upon entering, he nods to all present, finds a seat on a bench, and looks around for another pair of shoes. He wiggles his large toes before he slips on the dry shoes.

Blooming Rose smiles to herself, as she takes in the cozy scene from her corner by the indoor hearth. Pleased and feeling an overriding sense of peace, she adds more water to her kettle for additional tea making. Her house was larger than many in the village because her husband, who is now in the Spirit World, was of the giant people with red hair. Her two children inherited these characteristics.

Nestled in for the stormy afternoon, the eclectic members shared stories, laughed, and enjoyed their time together.

Water Dog shares his sense of success as a flint knapper, "I'm so enjoying the work I'm doing. It's what I now feel that I am. Rising Wolf is a taskmaster, teaching me what he knows. His skills are wondrous, and he's taken me under his wing as his apprentice. I've been learning how to spot places to dig and what to look for when seeking new sources of flint to work.

"What I find intriguing is that I've been honing my intuitive sense of where to dig. Rising Wolf is good at detecting the places to dig for flint this way. He's encouraging me to tap into my unity with Mother Earth and let her direct me to where the best flint source is. Since we have to dig ten or twenty feet down to find it, we want to be sure that it is the right place to start. I find it such an incredible experience to tune in to Mother Earth and follow her direction."

At this statement, Blooming Rose smiles wistfully to herself. At last her son has found himself and can settle down doing what he enjoys.

Water Dog adds after a few moments, "As we dig, we take the flint out from the vein to shape later into arrowheads, spears, knives, and so forth. Then we move on to find another source, always leaving the rest of the vein of flint with Mother Earth. Because she is so generous in providing this resource for us, we do not want to take everything from her in any one spot." Having spoken, Water Dog sits back folding his large arms across his chest in satisfaction.

I keep an extra sense out for the weather and possible waning of the storm. I get up several times to look outside the front door for changes, and see only serious rain and the blowing of a cold wind.

"You know, I've some sweet cakes left over from yesterday. Would anyone like some with their tea?" Blooming Rose asks as she sees me check on the weather for a third time.

Little Otter nods in acceptance of her offer. Blooming Rose rises to sort out the cakes and pour more tea.

As she serves the cakes to Little Otter, she looks him in the eye, lowers her voice, and says, "I guess I'll be needing a large measure of drilled pearls for a special dress for Bluebird Near the Lily. Why don't you take word back to Seip when you return there. She's tiny, you know. I want her to be covered in pearls. The radiance of the pearls will match the radiance of her soul." Little Otter purses his lips and nods in affirmation, and then adds a wink and a smile.

Warm Stone shifts his weight, feeling stiffness set in. As he sits up a bit, he shakes his head slightly, furrows his eyebrows and then says, "I've never seen red-haired people before, not to mention giant red-haired people. Turning Rabbit told me about them and introduced me to Floating Lily when we first arrived. Are there more?"

"We have entire villages of them," I respond.

"Who are they?" Warm Stone asks.

"Maybe it's not so much who *they* are as who *we* are," I say. "We are one as The People. Together we have lived here in the Ohio Valley in peace for over a thousand years. Before that, wars occurred off and on between the dark-haired people and the red-haired people. Together, over the millennia, we have evolved into a single People. Maybe the question might be where did we come from?"

Warm Stone nods, "Yes, I guess that's what I'm asking."

I gladly tell the story, "The ancestors of the smaller black-haired people migrated from their land across the sea in the west. Gradually, their land sank. As that happened they journeyed over the water to the land where you are from, like Mexico, and further south and further north.

"Some settled on the coastal shores about twenty or thirty thousand years ago or more. Some migrated across this land and settled north of here, and south of here. Our particular set of ancestors found this part of the country especially beautiful and inviting. Mother Earth spoke to our ancestors here. Our legends give us great detail about how Mother Earth agreed to provide for us lavishly as long as we honored her and kept our promises to her.

"In the sea to the east of here existed another land. The people of that land were quite tall and many had red hair or yellow hair. These people were even larger than Water Dog. Actually, Water Dog is small compared to them." At the mention of his name, Water Dog opens a sleepy eye and nods. "Some of those people migrated to our land here. Then their land also gradually sank. Neither of these ancient lands exists today.

"Over time the people from each direction combined and became our ancestors. As a result we are a mixture of these two peoples. We've flourished because of the mixing and inter-relating, the sharing of ideas, skills, and knowledge. With the blending of the spiritual knowledge from the west and the technical knowledge from the east, we've developed a belief system that recognizes that an elegant intelligence guides the processes of the Universe.

"For example, our People live in the sense of oneness with Great Spirit. As a result, we practice our oneness with each other and in our relationship with Mother Earth. She is a living being such as we are. She provides us with everything we need to live. The plants and animals come from her too. Our bodies are from her as she provides the food, water, and air that we need to sustain ourselves.

"We do not compete with each other for more of anything. Our entire way of life is based on cooperation, collaboration, and sharing what we have with everyone else and that includes you."

Then Warm Stone asks, "But what of the traders? You trade with us."

I continue, "Yes, that is your way. You and the other traders bring us items from your land and from other lands where we don't go. We give you items you find valuable to take back with you to other villages far away. You bring us news of other places. We give you food, shelter, and provide healing when needed. Now isn't that right?"

"Yes, I see that. It is so," Warm Stone says.

He paused a moment, then said, "Tell me more about the red and yellow-haired people. You also mentioned black-haired people. Tell me about them also."

I say to answer his curiosity, "The red and yellow-haired people came to this land with much technology. They knew how to build great monuments. They had engineering skills and mathematics. They had knowledge of the stars. They comprehended the physically manifested world.

"The black-haired people understood how the unmanifested world works.

"We know both. We are one People now. Does that answer your question?" I ask.

"It does for now," Warm Stone replies. "I'm getting a little stiff. How long do these storms usually last?"

"I'll check the sky again," I offer, getting up and moving toward the door. I step outside for a moment taking in the weather conditions. The rain has lessened somewhat, and I spot lightning in the clouds. Stepping back in, I look around at my friends, appreciating the intimacy of the past hours.

"Blooming Rose, I thank you for your hospitality today," I say as I smile at her. "It appears that we have a break in the storm momentarily. While the rain has eased off a bit, I see lightning and suspect that the storm will continue to rage on into the evening. The wind is still blowing and may get worse. I think maybe it's best to take Warm Stone back before we are all stuck here for the night."

Warm Stone raised his eyebrows at the anticipation of moving, feeling stiffness from walking a distance then sitting for hours with little or no stretching.

Water Dog gets up and says, "I'll help you get Warm Stone back. Floating Lily and Little Otter can stay here." Turning to his mother, Water Dog adds reassuringly, "I'll be back after I help with Warm Stone."

With that, Blooming Rose pulls out turkey feather cape-like wraps from under another bench, and wraps one around Warm Stone as he rises. She hands me one, and I throw it over my shoulders. Water Dog steps outside and reaches for his cape from where it was hanging.

We step out into the rain. Both Water Dog and I put our arms around Warm Stone as he struggles with his crutches on the wet ground.

We find that the regular path to the Healing House is blocked by fallen trees.

"What a storm," Warm Stone comments.

We look around for another path back to the Healing House. As a trio we stand there a few moments to get our bearings as the rain continues.

Flash. The lightning strikes a tree a distance away.

Crack, sounds the thunder.

Flap. Flap. Flap.

Again, flash, flash. Again crack, boom sound the darkening clouds.

With the wind picking up, I feel the need to make a decision as to which direction we go. The rich soil has been absorbing the moisture, making it treacherous for Warm Stone to walk, even with help.

"The hill up to the Healing House is too steep in the loosening mud for us to go back there. Let's take Warm Stone to my house. We have room. As big as your house is, Water Dog, all of us would have been cramped there, especially if we ended up spending the night." Water Dog shakes his head in agreement, and we head toward my house, a much easier trek.

Flap. Flap. Flap.

Annoyingly, the flapping continues.

Warm Stone looks around to find the source of the flapping. As he focuses his eyes on the source of the flapping, I look in the same direction. The doors to the wooden birdcages had become unbound in some way and fell victim to the blowing wind.

Flap, flap, the flapping continues.

"Floating Lily," explains Water Dog.

Warm Stone asks our giant companion, "Did she trade something to get the parrots? Too bad she lost them."

"She didn't lose them," I say shaking my head.

"Yeah, but the birds are gone. You mean she had them cooked?" Warm Stone asks in disbelief.

Smiling, Water Dog, responds, "No. She set them free. She could not stand to see a creature caged that is supposed to be free."

". . . Right," I say. "Their nature is to be free. Those beautiful birds are one manifestation of the myriad of life forms on Mother Earth. Their nature and purpose is to be who they were meant to be, which is to say, not bound, not restricted, not enclosed in a cage for us to marvel at. We can still admire their beauty when we see them living their lives freely as they were designed to be."

Rain begins to pelt us while we stand there talking. So, we turn and begin to make our way to my house. As we approach, delicious aromas drift toward us.

The outside shelter around the front of my house was built larger than most as my mother spends much of her time cooking outside on the enlarged new oven and cook center. The half walls of this open cook center provide some protection from this kind of weather. I notice that my mother had hung thick woven mats from the eaves and fastened them to the top of the half walls, thereby granting dry space for protection from the blowing rain. Despite the wind, my mother is preparing a large pot of stew with other steamed vegetables, and a large pot of wild rice, and biscuits. Under this shelter, we remove our borrowed wraps. I set them aside so that Water Dog could take them back with him.

As Warm Stone and I enter, I see my mother bending over her inside hearth pouring hot tea into pottery cups. Smiling at Warm Stone is Grandmother Shining Moon, sitting across the room wrapped up in robes, obviously enjoying the return of health and strength of her patient.

"Greetings, Grandmother Shining Moon," Warm Stone says with a broad smile, recognizing her as the one who treated his leg.

"Mother, this is Warm Stone. The storm is such that we found it best to bring him here," I introduce my new friend to my family.

"We?" she quizzed.

I look around and realize that Water Dog had already left without ceremony. "Yes, Water Dog and I. I guess he felt the need to get back home right away. We've got quite a storm. I expect it to last another day at least, maybe more," I finish then add changing the subject, "sure smells good. Oh, I'm forgetting my manners. Warm Stone, this is my mother, Raven's Wing, and of course you know my Grandmother."

Warm Stone stands weakly, nods his head in acknowledgment of Raven's Wing. She holds a cup of tea for him and touching his arm turns him toward a bench to sit. "Drink up," she encourages. "This tea is especially prepared for you to promote your healing after your long walks. I've prepared a meal for you that will help your strength return. You've walked a lot today. You still need to walk more. For now, I want you eat and rest," she dictated with absolute finality.

Warm Stone looks at her puzzled. *What an intriguing people these are.*

12

HAL TAKES ACTION

Hal struggles to put his jacket on straight as he rushes past the receptionist.

Hal stops briefly and says to the receptionist, "I'm leaving to find out what's going on with Tom. I feel it is something weird or trouble of some kind. Would you lock up the office when you leave?"

Hal stops for a moment checking his pockets. "My phone," he says, "I need to keep calling him. I won't rest until I reach him or I know what happened."

He finds his cell phone then rushes out the door.

13

RED FOX AT SEIP

The Seip workshops lay ahead for Red Fox and Soaring Red Hawk. It was the next stop on a tour. As they approached the workshops Red Fox discovered they were near Paint Creek. Red Fox noticed many buildings with open-air working areas shaded by large canopies.

Large clay pots boiled while suspended above pit fires. Both men and women were hard at work. As the two approached, they passed several large hardened clay-lined water pits holding stalks of milkweed, dogbane, hemp and other fibrous plants and tree barks. The cloth makers processed the plant fibers through several more stages than were used in any other village, especially for the more delicate fabrics.

Soaring Red Hawk began, "These first several pits soak the plants in water for several days to soften them. Then we move them to these other pits over here where various substances are added to further refine the fibers. As you can see, some of the fabrics are dyed into a broad range of hues. Finally, they are dried and further prepared for our weavers."

Walking past the pit area Soaring Red Hawk said after a pause, "Over here," Soaring Red Hawk pointed as if enjoying leading a guided tour for a dignitary, "the workers grind colored soils, minerals and plant products to make the dyes and paints that we use to decorate the finished fabrics." He paused a moment to reflect, then continued, "Each village has similar ways of making their fabrics. As you know, it was decided by the Great Council of Elders that Seip village would specialize in ceremonial garments." The pair stood for a few moments to take it all in.

Walking over to another workshop, Soaring Red Hawk said, "We also work with leather made from the hides of deer, elk, buffalo and other fur bearing animals. Most of these are made for Elders, Shaman and Healers. Later I will take you to the mica and pearl workshops. All of these other ornaments and decorations are brought here to the weavers who weave and sew them into the fabric as each garment is made." As they entered an enclosed shop, Soaring Red Hawk acknowledged the artisans at work as a few looked up to smile at them and then he looked for the costumes in inventory.

"A ceremonial dress is over here. It is almost finished," Soaring Red Hawk said.

Hanging in elegant splendor within a large wooden weaving frame radiated the dress Soaring Red Hawk wanted to show.

"It's one of the most beautiful dresses I've ever seen," Red Fox exclaimed, unable to hold back his admiration. "There must be hundreds of pearls and dozens of grizzly bear teeth. Are the copper breast plates suspended on a necklace of silver orbs?" he asked.

"Yes, Red Fox," Soaring Red Hawk assured him with a nod. "The silver was brought here from near and far. The grizzly bear teeth came from the great mountains far to the west where the obsidian comes from. The copper antler headdress was made by copper artisans near Chillicothe, who also make other ceremonial copper objects," Soaring Red Hawk said with great pleasure.

"Are you Red Fox?" asked a voice from behind a weaving frame.

"Yes."

Silver Thread smiled broadly as she moved out from behind a wooden structure. "Thank you for your wonderful compliment on the dress. Grandmother White Eagle will be wearing it when she marries your friends, Water Dog and Bluebird Near the Lily, as well as many others, at the High Bank Southernmost Moonrise Ceremony later this year."

She smiled again, "My name is Silver Thread. I've heard much about your village and you. I have some samples of the other types of weaving we do here," she said with pride. "Once in a great while traders bring us wondrous cloth from South America which we use in many of our garments."

Silver Thread then turned away for a moment and rifled through several storage areas and brought out several more samples of other fabrics and a few leather garments to show Red Fox.

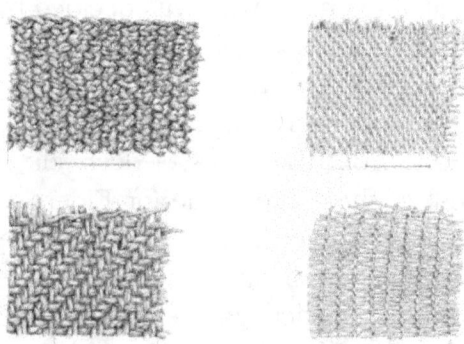

Figure 1.2: "Drawing of Charred Fabric from Mounds" Holmes 1896: Plate VII

After the two finished looking at the samples, Silver Thread said, "Follow me over to this other work area. We're working on quite a few garments and costumes that I think you will be very interested in."

As they were walking Soaring Red Hawk explained, "Each year the farmers at Baum have a renewal ceremony to express gratitude for the many insects that pollinate the crops we raise. We're just about finished getting them all prepared for the ceremony that will be happening right about the time you are at Baum. This is a very special ceremony which allows The People to express their gratitude for the bountiful crops that are raised at Baum and throughout the lands in which we live. Were it not for the bees and other insects that pollinate our crops, we would starve." He paused to let the meaning of his statement sink in for Red Fox.

"The bees are very precious to The People," Soaring Red Hawk commented. "They're very much like the Ant People who saved us from destruction by sheltering us when the prior worlds were destroyed. They live in harmony. They perform their work with a collective frequency in joyful fulfillment of the fertility energy from Mother Earth. Even though these insects are very small and fragile, the work they perform is vital to all plant life and humankind. Each spring we participate in the fertility dance of renewing life on Mother Earth. The dance honors them for bringing a fruitful life back to all our crops."

Red Fox nodded, even though he was not quite sure what that meant exactly.

Soaring Red Hawk seeing a slightly confused look on Red Fox's face waited a moment and said, "We, here at Seip, weave and maintain the special garments for all the men and women who represent the bees, the butterflies and the moths in this ceremony held at Baum.

"Distinctive copper headdresses are worn by the dancers who perform the central ceremony. We also make the costumes for the women who represent the flowers of all plant life. The bee dancers honor the bees that pollinate the flowers. The butterfly and moth dancers honor those insects that pollinate our tobacco crops.

"The main dancers will be on the top of the special flat topped mound where the ceremony is centered. Yet, there are many, many more dancers who are involved and who circle around the mound as the ceremony unfolds. They're dressed in colored costumes representative of those worn by the main dancers. As you will see, the fertility dances are very beautiful and stirring. They remind us of the blessing of new life, renewal and the Oneness that connects everything."

Silver Thread, who had been attentively listening as she moved in to contribute to the presentation, handed Red Fox a bee headdress. It was something he had never seen before.

The copper plate headdress had been fashioned in the shape of a large bee. Atop the copper plate was affixed a bee made from fabric. The fabric bee was very realistic in color and shape with copper antennae.

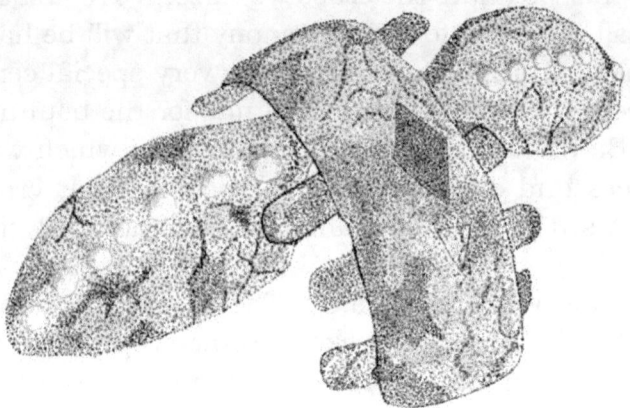

Redrawn and adapted from Shetrone 1930: 115, Fig 61. Copper, pearl and mica headdress.

"See how the wings move?" she asked.

"Yes, that is very clever," Red Fox remarked as he examined the intricate craftsmanship.

Silver Thread continued, "The mica wings are mounted on copper hinges attached to the fabric body, and nearly invisible threads are attached through the hinges to the top of the wings. The threads will be attached at the ends of the shoulders of the costume, so when the dancers raise and lower their shoulders, the mica wings move in rhythm. The bee costume is colored like a bee's body, in yellow and black stripes.

"See?" announced Silver Thread, "here is a full-body costume of the bee." She held up another costume for him to admire, "See, here, it is about the length of a human body, and made into concentric circles fashioned from willow branches. The alternating yellow and black fabric holds the circles together." Red Fox nodded.

"The smallest circle goes around the neck and shoulders, and the circles get larger in circumference toward the middle, then smaller again at the end of the body. When the dancers wear this and the headdress, they dance representing the bees. Because it's all made of light fabric and wood, they are not too heavy for the dancers as they participate in the ceremony." She finished happily and put the bee costume back.

Red Fox just stood there in awe of the art he was witnessing. All the costumes and headdresses he saw there impressed him due to their degree of intricacy and sophistication. He remained standing there when Silver Thread returned with a hand outstretched. She reached for one of Red Fox's hands and led him into another part of the workshop.

"Here are some of my favorite costumes, Red Fox," she said as she resumed her tour. Letting go of his hand, she moved one arm in a sweeping gesture to direct his gaze to focus on the rich display of splendor in the form of delicate costumes. "The costume of the butterfly's body is here," she said as she pointed. "Attached to it are the colored cloth wings which move," she said as she pulled on a wing and held it up for him to see. The wings are made of sheer fabric which extend downward for the full length of the dancer's arms, and are attached at the waist in the back."

Silver Thread lowered her voice and spoke gracefully as if in awe of the costumes, "As the dancers move their arms, the wings flap in response. The wings are dyed and painted to look like butterfly and moth wings. All of the dancers wear facemasks of the insect they represent." Silver Thread smiled holding two of the masks in her hands.

"Silver Thread, thank you," Red Fox said graciously, "I so much enjoyed seeing the beautiful fabrics and the many processes required. While the garments in our village are very well made and serve our purposes well, these are indeed elegant. I now know that great skill is required to produce such fabrics and garments and how the name Seip village garments had become known throughout The People." "Silver Thread, I've always wondered how the fresh water pearls and shells were attached to the fabrics with no thread visible?" Red Fox asked.

Silver Thread now took charge of the tour and said, "Come with me over to these other tables in this next workshop where you will see how our pearl and shell artisans attach these ornaments to the fabrics."

Soaring Red Hawk followed along giving Silver Thread the opportunity to take the lead. Seeing that Red Fox was in good hands, he signaled to Red Fox he would meet him later. Red Fox tossed his head back slightly in acknowledgement.

"Oh, what are these?" asked Red Fox curiously. "I've never seen shells like these before."

"Aren't they beautiful? So exotic," Silver Thread beamed. "The traders brought them to us. I think they said they come from off the coast of Africa, across the eastern ocean. I truly love working with such exquisite items. They so enhance the garments and jewelry pieces we make here."

After he and Silver Thread approached the next workshop, she picked up some pearls and shells from several of the containers on the workbench.

"As you can see, Red Fox, some of the pearls have been flattened on one side and notice the two little holes.

"The pearl artisans will carefully drill two diagonal holes into the pearl until they meet in the middle. Then they can be threaded onto a strand of the fabric or sewn onto a garment and they will lie flat and firmly held to the garment. Depending on where the pearls will be placed, it may not be necessary to flatten one side. They are attached just using the two holes. Here are some of the needles we use. These are three to five inches long, although some are over nine inches long. Notice the eye in each needle where the thread goes through.

"The crested mudalia shells are routinely ground down on one side and the marginella shells are drilled with two holes and then a thread is passed through to attach the shells to the fabric. We have found over many years that these techniques provide the best attachments for durability and retention of the ornaments on the various ceremonial garments that we make," Silver Thread said with a smile.

Red Fox enjoyed watching and learning more about the decoration of various garments.

Some of the finished fabrics were given to other workers who used large clay stamps that had been soaking in clay trays filled with various colors: reds, yellows, brown, copper, and turquoise, black and white. The stamps depicted a variety of geometric shapes, curving lines ending in circles, squares and other symbols familiar to The People.

It was now time for Red Fox to meet Soaring Red Hawk before the afternoon was over.

"I can't thank you enough, Silver Thread. I really appreciate this opportunity and I have learned much," he said before he left.

"No, dear, the pleasure was mine" smiled Silver Thread. "Good luck on your presentations and journey. I will see you tomorrow night when you make your presentation for our village. Do you know where the pearl workshops are?" Silver Thread asked.

"Yes, thank you. Soaring Red Hawk pointed them out to me and he is waiting for me there."

"Before you go we have something for you that all of us made for you," Silver Thread said smiling as she handed the young man a bundle of finely woven fabric.

Red Fox unfolded the bundle. Much to his surprise, the artisans had gifted him with a beautiful ceremonial shirt and leggings. Suspended by a leather cord was a cutout of a red fox made from the rare ruby mica, mounted on a same-shaped brightly polished copper mirror. It was to be worn as a chest plate.

"I don't know what to say," Red Fox fumbled his words with eyes wide with wonder. "They are wonderful. Thank you, thank you so very much. I am amazed. These are beautiful. I'll be so pleased to wear them. How did you know my size?"

"A little singing hawk told me," Silver Thread said with a smile and a wink.

As he walked back to the central area of Seip village, Red Fox thought about his gifts and how much he appreciated these ceremonial garments.

"Well, Red Fox, did you enjoy your time with the textile artisans?" Soaring Red Hawk said. "Oh, I see you have something."

"Yes, look at these ceremonial garments that Silver Thread, the weavers and the other craft people, created for me. They are beautiful. I will wear them at my presentation tomorrow night and at other villages. I am especially pleased with the namesake adornment. I've only heard of the rare ruby mica. I can't thank you enough."

"You're certainly welcome. Come now, let me take you over to the pearl crafts house and I'll meet up with you later. There you can see what they do. People from villages throughout our lands collect the pearls which are brought here." Soaring Red Hawk said.

Large clay vats sat outside the huts holding thousands of pearls soaking in water. Elsewhere deer hides boasted hundreds of pearls as they lay drying in the sun.

"Good afternoon, Soaring Red Hawk. This must be Red Fox. Greetings, thank you for coming to our village. We've heard a great deal about you. My name is Grandmother Blue Heron. I'm so pleased to meet you." Grandmother Blue Heron smiled as she bowed her head to her guest and Soaring Red Hawk as Soaring Red Hawk left.

"Thank you, Grandmother. I too have heard of you from my Grandmother Blue Lightning. I've seen many of the strands of pearls that have come from Seip at ceremonies in our village. The pearl work on my ceremonial garment is beautiful, I'm so very moved," Red Fox said giving Grandmother Blue Heron a hug.

"Thank you. I'm pleased that you like them. Now let me show you how they came to be," Grandmother Blue Heron said as she went into the first workshop.

"This is where we drill the pearls that will be made into necklaces, bracelets or sown onto clothing. As you can see this is very exacting work even for our most skilled workers," Grandmother Blue Heron said.

Several tables were arranged so that sunlight embraced the workstation. Impressed by the clever devices used by the artisans, Red Fox noticed that most tools were made from wood, and several were made from pottery clay. As an apprentice architect, he appreciated the precision of good tools. The base of each devise had a hole in the bottom that was lined with buckskin. The fresh water pearls were irregular in shape unlike the almost perfectly round pearls brought in by the traders from the oceans to the south. However, some of the local pearls were nearly perfect and highly prized.

Not all the pearls were drilled, only the amount necessary for necklace making or for use on garments. Red Fox had been informed that many of the finest pearls were destined to be gifts and offerings at burial or cremation ceremonies throughout the many villages of The People.

He saw basket after basket of pearls that had been sorted as to size, shape and color.

"Would you like to see how the holes are drilled into a pearl?" Grandmother Blue Heron asked.

"Yes, that would be interesting to see," said Red Fox.

The two of them moved over to another table where an artisan was mounting a large almost round pearl into the drilling devise. The artisan secured it in the drilling platform, centered the drill and began the drilling process using great care to avoid splitting the pearl. Once she finished she handed it to Grandmother Blue Heron.

"Very nicely done. Would you like to have this, Red Fox?" Grandmother Blue Heron said as she threaded the pearl with a long string.

"Oh yes, my mother will love it. Thank you." Red Fox said as he admired the iridescent pearl. "Let's go over to the next workshop which I think you'll find interesting." Grandmother Blue Heron said as she motioned to another workshop a short walk away.

There on the hardwood plank workshop bench sat a balance scale delicately made from wood and copper. Grandmother Blue Heron told Red Fox that the artisan was weighting a series of pearls searching for an exact match both in number and total weight. He had been asked to fashion two pearl bracelets that would each weigh four ounces. He had already finished one bracelet.

Looking up from his focus, "You must be Red Fox," Kicking Rock said with a gleam in his eye.

"Yes," Red Fox replied. "I'm very interested in the scale you're using. I've heard about them from Singing Hawk but have never seen one before."

"Well, let me show you how it works," Kicking Rock said as he stopped his work to engage in the conversation, "on this side I have placed a copper weight that weighs exactly four ounces. I'm going through this assortment of matched pearls looking for the same number of pearls in the completed bracelet to make a matching bracelet that will also weigh exactly four ounces. I received an order from a husband from another village who wanted them as a gift for his wife." Kicking Rock selected additional pearls until the scale balanced. He then asked Red Fox if he would like to use the scale.

"Thank you, I must decline. I'd love to stay longer. It's getting late and I need to clean up and get ready for dinner. Again, thank you. I had not seen a scale before. I enjoyed seeing how it worked," Red Fox said.

Running Bear, Morning Star and Red Fox were invited to eat with Soaring Red Hawk and the village Elders, Grandmothers and Grandfathers. At dinner the traveling trio enjoyed hearing the many stories that were told of the Ancient Ones and the adventures of those who lived in Paint Creek Valley. The group talked until very late.

Red Fox felt a change coming over him. He sensed a change in his awareness of all that was around him . . . the beauty and oneness of The People. Nodding to himself as he walked back to their guesthouse to sleep, he especially felt the joy of living in the fellowship of The People.

The next morning, Red Fox was scheduled to visit the Seip mica work areas. The mica artisans at Seip typically worked on ornamental pieces.

As he walked around, he saw hundreds of pounds of mica sheets that were neatly stacked as to size. Nearby he saw ovens where the mica sheets were gently warmed to the right temperature, so that it would be easier to cut into the desired patterns. The workstations were made from large hardwood planks smoothed and polished with oils. Some of the mica was fashioned free hand while other pieces were placed under copper templates.

When a copper template was used, the warmed mica was placed on the hardwood surface and held in place by drops of warmed tree sap. Then a warmed copper form was placed on top. The artisan used just the point of a flint bladelet to cut the mica. Finished pieces of many kinds of beautiful objects of art, parrots, birds, human figures, stars, geometrical shapes and scrollwork, were laid out on another table.

After that, Red Fox left the work area and began to wander off by himself. For the moment he felt over stimulated by everything he had seen and experienced over the past several days. He also felt overwhelmed by the size of Seip and its complexity, not at all similar to the quiet little village he called home.

"Ah, home," he thought to himself, taking mental inventory of what his village looked like, his home and family, and the homes of his friends.

"Dear friends," he continued in his thoughts while walking alone, "how I miss you. Gray Wolf, what are you doing now? Shining Bird, are you still teaching Gray Wolf at Singing Hawk's? Grandmother Blue Lightning, how much I owe you for all that you've taught me. If you could see me, you would see how well I give my presentations with all the power and responsibility given to me by Great Spirit. I am doing. I am learning much. I will continue to do well and to learn much on this journey. I can see it is a journey of a lifetime." Heaving the sigh of a boy on a man's errand, Red Fox squinted his eyes in the attempt to prevent tears from coming. They rushed forth anyway. He paused in his reverie to wipe away the tears of his soul that burned his face.

Then Red Fox continued in his thoughts, "Water Dog and Bluebird Near the Lily, how I miss you, you and my dearest friends, Gray Wolf and Shining Bird. I see your love for each other. As I feel myself changing, growing, evolving from a boy into a man, I now feel the need for a life companion, such as what you have.

"Before this journey, I had never felt lonely. And, I had never even thought about looking for a woman who would be my beloved. Even though I am surrounded by people, and strong supporters of what I am doing, I am sensing something new within me. I feel busy. I feel productive. I feel like I am contributing to our society through what I am doing. Yet . . . something is missing from my life. I feel alone."

In a prayer, Red Fox closed his eyes and within a deep part of his soul felt a thought not quite articulated into words, "Oh, Great Spirit, I thank you for this opportunity and for the opportunities to come. In spite of all of this, I ask for a life companion. Oh, beautiful beloved of mine, I know you are out there somewhere. When will we find each other?"

With that, Red Fox could only hear the beating of his heart. His thoughts again turned to his own village as he mentally pictured friends and family as they might be going about their daily business. In his reverie about back home, Red Fox found himself walking the inside perimeter of the great square.

As he continued to walk, his attention pulled away from his feelings of homesickness and toward what he was now experiencing.

Red Fox At Seip

"It's a perfect square," thought Red Fox to himself, as he noticed the 90-degree right angles.

Red Fox looked back over his shoulder at all the workshops populating the square. Then appreciating the respite he received from his solitary walk, he turned looking forward. The new sights he saw enticed his mind and his budding architect senses. As he left the area of the square and walked into the conjoined square and circle area, he stood there marveling at a huge oval in the ground. Its perfectly flat surface was made from hardened clay fired to seal it as it was designed to last forever.

He noticed several rectangular and circular basins that had been placed into the floor of the oval. Each of these basins contained pieces of charred objects along with evidence that these objects had been part of a ceremony.

"There you are!" said a booming voice behind him. Red Fox turned to see Soaring Red Hawk walking toward him carrying something in his hand. "Have you learned more today?" he asked.

"Yes, this visit has been one of great learning and experiences for me. I'm curious about this specially prepared area of ground in the shape of an oval. I've never seen anything like this before. I believe it's a sacred ceremonial area from what I can tell."

"You are correct," Soaring Red Hawk said with a nod.

"What are these rectangular and circular receptacles for?" Red Fox asked.

Soaring Red Hawk replied, "The rectangular and circular basins are designed to accommodate the release of the energy fields of each object placed there. These objects had belonged to those who have walked on into Spirit. They were placed there by family members and friends as part of the ritual of letting the dead and ourselves move on."

"Ohhh," Red Fox responded. "I see. What more can you tell me?"

Soaring Red Hawk said as he began walking and stretched out his arm in a sweeping motion, "The earthen walls of this complex enclose approximately 121 acres of land. You may have seen several of the other burial mounds contained within the enclosure and others that are outside of it. The hardened clay oval that we're standing on is a sacred ceremonial site. This area honors those buried here at Seip whose lives represented the principle of *'as in heaven, so on earth'* as they journeyed on Mother Earth."

After a moment's pause, Soaring Red Hawk said, "It was decided by the Council of Elders that Seip would be another burial site for those Elders of The People who wished to be wrapped in the arms of Mother Earth. It will also be the resting place for those who choose to be cremated in the Fires of Creation. Eventually my cremated remains will be buried here. You will visit some of the other Elder burial sites in and around Chillicothe on your journey."

As they walked Soaring Red Hawk continued his lecture while Red Fox listened.

"This entire oval was specially prepared in accordance with our traditions. Similar areas have been constructed elsewhere. Some are now covered with earthen mounds. Of course, here at Seip, many generations will pass before an earthen mound is placed over this oval," Soaring Red Hawk said as his eyes gazed into the distance of time.

Red Fox stopped walking to turn and look at the oval again, mentally associating the information he was receiving with what it looked like.

Soaring Red Hawk continued, "For now we are using this area for the burial rites ceremonies prior to a cremation or an internment. As time goes on, burials will be placed within earthen mounds that will be built on this oval. There is enough room for three such earthen mounds. These mounds will be used for internments or for the ashes from cremations."

Red Fox nodded in acknowledgement.

Following Soaring Red Hawk's lead, Red Fox turned back again to look at the sacred space under discussion. They both stood there without speaking for several moments feeling the sanctity of the grounds and the efforts planned for those who would be walking on into Spirit.

"Yes, my Grandmother has told me about the burial ceremonies she has attended of revered Elders and others who have served the Great Oneness in ways beyond the ordinary," Red Fox said. "Yet, since there is no death of the soul are we not just honoring our memory of the person and what they contributed during their life on Mother Earth?" Red Fox asked.

"That is true," responded Soaring Red Hawk. "I can tell your Grandmother has taught you well. Yet the grieving process is an expression of a human emotion that is essential to maintaining balance within our lives. And, it is an energy field we must move through. It's also a time when people from near and far will gather to honor the memory and celebrate the lives of all of the Elders, as well as their beloveds, who have walked on into the next world. We gather many sacred objects made from copper, pearls, carved beads, effigies of the person's spirit guides, colorful flint, obsidian, teeth of many creatures, bear claws and teeth, mica sheets, pottery and more to honor the memory of those who have walked on."

Red Fox asked, "So why does grief hurt so much?"

The shaman replied, "Grief is experienced as physical pain. The pain we feel is the tearing or dissolving of the energy field we shared with our beloved ones or others who were significant in our lives in one way or another."

"Wait a minute," Red Fox said, "even after death, are we not still connected to our loved ones?"

Soaring Red Hawk said, "Yes, we are indeed. The field of energy that still connects you is different though as our loved ones are no longer on the physical plane."

Red Fox asked Soaring Red Hawk, "I haven't thought much about death. Can you help me understand it?"

"Death is a change that is part of the ebb and flow of life, the flux that challenges our perception of the constancy of life. Because of death, we can more fully appreciate and understand the purpose for our physical life. Our physical life appears to be real and death informs us otherwise. In death we return to our Spirit form, which is our true nature. We are expressions of Great Spirit experiencing a physical manifestation. So death also reminds us that what appears to be so, is not."

Moments of silence passed between them. This gave Red Fox the opportunity to contemplate what he had just heard.

Then Soaring Red Hawk thought to add a little more about the ceremonial traditions and said, "According to the traditions within a family, objects may be placed undamaged in the grave, while other families will release the emotional energy attached to the objects by breaking them or burning them in the Fires of Creation before placement in the grave. The receptacles and basins that you see here are used for such purposes during the honoring of the dead ceremonies.

"Now there is another important aspect of the Seip Earthworks that you should know about," Soaring Red Hawk said with a smile to his young student. "As you know Sister Moon is an important part of our daily lives and ceremonies." He paused to ensure he had Red Fox's attention before going on, "I have a diagram here. It's a drawing on birch bark. As you can see from the drawing, there are many lines of sight from various points of the Seip Earthworks," he said while pointing to parts of the drawing.

"These align with the northernmost rise of Sister Moon on the eastern horizon. Other viewpoints align with her northernmost setting on the western horizon. At those times, which occur on her 18-year cycle we hold special ceremonies to ask her to remain on her journey and return on her path to the south. Should she not, then Mother

Earth would spin out of balance and our world would end." Soaring Red Hawk said.

"Yes, I have some understanding of this from my lessons with Singing Hawk and, of course, the teachings of my two Grandmothers." Red Fox acknowledged in a somber tone.

"Our ability to align the Seip Earthworks to Sister Moon's journey came from the ancient knowledge which has been passed down from generation to generation for thousands of years. You have been selected as one of the chosen ones to possess this information for your generation," Soaring Red Hawk said to Red Fox placing his hand on Red Fox's shoulder. A surge of energy entered Red Fox's body like a current of electricity washing through him.

For a moment he could not speak. Recovering, Red Fox looked Soaring Red Hawk straight in the eye and said, "At times my mind swims with all this information. I worry that I will not remember it all. At times it seems almost overwhelming."

"Do not let fear cloud your mind. Your talents are extraordinary, and you will provide a safe haven for the ancient knowledge which you will use properly for the good of all concerned." Soaring Red Hawk said without doubt.

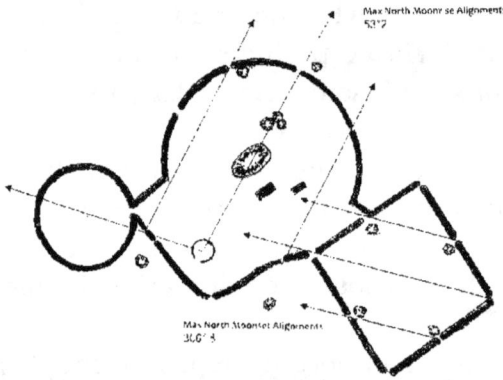

Redrawn and modified after Romain, 1992b, Fig. 6.

As they continued their walk, Red Fox looked at the drawing Soaring Red Hawk had given him.

Then he asked a question, "Soaring Red Hawk, I noticed a large amount of red ochre near the northeastern wall of the large circle. I've never seen so much red ochre in one place before. What is that for?" Red Fox asked.

"Yes indeed, Red Fox. Red ochre is mined near here. Many of our villages do not have easy access to the red ochre. So we have collected it here to make it available for all of The People. As you know, this is one of the honored minerals from Mother Earth that we use to make paint, dyes for our garments and for use in burial ceremonies. I imagine that

Silver Thread told you that we also made leather garments here. Have you heard of Red Coat?" Soaring Red Hawk asked.

"Yes, my Grandmother mentioned to me that it was possible I might have the opportunity to meet him on my journey. I've heard he is a great teacher and Elder of The People," Red Fox said.

"Well, when you do, you will see him wearing his elk skin vest which was made here. We also made his full-length buffalo coat which he wears in the winter. Both were dyed with the red ochre that we are talking about. At his request the hair was removed from the elk hide for his vest, and then the very soft leather was hand-tooled and fashioned to fit his muscular body. The buffalo coat was made with the hair facing in. The outside of the hide was then dyed red. He is a very powerful man both in body and spirit." Soaring Red Hawk said.

"Well, you will learn more on your journey as you travel to other settlements. Now it is time for dinner and afterwards preparing for your presentation tonight. Tomorrow morning your journey to Baum will be short as it's only about four miles from here," Soaring Red Hawk said as they turned to go back to the village outside the earthen walls of this enclosure.

Dinner was luscious with many cooked meats, sweet cakes, dried plums and teas. Red Fox's presentation went well, and his new ceremonial garments felt very comfortable. It seemed like Red Fox had just gotten to sleep when his uncle woke him up the next morning.

14

RED FOX AT BAUM

Early morning fog blanketed the landscape as the trio, travois, and dogs left Seip heading for Baum. Walking in silence, they witnessed the early rays of Father Sun glistening here and there through the shroud hindering their view. Stillness screamed through the chilled air. Otherworldly thoughts pervaded Red Fox's mind as the travelers each participated in their own silent meditations. Memories of all his experiences since leaving his home near the Great Serpent tumbled over and over as Red Fox pondered them.

The well-worn path stretched before them for the four miles to Baum. Mists insisted on maintaining a cloak of invisibility over the land around them making it difficult to see the landscape. They continued to walk without talking, nodding to those passing them by who could travel faster. Some stopped to chat briefly before going on. Those they met along the way eagerly anticipated the Bee Ceremony at Baum.

Off to their right they could hear the sounds of Paint Creek winding its way down to the Scioto River near Chillicothe. They would soon have to cross the creek to get to Baum. This time, however, they would not have to ford the creek as a wood bridge provided access to Baum village.

Approaching the bridge, the travelers could see the mist dissolving reluctantly into the warming rays of sunlight. It filtered through brewing storm clouds to reveal a gently rolling land that undulated like waves as far as the eye could see. A cooled breeze occasionally kissed their faces as they peered into the landscape that had been farmed for thousands of years.

It was a fertile land. Most of the trees had been cleared for the crop fields, except for shade oases located here or there for those who worked the land and traveled here. Red Fox noticed something that piqued his curiosity as he gazed across the fields just beginning to green from the early spring planting.

"What are all these small channels of water leading away from the creek?" he asked his uncle.

Nodding his head, Running Bear replied, "These are irrigation channels . . . which you've seen before, but not on this grand scale."

"Oh," responded Red Fox. "You mean *all* these fields are irrigated?"

"Yes, indeed. They stretch for miles."

"You mean *all* of this land is farmed?" Red Fox asked incredulously. "What do they grow here?"

Running Bear sighed before answering his nephew, "Corn, and other grain crops, kidney beans, squash, sunflowers, tobacco, plus other crops we also grow near our village. Oh, yes, some of the other crops include plants that provide the fibers for the weavers at Seip." Running Bear stopped and pointed to the farmed land with his arm outstretched and added, "They will plant in stages, so that they don't have to harvest it all at once."

Red Fox continued looking at the cropland and said, "This farmland must go on for miles."

After crossing the fields, they saw houses on the outskirts of the main Baum village. A few villagers saw the trio coming, pointed to them and beckoned to other villagers to come out and greet Red Fox and company. Dozens of other people milled around. Some Red Fox recognized from Seip.

The trio was guided to a guesthouse where they settled in. As usual, Morning Star looked after the dogs.

"We weren't expecting you so soon," announced a village greeter. "I am Laughing Cattails. Most of us are preparing for the upcoming ceremony. We won't be ready to have you give your first presentation until tomorrow night."

He looked at Red Fox for acknowledgement before continuing and then said, "I'm sure you've heard of our Bee Ceremony. Nearly all of the costumes are made at Seip. We have several ceremonies a year. This one is my favorite. It's about recognizing and celebrating renewal." He paused momentarily as if distracted and then said, "Maybe you'd like to take a look around? We could show you Spruce Hill. How's that?"

Red Fox smiled and then turned and looked at his companions before accepting. Both Running Bear and Morning Star waved indicating Red Fox should go on without them. Then Red Fox turned back to his host, still smiling, and said, "I really want to see the furnaces. I want to see how they are built."

"I'll take you to Great Owl, an Elder, who would like to meet you. He will be organizing your visit here," Laughing Cattails said.

"Red Fox," Great Owl warmly greeted the young pilgrim. "We've been waiting for you. I trust you and your companions will find your accommodations suitable."

"Yes, thank you, Great Owl," Red Fox said. "I'd really like to see those furnaces. Laughing Cattails said I won't be giving my presentation until tomorrow, so maybe we would have time for me to see them today."

With raised eyebrows, Great Owl smiled and nodded then said, "Of course. I'll take you up there myself." Looking around the village in his mind and mentally checking on the progress of the preparations for the ceremony, he said, "I think I can take some time right now. Are you ready to go now?"

"Sure," Red Fox said emphatically then looked around to see in which direction they needed to go.

The village of Baum appeared much larger than Red Fox had imagined. Houses were spread out for miles. In the central area the homes clustered together on more than ten acres and in closer proximity to each other than in his own village. They walked through part of the village as they made their way toward Spruce Hill some distance away.

"Red Fox," Great Owl initiated a commentary as they walked, "Did you know that Baum, along with Gartner, supplies most of the food for our large ceremonial gatherings?"

"So how do you do that?" asked Red Fox. "I mean, I can see you have the ability to produce a lot of food. I saw miles and miles of cropland just as far as I could see. So what do you do with it all? How do you keep it?"

"All around the village and even beyond," Great Owl proudly explained, "we have food stored underground."

"Underground?" asked Red Fox.

Great Owl nodded, pleased that he seemed to be impressing his guest. "Yes. We keep hundreds of storage pits full of grains, corn, beans, dried plums, and more, even tobacco."

" . . . All that underground?" asked Red Fox again. Then he asked, "How do you keep the food from spoiling? Or, how do you keep the underground bugs from getting into them?"

"Simple," explained the Elder looking at Red Fox, "We plaster the sides with clay, the kind we use for flooring in our houses." Red Fox nodded. Great Owl continued, "Then we fire the clay so it hardens into a ceramic shell. Then we seal the top. Food keeps for years like that."

Walking through the village, Great Owl waved to several men and women standing about or sitting at workbenches in the covered areas of several structures. Most of the visiting crowds were in other parts of the village, although, a few entered this area to speak to local artisans.

"What are they working on, Great Owl?" Red Fox asked curiously.

Great Owl changed the direction of their walk so they could go over to speak to the artisans.

"Baum village artisans are known for their exquisite fishing hooks made from deer and turkey bones," the Elder said. He introduced Red Fox to those who were there. Red Fox looked on as several artisans continued working uninterrupted. Red Fox noted the detail and the high polish of each finished item.

Gusts of wind picked up. The artisans noticed the slight buildup of pressure from the storm that appeared to be brewing. Not wanting to get caught up in a storm that might scatter their labors of the day, the artisans elected to put away their works. Taking leave of Red Fox and Great Owl, they began closing down their open-air workshop.

Great Owl graciously nodded and signaled Red Fox to turn and move on. As they made their way toward the hill where the furnaces were, they chatted casually. As they walked, Red Fox noticed a house with what looked like several dozen canoe oars propped up against an outside wall.

"Oh, so you make canoe oars here also?" asked Red Fox.

Great Owl looked in the direction Red Fox was looking. At that moment, another artisan came out, nodded to the two, and began bringing the items inside.

"Well, yes," Great Owl said, "while we do make oars here at Baum, and good ones too . . . those are not oars."

"But they look like oars," insisted Red Fox.

"Yes, I guess they do," replied the Elder. "They are not oars. They are shovels."

"Oh, I think we have a couple of shovels back home, but they looked a little different," Red Fox said. "I didn't realize villages needed so many."

Laughing, Great Owl said, "The villages don't need too many. These shovels are for the copper mines up in the Michigan area. The People up there who dig for copper and copper ore need these shovels. They mine the metal and need the shovels to dig deep tunnels into Mother Earth, so they can extract it from the ground."

"Oh, you mean for the copper ornaments we have, like our breastplates, ear spools and such?" asked Red Fox.

"Yes, that's it," the Elder said. "However, we get only a little of the copper. Nearly all of it goes to traders."

"Traders?" Red Fox asked in surprise.

"Yes," Great Owl answered then explained, "traders, who sail on large ships across the great ocean to the east, come in to Canada, and sail up the Ottawa River into Lake Nippissing. From there they sail into Lake Superior where the copper mines are. Once they have loaded copper from the mines to their ships, they take the Illinois River off of Lake Michigan, and sail down the Mississippi River and back to the ocean to the east. Or, depending on the weather, time of year, and ultimate destination they return the way they came, down the Ottawa River."

Pausing to think about what he had just heard, Red Fox said, "I never knew about that. How long has that been going on?"

"I really can't say," said Great Owl. "According to tradition, it's been going on for thousands of years. Traders have been transporting our copper for that long, taking it far, far to the east. What they do with it there is anybody's guess."

The wind picked up. Cloudbanks formed in the sky, sometimes appearing threatening, then backing away in a dance, tantalizing Mother Earth with promise of rain. As the two continued their hike up to Spruce Hill, several groups of men and women walked past them.

As they went by, Great Owl remarked to Red Fox, "Those are furnace workers. You may see some of them working, because the wind is picking up."

Red Fox asked, "The wind is important to the furnaces?"

Great Owl nodded and said, "Yes, the furnaces are built on this hill facing the west side, so they can capture the wind which feeds the flames. The fire in the furnaces burns hotter this way. We need very high temperatures to melt the copper."

As Red Fox and Great Owl followed the trail up to the ridge top where the Spruce Hill furnace complex was located, Red Fox got his first glimpse of the stonewalls and the arched stone gateways that greeted those entering its walled enclosure. Red Fox suddenly stopped.

THE CAMP OF GOD'S TEARS

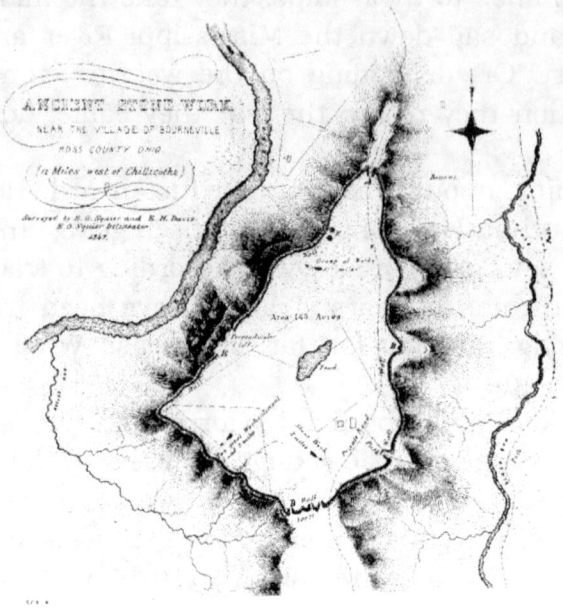

Diagram of Spruce Hill - Squier and Davis 1848

Even though Red Fox had never seen any of The People's hill top enclosures, of which there were many, the immensity, and the arrangement of the stones seemed so very familiar to him. He could not move. He could not speak. He stood there mesmerized barely able to breathe.

Moments passed in silence.

Finally Great Owl spoke, "Red Fox are you alright?"

When Red Fox finally was able to speak, he choked out, "Yes, it's just . . . I don't know . . . I am not sure . . . I've never seen anything like this before. It is magnificent, and somehow, in some way, it is so very familiar to me. I'm not sure what is going on. I felt a surge of energy, a surge of recognition."

Great Owl stood with Red Fox for a few moments more to make sure Red Fox was indeed all right before moving through the gateway.

After entering the enclosure, Great Owl led Red Fox over to the viewpoint on the western wall. He showed Red Fox the view of Baum from Spruce Hill.

"As you already know, Baum Earthworks are near Paint Creek," Great Owl began his telling without asking Red Fox if he wanted to know. "However, Baum has no burial mounds within its enclosure. It is shaped differently than Seip and still incorporates two circles and a square." Red Fox listened politely.

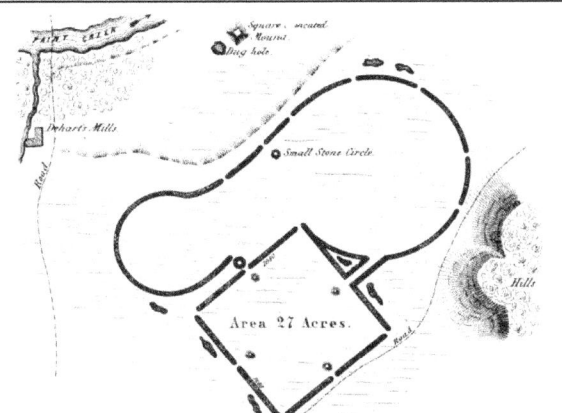
Diagram of the Baum Earthworks - Squier and Davis 1848

Great Owl spoke in a lecturing tone, "The design of Baum is somewhat similar to the earthworks at Seip, Liberty, Works East, and Frankfort in that it's made up of a large circle, small circle, and a square.

"As you may know, Red Fox, there are levels of meanings attached to the symbols used by The People depending on the context, the intent, circumstances or occasions when they are being displayed or used. The small circle represents the circle of life for all the people living and working at Baum. The People are represented by the larger and conjoined circle of life. From the large circle there is a walled pathway leading into the large square that represents Heaven. This pathway connects the square to the circles signifying that The People are connected to Heaven, *as above so below.*

"Outside our main earthwork is the ceremonial pyramid shaped mound with a flat top. It is located to the north just outside the earthen walls near the creek. As you may or may not know, it is used for our ceremonies."

Striking for the *piece-de-résistance,* Great Owl raised his voice to declare,

". . . and *that* is where our Bee Ceremony is being held. Right there on top of the ceremonial pyramid." His eyes glistened as he spoke. Pausing a moment to see if he still held Red Fox's attention, the proud Elder smiled broadly unable to hold back his passion for what appeared to be a greatly anticipated ceremony.

Red Fox nodded and said, "I'm really looking forward to seeing it. I heard about it at Seip when talking with Silver Thread and Soaring Red Hawk."

Just then a young man about Red Fox's age came running up to them. Out of breath and gasping, he stopped abruptly where the two were standing.

Great Owl asked him, "Yes? Am I needed?"

"Yes, Great Owl," the boy responded, still out of breath, "so sorry to interrupt you. However, you are needed back down in the village right now."

The Elder took a breath, looked at Red Fox, then back at Little Elk. He nodded acknowledgement and then said, "Little Elk, you're familiar with the furnaces and what goes on up here since your parents work up here. Why don't you finish showing Red Fox around?"

Little Elk smiled broadly at Red Fox and said, "That would be great!"

At that, Great Owl turned and headed back to the village.

"You know," Little Elk said to Red Fox, "the furnaces won't be ready for a while yet as they are just now getting the fires built up to make the coals they need. Since we have time, why don't we visit the Great Bear Paw at Black Run? It's just down the hill."

Red Fox asked, "The Great Bear Paw? What's that?"

"If you like to see something quite different, then you'll like this," Little Elk said. "It's shaped like a huge bear paw with five claws, and made out of stones piled up."

With his interest piqued, Red Fox said, "Yes. Let's go."

"Okay," Little Elk responded, "It's this way. It points directly to the Great Bear constellation, and the pole star."

The two boys scrambled down the other side of Spruce Hill.

Once they were about halfway down the slope, Little Elk pointed towards the southeast.

"Look," he pointed as he spoke to Red Fox, "can you see it from here? It is over a mile from where we are standing. That's where we are going."

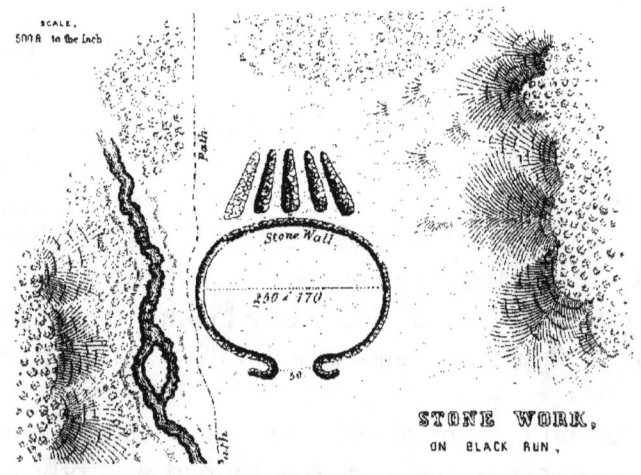

Diagram of stonework on Black Run - Squier and Davis 1848

Red Fox took a minute to focus on where Little Elk pointed. Then they made their way down to the stonework.

While walking around the Great Bear Paw, Red Fox could barely speak, feeling an intense sense of awe. Little Elk just kept smiling as they walked around.

"This is amazing. I've never seen a stone structure like this. It's huge," Red Fox exclaimed.

"Like I said earlier, at certain times of the year it points directly to the Great Bear constellation," explained Little Elk.

Boldly Little Elk began climbing the large stones and waved for Red Fox to follow. Just then the two felt several drops of rain hit their faces.

"Let's go," signaled Little Elk, "it's time we get back to the furnaces."

Upon their return to the top of Spruce Hill, they could see a cloud of smoke over the pond inside the enclosure.

Little Elk said, "If there is smoke over the pond, then some of the furnaces are operating. Let's see what they are making."

Red Fox nodded in agreement. The boys walked over to where the furnaces were located. Gusts of winds continued to blow accompanied by a few drop of rain.

As they approached one of the furnaces, Red Fox felt glad to be out of the chilling wind and under the protective shelters built in front of each furnace. Red Fox noticed several men and women working each of the several furnaces. Looking down into one he saw hot coals producing the heat necessary for changing the lumps of copper into a liquid.

"Hello boys," greeted one of the metal workers, "Come to see how we make our copper items?"

Little Elk replied, "Yes, I'm showing Red Fox around."

"I'm fascinated by the furnaces, how they are constructed, and how they work," said Red Fox.

"Okay, well," offered the worker, "as you can see, these pits are fortified with limestone bricks put together with clay mortar. If you notice," he said as he pointed, "they have a glaze on them, so they don't look like the limestone when we first create the bricks from the quarries. The excessive heat changes their surface. Melting copper and copper ore requires such intense heat that it transformed the limestone. Of course, making iron requires even hotter temperatures and a little different process."

Red Fox just stood there absorbing the information. He took note of the physical construction of the pits and how even the walls were. He noticed the chimney over each pit.

After a while, one of the other workers pointed out, "See how the copper in the crucible is now liquid?" She waited to see she had their attention then added, "It's now ready to be removed from the heat and poured into a mold."

Using tongs to lift the crucible out of the intense heat, one of the workers lifted the hot crucible out. Another worker had several molds ready. He grabbed a mold that looked like a large ceremonial axe. Red Fox watched the small team as they carefully removed the crucible from the furnace hearth, turn, and move it toward a workstation nearby. Together they poured the liquid copper into one mold then smiled happily. Clearly experience was required to manage this process.

Impressed, Red Fox asked, "So, how does this work exactly? . . . I mean . . . the furnaces? And how does the wind make a difference?"

"We need the wind to fan the coals so we can maintain a high degree of heat," responded the woman. "See the chimney?" she asked as she pointed. "We drop charcoal down from the top into the hearth after we've already got a fire built up. The wind funnels through air ducts that are designed to speed up the flow of the air as it enters the hearth. Does that help?" she asked Red Fox.

"I see," Red Fox again responded, then asked, "I see a stack of red bricks over there as well. What are they used for?"

One worker answered, "That brick is made from nearby clay deposits to help maintain the White Road of Sister Moon."

Surprised by this, Red Fox asked, "The White Road of Sister Moon? What do you mean?"

The worker answered, "Parts of the walls of the White Road of Sister Moon are made from bricks like these. That road is ancient and needs repair from time to time. Villagers along the sixty-mile route help maintain it. It is used almost constantly. We don't want to let it fall into disrepair."

Red Fox nodded and said, "Oh. I guess I never thought about the road needing maintenance. Of course, I haven't seen it yet, and expect to on my journey."

"It's getting dark, and it's starting to rain again," said Little Elk.

"Thanks for everything. I had a great time," said Red Fox.

"I had a great time too," said Little Elk. "We need to go. The trail down to the village can get tricky in the dark.

"So, there you are," Morning Star said when he saw Red Fox at the door of the guesthouse. "You're wet. You should probably take off your wet clothes, so they can dry by the fire. We brought some food back for you in case you are hungry."

"I'm not too wet. The cloak my mother made for me helped to keep much of the rain off. . . Fish?" Red Fox asked as he looked down at the food. "They look wonderful. I'm hungry."

Watching the young man eat heartily, his uncle, Running Bear, sat down across the table from Red Fox.

"You must have done something really interesting to come back with such an appetite," Running Bear said.

With a mouth full of food, Red Fox nodded enthusiastically. After he had stuffed several more bites in, he was finally able to speak.

"Oh, yes, let me just tell you," Red Fox said. Then he went on to describe his day's adventures, talking between bites. Running Bear and Morning Star just sat and listened fascinated by Red Fox's excitement. The two older men sat enraptured by Red Fox's ability to tell his tales. At times they winked at each other, sometimes making jokes, and sometimes asking him questions. All in all the three companions enjoyed each other's company, grateful to share the adventure together.

Then, with a change in tone, Red Fox added, "Morning Star, I had an interesting experience today when I first saw the Spruce Hill stonework." Morning Star cocked his head to one side, sat forward slightly, and listened.

"When I first saw the Spruce Hill walls and arched gate entrances, I experienced something very . . . powerful. It was like . . . I really don't know how to say this . . . I felt so very familiar with the way it was constructed . . . like I had been involved with its design or something. I felt frozen in time for a few seconds. Then the same thing happened when I saw the Bear Claw structure . . . I felt like I knew it somehow . . . like I had helped build them . . . I could not move or even speak for a while. I can't explain it to myself. What does it mean?"

Pondering the question, Morning Star thought a moment, and then said to Red Fox, "You've experienced something today that is very interesting and for which you have no explanation. You've seen things that you've never seen before, yet they are so familiar to you." Red Fox nodded and Morning Star continued.

"Many of our people have had similar experiences. They are drawn to do certain trades like making pottery, working in flint, mica, copper or other trades like weaving, planting or healing. Even though they had no formal training, it just came naturally to them. When we see such things we know that it comes from skills we developed in our prior lives, surfacing again in this life to help The People and themselves on their path in this lifetime. Be aware of such feelings and be open to knowing and allowing this energy to guide you as you master the ways of becoming who you are." Morning Star smiled as he spoke to Red Fox.

As he went to sleep that night, Morning Star noted how Red Fox was developing.

Red Fox awoke late the next morning, feeling a little stiff with a few muscle aches. He found food left out for him and a pot of warming tea next to the hearth of their guesthouse. Walking past the food and the tea, he went outside looking for Running Bear and Morning Star. He did not see them anywhere, but he did see the dogs tied up outside where they had been left for the night. They wagged their tails and showed they were glad to see him, even though he found evidence that they had already been fed.

After going back inside to eat breakfast, he poured a cup of tea and took his cup outside. Leaning up against the wall of the house, Red Fox felt glad he had nothing to do that morning. He did not know where his uncle and Morning Star had gone to, and right now, he did not care. Yesterday's climb had been strenuous.

He felt grateful that he had all morning to rest until later in the afternoon. He knew he was scheduled to give an afternoon and evening presentation. So many people were coming to Baum for the Bee Ceremony that he needed to give more than one presentation that day. That was fine with him.

He enjoyed giving the presentations. Often he would feel Presence of the Great Oneness. He found he liked the story-telling and imparting the meaning of all he had to share. He found that when someone asked a question, he was able to call upon Spirit to provide the appropriate response. His sense of being in at-one-ment with Spirit, as defined by his Grandmother Blue Lightning, increased with each presentation. Red Fox's experiences of oneness grew into his consciousness and created a sense of well-being.

By the time Running Bear and Morning Star returned, it was time for Red Fox to gather up his model of the Great Serpent in preparation for his first presentation at Baum.

"Hold on there, boy," Running Bear announced on his return. "We'll help you with that."

Red Fox felt relieved they returned in time to help him get the model over to where the presentation would take place.

"Where'd you guys go, anyway?" Red Fox asked, curious as to what they had been up to all day.

The two men looked at each other before responding. Morning Star finally replied, "Fishing."

"Fishing?" Red Fox asked.

Breaking into a big grin, his uncle, nodded, then explained, "Paint Creek. They carved four large cisterns in the bottom of the river rock." The two men looked at each other and grinned again reliving the day's adventure. Running Bear continued, "We bate the water in the cisterns and wait for the fish to swim in, then we catch 'em." Smiling broadly again, the two grown men behaved like children having had a day full of untold fun.

Chuckling to himself, Running Bear continued explaining to Red Fox, "We were given a supply of fish hooks and line. We spent all day yesterday, and all day today fishing! How great is that?"

"Did you catch any?" asked the Red Fox.

"Did we catch any? What a hoot!" retorted his uncle good-naturedly. "We caught so many we had to have some of the local villagers carry them all back for us."

"I don't know whether to believe you," Red Fox said with doubt. "It all sounds too fantastic, like a great story you want me to believe."

"Well, okay, don't believe us," Running Bear offered with a twinkle in his eye and a half grin on his face. "But when the feasting begins tomorrow, just know that a lot of the fish everyone will be eating were caught by us."

By the end of the evening, with his second presentation finished, the trio returned to their guesthouse to turn in. Red Fox's presentations had gone well. By this time Red Fox felt he was getting more polished at it. He felt more fluid and spontaneous. He much preferred the building of the model over talking about it, but talking about it was the reason for it to be built in the first place.

Much feasting and laughter prevailed throughout the afternoon of the next day. All morning Red Fox could smell the delicious aromas carried on the breezes. With the throngs of people in and around the village of Baum, food had been served up in courses and in various places, to accommodate the crowds of people. Red Fox, smiling to himself, noted the amount of fish presented and how quickly the fish were eaten. In addition the feast also included roasted ducks, geese, possums, venison, as well as various stews. Side dishes abounded adding to the color, texture, and variety.

The entire day was given over to joyous expressions. Musicians who would be playing later in the ceremony played during the day as individuals or in small groups. This gave opportunity for both visitors and villagers to dance wherever they found themselves, either alone, with a partner, or in a small group. Storytelling, joke telling, and just plain visiting dominated the interests of those not otherwise engaged in some pleasurable activity.

This was more than a day off from their ordinary labors. The People treated the entire day as a celebration, a celebration and acknowledgement of life itself. The Bee Ceremony would begin toward dusk, twilight, at just the time of day between day and night, a magical time, betwixt and between.

Torches would be lit and held on posts around the ceremonial mound. Some torches would be placed on the four sides of the flat top mound to provide light for the dancers in the ceremony, as well as light for the audience to see the event.

Red Fox noted that with the heavy consumption of food, some folks found places to nap, while others busied themselves with cleaning up. Others focused on the last minute preparations for the ceremony.

He could not help but feel the anticipation as energy ran high in the village. This energy produced a feeling of grandeur and eloquence coupled with high expectations. By this time, he could hardly wait for the ceremony to start.

As Red Fox sat in the audience for the Bee Ceremony, he could see that it met, no, exceeded all he had imagined. So graceful and accomplished were the dancers, the ceremony was not something to be watched, but experienced.

From the beginning moment until the very end, a symphony drove the dance. Notes floated across the stage timidly at first, and then gained confidence as gradually other notes from other instruments joined the concert. Music came from the different sized flutes that offered various tones. Bells and small cymbals, obtained from traders, sounded at just the right moments accenting the constant beating of drums in various tones and rhythms.

The costumes of the flower and insect dancers spoke to his imagination as the flowers and insects flowed in circles around the stage, back and forth, in and out, and around each other.

Several principal dancers adorned with the most elaborate headdresses and costumes performed on the stage.

Dozens of other dancers performed around the stage. The bee performers had whorl sticks with large ribbons attached that they twirled around making a bee sound.

These dancers reflected the actions of the principal dancers on the stage, and embellished the movements because they had more space. This added a multi-dimensional effect to the ceremony.

Red Fox remembered the costumes and headdresses from his previous visit at Seip. When he saw them in the workshop, they looked beautiful, but still limp and unaffected as they sat on display.

However, these same costumes came to life adorned by the energy field of each dancer who then transformed into the image of the costume. Each flower and each bee or butterfly breathed a performance of grace and life. Each portrayed a piece of choreographed cosmic magic. Red Fox had never experienced such beauty of dance as he watched them swirl in flourishes, couple and re-couple, pulsating together with each partner, and together as one with the music.

Being driven by the music, the dancers performed in a heightened energy as the dance continued. Then each bee and moth dancer moved gradually in sync as the music increased the intensity. Dictated by the music, each flower curled down, down to the ground. Then each in turn, led by the music, leapt up showing some kind of bundle as part of their costume, indicating the renewal of life process after the conjoining of insects to flowers had occurred. The symphony of sound and movement rose in a crescendo of nearly unbearable stimulation to the senses until, like life giving life, orgasmic explosions burst over and over.

At some invisible signal, the audience members stood up cheering the symbolic renewal of life with many dancing in place as part of the total celebration. This continued for a while with a frenzy until the energy waned as the music slowed. The audience-dancers slowed too and eventually resumed their seats.

The ceremony ended with the tiny sounds of bells twinkling and a lone flute settling over the evening. Light flickered against the costumes and adornments of the flower-dancers as they slowly came to rest on the ground. With all the dancers resting on the ground, the music stopped signaling the ceremony's end.

Stunned by the impact of the ceremony, Red Fox could hardly move. As the night had taken over, audience members drifted away lazily or scurried home in anticipation of the rest of the evening. Night had fallen. Sister Moon shone brilliantly providing enough light that enabled folks to see their way. Red Fox took his secret longing for a companion off into the night.

Villagers and visitors moved ever so slowly the next day, many not arising until late. After a relatively lazy day, Great Owl approached the guesthouse where the trio stayed to inform Red Fox that he would be giving another presentation toward evening.

After that presentation, Red Fox joined villagers and guests in sitting around a campfire. Red Fox discovered that many children had enjoyed his Great Serpent story. Audience members continued to sit around the fire entertaining the children with traditional stories inspired by Red Fox's presentation.

Then one youngster, Skipping Stone, said to his grandfather, "Grandfather, when Red Fox told of how the Ant People protected us, it reminded me of another Ant Story you used to tell. Would you tell it again?"

Murmurs rippled out among the other children as they sat alerted in anticipation.

Grandfather Standing Tall acknowledged his grandson and the rest in agreement. Everyone waited. The adults in the audience already knew the story and enjoyed hearing it again. The children nestled among their parents with full attention on the Grandfather.

Grandfather Standing Tall began, "Twice the Creator had asked the Ant People to shelter The People when the First and Second Worlds were destroyed. The Ant People had learned to live in harmony. The People saw how they all moved in unison, in cooperation with each other, to move large amounts of dirt, rocks, and other debris to re-open tunnels, and build new rooms and chambers.

"It was as if they all had the same vision of the overall plan. Only rarely did they speak. They remained focused on the desired outcome. Each in his or her own way worked the task they had agreed to perform or for which they were especially gifted. The People were truly amazed at what they observed. The Elders saw a great lesson to be learned but were unable to discern the secret of the ways of the Ant People.

"At dinner one evening an Elder of The People asked one of the Ant People Elders how it was that they lived in such harmony and with such unity of purpose, intent, and perception. The information that followed forever changed The People.

"An Elder of the Ant People answered in this way," continued Grandfather Standing Tall, "'In the ancient times, the Ant People were disorganized. Each sought only his or her personal interests and well-being. There were fights, disharmony, jealousy, greed and sometimes, great wars. Some entire ant villages were destroyed by those living there or by other villages. The Ant People themselves were almost destroyed.

"'However, a few great ones had gathered with those who shared their visions and moved far away from the other villages. They created their own villages becoming successful and prosperous. They taught their young ones that there is a Great Oneness, a Presence, which transcends the illusion that each ant was just an individual with no responsibility toward others.

"'This awareness that one's consciousness should be used for the benefit of all, and not just for the individual, was one of the great teachings. To think that we were mere individuals was an illusion. This illusion created the false image that we were separate from one another. This illusion was a negative thought-form that led to disharmony, separations, fear, anger, and other emotions that did not benefit the social order of the Ant People.'" Grandfather Standing Tall paused briefly to look around his audience then went on.

"The Ant Elder continued, 'We are not separate from each other, and we are not separate from Spirit. Everything and everyone is connected with everything else. It is this awareness of the Great Oneness that these great Elders of the Ant People taught.' The Ant People used this principle to teach how to behave within the society.

"As each individual practiced living according to the Principle of Oneness, their level of consciousness lifted, expressing itself in specific actions as compassion, kindness and unconditional love for one another.

"Their collective frequency as a society rose which manifested into the betterment of the Ant People as a whole. They could transcend the illusion of separation and the negative energies that had caused so many disharmonies in the distant villages. As this practice grew, problems within their own village began to disappear.

"This was not to say that the individual ant was unimportant, a mere slave to the greater community. Quite the contrary, the sanctity, value, and inherent beauty of each individual ant was at the core of this way of life.

"Each ant was bestowed by the Creator with intrinsic dignity, possessed the freedom of choice and intent, sovereignty and self-determination.

As each ant participated, each achieved greater awareness and compassion. By so exercising individual free will, they chose to contribute their energies to the good of all. Then, by so doing, they perceived that self-serving purposes merely distorted the truth that all things are connected.

"As this enlightenment increased, it became less and less necessary for them to communicate by using words. Joy, peace, harmony, humility, and gratitude manifested into the new world of the Ant People.

"Having learned these lessons from the Ant People," Grandfather Standing Tall looked around again to bring his point home, "our People began practicing these new ways. Creator was pleased when many villages of The People chose to join in this way of life. In so doing they transcended the 'social problems' that had challenged them in the past. Unity of Purpose, Unity of Intent, and Unity of Perception, and Unity of Consciousness were some of the gifts the Ant People gave to our way of life, in this, the Fourth World."

Grandfather Standing Tall finished by saying, "We must remember that true consciousness of our alignment with the Great Oneness does not recognize separation. A sense of separation limits perception of what choices we have."

15

RED FOX AT MOUNDCITY

Mist-laden cool breezes swirled around the fog-tinged valley. The trio greeted the rising of Father Sun with their usual offering of tobacco and prepared for their day's journey. It was only about fourteen miles or so to the village that rested at the confluence of two waterways, Paint Creek and North Fork. Moving at a slower pace than usual, the pilgrims did not reach the next village as late afternoon turned into evening. They elected to camp out that night rather than pushing themselves farther that day.

Morning Star attended the dogs as was his custom, giving them much playful attention as well as their food. As the other two travelers prepared the fire and evening meal, they made camp for the night. Red Fox noticed Morning Star seeming more animated than usual. The young man even detected a light coming from the beloved Grandfather's countenance that Red Fox had not remembered before. Looking up at Morning Star from a position seated around the campfire, Red Fox wondered what was going on with Morning Star.

Hearing the unasked question, Morning Star responded, "Getting closer to the sacred sites where I grew up, getting closer to the sites that I have spent so many years studying, I can't help feeling excited." Red Fox looked at Morning Star with eyebrows knitted asking for more information but without words.

Morning Star went on, "Red Fox, you have begun studying the ancient knowledge about the Great Serpent. You know much about it, how it was constructed, its applied mathematics and geometrics. All of that is sacred knowledge. Actually, that is only the beginning." Red Fox cocked his head indicating increased interest in what the Elder was disclosing.

"We've visited several sites already. Yet, there are many more. In fact every village has its mounds of ceremonial artifacts and burials, especially of those items left behind by individuals no longer living. The larger complexes we are soon to visit hold even more ancient knowledge. I am anxious to encounter them again.

"That's why I'm beginning to feel excited about the next part of our journey. So now that we've visited Seip and Baum and we are headed into the Chillicothe area, I have something both to tell and show you before our campfire light fades," Morning Star said as he got up to put more wood on the fire.

As he sat back down a birch bark scroll suddenly appeared in his hand. "I think you'll find this quite interesting," Morning Star said as Red Fox drew closer to see the image.

"When our People began building the earthworks in this region, the location of each was by no means randomly selected. Each earthwork was placed in a precise location. In addition to considerations of soil type, proximity to water, and types of vegetation surrounding each proposed new earthwork, there was a master plan based on the travels of Sister Moon.

"The placement of each one was built according to a grand matrix. Due to the distances involved between the various earthworks, you can't see this design with the naked eye. To appreciate the relationships among the earthworks, you need to see this scroll. It shows the design of these fourteen earthworks and their relationship to the travels of Sister Moon. Something to think about, is it not?"

Morning Star then traced with his finger all of the interconnecting lines as he described each alignment displayed on the scroll, "As you can see here, Seip, Baum and Works East near Chillicothe are aligned with Sister Moon's minimum north rise even though they are over sixteen miles apart from each other with hills and ridges in between.

"Junction Group, where we are headed next, and six other earthworks are aligned to Sister Moon's minimum south rise.

"As you can see here, these other earthworks are aligned to location on the horizon of the rising points of Sister Moon."

Morning Star paused to see if his student had any questions. He saw that Red Fox comprehended the information. He then continued, "Finally, three of these earthworks are aligned to the North Star."

"This is amazing," Red Fox said. "How is this possible? . . . I mean, this is very complicated as these earthworks are so very far apart. Even with what I've studied and learned the precision involved is remarkable.

"I see why you are so excited about re-visiting them on our journey."

With no immediate response from the Elder, Red Fox just continued to focus on the images as his mind raced with thoughts of how this was all calculated and the complex planning required to accomplish the visions of those involved in the master plan.

Morning Star looked down again at the scroll then at Red Fox who was completely focused on the diagram and said, "We'll not be visiting all of these earthworks. As there will be no renewal ceremonies held while we are in the Chillicothe area, I wanted you to be aware of this information. This is another layer in the application of the principle of *as above so below* that comes from the Ancient Knowledge."

While Red Fox had more questions, he did not pursue them as the hour was late. Morning Star neatly rolled up the scroll and replaced it in his bundle.

With that Morning Star arranged then re-arranged his sleeping blankets and lay down to sleep, leaving Red Fox more wide-awake than ever. Red Fox wanted to know more, and felt increased honor for the Grandfather, now lightly snoring as the night air embraced the troupe.

The next day they reached the confluence of two waterways, Paint Creek and its North Fork. As they approached the Junction Group village nestled there, they could not help but witness a small, but steady, stream of people flowing into this village.

"Do all those people live here?" Red Fox asked, after being welcomed by several villagers.

"No. They are coming in to hear your presentation, my son," remarked an Elder who was showing them to a guesthouse within the village. "They heard you were coming. It seems that your reputation precedes you on your journey, Red Fox," said the Elder.

"Thank you for your hospitality," Red Fox said.

Nodding, the Elder responded, "Yes, and we are providing a feast in your honor, and everyone will be sumptuously fed before your presentation later. I trust you and your companions will be comfortable here." With that he bowed his head slightly, turned and left.

The next stop on their journey, as they approached the Chillicothe area, was to first head north to a village known for its burial mounds, affectionately referred to as Mound City. The village provided an enclosed area of burial sites for many celebrated in their trades, as well as, other honored Elders.

During the burial ceremonies, The People did not routinely distinguish between shaman or others who were revered for a variety of reasons. However, occasionally a few individuals were buried with items that showed they had been honored at death as they had been honored in life.

As they approached the village near Mound city, Gazing Raven, an Elder, greeted them, "Word about you has come to us, Red Fox. We are honored to have you visit our village. Would you like me to show you the burial mounds?"

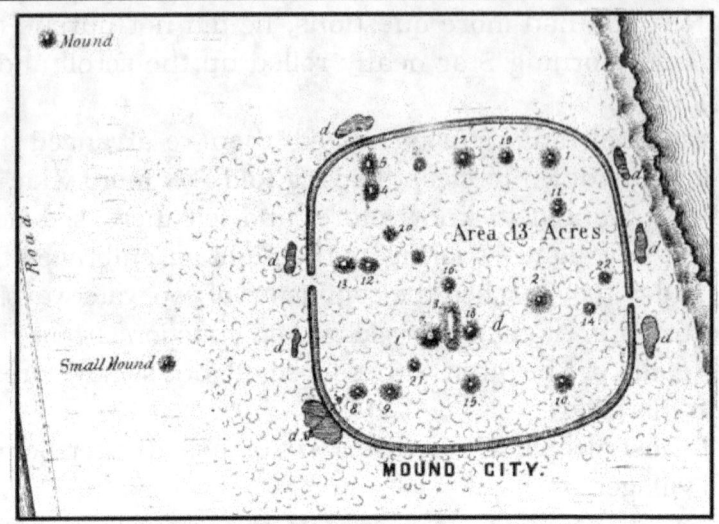
Diagram of Mound City Earthworks Squier and Davis 1848

Red Fox looked at his companions then back to Gazing Raven and responded with a slight bow of his head, "Thank you. I'd love to see Mound City." Morning Star and Running Bear took that as a cue to tend to their packs and dogs as Red Fox walked off with the Elder.

Gazing Raven said to Red Fox, "this is ancient site that is still being used for burial and cremation ceremonies. The People buried here had received special gifts from the Creator, which they used to benefit of the community. They were Healers, Rememberers, Dreamers and Shamans of various kinds."

"What about the Elders? My Grandmothers have told me about some of those buried here," asked Red Fox.

"Well, there are certainly some things that I wish to tell and show you," said Gazing Raven.

Just then, Morning Star quietly drew near. "Oh, there you are, Morning Star, I was hoping that you would be able to join us," Gazing Raven said.

Morning Star had been quietly standing a short distance away not wanting to interrupt.

"I was wondering how the two of you were doing," said Morning Star with a twinkle in his eye.

Red Fox sensed that more was going on than just a walk around this impressive place.

"We were just heading over to the burial site of the Elders of the Four Directions. Red Fox mentioned that he was interested in hearing about those who are buried there," Gazing Raven said with a broad sweep of his arm.

The trio walked the short distance from the entryway toward two large round earthen mounds.

When they arrived in front of the mounds, Gazing Raven said, "Red Fox, the mound to your left contains the earthly remains of well-known Elders who lived before your time. You might remember them from the ancient stories, Woman Who Shines Brightly, Eastern Star Rising, Sundown Quietly and Pointing Bear Star. They have become known as the Elders of the Four Directions," Gazing Raven said in hushed tones.

"What happened? How did they all die at the same time?" asked Red Fox apparently confused.

"No, no," smiled Gazing Raven, "they all walked on at different times and places within the lands of The People. They each had distinguished themselves in service to The People. The Council of the Twelve Plus One decided to bring their remains here.

"How did they become known as the Elders of the Four Directions?" asked Red Fox.

"Good question . . . Each of them was born at the far reaches of our lands, from the north, south, east, and west. The Council realized that each of these Elders had brought new layers of knowledge and awareness of the Great Oneness.

"In their discussions, the Council of Twelve Plus One saw that although each were given different skills and were very different people, they had one very special and rare gift in common," Gazing Raven paused to make sure he had Red Fox's full attention and continued, "their connection to the Great Oneness was exceptional. For each of them the Veil of Forgetfulness was very thin.

"They, each in their own way, were able to tell us much about our purposes here and what we can learn from our experiences.

"In addition, they showed us that from time to time, some individuals have appetites in an obsessive way. Or some have a longing inside which they try to satisfy with material things or though many unsatisfying relationships. Some try to have power over others. They exhibit these and other out-of-balance behaviors in their effort to fill a perceived void or emptiness in their lives.

"These individuals suffer from a mistaken belief that they are not whole in some way, or not worthy enough to feel whole or complete. Those with that sense of these mistaken beliefs or emptiness inside try to fill it from the outside in . . . from the seen world, so to speak. They are really, in effect, longing for their sense of connectedness and the remembrance of our true Home.

"The teachings reveal that the only way to satisfy that longing or to fill that emptiness is from the *inside* . . . through connecting with the unseen. Connecting with the unseen provides us alignment with the Great Oneness, or at-one-ment with the One.

"With their teachings, many of those of two hearts or those who were experiencing unhealthy appetites or those feeling a sense of separation were brought back to the Oneness and felt the connectedness. These Elders accomplished this through their teachings.

"For most, the individuals who sought their guidance got to experience the knowing that our physical body is merely a projection of our spiritual identity as an individualized expression of the One Creator. Our true being is the same Being as our Creator, the One.

"In honor of their dedication to continually lift others in this way, their cremated remains were placed together here in this mound along with special selected offerings. This honoring is actually a way we remind ourselves of what they did for us as a People. We honor their honoring of us by their teachings and willingness to help.

"A copper headdress was made for Woman Who Shines Brightly as she was from the copper mines area in the north.

"When the re-burial ceremony was held, people from far and wide came to pay their respects leaving offerings of gratitude.

"Their remains were placed on top of a layer of mica which formed a large rectangular area.

"Mica, as you know, represents, among other things, the Veil of Forgetfulness. This Veil occludes our ability to consciously remember what it was like before our return to a physical existence.

"Placing their ashes on the mica in this way, we show and we recognize that while they walked on Mother Earth, they clearly saw beyond the Veil and worked to strengthen our connections to Great Spirit." Gazing Raven finished his explanation and saw that Red Fox comprehended.

Red Fox looked silently around and back again at Gazing Raven then nodded in acknowledgement.

Morning Star was also very pleased with Red Fox's growing understanding of the Ways of The People. During the next few moments of silence Red Fox noticed that Gazing Raven and Morning Star had focused on each other's faces. Something unsaid passed between them. Then they each smiled.

"We have something to show you that you might be interested in," said Gazing Raven to Red Fox as he turned and started walking. They remained in silence until Gazing Raven stopped.

Floating overhead riding the thermals, several hawks called to each other. The gentle fragrance of blooming wildflowers and trees filled the air.

In front of them rested a large oblong mound with two round mounds on either side. The one on the west side was larger. Red Fox realized that this was their destination when they stopped there.

"While we are on the subject of mica . . ." Gazing Raven continued, "this mound also has a large mica feature resting on its floor. A crescent moon was formed from round disks of silvery mica," Gazing Raven said tracing a crescent shape in the air with his hand.

"So who were the Elders whose remains were placed on top of this mica moon?" asked Red Fox.

"It is not about what's *on* the mica moon but *what's below it*." Gazing Raven said with a hint of mystery in his voice.

"What do you mean?" Red Fox pressed.

"You will soon see," said Gazing Raven smiling.

Meanwhile, as this conversation engaged Red Fox, Morning Star had vanished behind the far side of the mound. A musky dank smell began to compete with the sweet fragrances in the air as Morning Star removed a camouflaged doorway.

"We're now ready," said Morning Star as he reappeared, "follow me, Red Fox."

The trio moved to the other side of the mound. Red Fox stood at the entrance.

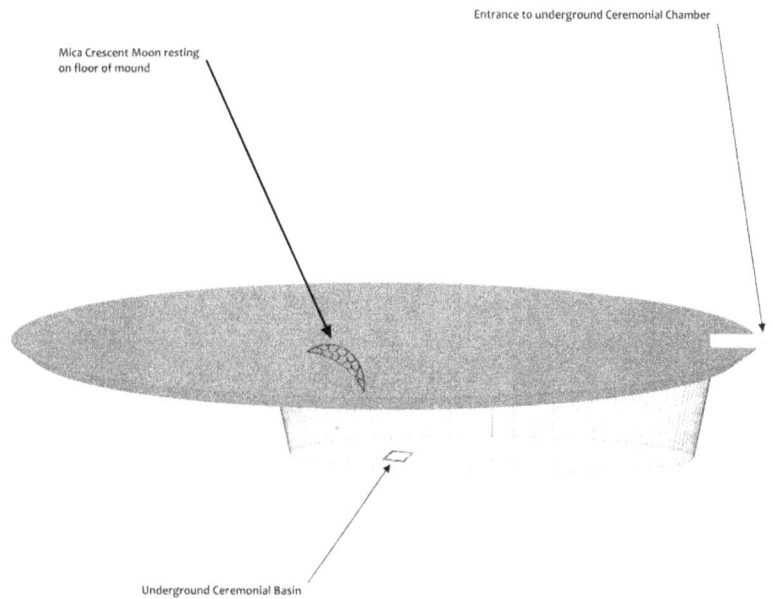

Cutaway view of **Mound 7, Mound City, showing floor of mound and underground chamber.**
Redrawn and modified from Mills, 1922, Fig. 25.

"Is this . . . a . . . ceremonial chamber . . .?" stammered Red Fox eyes wide open.

"Indeed" Gazing Raven and Morning Star said together smiling at the young man.

"Oh my," was all Red Fox could muster.

At that point Gazing Raven took a bundle of herbs that had been tied with string from a pocket in his tunic. He also pulled out a crystal lens. He held the crystal lens over the bundle using the rays of Father Sun to ignite the herbs. As the smoke came forth, he smudged himself by waving the smoking bundle over and around his body. He then repeated this ceremony for Morning Star and finally Red Fox.

"We must be purified of any negative energy before we enter the chamber. Watch your head as we proceed in so that you do not hit the timbers that support the chamber. I will go in first and light some oil lamps, so that we can see," Gazing Raven instructed as he started down the timber lined entry ramp whose walls and floor were made from clay and sand mixed together to form a very hard surface. As each man stood over six feet, they each had to stoop slightly to enter the chamber.

The chamber was oriented southwest to northeast. Its oval shape was 40 feet long and 30 feet wide. Timbers lined the ceiling chinked with the same clay/sand mix that covered the walls and floor.

The interior height was sufficient to allow the three men to stand upright with room to spare. Oil lamps made of pottery backed by shiny copper reflectors with a rounded mica casing offered more diffused light. Decorated woven mats lined the walls, painted with symbols in different colors, and writings from the Ancient Knowledge that Red Fox could not decipher as he looked around. Toward the southwest end gaped a large ceremonial pit dug into the floor of this subterranean room. The pit boasted six feet long and four feet wide. A mica crescent moon hung from cords above this pit.

"This must be a significant ceremonial site," observed Red Fox. The two Elders stood in silence watching Red Fox as he reacted to what he was seeing. Red Fox added, "This must be a site for some kind of ceremony. That pit appears to be large enough for a person to curl up in."

"Good insight, Red Fox . . . this ceremonial room," Gazing Raven said, "is where we bring those who have accepted the path of initiation into the Great Mystery. This is where some of the tasks take place for an initiate to complete. The pit you see there is where an initiate lies for a deep and powerful meditation, away from all distractions of ordinary life. It provides a place, like the womb, where the initiate can dream and or even leave the body to accomplish whatever tasks are presented." He noticed Red Fox wrinkling his forehead bringing his eyebrows together. "Do you have a question?"

"The Great Mystery? I'm not sure what you mean exactly," Red Fox asked.

"The Great Mystery, or the Great Oneness, is Great Spirit and our conscious connection with Great Spirit," was the reply. Red Fox tilted his head to one side listening for more information.

Gazing Raven seeing this as a cue to offer more information added, "It's about vividly connecting with Spirit, so that you experience your Oneness. Because you do it consciously, you then get the opportunity to experience the Knowing. It's all One. The Great Oneness offers different dimensions. When you go through the different stages of initiation, you experience Great Spirit in many facets of the One. Experiencing the Great Mystery and becoming aware of your connection then makes it easier for you to assist others to feel their sense of Oneness also.

"Nearly all of our Elders whose remains are here at Mound City completed the process of initiation. This process also augments the talents of each individual, so each can contribute that much more to our civilization as a whole. It also amplifies the vision for those who can see through the Veil of Forgetfulness.

"Of course there are many initiates living among The People today who have fully completed the process. I think you might have heard of Red Coat. Red Coat is a powerful shaman who continuously works to stay in touch with the Great Mystery. He now lives in the Chillicothe area."

Red Fox remained silent. Finally he asked, "So, what exactly are the steps someone goes through in this initiation process?"

"Good question," responded Gazing Raven. ". . . And that is something I am unable to tell you. Because this process can be harrowing, as well as uplifting, and because each individual entering this process must be prepared spiritually to accomplish certain tasks, that must remain unknown before presented with them. The steps must, by their very nature, remain in secrecy."

After a few more moments of silence, Red Fox asked another question, "So why here? Why in this chamber?"

Gazing Raven nodded a moment before answering and then said, "Another good question. Our bodies come from Mother Earth. This chamber is constructed within Mother Earth. It provides a sacred space for the spirit of each individual to begin the journey of unfoldment from the physical body and enfoldment into Spirit . . . from darkness into light."

Red Fox interjected wistfully, "That sounds fascinating."

"This sacred space is not entered unless by intention for the purpose of ceremony," Gazing Raven continued without acknowledging the interruption. "Much of our artifacts needed for ceremony can be stored here. The pit is here. Everything here remains undisturbed by wind or rain or other elements. It is safe, sacred, and protected and it is not the only ceremonial chamber we have."

"You mean, there's more?" asked Red Fox.

"Yes," came the response. "Usually, their locations are known only to a few Elders, and their entrances are kept hidden."

Red Fox looked around again. He noticed the mica crescent hanging directly above the pit.

"And this?" Red Fox pointed to it. "Is this Sister Moon?"

Gazing Raven replied, "Indeed. She is waxing in strength as do the initiates in this progression. Because we usually begin in the dark, Sister Moon figures prominently in the beginning processes. She lights our way out of the darkness as we move into light. Additionally, the other crescent mica moon *just above this room*, the one that rests buried in the dirt floor of this mound, is positioned to the southeast of this pit. At certain times there is an alignment between these two mica moons and a waxing crescent Sister Moon."

Inhaling deeply, Red Fox, fascinated by this information, continued to look around without speaking or needing to ask further questions. Morning Star noticed that Red Fox's attention appeared to be drifting off.

After a while, Morning Star silently signaled to Gazing Raven with a nod that it was time to leave. When they had entered, the chamber had been dark and forbidding and now seemed full of embracing energy and light. Gazing Raven gradually put out each of the lanterns as they drifted toward the opening. Red Fox followed absent-mindedly.

On the road again after the presentation given at the village near Mound City, the trio and dogs continued south into the largest settlement known among The People, Chillicothe.

Raven's Wing kept herself busy cooking and baking for the differing needs of her community. With Warm Stone as a semi-permanent guest, she found herself appreciating his attentiveness, fetching and carrying for her. His leg was healing nicely as he remained in the village for Turning Rabbit's return.

"Gray Wolf," Warm Stone turns to me one afternoon outside my home after a mid-day meal, "My leg is better than ever. Yet, I feel I must wait here for Turning Rabbit to come back." Warm Stone sounds wistful almost apologetic.

"You're contributing here. That's all that matters. You're welcome to stay with us as long as you need to. If you took off to find Turning Rabbit, you'd probably get lost, not really knowing the country and not really knowing exactly where he might be. No, it's best you stay put 'til he shows up," I offer encouragingly.

"Besides, he could've gone way up north or far east all the way to the coast for all we know. He doesn't just visit The People here in the Ohio Valley area."

At the thought of Warm Stone leaving, I realize that I was missing my two friends, Water Dog and Red Fox, more than I wanted to admit. "Besides," I add, "I don't want to see you go. We are becoming friends, and I enjoy your company."

Warm Stone responds, "Gray Wolf, you are such a good friend to me, much like a brother. I shall always remember you and your family. How good everyone is to me, and how your healers saved my life and saved my leg. I'm indebted to you forever. Someday I'll find a way to repay The People for your constant kindnesses," he adds putting his hand on my shoulder with a serious look on his face.

"Let's walk," I suggest. "I'd like to get back to Singing Hawk's to continue my studies. Come with." My mother catches my eye before we leave. "Oh, I guess I'd better get some more water before we go."

Warm Stone looks up at Raven's Wing trying to figure out the communication that he sensed had taken place beyond his notice. "I'm trying too hard to catch on," he confesses. "I've noticed a level of communication that occurs around here without words, yet it's just as effective."

He grabs a water basket, and we head toward the pond. He continues, "I've been noticing it more and more lately. Floating Lily shows up at your house with information your mother needs in time for her to prepare dishes for whomever. When she shows up, your mother acts like she's expecting Floating Lily. Shining Moon shows up at the Healing House with just the right herbs and stuff to help me without Speaks With Plants sending a messenger. How does it work? I should like to learn this."

"I'm not exactly sure," I confess. "We live with it and don't even think about it. It's just a natural part of who we are." I screw up my face as I search for a better answer. "I guess it's something I can work on this afternoon with Singing Hawk."

I am so deep in thought at this comment by Warm Stone neither of us speak as we retrieve the water for my mother.

Warm Stone joins me as I head back to Singing Hawk's house for more lessons and contemplation. I had set my mind on examining Warm Stone's observation. As we saunter across the village, for some reason we take the direction that goes by the edge of the forest where Lone Tree lives and works.

"Hello boys," shouts Lone Tree, as he is carrying an armload of logs. Sweaty and out of breath, Lone Tree puts down his load in a particular spot near his smokehouse, before coming over to greet us. Even though we had not planned on stopping, his enthusiastic greeting catches us off guard. So we stop momentarily to accept Lone Tree's greeting.

"Are you sure you are up to carrying heavy loads of wood, Lone Tree?" Warm Stone asks.

"Oh, yes," says Lone Tree as he shrugs, "I just need to take fewer logs as I move them. I'm not as young as I once was. Ever since I was a pup, I've been hauling wood to the smokehouse. My hair is gray and white now," he adds, flapping his ponytail hanging down his back. "It used to be black like coal. That's when my back was strong and solid. My, how the seasons pass." He wipes his forehead again as if wiping years off.

"Looks like you need some help," observes Warm Stone. "My back is strong and so are my legs. I can help you if you like? . . . Besides, what's coal?"

"Sure, I'll take your help, Warm Stone. Word is you're blending in nicely with The People," Lone Tree comments in response to Warm Stone's offer of help.

"Coal? Oh, yes, we don't get much of it here. It's a fuel source provided by Mother Earth. It's good for heating, but I don't use it in the smokehouse. I've heard they have used it at Spruce Hill sometimes, but wood still works better for the furnaces there. It tends to release black soot, not good for smoking meats. I much prefer wood." He turns as he finishes. "Well, come on then," half waving an arm as he walks away.

"Gray Wolf," Warm Stone turns back to me, "I guess I won't be going with you to Singing Hawk's, today. I'm needed here."

At that, Warm Stone takes several quick steps to catch up with Lone Tree, leaving me standing there by myself, not really knowing what just happened. I turn and wind my way to Singing Hawk's house.

All afternoon, Warm Stone carried short cut logs from the pile neatly stacked up and around several hills away to place them in yet another neatly stacked pile near the smokehouse. He did not mind the hard work, and in fact, felt invigorated by the steady rhythm of the walking, lifting, carrying, and walking. As the day was coming to a close, Warm Stone finally spoke to Lone Tree as they were making their last trip, "Something's bothering me."

Lone Tree looked up, surprised by an anticipated complaint. "Is the work too hard for you?" he asked Warm Stone.

"No, not at all. In fact I've enjoyed myself. Due to my injury I was laid up for a while. So now I enjoy the physical exercise," clarified Warm Stone. Lone Tree nodded one nod in acknowledgment as they trudged their final trudge.

"I got a question about these logs," said Warm Stone.

Lone Tree threw his head back in surprise, not at all comprehending what his companion was talking about.

"I mean," Warm Stone continued, "I don't believe I have ever seen logs shaped at the ends quite like this. They are so perfectly sliced to just the right size for carrying and burning in your oven at the smokehouse."

Reaching the smokehouse with the last load, Lone Tree said, "I'm not sure what you are talking about. But if you mean the sawed ends of these logs, that's easy. A team of villagers take saws and cut down the dead trees or those blown down by a storm. They saw them into sizes appropriate for burning in either the cook stoves or my smokehouse," Lone Tree explained.

Warm Stone interrupted, "What's a saw? I don't know what that is."

"I don't have any saws around here to show you. But they are like very large knives with large teeth and sometimes handles on both sides. Very handy for providing the right sized wood for the village," Lone Tree responded.

"Now before you go, be a good fella' and fetch me a bag of salt from the storehouse? It'll save me a trip," Lone Tree said showing some fatigue from the day's labor. "It will be in bags in a large clay vessel about this size with a lid," he shaped his hands to show the dimensions to Warm Stone. "Thanks. I only need one bag for now."

"Salt! Salt? You have that much *salt*?" asked Warm Stone incredulously.

"Well, of course, we have salt," Lone Tree responded as he sat down on a bench outside next to the smoke house. "Don't you find the food here to your liking?" he asked rhetorically. "Why, with the herbs and the salt, our food is pretty good, seems to me anyway. Haven't you noticed just how tasty Raven's Wing's stews and other dishes are?" again he asked rhetorically.

With that, Warm Stone turned and walked over toward the storage house. After a short while, he returned, handing Lone Tree a bag of salt neatly tied at the top to prevent spillage. "I've never seen so much salt in one place before," he commented after sitting down next to Lone Tree. "It's like having great riches to some people I have met on my travels. I've been to places where salt is dear and comes with a high price. How do The People get so much salt?"

Lone Tree held the bag of salt for a while thinking about the possibility of people not having salt or enough salt, making it a valuable commodity. After being lost in thought for a moment, he said, "Off to the east several settlements over, there's a brine spring.

"The People take water from the brine spring and place it in large open pottery vats built into the ground. Then over several days the energy from Father Sun evaporates the water leaving the salt behind. Then, what do you know . . . salt," he smiled half-jokingly

"In the winter the water is poured into large pottery trays which are placed over a fire to evaporate the water. Either way, the salt is then collected and placed in these woven bags and distributed to our villages. Once a bag is empty, we save it. When the next shipment comes, the bags are sent back to be re-used."

Crunch, crunch, crunch.

They both looked up in the direction of footsteps sounding from the falling shadows of dusk.

"Raven's Wing sent me," announced Floating Lily to the two surprised men. She stepped up closer carrying a large covered pot warm to the touch. "She said you would be hungry." She set the pot down on an outside table and stood looking at the bewildered Warm Stone before turning and escaping back into the shadows.

Meanwhile, as I continue to walk towards Singing Hawk's house, I reach into the ethers to solve the riddle of the wordless communication that Warm Stone brought to my attention. When I arrive, I am surprised to see Shining Bird sitting quietly at a table with scrolls in front of her. She looks up with a smile as I enter.

"Where's Singing Hawk?" I command. "I need to discuss something with her."

Shining Bird taken aback by my abruptness, sits up erect on her bench. "What's wrong?" she furrows her brows, anticipating some kind of emergency.

"*Where* is she?" I demand.

"Oh, my," coos Shining Bird. "What is it, may I ask?"

"I need to speak with her right now. Where did you say she was?" I ask again, not really listening to my dearest friend and lover.

"I didn't say, my beloved. She left here only a few minutes ago and don't know to expect her back any time soon. Hmmm, what's going on? What's up?"

"I have to speak to her. I have to speak to someone about this. My mind is tied up in knots. It's a puzzle, you see," I admit reluctantly.

Eyes lingering on the birch bark scrolls she had been studying until I arrived, Shining Bird moves gracefully up from her bench over to where I had plopped myself down in a huff. As she sits next to me, I can see her eyes fixed on a light not there, pupils dilated. "What is it?" she asks again with infinite patience.

Screwing up my mouth trying to not talk, not ask, not state the problem, I finally give in to her presence and say, "Warm Stone mentioned that on many occasions he had noticed a form of wordless communication among us over many instances." I relate my recent conversation with Warm Stone. "I need an answer." There, finally I say it out loud.

"Oh, is that all," Shining Bird softly replies, leaning in toward me. "I can help you with that, I think."

I pull backward still resisting.

Undaunted, my lady pursues the issue, "Yes, it's really quite simple, you see."

I swallow hard needing to readjust my esteem of Shining Bird.

She continues, ignoring my discomfort, "It's always about frequency." She pauses to let my energy field shift into one of listening rather than one of fighting an idea.

"We, as a group of people, we, as family members, we, as The People, participate in a field of frequencies in which we operate most of the time. We 'tune in' so to speak to each other. We 'tune in' to others within our scope. As we talk and as we think thoughts, our minds send out frequencies. Others of us 'tune in' to those same frequencies. It is wordless as words are not actually spoken. Yet, they are thought energies. They are thought with such definition that the energy of them goes out and is picked up by others of us. We are and remain in tune with each other because we live in a communion with each other. This communion unites us in unseen ways. It's another way of communing or staying connected."

She pauses, turns slightly and adds, "Of course, some are better at it than others. And, some are more in tune with specific individuals than with others in general, but you get the picture."

Turning toward me again and putting her hand on my arm to comfort me as she lectures me with the softest of tones, "You see, it should be no mystery that this kind of communication occurs with us. For us, it is natural, and normal. I can see why strangers might think it unusual. Warm Stone can learn it. His frequency is increasing, becoming much more compatible with us."

Completely engrossed in the mental graphics in my head, I forget where I am. I begin to sense her very near presence, smell a honeysuckle scent coming from her. She moves closer to me pushing her center into my center. The pores of my face open, my eyes roll back, and I am lost in a paradise of lust, love, and spiritual admiration for my friend, my beloved, and once again my teacher.

16

RED FOX AT CHILLICOTHE

Despite the contributions made by other villages among The People, Chillicothe stood out as the center of our culture. Not only were the various trades practiced here, but also here was the center for the exchange of new methods of artistic endeavors. More importantly, it was the place for the exchange of ideas and support throughout our lands. As a result, Chillicothe had become a place of prominence. Thousands of people lived in the area.

It was the place where the Council of the Twelve Plus One met.

The Council of Twelve Plus One met in the large meetinghouse. The Twelve were representatives of various outlying areas of The People, many from very far away. They would travel here to discuss issues important to The People.

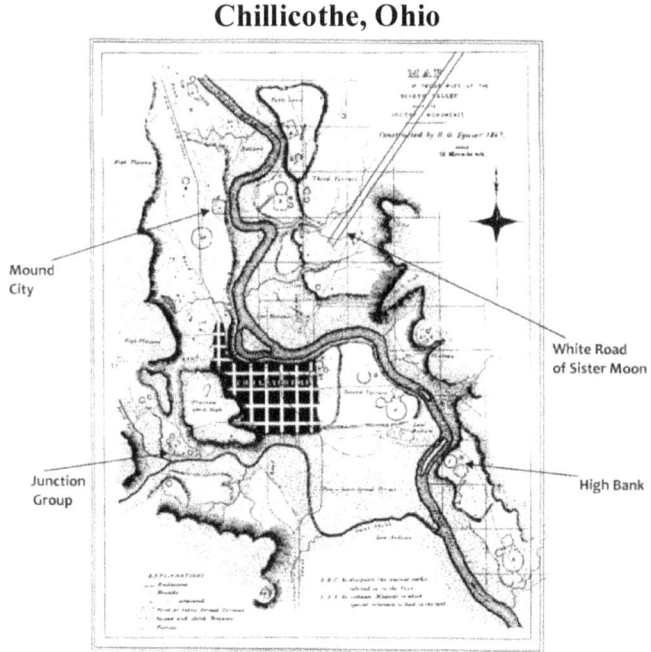

Diagram of Chillicothe Ohio area Squier and Davis 1848

Representatives came from lands near the far eastern ocean and the southern ocean. They also came from the Mississippi River area, plus from the Great Lakes and Canada.

When the Council met, the differing perspectives shared offered different ways of seeing an issue.

The Council of the Twelve Plus One was a tradition centuries old, which reinforced a larger sense of community.

The Council of the Twelve Plus One always met in Chillicothe. Sometimes, representatives would come there even though no official meeting had been called. It provided a place of great sanctuary for repose. Because of this ongoing practice, citizens of Chillicothe set aside housing dedicated especially for such guests. In this way, the physical needs of pilgrims were provided for.

Because this city thrived with its enormous population, Red Fox gave several presentations a day for several days moving from one local earthwork complex to another.

As he continued his many presentations in this cultural center, he noticed many familiar faces in the audience. For a brief moment, he thought he recognized a certain feminine face in the crowd. Each time he gave his presentation the audience grew in size as previous listeners returned bringing with them more and more friends and family members. Red Fox performed each time with the same delivery and with the same straightforward style. He never varied in style, and he felt he had become one with the message. He spoke from his soul.

One evening the crowd was larger than usual. He noted that a small band of men wore a different style of clothing than that worn by The People. He assumed they must be travelers from some distant place as their demeanor and appearance differed from The People. One had a noticeable scar across and down his left cheek.

Red Fox delivered his presentation with as much emotional and uplifting appeal as ever. As usual, after he ended, he looked straight out into the audience as if to ask if there were any questions or comments. The People sat silent. Then the one with the scarred face stood up. Faces turned toward him waiting for him to speak.

"You tell these stories like they were *true*," he said defiantly with a toss of his head and throwing his hands upward.

Red Fox focused his attention on the challenger and nodded in affirmation.

"You learned those stories from an old woman," Scarface continued his challenge. "You stand there telling stories you learned from old women. How can you believe such stories? What a bunch of weaklings all of you are. You listen to old women. You let old women lead you," he snarled with distain.

Shocked silence seized the audience.

After a pause and seeing an opening to continue, the scar-faced man spoke again.

"Where I come from, men are the leaders. Men have the power. Where I come from everyone knows who the leaders are by their rank. Everyone knows that the leaders have the power over the land and the social order. We know who is in charge, and . . . it is not women. Women are not allowed inside the temples. Women have no power. You don't even have temples to honor the priests and the gods. What kind of people are you?

"You don't have temples. You don't have priests to speak to the gods for you. You let women lead you. You don't have a ranking of men for organization. Back where I come from, we all know where each man ranks by their dress, by how great their houses are, and by how much wealth each one has. That tells everyone how much power each man has over others. None of the men who live here show power. You let the women have power over us visitors and over the ways of doing things.

"How backward you are! Why don't you wise up and see how much better our ways are? Why don't you change to our way? Our way is better, because it is the men who lead, the men who can fight, and the men who are in charge. Our priests are men, and they are the ones who speak to the gods for us. Can't you see how much better we are than you? Can't you see you should be more like us?"

The audience remained in shock.

"You are all cowards!" Scarface exhorted. "You have no leaders, but listen to old women. You do not war against anyone! What kind of people are you?"

Gasps.

Murmurings.

Red Fox unabashed and undaunted by the challenge continued standing looking at Scarface, then through him, seeing something beyond him. Then he looked up to the sky.

At that moment, Red Coat stood up.

Gasps . . . then awkward silence.

"And, who would you have us war against?" Red Coat boomed with authority.

Red Coat had joined the audience at the beginning of the presentation. However, he sat on the outside perimeter of the audience and on the opposite side from Scarface and his companions. Red Coat's large robust frame imposed an image of authority, exuding power. His red vest screamed the knowledge, power and sense of connectedness that Red Coat represented. When he spoke, people listened. When he spoke, listeners knew his words came from the Great Oneness.

Red Fox had occasionally seen Red Coat coming and going, from across a distance during his stay at Chillicothe. Chillicothe was such an expansive settlement that Red Fox had not crossed paths with him yet. Red Fox remembered seeing this tall shaman entering and leaving a meetinghouse several times over the past several days. Red Fox had not yet met this great shaman. Now was the time.

At the posing of that question by Red Coat, Scarface turned away from addressing Red Fox and the crowd, so he could focus on Red Coat. The two adversaries stood facing each other with over a thousand people between them.

Red Coat stood tall, taller than many, and alert, and comfortable in his imposing muscular body, wearing his vest dyed deep red. The red vest contrasted against his heavy tan woven trousers, fitting his waist tightly. Bare arms exposed his bulging muscles. He wore few adornments, only a few shell necklaces, a pendant of a small copper six-pointed star within a circle, and no ear spools. His long black hair worn pulled back and tied with three eagle feathers set with pearls.

In contrast, Scarface stood nervously, shifting his weight back and forth from left to right and back again. Brief in stature, he appeared shorter than many. A wiry frame clothed in tanned leather pants fitting tightly with an over-shirt opened at the chest and a sleeveless jacket of mixed colors woven in designs foreign to The People.

Repeating his question, Red Coat boomed again, "And whom would you have us fight?"

Feeling slapped in the face by this question, Scarface hesitated slightly, stumbling over his words. "Uh, uh, each other," he responded indignantly with a wide gesture indicating the audience members.

"Why would we want to do that?" asked Red Coat loudly.

Now standing with his weight on both feet, Scarface rose to the challenge of the debate and confidently answered, "To win over each other. That's how you establish ranking and power. The one with the most power and wealth rules. The one with the most wealth and power has the highest rank. That way everyone else knows who makes the rules."

"And what are the rules?" Red Coat asked again.

With a condescending attitude, Scarface replied, "The rules are whatever the leaders say they are. That's why you need to know who the leaders are. Then everyone knows what to do."

After a few moments, Red Coat inhaled deeply before speaking, "You have come from a faraway place where the ways of doing and being appear very different from The People. Your ways are set, and you probably have been living in your ways for a very long time. That is just fine . . . *for you.*

"You come here to where we are. We, as The People, have our ways of doing and being. You come to where we are and want to bring your ways with you. You wish to establish your ways of doing things here. It seems that you wish to re-create your traditions in a place that does not recognize your traditions. You find yourself uncomfortable with our ways and seek to change them to suit you.

"When you come to a new place, consider honoring the ways of the people where you find yourselves. No one is asking that you give up your ways. Consider keeping your ways to yourselves, but behave in the ways of the place where you are.

"While there may be nothing wrong with your ways, they do not fit with us. Your ways of doing would not serve The People here as they appear out-of-order to us. If you wish to live among us, you and the others with you are certainly welcome.

"However, for you to become successful while here, it would serve you to integrate with us and honor our ways. We do not seek power *over* others as you describe. We do not seek power at all, nor do we need power."

Scarface scoffed at Red Coat's remark, "*Hah!* You just used the word 'power' so you know what I'm talking about. Power is used by our leaders to force others to do their bidding."

Red Coat breathed deeply in before responding and then said, "Power in your sense means *force*, subjugating others to satisfy ego-driven desires. You justify force to create a sense of well-being for those who can compel others, and that sense of power is only a mere illusion. Using force over others fragments the community. Ego-driven exercise of force provides only a temporary sense of satisfaction, much like an appetite that can never be satisfied. The ego-driven desires cannot fulfill the soul's desire for expression.

"Force is not something we consider, because it is self-serving. We see power residing within Spirit and within each of us as individuals. Power, as energy, resides in everything. When we wish to accomplish a common purpose, it is for the benefit of all concerned. The power to do that comes from within our community, much like harmonizing tones. Power is harmonic energy that manifests, because it creates. In other words, it is our collective frequency that serves us to complete any task. Power serves, force savages. It's not about power *over* others, but power *with* others."

Agitated by Red Coat's argument, Scarface interrupted with contempt and announced, "Our ways are right!" He pounded the air with a fist. "Your ways are wrong. You have no leaders to follow. You let women lead you . . . *spagh*," he spits on the ground. "You hunt like women. You don't take everything you can. You leave more than you take. How can you win when you take only what you need?

"You don't have temples. You don't have priests. How can you live like you do, with no leaders, no rules, and no temples?"

Looking down then back up again, Red Coat delivered his response with silky smooth power like an arrow in slow motion. "We are one with Great Spirit. We live in a sense of oneness with each other and with Spirit. Each of us is a flamelet of the great fire, of the essence of all of life that we call the Great Oneness. We treat each other with the honor we would treat Spirit.

"We hunt and take only what we need, because Mother Earth provides for us. We do not savage her, but serve her. She is our Mother in a sense."

At that remark, Scarface reacted against it by giving a huff, and jolting back, and then stood with most of his weight on one leg and arms akimbo and hands at his hips. His posture showed he objected.

Red Coat saw the objection and continued uninterrupted, "That's right. Our essence is part of Great Spirit. Each of us is Spirit, individualized for the experience of experiencing in the physical. Mother Earth provides our bodies, a covering of our spirit, so to speak, so Spirit can experience through our experiences."

Red Coat looked around and saw that the audience was frozen in wonder at this confrontation. They were not used to having their values and culture challenged in such a contemptuous way. At the same time they were struck by Red Coat's clarity in articulating their tacit beliefs. Red Coat's message resonated deeply at their core.

Red Coat continued, "Yes. That's right. As individual spirits, we enter the physical world through the woman's body. The woman breathes air from the Earth and gives that air to her baby growing inside her, just as she does with the water she drinks. The food that she eats for herself also nurtures her growing baby, and it comes from Mother Earth as well. The water surrounding the baby while it is in the womb comes from Mother Earth. In that sense Earth is a mother to us, . . ." Red Coat trailed off in thought then returns to add more.

". . . and by the same token, our physical bodies become the temple of Great Spirit."

With that remark, Scarface cocked his head, yet he remained standing in opposition.

"Yes, indeed, again, we need no other temples. We do not need to worship in a physical temple, built of stone, or wood, or earth.

"When we comprehend that we are Spirit, then each of our physical bodies automatically are temples housing that part of Great Spirit we acknowledge as each other. This is also why we don't need anyone else to intercede with Great Spirit on our behalf."

Red Coat shrugged his shoulders, arms and palms open toward the listeners and added, "No priests needed.

"This is what makes us one in the One. This is the only rule we need. There is no other rank to achieve. When we treat each other as if the other person is us and part of us, we need no other law or rule to live by. We are all connected to each other in a collective energy field that continues throughout the Great Oneness. We are all related within the Great Oneness, seen and unseen, spirit and earth, constancy and flux. We cannot compete or war against each other. We, as members of a collective, are not separate from the whole as we live together in deep communion. We live in a sense of unity that is spiritual or unseen. Every person is part of the Whole or the Great Oneness, and we feel our connection to each other. Because we see the connection to each other, we do not behave like the other person is separate.

"We cannot dominate anyone, because that anyone is also us. What one person does impacts all of us. We share everything, so accumulation of wealth or force is not a concept or frequency in which we participate. How we behave toward each other and toward Mother Earth is ultimately how we behave toward Great Spirit. This is why we do not war on anyone or fight anyone. The way we see it, we would be fighting ourselves. Warring against another is the same as Great Spirit warring against Itself.

"When you fight others, you must do so in a way that causes you to become as bad as or worse than they. When you lose, you remain a force against your conqueror. When you win, look at what you win. Is it something that soothes the heart? Does winning beget serenity? Does inflicting force over someone else bring you peace? Or, when you win is the victory temporary because the ego must continue to exert force over someone or something more? Does winning satisfy the soul? And then do you consider that you still have an enemy who could still turn on you later? So, in the end you become what you fight."

Scarface frowned at the expression of this thought. Red Coat noticed this and continued, "The People do not have the concept of fighting, especially fighting each other. In our ancient past, wars did occur among segments of the people who lived here. Yet at a point the segments joined into a whole, and we became The People. War and fighting is simply not in our vision of ourselves."

Interrupting impatiently at this point, Scarface intruded with a sneer and an objection, "Yeah, but you still let old women tell you what to do. What kind of leadership is that?"

Putting his hands together in front of him, Red Coat looked down again, pursed his lips, looked up, unclasped his hands and spoke with hands open, "We have no leaders who tell us what to do. We need no leaders, as each person is a leader in his or her own life.

"Women are part of us, just as men are part of us. No one is lesser or greater. Women cannot be ranked lower than men, because we all come from the same essence, simply expressing either a masculine or feminine energy in the physical."

He paused briefly to let that sink in a moment and to give emphasis to his next comment and then continued, "Yet, women have been given a special assignment. That is the nurturing and birthing of new individuals coming into this physical experience. It is the feminine energy that nurtures. Their assignment is special, because special construction of their bodies is required to make this happen. Entering this world through the birthing process is the only way new spirits can arrive here if it's their intention to experience experiences in the physical.

"Women are in touch with the Great Mother, in particular. What this does for women is it gifts them with a powerful connection to the sense of nurturing. The wombs hold the wisdom, the nurturing. As women grow beyond the years for producing babies, they accumulate increased insight and perspective. Their wombs, while no longer nurturing babies, grow with wisdom to continue nurturing The People. Much to your objection, it is the women, the *old women* in particular, who provide us with direction, insight, and support. Our beloved Grandmothers are the keepers of our ways, the keepers of our applied wisdom, the keepers of our identity as The People. They position present-day events and experiences of The People in relationship to our ancient knowledge . . . not ancient times . . . Ancient Wisdom. This keeps the balance." Red Coat paused to breathe then added, ". . . and it is our beloved Grandfathers who do the same, as they stand in support for all of us."

"Humph," was all Scarface could muster.

Red Coat finished with, "From what you have said, your leaders require blind obedience from their followers. Such blind obedience can be fatal to a people. It becomes clear to me that the harmonics of our two cultures clash, rather than blend."

Without backing down, but no longer willing to confront Red Coat, Scarface turned his back to Red Coat, snarling while doing so. He realized he lost the debate, and felt unwilling to signal the loss. With his back to the audience, Red Coat and Red Fox, Scarface did not retreat, but moved away from his verbal battlefield, not to be seen again for a long time. Only several of his companions left with him. The rest stayed to become part of The People.

The audience remained seated for a very long time after the debate ended. They felt awed by what they had just witnessed. Red Coat was the first to leave. Then, gradually listeners stood to leave also. Many sent a mental salute of a nod or toss of the head to Red Fox, who had remained at his spot until the meeting area emptied.

"That was pretty interesting," commented Morning Star as he accompanied Red Fox back to their guesthouse.

"After that encounter, I felt speechless," said Red Fox reeling in the sobering aftermath.

"I suspect that you might have been feeling a little heady by the time you got to this last presentation. I was worried that your ego might be starting to get the better of you . . . that is until tonight." Morning Star went on, "Red Fox, you have experienced enormous success in giving your presentations over these past weeks or so. Here, at Chillicothe, I noticed some of the same people coming back to hear you again, each time bringing more friends with them."

Red Fox grimaced at the observation but kept quiet.

Grandfather Morning Star continued uninterrupted, "Misuse of ego is fatal, or at the very least, crippling. Those people came to experience how you presented the grand story you spoke about. It actually was not about you, but about their experience when you speak to them. Be careful, little one, that you do not fall into the trap of allowing your ego to run you." He smiled at Red Fox and then added, "You are doing so well, son. I trust you will keep up the good work and keep your ego in check."

"Right," Red Fox answered humbly.

"By the way, what would you have said when Scarface challenged you?"

Red Fox smiled and answered, "I asked Spirit for help. When I looked up at just that moment, I felt reassured that all the right words would come. And they did . . . through Red Coat." Red Fox paused momentarily to change the topic. "I'm not sure about Scarface and his band of followers."

The Grandfather nodded and commented, "Right . . . they do have a different energy about them . . . and it does not work in harmony with The People. I'm not sure what they are up to or where they are going, but I must tell you I don't trust them. My sense is they may never join The People. It seems to me, their view of the world is hardened and aggressive. I would not want to meet up with them alone on a road."

Red Fox agreed by saying, "I feel the same way. I don't trust their energy and can't figure out what they want to do. I feel Red Coat was able to speak to that. Other than that I really don't know how to comment on it."

"You don't need to, son," assured Morning Star. "Red Coat pretty much said it all. Nothing more to say, really."

17

RED FOX AT HIGH BANK

With the presentations concluded at Chillicothe, the trio decided to stay another day before heading out. After Morning Star had taken care of the dogs, as was his custom, he returned from a romp with them to find Red Fox sitting alone on a bench outside their guesthouse.

Morning Star said, "I certainly have enjoyed myself here at Chillicothe. While you've been busy with your presentations, I've spent time walking around the entire complex here remembering ceremonies I participated in long ago. Why don't I show you some things? Your architect mind might appreciate it . . . not to mention your appreciation of ancient knowledge."

With head down thinking over the offer, Red Fox looked up at the Grandfather with a grateful smile and said, "Sure, I'd love it."

The Elder and the young man strolled around several nearby earthworks. Morning Star reveled in discussing many points of interest with Red Fox. Then they started walking toward the Scioto River. Red Fox noticed several canoes pulled up on the bank.

"Are we going for a canoe ride? Where are we going?" asked Red Fox.

"You'll soon see. Help me get the canoe into the water then hop in," Morning Star instructed. "We'll head over to that landing over there."

"But I don't see anything over there, just the landing and a tall cliff," said Red Fox.

"Sometimes important things can be just outside our vision," Morning Star said in a way that invited no questions.

As they paddled across, Morning Star broke the silence asking with a lowered voice, "You haven't participated in the Sister Moon Ceremony yet, have you?" Red Fox turned and just looked at the Grandfather. "No, I guess you are not old enough."

"Oh," said Red Fox, "You mean the Southernmost Moonrise Ceremony? No, I haven't participated in it, but I studied it when I worked with Singing Hawk building the Great Serpent Model. It occurs every 18.6 years." Grinning at the Elder, Red Fox added, "Is that where we are going? High Bank? Wow, I've heard about it and knew it was near Chillicothe when you showed me the scroll, but I didn't know exactly where it was."

THE CAMP OF GOD'S TEARS

The two reached the shore and pulled the canoe up on the sand bar landing, "That's right," said Morning Star, "you would've studied it to build the model you're using in your presentations. One of the curves of the Great Serpent also aligns perfectly with the southernmost moonrise.

"When we get to Newark, an Elder there will show you its great earthwork complexes and how everything all fits together there. That complex aligns with the northernmost moonrise. In addition, I've already shown you how the different earthworks in this region all fit together in alignment with each other despite how many miles apart they are.

"So you now know about the interconnection of the earthworks in this region. Back home the Great Serpent is a wonderful gauge of cosmic events. We all know precisely the sunrise day of both the Summer Solstice and the Winter Solstice. We also know precisely the day, or rather evening of the southernmost moonrise. The Great Serpent reaffirms that for us. In another month or more, we'll be back at our village getting ready for the Summer Solstice Ceremony about which you have been speaking.

"I expect after this journey, you will find many more of The People will be attending it, although, other villages do have their own ceremonies that day, as well." As they continued walking, Red Fox listened and nodded at appropriate moments, expecting something more to be revealed as the conversation ensued.

Grandfather Morning Star continued, ". . . I do so enjoy the Summer Solstice Sunset Ceremony that we have at the Great Serpent. The whole thing is about renewal . . . anyway, renewal and rebirth. I guess I like the Summer Solstice Sunset Ceremony the best."

After several moments spent in thought, Red Fox said, "I believe White Eagle is planning a much more elaborate Ceremony than usual this year. It's part of the whole reason the Elders asked me to make a model of the Serpent and take this journey in the first place."

"Right," acknowledged Morning Star, ". . . and in about three months after that we will be back here at High Bank, right where we are now, to celebrate the southernmost moonrise. It's a celebratory time and quite the ceremony as well.

"Now we need to follow this trail along this creek which lies just north of the earthworks. Then we will follow a path up a ravine that will lead us up to a plateau that overlooks the High Bank earthwork complex. This complex sits sixty feet above the river . . . and that's why you couldn't see it earlier," Morning Star said with a smile.

With his interest piqued Red Fox cocked his head then asked, "What do you mean? Is it more of a special ceremony than usual?"

"Of course," said Morning Star, "we all participate in the prayers and affirmations in seeking the renewal of Sister Moon's orbit around the Earth. We don't want her spinning off, out of her path, you know.

"It's not that we think our prayers actually keep Sister Moon in her orbit. It's about our prayers of affirmation and gratitude to her for staying with Mother Earth and us in our recognition and appreciation for their constancy. When all remains in balance, each moving within their individual rhythms, it is easier for us to count on the present, harmoniously leading us into our future. It all plays into the motif of our sense of renewal."

The Elder paused briefly to shift his attention to the scene below.

"Many of us go down to the water there," he pointed to the nearby creek they had just climbed up from.

"Why would we do that?" asked Red Fox.

"It's all part of the rituals and traditions we practice. Not everyone goes into the water, but many do. Going into the water and pouring water or splashing water over ourselves, becomes reminiscent of being born again, as it were, from the waters of the womb. This act reinforces a sense of renewal of our individual selves in our pursuit of staying in touch with the Great Oneness. The People have been practicing this tradition for thousands of years.

"It's spiritually uplifting, especially after a time of quiet self-reflection, introspection, or meditation," Morning Star finished as they approached a meaningful spot.

"Ah," he declared changing the subject. "This is where I wanted to bring you." He stood and pointed with his entire hand and arm outstretched. "Here it is. Here is the view I wanted to show you."

Red Fox looked across and took in a deep breath. For a while he just stood there appreciating the symmetry, proportion and design of the High Bank complex.

"It may just be my perspective from here," Red Fox said, "but there appears to be some irregularity on the western walls of the octagon. And, oh . . . I think I see an opening in the main Circle there on the eastern side. Is that an entrance?" asked Red Fox.

"Well, you're certainly demonstrating your architectural eye for things. All in good time," smiled Morning Star.

Although frustrated, Red Fox did not pursue the question knowing that Morning Star would answer his questions when the time was right.

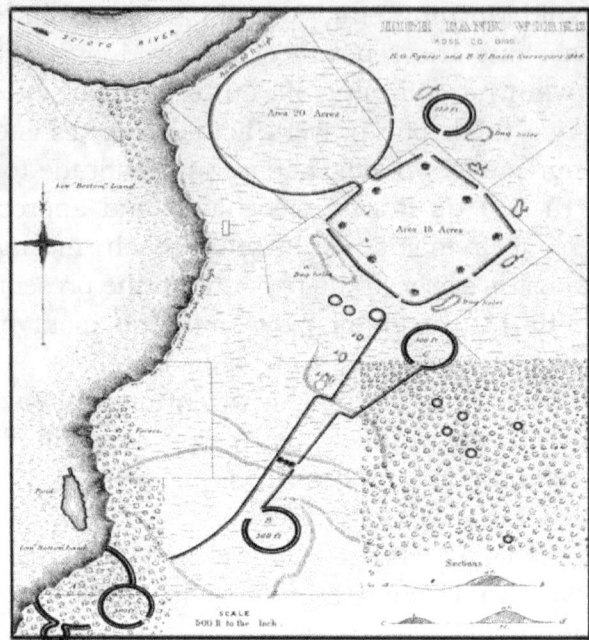

Diagram of High Bank Earthworks Squire and Davis 1848

"Now that you have seen the earthwork complex from the higher ground that we are standing on, let's go down and walk the perimeter," suggested Morning Star.

Once they got down to the complex, Morning Star proceeded toward the base of the Circle located near the cliff. As they walked they discussed more details of the earthworks, how they were built and what materials were used. Once they climbed up the wall and faced the avenue axis that joined the Circle to the Octagon, Morning Star began.

"As you can see, Red Fox, a wide concentric circle of water-worn cobblestones borders the interior wall of the Circle. Since there is no readily available water source, the stones represent the Waters of Life, you know, the amniotic fluids in the womb, which we remember to remember in our renewal ceremonies. This is demonstrated in a more obvious way at the Great Circle at Newark.

The Elder paused for a moment and then continued, "The interior surfaces of the Circle and Octagon walls are covered with a bright yellow clay and silt mixture and the exterior with a red clay and silt mixture. Most of these special soils were brought from distance areas for this earthwork. The caretakers renew these surfaces when necessary, and they are fairly resistant to the elements."

"So why did they decide to construct an Octagon? I am aware of only two, this one and the one at Newark," said Red Fox.

Morning Star said, "Well, there are several reasons for this. First of all the eight sides represent the eight phases of Sister Moon. She waxes from the new moon to the full moon and then wanes back to a new moon.

"Eight also represents the significant rises and sets of Sister Moon which we follow on her 18.6 year cycle.

"Now from where we're standing," Morning Star said, ". . . we will be able to witness Sister Moon's southernmost rise. That night will be one of great awe and reverence as an acknowledgement for her renewed relationship to our Mother Earth. Mother Earth and her sister have quite a relationship. Sister Moon influences so much with regards to Mother Earth, all of which impacts our lives. We cannot do without Sister Moon . . . which is why . . . of course, we honor her and have our ceremonies about her."

After a few silent moments, Morning Star commented, "Then, naturally, we celebrate." He smiled at his own memories before going on.

Then he continued, "We celebrate with great feasting, music, dancing and marriages . . . and *consummation* of marriages," he emphasized with a grin, eyebrows raised and eyes twinkling. "Thousands of people will be here, all participating and celebrating." He paused a moment then asked, "Say, aren't several of your friends planning on participating in the marriage celebration at the next Southernmost Moonrise Ceremony?"

"Ahhh, yes," Red Fox affirmed with a pained expression. "They will be. I'll be here for them, but I won't be participating in the dance."

"Not dance?" asked Morning Star emphatically. "Not dance?" he repeated. "Of course, you'll dance. This is where many of our young people meet each other and find life partners. How silly of you to think you won't dance. Of course, you'll dance."

Not comfortable continuing that conversation, Red Fox remained silent as he had recently experienced an encounter with a young woman. He had allowed his dreams to get the better of him without being able to bring a potential relationship closer to fruition.

At that moment he did not feel in the mood to share his experience or feelings about it. He felt much disappointment at not being able to create a liaison to satisfy his heart-felt desire to find a partner. Wishing to avoid the unresolved emotional pain, Red Fox changed the focus back to the High Bank complex.

"So this is where we stand to see Sister Moon rise?" Red Fox asked. "So do we look in this direction? . . . using those walls that connect the circle and the octagon as a sightline as we face the southeastern horizon?"

THE CAMP OF GOD'S TEARS

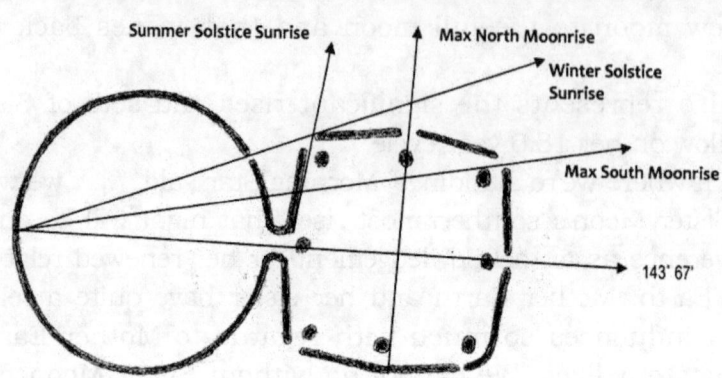

Redrawn and modified after Hively and Horn 1984

"Actually . . . no," responded Morning Star.

"Wait a minute, now I am really confused," Red Fox objected, "didn't you just tell me this complex is where we acknowledge the rise of Sister Moon on the southernmost moonrise? That this was built as part of that celebration? That from where we are standing we can look straight ahead through the walls that connect the circle and the octagon and witness the Southernmost Moonrise on the southeastern horizon in perfect alignment with the main axis of this earthwork?"

"No, that's not exactly what I said," responded Morning Star. "What I said was, that at Newark, the Circle and Octagon avenue axis was built in perfect alignment with the northernmost moonrise . . . and that we come here to High Bank to celebrate the southernmost moonrise."

Interrupting Morning Star, Red Fox challenged again, "You told me that the Newark Complex was built long after the High Bank Complex. And you told me that Newark Complex is rotated 90 degrees towards the northeast as compared to the angle of alignment of the High Bank Complex. Didn't you tell me that they are exact replicas, except for the size of the two octagons?

"All of that is true, my son," reassured Morning Star. "That is all true. Yes, indeed . . . all true. But I didn't say that the axis alignment of the High Bank earthwork was built to align with the southernmost moonrise."

"What?" Red Fox shouted softly, "I'm confused." He swallowed hard before asking his next question, "If the High Bank complex is not directly aligned with the southernmost moonrise, then what does it *align* with?"

Silence.

Impatient for a response Red Fox exclaimed, "You mean to tell me that they built this huge complex with such precision and it points to *nothing*?"

"That's part of the Great Mystery," Morning Star commented with a grin.

Shaking his head at the Grandfather, "Don't give me that. You know, don't you?"

Silent pause.

Morning Star half closed his eyes as if dreaming before he began speaking, "I told you these earthworks are ancient . . . very ancient structures. Our Ancient Ones built them. We did not build them. We use them in our ceremonies, and we maintain them, but we did not build them."

Red Fox folded his arms across his chest with his head held back a little. He inhaled and waited for the mystery to be pronounced before breathing again.

"Ancient . . . yes, ancient," continued Morning Star. "When they built High Bank, it aligned perfectly with the autumnal rise of the constellations of the Pleiades, Orion and Sirius."

Red Fox exhaled so hard he almost choked. "Oh," was all he could say before asking, "The Pleiades. The Pleiades?" Then he asked, "But it doesn't now, though, right?"

"Well, actually, it's spring now," replied Morning Star. "So you won't see them on the horizon while you are here.

"Our Ancient Ones positioned this earthwork in precise alignment, so they could stand right where we are now standing as those precious constellations and Sirius rose on the southeastern horizon *in the fall at the time when they lived here.*"

Red Fox looked at Morning Star, then at the alignment of the earthwork, then back at Morning Star.

Then Red Fox asked, "So, can we see them rise on the horizon right here every fall but not in alignment with this earthwork?"

"Actually . . . yes," said Morning Star. "However, standing here, the Ancient Ones saw them rise on the horizon in precise alignment with this earthwork in the fall about five thousand years ago."

Red Fox worked at comprehending this last piece of information and asked, "What do you mean, five thousand years ago?"

Nodding in affirmation, Morning Star said, "We are an ancient People . . . very ancient. In fact, some of us are of the understanding that some of these earthworks are even much older than that. These earthworks, which were built by our Ancient Ones, acknowledge the rhythms of the cosmos.

"Their knowledge has been passed down to us. Many of us are keepers of this knowledge, like Singing Hawk, for example. All this information, including the math and engineering principles, plus the knowledge about the stars and their movements are written down in the ancients texts, like on the birch bark scrolls you studied."

"Yes," Red Fox said, "Singing Hawk showed me many of those mathematical formulas on the scrolls. I did see she had more scrolls that she did not show me. I guess she taught me a lot, just not everything. After thinking about it, I didn't have a lot of time to study more than I did, because I had to get the model of the Great Serpent made."

Morning Star nodded silently.

The two of them, student and teacher, just stood there for a while without speaking.

Finally, Red Fox turned to Morning Star and asked, "Okay, if the autumnal rise of the Pleiades and Orion could be seen rising in alignment here five thousand years ago, why can't we see this alignment every fall now?"

Morning Star smiled broadly glad that Red Fox was thinking intelligently by asking such a cogent question. Responding, Morning Star said, "Glad you asked."

Morning Star thought for a moment then said, "Mother Earth has a spine that goes through her middle. It's a straight line, an axis. Aligned directly under the pole star is the top of this axis."

Red Fox lifted a finger up to signal he has a comment, "I know all this. What does this have to do . . .?"

Morning Star nodded, patted his student on his arm, interrupting him, and said, "I'm getting there. Just needed to provide a context for what I'm about to tell you."

"Oh."

"All this speaks to the rhythm of the cosmos. What I want to point out is that while Mother Earth's axis rotates, yes, but her axis also wobbles."

"Wobbles?" Red Fox asked. "What do you mean, 'wobbles'?"

"Wobbles, yes," Morning Star affirmed. "Imagine yourself holding a straight stick. Imagine that stick turning constantly in one direction." He peered into Red Fox's face to see if he was following. Then he continued, "Now imagine that stick also twisting as it rotates . . . So that if you continue an imaginary line from the tip of the stick into the sky, you would see that it draws a large circle. Can you see that in your mind's eye? Here let me illustrate this for you." Morning Star picked up a long stick and drew in the dirt.

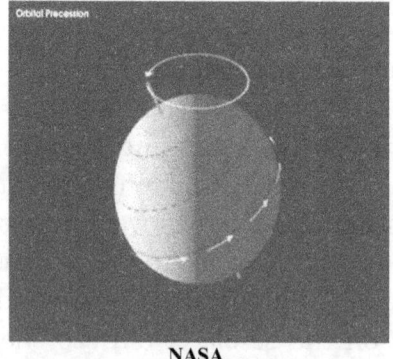

NASA

Red Fox nodded with his eyes half closed.

"Okay. Now pretend in your mind's eye that you are looking out into the cosmos at all the stars and constellations. Can you do that?"

Red Fox again nodded with his eyes still half closed.

Morning Star continued with additional sketches in the dirt, "Can you imagine that you would see a specific constellation when the end of the stick or axis is pointing in one direction? As the tip of the stick, the axis, traces its way around that circle *very, very* slowly, it will point to a different one of the twelve constellations that border the circle. Can you see that?" Morning Star used the stick in his hands to demonstrate this concept.

After a few moments, Red Fox blinked his eyes wide open then exclaimed, "Yes. Grandfather, yes, I do see that. Now what?"

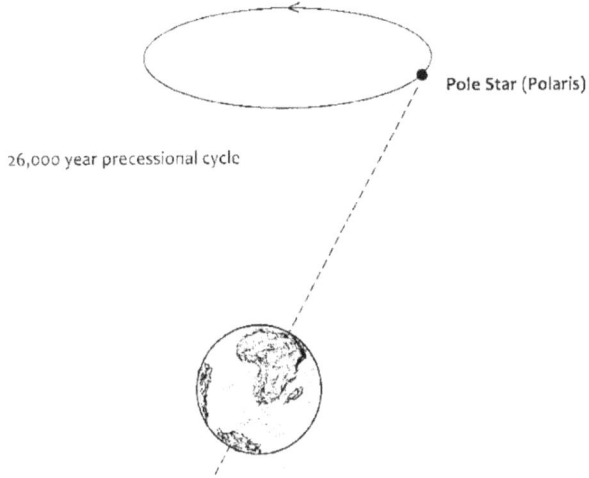

"Okay, we are almost there," Morning Star confirmed. "That's what we call a wobble. Now, see yourself standing just where you are standing, and see yourself looking up at the night sky. What you might see tonight, for example, is a specific constellation or star rising at a specific point on the eastern horizon. It would be a different constellation or star rising there, if you were standing on this exact spot at night, say five, ten or twenty thousand years, either into the past or the future."

"What do you mean, Grandfather?"

"It takes about twenty-six thousand years for Mother Earth's axis to complete one revolution of the great circle in the sky which is traced by her wobble. So . . ."

Interrupting, Red Fox exclaimed, ". . . So that's why the Ancient Ones could see the Pleiades, Orion and Sirius rise on the southeastern horizon in alignment in this very spot about five thousand years ago. It will be quite a while before this alignment returns, and it will eventually." Smiling, proud of himself to have put it all together, he looked straight into Morning Star's eyes.

Smiling back, and affectionately tossing Red Fox's hair with his hand, Morning Star nodded in affirmation. Then he said, "That's what we call 'precession'."

"Precession?"

"Precession!"

"Oh, and by the way," Morning Star noted, "When we get to Newark, you'll visit the Great Circle. It is now aligned with the spring rise of the Pleiades and Orion at the horizon."

Red Fox nodded in acknowledgement.

"Now, this is just the beginning," Morning Star said to his inquisitive student. He paused and then continued, "As you know there are many layers in the Ancient Knowledge. While precession appears to change the reference point location of the stars over the ages, Father Sun and Sister Moon are not so greatly affected. So when we observe their movements here, we are virtually seeing exactly what our Ancient Ones saw." Morning Star paused as he took a birch bark scroll from a pocket in his tunic.

"While you cannot see all of these alignments from where we are standing right now, this will help make it all clearer to you." Morning Star held the scroll so that Red Fox could see the images.

"This drawing shows the alignment for the southernmost moonrise. We can also see Father Sun's rise on the winter solstice from where we are now standing. As you noticed earlier, there is a gap in the Circle. While it is not an entryway, it can be used as one. Actually, it is used to make a more accurate alignment from where we are standing now for the Winter Solstice sunrise." Morning Star said as he traced the sight line on the drawing with his finger. He also explained to Red Fox the reasons for the other modifications to the west wall of the Octagon and that similar modifications had been made to the Octagon at Newark. These modifications permitted additional celestial alignments to be observed while not interfering with the overall astronomical function of the complex.

Red Fox nodded his head and said, "Thank you, Grandfather. I guess what looks like a mistake from one perspective is in fact the result of someone else's careful and considered design."

"Very good, Red Fox, I see that you're beginning to see things from a wider viewpoint." Morning Star was pleased with his student and said, "Now let's head down into the Circle and through the avenue into the Octagon where I will show you more of the alignments and finish answering your questions."

Proceeding around the Octagon enclosure, Red Fox was shown how the Winter and Summer Solstice sunsets and the significant rises and sets of

Sister Moon were marked. He listened to Morning Star explain how the Ancient Knowledge and the careful observations of their ancestors led to the design and construction of the High Bank complex thousands of years ago.

Having now walked around the entire Circle and Octagon complex they began their walk back up to where they first saw the complex. After they crossed the river they stopped at the house of one of Morning Star's friends for something to eat and drink.

Returning back to their guesthouse, the two of them walked the entire way in silence. Red Fox felt he had grown another foot or two from his daylong experience. It was now late afternoon.

"If we pack up now," announced Running Bear to the two of them as they arrived, "we can just make it to Gartner Village which is about six miles north of the entrance to the White Road of Sister Moon."

Without speaking the trio packed up their belongings, the dogs and the travois, and marched off to their next adventure.

The People of Gartner village were anxious to have them arrive, greeted them generously and gave them a place to stay.

The next day The People had planned a feast in their honor. For this feast many of the villagers collected hundreds of mussels from the waterways that flowed by. The trio could hardly think of anything more enjoyable than an outside feast of mussels steamed in a deep pit. They also enjoyed many favorite side dishes.

Afterwards, they all retired for the night feeling joy from the raucous celebration at Gartner along with the fun, laughter and conviviality of a content People.

That night a familiar dream returned to Red Fox.

18

ON THE ROAD AGAIN

Red Fox felt himself changing on this journey. He felt himself evolving. He felt he was growing. At the beginning of his journey, Red Fox was an adolescent, feeling the anticipatory excitement at the verge of the adventure of a lifetime. Indeed, his journey proved to be a maturing experience, one that he expected to be a highlight of a lifetime.

At each new village, with each presentation, he felt himself grow in awareness of his connection with Spirit. He remembered his battle with ego at the outset of his being selected to build the model of the Great Serpent. He remembered his conversation with his Grandmother Blue Lightning about ego. He remembered ego wanting to come up at Chillicothe and Morning Star cautioning him about it. He appreciated the Elder's comment to help him remember to remember.

Yet there was another energy tugging inside. While he was growing spiritually and manifesting his life's purpose in ways that he never imagined, he still felt something missing. He questioned whether he would ever experience the joy of a loving relationship with a life companion. His close friends were in loving relationships. He felt an ache of not being able to share a deep bonding with a partner, particularly as he traveled from the Chillicothe area.

Many times in his presentations, especially at Chillicothe, he made eye contact with a lovely young woman his age. He would feel a connection as she watched him make his presentation. He would notice a change in her posture, a change in her expressions, or a smile rising on her face.

This happened several times during his many presentations. He would note a sparkle in her eye, and that would send him into the realms of elation, something that he had not experienced before.

Occasionally after a presentation or while walking around in the various places where he spoke, he would encounter one of them. While on each occasion, they would engage in a conversation. During the conversation, he would then witness a sudden and unexplained reaction of aloofness. At that moment the young woman would indicate no real interest in him as a person. He felt confused by this. When experiencing the stage of elation with the feeling that a young woman was attracted to him, his ego expanded, and then deflated as the potential of a relationship clearly vanished within minutes.

Then he met Meadowlark. He first saw her at one of his afternoon presentations near Mound City, and her eyes never left him. After that presentation, she waited at a discrete distance to meet him, and greeted him with a smile. His heart simply leaped at the sight of her standing there, waiting for him. He felt a stirring in his loins. He wanted to run up to her and hold her in an embrace.

They spent the remaining hours before sunset together walking by the Scioto River. He told her of his life experiences and they generally got to know one another. She spoke of how his words touched her heart and her amazement at how much he had learned and the skill that went into the making of the Great Serpent model. She seemed to want to know everything about him, his village, his friends and his adventures on this journey and said that she hoped her family would be able to come to the Summer Solstice Ceremony at the Great Serpent.

As they held hands and slowly returned to her village, they enjoyed an incredible sunset of billowing clouds against a deep blue sky immersed in brilliant reds, crimson hues, yellows and silver mirroring the ecstasy in Red Fox. Red Fox did not comprehend how physical arousal can enhance the pleasure of contextual circumstances.

Over the course of his remaining days at Chillicothe, they were able to see each other several more times. Red Fox noted how powerful the physical attraction felt, how drawn to her he was. Red Fox could barely contain his attraction to her and the delight that she had sparked into his fantasy during these moments.

A day before he was scheduled to leave, he went to her house with a gift he had made for her with the help of some artisans he had met. When he arrived at her home, he called out her name.

No response.

He called again, "Meadowlark . . . Meadowlark, I have a gift for you. A lovely bracelet of beads, shells and pearls that sparkle like your eyes."

No response.

He waited. He called out her name again.

No response.

Finally, now overcome by emotion, he said, "Meadowlark, I sensed something happening between us. Maybe, I was mistaken."

Silence

Red Fox's face was now stained with tears. His body shook with the emotion of disappointment, confusion, and rejection. He felt an overwhelming sadness, a torment that cut into his shattered ego, cut away his fantasy, and trampled on his desire to belong to someone special. He was unable to say another word. He set the bracelet down in front of her door and slowly walked away, stopping several times to look back hoping she would open the door.

The door remained closed.

He stumbled as he walked away towards the river to join his tears of a promise of happiness that was not to be into the waters of Mother Earth.

"I've been looking for you," announced Morning Star quietly as he approached the young man as twilight softened into the night.

"I felt the need to be alone for a while to meditate before turning in for the night," replied Red Fox.

"I don't mean to disturb you, Red Fox," said the Elder, "I'll leave you alone."

"Morning Star, no," said Red Fox as the Elder turned to leave, "I'd like you to stay awhile with me. I have many emotions crowding my mind and would appreciate a conversation about them."

At the invitation, the Elder turned back around, paused, then nodded, and approached Red Fox. He sat down near him sitting cross-legged on the ground. He sat for long moments before turning toward Red Fox. Then he spoke.

"First of all, your mind does not experience emotions. Emotions are energy in motion experienced within the body. They provide information. The mind can only process information. So your mind can give an interpretation to that information coming from your emotions. Once you have given the information an interpretation, then you can act on it.

"But, let's take a step back for a second," Morning Star said. "Emotions are energy produced by the body which serves to provide you with a status report, so to speak. That status report tells you where you are within the context of what you are presently experiencing. Your emotions actually say to you, 'you are doing great,' or they say, 'you are not doing so great,' or 'this is working for you' or 'this is not working for you . . . and to this degree,' depending on the intensity of feeling and the situation. So when you feel happiness or joy, for example, your emotions inform you of this, and it's a way of saying, 'you are doing well here.' And, when you feel frustration, disappointment, or anger, for example, they let you know that whatever it is you are doing or not doing is either working for you or not . . . maybe you should try another strategy or make another choice."

Red Fox tilted his head back looking up, not really wanting to hear this lecture.

Morning Star saw this and still continued, "You are experiencing something not pleasant, I take it. So let me ask you . . . what is in your heart, Red Fox?"

Red Fox silently turned his head from side to side.

"I can see that you're dealing with several emotions right now. What's troubling you?" Morning Star said as his gentle eyes focused on Red Fox.

"Well . . . it's hard for me . . . I mean . . . it's about . . ." tears were just below the surface as Red Fox struggled to find the words.

"It's about Meadowlark, is it not?" gently offered Morning Star.

"How did you know?" a surprised Red Fox demanded.

"Son, matters of the heart are often worn openly. I could see this emotional energy surrounding you along with the light that has grown in you since we began this journey." Morning Star paused then said, "As you know I'm now alone on my life's journey. I was grown by the time I met my companion Waters Run Deep. We enjoyed many years together, and I still miss her every day. And, even without her I chose to serve The People. Often times those choosing to serve The People are not always blessed with the same gifts as our friends. We're each invited by Spirit to walk a different path for reasons that are not always apparent at the time.

"This is the first time you experienced an attachment to a young woman, and you felt the exhilaration that I experienced when I first met Waters Run Deep." He paused a moment to breathe in and swallow and said, "She returned to Spirit . . . nor do I ever expect to meet another woman that would fill that space in my life . . .

". . . So I resolved that Great Spirit blessed me with her for a reason . . . My life with her allowed me to grow in ways that I could not have accomplished on my own. I have used the gifts she gave me to better understand the needs of The People.

"Your experience with Meadowlark does not mean that you will not find a life companion. I learned of this experience you had from another Elder. I asked her to tell me how you dealt with the situation. She said that you left the bracelet at the door and walked away. By so doing you acknowledged the free will of Meadowlark, honoring her choice . . . This too shall pass." Morning Star placed his hand on Red Fox's shoulder and they sat in silence for a time.

Finding more wisdom than comfort in Morning Star's words, Red Fox shifted his thoughts back to his recurring dream. This dream was not an omen about his experience with Meadowlark, although it certainly seemed that way when viewed though the disappointment he felt. He was so driven by the desire to find the love of his life, like Water Dog and me.

Red Fox thought perhaps he'd spent too much time talking to Meadowlark about himself, his accomplishments, his growth, the wonderful relationships of his friends and the adventures he had experienced on his journey and how grand they were. Did he assume too much? Perhaps Meadowlark saw their experience together differently. He would never know. Now the question was, does this recurring dream mean something far more profound?

"I'm not sure how to say this, Grandfather," Red Fox began. Then he related his conversation he had had with his Grandmother Blue Lightning. He described how he had experienced each of his presentations since the journey began, as well as what had transpired at Chillicothe.

"I'm now feeling much better. Thank you, Grandfather," Red Fox said. "Yet, I also feel humble about my service to The People. I feel good about what I am doing, and yet also feel an anticipation of something more to come. I don't know what it is. Several times I've had this dream where I am standing at the edge of a precipice with nothing but mists and clouds below me and the heavens and stars rising over me. I want to step off to move forward . . . I am holding my breath . . . perhaps to build my courage to take that next step, not knowing what is out there for me. Can you help me understand?"

After moments of silence, Morning Star looked at Red Fox and said, "Red Fox, at the time you started this project, you were little more than a growing boy with a talent and a passion for building and architecture . . . and with a good heart.

"You took to heart lessons from your Grandmother Blue Lightning and set aside your ego. That was an important move on your part. That allowed you to focus all your energy on learning the mathematics necessary to apply those design principles used to create the Great Serpent for the model you built. You committed your mind and heart to the lessons provided for you by Singing Hawk.

"You learned the stories associated with the Great Serpent. You tell them well. The reason you tell them well is because you align with Spirit to make the layers of meanings of the Great Serpent . . . represented by the model you built . . . come alive for The People.

"This entire experience is a journey in itself. You began as an apprentice, and now you have become a journeyman, on your way to becoming a master. I believe that your vision of standing at the edge of a precipice is an invitation to continue on to become the master your soul invites you to become.

"You feel afraid and hesitate, because it's an unknown as represented by the mists and clouds beneath. Fear of the unknown is still fear. Fear comes from your ego that fears its own destruction. It tells you if it dies, the self ends. This is because the ego has no awareness of being part of Spirit, which is your Creator. If you fear falling, you probably will fall, because your fear will draw that experience to you. If you should fall, you would fall into a vagueness or oblivion, or so the ego would have you to believe.

"If you step off that ledge without fear, aligning with Great Spirit, trusting in Great Spirit to lift you up, you will experience your destiny. You can't see it now, because you have not yet made that choice. It requires trust and faith, faith and follow-through as you live, and move and breathe, always remembering you are a flame in the large bon fire we know as Spirit.

"With this, your ego has no place." At that, Morning Star finished. The two sat in quiet for a long time, feeling the solace of those words, feeling their truth and feeling their power.

Red Fox stood in awe as the trio and their dogs reached the beginning of the White Road of Sister Moon the next day.

"I could not imagine how extraordinary this road is had I not seen it with my own eyes," Red Fox commented. "It's truly an engineer's dream to have designed and constructed it with such exquisite precision . . . straight as an arrow, linking the two major cultural centers." He paused for a moment as they began walking the road, nodding to those occasional pilgrims whom they met coming from the other direction.

He continued his commentary, "I mean, I read about it. I studied its design and the math applied to build it, but actually seeing it is an experience in itself. It's awesome," he said.

Red Fox assessed its perfection in construction, how it appeared mostly level, but slightly elevated in the middle to accommodate runoff from rain and snow melt. He noticed that the mixture of white sand and a light-colored clay was packed hard to give it a paved appearance.

Both Running Bear and Morning Star had walked this road before and just nodded in acknowledgement.

Red Fox added, "The white color is almost blinding as it reflects the sunlight."

"The white sand comes from several limestone quarries some near, some far away. When Sister Moon is full and overhead, the road is visible at night as it reflects her moonlight, so that walking it at night when the moon is high is not a problem," said Running Bear. "This road has been used by our People since the ancient days." He paused for a moment. "Since it's sixty miles long, I expect it should take us about five days or so to make the distance. Although," he added thoughtfully, "we just might be able to make more distance each day, because it's straight and wide and easy to walk. There are a number of hills and several narrow bridges over waterways that will slow us down from time to time."

They walked the rest of the day in silence. As evening approached, they stopped at a location along the road meant for travelers to rest or camp. The two to three foot high brick walls were held in place with a sand and clay mixture. Every several miles or so, an opening in the wall led to a walled-in circular area which provided a convenient place to camp.

Red Fox noticed that during the night other travelers had quietly joined them at the camp spot for the night, but left at dawn, leaving the three of them alone to break camp. Morning Star and Red Fox played with the dogs early in the morning, so they could get the attention they needed before moving out.

"Tomorrow night we will stay at a village near the road. You will be able to give your presentation while we're there," announced Running Bear.

That night the three pilgrims camped again at a spot provided by the ancient builders of the road. Lying on the ground at night with his legs extended and crossed at the ankles and his arms up and bent with his hands tucked under his head, Red Fox found himself admiring the star-studded night sky.

"Breathtaking, isn't it?" Morning Star asked Red Fox rhetorically.

Red Fox just breathed in the beauty as he watched the Milky Way reveal herself.

"The summer solstice will be coming in about two months from now," Morning Star said. "That's when she really makes a spectacular showing, right over this road."

"I remember Singing Hawk telling me about the cosmic alignments, particularly at that time," said Red Fox as he fondly remembered his lessons. "She told me how the White Road perfectly parallels the Milky Way at the time of the Summer Solstice. Then if you draw an imaginary line from the point of the summer sunrise to the point of the summer sunset, *on that day*, that line would cross the White Road and would perfectly intersect the sky, dividing it into four equal and perfect quadrants."

Reflective silence for a few moments.

"I'm so awed by this. With everything I've been experiencing, seeing the earthworks and learning about their alignments . . . well, I can hardly describe it, even to myself. I feel overwhelmed by it all."

More reflective silence.

Turning to Morning Star, Red Fox said, "You know, I appreciate the deep and intricate expressions of beauty by our People." Morning Star turned to listen. Red Fox continued, ". . . but I truly love the mathematics, astronomy, geometry, and trigonometry I've learned, and hope to continue learning . . . and I more truly love its application to our world . . . to our lives . . . like this road, for instance. The earthworks in the Chillicothe area and this road connecting Chillicothe to Newark are amazing. What I feel when I contemplate these things goes beyond my ability to describe."

With that comment from Red Fox, Morning Star turned his face again toward the night sky, and all fell silent. They slept soundly to Mother Earth's rhythm of night sounds joining in the symphony of stars as they played their rhapsody in a rhythm as part of a yet larger concert beyond the stars.

During the following day, Red Fox noticed that parts of the brick wall lining the road appeared under repair. He recognized the bricks piled up near a break point in the wall. He recalled seeing similar bricks stacked near the furnaces when he was at Spruce Hill. No one was tending to the brickwork on this particular day, and he saw that clearly it was a work in progress.

Running Bear said, "We'll be coming to the next village soon. I forget exactly where it is. I can tell we are getting close to it. I can see that the villagers who maintain this road have been working here, but are not here now."

"Why aren't they working today?" asked Red Fox.

"Because they know we are coming, and they all want to be in the village when we arrive," responded Running Bear.

At an opening in the wall where foot traffic had clearly worn down a path off the road, Running Bear signaled they would be turning onto the footpath. Red Fox could see some of their homes off in the distance.

"Those houses look bigger than our houses. Except for the meeting house at Seip, I don't believe I've seen such large buildings. They can't all be meeting houses. I don't understand," said Red Fox.

"You'll understand soon enough," Running Bear replied with a grin, "just wait 'til we get closer and see who lives here."

As the three approached the village, several Elders came out to meet them. They were all very tall people with long red hair. The Elder man, older in years with white hair salting the red also had a large red beard and mustache, both trimmed neatly. It was something Red Fox had never seen before.

So stunned was he that he almost forgot his manners at the introduction. He just stood there staring when he heard Running Bear say, "Red Fox. Red Fox, this is Flying Cloud . . . Red Fox?"

"Oh, yes, I'm sorry, I forgot my manners," Red Fox grinned sheepishly as he looked up at Flying Cloud who towered over him.

They were shown to a guesthouse. Morning Star attended to the dogs, while Running Bear and Red Fox settled in. Taking a cup of tea with him, Red Fox stood outside the guesthouse to take in the sights. He saw a village alive with its residents, bustling about finishing their chores or occupations in time to enjoy a meal before attending the presentation tonight. Nearly every one of the villagers had red hair of one hue or another. Several had very light yellow hair. A few had brown hair. All were taller than Red Fox, except for the children.

"So that's why their houses are bigger. Water Dog's house is larger than anyone's in our village," he thought to himself nodding in silence.

"I certainly hope you are comfortable," asked Flying Cloud as he approached the guesthouse. "I've come to invite you to have dinner with us."

"Thank you," said Morning Star, "Yes, we would be delighted to join you. Are you ready, Red Fox?"

As they participated in a sumptuous feast, different individuals told and re-told stories to the enjoyment of all. Laughter decorated the evening. Red Fox noted that these People were similar in all ways to his family and friends back at his home village. The only difference was their appearance. They looked hearty, ate hearty, and laughed hearty. He did notice that most had either blue eyes or green. A few had brown eyes. A few of the men had facial hair, something he had not seen much of. The men in his village shaved their faces if they had any facial hair. Few did, and it usually was dark.

Walking back to their guesthouse after dinner to get the model, Red Fox said to his two companions, "I guess I didn't realize that Water Dog and his family came from a heritage similar to these people." The two Elders only nodded without comment. "I think I see now," he added after a brief silence, "those folks in our village who have lighter hair or light colored eyes must have received a genetic inheritance from this strain. That's why Water Dog and Floating Lily are very tall people and have a version of red hair. Their mother is small with very dark hair. I guess I was just stunned at first. I had never contemplated an entire village of very tall, red-haired people as part of The People."

"Actually," said Morning Star, "we have quite a few villages of these taller people as part of us. Some live in their own villages. Some have scattered among all the other villages, like ours, inter-marrying. After all you have blue eyes. It adds to the strength of our heritage. It's been going on since ancient times."

Everyone in the audience simply sat in stunned silence after hearing Red Fox's presentation. As was his custom, he looked out into the audience checking to see if there were any questions. None were asked. After a while the children began squirming, so the adults gradually left. As Red Fox and company were preparing to leave, Flying Cloud approached silently from the dark.

"Red Fox, thank you for your presentation," he began. "Now I know why word of you came to us. I want to make sure you will continue to give more presentations. We have other villages close but up the road farther. You do plan on giving them your presentation, I trust?"

Running Bear interjected at this point, "Yes, indeed. We'll be stopping along the way at different villages until we get to Newark. Not to worry, Flying Cloud."

With a nod of affirmation, Flying Cloud stepped back into the night.

On the road again, the trio and dogs continued their journey. As promised, they stopped at various villages near the White Road, so Red Fox could give his presentation at each one.

Finally reaching Newark, Red Fox looked across the landscape to witness the broad clear stretches of land with earthworks visible. The entire complex covered about four square miles. As he took it all in, he felt his heart skip a beat, his pulse begin to race, and a warm wave of energy washed over him so intensely that the hairs on his arms and legs and back of his neck rose up noticeably.

19

RED FOX AT NEWARK

As had been the custom at all other village stops, they were greeted by Elders and shown to their quarters. In this case the village was a short distance away from the Circle and Octagon complex where the White Road of Sister Moon ends.

Newark was a highly populated area with villages scattered close and farther away. People from all around flowed into the Newark area to hear Red Fox. He spent several days giving two presentations a day in the surrounding villages.

One early morning Red Fox found himself with some free time. He decided to get a closer look at all the different earthen structures in the Newark area.

"Hold up there, Red Fox."

Red Fox heard a voice call to him from behind. It was Walking Eagle, one of the Elders who was a close friend of Morning Star.

"Would you like me to show you around?" Without waiting for a reply, Walking Eagle said, "The best way to start is to take the White Road back down to Geller Hill a little over a mile from where we are now."

As the two of them started down the road, Red Fox asked, "You're a friend of Morning Star, I think. Is that right? How long have you known him?"

"We go way back to when we were youngsters," the Elder said. "In fact, we went through initiation at nearly the same time."

"Initiation?" asked Red Fox. After a brief pause, Red Fox added, "Oh, yes, I learned a little bit about initiation at Mound City from Gazing Raven and Morning Star, and they allowed me to enter an initiation chamber. What's initiation exactly? Can you tell me more?"

After a few thoughtful moments, the Elder replied, "The easiest way I can explain it is to say that it is a process by which we bring to the surface that which is buried within.

"It is achieved by meditating deeply, usually in seclusion, and consulting within the self. It is a process of experiencing different stages at different times that can take a few years or a lifetime to complete. The goal is to *consciously* unite with Great Spirit . . . to *consciously* feel the absolute oneness with Great Spirit as our Source, that we call the Great Oneness."

Red Fox stopped for a moment and stood looking at Walking Eagle with eyes wide, staring at him, unable to speak. Walking Eagle took this as a cue to carry on.

"The issue is to experience the connection *consciously,* so that this connection pervades our awareness, and does so for the rest of our lives. The process is actually about renewal. It's about renewing more than our awareness . . . it's more like renewal of our experiential conscious knowing that who we are is Great Spirit expressed in physical individualizations.

"Many of our People have experienced initiation to some degree or another. Not all of us, of course, but quite a few of us have, including many of the Elders. Only some go through all the degrees. Not everyone needs to make it all the way through the different stages. The important thing is each of us lives our lives in accordance with the harmony that comes from our conscious union with Spirit . . . . And, of course, those who don't go through the process tend to feel the vibrational frequency and live in accordance with it as if they had gone through initiation themselves. And, that is a powerful way to live."

"Powerful? Powerful? What do you mean by powerful?" asked Red Fox.

Walking Eagle responded, "It's powerful, because living in that awareness empowers each of us at all levels within ourselves. As we make our choices, we act out or behave in ways that harmonize with each other. It's not just about remembering union with Great Spirit, it's also about feeling the joy of union. As a result, we get to live in the joy of it. The process of initiation renews our joy that goes beyond knowing. Experiencing joy is experiencing Great Spirit. Knowing Great Spirit is not just about the union. It's the joy of union that brings the joy expressed in our daily lives . . . and the peace within. If we *don't* have peace within, we *won't* have peace without."

They continued walking in silence.

After a while, Walking Eagle broke the silence, "I believe that's why our People, and our entire civilization for that matter, have lived over a thousand years in peace. It's about consciously being in alignment every day as we work through our physical experience . . . and feeling the joy of it."

Red Fox said, "I understand that. I've had many talks with my Grandmothers, and with my teacher, Singing Hawk. I'm starting to comprehend what they've been teaching me . . . and especially as I give my presentations. I guess the message gets reinforced."

Walking Eagle added, ". . . The initiation is a very specific process. It occurs in stages . . . and you go through it alone for the most part . . . and you start in the dark, in the womb of Mother Earth, much like when we began our physical lives in the womb of our mothers."

Red Fox nodded in acknowledgment and said, "Yes, Gazing Raven has already showed me the Mound City initiation chamber. So I ask you, how would I integrate the initiation experience into my daily life?"

"As we live each day, we make choices," Walking Eagle said as they stopped for a moment. "If we make a choice that is not in harmony with the Great Oneness, we experience the results of that choice. It may produce a sense of disharmony and a feeling of separation. We can then know it is not a choice we would want to make again, especially if it does not produce joy.

"When we make a choice that is in harmony and produces joy, then we will receive the results of that choice and feel the joy of it. Joy is the result of feeling uplifted. When we make such choices each day, we feel the oneness. This joy comes from aligning ourselves with the Great Oneness . . . and that alignment *feels* like we are connected with the Great Oneness," Walking Eagle explained.

Red Fox nodded as he listened then said, "I remember Grandmother Blue Lightning telling me about this and being in alignment. If I understand what you're saying, the way we can actually know Great Spirit is to make such choices that produce this joy and that becomes part of our knowing at the conscious level. That knowing or feeling can help us direct our thoughts and actions to help us to live in harmony, balance and peace. Is that right?"

"Precisely," exclaimed Walking Eagle with eyebrows raised and big a grin. "You got it.

"And, I'd like to talk to you more about the initiation process. This process helps those individuals who have gone through it assist the rest of us to remember the joy of who we are. Those initiates experience the Knowing at deep levels within. They assist our civilization to remain living in peace. Living in peace and in harmony with each other is not something we can take for granted."

"Why are you telling me this, Walking Eagle?" Red Fox suddenly asked. "Isn't that why I'm on this journey in the first place? . . . To help The People remember to remember? Isn't that what I'm already doing?"

"Yes, indeed," said Walking Eagle. "You are doing just that . . . and there is more. And, we are inviting you to that 'more', so to speak. We see in you the potential to benefit from being initiated . . . and then become a center of influence throughout our civilization. You don't ask for it. You can't volunteer for this. You must be selected by Elders. You must be invited.

We are inviting you. And, there is more that you should know about this process as you think about accepting this invitation.

"Some of the stages can be harrowing. At least it seems that way. Facing your ego, your fears and frailties, whatever they may be, using only your own inner resources to call upon . . . and really, that's what it's about . . . calling upon your inner resources, your deep reserves within provides an opportunity to experience your conscious connection to Great Spirit. This connection becomes a transcension from just a physical awareness into a clarity of spiritual awareness.

"No matter how many degrees or stages you end up going through, you still come out of it each time with a deep, uplifted and abiding conscious awareness of who you are and who you are in relationship with the Great Spirit . . . unless you don't. You experience the Knowing, and *knowing* at a deep level within yourself that everyone else is a physical extension of Great Spirit too."

It had been, in some ways, a long walk for Red Fox down the White Road of Sister Moon from the village near the Circle and Octagon earthworks to the highest point on Geller Hill. Red Fox was surprised by the pace set by the elder, Walking Eagle, especially as they began the climb up Geller Hill.

"Ah, here we are," Walking Eagle said as they reached the top, "This is the highest point. From here you can see the entire four square mile complex."

"This is incredible, said Red Fox. "From here I can see many of the earthworks and their connecting passageways. This is better than I imagined from what I learned from Singing Hawk about this complex," Red Fox said as he gazed at the expansive view.

It was still morning and Father Sun had begun warming the vast treeless prairie that supported the earthen structures built there to celebrate as above, so below.

Walking Eagle and Red Fox stood in silence as they listened to the breeze that carried the songs of the birds, their melodies drifting across the sculpted landscape.

"Indeed, Red Fox, there is more involved here than what meets your eyes," Walking Eagle said as he waved his arm across what lay below.

Turning toward Walking Eagle, Red Fox started to ask a question only to be surprised to see a large set of scrolls in Walking Eagle's hands.

"What I'm about to show you comes from those who designed this complex in the ancient times. While this complex contains a circle and octagon earthwork similar to High Bank, it was built at a much later time than High Bank. Let's begin with the drawing of this complex."

Walking Eagle explained the grand design and how each of the earthworks were used in various ceremonies. As Walking Eagle finished explaining the first scroll Red Fox said, "So Geller Hill does play an important role and vantage point for all the Newark ceremonies."

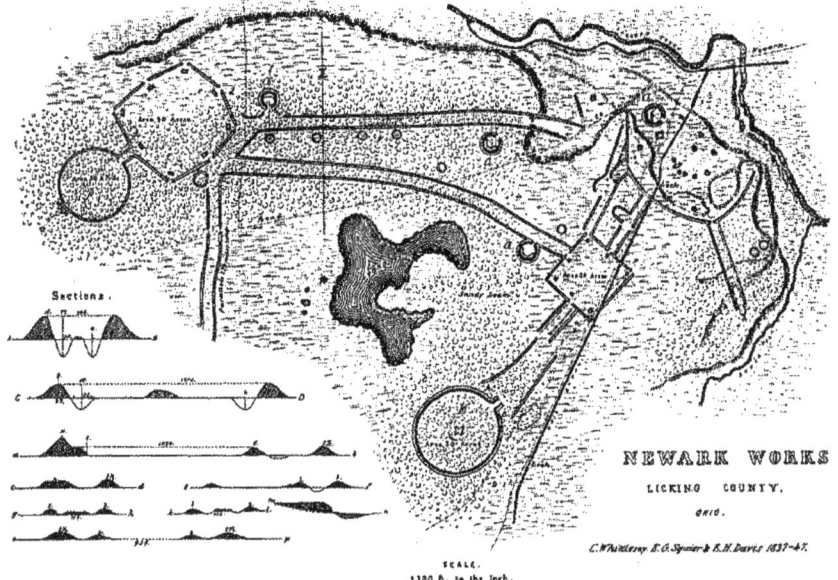

Diagram of the Newark Earthwork complex Squire and Davis 1848

"That's correct. This is where several shaman will stand at the time of the northernmost moonrise ceremony and at other renewal ceremonies that are held here at the Complex," Walking Eagle said and pointed his finger to the spot on a map to show where they were standing. Then he said, "There's more, a lot more. This gets a little complicated. This drawing will help you to see the grand design," Walking Eagle said and smiled as he unrolled yet another scroll.

Walking Eagle explained to Red Fox that while the individual earthworks in the Newark Complex appeared to be separate from one another, in fact, they were not.

Walking Eagle traced the "unseen" geometric lines with his finger on the scroll and then pointed to the corresponding earthworks where they lay on the land. In this way he demonstrated the invisible mathematical and geometrical design of each part to each part to express a harmonious Whole, a relationship of connectedness that could not be seen with physical eyes.

It became clear to Red Fox that the physical earth formations represented the 'seen' and the geometrical design used to direct the placement of each earthwork in relationship to each other represented the 'unseen' in a manifested complement of the 'seen' and 'unseen' in a world comprised of both.

Walking Eagle continued, "Also, as you can see on this drawing, the entire complex is bordered by and almost completely surrounded by three waterways, Ramp Creek, Raccoon Creek and the South Fork of the Licking River. So here we celebrate earth, sky and water as we acknowledge our responsibility to live in balance."

Red Fox nodded again as he processed all of the information that had been shared with him.

At the close of their discussion, the focus of their conversation shifted.

"Now there is a particular significance to the location of Geller Hill that relates to The White Road of Sister Moon, the Milky Way and Father Sun on the day of the Summer Solstice," Walking Eagle said with a bit of mystery in his voice.

"I think Morning Star may have told you some of this," Walking Eagle said. "On the day of the Summer Solstice, the White Road mirrors the Milky Way. The arc traced in the sky by Father Sun's movement from his sunrise to his sunset intersects the White Road and divides the heavens into quarters on that day. The point where Father Sun crosses over the White Road on that day occurs very close to where we are standing," Walking Eagle said as he pointed down the hill to the White Road near the base of the hill.

Walking Eagle paused briefly to let that detail sink in. Then he said, "Although other locations were considered by our Ancient Ones, this was one of the deciding factors in the discussions as to where to construct this Complex." Walking Eagle watched as Red Fox processed this information.

Silence.

Slowly Red Fox began to speak, "I . . . I . . . I never knew how complicated all of this was . . . I mean, just looking at the drawing of the Complex, then seeing it from this hilltop . . . I mean this is the largest Complex of The People which, in and of itself, is amazing. And then the layout of these earthworks is very impressive on its own.

"I just did not realize all the hidden layers of mathematical and design considerations that went into the planning and construction of this Complex. No wonder people travel great distances for the ceremonies that are held here."

Walking Eagle just stood and smiled at the soon to be initiate saying, "There is more, so let's move on. Our next stop will be the Great Circle."

The two then descended the Hill, crossed The Road and walked across the open prairie land to the Great Circle. Time seemed to pass quickly.

"Ah, here we are at the Great Circle," said Walking Eagle with his arm and hand outstretched. They stood in silence for a while at the entrance.

Red Fox breathed deeply as he took in the view of the Great Circle from its opening.

Walking Eagle began, "We are standing at the opening. As you can see, the outside walls are covered with brown earth and the inside with yellow colored earth. The circle varies in its diameter, so it's more of an ellipse, much like a womb."

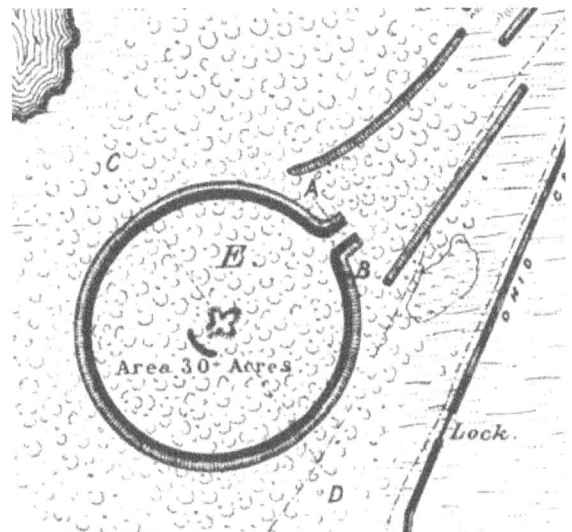

Diagram of the Great Circle Earthwork Squier and Davis 1848

Red Fox wondered how all of this was related, and remained silent and listened as Walking Eagle continued.

"It encompasses 30 acres. As we look at it from the inside, you can see a deep trench lining the circular wall. This trench is usually filled with water during ceremonies."

Red Fox asked, "Why's that?"

"Actually, you're an architect, so imagine that the trench and wall was sliced by a big knife. Imagine we are looking at it like it had been sliced open. Now imagine we are looking at a cross section of it.

Red Fox nodded. Walking Eagle went on.

"What do you see?" the Elder asked.

"A frequency line. Oh, I see, it's a sine wave!" said Red Fox.

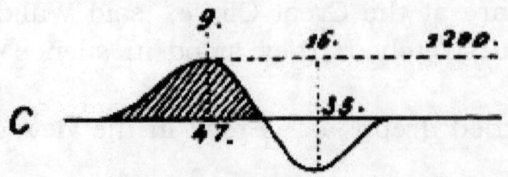

Cross-section of the wall of the Great Circle Squier and Davis 1848

"Exactly," said Walking Eagle with a big grin on his face. "Every one of our sacred earthworks is built as an expression of a vibrational frequency, and very few have an interior trench like this one. Very good."

Red Fox feeling that he had reached a new awareness, his eyes lit up with excitement, he began looking around with a heightened interest.

"And, what about the trench filled with water? What's that about? he asked.

"That's about ceremony, primarily," came the answer. "This is the ceremony place for observing the vernal rise of the Pleiades, then Orion, and then Sirius. This earthwork was built for that purpose, so every year in the spring we honor our connection to other worlds. It's part of celebrating a renewal in awareness. Star people from other worlds have given us so much in the way of knowledge. In fact, parts of the initiation process include connecting with some of those beings, so that you can go there in an out-of-body state while your physical body rests here in a deep meditation."

"So, you are saying that much of what I have learned in the way of mathematics and trigonometry and engineering principles was taught to us by our friends from the stars?" asked Red Fox.

"Yes. You're perceptive," Walking Eagle replied. "Much of the ancient knowledge on the birch bark scrolls that Singing Hawk has in her storehouse records has been handed down for thousands of years. She is one of our Keepers of the Ancient Knowledge."

"Okay. So what about the water? Where does it come from? " Red Fox pressed.

"Ah, yes, the water in the trench," Walking Eagle nodded as he answered. "Well, there is a small channel that leads to the lake that you have seen in the middle of this complex. This provides a supply of water, so we can maintain the water level in the trench.

"The water in the trench represents the waters in the womb. It represents the amniotic fluids that nurture us as we grow in our mother's womb.

"The trench is on the inside of the wall. This reminds us, as we participate in ceremony here, we come into this particular physical experience through the process of growing in our mother's bodies.

"This earthwork circle represents the womb, and the water in the trench symbolizes the waters we go through to get born. It reminds us we all come from the same Source, and arrive here individually through the womb . . . And it further reminds us that we are continually being nurtured and nourished by Mother Earth and Great Spirit, both physically and spiritually."

Walking Eagle paused speaking and stopped for a moment before continuing and then said, "Our ceremonies here are powerful. When we gather here in this earthwork area constructed to represent a sine wave, can you imagine the power generated as each individual focuses on honoring the sense of renewal and of our oneness?" Walking Eagle asked rhetorically.

"Thought has mass. So when we assemble and join our thoughts into a collective frequency that mass of energy impacts our world. We do this for the purpose of maintaining peace and harmony in our civilization. It serves to create and maintain balance and our connection to the Oneness.

"When I told you most of our ceremonies are about renewal, this is what I'm talking about. This mass of energy focuses on renewal and, as a result, raises our entire frequency field on several different levels . . . and this ceremony is not only done here, but elsewhere in our lands.

"The mass of our collective thought, intention and frequency is raised.

"The opening of the Great Circle points to the rise of several constellations on the horizon in the spring. Spring represents renewal. The water-filled trench represents the waters of the womb in this renewal ceremony."

Red Fox nodded silently as he looked around the earthwork.

After a pause that allowed for some reflecting, Walking Eagle changed the topic slightly as they walked toward the center of the circle and onto a set of conjoined earthen mounds.

"See this mound we are standing on?" he pointed to the ground. Red Fox looked down at it, briefly surveying in his head, then nodded, signaling for Walking Eagle to continue.

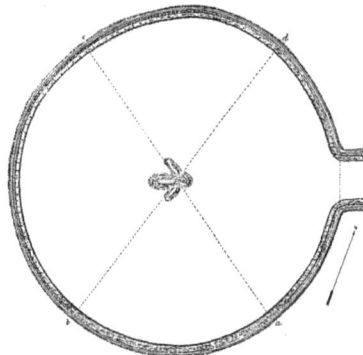

Diagram of the Great Circle and central mound Thomas 1889

"This mound is built in a tri-partite scheme. The three elongated mounds are joined here at one end." Red Fox looked at the particular shapes again, and then looked back to Walking Eagle.

The Elder said, "Each one of these mounds represents something different. The smallest one is for the mind, then one is for the body, and the last and largest is for Spirit. They all come together, here, where we are standing. This highest point is the most meaningful of them. It stands for the heart. Everything connects through the heart. I'm sure you have learned that it is through our hearts that we connect to Spirit . . . and that each of our other parts must serve the heart."

Red Fox remained silent as he again surveyed the conjoined mounds upon which they stood.

Walking Eagle then said, "These mounds have not always been here. In a more ancient time, we had a large ceremonial house here . . . and before that, we simply had a ceremonial center. This spot has served as a center for our ceremonies since the beginning. Ultimately, the ceremonial house was burned and these mounds were built in its place.

As it was late afternoon, it was time to leave the Great Circle and follow the walled pathway for nearly a mile to the west where the Great Octagon and Circle earthworks lay.

Once they arrived, Walking Eagle said, "As you can see, the octagon is large enough to accommodate thousands of participants for ceremony."

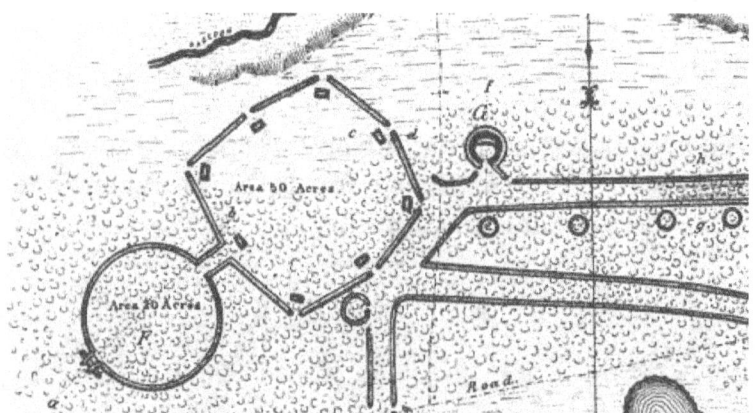

Diagram of the Circle and Octagon Earthwork Squier and Davis 1848

Red Fox looked around with the eyes of an architect.

Walking Eagle continued, "The squares and connected circles in all of our earthworks all over the countryside represent heaven and earth as being connected."

"I do see that," said Red Fox as they began walking inside the Great Octagon. "I'm aware of the squares connecting to the circles in other earthworks. But, my question to you is, why is this an *octagon*? A square has four sides, but the octagon has eight. What's that about?"

"Glad you asked," the Elder responded as they walked. "This is the place where we hold the ceremony for the Northernmost Moonrise. When we get to the back of the circle, you'll see the loaf shaped mound where White Eagle and Rising Wolf stand officiating at the beginning stages of the ceremony.

"Later as Father Sun sets, they will move forward to the much smaller mound within the Octagon in line with the wide gap in the walls at the top of the octagon. From there they will symbolically lift Sister Moon from the horizon into the night sky with their arms outstretched."

Heaving a sigh Red Fox asked again, "So what about the eight sides?"

"I'm coming to that," said the Elder with one nod of his head. "This structure, as I said before, is about Sister Moon. It's about other alignments as well, but the octagon provides the opportunity to observe and celebrate the eight phases of Sister Moon each month."

"In addition, on a grander scale it tracks her eight significant rise and set points of her intricate 18.6 year cycle. Here, this drawing may help you understand the alignments," Walking Eagle said as he unfurled another and larger scroll. Walking Eagle unrolled it to show Red Fox. He knelt down to set the scroll on the ground. Red Fox knelt down also to get a better view of the scroll.

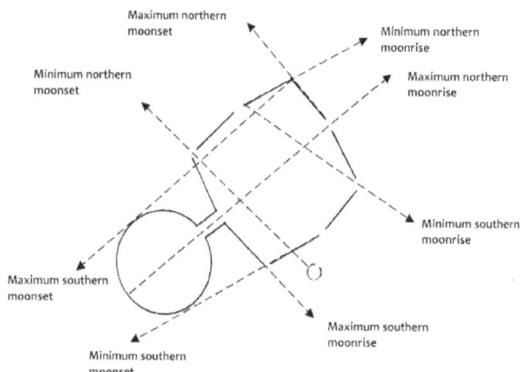

Redrawn and adapted after Lepper 2004

"Nearly all of our ceremonies are about renewal of one kind or another. Observing the travels of Sister Moon is just one of those activities that reinforces a sense of continued renewal.

"You're not old enough to have come to the last Northernmost Moonrise ceremony, but you'll have the opportunity to participate in the Southernmost Moonrise at High Bank this next fall.

"Just so you know, the circle connected to the octagon here at Newark is the same size as the one at High Bank, and they're both perfect circles encompassing nearly 20 acres.

"I want to share some more information about this octagon, especially since you are familiar with the High Bank octagon. As you know, the High Bank octagon was modified from the shape of an ideal octagon. The same is true here."

Walking Eagle continued, "Since the octagon encompasses 50 acres, it is difficult to see the modifications that were made to the lengths of the walls and the gaps between the walls. While our Ancient Ones could have designed an ideal and symmetric octagon, their desire was to establish accurate sightlines to mark the risings and settings of Sister Moon that we rely upon for our ceremonies at this complex."

They discussed at length the details of the construction of the circle and octagon complex and how the various sightlines were created.

Red Fox swallowed hard, working to comprehend and remember relationships he found fascinating.

Seeing Red Fox's reaction Walking Eagle said, "I imagine all of this might seem a bit overwhelming at first. After you study it a bit, you'll likely remember it better . . . yet there is even more. I think this is enough for today. You can study these scrolls for a while, and we can talk more later if you have questions.

"All we have discussed today will help you understand the information contained in the scrolls. The important thing to remember is that by using the sighting points here at the circle and octagon complex, we can, not only track, calculate and predict the occurrence of the Northernmost Moonrise well in advance, we can also calculate and predict those years when lunar eclipses will occur near the equinoxes or solstices."

Together they returned to the guest house in silence. Feeling the need to process so many details and what it all meant, Red Fox's thoughts felt loud to him even though he did not speak the entire way back. As Walking Eagle and Red Fox arrived at the village, Walking Eagle handed Red Fox a bundle of birch bark scrolls with a smile and a nod.

"Thanks is all I can say," said Red Fox after a few more moments of contemplation of what he had learned that day, comparing it to engineering principles, combined with his knowledge of astronomy. He marveled at the process of transforming a concept into a physical structure, moving a thought into a physical mass in manifestation of 'as above so below,' and the 'unseen' into the 'seen.'

When the two of them reached the guesthouse, Red Fox went inside, and Morning Star came outside to see Walking Eagle. The two Elders made eye contact and just stood there a few moments without speaking.

Finally Walking Eagle said. "I've invited Red Fox to begin initiation. Let me know what he chooses."

Morning Star smiled and nodded as Walking Eagle left.

Back at the village near the Great Serpent, Warm Stone has begun to feel a bonding with us. We had taken him in and taken him under our wing. He was beginning to feel like family . . . that he belonged with us.

Life hummed along for our villagers, each one performing whatever tasks were necessary according to their particular industry. The mat weavers wove mats. The pottery makers made pottery. The flint knappers created from stone. Harmony prevailed as it had always prevailed.

I, Gray Wolf, continue to assist my Grandmother Shining Moon in healing others and learning about herbs. My mother, Raven's Wing continues her cooking and baking and overseeing the nutting process, which produces oil for our lamps as well as nutmeats for flour. Shining Bird continues her studies with Singing Hawk. Laughing Willow, Red Fox's mother continues sewing costumes for the upcoming Summer Solstice ceremony at the Great Serpent. Numerous dancers who will be participating in that ceremony continue practicing.

During one warm sunny afternoon, many of us took a break from the routine and went to the stream. We picnicked alongside the water's edge, with the children splashing and playing in the water.

Many of the young people and some adults began diving and collecting mussels. Of course, we all knew that would result in an even larger celebration of the day. We would dig a large pit in the ground and start a fire and let it grow big enough and long enough to produce marvelous coals for steaming our mussels. These kinds of activities were always welcomed.

Warm Stone had never experienced one of these spontaneous celebrations and became curious.

He asks, "So what are they doing, diving in the water like that?"

"Mussels," Shining Bird says as she smiles at him. "They're collecting mussels. We consider them a delicacy and have acquired quite a taste for them. You remember eating mussels, I'm sure," she adds with several nods, encouraging him to remember.

"Ah, yes," Warm Stone smiles back, "I do, and I also remember that's where your pearls come from."

"Come on, Warm Stone," I say, "let's dive and I'll show you how. Swimming will be good exercise for your leg."

Not needing to be invited twice, Warm Stone readily agrees. I give him a knife and grab one for myself, and we go downstream a bit to find just the right spot. In the water, I show him what to look for and how to extract the shellfish from its underwater habitat.

Shining Bird watches us as we relentlessly dive and return with the precious supply of provisions for a late afternoon meal. She collects what we brought up and assists others in preparation for the grand mussel bake we so enjoy.

After a while Warm Stone begins to compete with me and several others for how many he could bring up. No one else wants to engage in a competition, so Warm Stone remains the last one to continue diving.

"There're several really big ones down there just out of reach which may hold really huge pearls," exclaims Warm Stone after he breached the surface. "I can't quite get to them, so I'm going after them again. I'd love to bring back several really big ones for dinner and use the pearls for trading once I'm back on my feet to travel," he adds raising his eyebrows several times punctuating his enthusiasm.

"No, Warm Stone," cautions Shining Bird, "there's no need for that. We've enough. We really don't need to take all the mussels from this part of the stream. We can leave some for Mother Earth. We already have plenty for everyone here. It's not about seeing how many or how big, it's about the enjoyment of it all."

"Well," Warm Stone replies in a cocky tone, "I'll enjoy providing the most and the biggest." With that he dives again.

He is underwater for an extraordinarily long time. Shining Bird grabs my arm and squeezes tightly.

As I turn to look at her, I see a look of concern on her face. Then I realize that Warm Stone must be in some kind of distress.

Just then we see what appears to be his body turning over and over in a deep part of the stream. He isn't swimming. His feet are pointed downstream and his arms trail over his head following his body. He appears to be caught in a turbulent current that is not releasing him. The current is taking him down stream. Then he disappears from our sight.

I gauge the speed at which his body is being ushered into the deep part of this stream, and I run downstream as fast as I can. Then I dive into the water to find him.

"Oh, Mother Earth," calls out Shining Bird loudly so all could hear, "I know you love us and honor us as we honor you. Warm Stone is becoming one of us, at least temporarily. He is in our care as he heals. If it is a blessing for him, and all the rest of us, to have him return to

Great Spirit now, then so be it. And, dearest Mother, if it is in the best interest of all concerned here to have him back with us, then please allow that blessing to occur. Then please release him and let him return back to us unharmed. And, so be it. Thank you, Mother." Having finished her prayer, she bows her head in deep respect for whatever the results would be.

At just that moment, as I fight the current, I touch the clothing and body of my friend. I wrap my arm around his mid-section under his arms and claw my way up to the surface.

Several men come to my aid and help lift him up out of the water. We place him on his stomach, and I pushed on his back to work the water out of his lungs.

He coughed and sputtered as he regained consciousness.

Back at Newark, Morning Star stood looking at Red Fox for very long moments. Red Fox looked up at Morning Star from his seat in the guest house after realizing that Morning Star was seemingly asking a question that he did not speak out loud.

"I guess you're wondering about what I learned from my tour with Walking Eagle," Red Fox said after a few moments. Morning Star shook his head slowly from side to side, still remaining silent.

". . . Then what?" Red Fox asked.

Morning Star breathed in deeply before responding then he said, "I am wondering about what you'll choose regarding going through initiation."

"Ah," was all Red Fox could say. "I don't know yet. I'm inclined to accept. I'm curious about what it would feel like connecting with the Knowing . . . it's just that I'm also hesitant to face my fears. I'm just not sure about that part of it."

"Remember your dream?" asked Morning Star, "the one where you are standing on a precipice?" Red Fox nodded. "Well, that is where I see you now."

Red Fox nodded again then said as he lay down, "I want to sleep on it. It's a big step, one that will impact the rest of my life."

For two more days, Red Fox gave several presentations a day. Again, he noticed different individuals and families returning to hear him again. Each presentation went without incident.

After the last one, Red Fox turned to Morning Star and said, "I sense that going through the initiation process is a chance of a lifetime, one that I do not wish to pass by."

Raising his eyebrows in surprise, Morning Star asked to confirm, "So, you've decided to take that leap?"

"Yes," the young man confessed, "I had mixed emotions about it at first. So, I asked about it every night before going to sleep. Now I feel a certain relief from that hesitancy. I really don't want to miss out on the experience. So I will accept the invitation . . . as much out of curiosity as out of trust that I will advance myself spiritually and then be in a place to offer greater assistance to The People as I work as an architect and builder."

Morning Star looked surprised at this comment, and Red Fox continued, "Yes, I saw myself designing and building homes and meeting houses all over the country. I felt thrilled at that prospect. If going through initiation will help me do that *and* assist The People in living in harmony, then, yes, absolutely, I want to do that."

Nodding and smiling, Morning Star replied, "That pleases me as I have had the same vision."

"You had the same vision?" asked Red Fox, "what do you mean?"

"I was shown in a vision a probability of what choice you might make . . . not an absolute choice, but a *probable* choice," responded Morning Star. "The future still remains a 'maybe,' not an absolute, because our future is always determined by the specific choices we each make, the intentions we set, and the way we form and order our thoughts to achieve those goals. We forge our own future, as it were, from the choices we make. Our future is always a result, or consequence, of whatever our choices are.

"Additionally, I noticed something else."

At that remark, Red Fox turned and tilted his head as if asking about the 'something else'.

"Yes," Morning Star said, "I saw you go through different emotions as you mentally processed the decision about initiation. Just so you know, as you might need to know while you go through the initiation process, our emotions are given to us to serve as a gauge."

"A gauge? What do you mean, 'a gauge'?" asked Red Fox.

"Yes, a gauge," said Morning Star. "There are many layers to our emotions. Our emotions inform us as to how much in alignment we are with Great Spirit, our Source of Being. When we feel afraid, for example, our emotional state informs us that we are feeling separated. When we feel any other emotion of not-happiness, these emotions tell us we are not experiencing our oneness."

Red Fox nodded as he listened.

The Elder goes on, "When we experience emotions of peace, or joy, for example, we are informing ourselves that we feel our close alignment with Great Spirit. Sometimes, however, we are presented with situations that might threaten our sense of peace.

"How we see the situation, the perspective we take, determines our emotional reaction. This is where our conscious awareness comes into play, in particular. It's really not about what is going on outside of you or what circumstances that are occurring around you. It's about what you feel, and what you choose to feel, regardless of the situation in which you find yourself.

"When you can experience your conscious awareness of your alignment with Great Spirit, regardless of what is going on outside of you, you mentally reach for your spiritual alignment. This changes your perspective. With a change in perspective you can see the situation differently and change your perception of the situation and then you experience it differently. Peace can then come to you."

"So, how do the emotions play out in this scenario?" asked Red Fox after he thought about what he had just heard.

"Again, your emotions signal to you where you are in choosing how you experience an experience. Your unhappiness, or frustration, or feeling less than others or better than others, or feeling disconnected, are emotional states that inform when you are off the mark, so to speak.

"When we are off the mark, we often make choices that might not be in our best interest or in the best interest of all concerned. This occurs most frequently when we make choices coming from ego, rather than from the heart.

"When we make our choices that come from our heart, we usually feel pretty good about the choices, and usually good about the outcome. That good feeling is an emotional state as well, and it informs us we feel connected to our Source."

Red Fox nodded again and remained in silent contemplation of this information.

After a brief pause, Morning Star said, "I've seen you go through several different emotional states, both now and a while back."

At this remark, Red Fox looked up at Morning Star again, and said, "Yes?"

"Remember, when you first heard you were selected for this project?"

Red Fox gave a nod.

The Elder continued, "You felt frustrated at not being able to get in to see Singing Hawk. That sense of frustration was an emotion that, if you were paying attention to it, informed you that you were not feeling connected to your Source. Also, when you felt 'better than others,' this same event triggered the feeling of wanting to pound your chest to announce your power. These behaviors were driven by your ego.

"You were not happy, right? Your unhappiness was an emotion that served as a gauge of where you were on a scale of alignment with Great Spirit." Morning Star paused briefly to let that sink in. Then he added, "When you are giving your presentations, you clearly demonstrate your sense of oneness by the peace and love that comes through you as you speak. Our emotions provide us with a gauge we want to pay attention to. So, when we are feeling an emotion that is not of the highest vibration, we should feel it, acknowledge it, and move through that vibration as we choose again.

"This is an important point to remember. As you go through initiation, just as you go through life, whenever you feel not-wonderful, you can choose again. You can choose a higher frequency of emotion. It's not about your circumstances. *It's about choosing how you wish to experience your circumstances.* This is what free-will is about. It allows you to make these kinds of choices. Your emotions inform you, as a gauge would, so you can make the choices you need to make . . . *if you pay attention.* Paying attention requires conscious awareness.

"When you go through initiation, some of the tasks or challenges will not be pleasant, just as in physical life. Some challenges are not pleasant, even ugly. It is up to you to choose how you wish to experience each one," Morning Star said as he placed his hand on Red Fox's shoulder.

Silence.

That evening Walking Eagle and several other Elders arrived at the guest house seeking Red Fox.

"Are you ready, Red Fox?" asked Walking Eagle.

"Yes, I am," responded the young man with his face shining in anticipation of the upcoming event.

Pulling out a neatly folded cloth, Walking Eagle announced, "We will blindfold you as we escort you to the place where the initiation will begin."

One of the other Elders took the blindfold from Walking Eagle and walked over to Red Fox and put the blindfold on.

The troupe walked for what seemed to Red Fox like several miles. Even with the blindfold on, Red Fox could feel the night air shifting in direction and in temperature as they traversed the countryside. The scents of the landscape changed as they distanced themselves from the village where they started.

Finally, they reached their destination. Red Fox could hear several of the others talking in hushed tones and then the scraping noises of an entryway being opened. A scent of underground dankness rushed his face still covered by the blindfold.

Then the scent of smudging herbs filled the air as a hushed prayer was said over him and all the others present to cleanse them of any negative energy.

"We are at the opening," Walking Eagle said quietly with a sense of the sacred in his tone. "You will need to step down a flight of steps to enter. When we get to the bottom, we will release you from the blindfold."

Once inside a large space underground Red Fox felt the blindfold come off. As he opened his eyes he could see only darkness at first. As his eyes adjusted to the dark, he saw several familiar looking copper and mica lamps attached to the walls of the chamber. His escorts led him to a large basin formed in the floor of the chamber. As he looked around, he noticed the walls covered with mats with symbols painted on them.

"To begin, you will meditate here in this room. We have water, dried fruits and nuts for you to nibble on should you need nourishment. We will watch your progression. When the time is appropriate, we will let you know, then you will climb into the basin and fold yourself into a pre-natal position. We will leave you here for some time. Yet someone will always be nearby just in case you find yourself experiencing something so unpleasant as to require being relieved from the initiation process. In that event, the initiation process will end and we will bring you back to your friends."

Red Fox nodded in affirmation.

"Once you enter the basin you will not be given food or water while you are in this state. We will not interrupt your process. You will meditate here for as long as you need to and will remain here until you return to your consciousness of the here and now. Before we leave you, we will all join in song of ceremony and prayer for you in affirmation of blessings on you and The People. It is part of setting the tone and vibrational frequency of this process. This is a very sacred event."

At that comment, Red Fox noticed about a dozen or more hooded individuals entering by the same entrance he had come through.

During the time Red Fox was gone, Morning Star and Running Bear played with the dogs and otherwise enjoyed their respite from their long travels. After five days had passed, Running Bear expressed concern for Red Fox.

"Does it usually take this long for the first stage in the initiation process?" he asked Morning Star.

"Not usually, if I remember correctly," came the answer.

Just then, they heard the dogs bark greetings to their third companion, Red Fox.

More of a maturing man than a youth, Red Fox appeared with peace shining from his face and entire countenance.

"I'm back," he said stating the obvious to Morning Star and Running Bear as they sat outside their guest house. They both stared at him in disbelief as they noted the changes. Neither of them questioned him on his experience, just grateful that he clearly completed the first steps in the sacred journey of initiation.

"Tomorrow we will head up to Flint Ridge. I believe you wanted to check in on Water Dog since we are already this far. It's only about nine miles to Rising Wolf's flint house," Running Bear said breaking the silence.

"Yes, I should like to see Water Dog. It's been a while since I've seen him. And, I'd like to see Flint Ridge, too. Thanks," said Red Fox.

After spending the remainder of the day preparing for resuming their journey, the three men worked in silence and remained silent until the next morning. Even though they got a late start, the three men and even the dogs enjoyed being on the move again.

The beautiful countryside was decorated with stands of hardwood trees and spring wildflowers in full bloom. Red Fox fairly floated as he journeyed to Rising Wolf's house at Flint Ridge, feeling a part of the beauty he was witnessing.

"I was wondering when you'd get here," said Water Dog with a huge smile as he took large steps toward his friends in greeting. Grabbing Red Fox's arms with both of his, Water Dog appeared happy to see his visitors.

"Look who's here," Water Dog shouted as he turned toward several Elders, both men and women, standing outside the Flint House. With smiles all around, the travelers greeted everyone. Just then the door to the Flint House opened and Rising Wolf came out with a very big smile for Red Fox.

"I feel honored that you, Red Fox, from my village, are the first of a new generation to begin initiation. Remember, initiation is one way individuals uplift their consciousness to experience at-one-ment. This is important so we can continually renew our spiritual communion with each other. In this way, our civilization remains living in peace and in conscious alignment with the Great Oneness," the Elder shaman grandly stated.

That moment became a ceremony.

Reaching into his bundle, Rising Wolf pulled out a small suede pouch with drawstrings. He put his large bundle down on the ground, still holding the small one. Then, raising both of his arms in the air, he began to chant a song of gratitude and recognition.

When he finished his song, Rising Wolf stepped closer to Red Fox. Then he reached his index finger and thumb into the pouch and pulled out a small square piece of fired clay, a tablet, with markings etched into it.

"This clay tablet is one of several tablets that have been passed down from generation to generation from ancient days. It was gifted to our ancestors from those that came across the great waters to the east to mine the copper in the far north. It is one that has stayed with The People for eons of time. It is one that is given in recognition of exchange.

"This exchange today for you is one of giving up the unreal for the real, surrendering the illusion that the physical is real for the knowing that what is of Spirit is the real and lasting. I give this tablet to you, Red Fox, in recognition of completing the first stages of initiation. Always keep it with you, so it can remind you of the oneness and of who we are as a People."

As the ceremony came to a close, happiness and smiles were shared all around. One of the Elders announced that a feast had been prepared, so that the celebration lasted into the late evening. During this time as twilight embraced the merrymaking, Red Fox and Water Dog spent time huddling together comparing notes and thoughts about life.

20

ON THE WAY HOME

Contemplating the return home, Running Bear and Morning Star consulted with others who had traveled to Flint Ridge as to the best water routes back to the Scioto River. Several men and women from Chillicothe had come to Flint Ridge to gather flint for knapping. They had come by canoes and had room to spare for the trip home.

"Judging by how many there are of us, plus the dogs, and the travois," offered Stalking Crane, "I think four large canoes would do it. We can have them already to go and waiting for us by the Licking River just a few miles north of here, so we don't have to go all the way back to Newark. South of Newark, we'll have a mile or so portage over to Walnut Creek that would take us to the Scioto River."

Those traveling in the boats began preparing for the journey home. Morning Star and Running Bear gathered together their belongings, the travois and the dogs.

While all this activity was going on, Red Fox's attention drifted to witnessing the house that had been built very long ago from blocks of flint-bearing rock cast off from the flint mining pits. Clearly Rising Wolf loved this little house. Red Fox circled the house several times, went inside, then back out, taking mental pictures of it, making imprints of it in his memory, his architect mind at work all the while.

"C'mon, Red Fox," called out Running Bear as those traveling together assembled to leave. Red Fox grabbed Water Dog with both arms, giving the tall man a hug as they said their good-byes.

Turning away from Water Dog, Red Fox affectionately slapped his friend on the shoulder and said, "See ya back at our village, good friend." Water Dog tossed his head in response, saying nothing, just looking at his childhood friend having matured into a journeyman, becoming a master, a shaman, before his very eyes.

In silence the travelers canoed their way down the Licking River toward the portage point and carried the canoes over to Walnut Creek and headed down towards the Scioto River.

The rhythmic sounds of the water added to the beauty of the landscape they witnessed as they made their way south. The dogs traveled well, occasionally wanting to stand up, a little unsure of the lack of steadiness beneath their feet. Morning Star sometimes cooed to them as a way of reassuring them on their ride.

Red Fox barely paid attention to his immediate surroundings. Even though he went through the motions of paddling, his mind was elsewhere. Often he would forget to paddle as his mind drifted back to his initiation experiences.

Once when Running Bear looked back at Red Fox, sensing he was not paddling, he saw the young man sitting in the boat physically, but elsewhere in his attention. Seeing that Red Fox's eyes held more than a faraway look, much closer to a glazed appearance, Running Bear said nothing, just returned to paddling, wanting to keep up with the other canoes.

It was the close of the third day by the time they reached the Scioto River. They paddled south for a while until one of the other boatmen began shouting to pull up to the bank. Evidently a village was close. It was a convenient place where they could stay the night, get a hot meal, and let the dogs stretch and run, and for the trio to stretch their legs as well.

Of course Red Fox was cajoled into giving yet another presentation, which he did most graciously.

The next day took them down the Scioto River to Chillicothe. The flint gatherers in the other boats had reached their destination. Yet the trio still needed two canoes and had only three people to paddle when a minimum of four would be required. After some unloading, the travelers stood around for a few moments. Red Fox sat off to the side still lost in his mental processing of what he had experienced at Newark.

Morning Star looked at Running Bear and spoke as if Running Bear did not know what the plan was, "You know, Running Bear, our destination is the Portsmouth and Tremper earthworks toward the Ohio River. Do you have any idea the best way to get there?" Running Bear just looked at Morning Star without speaking.

Then a traveling companion, Whispering Sun, from one of the other canoes stepped up and offered, "I could take you there. We would need two of these canoes though. I've been there several times and could lead you to just the right spot to put in. There's a spot on the east side of the Scioto River from where you could easily access the walled walkway that leads to the central part of the Portsmouth Earthworks."

"That'd be great, Whispering Sun. We'd sure appreciate your help. It's been a long time since I've been there," Morning Star said.

"Let's get going so we still have enough daylight to make it down to the village near the Liberty earthworks which is about eight miles south of High Bank," Whispering Sun said.

And, away they went, the three men, the four dogs, the travois, and Red Fox, riding the river south toward the Liberty Earthworks village.

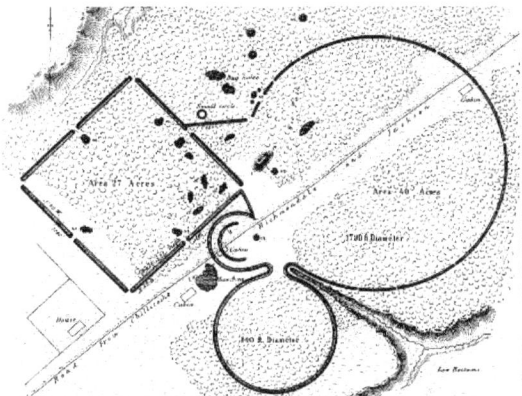

Diagram of the Liberty Earthworks, Squier and Davis 1848

Once they arrived at the village they were greeted warmly and given a meal and a place to stay.

Having been on the move for several days they decided to rest up for a few days. This gave Red Fox some time to make several presentations. Yet now as he spoke, he was taken by the words and mental images deeper into the history and significance of the Story of the Great Serpent, more as a participant than a teller of the ancient stories.

As they made their way down the Scioto River towards the Portsmouth earthwork complex, they stopped at several villages giving Red Fox several more opportunities to ask all to remember to remember the Story of the Great Serpent.

Upon arrival, north of the confluence of the Scioto and Ohio Rivers, Whispering Sun showed them how to maneuver into position to beach the canoes at the landing on the east side of the Scioto. They noticed several fishermen working the shoreline. A youngster among them ran up to the village, some distance away, to announce the arrival of the pilgrims.

Once they landed and unloaded, they said their good-byes to Whispering Sun. He started back up the Scioto with a canoe in tow hoping to reach the Fuert earthworks before dark.

"Where is he going?" asked Red Fox.

"He had mentioned earlier that he wanted to pick up a good supply of pipe stone from the quarries near the Fuert village, for the Chillicothe pipe artisans. Oh, by the way, the pipe artisans at Tremper also use this same pipe stone. We'll be visiting the Tremper earthworks on our way home," said Morning Star as he hoisted a pack on his back.

Having gathered their possessions and harnessed the dogs to the travois, they headed to the entrance to the walled road that headed in an easterly direction. This road was much different from the White Road of Sister Moon. Red Fox had heard about the Portsmouth Earthworks. However, he had never seen a drawing of them. The road followed the landscape for as far as the eye could see. Red Fox imagined that he was in for an adventure.

Well before they reached the end of the walled road, they were greeted by a village Elder, Swimming Turtle, who guided them to a gap in the walls and up a winding path along the cliff face to a village that sat on the plateau north of the complex. Once there Red Fox was transfixed by what he saw. These earthworks continued on the other side of the Ohio River and miles and miles of connecting walled roads.

"Quite a view, is it not?" whispered Swimming Turtle.

"This complex . . . it's huge . . . so very different in design from all the other earthworks that I know of," Red Fox exclaimed trying to take it all in.

"Well, yes it is," Swimming Turtle said. "In fact you can only see a small part of it from here. It spans both sides of the river for over eight miles. I have a map of it on a birch bark scroll. Let me go get it, so you can see the layout."

When the Elder returned, he unfurled the scroll for Red Fox. "Here let me show you this drawing," said Swimming Turtle after he had opened the scroll for Red Fox.

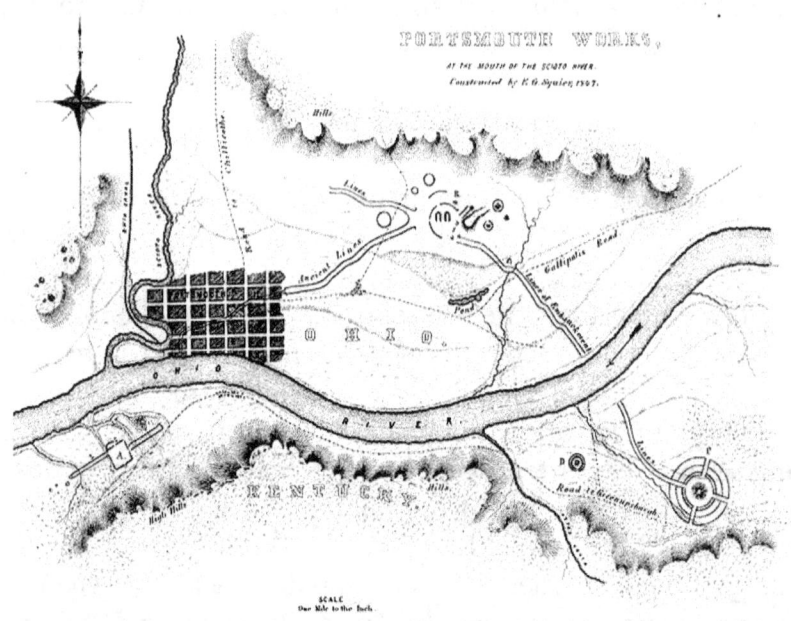

Diagram of Portsmouth Earthworks in Ohio and Kentucky Squier and Davis 1848

Red Fox studied it with a half-smile on his face, fascinated by the drawing he was reviewing. Before too long, it was time to eat.

During the meal Swimming Turtle outlined his plans for the tour with Red Fox, "When we are finished here, we'll head down to the central plaza and then take the walled road downhill to the Ohio River. That road is steep and is a little over three miles long. We'll cross the river and then follow the walled road nearly two miles up hill to the ceremonial mound.

"The ceremonial mound is ringed by four circular mounds. As we walk I'll tell you about the renewal ceremonies we have here at the Winter Solstice. That ceremony starts on this side of the Ohio River well before sunrise on that day."

"Do you use this complex for other ceremonies?" asked Red Fox.

"Yes," replied Swimming Turtle and added, "among other ceremonies, we also use it for a remember-to-remember ceremony focused on the migration of our People from the east before and during the sinking of those lands. As Children of the Law of One, we want to remind ourselves of the destruction that can occur when we forget who we really are in relationship to our Source, Mother Earth and each other."

After the sumptuous mid-day meal, Swimming Turtle and Red Fox followed the path along the cliff's edge to a trail down to the central complex. Swimming Turtle then led Red Fox to the crest of a small hill just to the east of the central part of this earthwork.

Waving his arm in a sweeping motion Swimming Turtle began, "Now here is the central plaza. Before sunrise on the day of the Winter Solstice, those who wish to participate in the ceremony will gather here.

"We say a prayer that reminds us that our physical lives are about experiencing experiences from which our Creator gathers the wisdom to better know Itself. As you already know, our Creator is not separate from creation created. Our Winter Solstice Ceremony reminds us of that."

After a pause, Swimming Turtle said, "The Ceremony begins at the symbolic end of our physical lives. In other words, at the point of gathering we move into the death-state, so to speak, before the moment of transition.

"Those participating will move down the walled roadway to the river and cross over the river. The river at that point in the Ceremony represents the actual transition that we call death.

"Canoes take us across the river, so we can then walk to the complex on the south side of the river. We then gather within the circular walls of the earthwork."

THE CAMP OF GOD'S TEARS

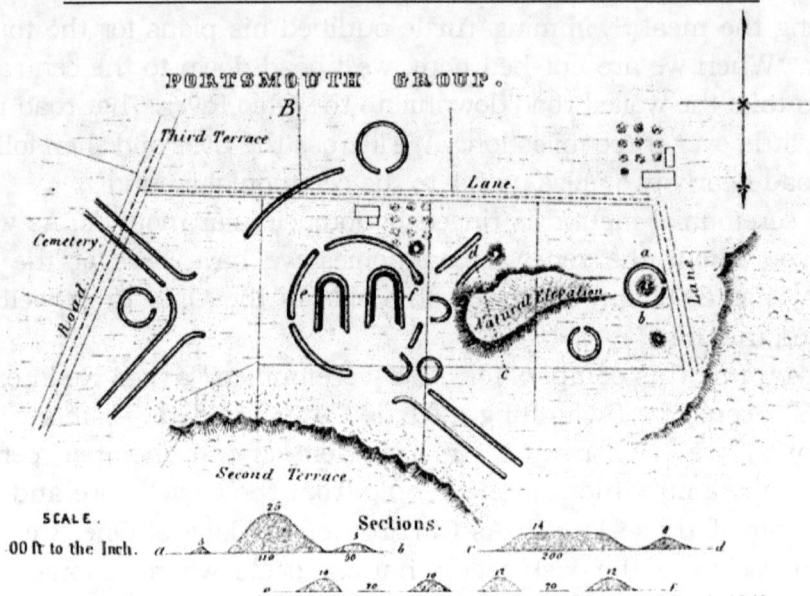

Diagram of the Portsmouth Earthworks Group B - Ohio - Squier and Davis 1848

After walking around inside all the earthworks in the central plaza, Swimming Turtle and Red Fox took the road down to the river where several canoes were beached. Swimming Turtle selected a smaller canoe for the two men to use to cross the expanse of the wide river. Red Fox noticed the hemp ropes and pulley system attached to each canoe. Swimming Turtle instructed Red Fox how to operate the system, and they pulled the canoe across the river to the other shore.

"It's been a convenient way to cross. As you can see, the Ohio River is very wide and powerful . . . and we've managed to make this pulley system work. We have the same system further down the river near the square complex which is also on the other side of the river."

After they reached the other side they beached the canoe and started walking up the walled roadway to the circular earthwork.

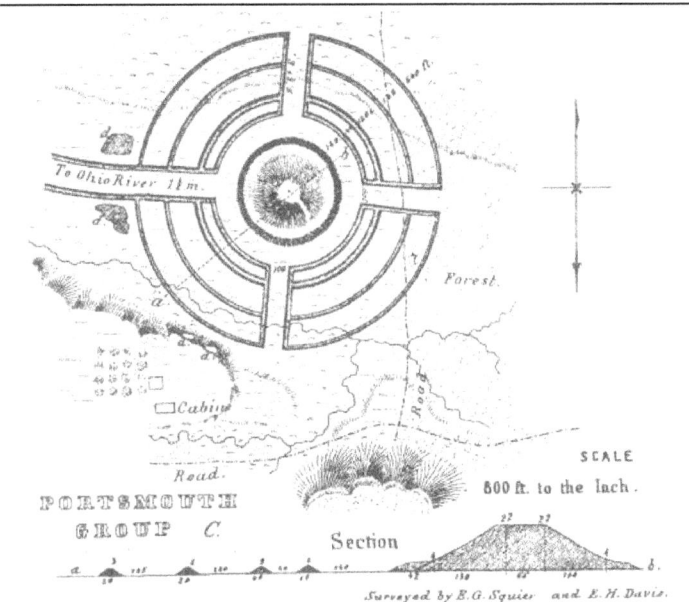
Diagram of Portsmouth Earthworks Group C - Kentucky -Squier and Davis 1848

"This is a replica of the capital city that existed a very long time ago. Many of our ancestors came from the land that sank in the ocean to the east. This site though is a much smaller version of that great city," said Swimming Turtle. "This was built for renewal ceremony and to remind us of what led to the destruction of the Third World."

As Swimming Turtle and Red Fox walked within circular walls of the ancient temple grounds, they ascended the truncated pyramid in the center. Red Fox gazed out to all the earthworks that comprised this feature of the Portsmouth Complex.

"Now the outside earthen ring is about a quarter of a mile in diameter. If you extend an imaginary line from the road we took from the river over the top of this mound we are standing on to the eastern horizon, it marks the point where Father Sun rises on the day of the Winter Solstice. On that same day Father Sun's path will cross directly over this central mound we are standing on."

As Red Fox wandered around the top of the central mound he made an observation, "Are those ditches supposed to be canals for water?"

"You've got a good eye, son," said the Elder. "Yes, indeed, they are designed to be filled with water. If you look over there," he pointed then walked toward where he was pointing, "you can see an auxiliary canal that was constructed to funnel water from several nearby streams into these water troughs that run along the inside of each circular wall."

He paused and they continued to look around. Then Swimming Turtle said, "The original city was a major port as well, for traders and such. So the canals were sufficiently large to accommodate the ships that traveled the oceans around the world. Here these water troughs symbolically represent the canals in the original city."

Red Fox said, "This one is so different . . . so different from all the others. I'm challenged to comprehend this one. Are there any others like this one?"

"Yes," was the answer. "In fact there are two more concentric circular style earthworks than I'm aware of," Swimming Turtle said.

"Two more? . . . where?" pressed Red Fox.

"Well, let me think," said Swimming Turtle. "You were near one when you reached the confluence of Walnut Creek and the Scioto River. That one is Circleville . . . and let's see . . . oh, right, the other one is at Poverty Point. It's very ancient."

"Where's Poverty Point?" asked Red Fox.

The Elder answered, "It's some distance north of where the Mississippi River empties into the southern ocean. It has served as a port along the Mississippi River. It's so ancient that some of it has been sheered away by the Great River. At one time Poverty Point was close to the river. It's not as close anymore as the Great River has shifted its course many times over the millennia. That's one place I've not been to, so I can't tell you more about it."

"What do you mean, 'a port'?" Red Fox asked curiously.

"The traders who transport the copper from the upper lakes and Canada often take the copper down the river system, and travel the Mississippi River to the southern ocean. Often they stop there at Poverty Point before continuing on to other parts of the world."

"Now getting back to describing our Winter Solstice Ceremony, with the rising of Father Sun on the Winter Solstice day, The People spend time here in meditation and contemplation of their lives. It represents the opportunity we have as individual beings to process information about the physical life we are experiencing. It's a time we give ourselves, as individuals, to feel our at-one-ment with the Great Oneness. It's a time to ensure our alignment with our Source.

"Actually, it's a general ceremony for many to experience a conscious connection with Spirit and to feel the joy of it. It's similar to the process of initiation. This ceremony is designed to reinforce what we already know and to re-experience the experience of connecting consciously. It's an opportunity for each individual to review his or her development, much like a life-review that often occurs after a physical death. To put it simply, it's a time for processing.

"The Elders perform rituals for those needing a little more structure in dealing with our present world. These rituals may be very personal and directed to individual needs and development."

Swimming Turtle waited patiently for Red Fox to spend time looking around and to feel whatever he needed to feel while he was there. Then when it appeared that Red Fox was ready to move on, he continued the tour, walking toward the square.

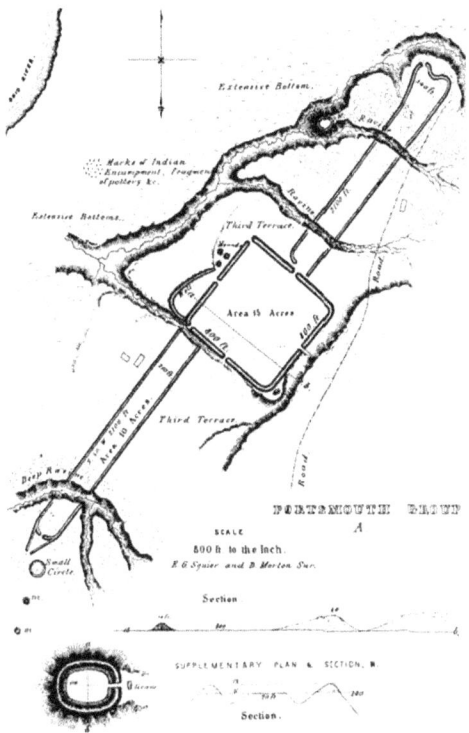

Diagram of Portsmouth Earthworks Group A - Kentucky - Squier and Davis 1848

When they arrived at the square, Swimming Turtle said, "When each individual is ready, they make their way down to the square. It's a distance from the circular mound, and each one must find his or her own way. And, that is symbolic also. No walled pathway leads to the square enclosure. The opening in the middle of the side that faces the river is oriented toward the Summer Solstice sunset.

"However, the walled extension of the square is aligned with the Winter Solstice sunset.

"The square is a symbol of the Absolute, or Heaven," Swimming Turtle said. "We acknowledge that the Absolute, or Spirit is not confined to any shape, nor constrained in any way. Yet, we as humans must deal with our physicality. So, in the physical, material dimension we find ourselves in, we use the square as a symbol for the Absolute in our rituals.

"Our rituals serve to enhance the underlying meaning of our symbols. Meanings of symbols are translated through the rituals to assist us in interacting with our true essence in the spiritual realm. They serve to energize us, not just mentally but spiritually as well. Through the use of our rituals, with the use of our symbols, we open portals in energy fields around us. In our rituals, we move through those portals that serve to uplift us, inspire us, and energize us. It's about re-connecting to our Source consciously."

Red Fox nodded in response. Then he asked, "So what happens in the square once The People are here?"

Swimming Turtle paused briefly then said, "Usually by this time it's dark. Nighttime is the most powerful time to finish this part of the Ceremony, especially at the Winter Solstice."

They walked through the square toward the western opening.

Swimming Turtle said, "While here, the participants meditate on what objectives they wish to accomplish in their next life. This is symbolic of course. It represents the time spent in preparation for the next physical life, and yet real preparation for the next year in the individual's personal life. Our individual life contracts are reviewed and agreed to, or not, as appropriate."

Red Fox nodded again in response.

Walking toward the western opening, Swimming Turtle pointed out, "These steps going down into this opening lead to a subterranean passageway which represents the birth canal that each of the participants use to symbolically enter again into the physical world. It's about a half-mile long. It leads to the Ohio River, again representing a re-birth or crossing from the realm of Spirit into the realm of the physical.

"We have also constructed a pulley system at this point on the river to assist everyone in crossing the Ohio River which now represents the 'waters of life.' This part of the Ceremony takes place at night as the womb and birth canal are dark. Then everyone makes their way up the gradual assent, to a walled walkway toward the central complex. And that represents a renewed sense of purpose, and a new life. Symbolically, this ceremony completes a life cycle, like Father Sun completes the annual cycle at the end of the Winter Solstice. Basically, it's a ceremony of renewal."

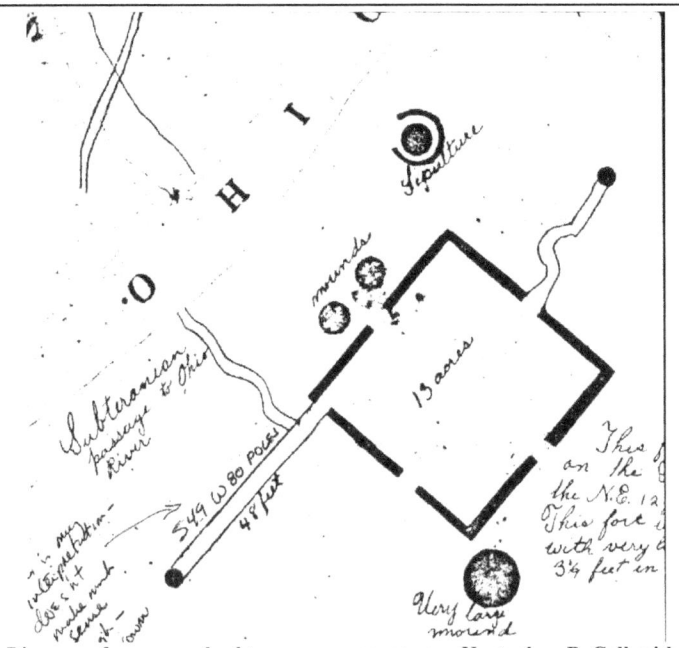
**Diagram of square and subterranean passageway - Kentucky - R. Galbraith.
Courtesy of the Cincinnati Museum Center**

"Now let's go back up and over to the Octagon." Swimming Turtle directed.

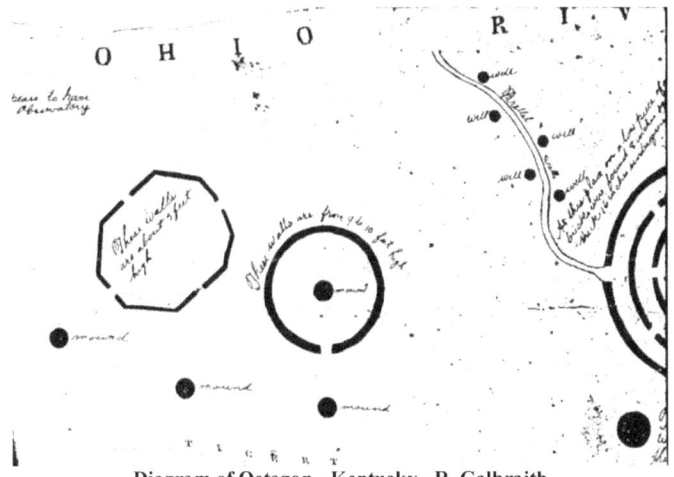
**Diagram of Octagon - Kentucky - R. Galbraith
Courtesy of the Cincinnati Museum Center**

Once they arrived at the center of the octagon, Swimming Turtle said, "Sometimes this octagon is a meeting place for Elders who travel up or down the Ohio River. I know you've visited the octagons at High Bank and Newark. However, as you can see, this octagon is not connected to a circle. Since the octagon honors Sister Moon, I have something for you which will complement the tablet Rising Wolf gave to you," Swimming Turtle said as he withdrew a sandstone tablet from his medicine bag.

"This is a calendar stone tablet. I will explain it to you and show you how to use it.

"While this might, at first, seem complicated once you understand how this engraved tablet functions, it will be easy to use.

"Now while this tablet is small enough to hold in your hand it contains a great deal of information. This particular size and shape is necessary to correctly establish the Solstice events. First you need to orient the middle of the top side towards the pole star."

"How can I be sure . . ." asked Red Fox interrupting.

Swimming Turtle pointed to a spot in the sky, "Right there day or night. You can always re-verify its location at night no matter where you may travel.

"This tablet marks three related cycles of the sun and moon that measures the lunar and solar year. The four basic phases of Sister Moon are depicted along the edges in such a way as to add up to one lunar year. The last depiction is the diagonal lines near the edges marking the series of 13 new moons that add up to one solar year.

Drawing of the Cincinnati Tablet, Squier and Davis 1848

Swimming Turtle explained in detail how the lines on the right and left edges of the tablet were used to count lunar months. Then he explained how to properly orient the tablet so that its four corners would mark the sunrises and sunsets on the Summer and Winter Solstices.

"In other words, this tablet allows us to mark the cosmic rhythms including the Solstices," Swimming Turtle finished and handed the tablet to Red Fox.

"This is quite a gift. Thank you Swimming Turtle. I so appreciate the knowledge that has come down to us from our ancestors," Red Fox said as he pointed to it, "I am really grateful to you for this gift."

"You are certainly welcome. You've traveled on your journey to many of our earthworks in this region asking people to remember to remember in the many presentations you have given. I have sent runners to Tremper, Fuert and other villages in this area and have made arrangements for your final presentation of your journey for tomorrow night.

"Since it's getting late, we need to get back to the canoe, cross the river and return to the village. Dinner will be awaiting us. Tomorrow, you, Morning Star and Running Bear are welcome to spend the day walking around this complex and feel free to re-cross the river and return to this part of the complex as I imagine both Morning Star and Running Bear would like to visit it," Swimming Turtle said as he placed both his hands on Red Fox's shoulders.

The following evening, during his presentation at Portsmouth village, several villagers asked him questions as many had received disturbing images during the last Winter Solstice Ceremony. At first, many had thought that they had strayed, in some way, from their at-one-ment with Spirit. Yet when they examined their daily lives, thoughts and behavior, they realized that what they were experiencing during the Ceremony was external to them. Something vague, something out-of-balance, something they had not experienced before at any prior Winter Solstice Ceremony.

In response, Red Fox reminded everyone that the Elders had selected young men and women throughout all the regions of The People to make journeys like this one. This effort was in preparation for the Summer Solstice Ceremony, and it involved asking all to remember to remember who The People are, our history, heritage and the need to restore balance and at-one-ment with each other and with Great Spirit. In this way the Elders hoped to restore the balance of The People. While his last presentation of this journey went well, Red Fox saw that a challenge to The People's way of life was making itself known.

Red Fox felt so fascinated by the Portsmouth complex, its schema and symmetry, the following day he wanted to revisit it. Morning Star and Running Bear joined him as they walked around it just absorbing its energy. The three of them with the dogs used the canoe and pulley system, to cross the Ohio River.

Once there, Morning Star took the dogs for a long run knowing they appreciated the sense of freedom. No settlements or villages existed near there, so the dogs could dash here and there without interfering with anyone. Red Fox spent his time there remembering what Swimming Turtle had told him. Later Morning Star joined up with him and shared more stories about information that he had learned about this very ancient complex.

After several hours had passed, Running Bear mentioned it was time to move on and head to Tremper village.

THE CAMP OF GOD'S TEARS

Once they collected everything, they paddled their canoes up the Scioto River about five miles to the Tremper village and its earthworks located on a plateau overlooking the Scioto River. The village of Tremper was known for pipe-making.

As they arrived and got settled in Red Fox went over to the pipe workshop area. The workshops were open on all sides and covered by a thatched roof. Several of the artisans had been to one of his presentations and said hello or nodded. One artisan had several completed effigy pipes on his work table. They were very detailed and life-like stone images of beavers, otters, hawks, owls, ducks and other animals and birds. Red Fox loved seeing the different styles of pipes, all works of art.

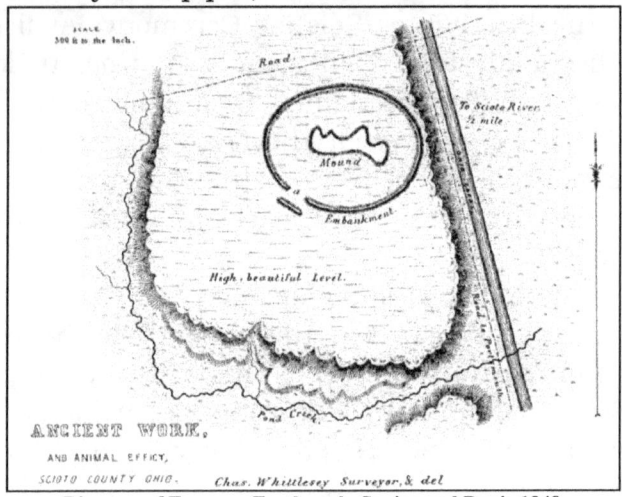
Diagram of Tremper Earthwork, Squier and Davis 1848

"Which one would you like, sonny?" crowed one of the older artisans with a wizened face.

"This one," responded Red Fox holding up his selection of a bear pipe. "I think my friend Gray Wolf's father, Black Bear, would enjoy smoking from such a pipe."

Courtesy of the Ohio Historical Society

"Then, this one is yours, sonny."

Red Fox smiled as he took the pipe, later tucking it in his bundle for the trip home.

The following morning the trio began their trip back to their village near the Great Serpent. The season had turned into warm days with hot afternoons as the pilgrims made their way home. Their homeward trek took several more days.

Weary of the journey by this time, Red Fox felt grateful to stay with villagers along the way each night instead of camping out. His mind had been continuously re-playing what he had experienced during his initiation, all the adventures and information he had gained on this journey that was now coming to a close.

As a result, he did not feel inclined to engage in conversation as they sojourned home. His two companions noticed this in silence. They more or less focused on each other, the dogs, all the while keeping a watchful eye on Red Fox.

21

HAL SEEKS TO SAVE HIS FRIEND

Entering the parking garage, Hal finds his car keys in his pocket. He gets into his car and drives toward the highway that leads to Tom's cabin. The weather is cloudy with intermittent rain showers. Low lying fog and mists sometimes cloud his vision.

Hal speeds up the same road Tom had taken. After he has been driving for a while, he desperately calls Tom again, and again, no answer.

Tom stands entranced by his vision of the most beautiful Native American woman who is wearing the intriguing necklace. He stretches out his hand to her as she stretches out her hand as well. Mists continue to embrace them. His vision continues.

WHITE EAGLE

The threat of our extinction looms ever over us.
We have exhausted our resources to stop the erosion of
our culture.
We still live the Oneness Principle,
and yet the darkness moves ever closer.
We do not know what it is,
but we do know it is the destroyer of peace.
That energy field comes ahead of the
foreigners who come to our lands.

Should we stay and fight for our lands,
our language, and our culture?

Or should we leave our ancestral lands,
where we have lived for countless generations?
Regardless,
we surrender to the All That Is
and find our journey into the Oneness.

22

HAL IS ON HIS WAY

Hal is racing up the highway, the same highway that Tom had taken several days before. This day has less rain but low-hanging mists blot out some of the road and scenery. Hal feels like his must dodge several of those low clouds. They appear to him almost like faces.

Hal remembers that Tom had spoken of seeing the face of a Native American woman in the clouds.

"Right," Tom insisted, "she was beautiful. For some reason I believe I've seen her before. She looks so familiar, but I couldn't have. It was just weird, that's all. It seems like she's the one in my dreams. Then her face faded when I said that it couldn't be happening. I just feel off kilter, I guess."

Hal responded, "Tom, I'm glad you are heading for your cabin. You really do need a rest. By rest, I mean not just from work, but rest from the woman who haunts you in your dreams. Take it easy, ole buddy. I'll take care of things here at the office while you a gone."

He continues to call Tom. Tom is not picking up the phone. This frustrates Hal as he fears for his friend, Tom. It could be nothing, but then again it could be something.

"Pick up," Hal insists but to no avail, "pick up. Please pick up."

Hal calls his wife to let her know he is on the road to Tom's cabin. "Hi, hon," Hal begins, "just wanted to let you know I might not make it home tonight. I was on the phone with Tom earlier today when he saw someone outside on his back patio. I don't know if it was a prowler or just what it was. The thing is he's not picking up. I'm worried and need to check on my friend. I couldn't live with myself if something had happened to Tom and I had done nothing about it.

"Yeah," Hal continues, "I know. We can do that another night. Right now I have to find out what's happened to Tom. I love you."

Hal wants to speed faster up the highway, but the clouds interfere with his visibility and force him to slow down.

"Ole, buddy," Hal talks to himself, I know something is going on with you. I just hope I get there in time.

23

HOMECOMING

"They're here! They're here!" several children exclaimed as the travelers approached their village near the Great Serpent . . . their home. Many villagers stopped their work and walked into the open area of their village to welcome the pilgrims' return.

Morning Star took the dogs back to where they belonged after dropping off the travois with the three-dimensional model of the Great Serpent at Singing Hawk's house. Running Bear helped get Red Fox squared away and re-united with his family then drifted out of sight, returning to his home.

Red Fox slept for days. It was as much out of exhaustion as it was part of his internal processing from his initiation. His mother made sure she had food available for when he woke up. He would eat dreamily, and then go back to bed.

In the meantime, many villagers were deeply engaged in preparing for the Summer Solstice Ceremony coming up very soon. It was actually only a few days away. Red Fox's parents didn't know what to think. They didn't want him to miss it since he had spent nearly four months of his life dedicated to its celebration and garnering support for it in many villages miles and miles away.

"He has spent his time away working to help everyone remember to remember. I just would not want him to miss the actual ceremony," Red Fox heard his father comment.

"Who? . . . who's going to miss the ceremony?" asked Red Fox scratching his head and squinting his eyes as he slowly emerged from a deep slumber.

"Oh, my son," exclaimed his mother breathlessly as she jumped up to reach for him in a hug.

Just then Floating Lily suddenly appeared at their home with an announcement. "White Eagle is waiting for you," she stated calmly as she looked Red Fox up and down.

Then she said, "Why don't you clean up before you go to see her. I'll let her know you will be there shortly." As usual, before anyone could reply, the tall red-haired beauty had vanished. It was difficult for them to view her as a child, because she was so tall and sophisticated in her demeanor, yet too young to be considered a young woman.

"White Eagle probably wants to see you to tell you how grateful she is that you completed the assignment . . . and for you to give an evaluation. After all, this was a big project for her and the Elders," said Red Fox's father, Whispering Rock.

"I think I need to eat something before I go," said Red Fox. Laughing Willow, his mother, poured some tea and set out a bowl of stew, with some nut bread on the side. After he ate, he changed his clothes.

Smiling, he put on the ceremonial outfit he had received at Seip. He had not worn it to every presentation he gave, but wore it to many. He especially enjoyed wearing the neckpiece of a red fox. His family gasped in admiration when they saw him.

"Where did you get that outfit?" asked his mother.

"The artisans of Seip made it for me, and even made this mica and copper necklace," said Red Fox. "I think it's appropriate that I wear it to see White Eagle."

In the warm days, few people stayed indoors much. White Eagle was not an exception. The gentle breezes brushed her cheek as she sat outside her home on the hill in the warming sunshine. The surrounding trees bent and swayed in tune with some music inaudible to the human ear. Floral scents wafted across the hilltop carried by songs of various birds each offering its gift of beauty to the landscape. She had set four chairs arranged in a circle just outside her dwelling.

I knew Red Fox had returned home. Shining Bird and I could hardly wait to see him privately to hear all about his adventures. We were both at Singing Hawk's house studying a birch bark scroll. Then Floating Lily waltzed in.

"I thought I'd find you here," she says. We both look up from our work bench. Singing Hawk had been in her back room. When she hears Floating Lily, Singing Hawk moves into the larger room where we were to hear the rest of the conversation.

The shaman and the messenger exchange nods in silent greeting.

"White Eagle is expecting you," Floating Lily announces to Shining Bird and me. Instead of suddenly disappearing as was her usual style, she stands facing Singing Hawk in reverent stillness. Something passes between them. I'm anxious to see why White Eagle wants to see both Shining Bird and myself.

By the time Red Fox arrives, Shining Bird and I have made ourselves as comfortable as we could, still not knowing exactly what this meeting was about. Red Fox smiles when he sees us as he comes up the hill. We both stand up in greeting. Both of us feel a little awkward seeing Red Fox after such a long absence. We just want to run to him and give big hugs, sit down on the ground and listen to stories. Since this is more of a formal occasion, we simply stand to honor him as he approaches. White Eagle remains seated.

"Greetings Grandmother," Red Fox says with a smile. Graciously he steps close to her and bends down to give her a kiss on her cheek. With that kiss, she reaches for him with both hands. He reaches back and they connect, both with their hands and their souls.

Immediately I notice something different about him. It wasn't just his clothes and neckpiece. The energy field around him feels calm and intriguing. It speaks to my heart.

I look over to Shining Bird to see what her reaction is. She is actively still, with eyes dilated working to pull in as much information as possible through her eyes, and indeed, all her senses. Her jaw drops open in amazement as she continues to look at Red Fox. It is like she was absorbing every sensation possible, both physically and spiritually, from the moment.

Dressed in his presentation best, Red Fox smiles at us glowing with buoyancy and confidence. This is not the same Red Fox who had left our village on a quest to share a remember to remember story. This is not the same Red Fox whose ego capitulated him into a humility. That humility led him to learn some Ancient Knowledge and to build the model of the Great Serpent. This was someone else. This was someone matured beyond his years. By now he is sixteen years old, and carries himself as an Elder of some maturity and stature. It makes me question that I even knew my childhood friend at all.

"Dearest Red Fox," White Eagle begins after a long silence prevailed over the four of us, like a blanket of ascetic reverence. "Dearest Red Fox, what have you to say to us?"

Without blinking, without even thinking, Red Fox replies, "Death, surrender, resurrection."

White Eagle looks down in contemplation for some time before looking up. Then she asks, "I understand that you began initiation. So, what have you experienced? What have you to say to us?"

Red Fox blinks a long blink, looks at each of us straight in the eye, and inhales a deep breath before speaking, "I was on a road. It was a path that led up to the celestial realms."

I swallow hard. I hold my breath. I can hardly believe what I was hearing. My childhood friend continues.

THE CAMP OF GOD'S TEARS

"At first I felt confused, not knowing where I was. I knew my body was in a sealed underground chamber that was pitch black. Even so, I could see there was a celestial light all around. I began to feel afraid, not really knowing what might happen or what might be my next step.

"Then suddenly a demon jumped in front of me. He was ugly and fierce with fiery eyes. I felt his intent to kill me. He wielded a knife in his left hand and a sword in his right. He was covered in heavy armor of some sort, with a helmet of many horns and sparkling jewels. When he opened his long snout to roar at me, toxic fluids dripped from his dagger-like teeth. I did not know where I was, nor did I know where to go to escape, except I only knew I was on a path that led to somewhere I did not know.

"I felt extreme fear at being confronted by such a demon. I had never imagined such ugliness or mal-intent could exist in the world I knew."

Shining Bird shifts her weight and leans forward. Evidently she wants to extract every detail of this experience by getting closer to the storyteller.

I sit hypnotized by the story I'm hearing. I couldn't move and feel rooted in my seat.

Red Fox continues, "He challenged me by swinging his weapons in my face, scowling in contempt for me. He would not let me pass. I realized I was going nowhere until I faced this demon. When that realization occurred to me, I suddenly saw that this demon came from within me . . . He was me . . . or at least part of me. He was my ego . . . my ego run amok."

Shining Bird sits partially back, shifting weight again as she processes this part of the story.

I remain in partial shock and in partial desire to know the rest of the story.

White Eagle sits unperturbed, yet wrapped in the listening.

Red Fox continues, "I did not know how to fight this demon. He had weapons. I did not. He appeared powerful. I felt unequipped to face this force that prevented me from moving forward. I thought about ways to fight. I thought about strategies to overcome this obstacle to my progress. Nothing seemed doable. Nothing appeared viable to me as I searched my knowledge base, as I searched my mind. My mind came up with nothing. My mind came up with no options, no ways of dealing with such a formidable challenge. I felt beside myself, in a quandary as to what to do."

At that moment, I hear Shining Bird suck in her breath.

He continues, "This demon threatened my extinction. My death appeared eminent as he raised his weapons in attack."

At this comment, Red Fox shows emotion. His face screws up for a second or two, and then tears well up and spill down his face. He speaks like he is re-experiencing the event with all the emotion inherent in that moment relived.

"With my death upon me, I surrendered to Great Spirit.

"At that moment, a light opened within me, and I saw the two triangles of the Great Serpent prophecy coming together. Then I remembered what Gray Wolf had said to you about the triangles when we spoke about the Prophecy of the Serpent before I left on my journey. Within this light I saw these two triangles joining as shown in your necklace, and I knew what it meant. The star in your necklace represents a gateway to the resources of the unseen."

Shining Bird releases her breath with a sound that accompanied a wash of tears streaming down her face.

I remain in partial shock and partial fascination.

White Eagle shows stoicism on her face, anticipation in her eyes.

Red Fox exhales then says, "With the surrender of my death, I felt extreme love come upon me. As the demon attempted to hack and swing at my body in bloody panic, like it was fighting for *its* life, I felt love encompass me. I felt a divine love embrace me. It was that moment that I reached out to my attacker with love. I totally embraced it with unconditional love, that love that had overcome me in my moment of surrender to Spirit, that same love came *from* me in such a way as to allow me to overcome my demon . . . and in that moment, the demon evaporated."

At hearing that, I suddenly sit forward wanting to extract every meaning, of every meaning possible, to comprehend at every level possible, the meaning of that event.

Shining Bird sits back, much more relaxed, breathing more normally.

White Eagle tilts her head back and smiles, content to rest on the back of her chair.

"In those moments," Red Fox says, "I experienced my death and then my surrender. I comprehended my death. I comprehended my surrender. What I did not yet comprehend was my resurrection. Just as I witnessed the disappearance of my demon-attacker, I was lifted up into a light of indescribable intensity. This light healed my sense of distress and torment of inadequacies. I felt whole and healed and resurrected.

"Any sense of separation I might have felt earlier disappeared in the audience of such divine love I was experiencing. It was then I realized at every level what oneness with the One actually *meant*, and the joy of what it *felt* like, and how important it is to keep that message pouring out in every activity and in every behavior I exhibit."

"You have mentioned 'surrender' several times. What does that really mean, Red Fox?" asks Shining Bird.

"Well, 'surrender' has many levels and meanings depending on the circumstances you encounter if you are in the presence of the moment. As I just mentioned, for me facing the demon, provided me with a new way of seeing my situation rather than surrendering to an overwhelming sense of fear. I realized that while this fear was ego driven, there was much, much more involved. A while back I said 'I searched my mind', 'I thought' and 'my mind came up with no options.' My mind was running wild, fearing death, fearing failure. What would happen if I failed the initiation and cried out to be released from the chamber? What would my parents, my friends say? Would I have to return home and abandon my journey of a lifetime in failure? In my mind, I saw no options but to surrender as a victim to the demon.

"It was then that the words of my Grandmother Blue Lightning and Walking Eagle pierced the darkness . . . 'Look to your heart, Red Fox . . . your spirit energy.'

"I realized that it was my mind, driven by fear and driven by ego that I must transcend. There *was* something I could do. The wisdom of their words allowed me to accept the 'is' of the moment, unconditionally, without judgment and negative emotions. I had to allow the death of the energy of my ego-mind-self and embrace my Spiritual energy. For you see, I learned when you have experienced and surrendered to this 'death' and realize there is nothing to fear, only the ego dies." Red Fox sighs a deep sigh and looks at each of us and then went on with his story.

"After this experience, I knew several things," Red Fox says with nods at each of us in the circle.

"I learned that the 'death' I experienced is a release. Death can actually be experienced as a release from obstacles or other attachments. Release from addictions or problems appearing as obstacles to our personal progress, or any issues that might hold us back in this life can be experienced as a kind of death. Then when we surrender to it, we accept what is. And . . . that leaves us 'free' to choose another way. A surrendering to what is, then, means a gain of freedom to choose a new way of doing, or seeing, or expressing ourselves differently, or a new way of living. Resurrection occurs as we actualize or become new in our sense of ourselves and how we relate to everyone else and the rest of the world."

"What more can you tell us, Red Fox?" questions White Eagle.

Sitting back, relaxing a bit, Red Fox purses his lips, thinking about what to say in reply. After a few moments of feeling his thoughts wanting physical expression in audible sound, he says, "Our physical, material world is not reality. It is merely an expression of a thought vibration we experience at a particular level of our consciousness."

Shining Bird sits halfway forward and challenges, "What does that mean . . . exactly?"

Red Fox pauses then replies, "Simply speaking, we experience our lives assuming our material world is all there is . . . Well, I'm here to say, it is not. It is nothing more than a physical experience we get to participate in. It is one we get to create, and to address any or all of our personal issues we see as challenges to feeling complete . . .

". . . and that is not all there is. More life exists beyond in the Beyond.

"In truth, we are not separate from Spirit.

"We are complete in the Great Oneness that is our Creator.

"It's just that while we are experiencing this physical experience, we sometimes feel separate. Sometimes, what we experience is not love, not forgiveness, not acceptance of who we think we are. Sometimes we can feel attacked or abused, criticized, undermined. That doesn't have to be a problem as long as we choose to allow that part of us to die and to surrender to the Absolute divine love that is our Source. When we do that, we are resurrected within ourselves, and then we heal our sense of separation and sense of feeling inadequate. I think this is what feeling 'reborn' must feel like.

"I learned so much about our People as I traveled. I learned that we have ceremonies of renewal over and over. I learned that many of us go into the waters to wash away our sense of separation or our sense of inadequacies, and to experience the feeling of renewing ourselves in Spirit."

Shining Bird interrupts Red Fox at this point, leans forward and asks, "So, why do we have to repeat our renewal ceremonies over and over?"

Red Fox swallows, turns his face toward her and says, "Between the time of each ceremony, we can change in many ways. Sometimes, we shift toward balance in our consciousness. Or, sometimes our awareness might become clouded with ego. These changes occur as a result of what we experience, the things that we do, the thoughts we have, the choices we make, the people we meet, the intentions we set, the emotions we feel, the challenges we encounter. All of these factors and how we have perceived, reacted to and engaged them requires us to renew our attunement and our connections to Spirit."

White Eagle furrows her eyebrows and asks, "So what can you tell us that is specific to you, Red Fox?"

Pursing his lips as he thinks about the question Red Fox says, "Well, I felt that I was justified in using my ego to help me make choices. I felt my ego was a vested part of me that I could use to rule my actions, uh . . . my behavioral choices, so to speak.

"What I got to comprehend is that the death of the ego, or the selfish-self, is a negative self that must 'die' to allow for spiritual transformation to take place. I realized that the selfish entity, often seen as the ego, would fight by any means possible to survive. We allow it to have power over us until we raise our consciousness to an awakened state. This causes the selfish ego-self entity to 'die' or, as I now prefer to say, to integrate with our heart energy. Then that allows enlightenment to take place.

"Letting go of the concept of the physical life as the 'true reality,' which it is not, is part of the transformation process. This is something the selfish ego-self entity refuses to let go of. It is tied to the idea that materiality is reality. It is afraid that if it lets go of its self-centered attachment to itself and to what appears to be real, it will no longer exist. As a result, it resists the concept of the 'letting go' process. It fights to the death, either its death or the death of our awareness of who we really are . . . and it is up to each of us to choose."

White Eagle raises one eyebrow and stares at Red Fox like she was seeing through him. A few moments of silence pass.

Finally, White Eagle asks, "What more is there that you can share with us, Red Fox."

Red Fox says, "Who we really are is an extension of Spirit, divine in origin and totally complete without faults or frailties. True Reality exists, but not in the physical . . . Perfection exists. In the experience of a physical life, we often do not see the perfection of the ongoing process of life's expressions. We only see the perfection if we *choose* to see it.

"On one of my journeys during initiation, I was shown other civilizations. I saw that not all cultures see the world the way The People see the world, so they experience life differently. So many people are treated by their rulers in such a way as to emphasize their unworthiness. Many others live their lives as if they were unworthy to experience happiness, or unworthy to handle spiritual truth. Often they accept the lie about themselves that they are unworthy . . . and believe that *untruth*. Since they are seen as 'unworthy' they are not offered opportunity to know the One or to experience the oneness of the One, or they do not allow themselves the opportunity.

"After realizing this, I knew that one significant reason *our culture* has thrived for so long in peace and harmony the way it has, is because we share with everyone the awareness, the knowledge that we are one with the One. No one is excluded from this. That's why so many of our People go through the initiation process. It's like sharing the wealth, so to speak, the 'wealth' is being in conscious awareness of who we really are. We share this sense of wealth openly and unselfishly. Sharing it does not impoverish us. Neither does withholding it enrich us. It is our inheritance, our birthright, so to speak. We see it as a birthright of everyone who breathes air."

Shining Bird finally relaxes back into her chair like it was made of soft cushions. She breathes easily as she listens, with a half-smile on her face. White Eagle nods from time to time as she listens to Red Fox. I am wild with internal excitement as I listen to these truths speak to my soul. I remain unruffled on the outside however.

After another pause, Red Fox blinks then goes on, "As I witnessed other civilizations on my journey, I saw different shaman, or priests, cry out for the need to sacrifice to get answers, or to appease the gods to whom they prayed. Typically they ceremoniously killed animals I didn't recognize, and sometimes killed humans for this same purpose, saying that blood sacrifice was required.

"What I comprehended was that any sacrifice, whether it was a human being, an animal, or just a part of our lives, was unnecessary to our healing or renewing or resurrecting. I saw that these kinds of physical sacrifices of the seen world were based on an illusion that such actions would, in fact, be effective.

"In actuality such ceremonies of sacrifice were, in fact, a very clever defense mechanism of the ego. That mechanism actually strengthens the belief that we are all separate from each other and from the One. That false belief deludes an individual into thinking he or she has transformed because of the physical sacrifice ceremony, when in fact that most likely is not the case.

"Truly integrating our ego into balance in our entire being renews us, brings us new life, and resurrects us into transformation.

"Each of the shaman or priests directing such sacrifices were themselves figureheads for an official, external, physically manifested ego. As such, they would not direct the giving up of our egos inside of us. They, themselves, designed to control our thoughts and intentions by physically demonstrating . . . uh . . . causing another to die physically in place of letting go of our internal ego. They re-directed attention to the external, physical life, requiring blood or a death, so that the sacrificial death could represent, *as a substitute* for allowing the selfish ego-self entity to 'die' and, as I said before, to integrate with our heart energy.

"From my vantage point in the ethers, I came to know that everything in life is sacred. It is sacred, because it is part of our experience from which we create learning opportunities. Sometimes they might be called failures or mistakes to be worked through, so I call them opportunities. These learning opportunities are about us as individuals progressing toward our connecting with Spirit, and even more, progressing toward our conscious connection as seeing and feeling who we really are as part of Spirit, or the One. Life is continuous and uninterrupted, regardless of any dying or killing that transpires.

"I came to see that blood sacrifice is a corruption of the true concept of 'dying' and surrender and resurrection. Dying in the physical experience is about translating into spirit. That is not death but translation into a higher frequency. So the concept of asking or forcing some person or animal to die to serve the larger needs of the population is not sacrifice. Sacrifice means to make sacred. If all of life is sacred, as it is endowed by our Creator . . . *everything* in life is sacred. Nothing we do, or can do, can make life more sacred than what it already is. So the corruption of some cultures that promote sacrifice in any form is really about power *over* others by cleverly feeding *their* egos. It certainly is not about resurrection, or transformation, or enlightenment. Rather, it is about perpetuating anger, despair, frustration and separation to feed the larger ego mind of their culture."

"Okay," questions White Eagle, "so what?"

"So what?" Red Fox asks quizzically.

"Yes, that's just what I asked. *So what?*" is White Eagle's response. "So what? So what does all of this mean to you?"

Looking down, Red Fox does not find the answers in the dirt. When he looks up, though, a light shines from his face.

He smiles and then says, "Okay, here it is," he pauses with a nod of confidence. His eyes focus on something we didn't see, "I realize that the ego is part of the mind. Our minds are wonderful. They can be used to invent, to solve puzzles, to analyze information. When working math problems, I use my mind to follow the logical sequence to arrive at solutions. I love it. When I use my mind in this way, I feel grand when I solve the problem or extrapolate the sequences into the next layer of implications. I feel successful.

"Then, because I feel successful," Red Fox pauses briefly to shift his eyes at each of us before continuing, "my ego steps out from my mind and stakes a claim on my success. If I don't shake the ego down, and put it back into the balance with myself or integrate it, it often puffs itself up, taking credit for the achievement, and begins to dictate orders or otherwise influence my behaviors. When this happens, this separation expands into a sense of separation from my inner self," Red Fox grimaces. With a half turn of his head he goes on, "separation . . . sometimes from others, and definitely from my connection to the One."

At this statement, White Eagle raises her eyebrows opening her eyes wide. She says nothing wanting to hear the rest of the story.

"Yes," affirms Red Fox. ". . . and this can occur even if I am not successful at something. It can occur when I did not achieve something. My ego can emerge in my defense of not succeeding at something, give excuses and laying blame on something or someone else outside of me .

. . really avoiding all responsibility . . . It all stems from not being in balance within myself."

I breathe in deeply, sit back and look over at Shining Bird. She is wrapped in full attention to what Red Fox is saying, sitting forward. I squirm in my hard chair. She floats in hers. She doesn't look at me, just floats there focused on something I don't see. Red Fox carries on without effort.

"The thing is . . . it's about staying in balance, staying integrated. That's what our renewal ceremonies are about . . . our sense of balance within. It's about feeling the oneness between our mind, our body, and our heart . . . and feeling the sense of oneness with the rest of the universe, the sun, the moon, Mother Earth . . . with All That Is.

"When the ego jumps out and influences our minds, then our bodies follow its orders. We physically behave or act out what is going on in our minds, influenced by our egos. That's why overuse or abuse of ego can be fatal. Eventually, if we don't keep it in check or balance, we start behaving in ways that are destructive to us and to our relationships.

"Fatality means death. This death can mean death of relationships or death of our sense of who we truly are."

I exhale. White Eagle breathes in deeply, exhales slowly and smiles and does not interrupt.

Red Fox says, "What I learned about the heart energy is critical, here."

At this remark, White Eagle raises one eyebrow and keeps her lips tightly closed, listening intently.

"Our hearts are our connection to the divine. Our hearts connect us to Great Spirit. It is through our hearts that we can know what is real and what is not. It is our heart that serves us as whole beings. Yes, our minds serve us as a physical tool would serve us. We use tools to make things. We use our minds to do the same. As long as our egos remain in balance with the heart, and mind, it can serve also.

"However, if the ego mind jumps out and conflicts with our hearts, then it no longer serves us. By allowing the ego to do this, we actually hinder ourselves in our progression along our life's path, journeying home to our Source.

"When we are able to listen to our hearts, we find our way home, so to speak. In an imagined, metaphoric sense, our lives represent a journey through experiences, from our birth to our death. Since we came from Spirit, since Spirit is our Creator, we return to Spirit, to our Source . . . *home* . . . resurrection . . . and that is best and most successfully accomplished by tapping our heart for direction and surrendering to our heart . . . and I mean, allowing our hearts to guide us.

"It is through our hearts that we are connected to Spirit. It is through our hearts that our Creator speaks to us . . . and . . ." Red Fox smiles as he speaks, ". . . and . . . it is through our hearts that Spirit breathes."

Stunned silence.

Red Fox then finishes with another smile, "death . . . surrender . . . resurrection." At this last statement, Red Fox finally leans back in his chair and breathes with a satisfied look on his face.

"As above, so below," White Eagle says.

"As above, so below," White Eagle repeats, her necklace reflecting sunlight, telegraphing its essence back to its source.

". . . Ah, yes," she adds, "It is upon this that the foundation of our civilization rests. I am saluting the three of you. I see this trio as capable of stewardship as we move forward in time. Red Fox, you have demonstrated yourself to be a true shaman." She gives a single nod of her head as she speaks.

Then she turns to Shining Bird and myself, looking through us as much as at us.

". . . and the two of you will stand in support of Red Fox. I don't know more than this. This trio is a significant combination of energies that will serve The People well."

We remain silent, stunned by this pronounce-ment. Nothing other than our immediate plans exist for us. In one sense we are all driven by our youthful desires, and at the same time, maturing in our sense of things, where we think we are in time, and our connectedness to each other. At that moment, nothing else matters to us. We have no sense of the future.

Little did we know how prophetic her words were.

White Eagle interrupts our individual contemplations as she says, "Now, the day after tomorrow is the Solstice Sunrise and Sunset Ceremonies. I expect each of you will want to join in. The costumes are all completed, and the dancers and musicians are ready. They have tomorrow off from rehearsal. I expect each of you to prepare in your own way. Now be off with you."

As we stand to walk away, I notice Shining Bird looking at Red Fox with wide-eyed admiration. I nod to him in a silent salute, putting my hand on his shoulder, giving a few pats in physical expression of my admiration. The three of us, each in our own way, are moving forward in developing our conscious connections to The One.

As we left the hill at White Eagle's, we feel so connected to each other that we find ourselves wandering over to the hill near the water where our conversation had taken place only months before. It was the conversation between Shining Bird and Red Fox that catapulted Red Fox onto his internal journey.

"It seems like it's been years since we were here last," says Red Fox. "So much has happened, so much has changed."

"Red Fox," Shining Bird says, "It is *you* who has changed. You have matured beyond recognition. You've grown in stature and it shows. You think the world has changed, when it's *you* who has changed," she adds laughingly.

We sit down. Just as we are getting comfortable, Shining Bird leans forward toward Red Fox and asks softly with her head tilted downward slightly and a wrinkled nose, "So what was it really like?"

"I had to quiet my mind," Red Fox says then pauses and looks at both of us. "I had to stop thinking and relax from the incessant noise of my ego telling me to fear, telling me that I had something to fear, and giving me a false sense of myself and that I would be destroyed if I went through with this. This false sense of self, created by my ego, told me I would suffer and created in me a false sense of separation and fragmentation. It was all just noise.

"As I continued to breathe through this as Walking Eagle, the Elder at Newark, instructed me, I began to observe my ego in operation from the position of a detached observer and *without judgment*. I observed how it distorted events that I had experienced in the past during incidents when I allowed my ego to rule my thoughts. It also distorted my thoughts about the future."

Shining Bird cocks her head to one side and knits her brows and does not interrupt him. He notes her look of confusion and offers an example.

"For example, what if I failed my initiation? That was a future event being clouded by fear. From my position of observer I could see that and look past it.

"It was then, as I continued breathing, that I began to feel I was entering a realm of stillness . . . my inner being . . . the I Am of Being. Through my breath I could feel my vibrational frequency rise. I became more alert and fully present in the consciousness and acceptance of the Now. I realized that the present moment was all I truly had." Red Fox pauses as the emotion of the memory of his experience courses through his body.

"But, Red Fox, you do have a past, a brief one, because you are so young, and because you are so young, you do have a future," Shining Bird says as she gently places her arm on him. "And, you are right. The present moment *is* all we really have."

Red Fox sits silent for a moment and then says, "I know. I think of it this way, the past and the future was where I mainly focused. Only briefly, did I focus on the present moment.

"I've since learned to focus on the Now. I've learned that when necessary I can use my mind as an effectual tool to deal with the practical aspects of my daily existence and to make future plans. In so doing, I briefly consider my past, my lessons learned and my future only to the extent required to make plans and set intentions for accomplishing my goals. I can use my mind to plan those things that I want to achieve or to accomplish, especially the desires of my heart. In this way I strive to maintain a balance between the energy of my mind and my heart energy as I walk a new path in this lifetime."

"Red Fox," I say, "sometimes our present moment might not be very pleasant and may be filled with pain, anguish or unhappiness. Sometimes we create these situations and sometimes we allow ourselves to get caught up in those events. We have all experienced such things."

"Yes, I know, Gray Wolf," Red Fox says as he nods in acknowledgement looking down. Raising his eyes to meet ours, he says, "Yet, it is how we *choose* to respond to such matters that determines how our mind interprets such events and feelings, especially when we come from a position of judgment as we look at the data. When I stomped outside Singing Hawk's house, which seems like so long ago now," Red Fox rolls in eyes back and around while titling his head back, "I allowed my ego to sit in judgment of the event. This generated emotions of pain and unhappiness. I resisted the present moment rather than accepting it for what it was in reality - *a mere event*.

"Sometimes we may not be able to immediately resolve the situation. I've learned, if I perceive myself as a victim or to react with force, anger or act out of fear, I create a downward spiraling sequence of negative energy to dominate that moment. If I let this become a habit, it would dominate my life. This throws me out of balance and continues the regeneration of victim energy, and down the spiral I go. I learned to allow the victim energy to die a noble death as having served to provide an alternative point of view from which to learn in the larger scheme of things.

"When such things occur, they must be faced head on and not with resistance. Resisting will ultimately fail and bring even more pain and really postpone the inevitable need to face it. I've learned it is better, rather, to come from the viewpoint of acceptance, surrendering, really, and be fully conscious in the moment.

"I am learning to feel the energy of the event as more of an observer and less as a judgmental participant.

"I've seen how this ego energy attempts to gain power from similar past experiences, fear for the present and fear for the future. When we allow the ego to get out of balance, it quickly gets out of control. I've observed the desire of my ego mind to strike out.

"How we perceive and deal with the challenges that life presents is the best gauge of our level of awareness . . . our level of consciousness.

"To be fully conscious, to be fully aware means being able to observe the emotion, to feel the emotion, to acknowledge and accept it and yet not to be taken over by it. It is important to realize, I believe, that we can change our emotions, what we are feeling from the event, by *changing our perceptions* of what we are experiencing."

Shining Bird nods at this comment in acknowledgment with a smile and says, "Right, changing our perspective and then our perception of an event provides us the opportunity to change our emotions we experience from that event."

The summer breeze picks up a bit, not too much, just a little. It lifts strands of Shining Bird's hair as she sits with her face toward the sunshine. Just then she turns and smiles at me. I melt . . . yet there was a thought I wanted to pursue. "Red Fox, you said something that I felt was interesting," I say, "I mean, everything you said was intriguing. There's something I'd like to understand more about . . ."

"What's that?" Red Fox replies.

"What did you say about 'love'" I ask.

Red Fox nodded his head once or twice before speaking.

"Ah, yes. We don't talk about love much. That feeling of being loved and accepted was not a new one for me . . . it's just I hadn't realized it is the power that joins everything in the universe together."

Shining Bird puts her hand out tapping Red Fox's arm and asks, "What do you mean?"

"I had a similar question during my initiation process. I questioned love also. So I was shown a review of life here, of how we live. By 'we' I mean The People. Our lifestyle, the way we consistently treat each other, in fact, our entire culture, pretty much lives in love. It's just what we do and how we are."

I interrupt, "Wait a minute. That really doesn't explain love."

"I know," Red Fox says. "Love is best felt when it is acted out in the way we live our lives and in the way we do things. So, the question becomes, how do we know love? How do we know we live in love? Is that what you mean?"

Both I and Shining Bird nod affirmatively.

He goes on, "I had the same questions. I then found myself visiting a stream with large bushes of wild roses. The blooms of the wild roses covered the bank of the stream. Clouds of their scent filled the air around me, swirled around me, and filled my lungs as I stood there breathing it in . . . and smiling, taking it for granted, not fully knowing it for what it was.

"Then I found myself at the edge of an old dump site where we would put our refuse, spoiled food and stuff. Usually it would be closed up, but this one was an opened pit, smelling of rotting something. It smelled so bad and so foul that I had to back away.

"Then in the next moment, I found myself back at the stream smelling the wild roses again. I realized that The People live in love all time, which is why we don't realize it consciously. It's like if you smell roses all the time, every day, day in and day out, how do you know you are smelling the scent of roses? In other words, how do you know you are living in love?"

Both Shining Bird and I look at each other with our faces showing question marks. As we turn back to look at Red Fox, he says, "Right! You don't. It was only after I smelled the foulness of refuse pit that I appreciated the scent of the roses. Only by experiencing the contrast, the not-roses, could I recognize and appreciate the beautiful scent of the rose. In that way, I could know the fragrance of roses, roses all around me . . . which is what it feels like to be in the divine presence of the One.

"Now, imagine that the scent of the rose is love experienced . . . and the odor of the refuse pit is something ugly, something so unlike love that we back away from its stench . . . now imagine that experience is not-love. By experiencing both do we bring into our awareness that love exists. That, then, makes it possible for us to actively choose the one we like, or the one that brings us joy . . . This is why we get to experience a physical experience . . . as individual- izations of Spirit, so we can *know* love, and wholeness and joy, consciously in this physical experience . . . In other words, we get to act it out in physical behaviors . . . or behave in a loving way as a physical expression of love . . . or as Spirit expressed physically," Red Fox stops and looks up at the clouds for a while.

Then he says, "The People typically live in this love frequency, collectively. Our lives are joyous for the most part, joy is love expressed . . . and for the most part we have chosen this frequency by how we behave toward each other, how we think and speak.

"Our collective frequency, the energy field we create and live in, is one that hums in a symphony at a comparatively high frequency on a scale of humanity. So did the other worlds when they first began. What happened to the three prior worlds is they let those higher frequencies degenerate and spiral down to a lower pitch until their worlds ended."

"How did they do that?" I ask, "I mean, how could that happen?"

Red Fox says, "If we are not conscious of our thoughts, intentions, and how we speak and act towards each other, *ourselves* even, and all other life forms, like Mother Earth, the quality of life can easily slip away from us.

"Harboring negative thoughts and feelings is part of the deterioration that can happen, because they have a mass. That mass is physical which can inflict physical damage as well as spiritual damage. When we hold on to feelings, thoughts, and intentions that do not serve us or humanity, they become expressed physically, which in turn spirals the frequency of the harmonic lower, and lower, and lower, until . . . well, no more world. The collateral damage speaks for itself . . . which is why we have had three prior worlds.

"That's why our ceremonies are so important to us. They help us renew our sense of who we are, both individually as well as collectively. They help us remember to remember that . . . that . . . that we are Spirit operating as an individualized spirit. We are Great Spirit expressed within a frequency or collection of frequencies that is physical in *perception*. That's the best explanation I can give right now."

The three of us just sit there for very long moments. I could see Shining Bird process her thoughts about what she had just heard.

She asks, "Red Fox, then what about . . . ?"

Interrupting her, he stands up and remarks, "That's all I'm up for today. I'm so glad to see you. I don't want to leave you now, but I've got to go. We can talk another time." Smiling, he turns and walks back down that same hill he had walked down months ago.

24

THE DAY OF THE SUMMER SOLSTICE

The next day was a quiet one as nearly everyone spent the day either in meditation or working on last minute preparations. I rarely saw my mother that day as she focused on directing food preparations for feeding the community before, during and after the ceremony.

Shining Bird and I spent the day reuniting with Water Dog and Bluebird Near the Lily. Because Water Dog had been spending so much time up at Flint Ridge working with Rising Wolf, we were glad to see him especially after a long absence.

In the pre-dawn hours on that summer's day of the Solstice sunrise, we join with many of our beloved friends. Most of the Grandmothers and many other participants wishing to join in assembled on top of the bluff where the Great Serpent effigy lies. We stand quietly on or near the one curve of the effigy that aligns with the Summer Solstice sunrise.

My mother stays in our village to finish overseeing the food preparations. So many visitors have come from other villages for the Summer Solstice Ceremony that mother feels compelled to ensure that plenty of food is available for all. We have several houses that we use as hospitality suites for those arriving. The rest of our visitors fill our campground that we reserve for other traveling guests, such as the traders, when they come.

I've always joined my parents and friends for the Solstice Sunrise. My father, Black Bear, and his mother, Shining Moon, routinely took me by the hand when I was little, and together we walked up the hill to honor Father Sun and Mother Earth.

Today, it is Shining Bird who takes me by the hand to walk up the hill to the ceremonial spot.

When the first rays of Father Sun reach above the horizon, a stillness blankets us as we silently thrill at the annual event. Being summer, the flocks of birds inhabiting the trees and shrubs along the streambed below the bluff send up a cacophony of songs and sounds as their regular greeting of the day.

Afterwards White Eagle and many others remain having found a comfortable spot on which to rest and converse, waiting for the next event. The next event of the day is observing the shadow of the large ceremonial pole erected in the area near the Great Serpent. The moment when the shadow completely disappears is the signal that the ceremony begins.

Few people leave the ceremonial area from sunrise through the rest of the day. I witness Floating Lily make her way back down to see what she can do to help my mother, Raven's Wing, with anything more.

Warm Stone appears drawn in two directions, one to help my mother, and the other to witness everything with wide-eyed anticipation of a ceremony eagerly awaited by many and planned down to every detail. Of all the ceremonies Warm Stone would witness, this one proved to be the most touching to the heart and the most opulent in presentation.

For the most part, nearly everyone else from the valley below gravitates up the hill as part of honoring the occasion. Shining Bird and I sit in silence as we watch the ceremonial space fill with spectators.

As the warm morning gradually spreads into a hot sunny day, I can feel the collective energy rise in anticipation. When the pole no longer displays a shadow, White Eagle rises and walks toward the pole with a small bundle hanging crossways from her left shoulder to her right hip. Nearly all the Elders in attendance sit in a circle around the pole.

White Eagle now opens the sacred bundle and removes the bowl of the ceremonial pipe with her left hand and holds it to her heart. Then with her right hand she removes the wooden stem of the pipe and points it to the East. She sprinkles a small amount of tobacco on the ground as an offering to Mother Earth and The East. She connects the stem to the bowl. As she loads a small pinch of tobacco into the pipe, she speaks a prayer of affirmation:

> *"The East is Red. The East is where the Morning Star rises, the Star of Knowledge. Red is for the Rising Sun which brings us a new day and another chance to learn. We thank Great Spirit for each day we are allowed to live upon Mother Earth under Father Sun. We pray for Knowledge, as from Knowledge comes Peace."*

White Eagle then faces the South and again gives tobacco to Mother Earth, continues to load the pipe, saying:

> *"The South is Yellow. Yellow is for the color of spring and the warm south wind. While we load this pipe, we give thanks for our strength, growth, and healing that is brought*

forth from the south wind. We use this as a time of planting so that the seeds may grow into new life."

White Eagle then turns to the West and again gives tobacco to Mother Earth, continues to load the pipe, saying:

"West is Black. West is where the Sun sets. West is where the Spirit Helpers live and black stands for the Spirit World. We will all go to the Spirit World, and we will all know one another and our deeds. We seek our spiritual wisdom in the West and give thanks for help from our Spirit Guides."

White Eagle faces North and says:

"White is for the North. The White Giant covers Mother Earth with the white blanket of snow. We stand here seeking and giving thanks for endurance and health from the North."

White Eagle then bends and touches the stem to the ground, saying:

"Green is the color of Mother Earth. We are all part of Mother Earth, each rock, every hill and mountain, all creatures, plants, trees and minerals. We are all related. We respect our Mother Earth and protect her. We give thanks to her for giving us a place to live our lives."

White Eagle holds the pipe above her head with the stem up at an angle, toward the sun:

"Father Sun, in union with Mother Earth, gives us our earthly parents. Father Sun gives us energy for our lives, for the energy to grow our food, and for the fire that heats our homes. We are thankful for Father Sun."

White Eagle holds the stem straight up:

"Great Spirit, Creator of us all, Creator of all things, Creator of the four directions, Mother Earth, and Father Sun, we offer this pipe to you."

Once the bowl is filled with tobacco and sacred herbs and with the prayer of affirmation completed, White Eagle lights the pipe, and takes a ceremonial pull on it. Then she passes it around the circle of

THE CAMP OF GOD'S TEARS

the seated Elders in the same direction as White Eagle's prayers, from East to South to West to North, returning to the East. Each Elder offers a prayer on behalf of each village represented, as each one in turn takes a pull on the pipe then lifting the pipe in the air as each prayer is spoken. This ceremony takes a few hours to complete.

By the time the pipe ceremony is completed, most of the dancers and musicians in the ceremony quietly arrive and position themselves in their respective places to begin the pageant part of the Ceremony. At some unseen cue, the villagers and visitors move into locations advantageous to watch the performance of the Story of the Great Serpent and the creation and destruction of the three prior worlds.

I notice Red Fox finds a spot near us in a front row. When he spots Shining Bird and me, he edges his way close to us.

"I can't believe how emotional I feel right now," Red Fox says to us under his breath. "I've told this story so many times now, I feel that I'm a part of it. Yesterday I visited with the dancers and saw their costumes. Now, I've been to Baum and saw the renewal ceremony there. I have to say that these costumes are every bit as exquisite as the ones I saw there. My mother, and the others who made them, did a wonderful job."

The music starts. The drums, various flutes and bells narrate the story through tones and rhythms. The dancers complete with make-up and dressed in their costumes work magic as they blend with the music and the Story.

I look over at Red Fox several times during the performance and see tears cascading down his face as he watches the enactment of each of the worlds rise and fall. Even though nearly everyone knows the Story, I can near hushed whispers from a Grandmother or Elder scattered here and there explaining the movements to someone apparently needing the details.

The grandeur of the ballet stuns the audience into a reverent silence afterwards. By the time this part of the Ceremony finishes, the day begins folding into evening. This summer's day is the longest of the year.

Food had been brought up from the village, so some folks migrate slowly in that direction. Others mill around conversing quietly.

In the meantime, several Elders have prepared a fire pit in the center of the oval within the effigy, stacking wood by size so when lit, the flames would catch and burn easily. The wood has been brought from near and far and from many different types of trees.

Several others have brought up the mica structure and placed it on the raised triangle directly in front of the oval. The mica structure is the same size and shape as the earthen triangle. Its two sides are right triangles joined at the top of their longest axis, the hypotenuse. The back panel is also formed from mica and includes clear crystals in the shape of a pyramid. Its entire design forms a prism lens to gather and split the rays of Father Sun. Copper seams and a wood frame holds the mica sheets in place much like a mosaic. Red Fox's father, being a window maker and having worked with mica for his entire life, is the keeper of this ceremonial artifact.

With the advance of Father Sun toward the western horizon, stillness settles over the tree covered creek below as the birds quiet in the long shadow below the bluff. With that stillness, the villagers and visitors mingle their way toward the Great Serpent. The hum of meditative minds prevails over the crowd sitting forward watching, with breaths held, as Father Sun gracefully aligns perfectly with the triangle, the oval and the Serpent's head.

As a parting shot while Father Sun taps the horizon, a magnificent spread of the sun's light caresses the mica structure. With that, the mica lights up like a giant lamp, spreading individual rays from its prism into the oval. The lighting of the mica lamp by Father Sun as he retires for the day triggers the Elders to light the fire in the center of the oval.

I overhear someone say to a visitor, "The light of Father Sun represents Great Spirit lighting our world. As in the rhythms of all of life, Father Sun sinks below the horizon, which is beyond our line of sight. The mica represents the Veil of Forgetfulness. So when Father Sun beams light into the mica, the light then refracts through the mica mosaic, and individual light rays from its prism spread into the world, represented by the oval. The individual rays represent each of us as individuals, or The People, all coming from the same Source."

Then I overhear another woman add, "It's up to us to maintain our respect for Mother Earth and each other, so that this, the Fourth World, is not ended. The Great Serpent can destroy the world, as represented by the oval. Should that happen," she swallows hard then continues emotionally, "three days of darkness will prevail, and Father Sun will rise in the west in perfect alignment with the Great Serpent, and the oval will return to its original circle form."

As the bonfire grows in light and intensity, everyone exhales with smiles in the confidence of life's constancy. The remainder of the night is one of total celebration. Some of the musicians begin playing for those who want to dance. Heaps of food appear for everyone. Throughout the night much merrymaking, conviviality, dancing, laughing and talking, occurs as the food and the black drink, specially formulated for this all night ceremony, sustains the partiers until dawn.

Even though many found themselves nearly exhausted from the elation of celebrating the night of flux, order re-introduces itself from the eastern horizon.

Sunset is the death of the day and season, surrender to the cycle of life that we honor. Sunrise is resurrection of a new day, new season and new cycle.

When the first beam of Father Sun gently reaches into our hearts, the beginning of a new day, a new season, and a new year reinforces the constancy of our universe.

25

AFTER THE SUMMER SOLSTICE CEREMONY

Everyone moved slowly, if at all, for several days following the Summer Solstice Ceremony, both villagers and visitors alike. Gradually, our community emptied of its guests, and our village settled down into its normal cadence of activities.

Not too long after the Solstice, Red Fox found himself invited to join with members of another village to help construct several new homes. That village was growing in population, as much from new families emerging within the population, as their growing need for guest houses to be repaired or new ones built. Red Fox fairly jumped at the opportunity to begin his life's work.

"I just stopped by to say I'll be back in a month or so. I was offered a chance to involve myself in building some houses," Red Fox says to us after a brief chat with Singing Hawk in her back room, his face glowing in anticipation. "I can hardly wait to get there," he nods to Shining Bird with a wink, "this is my calling, you know." Shining Bird nods in acknowledgement with a smile.

"We'll see you upon your return, good friend," I say as I grab his forearms with both my hands and squeeze tightly.

Red Fox's face puckers briefly. Then the glow returns as he shifts his thoughts and says, "Keep the faith, my good friends." Backing away toward the door, Red Fox stops still facing us and says with a wave of his arm, "Well, I'm off." Then he turns and leaves.

By this time Warm Stone's leg had healed nicely. He still lived at my parent's house and managed to put on some weight with full access to all of my mother's cooking. She enjoyed giving him samples of everything that wasn't already part of a meal for her immediate family, which included Warm Stone. Warm Stone and I felt like brothers, growing in attachment and fondness for one another.

After another month has passed, we had heard that Turning Rabbit was returning on his way back from Canada and the east coast territories.

Anticipation of the master trader's return filled Warm Stone with mixed emotions.

"Oh, Gray Wolf," he says one day as we walk through the hills nearby.

I am collecting healing herbs for my Grandmother Shining Moon and for use at the healing house. I am beginning to spend more time there than at Singing Hawk's house. It seems I am experiencing my calling too, in the healing arts.

"Gray Wolf," Warm Stone says again. "You know I must re-join Turning Rabbit, don't you?" He looks at me like he is expecting me to object in some way. I keep searching for just the right plants to pick keeping my head down.

After a long silence with that question hanging in the air, I stand up holding several sections of plants and finally say, "Warm Stone, you're a trader, driven to wander, to seek new peoples and new lands. I don't believe you are a *true* trader at heart. It's just that the business of a trader allows you to continuously partake in experiences of ever changing vistas." I could see he is taken aback by how profound and accurate my observation is.

I continue, "Warm Stone, I love you like a brother. The experience of loving someone incorporates letting that person follow his or her own path, without hindrances, without clinging attachments, and without expectations. That's what love includes."

I bend over sorting through several plants I am collecting while alternately looking at him and the plants and say, "I always knew that when Turning Rabbit returned, you would be more than happy to join him in his travels. There's no way I would try to hold you back or resent your leaving. In true love, I cannot do that to you or to myself. I want you to know that I've enjoyed you ever so much."

I stop picking plants, stand up straight, look him in the eye and say, "You have blessed me and our village. How could I possibly think to deprive you of any part of happiness you might feel as you journey yet ever onward?" Shaking my head I finish, "No . . . my brother, go on your journeys and take joy and my blessings with you as you go."

He just stands there in tears, so moved at hearing my expression of love for him.

When he finally pulls himself together, he says, "Thank you, Gray Wolf. I've not felt such love in my heart as I feel right now!" He chokes, wipes his eyes, and continues, "You, and your People, have saved me in so many ways. If ever I were to count anyone as my family, I would give that designation to you. You saved my life. You saved my leg. Then you saved my life again. You saved me in other ways as well by simply embracing me into your immediate family, not to mention embracing me as a member of your village. How can I thank you? I have no way of thanking you."

Reaching out to him, I place my hand on his shoulder and softly say, "Warm Stone, I don't need to be thanked. The People don't need to be thanked. Just live your life. Live in joy that you still can live, *walk* and travel and do what you do to fulfill your calling. That's *all* the thanks we need."

"But, not to sound ungracious, but . . . but . . . how will you know?" Warm Stone asks.

"My brother," I answer, "we don't need to know. Don't you understand that the fact that you came to us, and we tended you, and you healed and experienced joy . . . don't you know that's all we need to know?"

Stunned by this, he is speechless.

We return to the village in silence. By the time we get back to the village, Warm Stone touches my upper arm and we both stop walking. He looks me in the eye and says slowly, "One day, don't know when, I will repay you . . . don't know how, don't know when, but I will repay you . . . from my heart."

The next day, we hear several children shout, "They're here. They're here!"

This time when Turning Rabbit arrives, he is accompanied by only one other trader and two dogs. Taking long strides walking across the open area of our village, I go to greet him. I am glad to see him. As usual the traders stop in the middle of the village to allow the villagers to decide who would greet them and to let them know where they could stay. I am the first to reach them.

"Welcome, Turning Rabbit," I say in greeting.

Turning around to see who was speaking to him, he says, "Hello. I was sort of waiting for one of the Grandmothers to meet me." He smiles then says, "It's nice to see you, uh, uh . . ."

"Gray Wolf," I respond, realizing he might have recognized me and could not remember my name. We continue to stand there. He takes off his pack as we wait for a Grandmother to approach. After a few more moments, he unhitches the dogs from their packs. By that time, my Grandmother Shining Moon strolls over.

Upon seeing her approach, Turning Rabbit stands straight as if in a salute. She waves one arm at him to let him know he can relax. As he speaks to her, he leans slightly forward from the waist, "Grandmother, how is Warm Stone? Did he live? Can he walk? What can you tell me about him? I made sure to swing by this particular village to check in on him. How is he?"

Grandmother Shining Moon looks at him and snorts softly. Then with a single nod she put a hand on his upper arm and says, her steely blue eyes piercing his, "He's around here somewhere. Why don't you go make camp, and I'll have Floating Lily let him know you have finally arrived. He's been waiting for you."

Right on cue, Floating Lily shows up just as her name was spoken.

"C'mon," Floating Lily says to Turning Rabbit with a wave of an arm. Just as Turning Rabbit bends down to pick up a pack, several young boys rush in to help, easily lifting all the packs. As a troupe the mixed group makes their way to the campground reserved for such visitors.

After leaving the traders to make their camp, Floating Lily finds her way over to Lone Tree's to find Warm Stone. Warm Stone has been helping out the butcher and meat processor with his wood supply again.

Warm Stone has grown strong helping and participating in the daily chores around the village. Lifting and carrying heavy loads is enjoyable work for him. As soon as he spots Floating Lily, he drops part of his load of wood. Setting down the rest of the short logs, Warm Stone smiles broadly and doesn't even wait to hear what Floating Lily has to say. He simply starts running.

After a brief sprint, he stops and looks back at the young girl with his arms held out wide with a question mark on his face. At that, Floating Lily points toward the campground and smiles. He returns the smile and shifts around and begins running in the direction in which she had pointed.

"Warm Stone?" questions Turning Rabbit, seeing a tanned and robust young man running at full gallop entering the campground. "Warm Stone?" he questions again smiling, finally realizing that this healthy young buck was indeed the pale, fever-riddled, lying-at-death's door, skeletal, would-be trader he had left here many months ago.

Turning Rabbit's look of doubt stops Warm Stone before he actually reaches the master trader. At first Warm Stone feels confused as to how he is being greeted by his old mentor. Then Warm Stone blinks, inhales deeply and grins broadly. As Turning Rabbit stands frozen in disbelief, Warm Stone, still smiling, reaches for him with a hearty hug wrapping both his arms around the master trader. Only then Turning Rabbit melts and smiles.

As Warm Stone pulls back, still smiling, Turning Rabbit warms into a solid greeting clasping Warm Stone's arms.

"I can't believe it's you!" Turning Rabbit spits out finally. "They must have really worked miracles on you. That's all I can say."

"These People are really something," Warm Stone says. "I thought I was going to die, but they saved me. They not only saved my life and my leg, they saved me in other ways as well."

"I can hardly wait to hear about it," says Turning Rabbit. "First, would you help me get unpacked? . . . After all, I'm still a trader."

"Of course."

"I think you know Falling Rock," Turning Rabbit signals the other apprentice trader to move closer. "You remember Warm Stone, don't you?" You were with me when we left him here after he broke his leg."

Falling Rock nods silently, looks at Warm Stone for a brief moment, then turns and begins sorting through the packs the dogs had been carrying. As Turning Rabbit and Warm Stone unpack, Falling Rock frees the dogs and takes them for a run.

"Don't mind him, Warm Stone," says Turning Rabbit, "he's not happy being an apprentice trader without the rest of his gang."

"His gang?" questions Warm Stone with eyebrows raised

"Yeah, you remember, those ruffians who insisted on joining me on this trip."

Warm Stone pauses a few moments trying to remember.

"Oh, you remember them," Turning Rabbit insists, "they only agreed to help carry for me if I would guide them to the north. I can't imagine why they would want to leave that beautiful tropical country that is south near the western ocean. But, I guess they were out to conquer the world and needed me to take them there . . . wherever 'there' was."

"Oh, yes," Warm Stone nods. "I thought they were strange, but you meet many kinds of people on long journeys, I guess. So what happened to them?"

"They left me . . . or, I left them," says Turning Rabbit, "I don't know which . . . anyway, I'm rid of them. This one, Falling Rock, didn't like them too much either after a while. He's only with me now, so I can get him back home. I don't think he could make it on his own, having only come this way once. I'm glad to have him along, though."

"So, where did his gang go?" Warm Stone asks.

"Don't know . . . and really, don't care. I kept telling them over and over that every village or people we encountered, we were to honor their ways. We were their guests . . . and I wanted their business. Traders can only succeed at trading if they are welcomed by their customers, so to speak. We didn't see eye to eye, I figure," Turning Rabbit shrugs as he speaks. "So we parted ways. I was so relieved to not have them with me any longer. They were too much of a liability to me."

The two happily chat away in the campground until dogs come bounding back with tongues hanging out, ready to eat, and with Falling Rock following. Just about then, Floating Lily appears with a basket of offerings for the dogs.

"Thank you, Floating Lily," Turning Rabbit says as he takes the basket from her and divided up the food for the dogs. While the dogs were sumptuously gulping down their food, Floating Lily turns to the traders with an invitation.

"Shining Moon has asked that each of you join her and several others to eat in the dining house tonight," she says as more of a command than an invitation.

Turning Rabbit nods acceptance. With that, Floating Lily turns on a heel and leaves. Turning Rabbit sits in silence as he watches her exit the campground.

"Ever notice how she can just appear and then disappear just as surprisingly?" Turning Rabbit says aloud with an implied sense of admiration. "What a gal. She'd be quite a treat to have . . ."

Feeling protective towards Floating Lily like she is a younger sister, Warm Stone states as they both watch her leave, "Yeah, but she's all business, that one."

Later toward evening, the three traders saunter into the village heading for the dining house. As they cross the center of the village space, aromas bearing different seasonings drift out to reach them. They needed no enticement, since Raven's Wing is well known for the luscious dishes she offers.

Entering the dining house, Turning Rabbit looks around for Raven's Wing. He finds her setting up her food on a serving table.

"I made sure to swing by this particular village to give you these small packets of spices I picked up from my trader friends I met on the coast," Turning Rabbit softly says into her ear with great charm and a smile.

Raven's Wing stops what she is doing to stand up straight and look at Turning Rabbit with a twinkle in her eye, "More spices? These must be different from what you brought me last time. Those I believe, came from far south and near the western ocean. Where do these come from?"

"From across the eastern ocean," he says with a broad smile. "The ship that docked there was Phoenician, so I suspect that the spices came from farther east. They trade all over the world and had just come from the east."

By that time several of the Elders have entered and sit down at the long tables still engaged in their own conversations. Shining Bird and I arrive in time to hear one of the Elders ask Turning Rabbit, "So, you met up with other ocean traders when you were on the coast?"

"Yes," Turning Rabbit responds only too glad to begin telling his tales. Food is served and conviviality ensues.

"Several were long-time friends of mine I actually first met in Peru . . . ," the trader begins as everyone prepares to enjoy Turning Rabbit's stories.

Warm Stone listens enraptured by the tales of Turning Rabbit's adventures.

Some stories we had heard before, some are new. Warm Stone is unsure as to the veracity of each story, yet they lend a sense of romance, excitement, and incredible exploits that fascinate our imaginations.

Toward the end of the evening, Shining Moon finally appears standing in the doorway. Her sagacious presence permeates the room that causes everyone to quiet down, watch and wait.

"I hope all of you are enjoying the meal and the conversation," she says with a smile laced with authority. "I apologize for arriving late. I was attending to someone who required immediate attention." Entering the dining room, she floats over to where Turning Rabbit and Warm Stone are sitting. "I trust the meal met your expectations," she asks them.

Warm Stone always felt in awe of Shining Moon because of how completely she treated his ailments and how healthy he had become because of it. In his eyes, she could do no wrong. But then, again, that's how he felt about everyone in our village.

"It has come to my attention that you will be leaving us, Warm Stone," she says as she turns to him. "Is this true?"

Warm Stone first looks at me for a brief moment before looking back at her and says, "Yes, Grandmother. I am a trader and must continue my journeying. I am deeply grateful to you and your entire village for healing me, taking me in, and loving me like a family member. I will one day repay my debt to you."

"My son," Shining Moon softens her approach as she touches the back of Warm Stone's head, "there's nothing for you to repay. We are all one and part of the One. What we do for someone else, we do for ourselves." Warm Stone swallows hard, looks down and then looks back up at Shining Moon, with a tear hanging out of one corner of an eye.

She continues, "May the oneness you feel with us always remain with you. May the love you feel from us always stay in your heart. May your journeys give you joy and continuous rewards. You have become a part of The People, so know that you can come back to us at any time, so that we may embrace you again with our love for you. We wish you all the best on your journey through your life."

As she finishes, profuse tears run down both of Warm Stone's cheeks. He opens his mouth to speak, and no sounds come out. He chokes and tries again to speak and could not.

With that, my Grandmother, turns to Turning Rabbit, picks up one of his hands and commands, "Take care of him. Show him the ways to journey. Show him how to get from here to there. By doing so, you will have served The People."

And she walks out.

For the next several days, individuals passed by the trader camp to leave small gift offerings for Warm Stone. Then one morning when the sun was warming the summer's day, we realized that the traders had left early and Warm Stone with them.

Not too long after that Red Fox returns from the other villages where he had been engaged in building and repairing homes.

Water Dog and I had been roaming the hills together that afternoon.

Upon our return we see Red Fox working outside his Grandmother's home, replacing a door hinge for her. She didn't need the door closed in the summertime, so Red Fox thought he should fix it now before she needs it in the fall.

"Red Fox, you're just the man I'm looking for," Water Dog says. "It's sure good to see you again."

"Gray Wolf and Water Dog, my friends," comes the reply with a broad smile, "I can't tell you how glad I am to see you again. What's up? I'm sensing something."

Water Dog looks at me then back at Red Fox before he answers, "Red Fox, I need a house." Water Dog pauses briefly then repeats, "I need a new house built for my size person. Would you be willing to build me one?"

Red Fox first looks at me, then back at Water Dog, then back at me again.

"He and Bluebird Near the Lily will be needing their own place," I explain. "He can't move into her house, because it's too small, and she has her smaller sisters and brothers living there."

"I see," says Red Fox, putting down his tools and standing with both hands on his hips. He tosses his head back and says with a smile, "Water Dog, it would give me the greatest of pleasure to build you a house. You will be my first customer in our village!"

With a slow wave of his hand and a dreamy look in his eye, Red Fox adds, "I shall build you the most spacious house, complete with a second room at the back and a nice tall overhang outside the front door, so we won't have to think about adding to it later. Your house will be so tall as to accommodate any of your tall relatives should they come to visit. I shall double insulate the roofing with a layer of clay and bark between two woven mats over the solid frame and under the thatching.

That way Bluebird Near the Lily will always be warm even with only a small fire in the fireplace."

Water Dog just grins the biggest, broadest grin I had ever seen.

When Water Dog is finally able to speak, he stammers out a question,

"So . . . when . . . would you begin? . . . So I can tell Bluebird Near the Lily."

"My good friend," Red Fox says happily, "I've already started. I'll let you know where it should be placed after I've walked around our village a bit. Placement is very important, you know."

Water Dog almost explodes in joy. Then, he turns and heads to see Bluebird Near the Lily. From then on until Water Dog's house is finished, Red Fox devotes all of his time and energy into building a house for Water Dog.

Sometimes I'd go and see Red Fox while he was working on Water Dog's house. So focused was he that he barely took time to chat with me while he worked. Firing the clay he laid for the foundation hardened it. Each of the two rooms was much larger than a room in any of our other homes. This was partly necessary due to Water Dog's size, and I think, partly to experiment in designing and building.

He had the mat weavers come and measure the rooms after the foundation was ready to be walked on, so they could make their floor mats big enough.

He chose only the most appropriately sized supporting posts, and dug the postholes very deep to support their extra height. I watched him as he ensured every cross beam was level, using a clever device he had made. Red Fox's father came over to measure the window spaces, so he could create the right sized mica windows and fit them exactly.

"I walked over to see Water Dog's new house," Shining Bird announces to me one afternoon when we found ourselves alone, "very impressive."

I nod my head in acknowledgement, and then say, "Water Dog is thrilled to be getting his own home. He can hardly wait to move in."

"I thought so," she says. "So I took the liberty to take Bluebird Near the Lily with me to see the mat weavers. We ordered mats for all the wall space. There's a lot of wall space, so we ordered a lot of mats. Bluebird Near the Lily spoke to the artists who would be painting some of them and discussed what she would like on them."

"Isn't it a bit premature to be ordering mats right now?" I ask.

"It's a big order. It might take them longer than we think to get them all done for when they move in. I felt Bluebird Near the Lily a bit shy to be asking for them. That's why I took her there myself."

"Ah," I nod.

"She's so excited about the upcoming marriage celebration at the Southernmost Moonrise at the end of summer. In fact, she's so excited about it that she had to go over to Speaks With Plants to get another tea of his to calm her down.

"I think what adds to heighten her level of excitement is that Blooming Rose, Water Dog's mother, has asked for a special dress for her from Red Fox's mother, Laughing Willow. She got some beautiful raspberry colored fabric from Seip. She also got bags and bags of matching pearls to sew onto her tunic. Her tunic is specially designed, and it will take a while for all of those pearls to be sewn onto the dress after it is made. They are already drilled, so Laughing Willow can just sew them on without having to worry about drilling them. She's been working on it for some time now, so it will be ready for the Southern Moonrise Ceremony."

Lost in all these details, I just shake my head from side to side and smile at my beloved. Then I change the topic, "I'm just looking forward to making that journey to Chillicothe and High Bank with you, my dearest beloved, and participating in the marriage celebration with you." I smile into her eyes. She pulls me close to her making our bodies touch. She smiles into my eyes. We lose the rest of the afternoon in enjoying each other.

As the summer hints its passing, The People begin to prepare for the journey to Chillicothe and High Bank. It will take several weeks for everyone from near and far to assemble there for the ceremony.

Our village is busy getting ready and making plans. I find myself involved with my Grandmother's healing efforts. She is helping at another village and asked me to search for specific plants and herbs for her, some for the other village, and some to take with on the journey to Chillicothe. Because of this, I am away from our village so much that I barely see Shining Bird.

While I am gone, I miss most of the readying for the event. Shining Bird and Bluebird Near the Lily spend much time together and spend time with their families preparing. They also spend time at Water Dog's house with his mother Blooming Rose.

"Bluebird," Blooming Rose asks, "do you want to see your dress now? It's finished. Laughing Willow brought it over today."

Bluebird Near the Lily looks at Shining Bird then back at Blooming Rose and nods. As Blooming Rose lifts the long tunic up with both hands, Bluebird Near the Lily gasps.

"Oh, my," is all she can say.

"Laughing Willow made this?" asks Shining Bird with her eyes wide in wonder.

"Yes," replies Blooming Rose, "Isn't it elegant?"

Both young women glide closer to look and to touch it.

"I don't know what to say," says Bluebird Near the Lily.

"It is beautiful," says Shining Bird. "I've never seen a dress so exquisitely decorated. Look at all those pearls, and they all match. Blooming Rose, you must have been collecting and sorting for a long time to get so many that are so much alike."

"Thank you," is her response. "Yes, I love Bluebird Near the Lily, and I love my son. I'm so thrilled they are together."

With that comment, Bluebird Near the Lily steps closer to her mother-in-law and puts her thin arms around Blooming Rose for a gentle and deep felt hug.

"Let's see the dress again," Shining Bird requests.

Bluebird steps back and re-focuses on the deep raspberry colored tunic adorned in pearls. The front reveals the neck lined with fox fur in a graceful curve from shoulder to shoulder. Strands of pearls curve below the fur. They replicate the same graceful curve as they descend down the chest and stomach area.

"Look at the sleeves," Shining Bird points out. "They're connected at the shoulders to the wrists by a beautiful billowing fabric slit from the top of the arm . . . with how many strands of pearls linking from shoulder to wrist also? Oh, my."

"Well, you should see the back," says Blooming Rose. She turns the garment around to show off the back. "Do you see how the back plunges into a V-shape halfway down her back? Then we've got strands of pearls linking from shoulder to shoulder and down each side, followed by gradually smaller strands layered as they descend down the back."

"So what color will be your trousers?" Shining Bird asks, her eyes aglow with excitement for her friend.

"Dark blue, I think," Bluebird Near the Lily says as she looks at Blooming Rose, "right? Is that right?"

"Yes, dear, dark blue," the older woman says.

"Raspberry and dark blue will look good together," Shining Bird observes.

"Yes," says Blooming Rose, ". . . and Laughing Willow took several tucks in at the waist to give a slight emphasis to the feminine shape.

" . . . And for her hair," Blooming Rose turns away to pull out a wooden box. Reaching inside she pulls out several pearls with long silver pins in them and says, "These are for your hair. Maybe Shining Bird would help you with your hair. If you tie it up in several ways, you can pin the pearls into your hair. How 'bout that?"

"Oh my, thank you, Blooming Rose," Bluebird Near the Lily says through a tear-stained smile. "You've outdone yourself. I will be the most beautifully dressed young woman at the marriage ceremony event . . . oh my, I think I'm feeling faint. I need to sit down."

As both the young women sit down together, Blooming Rose begins carefully folding and wrapping the garments with a great tenderness. Then she says, "I'll carry your tunic and trousers with me as we travel. That way you won't have to worry about it. You'll need to focus on getting there. We'll meet up at Chillicothe, and I'll see to it that you get everything you need."

"Thank you so very much," says Bluebird Near the Lily, "I think I should get over to Speaks with Plants and get a cup of tea to settle my nerves again. Going to the Southernmost Moonrise Ceremony is so exciting. I'd better carry some of that tea with me, just in case."

"I'll go with you. I want to see that you are all right," offers Shining Bird.

"Before you go, I'd like to mention that it might be a good thing, Bluebird, for you to consider leaving with the first group. You may need to stop and rest longer at times, so it might take you a little longer to get there. The first group will be leaving in a couple of days from now," says Blooming Rose as the two young women move to leave.

As they walk together toward the Healing House, Bluebird Near the Lily asks Shining Bird, "So what does your tunic look like?"

"Well," Shining Bird says, "It's a large pattern of light blue, light green and dark blue. It's got long strands of pearls flowing down the front in a necklace style. It actually resembles more of a tunic than a dress as it has copper buttons across the left collar to the shoulder."

"Really?" asks Bluebird Near the Lily.

"Yes," smiles Shining Bird. "And Gray Wolf will be wearing a light blue tunic with copper buttons on the right side going across his right collar . . . and both of us will be wearing matching dark blue trousers."

"Oh, so you will look like a 'set'?" laughs Bluebird Near the Lily.

"Yes, I guess so," laughs Shining Bird in response. "I'll have copper trinkets in my hair and copper ear spools . . . and Gray Wolf will wear his copper gorget at his chest."

They walk lost in thought for a few moments. Then Shining Bird breaks the silence. " . . . Only my tunic won't be so close fitting as yours."

"Why not?" asks Blue Near the Lily. "It feels wonderful to accent the feminine shape."

"Yes, well feminine it is, alright," Shining Bird says with a big smile. "Instead of being tighter at the waist, it will be bigger in the waist."

"What? You mean . . . ?" Bluebird Near the Lily stops and faces her friend.

Smiling down at her mid-section and putting her hand on her side with a caressing movement, she replied, "Yes . . . I think it's a boy."

"Oh . . ." Bluebird says, "how wonderful. Does Gray Wolf know?"

Shining Bird shakes her head from side to side and says, "I don't think so. I haven't told him. If he doesn't guess by the time we get to Chillicothe, then I'll tell him at the marriage ceremony."

"So, when will he move into your parent's home?" Bluebird asks.

After taking a moment to reflect on the question, Shining Bird says, "Probably when we get back. That'll give him time to mentally prepare before we return home. He's so busy now working with his Grandmother Shining Moon and working his healing arts, I don't want to give him something more to think about until the time comes."

"Speaks With Plants tells me having children would be too much of a strain on my system," Bluebird Near the Lily says wistfully. "He said that it would be better for me not to get pregnant . . . so I don't know if I will have children or not."

"How do you manage having sex with Water Dog?" Shining Bird asks. "I mean, he's *so big*, after all."

Bluebird smiles at the thought, "Well, it's perfect actually. Yes, he *huge* in fact. And for some reason, my body can accommodate him . . . I know I'm tiny, compared to everyone else. It's just that . . . that part of my body works really well . . . and he fits into me like a hand in a glove . . . and am I glad for that." She ends with a broad smile.

By the time they finish their conversation, the young women reach the Healing House. As they enter they see Speaks With Plants preparing a tea for Bluebird Near the Lily.

"Thank you Speaks With Plants," Bluebird Near the Lily says to the shaman as she accepts her cup.

"I don't dare give *you* a cup of this," he says to Shining Bird, "it would not be suitable for you in your condition."

"Does it show that much?" Shining Bird asks.

"Not to most, dear," he says, "Don't forget, reading people's physical condition and knowing just what herbs are appropriate has been my life's work."

During this time, many others of The People joined our village as a stopping point on their way to the Southernmost Moonrise Ceremony. They camped out at the spot where the traders usually camped. It was spacious and provided what they needed as a place to take a breath and mix in with members of our village before continuing onward.

Late in the afternoon the day before White Eagle, Rising Wolf and the first group were set to begin the journey to Chillicothe and High Bank for the Southernmost Moonrise Ceremony, many children had gathered outside around a small fire with White Eagle sitting in a prominent place as was her story-telling custom.

"Tell us another story," Shining Bird heard one of the older children say as she sat on the fringe of the circle toward the back. Water Dog and Bluebird Near the Lily sat near her. They had all finished packing before beginning the week-long journey to Chillicothe and High Bank.

"Yes, please tell us another one, Grandmother," echoed several more children.

Not needing to be begged, but enjoying the enthusiasm, White Eagle nodded. She took in a deep breath, and then got up to pick up a stick near the fire pit. Then she began her last story of the evening.

"My children," she commented, "you and I, you and your parents, you and each other . . . are all one." She paused a moment before going on, looking around to ensure she had everyone's attention.

"We are Children of the Law of One. The Law says, 'we are one.' That is what we live by as a People. We all take care of each other. We know that what happens to one of us, happens to all of us. We are all connected.

"Do you see this fire here?" she asks as she points to the fire around which they are sitting. She looks around at all the children before continuing.

"Do you see this fire?

"This fire is like Great Spirit. Great Spirit is not something we can see with our eyes, though. Great Spirit is our Creator. It is the force that generates and sustains all life, life in every form.

"The force of the fire here is not something you can actually see. You can see the flames as they are the physical manifestation of the life force of the Great Oneness. It has no shape, no actual physical form. We can feel the heat of it as it expresses itself."

The children started to squirm. Noticing this, White Eagle continued.

"Pretend that Great Spirit is the fire we see here. Now see this stick I hold in my hand?" She looked around to see that all eyes are focused on the stick.

"I will put this stick into this fire. I will hold it there until it catches fire."

The children sat quietly as she did so, waiting for the next part of her story. As the stick caught fire, White Eagle gazed into it before lifting the stick away from the fire.

"See the flames on this stick?" she asked as she looked around again.

"This fire on this stick is identical to the fire in the pit here. Do you see that the main fire is not diminished as a result of this stick catching on fire?"

The children all nodded their heads.

"Remember that this fire in the pit is like Great Spirit. And, this fire on this stick is the same fire as the main fire. We are like the fire on the stick. We are made up of the same substance as Great Spirit. We are individual flames of the main fire, the same composition, the same essence, the same everything . . ."

One child asked, "But Grandmother, why do we all look different?"

"Do not let your physical appearance and the appearance of being separate individuals fool you. Great Spirit arranged with Mother Earth to give us a physical covering for our flames, so we can enjoy experiences at the frequency level of the physical. The physical covering is our bodies . . .when we are experiencing the life force at this frequency; our bodies appear distinct from each other.

"We each need to experience individualized experiences, so that Great Spirit can experience a vast variety of experiences to know itself. As a result, we have the privilege to experience our life force in the physical as individual flames of the fire that is Great Spirit.

"Because we all are individuals expressed from Great Spirit, we are one in the One. That is why we take care of each other. That is why we operate like the other person is us . . . because the other person is us . . . appearing as someone else

. . . That is why we call ourselves, Children of the Law of One. We are the offspring of the One, the Great Oneness."

White Eagle stopped and looked out at her audience. No one moved. No one spoke. While Eagle had finished speaking and simply smiled into her audience, like her audience was comprised of the very flames of which she spoke.

Finally, the children stirred and looked around for their parents who have been sitting on the sidelines. One by one, families found each other, and drifted back to their homes for the night before the journey began.

I missed out on the preparations for the journey to Chillicothe and High Bank as I was busy helping others. So the beginnings of the journey became a blur to me. I was called into so many directions, as I journeyed, I got there before I knew it. I hadn't seen Shining Bird until everyone began settling in their camp sites at Chillicothe.

The excitement level ran high among everyone. This was a celebratory occasion as the Moonrise Ceremonies always were. Everywhere I looked I could see The People smiling, laughing, moving about, and settling in. Since the Moonrise Ceremonies took place every nine plus years, this was the first for all the children, and the second for many adults. The Elders, Grandmothers and Grandfathers, of course, had celebrated the Moonrise Ceremonies several times.

One evening as Shining Bird and I are walking over to where Water Dog's campsite was, we see Rising Wolf sitting by a comfortable fire surrounded by many children, some of our village, and many more from near and far.

We stop momentarily as we hear one of the children ask, "Grandfather, tell us another story."

"Grandfather, tell us a story of the Ancient Ones," another one asks.

"Yes, my children, I will tell you one of the stories that my great grandfather told my father."

The children wiggle a bit to get more comfortable.

"We live on sacred ground. We do not own or possess that which Mother Earth has made for us. The land is not ours. The animals and plants are not ours. These do not belong to us.

"We take only what we need. When we do take, we must give back in some way. We say a prayer to the spirits of the animals and the plants and give blessing back for what they give us so that we may live.

"As I have shown you and told you in other stories we have shared, we must live in harmony with Mother Earth and that which she provides. The Ancient Ones told us stories of when humans lost their harmony with the world in which they lived.

"It is for these reasons, children that I, the Elders, your mothers and fathers give a prayer of gratitude to the deer when they have provided us with meat, to the plants for what the plants provide and to the earth from which all is given. This is why I teach you these ways, so that you will know to take no more than you need, and to give thanks to their spirits, so that they will return to us in the future to provide for us now and your children later.

"This is the way of harmony. This is the Way of Oneness in operation. This is the way of the Great Spirit. In so doing there will be enough for all and for our brothers and sisters who live apart from us.

"We have our great festivals to honor Father Sun, Mother Earth and all that she provides, when we plant in the spring and when we harvest in the fall.

"When the cold winter comes, we will have enough, and none will starve. We must treat the plants, animals and Mother Earth, herself, with respect and honor, and in so doing they will honor us. This is why we do not destroy or kill these things *just because we can*. You must never forget that we live only because we live in harmony with that which has been given to us."

Both Shining Bird and I are so moved by Rising Wolf's storytelling style that we feel riveted to the spot where we had stopped.

Rising Wolf pauses to look at his audience and then continues, "Now I remember seeing some of you at the Summer Solstice Ceremony. It is important to remember that there is an additional meaning to that Ceremony.

"As Father Sun sets in the West and enters the land of darkness, this represents the death of the day and the end of his northward journey. In our Ceremony we surrender to this cycle of life and honor its completion. We celebrate his resurrection in the East the following morning that brings a new day, the beginning of his journey to the South and the beginning of a new cycle in our lives.

"We honor the cycles of the days and nights, cycles of the seasons, cycles of Sister Moon, and the cycles of life on Mother Earth. All of these cycles are part of the Order of Life. The Order of Life prevails lending order and constancy to the flux in our lives.

"Grandfather, tell us the story of Sister Moon," says yet another child. Murmurs of agreement ripple out among the children.

"And so I will, my children. This will be the last story of the night. It's a very important story especially now as we gather to honor Sister Moon.

"It's a story about our world, Mother Earth and her Sister. This story comes from the long ago from our ancestors who lived in a land far away . . . a land that is no more. They learned this story from the Star People who brought them great knowledge of things that The People had observed but did not completely understand.

"In the ancient of days Mother Earth was alone. There was no one for her to talk to as men and women and all the creatures did not yet exist. She asked the Creator to bring her someone she could share her life with. The Creator said this was possible if she was willing to give of herself. Mother Earth said she was willing to do what was necessary.

"From far out in space the Creator selected a heavenly body to move toward Mother Earth. The Creator explained that this heavenly body would have to join with Mother Earth. From that union, a new heavenly body would come into being, which would circle around Mother Earth and be her companion. It would be made from a part of her and from part of this other heavenly body.

". . . And so it was. The heavenly body from far away collided with Mother Earth in an explosive joining of the two bodies. It resulted in a very large part of Mother Earth and the other heavenly body combining to create a third heavenly body, made up of both Mother Earth and the other. From this union Sister Moon was created.

"Sister Moon so loved Mother Earth that she always kept her face looking at Mother Earth. Sister Moon never turns her face away. She has eight different faces: the new moon, waxing crescent, waxing half, waxing gibbous, full moon, waning gibbous, waning half and waning crescent.

"We are here at this sacred place to honor Sister Moon. We will gather in the octagon, which has eight sides. These reflect the eight faces of Sister Moon.

"The new moon is the one we cannot see, because she is sleeping. As she awakens we first see just a very small smile. This grows with time until Sister Moon's face is full of light. Sister Moon helps us keep a record of the passage of days. It takes 28 days from when she goes to sleep, and then she grows until her face is full of light, and then goes to sleep again. When she does this 13 times, she tracks her year for us.

"You may have seen the turtle shells that we use to keep track of the passage of her days. The 28 little squares around the edge give us our month and the thirteen large squares on the back give us her year.

"Mother Earth was so very glad to have someone to talk to. And Sister Moon offered so much more. She helped create and sustain life on Mother Earth.

"Before Sister Moon, Mother Earth wobbled drastically on her axis in her journey around Father Sun. There were no seasons like the four seasons we have now: Spring, Summer, Fall and Winter. She could not bring forth life because her skin was barren. She could not bring balance to her days and nights, and the weather was ever changing. The oceans were in turmoil having no one to bring balance to their ever-changing storms and currents.

"As Sister Moon revolved around Mother Earth, Mother Earth's axis stabilized and tilted somewhat. The oceans developed rhythms that are called tides, and the tides created stable currents in all the great waters. The weather began to change and became stable. Because of the tilt in Mother Earth's axis, seasons came into being. And after a very long time, the Creator and Mother Earth began to bring forth various forms of life.

"At first these forms of life were very small. And with time they became larger and larger. Gradually new creatures came into being. Plants came into being and Mother Earth became very fertile with all the life that now existed on her skin. She was so very happy.

"Sister Moon had brought balance and harmony to Mother Earth. From this balance and harmony, the Creator and Mother Earth were able to provide all that we have today. All the animals, all the creatures that live in the waters and fly through the air, all the insects, the bounty of Mother Earth that sustains us, our seasons, our weather and our days and nights are gifts from the Creator for us to wisely use in balance and harmony in our daily lives.

"This is why we honor Sister Moon.

"High Bank and Newark are the sacred places where we give special prayers to Sister Moon. In her journey around Mother Earth there are times when she is further away and times when she is closer. She moves further North and then to the South. Every nine or so years, she reaches the northernmost point, and then again another nine or so years, she moves to the southernmost point. Should she decide to continue her journey on out into the stars at either of these two points, she would leave Mother Earth.

"If this should happen, life as we know it on Mother Earth would cease to exist. Mother Earth would once again wobble out of control, and the oceans would return to chaos. Our normal weather patterns and seasons would cease to exist, and we would be no more.

"My children, this is why we must maintain balance and harmony in our lives. This is why it is so important for us to honor Sister Moon. Make her a part of our daily prayers and always remember to follow the ways of the Creator. We must wisely use the gifts and blessings we have been given.

"If we take these things for granted and become separated from the ways of our Ancestors, we will lose our sense of Oneness with the Creator, and all that we have been given will come to an end.

"Now children, help me gather the earth to place on the fire, as it is time for you to return to your parents. May you sleep well."

As the children get up to help put dirt on the fire, Shining Bird and I move on, glad to have been reminded of the story of Sister Moon.

Many of The People participated in re-birthing rituals at the Scioto River's edge. Many also participated in other rituals of renewal during their stay here at Chillicothe. Nights were filled with music and dancing. The marriage ceremony was a special ritual, held for those who wished to find a partner, for those who had found a partner and wanted to experience a ceremonial joining, and also for those who wished to renew their partnership with their life's companion.

The marriage ceremony begins in the late afternoon. Shining Bird and Bluebird Near the Lily spent the entire day together. As the sun lowers in the western sky on this beautiful day at summer's end, I join Water Dog to wait for our partners to find us.

Red Fox is here again then gone again. He looks like he feels uncomfortable. He hasn't found a partner yet, and infiltrates the crowds of people still looking as if he had someone in mind. He does not find her.

Finally, our beloveds materialize from the throng of people. Water Dog almost drops to the ground when he first sees Bluebird Near the Lily. With so many pearls fairly dripping around her, their iridescence reflect the pink of the dark raspberry color of her tunic. She appears as a vision of raspberry pearlescence. Smiling, with eyes only for Water Dog, she approaches him. He takes her tiny, slender hands and clutches them together in his gigantic ones and holds them to his heart, pulling her close to him. His eyes locked on hers.

When I gaze upon my beloved, my heart pounds. I can see only Shining Bird amid the crowd as she emerges into view. Her face glows with the radiance of a new mother. As she approaches me, she lifts her left arm in greeting with a soft smile and love in her eyes.

She settles her left arm on my shoulder as I reach behind her with my right arm to pull her into a full body embrace.

Then she whispers sweetly into my ear, "This is just one moment in a lifetime of our love."

I can only smile as I lock my eyes onto hers. Then we turn toward the direction where the marriage ceremony is to begin, and I shift her body to my left side. We walked arm in arm, smiling uncontrollably, happy to just exist in that moment.

As late afternoon transitions into twilight, the marriage ceremony begins. I barely hear the words. I can only feel my exhilaration of recognizing my beloved as we celebrate life itself.

White Eagle and Rising Wolf facilitate the Southernmost Moonrise ceremony as Sister Moon rises majestically on the southeastern horizon. After that joyous ceremony, the music plays. We dance. We drink the frothy black drink stimulant made from ceremonial plants. Everyone there revels in the celebration of life. We make love as did most of the other couples. The physical joining reflects the spiritual and emotional joining during that night of celebrating, revelry and merrymaking.

That night ends as the music shifts from high intensity into a softer mellow greeting of Father Sun.

26

WHITE EAGLE'S DREAMS

Water Dog and Bluebird Near the Lily had happily settled down in their new home. They were grateful to Red Fox for the unusual design and solid construction.

Bluebird felt particularly pleased with her new surroundings, after moving out of her father's home with all the children she had helped raise since her mother's death. In addition, her father's house was not built for the size of a man that Water Dog was. A Grandmother from another settlement who needed a home graciously consented to move in and take over after Bluebird's leaving. Bluebird so enjoyed the quiet and peaceful energy of just her and Water Dog sharing each other's company in privacy.

I moved in with Shining Bird's family and began my work as a shaman under the apprenticeship of White Eagle with a little help from my own Grandmother, Shining Moon.

Fall was always a busy time for The People. Fall was a time of harvesting the wild rice. Some of our villagers participated in the reaping of this delectable staple. It was primarily a project in canoes in marsh country as that was where the rice grew. Corn and sunflowers had already been harvested in the larger fields near Baum. Some of the local settlements grew small patches of their own though.

Fall was a time for the nut harvesting everywhere. The nut trees spread profusely over the lands of The People, so that nearly every village spent time collecting and sorting the abundant resource. Nutting time was also experienced as a fun time. Small groups gathered around to separate the meat from the shells using nutting stones, laughing and talking, sharing stories as they did so. Nutmeats were used for so many different purposes. The meats were boiled, separating out the oil that was used for our lamps. The leftover meats were then dried and pounded into flour for baking and cooking.

Before too long, Rising Wolf found himself depending on Water Dog for maintaining organization of the flint mining. Water Dog took over when Rising Wolf returned home earlier in the Fall than expected. Rising Wolf usually spent much time up on Flint Ridge, happy as a clam in his house built from flint-bearing stone, knapping, teaching, coaching, and directing. Intuitively, Rising Wolf suddenly felt the need to return home to White Eagle. While she often traveled around the country visiting many of other villages, he sensed she was home and needing him.

Even though operations would soon cease for the winter months, Rising Wolf felt drawn to return home earlier than normal. He felt his lifetime companion needed him now more than ever. Something felt amiss. This turned out to be so.

Weeks passed by without notice.

Deep winter months passed.

As an apprentice shaman, as weather permitted, I traveled, to nearby villages getting acquainted with everyone, providing assistance as necessary. In these other villages The People asked me for help mainly because I was already there, which I gladly provided. That also gave me the opportunity to visit with The People not of my village and to get to know them more individually and them me.

It is just such a trip I was on when I get word from a messenger to return home.

"What's going on," I ask. "Is Shining Bird all right?"

"Indeed, she is, Gray Wolf," says the messenger with a broad smile. "You have a new son," he says happily. "She told me not to ask you to rush through your business here. Just when you can, if you could return, she wants to show you your son when you get home. I guess the baby came sooner than she expected."

"Your Grandmother was such a wonderful help. She does have a gift for healing and I don't know what all," Shining Bird reassures me after I arrive. As I gaze into the face of my beloved and that of my new son, I feel my heart expand beyond any boundary I had previously known. I find myself asking Spirit, "So this is what it is like to love broadly without qualification. What a feeling this is."

White Eagle soared above the clouds, gracefully and gently swaying this way and that. White Eagle noticed birds flying below her as well. Most of the birds she was familiar with.

She watched the birds as they began circling around her. Smiling, White Eagle enjoyed the flight out of body as she traveled eastward from her home in the Ohio Valley. As she continued to float and soar, she admired the landscape from her home toward the coast. The deep colors of the mountains contrasted against the lush green of the meadows outlined and circumscribed by pristine rivers and streams, glinting softly in the sunlight.

Its beauty touched her heart. As if hearing a whispering undertone of a threat from afar, suddenly all the birds disappeared. White Eagle looked up, squinted her aged eyes to better focus on the direction of the ominous rumble.

"What? What?" White Eagle cried out in breathless question as she wrestled with her bed covers in her sleep. Her husband, Rising Wolf, looked over at his beloved with deep concern.

When she awoke for the day, Rising Wolf spoke his distress, "I'm wondering how long your restless dreams have been haunting you. I've been away so much lately at the flint quarries." He sat patiently for her reply. She did not speak, but simply looked at him, then through him to someplace far away.

Rising Wolf sat patiently for her reply. As gruff and direct as he was with his team of flint knappers, he was that much more tender with his beloved. "You cried out in your sleep," Rising Wolf paused, then said again, "You cried out in your sleep again in apprehension of something. Tell me, my love, what are you seeing that is so alarming?"

She just sat with her bed covers and buffalo robes nestled around her, looking past him. He still sat patiently for her reply. Then, after waiting for a very long time, he got up and stirred the hearth embers adding fuel to the hearth, bringing heat to the frosty spring morning in their home.

Seeing that she remained fixated on her vision that he could not see, he prepared a morning tea with nut cakes on the side. After the tea was made he prepared her cup and handed it to her. She took it robotically, not leaving the place of her vision. After a while she took a sip, turned and looked at Rising Wolf who waited patiently for her response. Taking another sip, she looked straight at him without saying a word. He noticed a single tear. It hung there momentarily before reluctantly leaving its source and crawling down her cheek.

Rising Wolf continued to wait patiently for White Eagle to say something. While she was finally able to look at him and actually see him, she found herself unable to speak, to articulate her experience. She opened her mouth to speak but couldn't get any sound out.

After another long while, Rising Wolf moved over to the window facing the rising sun, feeling the sun's warmth as it passed through the mica glass. He stretched and remained standing there in thought, patiently waiting for her to speak.

She obviously was not up to eating anything as she left the nut cakes untouched. When he turned around from standing at the window, he found that she had set her cup down and fallen back into bed, not asleep, but not awake. He watched her eyes move beneath her closed lids. She moaned in heartbreak. He joined her under the covers, gently grasping a hand that she had left exposed, waiting patiently for her to return to him.

"Were you able to finish everything you had set out to do?" Shining Bird asks as she nurses her new son. "While I wanted you, I really didn't want you to rush through helping someone else. I would be here when you got home . . ." she adds, then lowers her head and confesses softly, ". . . even though I hoped you were able to get here right away."

"Not to worry, my lovely," I say reassuringly, "I was at a good place to stop when I got the message. I will go back later. This just gives me the excuse to return to that particular village and strengthen my relationships there."

Then after she lies down with my son, I feel impelled to comb her hair. I look around for her comb. It is a custom of The People for the husband to comb his wife's hair, usually early in the morning. Even though it is late in the afternoon, this dearest act of affection and honor feels especially appropriate at this moment.

Rising Wolf continued to wait patiently for his wife to return from her soul wrenching spiritual journeying. He knew she was distressed by the pitiful sounds she made in her sleep. He had witnessed her torturous slumbering for months now. By this time, it was getting worse.

He also knew she was not sick, so did not send for help from Grandmother Shining Moon. White Eagle had left for dreams before, but never for this long, and never had they been *this* disturbing.

By now Rising Wolf sensed a sickness of her heart, so deep that when she tried to talk to him, she could not. Eventually he gave up trying to reach her and left her to her dreams.

Water Dog and Bluebird, enjoying the privacy not afforded them earlier in their courtship, found each other's company delightful. They made love on every surface and available spot in their spacious new home. Despite their love for each other, no children proved forthcoming. Bluebird still remained faithful to her fragile body by her continued regular trips to see Speak With Plants and his apothecary.

Water Dog felt successful in his flint knapping. He enjoyed helping Rising Wolf in organizing and directing the systematic search for new digs. Water Dog certainly was adept at his actual knapping despite his long broad fingers. Many of the artists and artisans of The

People were small in stature and had tiny fingers. However, his work on the flint showed to be so exquisite as to amaze all others, especially because of his massive hands.

After putting down our son to sleep, Shining Bird and I melt into each other's space. I had finished combing out her hair and began putting a meal together for the two of us. We ate in silence, each appreciating the other.

Finally, I say, "I had some interesting experiences while away." Shining Bird nods encouragement for me to continue.

"Also, I heard stories of unusual happenings that occurred in other villages even farther away." Shining Bird stops eating and looks at me with full attention. "I'm not sure what to make of it," I say pondering the meaning of what I was about to share.

"You know late summer early fall is good berry picking time, for raspberries and blackberries, and so forth." I wait for her to nod acknowledgment, not really wanting to continue, feeling I must speak about some-thing that I felt was horrific. She continues eating for a moment. Then recognizing my hesitation, she pauses again to let me know she is interested in hearing what I have to say.

"Yes, berry picking is done in late summer, early fall. Yes, go on," she murmurs.

What I was about to tell was not something I understood. "Shining Bird, I'm not anxious to tell you this story, because it's so upsetting. Yet, it disturbs me so much, I must tell it in the hopes that it will make sense to me as I say it." I clutch her hand for support, then shake my head and lower my eyes as if the story will fall out of my head, so I won't have to speak it.

"Go on, I'm listening."

I let go of her hand, stand up and pace around the room, "I just heard about these incidents on my recent travels. Last fall a roaming group of young men attacked a young man from a village far away from here. They severely beat him, because they heard he liked men."

"Liked men?" Shining Bird asks raising her eyebrows.

"Yes, men, rather than women, for being in a loving partnership."

"What do you mean, 'beat him up'?" she asks.

"They ganged up on him, hit him over and over again, and kicked him when he was on the ground. They left him on the ground bleeding and helpless. He had to be taken over to a healer's house by other people who were just passing by where he was on the ground." My throat closes as I choke out the words.

After a pause I struggle to continue, "They just found him. No one had called for help. The gang of young men just left him there to die."

I feel myself challenged by the concept that anyone of The People would ever hurt or think of hurting another.

Shining Bird sits there blinking incredulously and says, "No, I don't think so. Are you sure? Are you sure someone didn't make this story up?" Then she pauses, reflecting a moment and adds, "If someone made it up, why would they spin such an ugly story?" she asks rhetorically.

"I don't know, but it actually happened. I spoke with someone who was there and helped the young man," I say shaking my head, "and . . . there's more."

"More? How could there be more? I've never heard of anything like this happening before. We've all lived in peace for a thousand years. This is not something that we do to each other!" Shining Bird says with power and passion. Her mother-bear energy emerges.

"Well, yes there is more, much to my utter dismay."

She tilts her head in question as to what more there could possibly be and says, "Gray Wolf, as you and I both know, The People have long known that these are two-spirit persons. We recognize that there are three gender categories, female, male and two-spirit persons. A two-spirit person can be either a biological male or female and engages in tasks usually associated with their biological opposite. Often they turn out to be dreamers, or a shaman of some kind, like Sundown Quietly. After all, we both know the teachings and life story of Sundown Quietly. He was one of our honored Elders long before we were born. He was a two-spirit person. So this incident is very disturbing."

"Later that same fall day," I struggle to get the words out, "that same gang of young men wandered across a young woman who was out berry picking with her family and friends." I cough several times.

"She had strayed a little too far from the group and found herself surrounded by these same young men."

Choking and coughing, as my throat tried to close off the words from being spoken, I am finally able to finish the story, "They threw her to the ground and raped her repeatedly, and each taking turns until her uncle came looking for her. When he came upon them, they scattered."

Tears run down my face as I finish. I look up at my beloved, imagining I would have to give her comfort after hearing these horrific events.

Hairs stand up on the back of her neck as she stands up hyper-alert, a tower of strength. "How *dare* they," she curses in a low breath. "How dare they treat people so! This certainly was an act of power over someone else, rather than the sacred sharing of personal energies."

With her burst of energy expressed, I suddenly find myself sitting down in surprise. "Cowards. Cowards, they are," she declares emphatically. Then looking off into the distance, she pauses a moment before continuing. "They are not of The People. They are not part of us. These young men are not two-hearted people . . . they are black-hearted.

"Their black hearts prevent them from knowing and feeling the connectedness of everyone to each other, that we are all part of the One. The Great Oneness is not included in their consciousness." Finally able to breathe, Shining Bird takes in a deep breath.

Sitting down again, she needs to unwind and let go of the tensions that had suddenly accumulated at her outrage upon hearing my story. "Oh my," she says, "we may not have heard the last of them. They may be roaming the countryside as they have no real home."

I then say to her, "I believe Red Fox ran into one or two of them while on his journey at Chillicothe. I don't know if they would be the same young men or not. But what I don't understand is . . . why should this be happening . . . at all?"

Later that same day, Rising Wolf felt glad that White Eagle was at last sitting up. She joined him on a bench outside their home soaking up the warming of a reluctant spring afternoon sun on their faces. Before too long they both heard the steady crunch of footsteps coming up the hill to their home.

"Hello, Floating Lily," Rising Wolf greeted the girl in a tone that smacked of both relief and warmth that took her by surprise.

"I've brought you something to eat, some stew and wilted goose foot greens. Oh, and some cakes. White Eagle needs something sweet to eat, at least according to Raven's Wing."

"Thank you, Floating Lily," said Rising Wolf, "but I'm not sure White Eagle is up to eating anything. She hasn't had any food all day, just a cup of tea."

"Just the same, Rising Wolf, I must leave the food for you," Floating Lily said as she tried to hand it over to Rising Wolf who refused to take it. Looking around, she left it on the table next to their bench. "You can eat it when you want." At that, Floating Lily turned and skipped down the hill and away.

With that Rising Wolf peered questioningly at his beloved to see just where she was. She returned the look but did not speak. Rising Wolf decided to continue to wait, patiently.

Grandmother Shining Moon had been away tending to another family farther down the stream from the village. Upon returning, she encountered Raven's Wing busy in her outside kitchen preparing stews and more.

"White Eagle," Raven's Wing said to Shining Moon in her succinct tone.

Grandmother Shining Moon nodded and took a seat on a bench outside the kitchen area. She folded her hands in her lap and bowed her head. Birds twittered in the trees nearby. A breeze played in the rays of the sun poking through the branches overhead.

Finally, Grandmother Shining Moon got up and began walking in the direction of the Healing House to see her brother, Speaks With Plants. As she approached the Healing House, Shining Moon stood in the doorway to announce her presence.

Speaks With Plants turned to face the door at the sound of her entrance with a warm greeting, "Hello, my sister, I was wondering when I should be seeing you again."

"Yes, well, it's White Eagle," she announced.

"I know she is not sick," his eyes opened widely and he blinked, and then asked, "What is it?"

"She's in a state of shock. Would you please make a concoction that will bring her out of it?" Grandmother Shining Moon looked around and sat down on a stool.

"Of course," he replied beginning to work at once. "Would you enjoy a cup of tea, while I put it together?"

"Yes, thank you, brother. I'd appreciate that."

Speaks With Plants handed Shining Moon a steaming cup of herb tea designed to invigorate, just what she needed after working so many long hours lately.

Meanwhile, Speaks With Plants finished his preparation and handed Shining Moon a pot of tea.

Carrying the warm pot of a tea of mixed herbs, Grandmother Shining Moon began heading toward White Eagle's home.

Again, Rising Wolf heard the crunch, crunch of an approaching someone outside. "Now who could this be?" he asked himself, not at all wanting to entertain company with White Eagle in this state.

Seeing no one outside, Grandmother Shining Moon announced, "Hello the house."

As he opened the door, Rising Wolf spoke with great relief, "Oh Grandmother, I've been waiting for White Eagle to speak. She can't. She's awake, but can't speak of the dreams she is having," he gushed and then felt self-conscious at having done so, not realizing just how worried he had been.

"Yes, well, Speaks With Plants worked up a tea for her to drink. I think it will help," she cooed to both of them after she entered. At that,

Rising Wolf turned to get a cup for his beloved to drink from. As he brought the cup over, he saw the two women seated just looking at each other with some kind of unspoken communication going on.

Rising Wolf was grateful that Shining Moon had come. He took the warm clay pot from her. He poured the unsavory looking drink into the cup he was holding. When he offered the drink to White Eagle, she did not respond, eyes still locked on Grandmother's eyes.

Realizing that White Eagle refused the drink from Rising Wolf, Grandmother Shining Moon took the cup from Rising Wolf and offered it to White Eagle. With that, White Eagle accepted the cup and began to sip the unknown beverage.

No words were spoken.

Outside, the sun gradually reached the horizon and the coolness turned to a chill. White Eagle just as gradually began to respond to her immediate environment.

"Ah," sighed Grandmother Shining Moon, "I think you are coming around. You gave us a little scare. Glad to see you back."

White Eagle blinked a couple of times then smiled. "Thank you Grandmother," then she bowed her head expressing honor to Shining Moon. White Eagle took Rising Wolf's hand in hers, then reached to his cheek and kissed him. "Thank you for your patience, dear one."

Rising Wolf nodded with tears in his eyes. Then to Grandmother Shining Moon, he turned and mouthed the words, "thank you," to her. That was as much as he could muster.

Grandmother Shining Moon got up to leave and as she closed the door behind her, she overheard White Eagle say to Rising Wolf, "We have much to discuss."

27

THE SWEETNESS OF THE PEOPLE

They sat up all night. White Eagle spoke of her dreams to Rising Wolf. They talked. They ate the food that Floating Lily had brought. They talked. They drank tea. They talked.

As White Eagle revealed her experience to Rising Wolf often tears streamed down her face. Sometimes she found herself choking as she spoke. As Rising Wolf listened in rapt attention, his body shuttered, shivered, and jerked, in silent response to the most horrific revelation he could never have imagined.

Not long after rays of the eastern sunrise stretched out at the horizon, Grandmother Shining Moon gently called out, "Hello the house."

White Eagle and Rising Wolf stopped talking instantly, alert at the sound of the outside world daring to intrude upon their sanctity.

"Hello the house." Again, Grandmother called, waiting patiently.

Blinking herself back to the here and now, White Eagle acknowledged, "Oh, it's Grandmother." Getting up from where she had been sitting all night in conversation with her beloved partner, White Eagle opened the door and stepped outside. "Good morning, Grandmother. Thank you for coming and checking on me. I've had quite a night."

"I believe you. I felt I needed to see how you're doing. You went into quite a state of shock. Looks like that drink that Speaks With Plants brewed up helped considerably. If you've been up all night, as I suspect, White Eagle, you will need at least another day and night's rest before you go to the sweat lodge for cleansing," prescribed Grandmother.

"You are so right, Grandmother," said White Eagle. "I need a three-day sweat. It's not just for cleansing of my body and my spirit, but also to get clarification. I seek clarity and direction. But, maybe not quite yet. Let me gain my strength back first, and I'm not sure right now when I'll be ready."

"Good, then, that's settled. I'll have a sweat lodge prepared for you when it's time . . . you let me know." Grandmother stopped suddenly as Rising Wolf stepped toward the door, his face ashen gray. Grandmother

Shining Moon stepped back to catch herself from falling backwards. "Oh my," was all the sound she could muster as she gazed at him.

Rising Wolf gave a nod to Grandmother, saying nothing, his gray eyes looking past the here and now.

Weeks pass.

Water Dog sighed contentedly. His life with Bluebird Near the Lily felt like a paradise. His house was big and roomy so the tall man felt comfortable and snug without being closed in. Despite children not forthcoming, Water Dog worshiped his beloved. He spent weeks up at Flint Ridge at a time, so when he was home, he forgot all about the world outside. They spent hours lounging together.

As a couple they matched in height as closely as a giant and a non-giant could. He stood by now, slightly over eight feet, and she not quite six feet. In all other physical categories they contrasted starkly with his flaming red hair and her straight black hair, his gargantuan size versus her petite frame. These differences made no difference to them. He folded his body around her, and she felt safe and adored. She wrapped her long legs around his girth, and he felt elevated and complete.

Even though no children blessed their lives, he felt self-actualized through his work. Due to his particular talent at shaping flint and other materials, such as clear quartz crystals and the black obsidian glass, his prestige increased as an artisan. This, coupled with his managerial skills working the flint teams successfully, served to elevate him in the minds of the team members, and most importantly in the eyes of Rising Wolf. Water Dog noticed that Rising Wolf returned to Flint Ridge less often and stayed home for longer and longer periods of time.

With another child on the way, Shining Bird and I felt that we were crowding her family too much in her parents' home. So I commissioned Red Fox to build us a home. Red Fox was only too glad to start right away to work his particular magic for us. By the time we moved in, our daughter, Star Rising, had arrived.

Even though life hummed along in its usual, satisfying rhythms of a contented daily life, everyone fitting into everyone else's life, each contributing to one another, I felt a subtle undertow, like energy being siphoned off. At first it was too obscure for me to identify. I noticed it then did not notice it. When I noticed it, I tried to grasp it, but could not hold on to it long enough for me to see it in my mind's eye. It felt foreign to the energy field of The People. I went to see White Eagle.

"As an apprentice shaman, you have served The People well, Gray Wolf," she says to me without smiling after we sit down inside her house. Her necklace reflects light, showing off the iridescence of the abalone shell and the glint of the silver and copper insignia of "as in Heaven, so on Earth."

She leans forward and speaks in a hushed but distinctive tone of authority, "it is now time that you begin another phase of your experience as a shaman of The People. There will come a time when the Council of Twelve meet, and you will join us."

Silenced by this announcement, I feel honored to be asked to join the highest circle of spiritual leaders of The People. They come from villages near and far away, each representing different locations and segments of The People. The circle is sacred and ancient and only designated individuals may participate.

"When that time comes, I suspect that we will consult The Knowing," White Eagle says as she purses her lips.

I nod in acknowledgement.

Silence.

My intent to see White Eagle had been to discuss my sense of something I could not grasp, an energy I find unable to identify.

As I begin to speak, my throat closes and I cough after getting only a few words out, "I am sensing something I cannot identify . . ." I choke before finishing.

Then I hear a gasp and a squeak from the corner of her home. Surprised, I looked over in the direction of the sound and see Rising Wolf sitting in the shadows. I had not noticed him there before. As I turn and focus my attention on him, he collapses down on the bed and sighs.

"It's time for you to go now, Gray Wolf," White Eagle commands as she stands up.

". . . But . . . but there is something I need to discuss with you, White Eagle," I beg.

"Yes, I know," she replies with one long nod, opening the door to move me out and end the conversation.

"Oooh, The Knowing," murmurs Shining Bird.

I had made a beeline to Singing Hawk's sanctuary of study and find my beloved there taking refuge from her daily routine.

"The Council of Twelve," says Singing Hawk with raised eyebrows after I finish my story of what White Eagle had said to me.

"I went to consult White Eagle about something that is bothering me. She never gave me a chance to speak about it," I say in frustration.

"Indeed," Singing Hawk says. "When the time comes you'll need to prepare. In doing so, you'll raise your personal vibrational frequency. This is required before consulting The Knowing." She looks directly at me and continues, "It requires practice. It's not something you can just do.

"If you consulted The Knowing now without preparation, all you would see is a wooden box with a lid and scrolls inside. The writing on the scrolls is in an ancient language. The language itself provides knowledge about the Universe, and provides portals to access knowledge of all the universes, as well.

"The Council of the Twelve consists of twelve individuals plus one facilitator. They tap into Infinite Intelligence as a way of seeking guidance for The People. We've been practicing this method for hundreds, probably thousands of years. It's not a place for debate." After a pause, she adds, "It is a select group of individuals. Gray Wolf, it is an honor for you to be asked to join."

"I wasn't asked," I respond. "I was informed."

"Just the same," says Singing Hawk, "it's significant that when the Knowing is consulted you will be there."

"Singing Hawk," I ask, "how do I prepare?"

"I recommend that you begin with a three-day sweat," she says. "When the time comes you will sweat out all toxins in your body, mind and soul. By the time you are finished, your mind will be clear, your body clean, your soul inspired. We will perform a ceremony for you as you begin to prepare and when you have completed the cleansing process." She looks at Shining Bird to let her know she would be included also.

Shining Bird blinks, and then nods agreement.

A pause.

Silence.

Months pass by.

On the other side of our village several women were talking.

"What?" Bluebird's eyes grew to the size of saucers. It was close to evening in late summer. She could not believe her ears after visiting with neighbors. Half running, half walking with great stride, she hurried home to her beloved to tell him the news. She could hardly believe it, how will he believe it? When she reached their home, she saw Water Dog and me standing outside chatting before going our separate ways for the night.

"Oh my," she blurts out in panic as she approaches us. We both turn to greet her and see the look of horror on her face. Alarmed, Water Dog gently grabs her arm.

"A murder," she breathlessly says trying to catch her breath.

Both of us stand there stunned at her pronouncement. "What?" We both ask at once, not wanting to hear what we had heard.

Needing physical support, Bluebird moves her arm out of Water Dog's grasp and reaches for the outside wall of her house to lean her weight against. With bowed head, she stands there gasping in disbelief at the words she is trying to form. Finally they come and she says, "Several villages . . . over . . . near the Scioto River, a man killed another man."

Stepping back and shaking his head, Water Dog asks, "Who was killed? Was it an accident?"

"No," she works up the strength to relate the story and says, "Evidently, a woman had been unhappy with her husband. I don't know who they are, but things were not right between them." Pausing to take another breath, she continues, "She found a loving partner to be with. When her husband found out, he killed her partner . . . He grabbed him and wrestled him to the ground and strangled him to death."

"What?" I ask incredulously, "what? You mean, a person actually killed another person?"

Still having difficulty breathing, Bluebird nods with tears in her eyes.

Stunned silence.

Several weeks after the incident, the council fire burned hotly one evening. White Eagle had sent for me to join her during the council meeting. Many people from the other village where the event had happened sat in attendance.

When I arrive, I see White Eagle sitting at the center. She signals me to sit beside her. After looking around, I discover that Rising Wolf is absent. Many Elders and Grandmothers sit in attendance from other villages, as well. The Council House is filled to capacity.

All came to hear Roaring Wind's story, the story of a husband killing his wife's lover. All felt compelled to participate in a returning to balance after this out-of-balance incident occurred.

After Roaring Wind presents his story in a manner that explained his justification, White Eagle asks the woman to stand and give her account.

"You know, my dear," White Eagle responds to the woman after hearing her side of the event, "you participated in this scenario by setting up the situation. You chose not to discuss your unhappiness with your husband. You chose not to bring your unhappiness to an Elder, a shaman, or a Grandmother.

"By making another choice, you might have prevented this from happening the way it did. By not addressing the conflict between you and your husband, by not speaking your unhappiness so something could have been done differently, you must accept partial responsibility for the outcome." The woman's face reddens with acknowledgment. Silently she sits down.

Then White Eagle says as she looks around at everyone she could see, "Is there anyone else who would like to speak here tonight?"

Silence.

Uncomfortable silence.

Nervous silence.

Shifting sounds. A cough sounds here and there. Shuffling sounds.

White Eagle closes her eyes and sits for a very long time before speaking. "We are Children of the Law of One."

She pauses to give silent emphasis to that thought.

Then she looks at Roaring Wind and says, "Each of us are individualized physical expressions of the One, the Infinite Intelligence. Since each of us is part of that One, none of us can sever our ties with It, as the One is in us. This alone drives our morality and ethics. We need no other law.

"We are in the Fourth World. If you recall, the Prophesy of the Great Serpent is as above, so below. Great Spirit is the energy of all of life, not only all of life, but specifically *in each life form* on this Earth.

"To hurt, to harm, or to kill another physical form of the One is to reject the Oneness of all of life, to reject your connection to It, to deny the Breath you have been given to be in this physical form. This you have done by killing another person.

"When we kill animals to provide ourselves with meat to eat, we do so with the permission of Mother Earth and the One. Together they provide us physical sustenance to continue in this physical energy field.

"Killing another human being is not part of our sustaining ourselves physically. It is not part of the energy field of maintaining our collective frequency. The act of killing another is an expression of feeling separate from the One, from your Source, from your Breath. You felt separate from yourself and from Great Spirit.

"Roaring Wind, you felt separate from your wife. You felt separate from her lover. Because you felt a sense of separation, killing your wife's lover was the answer for you. You didn't stop to think there might be a better solution or another choice. Perhaps you might have considered that your unhappiness could have been addressed in some positive way as to prevent such a violent choice.

"From what you said here tonight, you did not stop and give consideration to the thought that you should give her up and let her go her own way. Maybe you could find happiness either alone or with someone else. In fact, you did not stop to think anything at all. You chose instead to destroy someone who you felt had taken something of yours." White Eagle pauses, as if receiving inspiration and then continues, "No one person belongs to another as property.

"Because you acted on your sense of separation and violated the Law of One, you will be given the opportunity to continue to experience the separation that you chose."

Gasp.

Nervous silence.

"Starting tonight," White Eagle commands despite the gasps from the audience, "you are banished from The People."

Gasps from the Council House.

"You will leave here tonight. No one of The People will give you help or speak to you. No one will give you food or water as you leave. No one will see you. You are from this moment, not of The People."

Roaring Wind stands, obviously devastated by the declaration. He tries to move his mouth but no words form. He turns and walks out making his way through the nods of silent shock of those in attendance.

Another year passes.

Shining Bird and I loved our spacious home. At first we wondered why Red Fox had added extra rooms. However, with the birth of our third child and second son, Dancing Swan, his foresight was appreciated.

"Lone Tree, how are we doing on our winter meat supplies?" Raven's Wing asked after she had greeted the butcher. "I was getting the feeling that I needed to check with you. I know we still have possum meat, but that's usually fresh. I'm not worried about the fish as that usually can be supplied quickly when we are working the nets. Mussels are in good supply especially when the water is down and clear. I guess I am checking on the meat of larger game."

Nodding, Lone Tree then tilted his head as he said, "Let's take a look inside both the smoke house and the underground cooler." After touring the meat storage houses, he confirmed, "Raven's Wing, you are right. I'm thinking we should send out the word for those wanting to hunt that now might be a good time."

"In all the years I've been preparing food for The People and in the memory of before that even, I don't recall ever needing to check on meat supplies. We've always had hunters bring it in almost routinely and consistently. Of course, I doubt if we will ever run out of nuts for oil and for flour and so forth. Baum and the other agricultural areas always keep a supply for times when quantities of food are needed. Many of our vegetables are grown here also, so I don't worry about a supply of that nature."

Turning to go, she gets lost in thought, and then she said to him, while resting her arm on his arm for a moment, "It's just strange, that's all." Lone Tree nodded without adding more to the conversation as he watched her leave.

Some of The People enjoyed hunting. Men and women both took part in this activity, sometimes as individual hunting excursions and sometimes in small groups. It usually provided enjoyable times, but seldom lasted more than a day, maybe two. Game had always been so plentiful that getting provisions for the winter had never been a concern.

This time it was different.

Rising Wolf felt growing concern about his wife experiencing restless nights and especially her moaning in her sleep. After she woke herself up moaning in the early morning hours just before sunrise, she saw Rising Wolf already sitting up looking at her.

"Did you see it again?" he asked her after she blinked herself into focus.

"Yes, the brackish green hand, stained with a darkness, reached from its source across the eastern ocean. As it approached our land, finger tips narrowed, stretched out and touched down in different locations throughout our lands."

"This has been going on too long now, dear. It's time to call a regional Council of the Elders about it," Rising Wolf dictated.

White Eagle shook her head in disagreement, sucking in her lips to prevent further discussion from occurring.

"Yes, it is done," he said with determination. "I will send out word. While I know what you are seeing and experiencing is real and forbidding, we don't know what the others have been experiencing. It's time we ask them what they are seeing. We already know that Gray Wolf has picked up on it. He needs to be included in everything the regional council does now." Rising Wolf paused, looked down, then back up to White Eagle, then licked his lips once before speaking, and then took a deep breath.

"My dearest beloved," he spoke firmly, "it is something that must be discussed first with our Council of the Elders. If it is as prevalent as I predict it is, we will need to call a meeting of the Council of Twelve to consult The Knowing. I will tell you that I have seen it in my visions. It is insidious and final.

"My health has deteriorated much in the past year since your dreams first began several years ago. I must let you know that I will not live to see it happen to The People."

White Eagle stared at his pronouncement, unable to force herself to respond.

After Lone Tree and Raven's Wing had met to examine the village's meat supply, a call went out for a hunt to take place.

A group of hunters from our village had walked for several days and found not only no large game, but no sign of any. Befuddled by this experience, they stopped for a while sitting on the ground or leaning up against a tree.

"Do we go on today?" one asks.

"Maybe we should go back and get more provisions in preparation for a longer trip out?"

"I wish Gray Wolf were here. He'd call in the game for us so we wouldn't have to go so far." Several others nod in agreement.

"No need. I'm right here."

They all turn in surprise to see Gray Wolf standing on the outside of their circle.

"We need to go out farther. I brought more food as this might take longer than expected. We can also supply ourselves from the land as needed, depending on how long this takes," I say.

With their spirits lifted, each stands up and begins walking in a direction that would take us farther from our village and into unfamiliar territory. Not all the hunters carry weapons. Some members of the group were along just for the adventure, willing to lend a hand in the skinning and preparing the meat for transport.

Another day passes with no game in sight, and then unbelievably another day passes with the same result.

Managing to capture small game in the meantime to feed ourselves, some begin wondering where the larger game, prolific before, had gone. They start looking sideways at me. I had called in game before. My vision is clouded as to which direction to focus, frustrating the hunters.

One morning as the main body of our group is breaking camp, two boys come running back into camp. They inform us that they had been out scouting for animal sign. They tell us that they stumbled on a family living alone in a small opening in the wooded hills. They tell us that the family did not look well and might be in trouble.

When we get to where the family is located, we can easily see that the family is near starvation and suffering from dehydration. Several of the children appear in need of medical assistance, and the adults had festering wounds.

Where they were located is not a good place to camp, being that it is so far from a source of water. Herbs they needed for treatment do not grow close. It is such a barren spot.

Our group of hunters moves the family to our former camp site. All the children are picked up and carried.

Without discussion of any kind, immediately several of us fetch water. Others build a large campfire, partly for cooking and partly to create a sense of physical warmth as the nights are getting colder. Tea is brewed and poured for each family member.

Several others give them their coats and other pieces of clothing to help them restore body warmth. Those who parted with their coats and wraps then head back to our village to get more help, more supplies and to ask for a place to be prepared for the orphaned family.

I leave the group in search of herbs I could gather to tend to their wounds. It becomes clear to me that they not only needed herbs for their wounds, but also for their bodies to restore general health. I find myself in unfamiliar territory not knowing exactly where to look for the specific plants I need.

Sitting down at the base of a large tree, I open my thoughts and my heart with a prayer. "Great Spirit and Mother Earth, thank you for leading us to this family, so we may help them. We are indeed grateful for this opportunity. I ask that you show me to just the right plants that will perform the needed restorative energies. I ask all in Divine Order. As above so below. And, so it is."

After a while of meditating and listening, I get up and begin searching. Since I usually carry a medicine bag with me whenever traveling, I am able to gather many plants and carry them in the bag. Still one or two elude me. I look and look. Suddenly I hear something move through the bushes to my right. I strain to see what it was and see a movement of gray fur. When I stand up to see farther, I find myself looking straight into the eyes of a gray wolf.

"Ah," I say.

"Follow me," the wolf says as he turns and begins hopping over small shrubs and darting around others. In total confidence I proceed to follow him. After a distance, I see I am standing in the middle of a small meadow surrounded by beautiful trees all turning reds, oranges and gold in the autumn sun. The wolf disappears.

I look around and just listen. I hear a light harmonic sound coming from Mother Earth. The one medicinal herb I am looking for must be here I think to myself. I simply stand there in a soft quietness, opening myself up to Great Spirit. After opening my eyes, a sharp glint of the sun's reflection on a particular leaf, much like a sparkle, catches my attention. That's it. I stroll over to it and gather some of those particular plants into my bag.

As I return to camp one of the hunters informs me, "We've got a couple of large birds now. I'll pluck and clean them."

"One should be made into a soup as their systems probably can't handle solid meat right now," someone says.

"We can't make soup without a pot. We will also need a pot to make a stew with the several rabbits we just brought in," says another.

One of the young boys who had been bringing up water from a nearby creek offers, "I noticed some great clay down there. Why don't I dig up some, make a pot or two, put them in the fire to make it solid? Then we would have cooking pots, at least temporarily."

"I don't know if that would work," another objects.

"Well, we won't know unless we do it," the boy says and he bounds off down the hill toward the creek.

The family is well cared for, at least, given the limitations of the equipment we have.

Several of us still had some nut cakes and give them to the family to eat with a little nourishing tea. I manage to put several other herbs with water into the little canister someone had thought to bring and brought the decoction to a temperature just below boiling. I let it steep. When it had become just the right strength, I offer each family member a small cup to sip on until we finish other meal preparations.

Those remaining in our hunting group set up a shelter over them to help keep out the dampness. Since it looks like we will be staying longer than planned, they build several more for the rest of us. We use the buckskin tarps we had brought for packing and carrying meat home to cover the family for additional warmth at night.

The boy, with the clay idea, returns showing off two crude but possibly workable pots that are large enough to make a soup and a stew. We set them in the coals and put coals inside to help bake the clay to a proper hardness.

Using my training as a healer, and my spiritual intuition, I prepare several poultices and apply them to the infected wounds. Changing the poultices every several hours, I am able to reduce their fevers and pain. My entire focus is on them, rarely taking my attention away from my patients. By the end of the first day, we have medicine working, pots for cooking, fresh meat for stews and the tension lifting.

After several more days, the family members show significant improvement. No one is hungry. Our spirits lift. Since the different family members begin to move around a bit and talk with us, we enjoy sitting around the camp fire, especially evenings, telling stories, sharing personal insights, laughing, joking, and in general, acting like this was all done on purpose.

No one of the family offers any information as to why they were isolated in the middle of a forest with children, suffering from starvation and dehydration. No one of us asks as to their circumstances and why they came to such a state.

We have been here nearly a week before anyone from our village returns. And when they arrive, they bring food, much food, wild rice, cakes, vegetables, other supplies, best of all smiles and good news.

They tell us several Grandmothers designated an abandoned house for the new family.

Several other folks had begun to get it into shape for human habitation. New woven reed mats were laid down on the clay floor, beds repaired and outfitted with blankets, skins and buffalo robes. The roof over the kitchen area just outside the door was repaired and fenced properly. Furniture for both indoor and outdoor living was brought over by several other families. Waving Branches, the wood worker made a new table for them. Food supplies were stocked in the outdoor kitchen, complete with cooking and eating utensils.

Raven's Wing is planning a fresh hot meal for when the family arrives in our village. That way they wouldn't have to worry about food preparation right away as they got used to their new home.

Several more days pass before the family is capable of walking back to our village. With the additional help and supplies, they were escorted back to our village.

Additional supplies and more hunters joined our group to continue our initial plans of providing meat for the coming winter.

Now outfitted much more appropriately for a serious group hunt, we turn our faces toward seeking the game that has been so elusive. The energy field of the hunting group has noticeably shifted toward a sense of success now as we march across the wooded lands.

28

COUNCIL MEETING AT THE VILLAGE NEAR THE GREAT SERPENT

Never in the memory of The People had they had to work so hard to find game.

The group of hunters had grown with more volunteers after arriving with new supplies to help the destitute family. They walked for several more days before coming across a vast opening of grasses, larger than an extended meadow. They could see hills covered with tall grasses dotted only here and there with a tree or cluster of shrubs.

Before entering the open area, the group stops, and each individual says a silent prayer.

"Gray Wolf," one finally says. "Do you see that the cluster of shrubs on the one hill to the left is moving?"

Another says, "I don't think they're moving shrubs."

Alerted by an electric current running down my back, I stand facing the direction of the moving shrubs and focus on the beyond. I enter the realm of Oneness in gratitude and recognition of Spirit and Mother Earth providing for The People. Etherically, I reach out to the small herd of buffalo inviting them to provide sustenance for our People. As my spirit joins their spirit, in our oneness, they give their assent to contribute to The People.

"They're headed this way," a hunter whispers unable to believe his eyes.

"Get ready," another says. "We don't know what direction they will go in. Buffalo are unpredictable, so be ready for anything."

Nervous shifting of feet through the grass whispers among us as each member of the group positions themselves in tense apprehension.

Click, shuffle, knock, bump. Each hunter equipped with a weapon readies for just the right moment.

Watching. Waiting.

As the small herd wanders closer to the edge of trees hiding the hunters, the hunters begin to spread out from each other so as to create the advantage of approach from different directions.

As if knowing exactly where to stop to give the hunters the best possible position, the buffalo stop wandering and simply begin to graze contentedly.

Thwap.

Thwap. Thwap.

The bows of expert marksman could be heard above the trees silent in the wind.

Swoosh. Swoosh sound the spears thrown by the hunters of tall stature.

Flunk went the tonnage of buffalo as each hit the ground.

By the time a dozen or more animals are down and the hunters step out of the camouflage of trees, the remaining herd turns and trots in the opposite direction, soon to disappear.

Before the butchering could begin, I stand in the midst of these animals that had willingly given their physicality to us. Raising my hands to Spirit, I sing a prayer of gratitude and recognition for the meat that has been supplied to us and to the willingness of the animals to provide it. I thank the spirit of each animal as I touch each head in connection with the life energy now to flow into The People.

Anxious to get to work, several of the hunters pull out their knives in restless anticipation of the work ahead. After having to search so long for game, they had not anticipated such abundance all at once. Several of the younger boys stand nearby each animal watching the systematic cutting and slicing, learning as they help with smaller tasks as needed.

"This is a lot of meat and hides to pack back to our village," observes one of the hunters. "We should send someone back to the village to let them know. That way they can prepare for our return and also send us more help to get all of it back home. Also we should tell them all the travois dog teams would be useful. They will be necessary in hauling back the tremendous weight we'll have."

"Right," someone else says. "Two or three should go in case something happens on the way. Because it will take them several days or more, they should leave now."

I signal to several of the older boys who approach with smiles and say to them, "We need you to run back to the village and tell Lone Tree what we have here, so he can prepare for our return. Also have him call for more village members to join us here to help bring it all back. Lone Tree will give you the right equipment to haul back this quantity of meat and hides." I touch their heads with a palm of my hand as I say to them, "Now we've marked our way here. You know the trail markers."

I look straight into their eyes projecting an image and continue, "Remember them, so you can successfully lead them back to us. You'll need to take enough provisions with you to sustain you on your journey back to our village."

Eyes big as saucers, the boys nod, look at each other, and take off to gather up food stuffs for their traveling pouches.

"Wait," I call to them as they turn to leave, "I'll go with you to make sure you can find your way back. Besides, I want to return to see how my new son is doing." They smile knowing that I will be joining them.

I then turn to the remaining hunting party and say, "You know it would be best to start slicing, drying the meat and preparing the meat for travel as it may be several weeks before we get it all back to the village."

"Oooohhh," moaned White Eagle in her sleep. Rising Wolf opened one eye checking on his beloved suffering so in her sleep.

"On the next full moon," Rising Wolf began after they sipped their morning tea, "we will have the upcoming regional meeting of Elders and Grandmothers." His tone was one that was not to be argued with, "I've already called for it." White Eagle gave one nod reluctantly.

Raven's Wing consulted with Lone Tree at his butchering house about the upcoming council meeting. Because of the successful hunt, winter meat supplies were no longer as great a concern. It was then that she felt relief to see the first group of villagers returning with meat.

"Hello Water Dog," they both said to the giant of a man carrying what three or four average men could not.

He smiled as he set down his load and said, "We have a lot of meat on the way in."

"This is very, very good news, Water Dog," remarked Lone Tree now reassured that the concern over the winter meat supply was lifted.

"Thank you for helping," Raven's Wing said. "I sent over some nice cakes with honey to Bluebird while you were gone. I thought she needed them, and suspect you will enjoy them as well."

"No need to thank me, Raven's Wing," Water Dog said, wiping sweat off his forehead with his arm. "I'm only glad I was here and not up at Flint Ridge when the call came in from Lone Tree that the hunters needed help."

"You know," Raven's Wing said, "we'll be having a buffalo dance and feasting when everyone gets here and the meat is prepared. You're going to stick around for that before returning to Flint Ridge, I hope. It's important to celebrate and acknowledge how The People are provided for in our time of need."

The excitement of The People in the village rose as news of the success of the hunters spread. Several envoys from other settlements arrived in time to ask for a share as their supply of meat was noticeably low too. After properly preparing the meat for both storage and for immediate use, Lone Tree rationed out bundles to the folks from other villages.

"I've never seen Lone Tree divide out portions in such a non-generous way before," Floating Lily said to Raven's Wing. "I can't help wondering what's up."

Raven's Wing stopped what she was doing, turned and looked directly at Floating Lily. With all the freshly dried meat arriving, she had been busy preparing some of it for her village for immediate consumption. For the large portions, like the ones she was now handling, she often used the ovens and stoves in the center of the village near the meeting house. A number of women and Grandmothers assisted when the entire village was going to participate in a feasting.

The two of them, Floating Lily and Raven's Wing, had been a team for several years now. Raven's Wing now a Grandmother herself, medium height with long black hair trimmed with white strands, stood in contrast to the budding young woman of early teenage years standing taller than her with rippling red locks that reflected light like fire. It was the first time they had a conversation flavored by a sense of foreboding.

"I can't say, Floating Lily," said Raven's Wing. "I sense mischief, but can't put my finger on it. Maybe the upcoming council meeting will reveal something. White Eagle is haunted by something unseen. I've been led to prepare special foods for her. It's though she was sick, but not sick in her body . . . sick in her heart and in her mind." She paused to let Floating Lily digest the observations she had just shared and then said, "And, of course, I'm not sure about Rising Wolf, either. I don't think he is eating much of anything these days." Raven's Wing frowned disapprovingly.

"Well, I know one thing," said Floating Lily, "Lone Tree will be busy for a while. I think he has asked for help in the tanning of the hides. I don't know if you know this," Floating Lily hesitated as she saw Raven's Wing cock her head in surprise, "some of the hunters also brought in several deer they came across on their way back." Raven's Wing raised her eyebrows in acknowledgement of Floating Lily's observation, and then turned to continue her food preparation.

Council Meeting at the Village near the Great Serpent

Opening prayers completed in the Council House, White Eagle looks around at everyone in attendance. Each one is wearing the ceremonial garb of a formal meeting even though the invitation was for an informal meeting. The room fills with apprehension as silence prevails. Oil lamps flicker on the walls. The ceremonial fire darts and bounces in anticipation of a long-awaited meeting.

"We are the Children of the Law of One," White Eagle initiates the meeting's purpose. "I am asking each of you if you have been receiving visions or messages of something unexplainable, inexplicable in terms of what we all know to be true and right for The People."

"Ah, at last," Rising Wolf says to himself.

Uncomfortable silence spreads like a hand shutting the mouths of those in the meeting. No one speaks. No one wants to speak. Apprehension seizes the members by the throat to prevent the truth from coming out.

I stand up.

"Gray Wolf," acknowledges White Eagle relieved that someone is willing to show courage and begin what no one wants to begin.

"I am sensing a change coming," I say. "I don't know what this change is or when, but it's a definite something. I feel as if it means the end of the world as we know it."

Murmurings echo throughout the Council House.

"Our People have lived a thousand years of peace. We know of no other way to live." I continue. "Our lives are filled with each other, with love and laughter. We tell stories and bond with each other. We share all we have with everyone and still have untold wealth. We have wealth in the form of unlimited supplies of food, beautifully woven clothes, homes that provide a sense of substantial safety and nurturing.

"When a need arises for one of us, someone else provides the answer. Our People are healthy and well fed. Our children grow up healthy, balanced, and learn sharing and caring for each other by observing adults sharing and caring.

"Our ceremonies and pageants are deeply spiritual and meaningful at multiple levels. They are colorful, artistic and moving.

"We are wealthy with beautiful artwork, glazed pottery, painted mats and deer hides for hanging in our homes and much more.

"We have a history of amazing architecture, and monuments, like our Great Serpent, for example, and others around the country. Our traditions include coordination with the stars, Father Sun, and Sister Moon.

"Our prayers and our souls co-mingle with Spirit, the Creator of All, and with Mother Earth. We know who we are and how to live," I pause to catch my next breath, my next breath that I don't want to release.

"With all of our richness, with our deep spirituality and connection to the Great Oneness, with all of our experience with living successfully on Mother Earth, I am sensing a threat . . . a threat to all of it."

Rising Wolf leans back a little, exhaling as if he had been holding his breath for a very long time, murmurs softly, "Finally, it is spoken."

"So my question to you is," I say, "as I believe it is also White Eagle's question, what have you seen in your visions?" I sit down.

Murmurings.

Pan flute notes tingled on the breezes that drifted into the village. "They're here. They're here," called out several children. As was the custom, most of the villagers came to greet the traders wanting to see what was new. Whistling Wind and Blue Lightning, two Grandmothers stepped out first to check out who had arrived. The other villagers stood behind the gathering of children and others.

"Turning Rabbit," greeted Whistling Wind with a smile and warm grasp of his hand, "so glad to see you again. You've arrived with good timing. Tonight we're having a big feast in gratitude to Great Spirit and Mother Earth for the buffalo provided to us."

The aroma of well-seasoned meat roasting gently articulated the senses and the imagination for the upcoming celebration feast.

As usual, Turning Rabbit signaled to his companions, fewer in number than on previous trips, to set down their packs. "I've come to share what I have and to see Water Dog in particular." He noticed Floating Lily circling the group. He could hardly take his eyes off her as she had grown into a stunning beauty. It had been three years or more since he had visited this particular village. The last time he remembered speaking with Floating Lily was when she told him she was only ten years old. He blinked in disbelief.

"Close your mouth, Turning Rabbit," Blue Lightning softly commanded so as not to be overheard. "Release that thought. She's not for you." Turning Rabbit's attention jerked back to the present moment to see two Grandmothers standing before him.

"Oh, yeah, excuse me," he offered in apology, embarrassed at being caught in a private thought.

Floating Lily led the traders to the usual temporary camp reserved for traders and other migrating guests.

Later that afternoon, Turning Rabbit was glad to see Water Dog enter his camp. "I've got something I think you'll like, Water Dog," Turning Rabbit invited. After fumbling through several blankets, he pulled out several large pieces of obsidian. Water Dog's eyes attacked the black shiny stone with a passion that lit up his entire face.

"Oh, my goodness," Water Dog remarked. "What beautiful pieces." Then another, "oh, my goodness," slipped out from his lips as his hands reached out to hold the largest one. Several minutes passed as Water Dog was noticeably lost in fascination with the huge pieces of the glass.

"Uh-um," sounded Turning Rabbit clearing his throat.

Stepping back and shaking his head, Water Dog came back into focus. "What can I trade you for these?" he asked when he finally found himself.

Meanwhile, in the Council House, after much dialogue among the council members, Red Coat stands up and waits for everyone to stop talking.

"It does appear that many of us have had visions of something coming, something that feels dark and ominous. Some see it as a dark foreign energy field coming across the eastern ocean and covering our lands with a grip that chokes the very life out of The People. In White Eagle's dreams she saw the land dry up, die, and become barren as it sweeps over from the coast inland. Does that about capture the sense of what many of us are seeing in our visions?"

"There's more we have not shared, Red Coat," says a voice from the back.

"More?" Red Coat questions. "Then we need to hear it. This is the time and the place to have it out. This ominous feeling of impending doom has been with us long enough. Now is the time to speak about it."

"These are really interesting arrowheads, Water Dog," Turning Rabbit commented.

"There are times when I just feel like getting really creative," Water Dog responded. "I don't know if they would serve well as an arrowhead for killing game or not. I guess I got pretty carried away with the designs. Some of them might be better used as part of a necklace, I think."

"Well, I'll take them and trade them out as an experimental version. I'll be going south from here soon. If the hunters use them and later tell me they worked well, I'll let you know when I return back up here. How's that?" Turning Rabbit offered.

"I'm okay with that," Water Dog nodded. "I'm not really invested in these particular arrowheads. What I'd like to know, though, is about the obsidian you brought back. They are such great pieces. Where did you get them?"

"The place where this kind of rock occurs is very far from here," said Turning Rabbit, sitting down on a bench like he was beginning a long story. Water Dog sat down also on the bench, sturdy enough to hold the giant. The guest camp offered some accommodations. Benches like these were included.

Turning Rabbit said, "It takes me a very long time to make that specific trip. There is a place west of here, far north and west of here, a place where sometimes the mountains smoke. One river boils sometimes as it flows, and the land has many steaming vents. There are streams from springs of boiling water that issue from Mother Earth. In this place there are great stone mounds from which boiling hot water and steam shoot into the sky!"

Water Dog cocked his head as he listened, his imagination sparked, "So this black obsidian is there in this strange land?"

"Yes. This black glass occurs in various places around there. The land there has extreme mountains, not like here at all. The land here, while it has rolling hills, seems almost flat compared to the rugged mountains there. It can be a dangerous place if you don't know the area. In spite of the plentiful game there, I rarely encounter other people in that area."

"How do you get there? I mean is it a place I could go with my flint knappers?" asked Water Dog. "We search the ground for places where Mother Earth formed good flint stone. I've been pretty successful at finding those spots over the past several years. I think I'd like to try this new place."

"Uh, well, I don't think you heard me when I said it takes me many, many, *many* moons to get there," Turning Rabbit said. "You'd have to travel west toward the Mississippi River. You'd be in really flat land then, flatter than here. Then you'd have to travel up the Missouri River north, then west. Civilization thins out the farther you go. Then to get to this particular area, you'd have to drop down toward the Yellowstone River."

"Yeah, but it sounds fascinating," said Water Dog intrigued.

"I've been doing it so long, I don't think about how treacherous some of those mountains can be. There are trails that most of the traders use, so we don't lose our way." Turning Rabbit paused a moment, then asked, "Remember Warm Stone?" Water Dog nodded. "He now has his own trader group. He travels these areas. In fact he has gone all the way to the west ocean there."

Water Dog's face showed surprise. "Oh, wow," he responded to that new thought.

Turning Rabbit said, "I'm not sure I plan on returning to those very distant lands. That is where I got the obsidian, and knew I had to get it to you, which is why I'm here right now.

"I find trading more productive when I take a more southern route. Trading with the settlements along the Mississippi River tends to be more profitable. When I go into Mexico and even farther south the land changes so much I can hardly believe it is all one land."

As their conversation continued, the discussion in the Council House deepened.

"I saw savages coming to this land," one Grandmother bravely says.

Nods and murmurings.

"Yes, I saw the same thing. In my dreams I saw that they brought not just death to us, but much suffering. The devastating sicknesses were one thing, but the real threat was the poison they brought with them," another says.

"The poison you mentioned is what I saw as the way they treated Mother Earth, the way they treated each other, and the way they treated The People," says another Elder.

"Living in tune with Mother Earth, we live in the sense of Oneness," reaffirms Thunder Cloud. "The savages that are coming to our lands are a *godless* people, with no sense of connectedness. They represent a threat to The People."

Murmurings.

"That explains some of my visions, then," a Grandfather speaks up. "I keep seeing the godless savages systematically and deliberately strategizing to decimate The People. I keep seeing them herding The People in groups across unknown lands, making The People live in dirt, treating The People with less dignity than the dirt they walked on. I keep seeing them forcing The People to move and stay in lands not of their ancestors. I keep seeing the godless savages raping our women without retribution, taking away our children and beating the children into submission to take away the language of The People."

Nods and louder murmurings.

"Yes, thank you for speaking, Grandfather," one Elder comments, "I have seen the same thing and more. I saw them torture our children and sexually abuse them in the houses where they forced the children to live after taking them from their families. I saw too much of these fierce violators of Great Spirit stripping our men of all honor and dignity, not just once, but repeatedly over more years than I could imagine . . . I don't know . . . ," he finishes with tears running down his face while he chokes on overwhelming emotion.

There is not a dry eye in the house.

Choking, coughing, weeping, moaning.

Red Coat stands up again and says, "From my visions, I'm not sure they are godless."

"Perhaps, they have some kind of connection to Great Spirit. Maybe we are seeing the way they connect to the One is different than the way we connect.

"Maybe, it's just the way they interpret their relationship to Great Spirit. Perhaps they perceive their god as a force external to them. I think that their behaviors show us their sense of connectedness does not include The People, because they see us as different from them. They do not see The People as being connected to them or to the One.

"So perhaps it is their understanding of how all this works, of how everything relates that contrasts to our understanding. The understanding of things is acted out in behaviors. So, in our visions we are seeing how they behave toward us. This informs us that our sense of connectedness is in conflict with theirs, and sets up the physical conflicts that we are seeing in these visions. We see everyone and everything as connected. They clearly do not. That doesn't make them a godless people.

"What I do see in my visions of them is they are vested in being *right*. They come from a position of being right, even when what they do harms others, especially The People. So whatever they do, they determine what it is they want, then they call it 'right' and go forward, justifying what they do based on *their* sense of 'rightness.'

"In our visions, when we see them taking away our language, our cultural traditions, customs and lands, they interpret it as being 'right.'

"From their view, they were doing the 'right' thing. They have no understanding that stripping The People of their language, their customs, their homes, and the land of our ancestors diminishes The People of our humanity.

"But to them, taking away our humanity was the 'right' thing. In their interpretation of Great Spirit, they feel justified."

Council members squirm.

Red Coat pauses momentarily then continues, "For a thousand years The People have lived embraced in the arms of Great Spirit, at one with the Great Oneness. Living and being in such a way has given us a sense of Order to our universe, our world as we know it.

"We see them and their behavior as being out-of-order with Great Spirit, with the Divine Order as we know the Divine Order. That toxic energy that many have seen coming to our lands has touched some of us here already. The poison of this energy or consciousness has infected several of us with its fingers of the dark field touching down as it advances from the land across the sea to our lands."

Squirms and coughing.

"Yes, my dearest ones," Red Coat responds to the discomfort of his listeners, "Over the last several years, we can recall several incidents of individuals behaving in a way out-of-order with our sense of Oneness.

"For example, Roaring Wind killed his wife's lover. When he spoke at the council meeting before being banished, he eloquently defended his actions as being justified. While he gave a cogent argument, it was based on a faulty premise. To him, his reaction to his wife's infidelity was justifiable and therefore the right thing."

Red Coat looks around the room to see nods of affirmation. "Clearly his choice was made, not from a sense of being in at-one-ment, but from a sense of feeling separate. This sense of separation allows individuals to decide what they want, do it, and then call it the 'right thing to do' that comes from an out-of-order state of being.

"We are seeing in our dreams that the new people coming to our lands behave just like that. We see them as being in an out-of-order state, coming from a sense of being separate from the Great Oneness.

"I see them feeling justified in what they do and defending their actions as the 'right thing' *according to their beliefs*. To them, decimating The People and taking our lands is seen by them as the 'right thing to do' and therefore justifiable. They see it as the right thing, because they see themselves as superior to The People. A few of them can see The People for who we are. Most of them can't see us for who we are, because their perspective does not allow them to see beyond what they want and what they *want to see*."

After a pause, Red Coat goes on, "Now we are seeing in our dreams and visions an energy field coming to our lands in the air or space above us physically. It is deceptive. It *deludes* some into thinking it is above them and is an irresistible force. It preys on those most vulnerable. Those feeling a sense of inadequacy or having not-enough of something succumb.

"Fear then infiltrates into their consciousness. This fear-filled consciousness translates into out-of-order behavior that they defend as being justified and right."

Silence in the room as Red Coat again pauses momentarily before continuing, "Remember the Prophecy of the Great Serpent. Remember the meaning of the positions of the two triangles in the Great Serpent Prophecy. We all know the Earth triangle has been moved out and in front of the oval and the Serpent's Mouth. The triangle representing Heaven has been swallowed by the Serpent."

A Grandfather challenges, "But what does that have to do with our visions?"

Red Coat swallows and replies, "We are on the cusp of the destruction of the Fourth World. Our visions are warning us of a shift in consciousness which, if not properly addressed, may lead to the destruction of the Fourth World."

"What we are beginning to experience is the same energy that led to the destruction of the three prior worlds.

"This dark energy field, in our visions, represents, among other things, the belief that the *seen*, the physical, the material is more real, more important, more of a priority than is the *unseen* that is the spiritual. That is why our Ancestors placed the 'Earthly' triangle where they did, in front of the oval. It's a reminder to us of the Prophecy of the Serpent."

Murmurings.

"But, Red Coat," challenges an Elder, "we are in the Fourth World now. Are you saying that we are causing the destruction of the Fourth World?"

Silence.

"We are not causing it," Red Coat answers. "We are participating in it . . . not causing it. How we choose to act determines the outcome. If we let this negative energy field take over, we will see humanity celebrate materialism and physical life as a priority, while negating what actually uplifts us, what actually supports us in our endeavors, what actually inspires us to become and remain successful in the physical." He pauses to let the message sink in.

Then Red Coat adds, "What gets turned around is the sense of order. Right now we operate in Divine Order. That is where we live and come from in our thoughts and intentions toward others. We need no law as Order shows us the way.

"The reversing of the triangles of 'as above, so below' produces an 'out-of-order' state of being. What comes from this negative energy field is out of order beingness, which is what produces the behaviors and actions seen in your visions and dreams and the incidents, like Roaring Wind, that we discussed earlier this afternoon."

Then Thunder Cloud stands up and asks, "We all see that this energy field is coming. We see it in our dreams and visions. We see it in the stars. It is coming to take over our lands. Can we stop it? What can we do to prevent it? Or, what can we do about it?"

"Yeah. Yeah," sounds come from the council members with nods and a readjusting of their bodies suddenly alerted.

"With the energy field come other peoples who manifest disease, death and destruction of The People, our People," chokes out White Eagle, grateful that Red Coat had taken over.

She had suffered so much emotional stress over the past few months that her usual stamina had weakened.

"So, tell us, Red Coat, if you can," challenges another voice, "what can we do about this? Can we fight it? Can we fight the people invading our lands?"

Murmurings.

Louder murmurings.

"Fighting the people as invaders won't change the energy field causing them to take our women and children and our lands," responds Red Coat. "Fighting means killing other human beings, which is not part of the Children of the Law of One."

He pauses to swallow hard, and his eyes focus on something beyond the room. Then he continues, "If we choose to fight, then we would no longer be Children of the Law of One, because *you become what you fight.* If we fought, then we would lower ourselves to the level of the invaders and become like them or worse than them."

Uncomfortable silence prevails, punctuated by shuffling, shifting and grunting.

A long pause and Red Coat continues to stand, looking straight at those in attendance.

"May I ask a question?" asks another Grandmother who has been listening intensely. Red Coat nods affirmatively. "When is this happening?"

"Yeah," echoes another voice, ". . . next month? Next year? How long do we have to prepare?"

Silence.

Red Coat looks down for a long moment, folds his muscular arms in front of him, and shuffles his foot before answering. "We can't say."

Rumblings from the council members.

Red Coat lifts his palms to the audience to ask for their attention. "As you know, Sister Moon cycles around Mother Earth in her rhythm. Mother Earth moves in her cycles in her rhythm. Everything occurs in its own rhythm. No one can say 'when' this will happen."

"So what you are saying, Red Coat," another asks, "then, is we might have time to prepare in some way. If so, then we need to discuss what we can do and what we should do. Is that right?"

"We should leave! We should leave these lands and avoid all of this," shouts one from the back.

Objections and other vociferous opinions loudly rumble through the audience that begins transforming into a vocally unruly crowd.

"No, we should stay and see what happens," a difference voice shouts.

White Eagle looks panicked as she catches Red Coat's eye. Clearly she feels uncomfortable with this turn of events.

Then one Grandmother stands up in the middle of the council members and waits patiently for the members to settle down.

When all quiets down, giving her the floor, she says emphatically, "If we go," she pauses and turns to look at each individual, to ensure her words are received with power, "if we go, we will not be able to pass down our culture to our children and our children's children and their children.

"The land here is part of our culture. We are entrained to the land as part of Mother Earth. This land provides for us in unique ways. It accommodates us and we accommodate the land in a unique partnership. It is partially because of this unique partnership with this *particular* land that is responsible for our great abundance, continued health, and success as The People.

"Our People have lived here for thousands of years. Leaving this land is not an option. If we go, we will not be able to pass on our culture and *heritage* to our descendants. If we go, we will die."

Approving sounds affirm her declaration.

Another Grandmother stands up.

Faces turn to her.

She speaks, "If we stay, we will die."

Gasps.

She continues, "What has been said here is all true. We have a unique relationship with this land as part of Mother Earth. Yet, it feels like this land is being taken over by someone else or something else. It feels like this land is being taken away from us, forcing us to become separated from our abundance.

"If they take our lands, they take our culture. If we stay, we will be overrun as our culture becomes destroyed by those coming. If our culture is destroyed, we lose our identity. There will be nothing to pass on to our children and our children's children. If we stay, we will die. I say we leave before that happens!"

Murmurings.

After a very long pause, Red Coat stands up and faces White Eagle and Rising Wolf.

White Eagle looks up and beyond the meeting house before speaking, "Our ancestors who built the Great Serpent in the long ago had the same visions. Our ancestors felt much as we do tonight. The writings on the birch bark scrolls tell of conversations much like we have experienced this afternoon. A very large group of them left and headed west. We know they are living in lands west and southwest of us here, because the traders sometimes speak to me about them. According to the traders, they appear to be doing well.

"I cannot speak to whether we should go or stay. It is not a decision for me to make. That choice is up to each one of you and to all the other families in each of the villages across our lands. Nothing will be decided now.

"The purpose of this meeting has been fulfilled, which was to speak to the issue of the messages in our dreams and visions. We have accomplished that. What most of us have seen or felt is now out in the open. The problem has been identified. I'm not sure additional discussion is warranted at this time unless new information comes to light.

"What I propose at this time, is for you to go back to your villages and share what we have learned and discussed here.

"Now unless anyone objects, we should adjourn" she pauses to wait for an objection that did not come. "After that we will see."

"Is there anyone else who wishes to speak at this time?" she says.

Quieted voices and shuffling.

At that, everyone stands up stiff from sitting down for so long. They stretch and breathe. Little or no conversation takes place.

Each one files out of the meeting house, leaving the Council House empty of people, but still filled with the emotional energy of a people distraught and confused with the threat of extinction of a way of life.

29

THE DIALOGUE

The Buffalo Dance was a favorite dance among The People. While The People did not routinely seek the buffalo when hunting, they fully appreciated what the huge beast provided them. Buffalo robes often were acquired through trading with either traders or other villages to the west.

With the arrival of the huge quantities of meat, Lone Tree set to work. With a small team of volunteers, Lone Tree and the others made quick work of storing, smoking and setting some aside for feasting. His team also prepared the hides for tanning. In his storehouses he kept heads of animals, tanned and preserved for wearing during the celebratory dances of gratitude.

Feasting on the luscious meat, in addition to the plethora of side dishes, temporarily lifted the spirits of those visitors about to leave. Many decided to stay for the Buffalo Dance, because it was one of thanksgiving. With the small band of traders joining the onlookers, the energy of the dancers rose in excitement and anticipation knowing they would be performing for the larger than usual audience.

Floating Lily felt ambivalent about becoming one of the dancers. With encouragement from Raven's Wing, Floating Lily donned the massive head of a buffalo over her fur-cloaked body. Being tall, lithe and strong, Floating Lily gracefully performed the part of a lead buffalo ruling the grasslands and hills, then engaging with hunters only to fall to their spears and arrows for a successful hunt as the ceremony ended. The steady sounds of the drums, lyrical notes of the flutes, panpipes, copper sphere rattles and other musical instruments decorated the air, creating a composition of art, music, and drama with the chanting of the Buffalo Song.

The entire evening served to create smiles, laughter, and happy talk for the guests and council members who otherwise would have left for home the next day contemplating dread of an unknown fate of The People.

The Buffalo Dance proved indeed to be good medicine that day.

"You did well, my beloved," Rising Wolf spoke softly to White Eagle when they finally arrived at their home, the sounds of the celebration still wafting on the wind.

"Thank you," she replied. "I have not been myself for too long. It is time now that I open to Great Spirit to realize the returning of my strength. It will be needed in the upcoming years, and I do not wish to let my People down. I am grateful to Red Coat for his part during the council meeting since I was not able to manage. That is something I cannot let happen again."

As they nestled in for the night, they wrapped their arms around each other until sleep came over them. Much to Rising Wolf's relief, his wife slept peacefully all through the night for the first time in a very long while.

"Oh, you're already up?" asked Rising Wolf sleepily as he lazily moved through the bed covers.

After giving his morning blessing of tobacco outside the house, Rising Wolf returned inside to see that White Eagle had already prepared him morning tea. Smiling, she offered him a steaming cup. Rising Wolf accepted the offering, and stood still for a long moment. A long tear made its way down his check. Without speaking, he sat beside his lifelong companion to sip his tea in silence.

Upon finishing the morning drink, Rising Wolf looked around for her comb and reached for it. After shifting his body slightly to access the back of his wife, he began to comb her long white strands.

"I remember when I combed your hair as young lovers. Your hair was so black, I used to marvel at how it shined with a shimmering effervescent light that danced upon its blackness."

"What is it, my love?" White Eagle asked, wrinkling her brow, suspecting something. Turning to face her and reaching to hold her hand in both of his, Rising Wolf looked her in the eyes and said, "I will not live to see what's coming." He sighed. White Eagle's eyes grew large to bring in the sound of his words weighted with meaning.

He continued, "I will die soon. Aside from your companionship throughout all these years, my life has drawn significance from flint knapping and Flint Ridge. It is there where I found my connection with Mother Earth. It is there where I connected with Great Spirit, especially working in collaboration with Mother Earth and the flint she provided. I have directed the flint mining operation for decades. I have managed to keep the production and flow of flint for all of its many uses continuous for all our People, north of the Great Lakes, all the way to the eastern ocean and south to the south ocean. I have done well serving our People. So, my dearest one, it is there at my house at Flint Ridge where I choose to die."

"Oh," squeaked White Eagle.

Rising Wolf continued uninterrupted, "I see your strength returning. I will be leaving soon. I will take a small amount of supplies with me. It is my intention to live in my stone house up there, then lie down and die. After a while, you can send Water Dog up there to check on me. If he finds me dead, which is what I expect, then you can arrange for a quiet ceremony of only a few favorites. I wish to be buried in the house with the arms of Mother Earth wrapped around me.

"I know that many of our People choose cremation. But, my dear one, I have worked the earth my entire life. So, I wish to have my body remain in earth as well."

"Oh, Grandmother, it feels good to be going out tonight to spend time with friends. It's been a long time since we've all been together, just us," Shining Bird says as she finishes putting her three little ones into bed. "The five of us have remained especially close since we were children the size of my own children," she wistfully adds while admiring her brood of three and throwing a softly woven raspberry colored wrap around her shoulders. It nicely compliments her dark blue tunic. As they walk out of the house together, Grandmother Plum Blossom sits down in a chair outside to contemplate before turning in herself.

"I'm anxious to hear Gray Wolf retell the events of the last council meeting. He's already told me most of it, yet I'm interested to hear what our friends have to say," Shining Bird says to her Grandmother before leaving for Water Dog's home.

Water Dog's home, being more spacious than most, drew friends to meet and visit there usually in the evenings.

"Ha, ha, ha," Shining Bird hears laughter and bits of stories float through the air coming from Water Dog's home as she makes her way there.

"Oh, my lovely."

Shining Bird enters to hear herself being greeted by her husband with eyes shining only for her. She sees her childhood friends sitting around Water Dog's lovely home all grown up, living the lives they always knew they would. Gliding across the room before nestling next to me, Shining Bird assesses the success each of them had achieved. Nodding happily to herself, she appreciates the self-actualization each individual is manifesting, each in his or her own way. Their dreams have been realized and fulfilled.

Water Dog proved to be an amazing flint knapper to the point of being a true artisan, and was managing much of the flint mining operations. Bluebird Near the Lily ever in love with him, now is living a life unburdened by caring for her smaller siblings, and able to maintain a higher level of sturdy good health that she had not always enjoyed.

Red Fox, now an accomplished shamanic architect, was known across the entire Ohio River Valley. He was known even farther towards Canada for his abilities to design and build both homes and meeting houses with great skill.

Lastly, assessing herself, Shining Bird thought to herself, "I am pleased to be who I am, living the life of my dreams, with my adoring husband, Gray Wolf."

Just as she finished her thought, I turned to look at her as if I had heard or felt her last thought. Smiling at her, I reached over to Shining Bird's face and moved a wisp of her black hair that had been clinging tenaciously to her beautiful face.

"Welcome, Shining Bird," Water Dog says to her joyously after the raucous conversation died down. Shining Bird softly smiles and gives a nod of acknowledgement to each friend, again feeling her earlier assessment of each one as she arrived.

A momentary awkward silence.

"So tell us, Gray Wolf," Red Fox initiates the change of energy in the conversation, "What happened at the council meeting? What was said?" He leans forward to grasp more from my words than just my words. The circle of the five friends quiets.

"Many of The People have been having disturbing dreams and visions in their meditations for some time now," I begin. The circle of friends all nod in affirmation.

I continue, "While each of the visions or dreams is different, they all reveal a commonality."

My listeners sit in silent suspense.

I go on, "That commonality centers on our lands being approached by another people from across the great ocean from the east." I look around the circle, inhale, and then say, "Some of our people referred to them as invaders, because they are so different from The People. These foreigners are not from the land of our ancestors to the east. They are not from the land of our ancestors to the west across the great ocean to the west. They are from a land different from any of our ancestors."

Silent anticipation.

"Some of our Elders saw our lands dying. The death of the land of our People moved from the east coast, straight across the Ohio River Valley, and on and on to the west. No one saw a stop to it.

"Others saw these invaders intent on destroying The People.

"I do not wish to repeat the brutal and ugly visions many of the council members articulated as they were indeed heart-wrenching. I can't imagine human beings inflicting such atrocities on other human beings. I do not want to repeat it. I can't." I pause, choking slightly, to allow the emotion rising up inside me to settle down before going on.

"The discussion resulted in some advocating for migrating to someplace far away, while others argued that we should stay. Either way, destruction of our civilization seems inevitable . . . at least with the coming of the foreigners."

I pause momentarily, look up, put my hand up to my chin and rub it briefly. Each member of the circle suck in a breath and sit still, eyes wide suddenly alerted to an impending danger.

I then say, "The word 'foreigners' is an interesting way to describe them. I use it here, because it seems appropriate to name them something that means 'they are not like us.'" I look around the circle as I wait for another thought to formulate before speaking again.

Everyone around the circle silently nods.

"Someone even called these newcomers to this land 'a godless people.' I think that was said because most council members saw these new people as not comprehending the One, or the unity of the Great Oneness the way we do. We understand that the entire Whole exists in each part and in each part of each part," I say.

Red Fox interrupts, "I've seen some of this in my visions also. In my visions I saw these new people exploiting Earth, and exploiting each other. I saw them not serving Mother Earth but savaging her . . . not serving Life.

"I also saw them in competition with Life, in competition with each other and Mother Earth.

"In one of my visions, I realized they saw The People as savages who worship animals, not comprehending that we honor the Spirit of the animals as being part of Mother Earth, as being part of the Whole."

Each circle member turns, nods, and looks at each other around the circle.

Red Fox folds his arms and sits back indignantly. Then leaning forward, unfolding his arms as another thought occurs to him, he adds, "What I sensed is that they think they could actually own the land they walked on. Humph . . . as if land could be *owned*. I saw them building houses and fighting over land boundaries, behaving like the earth they strutted on was *ownable*. They perceived land as separate from them," pausing momentarily in thought, then he says, "In fact my visions showed me they behaved in ways that looked like they saw themselves as separate from everything, each other included."

Quiet murmurings of affirmation around the room.

"You know," Water Dog offers after a long silence, "when I walk the land seeking flint, I feel so in touch with Mother Earth. I hear her speaking to me. I hear the stone I am carving speaking to me as I work the flint, or quartz or obsidian. The rocks speak to me. Their heartbeat matches my heartbeat. My heartbeat matches Mother Earth's heartbeat. It's all in a rhythm, a grand symphony of entrainment. From what you are saying, these new people are not entrained to the Earth and that their hearts do not beat in the same symphony."

Everyone looks at Water Dog in surprise, not accustomed to hearing him speak so fluently, and much impressed with his observation.

"What it makes me think of," chirps Bluebird Near the Lily, "is our mica windows. Light passing through them is diffused. This represents a veil over the vision of our physical eyes, in not being able to see with our eyes the true light of the Oneness that lies beyond.

"Only through our hearts and our spiritual eyes can we see this true Light. This is the veil that Great Spirit made for this, the Fourth World. This is different from the ways of the First World when all were in the oneness, and there was no sense of separation."

Nods of agreement.

"Our mica windows are wonderful for letting in light. They are wonderful for letting in the sunlight or moonlight while keeping out some things undesirable like insects." We all nod. Bluebird Near the Lily continues, "Letting in the light, yes, they perform wonderfully at that. We are grateful for how the mica windows serve us. But, what they also do is preclude right seeing. Being opaque, diffusing light, the windows prevent us from seeing clearly through them. I guess it is up to us to see clearly using our spiritual vision through our heart energy."

Murmurings of agreement.

Bluebird Near the Lily continues, "It's like the foreigners look at us through opaque windows. It's not that they don't want to see us. It's that they can't see us. They don't know to see through their hearts."

Water Dog looks adoringly at his life's companion.

"One thing I have learned in studying the writings of the Ancient Ones," chimes in Shining Bird, "is that everything consists of energy. We move in and out of energy fields. I see these energy fields with my spiritual eyes, through my heart energy.

"Energy can appear to me as a wave, a sine wave, moving up and down as it flows rhythmically in tune within the harmonics of the field it occurs in.

"Energy can also appear as a particle or an object we can see with our physical eyes. Whether I see something as a wave or as a particle depends on my intent at the moment. In other words, what I see depends on my perspective.

"It's not that what I'm perceiving is one or the other. In fact, it is both at the same time. Yet it acts out as either one or the other depending on what I *want* to see and whether I *see* with my physical or spiritual eyes."

Red Fox furrows his brow, trying to understand how this relates to the visions and impending threat to The People and then asks, "I'm not following you exactly. How does this relate?"

Shining Bird swallows, sits up straight, then leans forward a bit as if to physically bring clarity to the moment and says, "The new people, the foreigners' worldview only allows them to see the world in fragments. It's like seeing, as Bluebird said, through mica windows as they see only with their physical eyes. Because they tend to look through only their physical eyes and rely on the 'seen', they see us as the particle only. They assume that is all there is.

"Their tendency is to fragment the seen universe and dismiss the unseen connectedness that flows through us and everyone and everything.

> *They do not comprehend that what ties us all together is a living, conscious essence which is the underlying fabric of the Universe.*

This unseen living, conscious *essence* is the Great Oneness.[2]

"They see everything as disconnected from everything else. They treat each other as though they were separate from each other. That's why they can exploit each other and other peoples. That's why they think they can lay claim to land and exploit it for what it can bring them. They disregard the damage done to Mother Earth or other people, not realizing that they damage themselves in the process too. When they hurt others, they hurt themselves. They deny that they are doing damage to themselves because of their actions. They only see what they think they can gain through their actions. Their world is a world of fragments and fragmentation."

Shining Bird swallows again, pauses briefly to see she still has an audience, and then continues, "It's about perspective. Their worldview comes from a perception of separation and fragmentation. They don't see us, The People, I mean really 'see' us, because they don't 'see' themselves.

---

[2] Please see the appendix to this chapter.

"They don't see themselves as part of the Whole, as part of the Great Oneness. They don't comprehend that the Great Oneness is in every particle and is not separate from it. The Great Oneness is the Conscious Essence that is found in everyone and in everything, that unites us all into the Whole. That is why the Whole is found in each part and in each part of each part.

"They can't treat us with dignity, because they don't see us as requiring dignity, something which, for most of them, is impossible to grant to anyone unlike themselves. We appear separate from them.

"It goes back to the particle or wave. When I see the particle, it *appears* solid. If I am looking to see a solid, I will see a solid. If I look for the energy wave of the same essence, it *appears* to me as a wave. What I see depends on my intention at the time.

"We each see the world from our own perspective. It is our *perspective* that determines what we see. Their worldview prescribes they see in fragments. To them, we are just another fragment.

"Their perspective determines they 'see' only people who are like *them*. When they encounter people not like them, they separate others in terms of people more like them, or less like them, or not at all like them. Because their perspective determines what they think they see, rather than what is actually there, they react to what *appears* to them as if it were truth." Shining Bird, raising her eyebrows with widened eyes looking at each of her beloved friends, pauses to allow that thought to sink in, hoping she had been clear.

"Which is why," I interject, "they come from a position of being right or justified. They react to appearances, believing them to be a reality. Not realizing that what appears to them or what is happening around them is created by their intention or perspective. They see us as a particle rather than as a wave of energy that connects all of us, including them, in the One. I see them as being trapped in the physicality of the *seen*, being out of alignment with the *unseen*."

"Does that help, Red Fox?" inquires Shining Bird, looking at her friend. He nods in affirmation.

Then Red Fox says, "So what you are saying is the harmonic of their collective frequency is out of phase with the harmonic of our collective frequency. This will produce a clash of cultures. The harmonics do not blend. Therefore, the clash of peoples is inevitable. Their perspective of reacting to the world of fragments conflicts with our perspective of the world of oneness. Does that about sum it up?" Each nods in agreement.

After a comfortable silence, I say, "Yes, that's right. They are emotionally attached to being *right*. In my visions, I saw them looking at us and seeing that we were very different from them.

The Dialogue

"They were challenged to distinguish between form and substance. Not too many of them could see substance, so most of them had to rely on the physical form of things to make a judgment. For example, what people look like, how people live and what their sacred objects are. They see our ceremonies as obscene, because to them that is true. Yet, ceremonies and sacred objects are only form. They rely heavily on the 'seen,' by that I mean what they can see with their physical eyes, rather than being in touch with the 'unseen' that connects all of us in the Great Oneness."

I cannot stop the flood of thoughts coming to me, and I say, "Because they are so immersed in valuing form, and believing form to be reality, combined with the need to be right, in their perceptions, and in their minds, *we* have to be wrong . . . wrong in every way. To their way of thinking, making us 'wrong' makes them more right. In their minds, because we are not like them, they feel it is permissible to destroy our societies, to attempt to abolish our identity and to do away with all those who rebel against them.

"They come from the position of being right. So when in time, they manage to move us to lands not of our ancestors, partly to control a population they wish did not exist, and partly for profit from the natural resources of our original lands, it is considered *right and just*. To them, we are wrong to even be. In their minds they are 'right' to treat us so inhumanely.

"In my visions I saw them work at making The People imitations of them. They want to impose their worldview and beliefs upon us. Those who refuse to become like them, believing like them, are dealt with harshly. Being right, so as to profit by it in some way, justifies the torture, the killing, the robbing us of our identity, our language, and our culture. All of this is sanctioned by their recognized powers as right and just.

"It is not in their scope of understanding that The People are another Expression of the Whole, the Great Oneness. All Life's expressions being connected in Spirit is not part of their comprehension.

"Yes, Shining Bird, their view of the world is indeed one of fragments, separated from all other fragments and each fragment isolated.

"It's like those colorful birds that Floating Lily got from the traders. Each bird, an individual life form was caged in a separate cage, as if each bird and each cage was a fragment of life, yet whole unto itself within that cage.

"The reality is those birds belong to Mother Earth. Their nature is to flock up and live in harmony and unison. From a distance, I watched Floating Lily open their cages and let them go. They each circled, challenged to fly by being caged up for so long. After they all circled in unison, they flew off together as a flock as if they were one. They needed to be free to be who they were, to express their identity as designed by Spirit.

"The foreigners we have been seeing in our visions would see us like those caged birds. They would work to deny our heritage, our connection to Mother Earth, to the lands of our ancestors, and our very purpose as designed by Spirit by placing us in cages of *their* design."

"But, Gray Wolf, how could they do that?" asks Water Dog.

"They forged the power to do so through the use of ego," I say, "because they devised the power to destroy The People, they used that power.

"Their belief system and their worldview constrained their thinking into mental constructions, much like these cages. Believing themselves to be right, they gave themselves permission to restrict life and its expressions, and to control the very Essence of Spirit. In their minds this gave them power over life and death.

"The cages they built in their minds to create their worldview actually encase and constrict *their* thought forms. These mental constructions actually prove to be cages for *them*, trapping them in an energy field of limitations. These cages of their minds prevent them from seeing clearly, from seeing beyond the limitations of the bars of the cages. They don't realize that just because they can't see the oneness encompassing all of us, doesn't mean it is not there.

"These limitations of thought prevent them from seeing all there is to see, prevent them from being who they are intended to be by the design of Great Spirit, and prevent them from being free to be. Freedom to be who they are and who they are intended to be came to only a few. This freedom, which we enjoy, comes only to a few of them. It is a concept not entertained by most of them.

"Their actions as seen in our visions come as a result of use and abuse of power driven by ego. Since they could not allow themselves to be who they were designed to be, they certainly could not allow anyone else to be either.

"They neglected to ask the question, 'what is our responsibility here?' . . . or maybe they did ask. Maybe they felt it was their responsibility to behave as dictated by their *ego*.

"Perhaps it was not within their understanding and perspective to see how responsibility works. They might not know that responsibility must flow from the question of 'what is the right thing to do in this circumstance?' This can only be answered as the question moves through the heart energy. As we know, power and responsibility must equal each other. Otherwise, imbalance and chaos are likely to occur as we are seeing in our visions. They wielded power over that for which they had no responsibility.

"The drive to be 'right' comes from ego. So I suspect that their ego-driven need to be *right*, or emotional attachment to be *right*, results in the demise of much of The People." I sigh, too pained to go on.

"Wait a minute, Gray Wolf. Could you back up a second?" Water Dog asks. "What exactly do you mean, 'driven by their *need to be right* and their *emotional attachment to being right*? What are you talking about? I'm not sure I understand that."

I really do not want to continue. Yet, I feel it is necessary to produce clarity.

"I get it," interrupts Red Fox. "In my talks with my Grandmother, Blue Lightning, I learned a few things."

We turn our attention to Red Fox as he says, "Clearly, they do not understand their connectedness to Great Spirit as we do. They talk like they do, but they do not act like it. Their view of the world somehow got formed into opposites, like a duality they created in their minds, good and bad, right and wrong. They interpreted themselves as being 'good' or 'right.'

"For them to remain in a perceived state of goodness or rightness, they require someone else to be wrong or bad. When they see us, The People, they necessarily see us as separate from themselves. From their perspective, we must be wrong or bad, not deserving of dignity or recognition of Great Spirit, the same as they are. For them to be 'right', someone else or something else must be 'wrong.' Making us 'wrong' in our beliefs and our worldview, helps to reinforce their sense of 'being right' and therefore . . . *righteous*.

"They are emotionally attached to being right, because they attached energy to their *need* to be right. That energy field of needing to be right takes on a life of its own. Because it must be constantly fed, and because being *right* does not exist, cannot exist, its appetite to gain constant reinforcement never gets satisfied. This ego based need to be right becomes insatiable. That's why it drives them.

"In my visions, I saw them as always seeking something, always uneasy and restless. It's as though they never get what they think they want, so they don't stop searching for it.

"I think what they are seeking is the Oneness that we experience as The People. We know that those of the First World lived in perfect harmony as in heaven, so on earth.

"The First World was a manifestation of the world of Spirit on the physical plane. As we say, 'as in heaven, so on earth.' The People have maintained that sense of unity and deep communion with each other right up through the now of time. Yet these foreigners behave as if they remember they forgot something important and can't figure out what it is. They feel an emptiness inside that they cannot fill.

"It's like they have some kind of inward pain that can't be addressed physically. I think it comes from a forgotten memory of being At-One with Spirit. They have come into this world seeking, yet unable to re-create that prior feeling of unity, that sense of communion."

"Red Fox," asks Bluebird Near the Lily, "what is this need to be right? I need a little more help here. Can you elaborate just a little more?"

After a few moments, Red Fox looks up then around at each friend before saying, "They come from the position of being right when they interact with The People." We all nod.

Red Fox says, "Coming from the position of being right is not the same as coming from the position of *knowing*."

Water Dog furrows his brushy red eyebrows, squints his eyes, trying to focus on the deeper meaning.

Red Fox continues, "When we come from the position of 'knowing,' we are aligned with Great Spirit, with the Great Oneness. Right or wrong is not in the equation.

"When we 'know' something, we feel it inside our heart as Spirit breathes through our hearts. We feel the inner-direction that comes with that alignment. It provides us with a sense of peace. That inner-knowing is peace inside. When we come from the position of *knowing*, we come from that peace, that alignment. Rightness and wrongness are not players in that energy field.

"When we come from a position of knowing, our choices and our behaviors are aligned with Great Spirit, and the result is whatever is appropriate in that instance. It becomes the appropriate action, because the source is Spirit. In this case, regardless of what appearances tell you at the time, the outcome will be the appropriate one for everyone concerned.

"What is appropriate in one instance, might not be appropriate in another, because the circumstances are not identical. What is right for one, might not be right for another, depending on the person, the timing, the state of affairs, and the circumstances.

"When we are aligned with Great Spirit, our response to an event will be appropriate. Our choices will be appropriate. If we let ego make our choices for us, and we insist on being *right*, we no longer find ourselves aligned with Spirit, and we have no sense of peace. And the outcome might not be as good as it could have been.

"So, not to put too fine a point on it," Red Fox concludes, "coming from a position of being *right* actually becomes a destructive force. While coming from a position of *knowing* leads us to peace within, to knowing what is manifested is for the good of all concerned."

Bluebird Near the Lily gets up from her place of comfort, stretches and begins brewing a tea to serve with cakes that Floating Lily had brought over earlier that evening.

Our conversation continues on into the night about the different options The People have before us, the advantages and disadvantages of staying or leaving our home, the lands that have so nurtured us at the behest of Mother Earth, the lands our civilization has occupied for thousands of years.

As fall flows into winter, Rising Wolf silently collected his things and some foodstuffs for the trip to Flint Ridge for his final journey on the Earth plane. White Eagle watched him gather his winter wraps and put his packs together without helping him, unable to participate in her partner's preparation for his transition.

Standing outside their home of a lifetime, Rising Wolf faced White Eagle, looked deeply into her eyes while softly resting his hand on her arm. No words were spoken. Rising Wolf sighed a heavy sigh. White Eagle did not turn her eyes away even as tears bubbled up and rolled down both cheeks. He nodded several times. She nodded once. With a final pat on her arm as a gesture of good-bye, Rising Wolf turned and trudged slowly away.

In his entire life he never trudged. Miles he walked around the hills and flint areas and he never trudged, never slowed. This time he trudged with great effort to distance himself from his lifelong companion, his home, his center. He had dedicated his life's work to Mother Earth, The People, and to the art of flint knapping. He knew his body would be wrapped in the arms of Mother Earth as he would begin a new journey with Great Spirit.

Several weeks later, in another village to the north and east, a woman killed her husband with a large flint knife. It had been known for some time that he beat her. When she showed up to get supplies or run errands, a black eye, or bruises about her face and arms were noticed. As a result of one beating, her arm was broken and not attended to. With an improperly set arm, the woman found chores difficult and received more blows from her husband because of her clumsiness. Recently, Grandmother Shining Moon had been called to re-set her arm that had been broken and had not healed properly.

"Gray Wolf, White Eagle sent me," Floating Lily announces as she arrives at our door. I turn and look at Shining Bird and my three offspring as they are getting ready for their day. I have just finished combing Shining Bird's hair as part of my morning ritual honoring my beloved. "Don't hurry, but she needs you right away. She will meet you by the meeting house."

Knowing how fast Floating Lily can make her getaway, as she was turning to leave, I catch her shoulder and stop her momentarily. My raised eyebrows ask the question.

Floating Lily answers, "She asks for you to accompany her to another village where a woman killed her husband. Rising Wolf is up at Flint Ridge."

I release my touch to her shoulder, and she disappears into the early morning mists.

"What a compliment," I say while starting to gather my winter garments together. Shining Bird tilts her head and looks up at me between handling and cuddling our smallest one. "What I mean is," I respond to her unasked question, "Rising Wolf is unable to go, so White Eagle is asking me to go in his stead. I feel that she must have confidence in me to give her balance as she attends to this business."

"Nice," Shining Bird smiles and nods in support and smiles as our children look at me.

The meeting house at the other village had not been designed for council meetings. Rather, it was one for feeding guests or for general gatherings of village business, such as this one. Most of the village inhabitants showed up making the room crowded with some standing against the walls. White Eagle and I sat in the middle. Her necklace glistened as it reflected the light from the oil lamps mounted high on the walls around the room.

"Many have testified here to what they saw and experienced between Sunflower and her now deceased husband," White Eagle summarizes. "Now I wish to hear from Sunflower. Would you please stand and tell us what happened?"

Polite silence reigns as Sunflower stands up from her place in the crowded room. Her left arm still in a sling, she stands and breaths a moment before speaking, working at keeping her emotions in check.

Then she says, "White Eagle, Gray Wolf, and all here, I am Sunflower. Many of my friends and neighbors have already spoken to you how my husband beat me, and how he treated me. Some of my neighbors would comment to me about my bruises and black eyes and feel sadness for me, until I explained to them my injuries were accidental." She pauses to allow the murmurings to subside.

White Eagle nods in affirmation, and says nothing allowing the young woman to continue.

The Dialogue

"He broke my arm in a rage. Even though I was in pain, he would not let me get to a healer to have it looked after for several weeks. When I did get to one, my arm had already begun to heal improperly. That's when my friends sent for Grandmother Shining Moon. Without the use of one arm, I found it even more challenging to take care of my normal activities," she says before pausing again.

As Sunflower inhales another breath to go on, White Eagle interrupts her, "My dear, did you speak about this to anyone? Did you seek help or advice in dealing with such a situation?"

Nodding and pursing her lips, Sunflower says, "I did speak to several Elders and asked them about how to work with my husband. I asked what there was about me that caused him to treat me that way. They said it was not what I was doing, but what I was *allowing* to be done.

"I begged my husband to join me to talk with a Grandmother about the energy field in our home, and he did once. He said nothing was wrong with him or the house, but much was wrong with me, and he wouldn't go again."

"I see," replies White Eagle. "When Grandmother Shining Moon came to see you and to put your arm back together, did you ask her about it?"

"Yes, I did," Sunflower affirms. "She asked me why I continued to allow him to abuse me. I told her it was to keep the peace. Then she asked me, to keep what peace?

"She said to me, 'There is no peace to keep. If you do not have peace inside yourself, you have no peace.' Then she told me that by allowing him to abuse me I was betraying the relationship, and that I was betraying myself.

"She said I betrayed the relationship by not requiring balance in the relationship, that I let him exert power *over* me as opposed to exercising power *with* me. She said I was responsible for my part in the abuse. She said it was a dance the two of us performed together. She said I betrayed myself by allowing myself to be abused. In so doing I denied the *worth* of my very essence. She said my essence is a manifestation of Great Spirit. She said that when I denied the worth of my essence, it was the same as denying the very existence of Great Spirit. That's why betraying myself was still a betrayal. It was a betrayal of the highest order."

"What else did she say?" asks White Eagle.

"Grandmother Shining Moon said to me, as long as I continue to allow him to abuse me, I was abusing him. I didn't understand all of this at first. I thought about it for a while. Then I realized I was hurting him because I was *letting* him hurt me."

White Eagle purses her lips and nods raising her eyebrows. Then, she says, "So please, Sunflower, tell us what happened that caused you to kill your husband."

Murmurings around the room, then quiet as Sunflower inhales another breath before saying, "I was standing in my kitchen outside under the canopy, chopping meat for the stew I was preparing for supper. Just as he was about to enter, I accidentally knocked over a ceramic cup, causing it to break with a loud crashing noise.

"This jarred his concentration, because he screamed at me with a rage on his face. With a roar he approached me with his arms raised as if to choke me." Sunflower swallows hard then says, "I felt surprised by the fact that I felt so calm. I didn't feel fear. I just stood there and turned toward him as he lunged at me. I still had the knife in my right hand from the food chopping. My left arm was still in the sling made for me by Grandmother Shining Moon. Her words still rang in my ears."

Sunflower pauses to breathe. She is the only one to do so. Everyone else in the room is holding their breath waiting to hear the rest of the story. Sunflower looks down then up before saying, "He kept coming in a rage. I just stood there with the knife in my hand . . . there was no place for me to go . . . my back was against the table where I had been preparing the food.

"Then I don't know if he tripped or what, but the next thing I knew he pressed against me with the blade of the knife sticking in his left side. That stopped him. The rage on his face turned to surprise and shock. I didn't know what to do next. I think I was in shock also. He fell to the ground yelling in pain. I just stood there with the knife still in my hand, blood dripping from it onto the floor and onto him."

Murmurings and affirming nods.

"Because he was yelling and roaring so loudly, I realized our neighbors could hear him. I looked up and out. I saw several of my friends and neighbors standing around watching." Sunflower clears her throat a moment, "I just looked at them . . . then down at him . . . and back up at them again. He was still writhing in pain as I dropped the knife and stepped over him to leave that space and breathe air outside.

"I walked away from him and the house while he was still on the floor yelling in pain. Several women friends came over to me, wrapping their arms around me and took me to one of their homes. Later he died. Then after several days, the house burned down with his body still lying on the floor."

Sunflower finalizes her story with one long nod.

Silence rules.

At the end of a very long silence, White Eagle turns to me and looks into my eyes, seeing past them to something only she could see. I look at her eyes to maintain the contact. Messages, thoughts and concepts wrestle between us as the two of us sit there staring at each other with all eyes on us. No words pass between us out loud.

Then, White Eagle turns to Sunflower who has remained standing.

Everyone draws in a loud breath, not wanting to hear a pronouncement of banishment.

White Eagle looks directly at Sunflower, smiles, and says, "Go in peace, my daughter."

The tension that had been building for the past several hours suddenly releases as people file out of the building with smiles and nods

30

SNOW FLURRIES

Snow flurries hampered Water Dog's view of the flint house.

Water Dog and Rising Wolf had spent much time together between trips around the country looking for good flint places. Rising Wolf, early in his career at Flint Ridge, had spent much time working on this house, repairing and maintaining it. It had been built ages before him from flint-bearing stone left over from the flint mining operations. From before his time there, the flint house had fallen into disrepair. Rising Wolf loved this little house from the instant he first saw it as a youngster.

Cold usually did not bother Water Dog much, but at this moment the icy fingers down his spine gave him a chill he did not welcome. By the time he got to the house, he could see the door closed, no lights flickering through the mica windows in the dark night, and no smoke up the chimney.

"Too cold not to have a fire," thought Water Dog as he budged the door open stubborn on its hinges. He felt an oppressive emptiness in the room he did not expect. As dark as it was, he still tried to see through the blackness. Knowing the little house as well as he did, he moved toward the stone fireplace to start a fire more for light than for heat. As he did so, his foot bumped something hard. Water Dog squatted down to feel what he was afraid to feel, to find what he did not want to find, to acknowledge what he did not want to acknowledge . . . Rising Wolf.

A blast of emotion hit him so hard that it knocked him over. The jolt of falling back hit the big man hard. Tears relentlessly poured down his face as he sat up, eyes adjusting to the dark, took in the scene of Rising Wolf's dead body lying with covers neatly spread over him like he had just gone to sleep.

Water Dog mentally processed his mentor's death and his life. He processed how Rising Wolf had taken him under his wing, taught him so much, bringing him into self-actualization. As he did so, the giant of a man humbled himself into as small an emotional lump as he could and bawled his heart out in gratitude, joy and sadness at the sense of loss of his friend.

Rays of the morning sun shot through the windows of the quaint stone house the next day. Morning found Water Dog still at Rising Wolf's side, still humbled by the emotional tide that had swept over him. Barely able to move, stiff from sleeping in a crouched position all night, Water Dog stirred to start a fire for a light meal before returning on the long journey back to his village.

Crunch. Crunch. Crunch.

White Eagle's cup she was drinking from stopped mid-air as she heard the sound of someone walking up to her house in the snow. She set her cup down on the table next to her where she had prepared herself a small meal.

Crunch. Crunch. Crunch.

She just sat and waited. Unable to move from her bench, she folded her hands in her lap and waited for someone to come through the door.

Knock, knock.

Then slowly the door opened. The threshold was too low for her guest to waltz in. He had to stoop down to poke his head inside. "White Eagle?" Water Dog asked.

With that, she put her face in her hands and wept.

After Floating Lily left our house, I turn to Shining Bird and say, "I need to meditate. I'd like to go to White Eagle's to use her meditation disks. A sweat in the sweat lodge would take longer than I want to spend in preparation. I feel at a loss and need some direction here. I'm not able to define my feelings, and I want to figure out what I need to do." She nods in acknowledgment as a tear finds its way down her lovely face.

I gather up my winter wraps and head up the hill to White Eagle's home. When I arrive, I find her just sitting at her table, eyes lost on some distant horizon. As I enter she stands stoically. Moving toward her, I greet her with a warm hug, which she returns. The top of her head comes to my chest, so she must look up at me to smile before turning down the ends of her mouth in sadness.

"It hurts," she sighs.

"We are all grieving, Grandmother," I begin, wanting to ask for a favor, but not wanting to impose. "As part of my preparation for our journey and the ceremony for Rising Wolf, I feel the need to communicate with Great Spirit in a deep way. I . . . ."

Before I could finish my next sentence, White Eagle walks over to some shelves and pulls out two beautifully engraved disks and hands one of them to me.

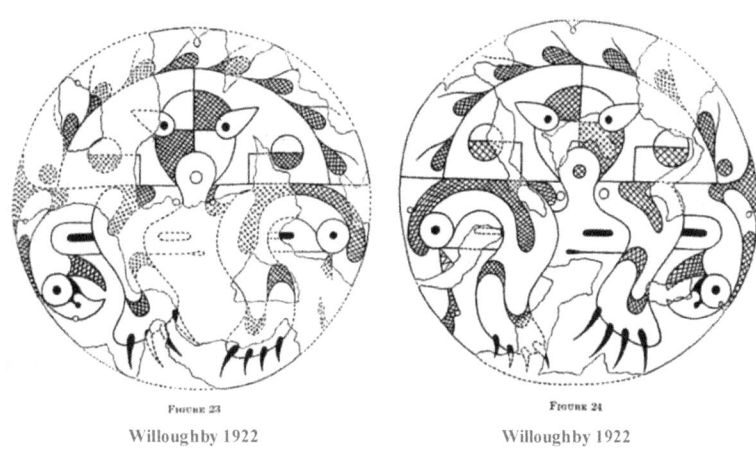

FIGURE 23
Willoughby 1922

FIGURE 24
Willoughby 1922

"I need help also," she murmurs. "Here, take one and I'll take the other. Let's sit here together in silence and focus on the disks." Grateful for not having to ask, I accept one and make myself comfortable.

I could not say how many hours passed in silence. What I remember from my time in meditation is clouds whispering around me, then Rising Wolf coming into focus walking along on his journey, walking straight like I would have imagined him as a young man walking, black hair hanging loosely down his back. I see him turn and look at me with a knowing of something I could not quite grasp. Clouds then swirl up and around as he faded from my sight.

Bounding into my view next appears my gray wolf guide smiling at me. After wagging his tail in greeting, he sits down and halfway bows his head to remind me of something he had told me earlier when we first met in the physical world. I strain my head forward to better receive the message.

"Oh," squeaks White Eagle as she returns to the here and now. I feel her presence in the room and slowly I return from my visions. She turns to me with a gentle smile, tension and grief gone from her face and says softly, "There, wasn't that nice."

I nod my head in affirmation. "Thank you, Grandmother," I say after a while. "Here is your disk back. I appreciate being able to use it. I feel much better, actually more directed."

This time she nods at me in affirmation.

I continue, "It's a day's walk at least up to Flint Ridge once we get to the Newark Earthworks. If we take the White Road of Sister Moon, the going will be much easier, but it will take about five days or so to get to Newark. And, it should take us at least a week to get to the White Road from here. When would you like to leave?" I ask politely.

"Hmmm," she rolls her eyes while searching the air for an answer, "How about tomorrow morning sometime?"

At about mid-morning, Floating Lily was just leaving as she finished delivering traveling foods to White Eagle's house. I had imagined us getting underway much earlier, but felt the need to be patient. Even though the air was cold, the sun felt warming to the skin as I chose to wait for Water Dog outside. As I look down the hill for Water Dog, I smile as I see Shining Bird on her way up to White Eagle's. I was secretly glad and grateful that she had been able to get away with me to attend to Rising Wolf up at Flint Ridge.

With each of us carrying a bundle or pack, the four of us head for the White Road which would take us most of the way. Small villages and hamlets along the way would take us in to sleep and to provide a hot evening meal for our trek. Even though we walked in silence after we had journeyed most of the way, during a noon break on the fourth day, we finally spoke of our feelings.

"He contributed so much wisdom to The People, of course we are going to feel a loss," Shining Bird says, initiating the conversation.

"He made me what I am today," exclaims Water Dog.

"Well, I disagree with you there, brother, Water Dog," I object. "What I saw between you both was a dance you did together."

"A dance?" Water Dog asks.

"Yes, a dance," I say. "When I brought you to Rising Wolf, you were in such a state. You felt lost and in a fog as to what you wanted to do with your life. All you knew was you wanted to marry Bluebird Near the Lily."

Water Dog's eyebrows lift as his eyes widen while listening and remembering.

I go on, "You had been making pots for a while and felt frustrated with that work. I was directed to take you to Rising Wolf."

". . . and so you did, Gray Wolf," Water Dog interrupts. "After that, it's history."

"Yes," I continue without noticing the interruption, "The two of you began your dance that afternoon. It continued ever since. As a master flint knapper, he became your mentor. He led the dance between you. You, as the apprentice, followed his lead. As you learned and developed your own mastery, the two of you partnered as leaders in the dance. The People are fortunate to have you as a master flint knapper following in Rising Wolf's footsteps, and now you are the new master. The dance is complete now. Rising Wolf could retire in peace, and you now lead the dance with other flint knappers. The cycle continues."

"Oh, I see," Water Dog says with his eyebrows knitted indicating he wasn't sure he saw at all.

Shining Bird says, "I think what Gray Wolf means, because you met up with Rising Wolf and he nurtured you and your innate talent, you found yourself."

Water Dog nods in affirmation.

"Then, because of your natural abilities, you combined that with what Rising Wolf taught you, you felt self-actualized, fully expressed as a person, then you transpersonalized yourself through your contributions to The People," says Shining Bird. "And for that you feel much gratitude and kinship. Is that right, Water Dog?" Water Dog nods with tears brimming in his eyes.

". . . and it still appeared to me as a dance the both of you performed together," I say. "I guess I'm looking at it from a different perspective."

"Of course, it's just a different way of seeing," Shining Bird says, while looking up at the sky as if receiving inspiration.

"Life is a series of cycles," Shining Bird adds. "It flows in and out, up and down, always complete, yet ever moving forward without any real stop or start. Life is like energy, more like frequency waves. It constantly moves forward, waxing and waning, yet never ending. Physical form as particles may change, but the energy of its essence does not. It simply goes on."

Water Dog looks at her in amazement.

Shining Bird says, "We know that life does not end at death. Although, we feel like it does sometimes as we suffer the loss of a loved one, like our dear Rising Wolf. We get to experience the sense of loss, even though he continues on. As he continues on, we never really lost him. We just think we did, because of our limited sense of our physical selves. We are more than our physical selves. Our essence can never be snuffed out because it is part of the One, part of Great Spirit.

"So what we are really about is a celebration of life," Shining Bird says gently and softly. Water Dog looks at her quizzically. "Our intent is to celebrate the life of the spirit we knew as Rising Wolf. We celebrate his life, because he is a part of us and part of The People.

"He contributed to The People, to our village, and to each of us individually. This journey we are making is our gift to him, to honor him. As we would honor him in life, we honor him in death, knowing that death is a passage to a different field of energy, a different experience of life in a never-ending journey, moving, flowing ever upwards back to our Center, Great Spirit."

"And, so it is!" White Eagle affirms with a nod.

A new layer of snow covers the ground around the quaint stone cabin. Stopping at the edge of the trees, before going across the open ground around the cabin itself, we all pause to take in the beauty of the moment. We stand for uncountable moments taking in the sense of poetry written on the scene before us.

Rising Wolf was a rock of the community. His life was spent with rocks. His face looked like it had been chiseled out of rock. Now his body lay like it was sleeping in a rock house. And, it was this rock house he chose to be interred.

On arriving we see that many of the flint knappers had been waiting for us, camping out in the cold. They have come to pay honor to their leader.

While waiting for us to arrive, they had already begun to dig up frozen dirt and section it into piles. They knew that Rising Wolf wanted to be embraced in the arms of Mother Earth.

Due to the cold of a hard winter, Rising Wolf's body lay frozen on the floor, undisturbed by man or beast. We light a fire in the fireplace as though the physical heat of the fire would warm the chill we feel by looking at him. Each of us unpacks our bundles we had so lovingly carried on our journey.

Each of us had found just the right piece of physical artifact to use in saying our farewells to a beloved friend.

At this moment I remember my dream from my childhood, when my devoted wolf guide offered his lower jaw as a sacred object to me. It was at this moment, the necklace I made from his lower jaw emerged from my pack seemingly by its own accord. The presence of my gray wolf guide and the energy of spirit wolves present attaches to the necklace, because it was also their gift to their beloved Rising Wolf.

I feel them around us as I hold the jawbone necklace up in the light for a long and tearful, heart-opening moment. Then I place the wolf-jaw-bone necklace in Rising Wolf's hand for his use in the Spirit World. I acknowledge the presence of the many spirits of wolves who guided and protected.

At the end of our ceremony, we all file out of the little house. Shining Bird and Water Dog exit first. As I turn to leave also, White Eagle says to me, "Just a minute, Gray Wolf. I need a word with you." Shining Bird looks back at me over her shoulder and continues to follow Water Dog out the door.

During what seems like a long wait for their companions, Shining Bird and Water Dog, and the rest of the flint knappers can hear muffled sounds of conversations taking place within the house. Finally, they heard a clear, "*I accept*," from me.

Moments later, White Eagle and I emerge with light beaming from our faces.

With that, the flint knappers, Water Dog and I begin filling the inside of the little house with dirt to fulfill the wish of a beloved shaman, leader, and friend.

When the house is filled to the ceiling with earth from our Mother, the four of us stand briefly looking at the stone building that now is a tomb.

The large group of flint knappers finish cleaning up their camps and begin to drift back to where they had come from.

By the spring the house would be completely covered with Mother Earth as an earthen mound.

The four of us turn and start our journey home.

31

GRAY WOLF IS CALLED UPON

Several years later, one summer morning I rise early, step outside to greet the day with my morning prayer and offering of tobacco to Mother Earth in gratitude.

Before the children begin to stir, I sit down on the bed next to Shining Bird. I reach for her comb, kiss her gently on her head before gingerly bringing the comb to her black locks.

"I think today is a good day to take Stalking Bear out with me to walk the land. It would be a good thing for him to learn more about some of the healing herbs I expect to find on our walk. My Grandmother, Shining Moon, asked me to gather several to re-stock her supply. We might even go as far as the next village. I would like to check in on several folks over there. It would be a good experience for him," I say.

"That would be great," replies Shining Bird. "I'll take the two younger ones down to the river and play at the water's edge. It's going to be a warm summer day, and some of the younger folk will be diving for mussels. It should be fun." She purses her lips and then says, "I'm feeling that we could use a little time by the water as a form of therapy to help lift our spirits. Sometimes I feel a little down." She frowns before going on, "The sense of impending threat sometimes hovers overhead. I don't like the feel of it. It has an out-of-order feel to it." Pausing to reflect a few moments, she adds, "Maybe we should have a ceremony to clear the energy field around us. What do you think?"

Grandmother Plum Blossom moves under the covers of her bed before arising for the day. Shining Bird and I look over to see our small brood begin to awaken. I move over to where the children lie and pick up my youngest son and tenderly hold him over my heart with loving masculine hands. My youngest son, not quite awake, continues to slumber in my arms. While still holding the sleepy child, I look off into an unseen distance before replying.

Then I finally say, "I think you are right. It sounds like a good idea. I think a negative energy randomly touches down here or there, and people act oddly, not at all consistent with their normal behavior."

Furrowing my eyebrows as I put down my still sleeping son and kissing him on his head, I add, "I'll stop by Singing Hawk's and have a conversation about it with her."

I smile at my youngest son seeing him begin to open his eyes and look around.

In the summer sun, Floating Lily's red hair glistened like flames sparkling as she sat with Shining Bird and our children on the shores of the stream. Raven's Wing sent Floating Lily to bring a basket of goodies to share among all the children that day. The women enjoyed themselves and the children as the day passed.

Hearing the celebratory sounds downstream from them, Floating Lily looked over to the source of the voices. She noted other young people and several men piling up mussels from their dives that would end up as part of a village feast later that evening.

Floating Lily said, "They look like they are getting a lot. We should have a great feast tonight. Raven's Wing told me she felt a bit concerned as to our meat supply. After I left her this morning, she went over to check on it."

Shining Bird did not comment on Floating Lily's observation as she smiled adoringly watching her children at play.

My son, Stalking Bear, and I thoroughly enjoy our walk through the forested hills. Our time together is decorated with sunlight filtering slanted rays through the trees, background music provided by the many birds, and cooling breezes swirling lazily between the undergrowth and the tall trees.

As we walk, I relish sharing insights and tidbits of information with my son of seven years. We talk about some of the plants and animals we encountered, and the relationships of all that we saw.

The bonfires had been built late in the afternoon. Shining Bird felt relaxed and refreshed after her day in the sun near the water watching her children happily playing. Our youngest son, Dancing Swan, too tired to walk the distance home, asked to be picked up. As soon as he was securely nestled in his mother's arms, he promptly fell asleep. Shining Bird walked the long distance home carrying him, feeling grateful that Floating Lily accompanied her holding the hand of our middle child and daughter, Star Rising.

Drums beat rhythmically accompanied with sounds of differing flutes in preparation of the feast soon to be experienced. After feeding our two children and washing up the dishes, she found herself putting them to bed early. They were only too eager to comply after having spent the day playing in the water and sand at the stream's edge.

Joyous music sounded throughout our village as a gratitude celebration unfolded. Many villagers danced in concentric circles and some just danced in a crowd. Feeling a happy tired, Shining Bird only too gladly sat on the sidelines to actively participate through watching, smiling and sometimes clapping. The meal proved to be luscious. The People so loved to eat mussels, and this turned out to be a feast of feasts. Raven's Wing had out-done herself of course by providing many side dishes. White Eagle spoke to the villagers during a quiet time when most were about finished eating.

"This is a time for gratitude for affirming our abundance of food, our abundance of meat to eat, and abundance of our love for each other. We thank Great Spirit for our breath, our love, and for our life. We acknowledge Mother Earth for being the avenue that Great Spirit uses to provide us with everything we need to continue living in prosperity. We give thanks to our Mother Earth for her partnership with us and for continuing to honor her promise to us as given to our Ancient Ones who lived here so very long ago. And so it is," White Eagle concluded with deep feeling.

"And so it is," murmured The People.

Drums began beating rhythmically again, and again the sound of flutes joined in. As some folks began clearing the space used for eating, and putting away leftovers, others began dancing again. Shining Bird sat a while longer, visiting with other mothers until she too turned in for the night.

Meanwhile, Stalking Bear and I in the late afternoon find ourselves wandering into a drying summer meadow dotted with a few flowers struggling to remain in bloom. As we walk around the meadow, I see ears pointing up over the tops of the tall grasses, sometimes followed by a furry tail. I smile to myself as I am reminded of my spirit guide, the gray wolf.

At one point the wolf moves into more open country, and I point it out to my son. Kneeling down, I stretch out my arm to ensure my son looks in the right direction so he too can see the magnificent creature.

Despite the fact that the afternoon was ending, we continue our walk. Just as dusk was shifting day into evening, we enter a village. Several folks are milling around. We just stand there in the middle of the village waiting for someone to address us.

"Gray Wolf," a soft voice speaks from behind me. I turn around and see a young woman carrying a basket of plants. "So good to see you, again," she adds after grabbing my arm. Then she bends down to greet Stalking Bear, smiles at him and touches his hand. I put my hands on each of my son's shoulders and say, "Crested Pearl, this is my oldest son, Stalking Bear."

Standing up after the introduction, Crested Pearl looks up at me and asks, "So, what brings you to our village, Gray Wolf? I hope no one is sick and needs your attention."

"No, no," I say with a smile, "nothing like that. My son and I just needed to take a walk and we ended up here. I'd like to know, though, how your mother is after I treated her last."

"She's much better, thank you," replies Crested Pearl. "Say, why don't both of you join us for the evening, have a little supper? Then spend the night before returning home? My mother would love to have you."

First looking down at my son, then back to Crested Pearl, I nod and say, "That sounds like a fine idea."

As the three of us turn to walk together toward her home, Crested Pearl says softly, "I'm so glad I picked these vegetables from our little garden this afternoon. We are a little low on our meat supply. I have wild rice and some biscuits. I think I'll drop you off with mother, and then I'll go on to see if some of the young men have some extra fish for us."

"Mother," calls Crested Pearl as the three of us enter their home, decorated similarly to all the other homes, "Look who I have here?"

I must duck to enter the low-beamed doorway. After entering I look around the room and finally spy a little gray haired woman who has been my patient for years. When I see her, she smiles a very broad smile and attempts to get up out of bed.

"No need to get up, Grandmother," I softly say. "May I introduce my son to you?" Again I put my hands on my son's shoulders to proudly display my offspring.

"Hello, Grandmother," Stalking Bear politely says.

As Crested Pearl turns to leave, I touch her arm and say deeply but quietly, "No need to go get meat for us. We are grateful for whatever you serve us."

Unable to resist the shaman medicine man who had treated her mother for years and had saved her life on several occasions, Crested Pearl shrugs her shoulders, looks at her basket of vegetables that included squash, green beans and goosefoot leaves and other greens, then nods and says. "Why don't I put some things together and see what I come up with? I think I have corn. With that and beans and the squash I just picked, it might be all right. That should go well with fresh steamed goosefoot greens and wild rice."

As Crested Pearl went about her business, I sit down and visit with Crested Pearl's mother. She sits up spryly enough, but remains in bed with blankets over her legs.

After the meal is served and the four of us sit around the room chatting, we bring each other up to date on all the latest news. Then several villagers come to the door. Crested Pearl greets several men and a woman.

"Hello there Gray Wolf," bellows one man. "I thought I saw you come into our village earlier today. And, who's that young man you have with you there, another shaman in training?"

As the evening passes, another older couple drops by with nut cakes to offer. We all appreciate the supplement to the meal. I heartily eat two of them. My son finishes only about half of his before leaning over on the bed he has been sitting on. The couple stays only a little while after they saw Stalking Bear start to fall asleep.

Later several other members of the village drop by, each with a little something of food as an offering. Once word is out that I am visiting their village, many want to see me if only for a little while. They feel honored that I am in their village, and they want to acknowledge me. The entire evening turns out to be so pleasant, with story-telling, and then retold stories told. The smiles and laughter feels good to me that evening.

At about noon the next day, my son and I prepare to leave the village of friends so warm they feel like family. This village is much smaller than ours, but welcoming and hospitable. Just after leaving the village heading for home, I think I hear my name called.

"Gray Wolf," calls a voice from far away, "Gray Wolf."

Wondering what that is about, I stop momentarily and turn around looking for the source of my name being called.

"Gray Wolf, Gray Wolf," hollers a young man running hard and very nearly out of breath. "So sorry to call you from such a distance, but I wanted to catch you before you got too far away."

I tilt my head as I anticipate hearing that someone is ill, or worse, injured. I grimace as I realize I had not brought all of my medicinal supplies with me.

"We need you at the next village over," the messenger says breathlessly. He stands there with his hands on his knees to catch his breath and to center himself before speaking. We wait patiently for the young man with the message to collect himself. Finally, he says, "There's been an incident."

I ask, "What do you mean, 'an incident'? What's happened?"

"There's been a killing!" he answers. "I've been running for a day and a half. So please forgive me for being out of breath." I nod puzzled about the 'incident'.

"Right," I say slowly, "now, let's start over. There's been a killing and why have you been running for so long?"

Taking another moment to catch his breath and his thoughts, the young man says, "A man from our village killed another man from a village three villages away from here. I was sent to get White Eagle at your village. She said you were over in this area here somewhere and that you should be the one to go. Shining Bird knows that you will not be home for a while."

I step back like I was pushed backward, not anticipating this. Then I ask the young runner in disbelief, "So what you are asking me to do is to go to your village and preside over the village meeting?"

"In a word," he replies and with one nod. "Yes."

I stop thinking. I stop talking. I stop seeing the here and now. I just stand there and listen to Great Spirit for a few moments.

"Well, son," I say to Stalking Bear, "I guess this trip will be an experience for you, and for me as well, I'm sure." Tossing my son's hair with my hand, I turn to the runner and say, "Show us the way."

Hushed voices can be heard as the villagers sit in a meeting space outside in the late afternoon. Most sit down in tiered concentric circles leaving one aisle open from the outside to the center. When I arrive, the voices lower and become silent as I walk to the center of the circles to sit down. Someone takes Stalking Bear by the arm and moves him into a space saved especially for him.

Most have known me as a healer whenever passing through their village from time to time over the past several years. They revere my Grandmother Shining Moon and knew that I was her student. Because of my success in healing people in their village, they know me as a shamanic healer, in touch with Great Spirit.

Now they are seeing me for the first time in a different role. White Eagle has always presided over any major issue that required great thought and application of the Law of One. This is one of those times.

For whatever reason, White Eagle has appointed me to preside over this occasion. These villagers trust me.

Many stand around the outside of the last circle. By this time, it is standing room only.

Hushed silence with breaths held.

"I am Gray Wolf," turning as I speak to the audience. "I am from the village near the Great Serpent. Most of you know me as a healer as I have come into your homes to do what I can for many of you."

Murmurings and nods.

I continue, "I am not here as a healer. I have been asked to come here this time as a leader to ascertain truth in this circumstance and apply a sense of order, balance, and harmony to it in accordance with the Law of One. I thank you for honoring me here today.

"Your elders and I have smoked the ceremonial pipe before entering into this circle of The People.

> *"We all acknowledge the Great Spirit, our Creator, as the Sacred Force in the Great Oneness. The Great Oneness is the Great Spirit manifested in the physical world. All of Heaven and Mother Earth birthed from Great Spirit. The Will of the Creator is as above, so below. Just as Great Spirit provides nurturing of our souls, so does our Mother Earth provide us with bounty for meeting our human needs. We live in Oneness with each other. As we help each other, we help ourselves. Should we by some act bring harm to another, we harm ourselves. As we remain in tune and aligned with Great Spirit and Mother Earth, we know our way is guided, our path protected. All comes from the Creator, all Life. Everything that is, is part of Great Spirit."*

"And so it is," softly and reverently the audience says in unison.

"Who wishes to speak first?" I begin addressing the entire audience.

Three young men stand up in one of the back rows. I look up at them as does everyone else. They each speak in turn, telling a similar story of how they and Thunder Bear were hunting for meat. The village had been low on meat for some time. They had been going out each day to hunt and each returned with very little or nothing for their efforts. Game had been scarce this year, and getting scarcer as the season progressed.

Finally, one afternoon, the four of them had spotted a deer and began tracking it. When they thought they were near it, they spread out with Thunder Bear out on point. By the time they caught up with the deer, they saw Thunder Bear standing over the dead deer and another man lying dead with an arrow in his heart next to the deer. That was all they knew.

"Thank you." I say nodding to them. Then I turn my head to look over the entire audience, and call, "Thunder Bear. Please stand and speak to us."

Silence.

Murmurings.

"Thunder Bear, please speak to us," I say with a tone of quiet power and authority.

THE CAMP OF GOD'S TEARS

Silence.

Stirrings among the audience.

Gasps and murmurings as Thunder Bear stands.

"I am Thunder Bear. I am a great hunter. I provide meat for my village," announces Thunder Bear with a boastful voice.

I look at him and through him for very long moments. Thunder Bear fidgets while he stands as everyone focuses their attention upon him.

Softly I say looking directly at Thunder Bear, "Speak."

Taken aback by this command so gently delivered, Thunder Bear attempts to speak. His throat catches on some of the words and they come out garbled at first.

Seeing his discomfort, I hold up my hand and say, "Why don't you breathe a few moments before you speak. Then maybe your words can come out."

Thunder Bear shifts his weight from one foot to the other several times, looks down, breathes several times then looks straight at me.

"My village needed meat," he is finally able to say. "We had been hunting for days. Some days we were able to get birds, turkeys and some ducks and geese. But what we really needed was a large animal, like an elk, or deer. We hadn't seen buffalo in so long, I didn't think we would ever see one again.

"So this one day we finally did spot a deer. It was a very large buck. We had to get it. It was too much of a prize not to take it back to our village. The People would be so grateful and would honor us for bringing home meat. We would be providers in a time of need."

Murmurings.

I put up my hand to signal everyone to become quiet again. "Please go on, Thunder Bear," I encourage. "Please tell us what happened next."

Looking around at everyone present before continuing, Thunder Bear takes in a deep breath and then says, "The four of us saw flashes of the deer as we walked through the brush and trees, and we began to track it. Because I went out on point, I saw the deer first. I looked around to see if I could see my companions. We didn't want to miss a good shot. Just as I was looking around, I heard an arrow zip through the air, and then I saw the deer go down. I just stood there in disbelief. My deer had been shot by someone else. *My* deer!"

Rumblings among the listeners.

Holding up a hand again to signal for quiet, I nod for Thunder Bear to continue.

Thunder Bear gulps and then says emphatically, "It was my deer! *My deer!* How could that man from another village take my deer from me? And now, my village would be without meat. Without thinking, I pulled an arrow out, put it in my bow, and before I knew it the other man fell dead. Dead. Right next to my deer!"

He pauses almost out of breath. "He took my deer. He killed *my* deer! He was going to take my deer that I was going to bring back to the village. We needed meat, doesn't anyone understand that? Doesn't anyone understand that what I did, I did for the good of our village? That I did it for the good of all?"

Gasps.

He says vehemently, "I should be considered a hero, not accused of murder. Why isn't that clear to everyone? Why am I even here?"

Thunder Bear continues standing.

I continue sitting at the center of the tiered concentric circles of villagers. I look down. Then I look up to a far distant plane of the heavens. I gaze into the Great Oneness. My soul consults with Great Spirit.

The villagers in the audience squirm in their seats. They feel a little uncomfortable with the length of time I appear to be contemplating the situation. After all they know that banishment is the typical result when one of us kills another of us. So they wait silently, not wanting to talk for fear of bringing me out of my contemplation.

Finally, I signal I am ready to speak.

"Thunder Bear," I say with a voice that sounds like it comes from somewhere else. "Thunder Bear, clearly your intentions were set to help the village by hunting for meat. You wanted to improve the meat supply as meat was becoming scarce."

Affirming murmurings.

I continue, "From what you said your ego was running you. You wanted to be a hero and to be seen as a provider in times when The People needed meat. Is that not so?"

"Yes, of course, what's wrong with that?" he says with his chin stuck out.

"We are Children of the Law of One," I begin. "As such, each and every one of us are heroes. We are heroes because we live here. We are the manifestation of Great Spirit and live in partnership with Mother Earth. We don't have to do anything to make us more of who we are. All any of us have to do to be a hero is to simply 'be.' We just are.

"By simply *being* we each become the greatest hero that ever lived. That is because, each of us are the individualized manifestation of Great Spirit. It's like we, that is each of us, are flamelets of the bonfire that is Great Spirit.

"We are spirits of Spirit endowed with a physical body by our Earth Mother, so we can experience experiences in this plane of existence. So, in reality, there is nothing we need 'to do'. Just be our divine selves as we journey through what we call this life. We already are what we wish ourselves to be, a divine expression of the Great Oneness. Our physical experiences provide us opportunities to gain reference points, to gain insights from what we experience, and again an opportunity to make difference choices."

Silence.

"In recognition of ego, we use our ego mind as a method for instructing our free will in choice making. We need our ego to help us function. Sometimes, however, we allow ourselves to think we are more important than others. Often we might think that our physical form is all there is of us. If we stay in that thought-energy too long, then it seems permissible to violate the Law of One. At that point, we then begin to feel we are a law unto ourselves. This is what I mean when I say 'your ego was running you'.

"Celebration of our individual ego in this sense brings on a feeling of separation from Great Spirit and each other. This divides us in our humanity. This further promotes a sense of separation and then fragmentation occurs. We then must compete against each other for everything and no longer operate as Children of the Law of One."

Silence.

I look down, then up again, and continue, "The deer that you claimed was *yours* is an interesting opinion.

"The deer you intended to kill for food for your village was part of Mother Earth. That deer did not belong to you. Mother Earth offered it as a source of food. Yet, please know, that she did not offer it to you specifically, but to us in general. She moved that deer into position for us to harvest as a food source. Yet, Mother Earth did not appoint which human being it would go to. She did not specify that it go to either you or the other man you killed. She simply provided it as a food source.

"As a result, you cannot claim it as 'your deer.' The People have no territorial claim on animals. You admitted to being far from home. We have no claim of ownership of wild animals, nor on any section of land. So, in the end, I must say, that the deer shot by the other man, was not your deer. He had a right to shoot it for food to bring home to his village."

Hushed murmurings.

Clearly, Thunder Bear feels uncomfortable. Despite the gentleness of my analysis, the truth feels prickly to him.

"And . . . by the way, Thunder Bear," I say, "If your village was experiencing a scarcity of meat, don't you think that the village that man was from may have been experiencing a scarcity of game as well? Don't you think that he may have been driven by the same need as you? . . . To bring back meat to feed his people? . . . The same People as in *Our People*?" I raise my eyebrows as I rhetorically ask this piercing question.

I pose additional questions, "Did you not pause a moment to say a prayer of invocation to our Earth Mother to provide another deer or other game to fill the needs of your village? Did you not know you can call in game when you have such a need?

"You said you didn't 'think,' that you just reacted. Did you not feel you had options, options other than killing that other man? You could have been generous with the other man and let him have the deer. Or you could have split it. Or you could seek other game. Did it not occur to you that killing someone for food that could have been shared is not part of who we are as Children of the Law of One?"

Not wanting to answer, Thunder Bear looks down at his feet. He does not reply.

I pause only momentarily to give Thunder Bear a chance to respond and then say, "And, then, that brings us to the matter of the killing of another human being."

Silence.

"In the matter of killing another human being, I must confess, I feel aghast. In my experience, I cannot visualize any motive or reason that would be adequate to cause me to kill another. On the other hand, we must consider you and the circumstances." I interrupt myself for a brief moment wherein I look again into the distant heavens.

Then I state, "In our opening prayer, part of it includes the affirmation, '*We live in Oneness with each other. As we help each other, we help ourselves. Should we by some act bring harm to another, we harm ourselves.*' That includes killing, taking the life of another person. You wish us to believe that you killed that other man for the purpose of claiming the deer for yourself and bringing it back to your village as a hero. Please understand that it appears to me that you did not kill the man so you could feed your village, as much as to feed your ego by the trophy kill. It also appears that you wish to be seen as a hero to your village by bringing back the deer for food."

Gasps!

Murmurings.

I wait for silence.

Looking around the audience from my center seat, I ask, "Is there anyone else who would like to speak?"

Village members look around at each other over and over. No one feels the need to speak, so silence speaks.

After waiting patiently, with the sun going down, I then gravely say, "Thunder Bear. You know the penalty for killing another is banishment."

Breath are sucked in and held.

"However," I continue, "You are not banished."

Gasps.

"You killed a man with a wife and three children. His wife is now without a husband. His children are now without a father. What you are to do, for the remainder of your life, is to provide for them. You are to ensure their needs are met in every way. You will see to it that his wife has all and everything she could possibly need. You will be her husband, in spirit, and in spirit only. You will provide for this man's children. You will see to it that each child has everything needed, included teachings, trainings, garments, visits to sacred sites and celebrations, and anything else needed to bring each child to maturity with all needs met, including spiritual needs. You will be their father in spirit and in spirit only.

"Do you understand, Thunder Bear?" I ask sternly with eyebrows raised.

Thunder Bear furrows his eyebrows, holding back his own emotions, and just looks sheepishly down at the ground.

I articulate clearly and deliberately with head tilted forward and eyes wide open, "If you don't know what that means, then members of this village are charged with reminding you, daily, if necessary, as to what that means. Also, you may decide to marry and have your own children. This is to be expected. However, your first obligation is to the wife and children of the man you murdered. Do you have any questions, Thunder Bear?"

Thunder Bear stands silently and shakes his head.

"Does anyone else have any questions?" I ask as I look around the audience.

After waiting an appropriate time for a response, I say softly, "And, so it is."

32

THE WALK HOME

Stunned by a shock wave that ripples from the center of the meeting place through the audience to its outer rings, the villagers at first freeze in their places without moving. Then signaling permission to breathe, talk and move, I stand up, smile at folks sitting nearby. My relaxed movements and my reaching out to touch some of them brave enough to smile at me and to reach out to me, set a tone of acceptance for what had just transpired. With that, a hum, then a buzz of voices ensues. They exchange perceptions and views with each other as they leave the meeting place. Dusk changes afternoon into evening by that time.

Stalking Bear and I have been given a little guest house to stay in that night. On our way back to the guest house, several villagers approach me with pats on the back and an invitation to join them around a small fire near their homes.

Although exhausted but feeling calm and in good spirits, my son and I agree to sit by their fire for a little while. Several other people from the village also join us. Someone brings food and shares it around the circle. Still wanting to process the afternoon's events, the villagers can't help but bring up in conversation the position that I had taken by not banishing Thunder Bear.

"That's always been the outcome . . . banishment!" emphasizes one villager. The others all nod in agreement.

"It's not that the outcome doesn't make sense," says another.

"It just feels strange, that's all," adds someone else.

"We're living in a strange time," I say, realizing they want to elicit an explanation from me. "I don't know how much you know about the visions and dreams that some, in fact, many of our Elders and shaman, and some others have been experiencing." They stop shuffling, sit very still and some lean forward to get closer to the information that is forthcoming.

"The feelings and visions, as seen in dreams, are distressing, not only by the dreamers, but those hearing about them. Even White Eagle sees a murky, forbidding cloud-like force stretching from a land faraway to the east. In her dreams that cloud forms a hand that reaches over to our lands and touches down with its malicious fingers. When its fingers reach down and touch our lands, strange things occur."

Quiet murmurings.

I pause briefly, looking around at each before going on, "This dark cloud, to me, is an energy, out-of-order, thought-form. As an energy field it appears to stretch from one continent to another. Where the fingers of it touch our land, it seems that some kind of disturbance occurs. Or, an incident, much like this one, occurs."

"Or," I take a deep breath, "some of our People act strangely or in ways not consistent with their normal behavior."

"I remember hearing something about that several years ago. Doesn't it have something to do with foreign invaders?" asks one man.

"What does this have to do with Thunder Bear not being banished?" challenges another.

I pause a moment, then I say, "It's really all part of the same energy field, at least, as I see it. We have lived a thousand years of peace, and now we foresee an energy field finding its way to us that is not in harmony with ours. Thunder Bear may have acted strictly out of his heightened ego and self-will. Or he may have been touched by the negative energy field. Or after having been exposed to that negative energy field, he allowed his ego-mind to run him, and he behaved in a way not consistent with The People. In any event, he remains accountable for the choice he made."

Stalking Bear yawns and leans up against me with half closed eyes. I put my arm around my son, and finish my thought. "While banishment is the norm for such rare abnormal behavior, in my opinion, this was more than abnormal behavior.

"Our awareness must be heightened, so we can prevent ourselves from becoming affected by such a thought-form. This requires our vigilance of the energy fields that we participate in.

"As Thunder Bear lives his life here and monitors the needs of the family he deprived of a husband and father, he will be reminded of his responsibility of remaining constant in his awareness. Both he and the rest of us will be reminded to stay alert to influences that may cause harm. You will be reminded every time you see him.

"This incident is not just about Thunder Bear. It is about The People. All of us. It is about our entire civilization. If more of this occurs, it would seem the survival of our civilization is at risk. The whole thing comes down to who we are, who we choose to be, how we want to live and how we choose to treat each other. Heightened awareness for the choices we make is a key factor.

"I've talked a long time tonight and feel like I'm talking in circles. I beg your forgiveness. I must take my son and put him to bed. It's been quite a day." With that I stand, nod to each one sitting around the campfire. I then pick up my sleepy son and take him back to the guest house.

After we left, the villagers remained sitting by the fire still unwilling to stop wrestling with the ideas under discussion. Looking down into the fire as if it could provide answers, one man finally spoke, "I remember conversations a while back about whether we should leave our homes in anticipation of the invaders coming to our lands. I remember that it was never settled, whether we should stay or go."

Another chimed in, "I'd heard descriptions of what might happen to The People if we stayed here after the foreign people arrive. It's hard to connect the two events. On the one hand, we have invasion by a people who do not know us or know who we are, and then on the other hand, we have an invasion of a thought-form influencing individuals to behave strangely."

"I think I understand it," said another. "I think Gray Wolf was saying that the invasion of the thought-form is preceding the invasion of the foreign people." The small group continued talking late into the night. After they let the fire die down, they all retired into their homes with the sense that a shift was occurring, with a sense that things might never be the same again.

I heave a sigh as Stalking Bear and I leave the village the following morning. Feeling free of my strong sense of responsibility to The People for a moment, I feel my spirits lift up as we enjoy our walk through trees and meadows along our return home. On our walk home, we stop at a stream to sit under the shade of trees for a brief respite.

While sitting, I breathe in the beauty of our surroundings, appreciating the summer blooms and the sounds of the brook rippling in harmonics with the environment. The sun's rays warm between the fitful gusts of wind that announce clouds gathering. My seven-year-old son finds entertainment playing in the water while I sit propped up against a large shade tree. Stalking Bear grabs a stick and begins making lines and circles in the dirt gradually edging closer to me.

"Dad," Stalking Bear says. I nod in acknowledgement. "Dad, can I ask you a question?" says my son looking at me, and then down at the designs he is aimlessly drawing.

"Sure," I say. "What do you want to know?"

"Well, if we're all part of the One and we're Children of the Law of One, then how is it that we look like we are separate?"

"Good question," I reply. I look down a few moments gathering my thoughts to formulate an answer that would help my son understand.

Finally, I say, "Great Spirit is the essence of all that is. This essence is the life-force or energy that can be found in all things, like that blade of grass over there. Or, in that rabbit over there," I point to a rabbit nibbling on some shoots a little distance away. My son looks in that direction and focuses on the rabbit for a few minutes.

I continue, "This life-force or essence is an energy that you cannot see with your physical eyes. It vibrates so fast that our physical eyes cannot see it. It's like watching insects when they fly."

I point to a bee circling around some flowers. "See that bee over there?" Stalking Bear nods. "When you watch a bee fly around, you see the body, but it's hard to see the wings. The wings move so fast, too fast for our eyes to see them move. We can't see them when they vibrate fast. When they slow down or stop, then we can see them. So we know that just because we can't see the wings when they vibrate fast doesn't mean they are not there." He nods indicating acknowledgement.

"But what about the Oneness?" Stalking Bear insists.

Again I look up as though the clouds overhead held answers, then look into Stalking Bear's eyes before I say. "The Oneness is the very essence of all creation. Because it is the essence comprising all things, it is One. We as human beings are individualized expressions of the One essence. The One essence is our Creator. We cannot be separated from our Creator, because our Creator is us."

The breezes blow a little harder and a roll of thunder sounds off as the clouds coalesce. I continue, ignoring the storm warnings, "You see, when we understand in our hearts that we are not separate from our Creator, and cannot be separate, we realize that we are not separate from each other either. As we go through life, we can acknowledge the unifying Presence in each person. The Law of One says we are One."

I pause a moment and then ask, "Am I explaining this okay? Am I clear?"

The boy nods big nods. "Yes, dad," he says. "I think I understand it. What you are saying is that even though different people look like they are separate from each other, they really are not. It's just that our physical eyes can't see the vibrational frequency that makes us connected."

Impressed with my child's response, I raise my eyebrows and open my eyes wide, then smile in admiration of my offspring. Then I grab him in a full hug. Still smiling I release him and say, "Very good, Stalking Bear . . . And not to test your comprehension too much, but I would like to add one more tidbit of information to what you just said." Stalking Bear pleased with the praise, waits for my comment.

I say, "Stalking Bear, take what you just said, and see in your mind. Let me show you a new way of seeing things. You can see the frequency of the energies of what is around you. Start with me, for example."

Stalking Bear squints his eyes and looks at me. A faraway look comes into his eyes with a light shining behind them. When I see this, I continue, "Now go higher in frequency. See the energies vibrate between each other. When you do, you will see how every physical thing is connected to an even greater field of vibrational frequencies."

Minutes pass.

Stalking Bear stays totally still while he takes the time to see the subtle energy connecting all things. By the time Stalking Bear finishes seeing beyond the beyond, a light shines from his face. "I see it, father. I see it," he says in awe.

The weather turns wet as rain begins coming down. Neither of us notices. We just stand up and begin walking the long way home, both of us smiling. Despite the rainy weather, and the lateness of the hour, and the darkness of the night, we arrive home safely.

Shining Bird had gone to bed but did not sleep. She felt restless, tossing and turning. In her prayers she tuned in to feel the confirmation that her husband and oldest son were well and safe. Yet, the recent information about a band of renegades attacking travelers and some tiny villages nagged at the back of her mind. She worked hard to push the fear away and replace it with sending a loving, protecting energy to her two men.

Scuffle, crunch. Bump, scuffle.

"Oh yeah. We are home," I announce gratefully but in a soft tone so as not to awaken anyone needlessly. Hearing us, Shining Bird jumps up out of bed to greet us. As she opens the door, she sees Stalking Bear and me standing in the covered area soaking wet and dripping water where we stand.

"Take off your clothes," she orders in low tones. "I'll heat up some water to wash you down with before you go to bed. I don't want you to stay chilled any longer than you have to."

The water boils for tea on the inside hearth as Shining Bird finishes working to prevent a chill from setting in on her two men, her husband and her son-turned-young-man. She wraps blankets around us. We sit silently as the warmth pervades our bodies. No one speaks.

My son and I just remain sitting grateful to be home feeling the warmth of the blankets and the warmth of a home filled with nurturing. Even as Shining Bird pours cups of herbal tea, still no one speaks. Silence screams in Shining Bird's ears while she stands watching us sip our tea, both of us holding both hands around our cups.

Knowing that something significant must have occurred, Shining Bird asks no questions. She turns and begins preparing porridge of cooked grains, feeling instinctively that we need nourishment after, not only such a long walk home, but what seems like a particularly draining event. We eat gratefully, but in silence.

Sleeping late into the morning, I awake to the sounds of voices speaking in hushed tones. Evidently Floating Lily had come by with nut cakes for me and Stalking Bear. Turning over under my covers I come face to face with my daughter, Star Rising, standing by my bed. She smiles at me. I smile back, feeling so proud of my family. After crawling out from the covers, I grab her, pick her up, swing her in the air while she giggles.

"Hi, daddy," she says after our joyous tryst.

"Hi, yourself. How's my little butterfly?" I ask her affectionately. She reaches forward, puts her arms around my neck and gives a squeeze, smiling. I hold her for a little while, standing and then walking around our home.

"We went to the stream and played there all day. Floating Lily came by with treats for us. It was fun. I like going there. I got to watch the bigger boys dive for mussels," says Star Rising. "Yesterday, mom took me over to spend some time with Singing Hawk. I want to go back and learn some more from her."

Star Rising is an inquisitive and unusually perceptive child for being almost six years old. She asks me, "What happened to you while you were gone? I knew you and Stalking Bear were all right, but I just couldn't help wondering. It felt a little strange, that's all."

Not really ready to engage in a deep conversation so soon after waking up, I put my daughter down with a pat on her head. "Let me wake up first. I'll be glad to tell you the whole story," I say looking up at Shining Bird. Stalking Bear has managed to stay asleep through this. I then sit down at the table, and Shining Bird takes that cue to pour me a cup of morning tea.

Setting several nut cakes on a platter next to my cup, she smiles at me. Then she pours herself a cup of tea and sits down across the table, wanting me to begin my story, but not wanting to ask. Then she says, "Floating Lily said that White Eagle will be by a little later. She wants to hear about what happened and how it turned out with Thunder Bear."

At that remark Stalking Bear wakes up, with eyes wide open in anticipation of hearing his father tell the story of the adventure he got to participate in. As he gets up and moves to the table, he says while rubbing one eye, "I want to hear it too."

The other two children alerted by the news that their father would be telling his story to White Eagle, raise their level of awareness as to the activities of their parents. Their anticipation of White Eagle coming to their house keeps them close to home that day. Neither of the two younger children wants to miss a single moment of the telling.

After what seems like hours and hours, Floating Lily arrives with a large pot of stew, full of a variety of vegetables, wild rice and plenty of possum meat in a rich gravy. Over her arm is a bag of warm rolls, made from corn and other grains, all prepared by Raven's Wing.

Shining Bird immediately sets about to make a nice evening tea to go with the meal. Stalking Bear clears the table and puts out ceramic bowls and cups with spoons. Plum Blossom, Shining Bird's grandmother, has already started to tidy up the house and helps the other two children organize themselves, bringing in more chairs from outside, and in general, preparing for White Eagle's visit.

Before too long, White Eagle appears in full formal dress, wearing her special necklace prominently. Just as she approaches the door, Star Rising dashes out the door, excusing herself to White Eagle and runs the distance to Singing Hawk's house to inform me that White Eagle had just arrived and that I am needed at home. I had spent the afternoon in conference with Singing Hawk, getting her views on my experience with Thunder Bear.

My daughter and I walk back to our home. When we arrive, we find White Eagle and Shining Bird sitting at the table cordially conversing as the other two children and Plum Blossom listen having glued themselves in their places in the background.

"Hello, White Eagle," I say in greeting as I enter.

"Gray Wolf, my son," White Eagle returns my greeting with an arm outstretched to me. She takes my hand as I sit down at the table. We look at each other with light shining from our faces. No one speaks. Then, Shining Bird gets up and begins serving the tasty stew and rolls made by Raven's Wing for this occasion. After serving White Eagle and me, Shining Bird ladles some into bowls for her Grandmother and her three children. Stalking Bear takes a serving over to Plum Blossom, so she would not have to get up from her place in the back. After eating in silence, White Eagle initiates the conversation.

"Tell me, Gray Wolf, tell me your experience. I want to hear every word you have to say, hear every thought and feeling you had from the moment the runner found you," White Eagle softly commands. "No, change that. I would like to hear your story beginning with the day you left to go on your walk. Start there and don't stop until you arrived back home. Don't leave out any details, regardless of how small or incidental they might seem."

I nod and begin. Everyone sits still as they listen enraptured. When I finish, White Eagle looks down and then nods in affirmation before speaking, "You did well, my son. I am pleased with how you conducted yourself and how you settled it. And, sadly, we are living in strange times."

"Thank you, Grandmother," I say.

"I am pleased that you looked to Great Spirit for your answers and for insight to apply to the situation," White Eagle says after a pause. "That, above all, is so important. Seeking guidance and direction from our Source, which is within us, is what helps us to say and do what is appropriate in the moment."

We all sit in silence for a few more moments. Then White Eagle gets up to leave. She stops at the door, turns around to take in the entire scene. After taking a few breaths, she says, "I will go speak with Singing Hawk." With that she left.

33

GRAY WOLF JOINS THE COUNCIL OF TWELVE PLUS ONE

Several months later, Singing Hawk asked to see me. When I arrive, I notice she is tutoring a handful of students with heads down obviously studying something. The scene reminds me of when Shining Bird and I were her young students.

Of course, I could not help but notice that one of her students is my very own daughter, Star Rising. Glancing over to her, I raise my head in a nod in silent acknowledgement to my daughter. I continue walking the length of the teaching room, passing all the tables I remember sitting at not too many years before as I smile to myself.

"Singing Hawk," I say as she appears from a back room. "You wanted to see me?"

"Yes, Gray Wolf," she says in a hushed tone, motioning me to sit down, "The Council of Twelve Plus One will be meeting at Chillicothe by the next full moon. Runners were sent awhile back to Canada and the east, as well as to the south and western regions. As you know, every section of The People is represented.

"You must prepare yourself and plan to leave at least a week before to give you enough time to walk there, get settled in, and to meditate before the discussions begin. You may bring with you several friends to join you on the journey there and to give you assistance while staying there. They will not be able to join you in the meetings. You will find that you will appreciate it if someone is responsible for bringing you food and seeing to any other needs you might have. Typically, the sessions can last from several days to a week or more."

"I recommend," Singing Hawk continues with a tone of seriousness, "you take a three-day sweat as part of your preparation for this meeting before you go."

I pause a moment then ask, "Do I get to know what the topics of discussion will be before I go so I can meditate on them in advance?"

"What's coming is the primary topic," she says and moves over to another part of the small room, straightening a few items before going on, "although, other topics may come up."

I nod in acknowledgement.

A few moments pass then she adds, "As you know, this Council has been meeting for at least a thousand years. Those chosen to sit in the Council of Twelve Plus One have contributed significantly as leaders among The People. Actually the word, leader, is misleading. Our leaders simply speak their opinions with no expectation that anyone will follow. The Council members return to their home villages and word gets out. The rest you'll just have to find out for yourself."

Back at home I ask Shining Bird, "So who should I take with me?" My life companion just stands there smiling at me, before a voice sounds at the door, "Anyone home?"

"Red Fox," I say in surprise. "What a surprise this is. We haven't seen you in way too long. What's going on?"

Entering our home, Red Fox grabs my arms in greeting as we smile at each other.

"You know, it's nice outside. Let's sit outside and enjoy the late summer sun," I say.

At that the two of us move outside and plop ourselves down on the chairs. We appreciate the lingering warmth of the sun's rays before the cool of the evening sets in.

"I've spent the last two months up in Canada building a lodge. Their trees up there are different, so I felt challenged to configure the building they wanted with the materials available," Red Fox says.

I nod. Both of us sit silently as several moments pass.

Red Fox continues, "I so enjoyed the challenge and feel a tremendous sense of satisfaction. When I came back I hung around a while and spent time with my Grandmothers . . . Then I felt directed to come and see you."

I cock my head to the side and look at Red Fox without saying anything. My children are playing nearby and run around in front of us before moving off toward another house not too far away. I notice the children, turn to Red Fox and ask, "In all your travels, have you not met someone who might be a companion for you, some young woman even up in Canada?"

Shifting his feet, hands placed on his knees, then relaxing his arms back again in obvious discomfort, Red Fox does not answer right away. He looks up then away from me. Finally, he says, "No. Not yet." Looking back up to the skies, he adds, "I know she is out there somewhere." Then wanting to change the subject, he says, "I'll be around here for a little while. Right now I've nothing scheduled."

"Really?" I inquire smiling broadly. "How would you like to come with me to Chillicothe? I have to make a trip soon with White Eagle and sure would enjoy your company along the way."

"Chillicothe?" asks Red Fox, "why, yes. That would be fun. It's been a long time since we've spent any time together. What a great idea! I haven't been there in a while and would enjoy consulting with a few artisans there, and this would give me that opportunity." Smiling broadly at me he says, "That's great! Sure, I'll go with you. How long do you plan on staying there?"

"I'm not sure exactly, maybe a week, maybe a few days more or a few days less, depending," I say.

"Sure. I think it would be great fun to join you," says Red Fox.

"Well, I'm not sure it's a fun trip, but going there with you would be fun," I reply.

As the afternoon turned into evening, my three children wandered home. Red Fox and I continued our conversation. Stalking Bear went to fetch water for his mother as she began preparing the evening meal. When Red Fox stood up moving to leave, I stood up also. The two of us stood silently for a few moments before Shining Bird came out to see what was going on.

"Ah, you still here, Red Fox?" she says. "Since you are still here, why don't you come in and share a meal with us. I'd so love to chat with you too and find out what you've been doing since I saw you last."

"I'd like that," says Red Fox with a smile.

Red Fox entertained the family, regaling us with stories of his adventures in other villages. Our conversations lasted well into the evening. The children had all gone to sleep and Grandmother Plum Blossom nodded off several times. After she went to bed, and all appeared to be sound asleep, our conversation shifted to the journey to Chillicothe.

"So when will you be leaving?" Red Fox asks me.

"I expect to take about a week to prepare myself, which includes a three-day sweat in the sweat lodge," I say. "I'd say in a about a week or so."

"That should give me plenty of time to get a few things done for my Grandmothers, as well as for several other friends," says Red Fox. "So, who else are you taking with you?"

Shining Bird looks me straight in my eyes waiting for my answer, anxious to be off on an adventure herself, but says nothing. I hold my wife's gaze, and then say jokingly with a half-smile, "Well, I just don't know who might want to go. Stalking Bear might be a little too young yet. Hmmm," I pause stroking my chin before going on.

Unable to hold it back any longer as the tension grows thick, I smile broadly and ask, "Shining Bird, you wouldn't by any chance be interested in coming with me, would you?" With that question, the tension broke and laughter ensues. Shining Bird beams with excitement.

On the day of departure the three of us hike up the hill to White Eagle's house. I knock on the door and say politely, "Grandmother. Grandmother, are you ready? We can wait if you would like." No answer comes. "Grandmother?" I inquire again, "Are you there?"

Muffled sounds come from within. After what seems like a very long wait, the door slowly opens halfway. White Eagle appears obviously not in traveling clothes.

"You have a good journey, my son," she says with a nod of her head.

"What do you mean 'have a good journey'? I am joining *you* in the Council meeting, am I not?" I ask incredulously.

"The Council of Twelve Plus One allows for only twelve members, plus one to facilitate. You are going in my place. I trust you will serve our People well," she says.

With that, she closes her door to prevent further conversation, leaving the three of us just standing there looking at each other.

After the shock wears off that White Eagle had stepped down from her Council membership, it becomes stunningly clear that I have been tapped as her replacement in representing our region at the Council meeting. Finding myself unable to speak, I look at White Eagle's door, look at my two closest friends, look to the trail we need to take, and just begin walking. The three of us walk in silence.

The five-day trek proved uneventful for the three of us journeying from our village near the Great Serpent to Chillicothe. The time spent walking provided an opportunity to rekindle our bond with each other. We found ourselves retelling old stories and laughing at our foibles that occurred while growing up. The time together also provided the opportunity to nurture each other as each spoke about questions and concerns, both personal and community issues.

This led our conversations toward sharing with each other personal insights and experiences that served to expand our own awareness. As each night fell different villages and hamlets welcomed us, providing us with comfortable quarters as we journeyed.

Upon arriving at our destination, a hospitality committee greets us and escorts Shining Bird and me, with Red Fox tagging along behind, to the guest houses long used by visiting dignitaries.

When we get to the guest house reserved for us, Red Fox says to us, "When you are ready to leave, send word to find me, and I'll be there."

We nod, smile and raise a hand to wave. Red Fox gives a brief wave back and turns to leave. Seeing that we were squared away, Red Fox looks at us again, and then drifts off in his own direction, seeking contacts he had previously established years before.

That evening Shining Bird and I were invited to join in a group dinner to meet the other Council members and their companions. As introductions are made, I realize that I am the only new member.

It was a time for the returning members to reacquaint with each other on events, and so forth, catching up on what had transpired in each of their lives and regions since the last gathering.

I discover that the Council of the Twelve Plus One met at various times, but not always to consult the Knowing. That is reserved for highly important circumstances, such as this one.

The next morning, I enter the Council lodge wearing a classic tunic and pants of linen-like fabric and color made for me by Laughing Willow, Red Fox's mother. She is such an accomplished seamstress that I felt honored to have her make me such a suit for this occasion. My long black hair is tied in back.

My meditations in preparation for this event had deepened my connection into Spirit. By the time the Council meeting was to start, I felt like I was floating as I entered the lodge to join the other Council members.

Some of the other Council members wore elaborately designed colorful garments, decorated exquisitely with pearls, copper and silver adornments. Others wore differently colored robes with hoods. Some wore copper and silver earspools or other jewelry. Some wore their hair bound up fashionably with jeweled pins and combs that worked for both red, blond and black hair. Others just pulled their hair back. No uniform style ruled as each member expressed their own individuality in their appearance. Both men and women dressed according to their own self-expression. Few spoke, and when they did it was in hushed tones. This was sacred space.

Not knowing the protocol, I observed what each of the others did and followed suit. The members sat on the floor crossed-legged. The seating design was shaped like a rectangle, with one parallel row of five members sitting across a five-foot measurement of space facing each other. Then at the two ends a member sat at each end completing the rectangle shape. The facilitator, draped in a linen-colored robe with a hood covering the head bent down so as to prevent identification, touched my arm and motioned for me to sit in a particular spot.

THE CAMP OF GOD'S TEARS

Placement for seating was designated by large comfortable down-filled cushions, each dyed in a different deep jewel tone color.

Incense smoked from several dishes placed in the center of the rectangle. After all twelve were seated and all were quiet, the thirteenth person wearing the hooded robe began the opening ceremony. She stood at a small table at one end of the rectangle.

Delicately and reverently, she unwraps a bundle that had been packaged in a brightly colored and finely woven fabric. Smoke from the incense fills my senses and I find myself expanding out of my body connecting with Spirit. The facilitator continues with the item she is unwrapping. Finally, she exposes two parts of a ceremonial pipe, the stem and the bowl. Deftly she puts the two together, then adds tobacco into the pipe's bowl and lights it. Confidently, the facilitator initiates the pipe by taking a few puffs and passes it to a Council member sitting at the end of the rectangle closest to her. No words were spoken as each member takes a few puffs and hands it to the next person.

Silence reigns over the peaceful setting as the pipe is passed around. When the last person finishes, the facilitator takes the pipe and sets it on the stand designed to hold it during the meeting.

Silence.

"AaaahhhhOoooooohhhmmmmmmmm," sounds the facilitator.

"AaaahhhhOoooooohhhmmmmmmmm," respond the members.

As a group we repeat the toning numerous times, raising the collective frequency of our group.

This toning came from the ancient of days from those who came from across the great waters to the west.

Then the facilitator standing between the table and the Council members begins:

We acknowledge the Creator or Great Spirit as the Sacred Force in the Universe. The Universe, created by Great Spirit, is the Great Spirit manifested. All of Heaven and Mother Earth birthed from Great Spirit. The Will of the Creator is as above, so below. Just as Great Spirit provides nurturing of our souls, so does our Mother Earth provide us with bounty for meeting our human needs. We live in Oneness with each other. As we help each other, we help ourselves. Should we by some act bring harm to another, we harm ourselves. As we remain in alignment with Great Spirit and Mother Earth, we know our way is guided, our path protected. All comes from the Creator, all Life, everything that is, is part of Great Spirit.

"And so it is," responds the Council members not quite in unison.

The facilitator continues, "We live in the Fourth World. We are the Children of the Law of One. Maintaining a sense of oneness requires awareness of our connectedness to each other and to our Creator and Mother Earth. We are connected to all that is through the frequencies of vibration that comprise the Universe. Our thoughts and emotions drive our words and actions that manifest into the world around us. What we experience results from that which we manifest."

The facilitator pauses briefly, breathing in deeply, and then says, "This is a meeting of the Council of Twelve. Each of you represent different regions and areas of The People from the north in Canada, to the edges of the eastern ocean, north of the Ohio River past the great lakes, south of the Ohio River to the southern ocean, and to the west past the great river and north and south from there. We are an ancient People living in these lands for thousands of years. Yet an imbalance of energy is appearing among us."

Nods and nearly silent sounds of affirmations.

"This meeting provides us with the time and space to consider an imbalance that is impacting The People. This meeting provides us with sacred space to discuss this and maybe yet other unidentified issues. We can share our observations, experiences, thoughts, feelings, and listen without judging each other's position. After our discussions are exhausted, and even between sessions, we will each spend time in meditation that will allow us to reconnect with Spirit. As most of you know, time spent in meditation, especially while here, will afford us the opportunity to raise our consciousness, awareness and our individual frequency so that we can access additional information through the Knowing."

Ever so quiet breaths inhaled.

She continues, "Then as each of you become ready, we will convene in a deep meditation to lift us unto the highest level of consciousness we can attain. At that time, I will bring forth the Knowing. Each of you will be given the opportunity to ask whatever question you wish to ask. It is also the time to set intentions." As she speaks, I recognize the voice but say nothing.

For days the twelve of us shared experiences, observations, and comments. I told my stories, which resonated with the others who in turn told their stories. Not all agreed with each other on shared insights, causes, influences and reasons. Not all agreed on solutions or on how to go about bringing balance to The People, the balance that had been lived for countless generations. Some members felt perplexed. Others felt peace and were not threatened by the experiences as told in the sessions.

Throughout the long days, a refreshing tea with fruit and other tidbits were served. Some sessions lasted longer than others. Some continued on into the night. Shining Bird awaited me whenever I returned from the Council House. I felt grateful for her support during this challenging time.

"Doomed! We're doomed either way. We go or stay," one council member says.

Another adds, "If we stay, it may not be the foreigners that destroy us, but quite possibly a disease for which we have no medicine."

"Well," another interjects, "some of my shaman saw just the foreigners coming to our lands, while others saw visions of diseases without people."

"That's interesting," another member says, "some of our shaman saw the diseases coming in advance of the foreigners. So, that by the time the invaders arrived, diseases had significantly diminished our numbers without mercy."

A Council member from the far west says, "I hear your words, but none of our dreamers, Elders, and shaman have experienced these visions."

"Either way, I must ask 'what do we do about it?' What is it that we must do?" asks another one.

"That's what we must ask the Knowing," comments one.

Another Council member says, "Several in my villages have reported a band of renegades who have occasionally accosted travelers. Has anyone heard of this?"

"Interfering with travelers or traders is not done. What do you mean?" asks another.

"Traders always have safe passage. Who would interfere with traders? Traders are sacred. They are an integral part of our civilization. Accosting traders is indeed a violation," comments another.

"I haven't heard that," interjects another, "but several villages in my region have been raided for food."

Gasps.

"No one should have to steal food. That is unheard of. We always have plenty," another member says. "Even when game is scarce, as in recent times, we always have food and plenty of it. Why would anyone raid for food, when we would always feed those who needed it?"

Such conversations lasted long into the night. I felt relieved when the time allowed for discussions came to an end. Deep meditation would begin the next day.

When I arrive at my guest house where Shining Bird awaits me late one night, I say, "I find it interesting that not everyone agrees with each other. While experiences may be similar, those experiences are interpreted differently. No decisions have been made and no proposals made for what The People should do. Maybe something will come out after the meditation time.

"I was told that we will sit and meditate for as long as we need to, in the effort to raise our individual frequencies. That will probably raise our collective frequency," I say. "Maybe that's what this is about. Maybe that's the process that will finally get us to a place where we all feel in one accord, if that is what is necessary."

Shining Bird just smiles and reaches for me in the dark, silently pulling my body close to hers. Without speaking, she strokes my head. With gentle touching, she persuades my body to give up its tension and give in to her. With my passion kindled, I abandon my mental struggles. Groaning in deep physical and spiritual pleasure, I surrender to the oneness between us. As I release myself inside my beloved, I feel space open up inside me.

That space becomes filled with a sense of oneness with Spirit the next day after I enter into my meditation.

Each day of meditation began with the same ceremony as the opening day. However, on this day events differed. The facilitator went into a small back room and brought out a large wooden box, stained a deep, dark red. It had a lid with metal hinges and a design carved on the lid. The energy field surrounding it shrieked its antiquity.

This catches my attention. Unable to focus on anything else, I just stare at it, turning my body to keep it in sight as it is carried into the room. Instinctively, I am drawn to it like it is a magnet to my mind and soul. Despite the fact that I continue to stare at the box, I still maintain my elevated state of meditative grace.

Realizing that I'm sitting in an awkward position, I finally let go of my need to hold the box in my sight. I turn back around to re-center myself and allow myself to deepen my meditation even more than before.

After hours sitting in deep meditation, I feel a tap on my shoulder. The facilitator motions for me to rise and follow her. The two of us walk to another part of the ceremonial room to where the box had been placed on a table. Standing next to me, the facilitator pulls back her hood. I gasp silently and step back a half step in surprise when I see my old teacher, Singing Hawk, now my new teacher as the Plus One of the Council of Twelve Plus One. Even though I recognized her voice earlier in the proceedings, protocol prevented me from pursuing the issue.

"Gray Wolf," she says intently in a hushed tone, "This is the Knowing."

My eyes open wide. I did not blink. I can hardly breathe. I wait for her to continue.

She says, "It is called the Knowing, because its energy field is connected to all the collective knowledge of humankind around the world and to the Akashic Records of the Universe."

I gulp.

Singing Hawk opens the lid to show me what is inside.

I see inscriptions carved on the inside surfaces of the box. I see it contains multiple scrolls, some of which had been made of materials I had never seen before. Each scroll is tied as if the tie secures the information contained within each scroll.

"Each scroll," Singing Hawk says quietly but intently, "is a portal. Each portal provides access to different planes of information and consciousness. Written on each scroll are symbols of the cosmos, formulas, numeric symbols, pictograms, and other forms that speak to different layers of knowledge. It links our inner visions to the consciousness within the fabric of the Universe."

I freeze in rapture of being so close to the threshold of accessing information gifted to us from those living in the Ancient of Days.

Singing Hawk says, "These scrolls were created by our ancient ones from beyond both the western ocean and the eastern ocean whose lands are no longer. Should an unenlightened person open this box, that person could see these scrolls. Should an unenlightened person open a scroll, little or no information would be imparted. The script would be unintelligible."

She pauses briefly to allow that to register before continuing. Then she says, "However, should someone, whose consciousness is attuned to Spirit at a very high frequency, open this box, and insert a hand to reach for a scroll, the person's hand will disappear. It disappears to the physical eye as the hand connects to the even higher frequency of the Knowing. At that moment the question in the mind of the questioner becomes answered. Or, the intention of the intender is acknowledged." Finally able to blink, I just stand there absorbing what my facilitator is saying. She continues, "You'll know when you have reached the level you need to be at to get your answer, or to set your intention, when you reach inside the box and you no longer see your hand. If you can see your hand while it's in the box, you will not hear or receive what you are looking for, and you must return to your meditations and repeat the process." Unable to speak and still frozen in rapture, I blink several times. "This is only for the pure in heart *and* only for those who seek the goodness for all concerned. This is not about ego or self-aggrandizement. These have no place in the Council of the Twelve Plus One. Do you understand, Gray Wolf?" she says looking directly at me.

I nod silently.

As she starts to close the lid, I put my right hand on her arm.

She stops and looks at me. "Yes?" she asks, "you have a question?"

Working to free myself from my state of amazement, I ask, "If we have access to the all-knowing, then couldn't just one person ask the question, and get the answer, then tell everyone what the answer is?"

"It does not work that way," she says.

"I don't understand this," I say. "What if each of the Council members asks the same question? Wouldn't they all get the same answer?"

She looks down then up again before answering, and then she says, "Even if each member asks the same question of the Knowing, the response for each would be different."

"So how does that work?"

"Since each is on a different journey within the river of time, and each may be attuned at a different frequency, the response will vary depending upon the frequency of the questioner, that person's filter in receiving answers, and how the question is asked."

So when you say 'filter' are you speaking of that person's life experience, ego, and biases?" I ask.

She nods affirmatively and continues. "We are asking to see around the curve in the river of time to access the multiple possibilities that exist. What becomes seen is influenced by the intentions of the person and how they position the intention or question. All of this impacts on what possibilities *could* occur in the future or how that possibility manifests. Our free will can change over time and can be influenced by our ego. It's a dynamic, interactive process, the outcome of which we create as we progress on our individual journeys in the flux and constancy of life. Our focus and intentions can shift as we move into our future." I listen, my attention locked on what Singing Hawk is saying to me.

She goes on uninterrupted, "We ask the question today, and we get an answer. But that answer may not apply several months from now as circumstances can change, exercise of free will can change, and our focus or our intentions can change.

"The future remains ethereal and malleable in many respects. When you receive knowledge, that information can impact your exercise of free will, or your intentions. That in and of itself creates possibilities, because it changes things, and that opens for additional potentialities and possibilities.

"The future is not set," she continues. "Since we influence everything all the time by all these variables, the only control we can have is over ourselves by staying centered within each moment. But, seeing around the curve of time can often help us prepare for a future event."

I scratch my ear, and then ask, "If the future is not set, then where are these visions coming from?"

"Good question," Singing Hawk comments. "When a future possibility gathers enough energy to become a potential manifestation, it may be perceived by those who are attuned. This energy can be either positive or negative. If it is a discordant harmonic, it may be perceived as ominous and threatening.

"That's why the Council of the Twelve was called, because so many were tapping into these discordant frequencies and the energy seems to be increasing."

"So," I swallow hard then breathe in deeply before saying, "now let me see what you are saying. If one person asks the question for all, that doesn't work. If all ask the same question, that still doesn't work. So how do we know which answer is right when it is different for each one?"

Singing Hawk purses her lips, looks down momentarily before looking up and commenting. Then she says, "First of all, the answer doesn't always come at the instant you ask the question. It may come later. It even might not come until the moment you need to know. Each will know what the right thing is for them, for example, to go or to stay, when you need to know it, and without doubt.

"This goes for setting intentions as well as asking questions. You need to know that setting intentions and asking questions are close in frequency. When we ask a question, we are in a sense setting an intention. That is because the question is a focus of what you are contemplating in terms of future actions. Should we go? Or, should we stay? Intentions are embedded in the question.

"Because, my dearest Gray Wolf," she softly says as she leans toward me embracing my hand in both of hers, "remember, what we are tapping into is the space between on and off, particle and wave, knowing and not-knowing, wherein all possibilities exist. Each of these possibilities are potentials available for realization into the material world, only waiting for the seer to see, the asker to ask, the intender to intend. This space is comprised of the omniscient, omnipresent, and omnipotent Force breathlessly waiting to manifest."

34

GRAY WOLF CONSULTS *THE KNOWING*

Waves of energy wash over me as I listen to Singing Hawk's words.

Feeling the tingling of truth as it touches my being, my body rocked slightly forward and backward. I nod silently at Singing Hawk, take in a deep breath and return to my designated seat.

Seriously involved within my own connection with Spirit at the deepest level I had not experienced until now, I did not notice other members, one at a time, leave their seats to approach the box of Knowing.

By the time I returned to the here and now, I realized several members had left the lodge. The Council member sitting next to me was just returning to his seat after approaching the box, unsuccessful in his attempt to connect with the Knowing. I turned around to see if anyone was standing at the table with the box on it. An older woman dressed in a brilliant red gown with many pearls sewn on to it around the chest area was standing at the table with her left hand in the Knowing looking thoughtful and serene. I watched her slowly remove her hand and close her eyes for a few moments before opening them. Then she moved away. Continuing to watch her, I saw her drift around the room, not in touch fully with the present, until she reached the doorway and vanished from my sight.

Still feeling in a deep, meditative state, I look around at the half dozen Council members still left. Summoning up the courage to approach the box and the Knowing, I stand up and walk over to it.

Standing a little to the left of the opening, I lift up the lid and let it sit back. Again my thoughts register on the symbols engraved on the insides of the box itself. My gaze rolls slowly over the several scrolls lying neatly in rows filling the box to about half full. Each was tied with a different kind of sash in differing colors.

At first I imagine I hear a kind of music as I stand there. By the time I lift my hand up to the box, I realize I am hearing a beautiful combination of tones in a harmonic that speaks to me in a mysterious code.

Breathing deeply with thoughts and questions weighing heavy on my mind, I look at my hand as it disappears inside the box. The music grows louder as I let my hand remain inside the box for a few moments, then a few moments longer, then a few more moments longer.

Finally, when I remove my hand out of the box, I find breathing difficult and my whole body clutches in a series of spasms. Stepping back then forward to prevent myself from falling backward, I am able to maintain my balance after the shock of the experience dissipates.

Afterward I wander out of the lodge into a full blast of the afternoon sun. I raise up my arm to shield my eyes then stagger slightly as I find my way back to the guest house and Shining Bird.

"I don't know if I can even talk about it now," I say to her as she looks at me with a question mark on her face. "What I do remember is that after all the days of discussion the twelve of us engaged in, no one really argued for a position. Each stated what they thought and felt, but no debate occurred."

"You already told me that. Then what happened?" prompts Shining Bird as she sits with me giving me her full attention.

"Then all of us meditated for several days. Singing Hawk instructed me on the Knowing and what it was about. I meditated for the longest time after that. Then the next thing I know, Council members are leaving!" I say with emphasis.

"They left?" asks Shining Bird.

I nod as I still could not believe it.

"Yes," I say. "Some just got up and left. Others left after consulting the Knowing. No discussion occurred after that. I guess the Council meeting was over."

The two of us sit in silence for a moment.

"Nothing was decided," I start up again. "I gather that this was not a decision-making body of people." Shaking my head, I say, "I think it was a time and place for us to share our views and experiences, so we could maybe see things from another perspective and identify issues before we meditated on them, and then ask the Knowing."

Looking down then up at me, Shining Bird says, "Seeing things from another perspective can be valuable when it comes time to make a choice about some issue at hand. When a People desire consistency in applying the truth of what they know, then it seems to me that sharing experiences and views are necessary."

I look at her, feeling that she is my teacher, again.

She continues, "Sometimes when we see an issue from one perspective, our own, then seeing it from the vantage point of how another might see it, can be fruitful in seeking answers to questions we might never have thought to ask." I sit back with full attention on my teacher.

She says, "Seeing from one point of view is not enough. It behooves us to see an issue from as many viewpoints as possible, especially if we are to make a decision or a choice about the matter. Seeing an issue from only one point of view blinds us to other possibilities and other vantage points unavailable from where we might be standing at the time we are looking at it."

"Hello, the house," a familiar voice rings out. "Anyone home?" shouts Red Fox.

Jolted out of our energy field of introspection, both Shining Bird and I jump up with smiles on our faces and run to the door. After the door swings wide open, we breathe in with joy to see our lifetime friend.

"Good timing, my friend," says Shining Bird.

"I thought I would stop by and see how you were doing and when you might be ready to go home," Red Fox says.

"I believe Gray Wolf has finished his business here," says Shining Bird. She looks at me and I nod an affirmation.

"If you don't mind then, I'll gather up our stuff, and we can be off. Are you ready, Gray Wolf? Or, do you need more time?" Shining Bird asks, unsure as to my state of mind before beginning our journey home.

"Oh, yes," I say with a grin while grabbing Red Fox's arm at the elbow, dragging him inside.

"I didn't know what your schedule was," Red Fox says. "I thought I'd take a chance and stop by to see what you were doing. If you are ready, then maybe we could get a bite to eat before we leave? I'm a little hungry."

"Oh, sure, sure," I say. "Yes, I do believe I have finished here."

After finishing a nice meal, the three of us packed some food for the trek homeward feeling glad to be off.

Even though our return journey home seemed uneventful physically, our conversations proved stimulating and continuous. On one particularly pleasant star-filled night we were camped near a stream. Red Fox listened eagerly to the tale I told of my time in the Council of Twelve Plus One. He especially felt intrigued by the Knowing and what I experienced.

"I thought Singing Hawk mentioned consulting the Knowing once or twice when I was her student," says Red Fox. "I didn't exactly know what that was. The subject was treated with awe and respect."

"Indeed," I say, "it certainly is something awesome." My two companions turn all ears toward me as I speak. "It provides access to the Universe." My two listeners draw in their breath and keep silent allowing me to continue. "Each scroll is a portal to a section of knowledge, complete and unabridged. Combined together, and with the energy of the box itself, one's mind can stretch into the farthest reaches of any library in all the galaxies, known and unknown. With your intention set or question asked, you can even go to the center of the Great Mystery, the Absolute."

Stunned by this information, both Red Fox and Shining Bird gulp and hold their breath as they process this information.

I pause briefly, and then continue, "Of course, the caveat is you must put yourself into a frequency high enough to actually connect while your hand is in the box. Then your answers usually come after, sometimes long after, you are done asking or intending."

Shining Bird is finally able to speak and asks, "What I understand from this is you have to get out of your mind to get into the box, which can give answers out of the box when you are back in your mind. Did I say that right?"

I nod in affirmation then say, "That's pretty much it." I shuffle my feet around the campfire as we sit processing the information I am sharing. "What I found intriguing was, the answer you get will depend on what question you ask and exactly how you ask it. When asking, the question must be framed so that you get the answer appropriate to your intention. Otherwise, you might get information you don't understand or is not suited to what you really thought you wanted to know."

"So what did you get?" Shining Bird asks.

"What I got was that accessing the Knowing can be accomplished without actually using the box itself. By itself, the box is a tool to get us there. We can enter the Knowing without the box, if we go through our heart energy with clarity of intent and purpose for the greatest good and *feel* what we desire, feel our attunement or connection to the All. The Knowing is really the realm of Spirit that we access. This realm is a living, breathing, intelligence that responds to our heart energy. It is part of the Great Oneness."

Both my listeners raise their eyebrows in response as they continue to listen.

"Another thing I learned is that when I work on someone to heal them, I use herbs and such to apply to the physical. But, I also have been going through my heart energy to access this field we have around us with the intent to heal, and I didn't realize that's what I did," I say with emphasis. "That's why I have been so successful at my healing efforts. I realize now that that's what I've been doing. And, that's also what I did at the different village meetings, especially when I had to preside. It's like I feel like I become one with Spirit, and that Oneness moves through me to accomplish whatever it is I am focusing on."

Again, both my listeners sit stunned at my descriptions of how the Knowing works.

"In addition, I believe that both of you, as well as others, especially the Grandmothers, do this also, often on a daily basis . . . routinely," I add. "That is how they *know*. You and they tap into that space, that frequency, that field of living intelligence."

Red Fox interrupts tapping his jaw with his hand, "Yes but where is this space, this field you talk about?"

I say, "It's all around us. It is the stuff of which we are made. We are actually a part of it and must become conscious of it in order to direct outcomes or materialize intentions. The way I see it, each of us has different talents, different strengths, and different frailties. That's as it should be so that Great Spirit can manifest Itself in countless myriad expressions. Because each of us has different strengths, and different filters through which we perceive the world, and quite possibly different frequencies of heart energy, we can each intend the same thing and it could manifest differently.

Shining Bird sits back smiling, nodding in quiet affirmation. Then she says, "Yes, I have always felt this is so." She pauses, and then demands, again suspecting I had not yet told everything, "So what else did you get?"

With a grimace on my face, and reluctance in my attitude, I say, "I'm not sure I can say the rest of it. I'm still processing it. Before I can speak it, I must be sure I understand it as much as possible. I intend to see White Eagle as soon as we get back."

"So, Gray Wolf," interjects Red Fox, "you are not able to say because you don't know? Or, is it you are not able to say because you don't want to say?"

I look directly at Red Fox and say, "Yes, that is correct."

"So, I take it," says Red Fox, "you are not going to tell us whether we as a People should go or stay? To leave our homelands, the lands of our ancestors, or to stay and fight the savages we feel are coming to invade our homelands. Is that right?"

Nodding in response, I do not speak. I poke the fire and spend the rest of the evening looking into it losing myself in my feelings.

"Gray Wolf, my son," White Eagle greets me at her door after my return home. "So good to see you. I was hoping you would come by sooner, rather than later. I am anxious to hear about your adventures at the Council." She sits down outside her house facing the late summer afternoon sun. "I've got my hearth fire started inside to warm up the place. But we can sit out here as long as it remains warm. If it cools down, we can go in if we need to. But please speak to me. Tell me what you experienced."

"Grandmother," I begin, "I hardly know where to start."

"Start at the beginning, of course," White Eagle instructs with her head turned toward me, eyes locked on mine as we sit next to each other.

We sit for hours. As the sun nears the horizon and glints through the trees, a chilling breeze that whipped into stronger gusts from time to time prompts White Eagle to insist on going inside. "My bones don't fully appreciate the cooling temperatures." Standing up as she speaks, "Why don't we go in and finish our conversation? I still have some things to discuss with you."

Following her lead, I join her inside her comfy home. I look around and see that it had seemingly become bigger with the absence of Rising Wolf.

"Let me make some tea for us," White Eagle says softly with a little smile. "Floating Lily left me some nut cakes for us that Raven's Wing sent over earlier today."

"I think I've told you everything that I can, everything that I remember," I say after eating half a nut cake and finishing my first cup of tea.

"I'm sure that is true," White Eagle responds raising her eyebrows, not at all ready to dismiss me.

"I have some things I wish to tell you, my son," she adds. "The ceremony for the Northernmost Moonrise is scheduled to occur in six months from now. Preparations must be made for it."

I furrow my eyebrows and ask, "Grandmother, are you still going to officiate?"

The Grandmother beams and nods, "Yes," she says, ". . . and so are you! That's what I want to talk about with you."

I sit back half surprised, half not surprised.

She continues, "As a boy, you started out as a healer, learning from your Grandmother, Shining Moon. Clearly she taught you well. And," White Eagle nods as she says to me, "indeed, you were a good student. You have the heart of a healer. As a young man, you began healing people in our village. Then you began traveling to other villages close by, then farther and yet even farther away, just as your Grandmother used to do."

I realize she is leading up to something and I just have to listen without interrupting.

She continues, "With the instruction of Singing Hawk, and I dare say, additional help from Shining Bird, you developed into a spiritual leader."

I ask myself, "Where is she going with this?" But I remain silent and respectful.

White Eagle then says as if she had heard my silent question, "Yes, my son." Then she asks, "Why do you think I asked you to join me during the several village meetings we attended together?"

Breathing in deeply, she pauses and then says, "You were a wonderful help to me during those times. That also provided me with the opportunity to see you in action, to enter into your energy field even deeper than you might have seen yourself."

I sit up alerted by this comment, remembering what I had learned from my experience with the Knowing at the Council Meeting.

"Oh, don't get upset by that," she says comfortingly as she pats my knee. "Since Rising Wolf's death, I have needed a partner in handling village business. You have proved to me that you are deeply spiritual and can be counted on to lead The People according to the original teachings of our Ancient Ones. As a leader, you are greatly needed . . ."

"Wait a minute," I interrupt. "What are you talking about? I only stepped in because you asked me to. I have no desire to lead. And, oh, wait another minute, what do you mean by 'lead' The People?"

A shadow crossed White Eagle's face as she pauses. After a long foreboding silence, she looks down, then up again at me. Finally she says, "Before Rising Wolf died, I had a vision of The People. No, I had visions that plagued me endlessly."

"I remember that," I say softly.

"Rising Wolf comforted me as much as he could. I told him everything that I saw. He was my partner in life. He was my partner in my grief from my visions. He was my partner in village meetings. He was my partner in conducting ceremonies."

I nod in agreement.

"Now that he has walked on into Spirit, I need a partner for the upcoming ceremonies. You are my partner, Gray Wolf. You know it, so don't try to protest. You have shown yourself worthy of the position, not just in my eyes, but in the eyes of The People."

I scratch my jaw on one side with one hand. After a moment, I scratch the side of my head with my other hand as I processed what she is telling me.

She continues, "With what you experienced with the Knowing, you are ready to conduct the Northern Moonrise Ceremony with me. Because this particular ceremony only occurs every 18 years or so, this will be the last one that I will lead. And, as you know, since it requires the balance of both male and female energies, both a woman and a man must lead it. You will be my partner in this."

Upon hearing this news, I gulp at first. Then taking a few minutes to think it over, I look down. After a while, I remember all the various experiences I have had during the past several years. Finally, looking up at her, I say, "When you put it that way, I can see that I would be the logical choice. I do sense a strong connection with Spirit within me and feel honored that I will be your partner for the ceremonies, especially for the upcoming Sister Moon gathering."

"There is much to be done to prepare, my son," she says, not at all surprised by my agreement to participate with her.

Lowing her voice as if to prevent the walls from hearing, she says, "So part of preparation includes knowing what I am about to divulge to you. I told only Rising Wolf. And, now I will only tell you. It is so grievous in nature that I must ask you to not tell anyone, including Shining Bird."

White Eagle pours more tea. After a brief pause, she says, "I realize that the question of whether we go or stay is one that our People have on their mind. I'm not sure I personally have an answer to that. However, in my meditations and looking into my heart, what I've been getting is that I will know. I will have a sign, and then I will know."

White Eagle shared her vision with me and we spoke until the wee hours of the morning. During that time, White Eagle pulled out her meditation disks, so we could both focus on an inner vision of what we both needed to see and do as part of what was to come.

In the late mists of the night's dark hours, I stumbled home. After I fell into bed, I slept past dawn, past morning, on until late in the afternoon.

About five months later Shining Bird says to our three children as they look at different items of clothing laid out on the beds, "We want to make sure each of you has all the right clothing for this event. We'll need traveling clothes. We'll need outfits for events during the day, and for that special evening at moonrise."

"Where are we going again?" asks our youngest son of nearly six years, Dancing Swan.

A cold wind blows through the village after a winter storm had just finished passing through our part of the country. Shining Bird adds a little more wood to her inside hearth before answering.

"Don't you remember, Dancing Swan?" Star Rising says, precocious as she was, unable to wait for her mother to respond. "It's the Northernmost Moonrise Ceremony. It's very special and occurs only every eighteen years, six months and two weeks."

"Yes," her younger brother replies, "but I wanted mom to tell me again," stealing a glance at his mother as she continues to assess different items of clothing belonging to our children.

"My dearest children," Shining Bird realizes she needed to stop looking at their clothes and give her full attention to them, "I've already told you several times. Why don't we get together with several other families at the meeting house and tell it again with you and your friends. That way we can all talk about it together. Maybe even White Eagle might come. How does that sound?"

"At the meeting house?" I ask stepping in from outside, having missed the previous part of their conversation. "That sounds official. What is it that we are doing?"

Standing there with our three children, Shining Bird smiles at me, her beloved husband, before saying, "The children are wanting to talk about our journey on the White Road of Sister Moon and the purpose of the Northern Moonrise Ceremony."

I nod in comprehension, and then say, "Ah, yes, it is an important one to understand. Having families gather together with their children to talk about it sounds like a marvelous idea. Let's plan it."

At that, Star Rising suddenly alerted to her own thought, stands up straight then runs out the door. We both are surprised by her rushing out without notice and we just look at the door after she left.

"She's going over to talk with Singing Hawk, I think," says Stalking Bear, her older brother. "She just can't leave a thought alone without wrestling with it over and over until she sees it from every angle and can get her arms around it."

We both look at our nine year old son astounded at his insight.

He responds to our unspoken question, "We both have been spending time with Singing Hawk. I'm in class with her and I can't help seeing how her mind works. She challenges everything and often frustrates Singing Hawk with her incessant questions," he explains further. We both nod. He continues, "Even though I am a year older than her, I admire her tenacity at wanting to grasp concepts with their details." We both look at him in astonishment at his clarity as he spoke. He adds, "I, on the other hand, find it easier to accept the larger concepts and maybe experience more faith in the knowing of them and in their application than she does."

At that Stalking Bear goes outside too, taking his younger brother, Dancing Swan with him. "C'mon, little brother," he says, "let's go see how our friends are doing and to find out how their packing is going."

After the two boys leave, I turn to Shining Bird and say, "Stalking Bear takes after you, my dear. He is so insightful and can phrase an idea in just such a way as to lay it out in absolute clarity." She smiles at me in my appreciation of her. Seeing her smile that way and with the children gone, I close the door tightly, and then reach for my beloved, still beautiful to me, and surround her in a sensual embrace. As we fall into bed in loving passion, we can no longer hear the wind, nor the sound of children, only the beating of our heart energy as our bodies convulse in harmonic unison.

Late one afternoon, families merged from all directions into the meeting house. Even though winter was passing, the spring warmth had not yet taken hold so the gathering could not be held outside. The meeting house provided the proper environment for the families to meet and talk about the upcoming journey and the meaning of it all with their children.

While many of the adults had participated in past ceremonies with Sister Moon at either Newark or High Bank, their younger children had not. They found it appropriate to imbue their youngsters with the meaning, importance, and reverence of this massive undertaking, the journey to the White Road, then the journey on the sixty-mile road itself to Newark, then the pageant and ceremonies of the actual event, and then the journey home.

Voices garbled in conversation with each other and their children dominated the air as everyone arrived and found seating. Suddenly a hushed awe struck the room as White Eagle entered. She wore her ceremonial garb, complete with her necklace, that reflected light from the copper and mica lamps lit on the walls. Quiet reverence now ruled as she stood silently acknowledging everyone attending.

After a few moments, she says, "The People had promised to honor and follow the Original Teachings given at the time of the Fourth Creation, which I will now say,

> *Take care of Mother Earth and the other colors of man and*
> *woman knowing that all on Mother Earth is interdependent, is*
> *alive and has a soul.*
> *Respect and honor Mother Earth and her creation.*
> *Honor all life and support that honor each day by your words,*
> *thoughts, deeds, and in your*
> *prayers and offerings.*
> *Be grateful from your heart for all of life.*
> *Remain pure in your heart. Thank the*
> *Creator at all times for all life.*
> *Love, and express that love through thought,*
> *word and deed. Be humble.*

Humility is the gift of understanding and wisdom.
Be kind with one's self and with others.
Share feelings and personal concerns and commitments as by so doing you will remain of good heart and in balance with the Great Mystery.
Be honest with one's self and with others in your thoughts, words and deeds. By so doing you will remain pure of heart and avoid the ways of the two-hearted.

Shuffling of small bodies and adult feet.
Murmurings.
Murmurings and hushing.
"And, so it is," she finishes.
"And, so it is," resounds the audience.

"As the time nears to leave our village on our journey to Newark and the earthworks of Sister Moon, we will see folks arriving in our village who have come from far way, especially from the west, to journey with us. Please welcome them as they are The People also. Many live to the west of us and some very far to the west. Some come from the south of us, south of the Ohio River. Their journey and commitment to the Original Teachings are great, so great it drives them to join us who only live a week or so journey to Chillicothe where the White Road of Sister Moon begins," says White Eagle.

Murmurings.

"We journey to witness the northernmost moonrise of our Sister Moon," White Eagle says. "The teachings have been given. Every 18 winters and six moons plus several weeks, Sister Moon rises at the most northern point of her journeys along the eastern horizon. This is due to her slow precession of her orbit around Mother Earth. During the last nine plus years Sister Moon has traveled from her southernmost rising point to the northernmost. This is her metonic cycle. This time she will rise as a full moon at the most northern point. We gather at Newark to observe and celebrate her return and continued journey to the southernmost point in her cycle.

"Our legends tell of what would happen should she continue on and not return on her journey to the south. Mother Earth would lose her balance, spin wildly on her axis, the days and nights would be disrupted and climates would forever be changing. It would be the end of the world as we know it.

"The People gather together to send their affirmations and acknowledgments to the Creator and to Sister Moon. We affirm and demonstrate that we have maintained balance in this world and are following the ancient ways and honoring the promises our ancestors had made when they entered the Fourth World."

"And, so it is," say many of the adults.

Sounds of squirming children and hushing of their parents.

White Eagle continues, "Winter is ending, but it is still a bit cold, so you will want to come prepared for enduring some cold weather."

Parents nod in affirmation.

White Eagle then says, "We will journey to Chillicothe, which will take about six to seven days or more, depending. When we get there, we will find the beginnings of the White Road of Sister Moon. It is sixty miles long but leads us straight to Newark. Once there, we will have places to set up camp and then participate in the many ceremonies among the earthworks there."

The children ask many questions and White Eagle patiently answers each one.

Once all the children's questions are answered, she explains to the group many of the practical considerations regarding food and so forth for the journey.

"Once we get to Newark," White Eagles continues, "as most of you might remember from past ceremonies, plenty of food will be available for everyone for the weeks we will be there. The farms at Baum and Gartner provide much of the food. Meat is provided by several teams of hunters who bring in game just for this event. No one is to be concerned about food once we get there."

She looks around the room and answers a few more questions. She then says, "Another interesting point I'd like to make. While some of the adults may have experienced a solar eclipse, I don't think the children have. We will get to witness a solar eclipse at about the time we will arrive at Newark. I expect to leave in a few days so I can get there in time to see it at Newark. I will let you know when I am ready to leave. Please know that any of you who wish to join me when I leave are indeed welcome. Otherwise, you can leave when you wish." With that she bows and leaves the meeting house.

The place buzzes with conversations between parents and their children, and among the children aglow with anticipation

.

35

THE JOURNEY TO THE NORTHERN MOONRISE CEREMONY

Today was no ordinary day.

As the eastern sky slowly changed color from black to deep purple, the clouds high in the sky glowed with the colors of the new day. Deep reds then orange then bright yellow, giving their promise that Father Sun was rising in the east.

White Eagle had been awaiting this rising of Father Sun. She was certain that he would rise behind the rock outcropping on the distant ridge. The travels of Sister Moon had already forecast the coming of this day. It was time to begin the journey to Newark.

The People were gathering from many directions to meet in Newark. Many would be traveling on the White Road of Sister Moon. This Road led to Newark.

Eighteen winters and six months had passed since the last Northern Moonrise Ceremony had taken place. A new generation had reached their adulthood, and it was time for them and others to honor Sister Moon and affirm with gratitude that she would stay on her path and not leave Mother Earth alone circling Father Sun.

Over nine years ago the villages to the north had traveled south on the White Road of Sister Moon for the Southernmost Moonrise Ceremony which was celebrated at the High Bank circle and octagon complex near Chillicothe.

The very top of the glowing orb was now visible. The rock outcropping centered itself right in the middle of the rising sun. White Eagle began the chant of the new day, thanking Father Sun, Mother Earth and all the creatures that Great Spirit had created for the Fourth World. It was now time to return to the village and announce that she would begin her journey, and anyone and everyone who was ready to go could join her. The rest could follow in their time. As she had announced earlier, she would be leaving a bit earlier than usual so as to be at the Newark Earthworks in time to witness the solar eclipse from the ancient monuments.

As the word spread, all The People were grateful the time was at hand to begin this great journey. Some older folks knew that this would be the last time for them. But they shared the joy of fulfillment knowing that they would once again have this opportunity to celebrate the Great Mystery before It welcomed their souls into Its Presence.

That day White Eagle began her pilgrimage from the Great Serpent village to Newark. Many joined her, including Shining Bird and our children. I had been called away to another village to help with someone who had suffered an injury and had asked for me. I would catch up after I had finished caring for my patient.

Anticipating that something celestial would occur, White Eagle kept an eye on the skies as they journeyed to Chillicothe. Few noticed except for Shining Bird. Little escaped her notice.

The journey to Chillicothe went without incident, yet the going was slow. With so many families, the large group of pilgrims took more days to get to Chillicothe than White Eagle had anticipated. Everything did not go quite as expected. White Eagle found that she didn't move as easily as she used to from her memories as a young woman. She found it just took longer for her to get from one place to another.

Everyone was fed and everyone slept well, whether it was in a guest house of a village or out camping along the trail to Chillicothe. Still something nagged at Shining Bird as the days passed. Mentally, she kept checking the subtle energies around her children, just as a mother bear would in anticipation of needing to protect her cubs. Something felt amiss, something sufficiently strong enough to catch her attention, but nebulous enough for her to be unable to identify it. She kept her eye on White Eagle for the same reason. And, for the same reason, she stayed close to the Elder as they journeyed.

As White Eagle had now aged beyond her own self-image, and with the small children along, the first group to leave the village on this journey took longer than expected. By the time they arrived at Chillicothe and the beginning of the White Road of Sister Moon, ten days had passed. White Eagle felt they had fallen behind schedule. However, her meditations had confirmed she was right on schedule.

"I don't know, Shining Bird," White Eagle confessed to her late one afternoon at Chillicothe. Shining Bird was all too eager to hear what the beloved Grandmother had to say as Shining Bird's inner direction had been to remain alert to whatever might happen, knowing nothing, suspicious of everything.

"I don't know," White Eagle repeated, "My thinking is, we are late. I don't like to be tardy to ceremonies. Yet, we still have plenty of time until the ceremonies begin. I don't know why I feel so unsettled about this. I know I will arrive on time to participate in the pre-ceremonial meetings of the Elders. My dreams tell me we are all right, but the stars portend something I cannot put my finger on. I just can't shake a feeling of something being wrong."

"Dearest Grandmother," said Shining Bird putting her hand on the Elder's arm, "I too feel something is not quite right. I just can't put my finger on it either. I keep checking in with my children. And, no it's not about my children. It's something else. Something else feels like a predator is near, but a predator in what form? I can't shake it." As Shining Bird finished speaking, she looked around in all directions looking for a mountain lion or a renegade bear threatening to attack. None appeared.

Finally, after crossing the Scioto River and climbing the cliff trail up from the river bottom, they reached the White Road of Sister Moon. By then, their group had grown since others from other villages had joined them. The People were now assembled at the entrance to the White Road. At the entrance to this Road, perched a stone tablet upon which was written,

> *A straight line is pointed out, upon which People are directed to walk. They are admonished that there should be no deviation, to the right or left, along other paths, but keep straight forward in the ways of honesty of purpose and forthrightness of intent.*

White Eagle and all the Elders of the all the villages who had joined them so far stood together. It was time for her to give the prayer for this journey. White Eagle standing on the wall, so more could see her as she spoke the words loud enough for the crowd within range to hear. They quieted as she began with both arms outstretched.

> *"Great Spirit, we are now beginning our journey on this White Road of Sister Moon to offer our prayers of affirmation and attention to the Great Mystery. We affirm that you guide and protect us, so that we may all arrive at the appointed time to honor Mother Earth, Sister Moon and our place in the cosmos. With the passing of the eighteen winters since we last made this journey, The People have honored the ways of the ancient teachings of peace and unity. Yet separations have entered the hearts of some of our people. Many have chosen to forget that being of two hearts removes the balance and the Oneness in this Fourth World. We affirm your blessings on those who have chosen this path of separation and to guide them back to The People, so that their hearts can heal. We honor You, Great Spirit, the Great Mystery and all that You provide. We honor Mother*

Earth who sustains us and gives us life in physical form. We honor Sister Moon who rules over the night and provides balance to this, the Fourth World. Thank you. Thank you. Thank you."

"And so it is," those within hearing distance said quietly.

And so the journey on the White Road of Sister Moon began. Entire families and those who were alone said prayers or gave gratitude before stepping onto this road, this passageway, both physical and metaphoric. By mid-afternoon many were still waiting to begin their journey taking their first steps upon this great road. Runners were assigned to keep the Elders informed of the progress, so that plans could be made for each night's rest to allow all to be present at sunset for the lighting of the fires and the evening prayers.

Many families had dogs with two pole travois to carry provisions, but most people carried their provisions on their backs in beautifully woven and colored baskets. These had been handed down for generations for use in this and other special journeys. Symbols were painted onto the surface of the baskets with colors from plants and soils. Each person also had their own medicine bundles filled with herbs, and carved and smoothed stones, beads, shells, and other objects for use during the Rising of the Moon Ceremony.

The People were blessed with fairly warm days, for this time of the year during the long journey. Eagles and hawks followed and circled above lending their support for the intent of The People.

Along the way more villagers joined in the large procession. Old friends who had not seen each other for many years shared stories and renewed their friendships. New friends were made when some grew tired and others stepped forward to lighten their burdens or to provide companionship. All shared the joy of the journey and the great anticipation of this Rising of Sister Moon Ceremony as this would be a celebrated full moon. Yet, in some hearts, foreboding visions caused anxiety without explanation.

Many hills and streams to cross slowed their progress. Narrow bridges had been constructed to allow passage over the deeper waters. The People knew to form two lines well before each bridge, so progress was steady. Venus shone brightly in the west and blessed The People as Father Sun went into the dark world at the end of each day. Under the blanket of night, brilliant stars twinkled in song, and some fell from the sky punctuating the harmonies.

At about mid-morning of the fourth day at a spot on a hill, the pilgrims, led by White Eagle, halted at a crest. Just below them was a fierce assemblage of young renegade warriors, representing the antithesis of The People. They appeared with faces painted to emphasize their power to anyone susceptible to images of terror. They rattled their weapons, spears and knives, which added to their primitive sounds of growling and roaring. It was like their guttural sounds and rattling of weapons could and should produce fear in the minds and hearts of more civilized people.

White Eagle, at the head of the procession, stopped. Standing silent at the top of the hill, she surveyed the obstacle to the timeless ritual of The People. Never in the memory of The People had this honored ritual ever been interrupted by bandits or renegades or anything else. White Eagle stood like iron, eyes locked on the renegades.

The traveling pilgrims stopped where they were and remained patient in faith that whatever White Eagle had encountered, she would resolve.

Shining Bird approached White Eagle from behind, along with several men and women. They each looked at the renegades blocking their way. Shining Bird studied individuals forming the blockade. She noted details, such as the prominent scar on the face of one.

Searching her memory, she recalled the scar-faced one who had come to their village with Turning Rabbit, the trader, many years before. He was standing behind someone she thought she knew from another village. The scar-faced one kept whispering into the ears of . . . "Oh, now, I remember who he is," she thought to herself. "He's Roaring Wind, the gruff, self-centered husband who murdered his wife's lover years ago. I often wondered what happened to him. It appears that after White Eagle banished him, he joined up with these rascals."

White Eagle just stood facing them without flinching and without expression. The desperate renegades felt confused. Neither White Eagle nor those standing with her did not react as they had expected.

Despite their threatening behavior and fierce appearance, they were unable to create a sense of fear as they had intended.

The bandits' behavior had no meaning to a people who had lived in peace for so long. In short, The People did not know they were supposed to be afraid.

Finally, Roaring Wind stepped forward, prompted from behind by the scar-faced one. He stepped forward and approached White Eagle with malicious intent and snarled, "Give us your food and all your valuable possessions or we will cut your throats and kill as many of you as possible."

Several of the bandits had already seized men and women as hostages and now held knives to their throats. By so doing they had violated the time-honored sacred right of safe passage.

White Eagle said to Roaring Wind, "If you need food, we can give you all we have. As you might know, we carry little in the way of food. We count on food being provided for us as we travel. But valuable possessions, we have none."

Roaring Wind turned to confer with the scar-faced one and others. They spoke for a long time. The bandits continued holding the hostages. During this time, White Eagle looked upward toward the sky. She then closed her eyes, and lost herself in a moment of prayer, while remaining standing with her arms outstretched, one arm supported by a staff topped with a large crystal hewn just for her by Water Dog.

The People waiting behind White Eagle in the procession grew restless. Shining Bird quietly sent a message to one then another for The People to settle where they were, as the journey appeared halted temporarily.

Roaring Wind, obviously not the leader, but posing as the voice, stepped up closer to again confront White Eagle.

"We demand food and valuable possessions. If you do not give us what we ask, we will not only kill those we have taken as hostages, we will kill as many of you as we can before you give in to us. Do you understand, *old woman*?" he shouted at White Eagle with an arrogance that said he believed what he had just pronounced.

White Eagle just stood still without flinching, her face emotionless. She did not back down. She never lost eye contact. Roaring Wind's attention riveted on her as if trapped by a force field beyond his control. As he locked eyes with hers, he thought he saw one of her eyebrows raise as she tilted her head slightly forward. Apparently, his intimidation tactics were not working here. He felt impelled to attempt another tactic.

Taking a step back, Roaring Wind turned to The People he could see from the hilltop advantage, and shouted, "You listen to old women. You let old women lead you. You still believe that the ancient ways are true. I tell you they are *not* true. They are nothing more than mere tales of old women. There is no Great Oneness. We live by taking or stealing what we need from others and trading sacred objects to those who are willing to give great value for such things. Can't you see that you are being misled? Can't you see that you are being lied to? Can't you see that there is nothing that exists but what you can see and touch? What fools you are to be led by women and old women at that. Ha. Haw," he laughed throwing his head back.

"Now," he demanded of White Eagle, "now, command your People to give us what we ask."

White Eagle remained standing, again locking eyes with the large man, twice her size, saying nothing, not turning her head in either direction, her necklace brilliantly reflecting the light of the sun by now high in the sky.

Because she felt that reason and argument would not prevail, White Eagle raised her eyes and arms to Father Sun saying as loudly as she could so that as many as possible could hear her on both sides of this hill, "Father Sun, we need your protection. Bring darkness to these lands and show these warriors that they will be taken into the darkness never to walk again on Mother Earth."

The bandit warriors began to laugh and mock White Eagle. She and Shining Bird and others heard them say, "What nonsense! Have you lost your mind? We are not afraid of your silly talk. Hand over all that we demand or we will slit the throats of those we have captured."

The birds silenced their melodies. Other animals stopped moving. A hush swept over the land. The face of Father Sun began to darken, the air became cold and the wind stopped blowing. Stillness stopped everything.

One by one each of the warriors looked skyward. Daylight had now become noticeably darker. Fear gripped the two-hearted ones. Some in the outlaw band fled in terror throwing down their weapons as they abruptly turned and left. Yet their leaders stood their ground with their flint knives still held to the throats of the hostages.

The sky had now become dark and stars began to appear. All in the same moment, the remaining warriors became filled with panic. Those holding the hostages released them, and they too fled into the woods, including the banished husband, Roaring Wind, and Scarface.

Now even The People were filled with some uncertainty. What did the darkness mean? Many had not experienced a solar eclipse before. But then, many remembered that White Eagle had mentioned a solar eclipse was scheduled to occur. Even so, many were filled with a sense of awe as they experienced the celestial event. Father Sun was gone and night had come early on this day. Some began to cry out.

White Eagle again raised her arms to Father Sun and spoke loudly for all to hear, "Father Sun and Sister Moon, thank you for your blessing and protection. We need to continue our journey. You have prevented the loss of lives and protected us from those that sought to bring harm to us. You have shown The People that those of two-hearts are lost from the ways of the Creator. They have chosen the path of separation and have rejected the ancient ways. Thank you for your continuing on your own journey as we continue on our journey." Slowly the darkness began to disappear and Father Sun returned.

A great cry of joy arose from The People. It was an interesting experience. It was as White Eagle's vision had said it would be. Only she knew that Sister Moon would pass between Father Sun and Mother

Earth *that* day. Her heart remained heavy though as this incident was yet another sign that the thousand years of peace and the unity of oneness was coming to an end and with it, the possible end of The People.

As the journey continued, there was much discussion among The People of what they had just witnessed and the need to remain pure of heart. This was something they had never seen and had heard of only in some of the very old legends. They had now become aware that this Rising of the Moon Ceremony was especially important to the future of their children, loved ones and Mother Earth.

The lighting of the fires on the fourth night brought forth renewed belief and special prayers from The People who were traveling on the long Road. They had seen that very day that there was a clear and present danger to the ways of their ancestors and to Mother Earth. A great healing, and indeed renewing, certainly appeared warranted.

Several days later, as White Eagle and the pilgrims approached the end of the Road at Newark, Elders assigned to welcome pilgrims as they arrived greeted them. A number of children accompanied the Elders. They could see families from other villages had already set up camp and had settled in

The next week or so was a time of great harmony and the joining of the vast number of different villagers who had traveled, some for months, to be present and witness this rising of the full moon at this sacred occasion. They shared stories, saw old friends and relatives and honored those that had walked on since the last Rising of the Moon Ceremony.

This Rising of the Moon Ceremony is now only two days away. White Eagle later joined by Red Fox and myself sat in council meetings with other Elders. White Eagle knew most of the Elders some of whom were from very far away. She signaled Red Fox to sit on her right and me next to her on her left.

For the next two days and nights, the Elders of all the villages attending sit in discussions, listening to each other, taking turns speaking the thoughts of their hearts.

Again, I find it interesting to witness the diversity of views and experiences based on geographic location.

One of the oldest Elders, from the east coast, spoke of more pronounced and frequent instances of out-of-balance behavior than experienced in our region. He says, "Many of us have had visions of changes coming. The changes we see coming are not good. The thing we need to realize is that these major changes we see coming in our visions can be disastrous."

Listeners nod in acknowledgement.

After a brief pause, he continues, "One thing we can agree on is we can work at preventing these changes from coming."

Murmurings.

Then he says, "I see, that through our collective consciousness, we can change the disasters from coming. As I see it, the issue is many of our People have strayed from Mother Earth and the Oneness with her. The consciousness in our region has been fragmented, and separations have occurred. This has been testified to here earlier in our discussions. And I have spoken of it many times in the villages I visit. My words have fallen on the ground. My words have not brought forth a harvest. We as a people through our consciousness can change what is coming. We have grown apart. Our wisdom has been lost. All of this could change tomorrow if we would be of one mind."

Murmurings and nodding of affirmation.

"We have spoken of this many, many times in our meetings," he says. "Our great Grandfathers, Grandmothers and the Rememberers told us of this time. And that these times would be coming. We are losing the oneness of ourselves and the oneness of ourselves with Mother Earth. The People are no longer whole. We have broken into factions among ourselves. This has come from disrespect for the teachings from our Ancient Ones. Unless we can re-unite ourselves in Spirit and in thought, The People will cease to exist."

"I agree with you, Grandfather," another Elder says. "My experience informs me that all of what you say is true. My question becomes, 'what do we do?' Do we stay and suffer the consequences of a people who no longer can live the truths we have lived for over a thousand years?"

Another Elder says, "Certainly, if we joined our consciousness into one mind, we could focus on changing what we see coming."

An Elder from the back stands and says, "Since so many of our People are already experiencing separation, the combining of our consciousness into one mind might not be workable . . . or even possible. So my question is, 'what do we do?' Is there something else? Do we stay? Or do we leave our ancestral lands, the lands that Mother Earth has promised would fulfill our human needs?"

The discussions went on endlessly throughout the night. The primary topic evolved into the question of whether to go or to stay as a People.

Finally, White Eagle says, "Clearly our visions and dreams are showing us that something profound is happening or is about to happen. They are showing us a 'death' as it were, death of our culture, death of our language, death of our way of knowing. To me, they indicate a pending death of The People.

"We can resist it if we choose. If we resist, we will be expending much energy opposing a force that is beyond our comprehension. If we do not comprehend it, how can we overcome it? Even if we continue to resist it, we would be battling an unknown . . . and we will become what we fight.

"However, if we surrender to our death, if we surrender to Great Spirit . . . if we surrender our resistance, we will release ourselves from whatever obstacles we might be attached to as a culture, release any obstacles to our continuing on or progressing in Spirit. If we do not fight, but surrender, we will free ourselves to accept what is. We can then move into acceptance, so we can be free to choose another way.

"I don't know what that looks like. I don't know what alternatives we would have from which to choose.

"The death of our culture, the death of The People, as it means to me, is a transition from what we know to something we do not know. So, what I am saying, to myself, as well as to all of you, is that I do not know what form The People will take as we transition. I feel in my heart that, as we surrender, we will find a freedom to find another or a different expression of Spirit. In other words, we will experience a resurrection.

As White Eagle pauses to get more comfortable, her necklace jets out reflected beams of firelight, flashing into the faces of those in the audience.

After a few moments of silence, she says, "Whether we should stay here in the lands of our ancestors, or whether we should leave these sacred lands is something I do not know. Either way, our dreams tell us a shift is coming, a shift that so far we find unable to stop. I believe we should not resist this shift, allow the death in whatever form it takes, to surrender to that release, and move on to experience our resurrection."

Uncomfortable silence.

No one speaks. Then after a long silence, White Eagle says, "Am I uncomfortable with what I just recommended? Yes, I am." She pauses momentarily to look around at each Elder and continues, "That means I am resisting. I also know that as long as I resist, I will feel uncomfortable."

Deep inhales and loud, tenuous exhales from audience members.

She continues with her final comment, "So, my beloveds, I choose to trust in Great Spirit to tell me what direction we should take.

In the sense of oneness, I give gratitude for knowing that I *will know*, that I will be given a sign, whether to go or to stay."

After a very long silence among the Elders, discussion continues. No decisions are made.

Binding group *decisions* were not typical of the Elders, nor of The People in general. White Eagle held her ground that she would know the moment she was supposed to know it. And, each person would make his or her own decision if such a moment should come.

While these discussions were going on, The People who had traveled from the Great Serpent village settled in among friends and families they knew or would come to know. For these several days, the children played with new-found friends, young people met other young people from other villages, and the adults enjoyed a festive conviviality among themselves. Musicians played much of the time. The music offered some the opportunity to dance in joy during this marvelous time of celestial celebration.

Raven's Wing accompanied by Floating Lily assisted the others involved with food preparation. Large cooking areas had been set up. We shared in the abundance supplied by the planning for such events with large quantities of food brought in from the neighboring farming areas. Black drink offered some an increased sense of the festivities.

During the days preceding the Moonrise ceremony, many entered into the various areas of the Newark complex and walked in contemplation and meditation. Many also engaged in a sense of renewal walking down to the water's edge of nearby streams to symbolically renew themselves in the water. The water acted as a reminder of the waters in the womb that nurtures prior to birth into the physical world. This ritual allowed for a symbolic renewal that endowed the individual with an increased sense of connectedness with Spirit.

As many walked, either in groups or individually, within the giant 50 acre octagon, they contemplated their heavenly origins as a spiritual being. Others, some distance away and near the lake, entered the Great Circle, complete with its symbolic waters of the womb encircling them. They also participated in a symbolic and often visceral experience of re-bonding with both the Creator and with Mother Earth.

Shining Bird took our three children through this renewal ceremony at the Great Circle to afford them the opportunity to have this experience. Water Dog and Bluebird Near the Lily followed along behind them walking hand in hand, smiling as they went.

THE CAMP OF GOD'S TEARS

This ritual of renewal felt so needed, especially by Shining Bird. At first many thought what had been happening over the past several years was merely affecting their own village. Now that there had been several weeks to talk and share stories, it was obvious to all that the disruptions from occurrences contrary to our ways were spreading throughout The People.

The sweetness and joy of having such a large assemblage of The People together in one place was darkened by the negative feelings of what they had been hearing from others. This saddened many hearts. There would be many healing circles and pipe ceremonies. Yet this gathering of The People presented an opportunity to work towards restoring peace and oneness in the minds and hearts of The People.

As Sister Moon gazed down upon the thousands of people gathered to offer their prayers to her, she too was saddened by what was to come.

White Eagle, Red Fox, and I, remain in council with many of the other Elders until it came time for the Sister Moon Ceremony to begin and our discussions to end. The Elders stroll back to their respective families in silence, brows furrowed, eyes moist, hearts heavy.

The Northernmost Moonrise Ceremony is always a celebratory occasion with spirits running high, potent and positive. On this night, however, few, if any, feel the renewal of life moving through them.

Late in the afternoon all The People gather in the circle and octagon complex. Multitudes standing close to each other give a silent sense of comfort. Some hold hands. Mothers hold their babies close. Young people stand arm in arm.

Potentially, this ceremony, by this one act, could turn around the entire energy field into one of joy and relief from a sense of pending doom. Hopes begin to lift as the ceremony proceeds.

The People watch, holding their breath, as White Eagle and I climb the observatory mound at the base of the circle for the initial portions of the ceremony on this late afternoon. I walk behind White Eagle as we take our respective places on the mound used for this same and other ceremonies for thousands of years.

We stand on the level surface of theloaf shaped earthen observation mound. It is located at the edge of the Circle in line with the causeway that connects the Circle to the Octagon. It is over a half a mile from where we are standing to the furthest gap of the octagon walls. Sister Moon will be seen rising directly through this gap in the wall.

White Eagle and I stand on the mound as the celebration of marriages and other ceremonies are conducted.

Then as twilight lowers its gentle veil over the lands, White Eagle and I leave the mound and walk around the walls of the Circle and Octagon. We position ourselves on a mound just inside the gap in the Octagon wall where Sister Moon will appear as she rises.

I stand to the right and just slightly behind White Eagle. I smile at my beloved Shining Bird when I spot her below and just to White Eagle's left.

Darkness is now almost complete. A glow on the eastern horizon announces the arrival of Sister Moon. Just the very top of the glowing orb is now visible on the distant horizon.

White Eagle, wearing the sacred necklace handed down from the ancient times, slowly raises her arms as if to help Sister Moon find her place in the night sky. To the audience now behind us, it appears as if White Eagle actually lifts Sister Moon from below the horizon to above the horizon as part of the ceremony.

But something is wrong.

Gasps of surprise come from the mouths of many.
Jaws drop.
Sister Moon is not a bright white light as all had expected. Sister Moon is *blood red in color.*
Anguished voices cry out. *What is this? What could this mean?*

White Eagle's vision that she had shared only with Rising Wolf and me is now manifesting for all to see.

White Eagle's soul cries out within her. The future of The People is now held in her arms.

Now the blood red moon is well above the horizon. White Eagle's arms are fully extended. She begins the sacred prayer that had been given to her in a vision.

>*Great Spirit, Creator of All that Is, the I-Am of All That Is, I am White Eagle. I speak on behalf of The People.*
>
>*We are here in acknowledgement of our alignment with the Great Oneness.*
>
>*Our physical experience both individually and collectively is You Manifested.*
>
>*Great Spirit, we are troubled by a growing sense of separation and fragmentation among The People. Our dreamers and seers see something coming that distresses us.*
>
>*We see an energy coming that carries suffering, death and destruction for The People.*
>
>*We are unable to see beyond it.*
>
>*We cannot see order within the chaos that is coming.*

> *We as The People only know our oneness with the One. We are caught at a cross-roads of what to do . . . stay in the lands of our ancestors or leave these lands and venture into unknown lands.*
>
> *Through our free will, we can make a choice. We understand that we must make a choice. We see our choices as either stay or leave. It is our intention to make the best choice for The People. What blesses one, blesses all. What harms one, harms all.*
>
> *We see death in staying.*
>
> *We see death in leaving.*
>
> *If what is coming means death to The People, then we surrender and go humbly into the All That Is.*
>
> *We will return with dignity to our Creator, and we then look forward to our resurrection in whatever form that takes.*
>
> *The People cannot prevent what is coming.*
>
> *We offer our forgiveness for what may be the death of The People. The deeply unconscious people who are coming to our lands are consumed by separation, ego manifested in their thoughts, words and actions.*
>
> *We must from within surrender to what is coming. Through surrender we see beyond their form to their true being that will awaken in them once they are aware that we are all connected.*
>
> *We must act, however, to preserve our way of life, our conscious connection to the Great Oneness. We set our intentions to preserve our ways. We ask for your protection, as in the past three worlds.*
>
> *We thank You, Great Spirit for hearing us. We trust Your Guidance, to stay or leave. Thank you.*

As she finishes her prayer with her arms still outstretched, she feels a silent snap.

At that, her heart crushes close inside her nearly rocking her off her feet.

She looks down to see the sacred necklace dangling on her chest, cord broken perilously close to falling to the ground.

Pearls and shells sewn onto her ceremonial costume had broken the fall of this sacred and very ancient symbol.

No one notices this during the ceremony. . . no one but Shining Bird.

Shining Bird had felt hyper-alert on the journey to the ceremonial grounds and that feeling had continued. When she witnessed the breakage and fall of this ever so ancient object, she knew why she had felt so vigilant. When she saw the snap and fall, she mentally lost contact with her children and her surroundings. Her eyes focused on the ancient artifact with her eyes opened wide and her jaw dropping. She gulped when she witnessed White Eagle noticing the fall of the symbol.

Feeling unobserved, White Eagle continues her ceremonial behavior, arms outstretched, but occasionally glancing down at her chest. Not wanting to make any sudden moves that would shake the necklace loose, she finishes the ceremony for The People.

With the deepest grief, White Eagle knows this is her sign, and that she will have to inform the other Elders that very night.

As everyone files out, Shining Bird catches White Eagle's eye. At that moment White Eagle knows there is a witness to the event that signals the end of our way of life as we know it, and had known it for a thousand years. She motions to Shining Bird to join us back at the meeting of the Elders.

White Eagle feels the weight of her long journey in this lifetime.

She knows for certain now that what has been can no more be.

The energy field of the separation has grown too great. She must gather those who are still faithful to the ancient ways and begin the long journey. This would soon take us to the great river, across the plains, through the great mountains beyond where obsidian and the grizzly bear teeth come from, and finally to the great waters that Father Sun dips into at the end of each day in the far west.

White Eagle knows within herself that she will not complete this journey as her body will return to Mother Earth along the way. Yet she finds comfort in the fact that all she has learned, all her knowledge, her powers, visions and the sacred necklace will be given to Red Fox who she will guide from the World of Spirit.

She willingly accepts this final task in this life. She will start The People on this journey. We will see many new lands, those that the traders have spoken of. Our way of life will change. She will caution The People that merely changing how or where we live is not enough. White Eagle knows that she must impart to us that we must see with new eyes, not just see new landscapes. Otherwise, the sense of being separate from Spirit will travel with us and all will be lost.

White Eagle looks back to me, her face ashen, holding the broken necklace in her hand. I see then what I didn't want to see and knew what I didn't want to know.

Together with Red Fox, who has just joined us, and Shining Bird, we all head back to the council fire of the Elders. As we walk White Eagle shares one of her favorite teachings.

It was a story of a Grandfather sharing wisdom with his grandson. The grandson was very angry with a friend who had done him an injustice.

"'A fight is going on inside you,' he said to the boy. 'It is a terrible fight and it is between two wolves. One is evil. He is anger, hatred, envy, sorrow, regret, greed, arrogance, self-pity, guilt, self-centeredness, resentment, inferiority, lies, false pride, superiority, and ego.

"'Being full of anger, the littlest thing will set him into a fit of temper. He fights everyone, all the time, for no reason. He cannot think because his anger and hate are so great. It is helpless anger, for his anger will change nothing. Hate wears you down, and does not hurt your enemy. It is like taking poison and wishing your enemy would die. I have struggled with these feelings many times.'

"The Grandfather continued, 'The other wolf is good and does no harm. This wolf is full of joy, peace, love, hope, serenity, humility, kindness, benevolence, empathy, forgiveness, generosity, truth, compassion, and faith.

"'The same fight is going on inside you, and inside every other person, too. Sometimes, it is very hard to live with these two wolves inside me, for both of them try to dominate my spirit,' said the Grandfather.'"

"The grandson thought about it for a minute and then asked his grandfather, 'Which wolf will win?'

"The Grandfather simply replied, 'The one you feed.'"

After the ceremony, the people dispersed to their camp spots. None felt like engaging in the normal activities customary for these special events. Usually this particular ceremony would end with joy and a strong sense of renewal. On this night, however, The People sensed something ominous and shuffled back to their campsites somber and sober.

A heavy silence rules.

36

COUNCIL FIRE OF THE ELDERS

Before the ashes of the last Newark council fire were cold, we began to disperse into an uncertain future.

37

THE WAY WEST

Most chose to leave, some chose otherwise. Those leaving ancestral lands tearfully hugged those staying. Small children, not comprehending having to leave their friends, cried out to each other as tears ran freely. Parents, on both sides of the leaving-or-staying decision line, coaxed their children back into their arms, tears staining their faces as well.

The People were separating. This time the separation was not spiritual or metaphoric. It was real. It was happening as we breathed the air. It was physical.

The emotional pain could be felt so keenly and so deeply that it felt physical. It was emotional pain triggered by grief and uncertainty. The air fairly choked with emotional pain of families and friends separating. The emotional pain lay so thickly in the air that it could be cut with a knife. Every face evidenced pain.

Many would be migrating, some would not. Others chose to migrate later. A few chose to migrate in a different direction. Most of us chose to migrate west . . . west by northwest. Some chose to go north by northeast.

None of our People in known times had ever migrated. Occasionally, families would change locations, change villages or territories, and not on a scale as large as this. We were farmers and mostly homebodies, tied to our land. In ancient times, a large segment of The People left the Great Serpent area to migrate southwest. We had heard they flourished in their new lands. That was of course, in ancient times.

Shining Bird and I packed up what we could carry, only hoping that it would be adequate to cover our needs. Shining Bird's grandmother, Plum Blossom, decided to stay, not feeling of sufficient strength or desire to migrate to lands unknown. Neither of my parents, nor my grandmother, Shining Moon, felt compelled to go, so they chose to stay.

With tears flowing generously down her round cheeks, Grandmother Shining Moon stood before us not speaking yet wanting to speak. Overcome with emotion, she handed me her trader's blanket, the red one with a wide black stripe down each of its shorter sides. Both my parents gave tearful hugs and left quickly.

Finally, Grandmother Shining Moon choked past her pain and said haltingly, "This blanket . . . should serve you well." She paused as she stuffed down a sob and added, "Take it in remembrance of me and in remembrance of our ancestral history." With that she bowed her head low to help shield her tears, turned and walked back to the Healing House and her brother, Speaks With Plants.

Singing Hawk and Floating Lily took their time to come to say their farewells. I spotted them standing at a distance watching with apparent concern, and slight apprehension, and with obvious reluctance. I waited to see if they would wave. When they saw me wave to them, they walked over to us. Both women, deeply in silent grief, embraced each of us before turning away and leaving. Good-by and fare thee well were utterances blocked by their pain. Tears ran profusely.

Red Fox joined Shining Bird, our children and me. None of his family chose to migrate with us, maybe later. Water Dog and Bluebird Near the Lily wanted to come with us. They both said they would join us later as Bluebird Near the Lily wasn't quite up to leaving on that day, her body so frail and all. I could see how anxious Water Dog was for the adventure of the migration, and I remembered his vision that he dreamily told me many years ago about traveling west on some unknown quest.

Water Dog's eyes brimmed with tears as he said good-by to us. He and I stood facing each other. As we stood there his emotions got the better of him. He fairly blubbered with sobs and torrents of tears. With that I reached for him with both arms and hugged him close until I felt his body relax from the convulsions caused by his sobbing.

"We'll catch up to you," he says motioning to himself and Bluebird Near the Lily as he pulls away. "We'll catch up. I'll find you," he courageously finishes with a half-smile. I nod small nods in acknowledgement, not feeling confident that I would see either of my two childhood friends again.

That day we joined White Eagle and began our journey westward bound, having no idea what might be in store for us before we arrived at the great western ocean. It was felt by many Elders that we should follow the Ohio River westward. By staying relatively close to the Ohio River, we would be within close proximity to a source of water, fish, game and other natural resources. We could follow trails established for centuries by traders that would lead us eventually to the great river, the Mississippi.

Off we went, carrying what we could, people dragging supply-laden travois, and dogs pulling travois as well. We moved westward leading tens of thousands, each one carrying what they could.

A few of our People and several traders had taken boats down the Ohio River towards the Mississippi River to inform villages along the way that we were coming. That trip took several weeks by canoe. Our People traveled on land walking with their children and some Elders, Grandmothers and Grandfathers. Everyone carried something. The stronger carried more. Many of the children looked like they were in shock at the sudden and severe change in lifestyle.

The children walked along with glazed eyes appearing as if they were in a bad dream from which they would gratefully awaken to find themselves in their own homes, their own beds, and with their friends available to play on a moment's notice.

This trip had not been planned with the same anticipation that journeys to the moonrise ceremonies were. In fact, this trip had not really been planned at all, and only vaguely mentioned now and then for years as the visions continued and deepened for many. The pilgrimages made to High Bank and to Newark were always planned and executed to perfection. Everyone knew about it months in advance, which allowed for months of preparation.

We had little preparation time, no anticipation of glorious and uplifting ceremonies, and no anticipation of the great social occasions of those ceremonies. This trip was one thrown together quickly within a few weeks of returning from Newark. Many who attended the Moonrise Ceremony wanted to return home first to gather their family members, spread the news to others who may wish to join the migration, say their farewells to those who didn't, gather their necessities for the journey of a lifetime, and then travel to Serpent Mound village which had become the rallying point in our region.

The journeys to the moonrise ceremonies included having provisions stashed along the Great White Road of Sister Moon, or having hospitality provided by villagers along the way. This event included none of that. Those holy journeys brought us together with Mother Earth, with Sister Moon, each other, and the cosmos.

This journey offered separation from our kindred, from our homes, our history, and from the lands of our Ancient Ones. Our moonrise pilgrimages promised continuance as a People. This pilgrimage promised nothing.

This journey demonstrated our desire to safeguard our culture, our beliefs and practices as a People from the threatened onslaught of an unknown, and as yet, unrealized, menace.

Sister Moon journeys occurred several times in a lifetime. This journey was one of a lifetime.

The Sister Moon journeys were about sustaining cultural renewal. This journey was about preventing cultural eradication.

The migration began slowly at first. Having been farmers and craftsmen for longer than anyone could account, The People for the first time experienced unaccustomed hardships. We had been used to a comfortable life, luxurious compared to the days and nights camping among hundreds and thousands of others, without the richness that life in our beautiful homes afforded.

Being early spring, the unpredictable weather caused us, the migrants, to get creative regarding building shelters and cooking styles. We learned from each other and depended on each other to help each other endure the elements, even though we had not gone very far yet. Many brought with them the shelters made from wood frames and hides they used for the campouts at the Sister Moon ceremonies and other ceremonies. These were not always sufficient for the population that was migrating. Our migrating population included those who did not usually travel to distant ceremonies, including the smallest of children, some nursing mothers, and many of the oldest Elders.

Movement proved slow going for the tens of thousands of us. Few were used to walking all day. Not all of us started on the same day. This made the migration spread out much like a snake creeping slowly westward across the hills and dales along the northern side of the Ohio River. Impact upon the land, the natural resources and the wild animal population, could not be measured. Mother Earth provided easily for us though.

Before we had traveled too far, Red Fox came to me with a wild idea. He had heard of another earthwork not too far from where we camped while we were still in Ohio.

"Let's go," he says excitedly. "We should see it before we leave this part of the country. Several of us want to go. Why don't you join us?"

"Umm," I say, "I don't think it was made by *our* Ancient Ones. From what I understand the style is quite different. This particular earthwork was built by others, perhaps those from lands across the great waters. I'm not feeling drawn to explore right now. It doesn't feel right. I've got my family here, plus several people have injuries I must attend to. My sense of responsibility is to them." I pat his shoulder as I say, "You go, my brother. Go and come back and tell me about it." Red Fox frowns and nods as he turns and leaves.

Shining Bird looks sad at hearing our conversation. Then she tilts her head and says, "You do know, we will be here at least another day. Why don't you go with Red Fox?"

I look at her for several long moments then smile and say, "I know. I don't have a good feeling about it. In fact, I feel something, like unsettled or ominous or questionable I'm not sure how to identify it." I shake my head as I pick up my medicine bundle to go out and find my patients. "I'll be back," I say, "after I've attended to several folks who need my help." I throw my head back in a salute to my life's companion as I leave our shelter.

Red Fox and company hiked up to the earthwork from our camp that was a distance north of the Ohio River. This indeed was a very strange earthwork. Part of it looked like one of the copper trader's oil lamps that Red Fox had seen on his travels near the copper mines up north. The earthwork also contained an unfamiliar configuration of nine straight and narrow earthen walls. Its entire design was unlike, and in fact, foreign to anything constructed by The People.

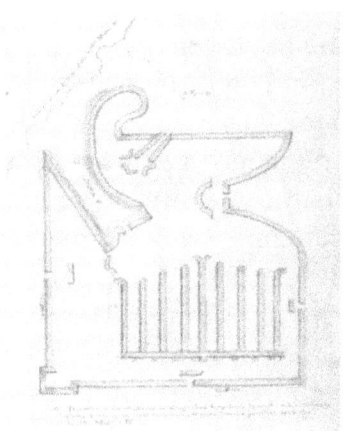

Diagram of the East Fork Earthwork near Milford, Ohio Squier and Davis 1848

Red Fox and his companions climbed all over it, walked around it, feeling amazed at its beauty, and sense of the profound.

On their way back, Red Fox spied an outcropping of rocks jutting out from a bluff surrounded by tall trees. As the troupe stopped on their way home to appreciate the splendor of the landscape, an eagle flew overhead and landed in one of the treetops there on the side of the bluff at the edge of the rock outcropping.

Red Fox's eyes filled with light and wonder as he said to his companions, "Let's go up there and check that out. Perhaps there is a nest up there. I can't tell from here" Each of his adventurous companions looked at each other then back at Red Fox.

One said, "Red Fox, it's getting late. It's getting cold. Look at the clouds . . . and off in the distance what looks like a fog moving in. You know how spring weather can change quickly. I think we should head back now." Then he added as he looked at the rest of the gang, "What do you think?"

They all nodded in agreement.

Red Fox murmured in reply as he continued his gaze at the treetops where the eagle flew in and landed, "All right. Why don't you go back to camp. I'll be along shortly." They hesitated for a few moments looking at each other and then at Red Fox who obviously was not returning with them. Then they turned and left for camp.

Late that evening those same adventurous lads approached my shelter as my little ones were just about asleep.

"Gray Wolf," one says, "may we speak with you?" I nod noting the seriousness of their demeanor. They motion for me to step out beyond the confines of our makeshift shelter.

I stand towering over them waiting for them to speak. Finally one says, "Red Fox hasn't come back yet."

I just stand there and look at them not knowing what exactly they were trying to say to me.

"Red Fox hasn't come back yet," he repeats.

I wrinkle my forehead that must have indicated confusion on my part. I ask, "Red Fox hasn't come back from where?"

"We went with Red Fox to see the earthwork that Red Fox told us looked like a copper trader's oil lamp. The whole earthwork was very different from any we had seen before," another says.

"I'm not sure I'm connecting here," I say trying to put pieces together.

Another says, "We all went to see it, but Red Fox didn't come back with us."

"What do you mean 'he didn't come back with you'?" I ask feeling a rise in apprehension about Red Fox and this conversation.

"Well, after we started on our way back, Red Fox saw an eagle fly to a treetop by some rock outcropping near a bluff. We wanted to come back to camp, and he wanted to climb up the bluff and check out the eagle's nest in the treetop. We don't know where he is. All we know is he didn't come back with us," says one.

Then another adds, "After a few miles on our way back clouds covered everything and later a fog rolled in. The last I saw as we started hiking back was that Red Fox had climbed the rocks and stood at the top looking down at us and waving. That's the last time we saw him."

I stand there for a few moments not wanting to hear what I'm hearing. I don't want to feel what I'm feeling. I just stand looking at the ground.

Finally, I say, "All right, boys, why don't you call it a night? Go back to your shelters and go to sleep. It's very dark tonight and windy, and there is nothing we can do now. If he doesn't show up by morning, we'll send out a search party."

As Father Sun came up in the east, the previous day's clouds had all but disappeared. A chilled breeze whipped around our shelters. The group of young explorers and several adults showed up at my shelter early just as I was giving Mother Earth my offering of tobacco as part of my morning prayers.

Clearly, concern covered their anxious faces. Without speaking, I went into my shelter to gather my outer wrap and my medicine bundle just in case we found Red Fox needing medical attention. I turned to signal a good-bye to Shining Bird and my children and left in silence.

After a couple of hours of hiking, the boys brought me to the bluff where they had last seen Red Fox. We stood on the bluff and spotted the outcropping of rocks that had apparently fascinated my good friend. The tops of very tall trees peered up at me from below the bluff. I just stood there wondering where to look, wondering where my closest friend went after he left this bluff.

Feeling nothing, I say a prayer to Mother Earth, "Mother, I am here with you. I seek my friend, Red Fox. He honored you in his daily practices and in his work. He honored Great Spirit with each breath he took. Would you please show me where he went? My heart is grieving for him. I thank you for your help." I continue to stand there with my hands and arms outstretched from the elbows, feeling my unity with Great Spirit and with Mother Earth.

After a few more moments, I hear the screech of an eagle. She circles overhead emitting several loud cries and then lands at the top of one of the trees. My eyes focus on her sitting in the top of that tree. Then suddenly I'm moved to look down once again into the trees below.

My heart jumps into my throat when this time I spot a piece of cloth waving in the spring breeze like it is trying to get my attention.

"Down there," I choke out a yell pointing down into the trees to the group of rescuers still standing around below. The boys and I scramble down from the bluff to join the others.

Finding our way into the group of trees that boasted the cloth flag I had spotted from the bluff above proves more challenging than anticipated. Thick undergrowth blocks our entry to the stand of trees we are seeking. Finally after much hacking and determined pushing our way through, I look up and freeze.

Much dark blood had stained the trunk of one tree and some surrounding branches. Parts of Red Fox's torn clothing caught our eye as the breeze wrapped itself around the tree where Red Fox hung upside down. My heart sank into my stomach when I gazed up at the body of my friend hanging amid several snapped branches.

It took several more hours of work to get Red Fox's body down from that tree. When we finally did, I knelt down next to his body and mournfully examined him, hoping against hope that he was still alive. His body was stiff as rigor mortis had set in telling me he had been dead for some time. I looked into his glazed eyes searching for a flicker that would tell me this was a bad dream and that he was alive, injured, but alive. Nothing.

"He must have fallen from those rocks up there," someone says.

"He has several broken bones," I finally say, "but the fall didn't kill him. Look at his upper left arm," I point to it. "See the deep lacerations? See all this blood? He bled to death . . . He bled to death." I lean back in severe emotional pain and grief. "I could've saved him." My face screws up to hold in the deep emotion I am feeling. "I could've saved him . . . if I had just gone with him, I would have gotten to him in time . . . if I'd gotten to him in time . . . he would still be alive . . . if we'd have gotten to him last night . . . "

Awkward moments.

Then one of the rescuers says, "It was too dark last night. We'd never have found him in the dark." Several others nod in agreement.

"Yes," another says, "we would never have seen him here in the dark last night. It was hard enough in daylight."

Still another puts his hand on my shoulder and gives a squeeze, "Don't blame yourself, Gray Wolf. Evidently, this was something that was about Red Fox."

With the death of Red Fox, The People delayed moving again for several days. At every delay such as this one, those intending on keeping our meat supply fresh would take the opportunity to bring in game or fish. We had packed all the smoked meat we could, and fresh meat, though, became very welcomed and appreciated.

Because Red Fox had worked with Mother Earth, utilizing natural resources for constructing his buildings, we agreed to bury his body in the land he worked with so lovingly and with so much talent.

In the eyes of The People, Red Fox had been the heir apparent to White Eagle. He had completed initiation. He studied intensely with

Singing Hawk and many other Elders in Chillicothe and Newark and other places in Canada.

His encyclopedic mind held a virtual library of ancient knowledge, sacred geometry, knowledge of the stars and their alignments with each other and with our earthworks here on Mother Earth. His spiritual journeys enriched his character and The People as he shared his insights and application of his knowledge with others while on his physical journeys throughout our lands. He was known among many villages across vast distances of our People. Red Fox was beloved by our People.

With the death of Red Fox came the death, for those on this journey, to our access to much ancient and sacred knowledge. He would be sorely missed as a beloved person, and well-known shaman. No amount of figuring could calculate the extent of this loss to The People. The loss of Red Fox was immeasurable.

"I cannot describe the depth of my grief," I say to my life's companion, my beautiful Shining Bird. She gives me as much comfort as she can while still keeping our children active and interested in daily activities. She's the one who sees to ensuring we all eat and sleep and work at our daily tasks.

For those several days before we completed our ceremony for Red Fox's body, I simply sit alone, half in grief, and half in meditation, ignoring most of the goings on occurring around me. That luxury is provided to me by my devoted Shining Bird. She too grieves heavily. Her position as mother does not allow her respite to grieve as I do. Her mother-bear energy keeps everything else flowing smoothly without my help.

At one point she hands me Red Fox's sacred bundle that includes the engraved clay tablet in it. She says, "I think Red Fox would want you to have this." I nod and accept it.

"Mica," I blurt suddenly out of the blue to her, "mica. Where can we get mica? Mica and shells . . . that's what we need for the ceremony."

Shining Bird sent word out to spread among the many migrants asking for pieces of mica that anyone had thought to bring. Not really knowing what such a migration would entail, many had tucked away small sheets of mica or odd pieces of the glassy material, not really knowing how it could serve in the future of a migratory population. After the call went out, The People provided sufficient amounts of mica and shells for the burial ceremony offerings.

THE CAMP OF GOD'S TEARS

Red Fox's body had been wrapped in cloth and placed on a slightly raised earthen platform. Once the ceremony was over, his body and offerings would be buried under an earthen mound, wrapping him in the arms of Mother Earth. The real ceremony took place within the privacy of thoughts and feelings, for those who chose to attend. White Eagle began singing at midday standing over his body, her arms outstretched as she did so.

Many of The People knew and loved Red Fox since he traveled far and wide making friends wherever he went, helping repair homes or other structures as he made his way around the country. As a result, many approached the site with tears as they stopped briefly to listen to White Eagle's chanting.

Those not already carrying a shell or a small water-worn stone helped themselves to a piece of mica or a shell from the piles standing near his soon to be grave. It took hours for The People to file past and set down their contribution of mica or shell or water-worn stone. Soon his body and the area around it were covered with items representing water for renewal and rebirth.

With darkness closing in, fires were lit to provide light for those still wanting to honor their beloved Red Fox.

I had not yet participated. Shining Bird and I stood in the dark hours waiting for the last of The People to complete their ceremony. By then the mica covering his body reflected light from the surrounding fires like it had a light of its own.

I waited for the last person to finish. Shining Bird looked at me and handed me a clay pot filled with water from among the several she had brought to the ceremony. I fell on my knees at the edge of his grave. My heart pounded as I felt my consecrated prayer move through me like a river of intention. As I rose slowly I methodically poured water over and around his body and the offerings, my tears replicated the water pouring out of pot after pot. Shining Bird watched me solemnly witnessing my expression of grief.

When I finished my prayers and my sacred water offering and now on my knees again, Shining Bird could hear me utter ever so softly, "May the waters of birthing resurrect your spirit, so that you come back to The People."

Spring began producing warmer days between storms. After another two months or more of travel, travail of living off the land with all of its hardships, began to press against The People. We were accustomed to an easy-going life-style with few, if any, deprivations. Our clothes of finely crafted fabrics made by skilled weavers then artfully sewn by tailors and then decorated ever so beautifully with pearls and shells showed wear. Typically whenever that occurred, new clothes were created and supplied. Now being hundreds of miles from home, getting new clothes was not an option. Life felt harsh.

White Eagle felt, rather than heard, the discontent with life on the road. She sensed the vibrations of some feeling disgruntled and disillusioned with the romantic idea of saving our culture by escaping into unknown territory from an unknown force set on our destruction. The idea was uplifting. The reality was not.

I said nothing to White Eagle. As I tended those in need of medical attention, I caught whiffs of dismay and occasionally overheard complaints spoken loud enough for me to hear but not said to me directly. I would comment, "If you notice the land is changing. We're getting closer to the Mississippi River. We can hold out just a little longer. Remember, this journey is one we all thought best to take given the alternative. We are one with the One . . . and that's what we want to maintain, our sense of unity with each other, the land and Great Spirit." I would smile and give a pat on a shoulder of any person standing or sitting close to me.

Another month went by in much the same way as the previous three months had, and now we were closer to the Mississippi River. We had sent runners up ahead to see how close we were to our destination. When they returned, they said that several encampments of other members of The People had been set up at various places, some near existing villages, along the way and some close to the great river. They also had heard reports of the existence of a large settlement populated mostly by The People. That settlement included others from varying locales not of The People but still quite some distance north up the Mississippi. This was where we were heading. Such news lifted the morale of most and quieted those unhappy on the journey west. At last, we knew we were more than half way to the place we would winter *and* a place of civilization.

Because of this news, The People picked up their pace. Many began pushing harder than before, anxious to get to what they thought was our destination, forgetting that our ultimate goal was the western ocean. So rigorous, so harsh was their experience thus far, many conveniently failed to remember where we had originally set our sights and were seeing this as their ultimate destination.

The pace of many increased, as they hastened to rejoin civilization at a site on the Mississippi River composed of long established villages of The People. White Eagle's pace slowed.

For some time now she had tried valiantly to keep up, and only fell further behind. I noted it only briefly as I was kept busy caring for anyone and everyone else, from cuts and scrapes and other minor ailments. Finally, one day a runner came to find me as I was wrapping a sprained ankle of a young mother.

It is late afternoon and a very long way from White Eagle's shelter. The young man abruptly approaches breathing hard and out of breath. I'm just finishing tying the leather binding and say to her, "I know you need to keep walking as we journey, so see if you can stay sitting with your leg propped up as much as possible when we are not moving." She looks at me sadly as I say that. I continue, "I've prepared a mixture for tea that should help you. I'm sure we can find several other mothers to look after your children while you rest and heal. Your husband can make the tea for you and help with the children as well. He's out getting a walking stick for you to help support you when you do need to walk." I smile at her and then she smiles back.

"Gray Wolf," the runner says thinking he had remained polite long enough, "please come. Please come, right now!"

"Now, now, what's the trouble young man?" I ask patiently.

"White Eagle . . . it's White Eagle . . . she's . . . she's asking for you," he answers still catching his breath.

I found White Eagle lying there in her shelter, comfortably resting on a bed of buffalo robes in one of the makeshift shelters. A fire softly crackled as it warmed the rustic space and the pot of healing tea sitting near it. The shelter was open on one side so as to allow those attending her to keep an eye on her at a distance as evening faded into night. They felt her conversation with me needed to be a private one, so they honored her privacy by stepping outside.

White Eagle had been our spiritual leader for as long as anyone could remember, at least among all those electing to migrate. Our People, including the small children, had always loved her. The children so enjoyed sitting down around her feet in the late afternoons or early evenings to listen to her stories. She told them stories about Sister Moon, the Great Serpent, stories about creation and Mother Earth, and even about the star people. She had traveled from village to village over the years and always made time to sit with the children to simply talk and tell and retell the cultural stories.

Over the years, White Eagle had addressed several generations, so that nearly all the adults on this journey had at one time or another enjoyed her presence and entertaining stories as children. Her tales and time spent with them as children had become part of their growing up and part of their cultural traditions. She helped make the glue that sealed The People to the forces significant in their lives. They saw her and experienced her as a treasure they maintained in their fondest memories and heart energy.

"Grandmother," I say under my breath, not wanting to wake her if she is sleeping. As I gently approach my mentor, she slowly opens her eyes to reveal beams of light that appear to be dimming.

The fact that she appears close to death sent gasps of emotional choking and breathless alarm to those people encamped around her. The fact that we are away from our homeland, away from our homes of lifetimes, away from the ground occupied by The People from ancient of days, causes many to feel isolated and distant from their core.

Even more, many of us are feeling abandoned by their one spiritual leader whom they would follow to the ends of the earth. Indeed, they are on their way to the ends of the earth as they knew it. It is hard to take. They find themselves suffering the sense of losing their bearings in the middle of a benchmark journey. They find themselves having to face the potential loss of their leader who they believe would lead them to a promised land. Dismay and a sense of abandonment, first by Red Fox and now White Eagle, prevails.

"Grandmother," I say again. "What happened to you?"

"My dearest, Gray Wolf," White Eagle says with a long blink. "It's nothing, my son. It's nothing more than my time to go."

"Oh, no, you are not leaving me now!" I say with a smile. "You need to . . ."

She interrupts me by putting her hand on my arm and locking eyes with mine. "Dearest one," she begins, "Both you and I know that I would not complete this journey."

I listen patiently allowing her to say what is on her mind.

"It was my responsibility to get The People moving. They would not have gone without me."

"Why now, Grandmother?" I ask with tears in my eyes, finally unable to hold back my grief. "It certainly is sooner than even I had anticipated."

White Eagle grips my arm with surprising strength, "Let me say what it is I need to say without you interrupting me. Besides my passing is merely a change that is part of the ebb and flow of life, the flux that challenges our perception of the constancy of life. We have spoken of this before.

"Remember that this transition allows us to more fully appreciate and understand the purpose for our physical life. While our physical life appears to be real, death informs us otherwise. In death we return to our Spirit form that is our true nature. We are extensions of Great Spirit experiencing a physical manifestation. So death reminds us that what appears to be so is not."

I bow my head at the chastisement and nod.

Moments pass between us.

She continues, "I have already told you much. Now I am asking you to remember what we have already spoken about. You must remember the purpose of this journey. It will be so much harder than what many can bear, and The People might forget it. It is your responsibility to remind them when their spirits are low, and this *will happen* from time to time."

I look into her face. My eyes widen to capture all the meaning available beyond the words that she speaks. My senses heighten, and my mind feels alert to what I am about to hear from my beloved White Eagle.

"My son," she begins again, "the purpose of this journey is to preserve The People, and our way of seeing the world, and most importantly, our sense of connectedness with all things.

"This includes the sacred knowledge of our ancestors, the sense of oneness with each other, Mother Earth and Spirit. This journey is necessary to preserve this as what is coming is bent on destroying all we have and all we know to be true.

"My visions, as you already know, have shown me the difficulties The People will encounter." At this, White Eagle closes her eyes and heaves a sigh. Her grip on my arm relaxes somewhat, and I breathe a little freer. When she feels me move back, she opens her eyes again revealing a look into a distant place unseen by me and those watching from a distance.

"My visions have shown me something I must tell you," she begins again. "Another characteristic of the people who are coming to our lands is one that is contrary to our ways."

I look at her quizzically but say nothing.

She says, "Many of us acknowledged in our conversations that these people do not feel connected to each other." I nod, wondering where she is going with this.

"Many of them have a sense of being connected to their family members and sometimes their closest friends. It's like you could draw a circle around them, enclosing them within that boundary as it were. Then I was shown they have another layer of relationships that tend to be close but only a semblance of connectedness exists. Then I could see another layer, and then another layer extending out in concentric circles. What I was shown is the farther out in the layering the relationship is, the less connected is the feeling among them. Each person or family has their own list of concentric circles of relationships. Sometimes they intersect." I listen while trying to grasp what she is saying.

"I think I see the diagrams you are describing, Grandmother," I say interrupting her. "They are all a series of concentric circles moving around. Sometimes they touch other circles and sometimes they don't. What does this mean to us?"

"Hush, now," she warns patting my arm, "I'm getting to it. Each and every person or family behaves as though they were the center of universe. Their sense of being connected to everyone does not exist, cannot exist under this view of the world. The problem occurs especially when someone makes a choice about others, or for others, or against others, who are at a distance away. The greater this distance, the less personal involvement occurs. The greater the distance from the relationship, the more reduced the sense of being directly connected is felt. The point is these people who are coming to our lands do not comprehend that everyone is directly connected to each other no matter what."

"I see what you are saying, Grandmother," I interrupt again, "they don't see that each person is directly related to every other person, and that can influence choices made. Is that right?"

"Yes, my dearest one," she says granting me a smile. "They don't see the Oneness in all. It makes a difference in what they choose to do and how they choose to do it. Regard for outcomes lessens, especially when the outcomes are far reaching or have long range effects."

"But how does this . . . ?"

"I'm getting there. I'm glad you see," she says then licks her dry lips with her tongue. She continues, "I want you to see the meaning of the information in my visions about those who are coming. Because of the way they see each other, most will not even *see* us. At first they will, in a way, because we are many and they few. But as time passes we will be merely in their way, an inconvenient factor that will stand in the way of what they want, what they seek.

"They wish to take the lands we live on and make them their own. We will be in the way, and they will seek to eliminate us. This is the reason this journey to protect our ways is so very important. Our journey is a sacred one. It is critical that you comprehend this concept." I sit up a little straighter. I have been bending over her while kneeling beside her. At this remark, I feel alerted to a warning I sense is coming.

"Gray Wolf, this journey has been difficult just getting this far," she says. "What is ahead is still even more challenging than you or anyone can imagine. I want you to consider that the homeland we are leaving is like the center of our universe," White Eagle pauses to breathe. She takes shallow breaths as she feels herself weakening. I can see that she is straining to tell me something so important that she does not want the night to pass without imparting this message.

The onlookers begin a low chanting. They feel instinctively that their beloved leader is fading. Their chant is one of both grief and support. More gather outside, some bringing small torches as the night has set in. Many hold their vigil with faces tense from holding back tears.

Looking straight in my eyes, without flinching, she says, "Because the journey will be so extremely arduous, and because The People are journeying farther away from our homelands, away from our center, the lands of our ancestors, and the core of our culture, it will be all the more challenging for everyone to remember who they are. Many will feel challenged to remember their connectedness."

At this last remark, my jaw drops and I say, "I hadn't thought of that."

"When The People lived their lives in the extreme comfort of our villages in the place where The People have lived for thousands of years, it was easy to remember we are all related through Great Spirit. We didn't have to think about staying connected. The hardships The People have suffered so far, and the extreme hardships yet to come may prove how solid we are in our knowing that each of us are indeed individualized members of the Great Oneness. That's how we are connected."

I nod in affirmation.

"Yes, my dearest Gray Wolf," she pats my arm again and says, "I am entrusting The People to your guidance. Their spiritual strength is what will get them through. You will now be their spiritual leader in my absence.

"Some of our People will fall away. Some will change direction. Some will simply stop and settle. Regardless, it is your destiny to lead our People to the lands we have been shown in our visions.

"This land rests on the edge of the western ocean. You will encounter rivers, lands of grasses, deserts, and mountains larger than you have ever seen, and then still more rivers and lands of grasses, and mountains before you get there. I believe that the deadly sicknesses that will be coming here might not reach you there."

My eyes lift to see beyond the low roof of the quaint shelter, and I breathe in a deep breath as I process this information.

Lifting her head with great effort and grabbing my arm to pull herself up half way, using all her strength, White Eagle cautions me with a voice intense with command, "In your efforts to guide The People, if you resort to ego or if you allow ego to slip in and take over your decision-making, you will die and take everyone with you."

Taken aback and caught off guard by this utterance, I open my eyes in surprise and jerk back my head. She continues, "Yes, Gray Wolf, everyone can become susceptible to ego. I tell you this. Misuse of ego can be fatal. Abuse of ego is worse. I tell you this, because the stresses and strains of the journey will make many of our People either challenge you or fall away. Use of ego comes from a sense of separation, the opposite of connectedness. Keeping The People aware of their connectedness with each other and with Great Spirit, as well as Mother Earth, is what will strengthen the dedication to complete the journey as The People. This means you must remain constant in your attunement with Great Spirit and Mother Earth. Only then can you help The People stay on course. Lead by example."

Falling back as she lets go of my arm, White Eagle pauses. Clearly her strength is failing her and this conversation appears to exhaust any reserves she had. At the moment she fell back, those waiting and watching jump as if wanting to catch her despite the distance. All eyes remain focused on the both of us.

"Before you go, Gray Wolf," she finally says after several tortured breaths, "there is something else."

"Yes?" I say reluctantly, not wanting to hear what that something else is.

Before speaking, White Eagle lifts her head up then turns to see the audience assembled outside her shelter. Turning her head back toward me, she grabs me and pulls me closer to her. Evidently she does not want to be overheard. I lean down and turn my head facing the onlookers so I can put an ear closer to her mouth. She speaks for several minutes.

All the while, all eyes from outside never leave my face as I listen. They watch my eyes open wide, then close, and then open again. They witness tears finding their way out of my closed eyes only to fall upon White Eagle. She does not notice so intent is she in giving what appears to them to be critical information to her successor.

Finally she finishes speaking. I look White Eagle in the eye. The audience outside in vigilance softens their chanting and pause to hear me say, "*I accept*," as I weep openly.

At that, they witness White Eagle struggle to pull off her cherished necklace. As she holds it momentarily, it reflects the firelight from the little fire and all the torches, flashing beams of light across everyone's faces. The onlookers feel the message it holds within its symbols. "As above, so below," becomes embossed on each face.

Choking.

Silent tears accompany several ever so quiet moans.

As they see her put the necklace over my head, tears run openly like rivers on the faces of all in attendance.

"Now, go," she commands me choking as she did so.

I get up slowly, tears running down my face unashamedly.

As I move through the grief felt inside that little shelter, I stop at the edge of the crowd momentarily. Those witnessing the painful scene part allowing me to pass wearing the treasured necklace, saying nothing.

Having passed through the crowd, I stagger across the camp finding my way to my own shelter. Upon my approach, I see Shining Bird stand still and drop whatever is in her hand when she sees me.

Our three children felt instinctively that something important had occurred and suddenly fell quiet. Eyes of their parents connected. They saw their father stumble inside and fall, caught in the arms of their mother. The children's eyes grew wide in awe as they witnessed their father, such a tower of strength and assurance to them, break down and sob uncontrollably. No words were spoken.

That night while my family slept peacefully, I awoke startled. Immediately I connected with White Eagle. "Remember the story of the two wolves, my son," were the words passing through my heart spoken in White Eagle's voice. I heaved a sigh and knew that she was gone from this life.

At that moment, White Eagle finds herself in a dream state. Then she sees Rising Wolf appearing to her as he did as a young man. She sees him smile at her. Then he extends an arm toward her and says, "I have come to escort you on your journey as it continues into the Absolute." She smiles at him. As she does, she lifts out of her shrunken form that had served her so well, and sees herself as the young beautiful woman she had been when first a bride to Rising Wolf.

Mists.
Fog.
Clouds.

38

THE GATHERING OF MIGRANTS

It took us two more months to travel north along the east side of the Mississippi River to the established settlements that existed on both sides of the great river. A large number of People migrating from other areas chose to meet up with us here. Those in our group, plus those who already lived here, realized we needed to establish new villages around the area. Most of our group decided to cross the river to the west side.

Crossing the Mississippi River during late summer, early autumn, had not been a serious problem. It was wide and shallow in most parts with sandbars interspersing themselves between deeper currents. Most of us walked across part way and appreciated the use of canoes of the people who lived there to help us cross completely. We also gladly used canoes to transport the very young, the very old, some of the dogs and all of the travois carrying our blankets, hides and other possessions. It took days for all of us to cross, and eventually, we all made it intact, smiling as we finished that leg of our journey.

The established communities on both sides of the river were simply too small to accommodate our great numbers so new villages were created on both sides of the river.

By this time the season was changing into autumn. We knew it was time to prepare for winter. We chose an area near forests and game in close proximity. The land we occupied undulated softly, so our winter shelters were far enough apart to avoid a sense of congestion. We built our winter shelters with enough distance to feel close, yet not feel completely exposed to each other. Unlike the temporary close placement of our temporary shelters while on the journey, we knew we were settling in for the winter.

Those who felt like hunting for fresh meat to supply us were provided ample opportunity to do so. Those who felt drawn to fish did so. Families grouped themselves together for cooking and food preparation. With our high degree of cooperation, despite our numbers, it was not long before we regained the sense of a community, or rather an expanded community, as we prepared for winter.

More of our People continued to migrate into this new territory despite the weather and the season. We were among the first wave to arrive. Subsequent waves of our People streamed into the area. Some came from the northeast, others came from the southeast. Many of them chose to take up residence on the east side of the Mississippi River, and some joined us on the west side.

By spring at least a hundred thousand or more of us resided in temporary quarters spread on both sides of the great river. The impact on the land's resources revealed itself as game became increasingly scarce. Hunters had to go farther and farther out. The People scoured the area for other kinds of edible foods and roots to supplement our diet. The great river continued to provide fish.

The land was not as hostile as it was strange to us. The People found themselves having to learn new plants for both food and other needs and new ways of surviving. As winter lessened its grip on the land, social pressure was building to either settle permanently or move on quickly.

Throughout the winter season and on into the spring, shaman and Elders from many parts of our civilization met in council meetings near the settlement on the east side of the river which had a large meeting shelter constructed from tall poles covered by a coarse canvas cloth and hides. Some meetings went on for days and nights.

I spent my time primarily between attending council meetings and taking care of The People who knew me, or those who did not but needed a healer. Between attending to newborn babies and their mothers, attending to all other minor ailments and attending council meetings, I didn't see Shining Bird and my children as often as they needed me.

I sensed that participating in the council meetings was important. I felt out of my element in this new land and needed a sense of direction. I also desired to know what others knew about direction, conditions, what to expect, and basically what all these different groups were feeling, the visions they had received about where to go from here and when.

I wanted to feel attuned to what others were thinking and feeling. I searched for knowledge of how to get from here to there never forgetting White Eagle's visions and staying focused on her last words to me.

With much new information and viewpoints to consider, I still lacked the clarity of a vision I could have confidence in. I felt an obligation to keep my mind open, as there was general agreement that to preserve our way of life, relocation was essential.

After much listening and asking questions, I discovered that going straight west to the ocean was simply out of the question. Local knowledge of the area to the far west was sketchy. It was known to be relatively flat for a distance, but then became mountainous and dry for a long distance with little access to water, not a good choice for the tens of thousands of us. Healthy and strong men and women could easily march ten, or twenty, or more miles in a day. Yet, we had infants, nursing mothers, small children, travois with foodstuffs, supplies for making shelters, and older adults, packs and bags. None of these added up to covering long distances fast or long distances without water. Straight west was clearly not the appropriate direction.

We originated from the east, which left the directions north or south from which to choose. I learned that we could reach the western ocean by going either north or south first then by turning west.

The long winter provided time and opportunity for much discussion. Now with this vast number of people from all reaches of our lands, opinions differed about when this devastation was coming and what to do about it. Now that so many had committed to and invested in leaving their homelands, I detected a strange and unsettling energy echoing quietly from an unknown source that was gaining strength.

South, south, south, south, south, south, south.

Endlessly the council meetings continued. Sometimes, we all sat and listened to one speaker after another after another say their peace long into the night. Some of the shaman used hallucinogens of one sort or another to achieve clarity in and to enhance their continued visions and persuasive rhetoric for their descriptions of what they saw coming and what we should do.

I was not inclined to participate in the use of drugs, as my vision was clear enough to know the purpose behind our migration. Focusing on a potential distant future was not my issue. My concern was focused on our immediate future, specifically what direction should we go and *when*.

In the council meetings, sometimes, many of us sat and visited in small groups. Many shared and discussed our visions and dreams of the strangers coming to our lands, only to cause devastation of The People by one type of death and suffering or another. In their visions, differences occurred as to what form the devastation or atrocities would take. Many disagreed on the impact. Some never saw clearly the source of the potential demise of The People. However, the reason for our general migration was abundantly clear. Something was or would threaten our way of life. Thousands upon thousands of The People waited for the decision to move . . . but in which direction?

South, south, south, south, south, south, south.

Typically we debated the virtues of which direction would be best, north or south. As days moved into weeks, and weeks moved into months, I noticed the feeling to go south infiltrate the conversations. By going south, we could not only reach the southern ocean and then follow its coast until we found a way across land to the western ocean. Reports indicated that the land there held much promise for its rich soils, available native plants, both for a food source and for other practical uses, plentiful game, and stone for building. Winters there tended to be mild with no snow.

South, south, south, south, south, south, south.

The talks and discussions seemed endless to me. The People were getting restless to build permanent homes and permanent farmlands. Coming from countless generations in a farm-based culture, living as migrants in temporary housing for any length of time, simply, did not fit our sense of who we are. I could feel a generic need pervading the consciousness of many to put down roots, both physically in the way of farming, and metaphorically for making this crossroads a place to stay. As the land blossomed into spring, I could see that many would not be moving on when it came time to leave.

"North or south," I say in a discussion with Shining Bird and several of our neighbors, "which is best for us. I don't know. I've been asking in my prayers and have not yet received an answer." Shining Bird gives me a supportive look as she rocks our youngest son in her arms.

We talked about White Eagle's vision of heading toward the places where the obsidian and grizzly bear teeth came from. White Eagle was most clear on this point.

In my private conversations with Shining Bird, I told her that I had noticed something strange over the past months. I had noticed that during this time, one by one Elders and shaman who had always attended the large council meetings showed up less and less frequently. Typically they were the ones who used the hallucinogens and typically were the ones who tended to speak the loudest and longest . . . and that I was detecting a troubling energy . . . .

South, south, south, south, south, south, south.

"What I have received is 'I will know' . . . and as soon as I know, we will go," I say as I look at each listener in a small group gathering near our shelter. "I tapped into the Knowing in my meditations," I say, "I was given that when I knew which direction is best, I would know, *in no uncertain terms,* and that I would be clear about it."

One of my neighbors says, "Why don't we look for traders?" We all stop and just look at him. "Yes, I know that sounds crazy, but traders pass through here. Maybe we should look for a trader or someone to guide us. Traders know the land and what to expect in this part of the country. Gray Wolf, when you go into the council meetings next, why don't you start asking around? Why don't you see if you could find a trader or someone else and ask them which is better, north or south?" Everyone in our group nods or grunts in agreement.

South, south, south, south, south, south, south.

"Well, I too have seen others in the settlements, I mean, others not of the People," I say thoughtfully, "they came from somewhere. I heard that they come from far to the south and west, but they don't look like traders and have not been at the council meetings. It makes sense what you suggest.

"If they have come here from the south, then they would know the way and the territory," I say. "Why don't we all go together next time I go to the council meetings? This way all of you can hear what is said among those outside of the council meeting. Talk to different folks and ask questions. Maybe we could find one or two of these other people, and we could all listen to them and ask questions?"

Several nod silently. Shining Bird smiles like she suddenly knows something I do not.

By this time spring had melted into early summer.

"I'm all ready to go," Shining Bird says as I am preparing to attend the next meeting. "One of the Grandmothers will be staying here with the children, so I can go with you."

I didn't know what to say. I wasn't going to say she shouldn't come. In fact I was grateful for her support during these trying times. We were stuck, as it were. She knew I was in a quandary and needed help. I smiled at her in response. As we left, more than several of our neighbors joined us. Evidently they thought I needed help also.

"The river is high this time of year and much more turbulent," I say aloud for the benefit of my companions. Getting across proves to be more of a challenge than during the winter or early spring as the river is swollen with snow melt runoff from the north. The boatmen adroitly handle their canoes, and we reach the other side in safety. We are all glad to have our feet firmly on the ground as we walk toward the main settlement looking for traders.

As we head toward where the council meeting is usually held, the others lag a little behind. I notice their attention is on a large audience that is listening to a speaker who does not sound like he is one of The People. I turn to see which direction Shining Bird would be going in, and I see that she has stopped suddenly, frozen in fierce determination, her jaw and closed mouth set hard, her eyes wide open and not blinking, focused on someone or something across the way. I have never seen her behave like this before. I look at her incredulously. When she realizes I am paying attention to her, she lifts a hand up and points.

I looked into the direction she is pointing and just could not see what she was seeing. I move close to her and touch her arm and ask, "Shining Bird, what is it?"

All I can see is a small group of men standing around on the top of a sizeable flattened earthen mound with one speaking intensely. Those standing on the mound are all visible to the large crowd that keeps growing. The other men with the speaker are looking out into the audience as if waiting for something to happen. I recognize the speaker and these others. They are the Elders and shaman who had gone missing from the council meetings.

Shining Bird remains silent for a long time. Finally I say, "Shining Bird, all I see is a group of men, some of The People, some of the others, standing and talking. What is it?" I ask impatiently.

She says to me in almost a whisper while not taking her eyes off them, "See the one with the long scar on his face? He's the one who told the band of renegades what to do when they accosted us on The White Road of Sister Moon. He stood behind them whispering orders to them to seize hostages and to hold knives at their necks. They were an ugly bunch. That was an experience I do not wish to have again."

"Him?" I ask incredulously, "I've seen him around here many times on my way in or out of council meetings. I wonder what he's up to? My guess is he would be one to steer clear of while we're here." For the moment, attending the main council meeting became irrelevant.

South, south, south, south, south, south, south.

Shining Bird and I, along with our companions, gravitated together and moved toward the outer edges of the crowd. I noticed another group of men standing around just behind the mound with

The Gathering of Migrants

several turkeys bound with ropes. Scarface stood among them whispering something into their ears from behind.

Finally, as the crowd multiplied, one of the others stood and moved to the front of the flattened mound and took a turn speaking. We weren't close enough to hear. As he continued to speak, the audience grew and drew closer. As he spoke, he raised and lowered his voice, sometimes waving his arms, sometimes pacing on the narrow ledge he used as his platform from which to exhort The People to go south.

As he continued in this way, we moved in closer, so we could hear what he was saying exactly. As we did, several glassy-eyed shaman of The People got back up onto the platform and each began speaking in an effort to persuade The People to go south. As I peered closer at those shaman, I noticed they showed signs of being in a drug-induced state. I noticed one shaman that I had not seen before. Their different presentations appeared partly prayer, partly as incoherent chanting and partly talk.

South, south, south, south, south, south, south.

I stood there only half-listening to their speeches, seeing my own visions produced with clarity within myself. I needed no toxic hallucinogenic substances to elevate my inner sight. With great clarity, I resolved to search diligently for a trader or guide to take The People . . . .

". . . and so, we will make a sacrifice to the gods of our fathers," I hear the speaker say, "to make our way right as we go south, south then west to create the next heaven on earth." Many in the audience raise their arms and shout in approval and support.

We react with gasps and shock at hearing this.

At hearing this, Shining Bird mutters under her breath softly yet with sufficient potency for those standing around us to hear, "They've forgotten their *at-one-ment* . . .their sense of oneness with the One."

I look at Shining Bird. Our eyes meet in a mutual understanding. Then I also softly say in a way so our companions could hear, "Sacrifice means to make sacred. There is nothing we need to do to become more sacred than we already are. These shaman are frauds, or at the very least, not conscious of the Law of One."

As I stand there in a partial state of shock, I overhear several men of The People standing nearby us saying to themselves, "Yeah, south, then west, then south again."

Another nods and says, "That's where those colored birds come from."

"You mean, it's not straight west to the western ocean?" a third asks.

"No," is the response, "I've heard that they actually turn south again before turning west to get to the western ocean."

Then my attention diverts back to the speakers again. Several shaman of The People, and several of the others all stand up with arms raised to gain silent attention from the much expanded audience.

Then one of the shaman shouts, "A blood sacrifice is what we need. A *blood* sacrifice to appease the gods to grant us a successful journey south."

I could not believe my ears. I turned and looked at Shining Bird. She turned and looked back at me with her jaw dropped. We both felt speechless. I turned and looked at those who had accompanied us today. I saw they each stood with eyes wide, speechless also, not quite believing what they were hearing.

Stillness dominated.

The speakers moved around and someone brought one of the bound turkeys on to the stage. As I riveted my attention to the scene unveiling before us, I noticed Scarface skulking around in the background. He was one of those who helped bring up the turkey. He didn't get on stage, just stayed in the background.

The shaman renewed their incoherent chanting rocking from side to side, shaking rattles or beating small drums. The rhythmic sounds added to the drama. As they increased in their volume, I felt the tension coalesce throughout the audience. It became hypnotic.

Chanting.

Rhythmic sounds.

Louder chanting.

The entire audience began to sway to the rhythm and chanting also. This further increased the volume and the hypnotic affect.

As this was going on, one of the speakers raised a large knife and swayed with the chanting.

Suddenly, he lifts the turkey and firmly grasped it just below its head. With one powerful stroke . . . .

Swack!

The turkey's head rolled in the air landing among those standing closest to the stage. Blood spurted like a fountain. In celebration of the blood spouting upwards, those on stage stopped their chanting and raised their arms into the air, giving shouts of exhilaration, many audience members doing likewise.

Turmoil ensued.

My face paled.

My stomach turned.

I looked at my companions and Shining Bird. We all looked sickened by what we had just witnessed.

Evidently the erosion of our culture didn't have to wait for a future day, or even a future moment. The erosion of our culture had already begun.

I did not attend the council meeting that day, nor any other day.

As a group, Shining Bird, the others and I returned to where the boatman could take us back across the river, back to our temporary homes. While we waited for the boatmen to get organized and prepared to go across the great river again, the group of us stood in tortured silence.

In the quiet of the wait, while standing close together, I say with absolute finality, "We go *north* . . .*north* and then west, just as White Eagle saw." Those in our group nod in solid affirmation. Then I say, ". . .

> *I have wrestled all winter during the council meetings to answer the question which way to we go? Which is the best route to follow? Others have answered their question by going south and others elsewhere. I guess we never really solve anything. We just rearrange the mystery of how to deal with what is coming. We will head north then west."*

Within days, many, many thousands of The People, including many shaman and those who had gone through initiation or had been schooled in the ancient knowledge, packed up and headed south.

It was now clear to me that the out-of-balance energy I was sensing had been generated from the scar-faced one and his band of cohorts. Remembering all that Shining Bird told me about him, I realized he had worked to corrupt the minds of the Elders and shaman and convinced them and their followers to go south with him.

Late one evening after our children were asleep, I say to Shining Bird, "You remember, I think, what Red Fox told us when we were with White Eagle after his initiation so many years ago."

Shining Bird replies, "Yes, of course. Scarface took advantage of the Elders who officiated the sacrifice ceremony and persuaded many, including the Elders, to go south. Scarface used the sacrifice ceremony as a mechanism to persuade what he wanted them to do. Such ceremonies of sacrifice, as Red Fox said, are a very clever defense mechanism of the ego. Clearly, the Elders were just as confounded as you were regarding which direction to go. They used the sacrifice ceremony to protect their egos, because they did not really know, and they did not want to appear weak and undecided. The blood sacrifice appeared to provide the answer. It was based on the idea that the illusion would be effective. It became the *substitute* for going through our heart energy."

I listen to what Shining Bird said, and then I say to her thoughtfully, "I think I see what has happened. I believe that these Elders have chosen to abandon our ways of *power with* for *power over*. They appear to want to be rulers rather than leaders with their egos directing choices. They appear to be unable to make a choice based on *knowing*. You know, blind obedience to the Elders here will be fatal to our People who follow them."

Shining Bird says, "Yes, I see that happening also."

Word went out to prepare to leave and continue our migration. Only a few thousand of us agreed to go north. The rest determined to remain in the St Louis area.

"Gray Wolf," someone asks me, "why don't you go out and convince those others to come with us. Why don't you go out and tell them they must join us?"

Another says to me, "Yes, Gray Wolf, it's your job to enforce the cohesiveness of our People. It's your job to *make* them come with us."

Finally, I turn to all of them and say, "I can see that the turmoil of being unsettled for so many months has affected all of us. If we have no peace within each of us, then we will not have a peace among us as we journey. It is the responsibility for each person to determine in which direction to go and have peace with that choice.

"It is up to each person and each family to make that choice. It is not up to me to say which direction any person should go. I do not have the power *over* others to make them choose to join us. The consequences or results of each choice are up to each choice-maker to experience. I do not have the power to take away consequences of choices made. I do not have the power to take that away from anyone. I do not have the power to make those choices for others . . . where I have no power, I have no responsibility. I can let others know my personal choice, and each one can make their own choice based on that information."

As The People prepared to journey, I went back into the settlement across the river searching for a trader who would be willing to guide us north across the maze of waterways, and north along the east side of the Missouri River.

And I did.

I found Warm Stone.

Even with Warm Stone guiding us part of the way, it took us many years of struggle to move up the Missouri River then west toward its source.

39

TOM'S CABIN

Abruptly stopping as he pulls up at Tom's cabin, Hal gets out of his vehicle feeling wary. He furrows his brows as he feels a presence he cannot identify. He is afraid for his friend.

Seeing the cabin again, he remembers how happy Tom was when he built it.

"Hal," Tom said, "you are going to love this place. It is situated in just the right spot here, kinda like it's in a vortex of energies, I think."

"Just as long as you are happy with it, my friend," Hal remembers responding.

"You can bring your family up anytime and experience a nice change of pace. I know I need a change of pace sometimes. It's gonna be great," Tom said. "the lifestyle up hear is easy and calming. The environment offers so much. The outside world fades and I feel a oneness here."

WHITE EAGLE

The Oneness Principle never dies.
Sometimes it lies dormant.

The Oneness Principle can only be
lived when there is peace in the heart.

When it is lived, resurrection emerges.

40

TOM'S RESCUE

Hal cannot imagine what might be happening to Tom. So, Hal slowly stalks up to the front door and knocks. No answer.

The air is suddenly very still with no birds singing. The rain stopped a while ago and left only mists in its place. He tries the door and finds it locked. So he enters his own key into the lock. As the key turns, he hears the tumblers move. The sound they make feels like thunder to Hal.

He remembers Tom saying, "This cabin is the best place ever. I can't stop smiling just thinking about it. What do you feel, Hal?"

Hal replied, "I don't know, Tom. Clearly you are happy with it. I'm sure we will get a lot of use out of it."

"Well, I just think it is the best place ever," Tom said, "it's like it belongs to a different world, like a different dimension. You'll see. Just wait. You'll see. This is probably the best building I ever created."

Hal said, "Coming from an architect, that's saying a lot. You've built whole sections of cities all environmentally compatible. Now that's a lot." Hal smiles, and adds, "To say this is the best building you've ever built, now that's saying something."

Hal slowly and carefully opens the door. Stepping across the threshold, Hal feels as if he truly is entering into a different dimension.

Hal feels like he needs to sneak into the cabin. He roams about looking for Tom. When he makes his way into the room that goes out onto the patio, he spies Tom's phone lying on the table, just where Tom left it. Hal moves toward the sliding glass door that has been left open. He sees Tom and someone else. Hal steps outside to see what is going on.

41

THE VISION

I completed my morning prayers and offerings to the Creator, Mother Earth and Father Sun. I left before sunrise to walk, from the hide-covered shelters that had become our temporary village, to the hill top from where I could witness the vastness of the land. From where I stood I could see the Missouri River run through the great falls as it rushed away from the towering mountains on its way toward the east.

Thoughts of homes long left behind haunted me as I trudged through the snow. Rabbit fur-lined deerskin boots broke the cold-hardened crust of the foot deep snow. Father Sun rose with no warmth behind the layered mask of deep winter clouds that blanketed the horizon and covered the sky.

The chill I felt was reinforced by my thoughts of the council meeting set to begin later that day. Pulling myself out of the torturous grip of the memory of my recent meetings with individual members over the past several days, I sought guidance from Great Spirit and from my wolf spirit guides. I must find a way to bring renewed strength and reassurance to address the growing dissention among The People. Many were wavering in their decision to start a new life in strange lands far from the beloved lands of our ancestors. Many were questioning White Eagle's vision that this was the way to preserve our ancient promises to the Creator.

The journey proved far more challenging that anyone had imagined. The journey so far had been one of many deaths. We had faced untold hardships. Many had chosen to remain in settlements along the way, not wishing to go forward into an unknown beyond. Some even chose to return home. Many had walked on into Spirit. Mothers lost their children before birth, and those that were born on the journey did not survive. With no babies, with no new children and with none forthcoming to ensure continuance as a People, our sense of having a future significantly diminished.

This winter had been difficult, more difficult than the past seven winters. As a diminished band, we found ourselves farther north than anticipated, where the winds were stronger and the cold deeper. This added to our sense of desperation. Despite the intense hardships, the decision to make winter camp here near the river at the place of the great falls where the black eagles gather had been a good one.

The fall harvest of local resources had been good to us. The People had been able to gather other foods that Mother Earth provided. We had an ample supply of dried and smoked buffalo, antelope, fresh deer and elk meat, combined with a steady supply of fish from the river. Starvation did not come to our camp this winter.

Our small band of The People acutely felt the sense of feeling lost and isolated. This combined with their sense of deprivation of stability of home, prevented us from experiencing a sense of prosperity. Death of hope, death of a dream, and death of a heart felt vision loomed starkly in front of us.

Memories of creature comforts contrasted harshly against our rudimentary migratory lifestyle. I merely had to look to the west from the top of the hill where I was standing to understand the concerns and fears now coursing through the minds of those who had survived so far. We saw ourselves pitted against a walled barrier with no other direction to go, slammed against stone monoliths preventing our trespass.

The wall of mountains to the west indeed loomed threateningly as I heaved a sigh tinged with a sadness felt deep in my heart. In the gray late winter morning light stood the barricade of mountains, jagged, forbidding, offering no promise, only more challenges to those on this journey. Was a slow death of dreams, morale, and of a People to be our destiny?

Hearing me returning, Stalking Bear, my oldest son, was waiting with a cup of hot tea and a plate of roasted meat and bread that Shining Bird had prepared. I embraced my son and sat down on the dirt floor giving a blessing for the food I was about to eat.

The Vision

Shining Bird gazed upon me, feeling the burden I so deeply carried. Even though we both had grown older and the journey had taken its toll, when I looked up to thank her for preparing this meal, she could see the light in my eyes still shone brightly. Shining Bird could tell that the message I had been seeking for these past several days had not yet been received. As I rose to leave for the council meeting, we embraced feeling the love between us that had begun so very long ago.

I was the last to enter the council meeting. As I approached the large shelter I could hear many loud voices rife with concern and doubt. All became quiet as I unwrapped my gray wolf hide bundle. I removed the ceremonial pipe and prepared it for the opening prayer so that all could speak what was in our hearts and minds as we met.

"We have all smoked the pipe" I begin. "The smoke lifts our prayers to Heaven.

> "We all acknowledge the Great Spirit, our Creator, as the Sacred Force in the Universe. The Universe, created by Great Spirit, is the Great Spirit manifested in the physical world. All of Heaven and Mother Earth birthed from Great Spirit. The Will of the Creator is as above, so below. Just as Great Spirit provides nurturing of our souls, so does our Mother Earth provide us with bounty for meeting our human needs. We live in Oneness with each other. As we help each other, we help ourselves. Should we by some act bring harm to another, we harm ourselves. As we remain in tune and aligned with Great Spirit and Mother Earth, we know our way is guided, our path protected. All comes from the Creator, all Life, everything that is, is part of Great Spirit."

I pause for a moment, look around at everyone before continuing. "Speak," I say. "Speak what is on your minds and in your hearts."

A long silence prevails.

No one wants to put his or her thoughts into words in the presence of what is felt to be Great Spirit in attendance. Finally, someone chokes, looks around timidly before speaking and then says, "Gray Wolf, this journey is not what we thought it would be."

Nods occur around the room as forces mustered against an unseen enemy.

THE CAMP OF GOD'S TEARS

One woman member reminisces with regret, "I just want one of those warm nut cakes that Raven's Wing would make, or the stews she would bring over to us. I miss all the vegetables and cakes we all so enjoyed. Oh, and all the beautiful garments we wore, instead of these animal skins we are now forced to wear." Weeping she bows her head and stops speaking.

Another woman echoes similar sentiments and says, "I miss the variety of foods. Oh, and sitting on furniture. Remember when we had nutting parties? When we nutted together? While it was work, we turned it into social events. I so enjoyed eating our mussels . . . ummm. If I had known I would never eat one again, I think I should have eaten more of them. I miss Floating Lily and how she would always bring the news . . . ." Her voice trails off as emotion grabs her throat.

A man complains bitterly, "I feel lost and isolated from life, and so does everyone I know. I want to turn back. I feel betrayed. All my children have died on this forbidden journey of ours. We have suffered blinding mosquitoes, unknown insects, accidents, fatigue, hunger and too many deaths. My wife is sick and I am tired. What could White Eagle possibly have had in her mind as to send us out into the wilderness like this?"

Supporting sentiments are expressed around the room as the energy of opposition coalesces. A sense of hopelessness strangles their vision.

Another challenges, "Gray Wolf, you are leading us. Why did you lead us to such an inhospitable land as this? We have suffered too much to bear. What is it that is preventing us from turning back? I say in the spring we return, go back the way we came, and forget this nonsense about saving our People from imagined foreign invaders coming to take our homelands."

Affirming sounds come from those present, louder than before.

Then feeling braver to risk saying more by the shift in the group support, the challenger continues, "We look at those mountains ahead. There is no way over them. After all the deprivations for these seven years since we left our homes that we have tolerated, now we must face an unfaceable foe. Those mountains are impossible. How dare you, Gray Wolf, think to take us here? Just these winters here on the plains are too much for us. We have been fools all along. Haven't we suffered enough?

The Vision

I feel like you are wanting us to follow you on a pipedream of yours just to ridicule us and create pain we cannot endure." He stretches out both arms palms up, then asks, "Great Spirit, how can we be abandoned like this?"

Stunned silence. The challenger had gone too far.

I look up over their heads as if listening to some voice unheard by the others. Then, turning back to the group, I say, "The choice to leave our homelands was not White Eagle's. It was ours. Each of us made the choice unencumbered by pressure from anyone else in our village. Each of us simply chose on our own.

"This is not my dream we are following. If you choose to leave, then you choose to leave, remembering that all of us only have each other for support. So if half leave and half stay, each half is reduced in strength to help each other.

"Indeed, our journey has been arduous. I expect it to remain arduous until we get to where the sun and the great waters meet."

Rebellious sighs.

I continue, "Because we left our homelands for the purpose of preserving our identity as a People, we no longer can claim that land, the land of our ancestors, to be ours. It was the home of our ancestors and remains so. Yet, no longer is it *our* home. We have no ties to what no longer serves us. I agree. This feels like a death we are experiencing.

"We make our home wherever we are, regardless of the hostility of the land. Some of our ancestors left those very lands we have left. They traversed to unknown lands south and southwest of here and settled in lands that at first appeared inhospitable. They have endured and prospered in their new homelands.

"We travel to new lands also. Spirit goes before us, guiding our way. Despite the hardships put before us, we continue following the torch of Spirit lighting our way as we progress ever westward. Great Spirit does not require us to suffer, nor to suffer needlessly. Quite possibly we need this experience of deprivation and toil to appreciate how highly we had flourished before and how we will flourish again once we arrive at our new home in the west.

Half nods reluctantly around the room.

"Now I ask of you . . . *surrender.*"

Everyone looked around at each other seeking a clue as to what more was available to surrender.

"It is time, right here, right now, to *surrender* the death of hope to Spirit. Know that Great Spirit cares for us, embraces us, and holds us dearly to Her Breast. See the flowers how they grow. We know they are cared for by Spirit and Mother Earth. See the fish. See the birds. See all animals. See how they are cared for by Spirit and by Mother Earth. See yourselves embraced by Spirit. See the wings of Spirit's dove held up around you, protecting you, loving you and supporting you. Surrender your anger. Surrender your pain. Surrender your ego to the Great Oneness. Make it a sweet surrender to Spirit, knowing we are guarded and guided every step of the way. Know you and each of us are loved."

Silence.

"I ask once more, surrender. Surrender to Spirit in the knowing that our resurrection is on its way to us."

The meeting lasted until very late in the afternoon. Exhausted, each left in silence, leaving me sitting alone with the dying embers of the council fire. While the meeting allowed all to freely express his or her views, no vision had come. My heart was heavy with all that I had heard.

The fear of heading into the mountains, the fear of entering lands so formidable, so foreign from anything ever encountered in the history of The People had gripped the hearts and minds of nearly everyone who had made it this far. I found it challenging to shut out the voices of the people as their words kept ringing in my ears.

"We must turn back when spring comes!" "How can we continue this journey?" "How can we trust the vision of White Eagle that was given only to her?" "We abandoned the lands of our ancestors." "We abandoned the lands blessed for us by Mother Earth, and for what?" "This journey has only brought hardships, death and a way of life so contrary and so out of balance with the bountiful riches of the lands of our ancestors." "We must turn back before we lose everything."

Their words continued to echo through my mind as I opened the buffalo hide covering the door to the council shelter on my way out. Only in my distant memory could I hear the sound of the hinges from the door in my parent's home and the home that Red

The Vision

Fox had built for me and my beloved Shining Bird. The tears from my eyes burned as the chilled wind hit my face.

I turned to look north towards the river hearing the sounds of the rushing water as it fell from the great falls some distance away. In the fading light of late afternoon, I saw movement in the distance heading toward the river. As my eyes focused, I saw a gray wolf that had now stopped at the edge of the cliff above the riverbank. He looked back at me, then pointed his face toward the falls and then disappeared. I knew I must follow the wolf.

Reaching the edge of the cliff above the river, I saw many great black eagles roosting on the trees on the island just below the falls. Calmness came over me as I gazed at the beauty unfolding before me, the water hurrying toward its eastern destination, the cries of the assembled eagles. My gray wolf spirit guide had brought me to this moment.

Finding a comfortable place to sit, gently I laid my gray wolf hide bundle on the ground. I prepared a small fire, not so much for the warmth, but to prepare for my journey entering The Knowing for the message I so desired.

Methodically I removed the ceremonial pipe, gifted to me by White Eagle, from its two pouches. I joined the stem to the bowl and prepared the tobacco mixed with special plants and placed the mixture in the bowl of the pipe. Lighting a twig from the fire brought the light of the Creator to the tobacco.

As I lit the pipe, a shaft of sunlight touched my left shoulder like a spirit hand bringing reassurance to my soul as I entered The Knowing. I knew I was no longer on the physical plane. The unseen was now seen. Still sitting on the cliff edge, I entered a different dimension.

All was not what it had been a moment ago. Below me was a clear pool of water, eddying around and around. As I gazed upon the pool, it transformed into the primordial waters of creation and an image of the face of a gray wolf appeared. Its golden eyes, glowing with knowledge, locked on mine. Slowly the image transformed into millions of particles of light that began swirling, in wave-form, into a beautiful spiral galaxy. It matched the one Singing Hawk had shown me in the birch bark scrolls so many, many years ago.

The Great Mystery began to speak.

> *Gray Wolf, two children will be born on the*
> *journey through the great mountains.*
> *They are a sign that The People are on*
> *the right path in fulfillment of The Promise.*
> *One will be a boy.*
> *He will be born in the spring when the*
> *turtles hatch and begin their new lives in the*
> *rivers and lakes.*
> *He will bring strength, endurance and longevity to*
> *The People. He will be a great leader of The People*
> *and will bring new ways, new ideas and guide them*
> *to a successful, full life in the new lands in which The People will*
> *settle.*
> *The other will be a girl. She will be a great*
> *spiritual leader, one of vision, one who will bring*
> *great wisdom and knowledge to The People in fulfillment of The*
> *Promise. A great sign in the*
> *heavens will herald her birth.*
>
> *Together they will lead The People to a*
> *manifestation and realization of The Promise.*

The swirling galaxy faded. Sounds of the waterfalls and the cries of the eagles pulled me back into the present. My body tingled with new energy. My mind and soul were now at peace with clarity. I was surprised to see that most of the sky had become clear as I blinked my way into focus with the here and now. On the far western horizon, above the range of mountains, hovered golden and crimson clouds pierced by brilliant rays of white and golden light.

Darkness began setting in. Half way back to what passed for home, I saw figures moving toward me. Feeling an overwhelming sense of peace as I returned, I smiled as I recognized one of the figures as Shining Bird.

"There you are," she says with a broad smile. Tilting her head from side to side, she adds, "I see a light coming from your face. You must have received a message. I thought so." The two men accompanying her had been at the meeting earlier that day. Their eyes grew like saucers, and their mouths drop as they look at me.

One finally says, "What message did you get, Gray Wolf? Clearly you got something as I can see it on your face."

As we all walked back to our shelter, I described my experience and the message in detail. The men made no comment and left when they reached our shelter. Shining Bird lifted the buffalo hide to go inside where she knew several others were waiting for us. After sitting down on the floor, I acknowledged the man and two women, and again retold my story. They listened intently, stared off into space for a few moments before rising to leave without conversation.

After the energy field in our shelter quieted down, I whispered softly, "It's a promise."

42

THE REUNION

Dogs barking.

Day breaking.

We wake to the sounds of the dogs barking. I sit up, listening to the sounds of the dogs.

"Strange," furrowing my eyebrows, I whisper to myself. "When wolves come threatening the camp, the dogs growl. Must be something else." I could not fathom what could be the problem. Fascinated by this unknown reason for the dogs barking, I get up and put on warm wraps and boots.

This spring was a wet one. The People had wanted to leave this camp by the great falls earlier, but the late melting of the snows, combined with the recent rains prevented us from moving westward too early in the spring. My People's despair matched the cold, cloudy season.

Motivating ourselves to move in any direction proved to be a challenge that only increased the level of frustration. Many still spoke quietly about going back. Some said nothing. Others hoped to go forward, and found little open support for traversing in the original westward direction. The giant mountains pointing so eloquently towards heaven daunted even the most courageous of heart.

Barking dogs.

Stepping out of my shelter, I see several others standing outside looking in the direction the barking dogs are pointing . . . eastward with tails wagging. Rays of the east rising sun struggle to make themselves seen and felt behind the damp mist covering the ground. The veil of fog lying low to the ground, created by the dewy dampness warming to the sunrise, prevents everyone from seeing beyond.

As we stand and watch, I must shade my eyes with my hand as the sun continues to kiss the camp with its warmth. More people step out of their warm shelters to stand facing east, as now even more dogs are barking. No one knows what to look for.

Through the foggy mists wavy silhouettes begin to form. My eyes stay riveted on the mirage-like apparitions emerging from the gray cold.

As the shadowed silhouettes materialize from the mists, I catch my breath, choking on emotion. My heart leaps as tears run relentlessly down my face. Smiling broadly, I cannot prevent my body from springing into a run with arms outstretched to greet my old friend, Warm Stone.

Without warning the mists and fog disappear to reveal the brightness of the east rising sun embracing the camp and The People.

Nearly everyone who had waited and watched outside this morning recognized the trader who had lived among us for a summer so very long ago, and who had graciously guided us north by northwest in the early stages of our migration up the Missouri River.

Despite the clumsiness of bundles on their backs and on their dogs, the small group of traders found themselves greeted ever so enthusiastically by The People, much like a group hug.

Traders usually were greeted happily by villages and settlements wherever they went. Never before had these traders been welcomed so warmly and openly. It wasn't Warm Stone's imagination when he witnessed a sigh of relief expressed from our camp as he stood smiling, nodding, touching hands and faces of The People he knew and had grown to love years before this adventure began.

Companions to Warm Stone had never experienced anything like this, and looked to Warm Stone for a cue on how to behave at this greeting. He just stood there smiling, weeping in happiness, arms outstretched receiving love and heart-felt gratitude.

The People then began to unhitch the packs the traders and dogs were carrying, helping them unload. Various members of The People began carrying the packs to where the traders could set up their camp. Warm Stone looked over at me as he was ushered into camp by the welcomers. Our eyes locked. Now was not the time for us to talk.

The Reunion

The mood of everyone was celebratory. Instinctively, many members of The People began making preparations to provide a feast in recognition of a connection with the past, and a sense of reassurance for the future.

I noticed women consulting each other, while a large component of the men and some women grabbed their hunting equipment and made off toward a likely source of game. Several other men and women grouped together to search for edible plants to enhance the celebration meals.

All winter we had kept a pile of wood stockpiled near our camp to use in keeping our shelters warm through the bitterly cold winter. The stack, while not depleted, needed to be replenished. Other members of our camp headed off to gather more wood. With what the wood gatherers brought back, our supply for daily use would be supplemented, plus more to cover the big bonfires we intended to create for the upcoming celebration. The extra firewood would be useful for cooking large quantities of fresh meat, for warmth on a spring night when most of us would be dancing around it outside. And most importantly, it would serve for lighting the way for our souls to uplift out of the sense of desperation that so strongly gripped my People.

My heart opened and released tension that had built up during the past year and longer. The People were now smiling with the same release of tension. Now they were remembering who they are. Just the appearance of Warm Stone gave them that gift.

I stood looking intently at Warm Stone from a distance. I knew he could feel me watching, waiting for the most appropriate moment to share experiences with story-telling.

All day long our camp hummed with anticipation. The traders spent the day unpacking with the help of some volunteers. Other onlookers stood around watching the traders and Warm Stone who reminded them of a past life so fondly remembered.

Some brought food or food dishes for the band of traders and Warm Stone. These traders were perplexed with the idea that individuals deliberately brought food to them without asking for something in trade. Traders were unaccustomed to this kind of hospitality.

Those bringing the gifts of food came with a hunger. They were not hungry for food, but hungry for information.

THE CAMP OF GOD'S TEARS

I watched from a distance aching to speak with Warm Stone myself about what he knew of our People we left behind. I asked myself, *Was there a 'home' to return to for those who felt the oppressive despair of migrating to a new land?* Many wondered about the land left behind. The primary source of oppression felt by my People was the unexpected hardness of the struggle to survive in a foreign and often hostile land. The pain of living through facing the unknown and often terrifying events of this migration clouded the reason for the migration. It also clouded the resolve to go the distance . . . no matter what.

Our camp by the great falls proved to be a crossroads in choosing our way west. The sky-high mountains intimidated The People from wanting to press onward. The arrival of Warm Stone, propitious in timing, surely was an answer to prayer.

All day I stood and watched the activities of the day. Despite the fact that we were migrating, the energy field felt like we were a village again, or almost. Everyone busied themselves with a purpose of creating a celebration marked with gratitude.

By the end of the first day, several hunting groups returned with something to contribute, some greater than others, but something nonetheless. The several elk and deer, along with the grouse and turkeys, added up. Then those providing fish complemented the meat supply. Others set to work skinning, butchering, and roasting in pits in the ground already prepared by those who stayed in camp. Aromas rose up and drifted throughout the camp with enticing scents from other dishes in preparation.

Of course the variety could not match that produced when we lived in the Ohio River Valley. Along the journey, and especially here in this camp, The People did the best they could under the circumstances. But, then again, nothing on this journey regarding lifestyle pleasures, conveniences, foods, art, music, clothing, tradition, and just plain living could compare with the luxury of that life.

As I pondered on the wealth of that life, it seemed so very long ago. I sometimes felt that our life in the Ohio River Valley was a beautiful dream. This present migratory life was an ugly reality. I asked myself, *Is this reality just an ugly nightmare and am I still actually living a life ever prosperous and beautiful?*

Clearly The People, when living there, took for granted the safety, security and prosperity. These were just a few basics that came to my mind when I compared that lifestyle to the constant threat of physical survival on this journey.

With the meat roasting in the ground, we knew we would all be feasting by tomorrow. Spirits ran high. The evening of the second day after Warm Stone's arrival got started with feasting. Music began as some of The People brought out their flutes and drums, packed and carried as precious cargo. Dancers began spinning and moving around the bonfire accompanied to the sacred sound of music not heard nor played in far too long. Warm Stone finally was able to amble over to a sitting place near another smaller fire where I had been waiting.

"After my heart leaped, I finally breathed, when I realized it was you, Warm Stone. You can't know just how important you are to us at this moment in time," I say in greeting as he sits down.

"I was driven by Great Spirit to get here as fast as possible," he says without smiling. "Somehow I knew I needed to be here." After a pause he asks, "How long has it been, anyway?"

I reflect a few moments before saying, "So far, since leaving our homes in the Ohio Valley, it's been over seven years. From the time we left Ohio and set up winter camp on the west side of the Mississippi River until we met up with you about a year had passed. So I'd say, it's been five, no six years since when you had to return to the east from the Missouri River where you left us. It's been quite a journey since then."

Warm Stone nods in affirmation.

Silence.

"I saw the graves along the way as I followed your trail here," says Warm Stone breaking the silence.

Holding back tears in my eyes, I nod, then say, "Yes, too many."

Silence.

During the silence, several others quietly approach and sit down around us. No words are exchanged.

As the evening deepened and the sounds of celebration quieted, others joined our campfire. I got up and threw several more large pieces of wood on the fire. Flames shot up accompanied by sparks reaching for heaven.

As I sit back down I noticed that even more people had slipped quietly into our audience. I suspected they had their questions too and voiced them silently through the evening air. It seemed they were allowing me to address Warm Stone singularly without competition.

"As I remember," Warm Stone says, "you were preparing to head north from St. Louis. You really wanted to head straight west, but that was out of the question. I believe you were asking around for ideas and directions as to what path would be best to reach the western ocean. I remember seeing you standing in the middle of that village talking with different traders. I could not believe my eyes."

"Yes," I smile broadly and say, "it felt so good to see not just a familiar face, but someone I knew and trusted. What a relief I felt at that moment."

Smiling back just as broadly Warm Stone says, "I never thought you would leave your home in Ohio. But there you were, and was I glad to see you. Since I was heading part way up the Missouri River anyway, it certainly was no problem acting as a guide for you, at least as far as I was going in that direction. My main concern was that I guide you through the confluence of rivers, so that you would take the right one."

Then Warm Stone's face clouds with concern and sadness as he says, "At that time, I counted several thousand of you. What happened?"

Murmurings and nodding among the audience members.

After a moment to reflect on just how to phrase it, knowing I have an audience, I say, "We were many when we started. A large portion of our group chose to either stay in St. Louis, or go south. I didn't understand it. The others there were different from The People. I discovered they presented their ideas and themselves in such a persuasive way, that many of our People went south with the others. So, our original group had lost many already at that point.

"After you left us and headed east, we followed the Missouri River north then west, as you recommended. As we began north, moving several thousand people proved challenging partly because we experienced new landscapes. The land was different. The march proved too much for so many. Sometimes we would reach small settlements of The People. We would stay for a while to acquire game and other foodstuffs.

"Each fall we had to set up and prepare for winter camp. Some of The People who lived along the Missouri River built homes out of mud bricks. That provided excellent shelter from the harsh winter winds and snows. At several of the settlements along the way, some of our People chose to stay. They just couldn't make themselves go on.

"This journey proved especially hard for the women and children. Some families chose to stay so their children would live. When the women died, some families had to join together. The stress and deprivations of the journey proved so challenging that nearly all the women who were pregnant lost their babies before the end of their term. Those babies who did live to birth died soon after."

I begin to choke and say, "I still feel the pain at not being able to save them even with my herbs and knowledge of medicinal treatments, and with the skills and knowledge of Buffalo Cloud and his People."

"Oh?" Warm Stone ask in surprise, "You know that giant of a man, Buffalo Cloud? He must be at least nine feet tall."

"Yes. Had it not been for him and those who were with him joining our journey, we would not have survived. They stayed with us until last winter a year ago when they had to go back. Many of our People returned with him.

"I did everything I could think of to help those women and their babies," I confess as I swallow back emotion. "As we pressed on, the journey was so hard for them with the physical stress, the emotional stress, and the uncertainty of it all, the women stopped menses altogether. No more babies.

"I tell you, Warm Stone, I don't think I ever felt so lost and alone on that almost forgotten stretch of plains heading west along the Missouri River after Buffalo Cloud and his people had to leave us. I had to come to terms with the fact that our women could not bring forth new life, new generations. I was disheartened to realize that we were no longer physically able to bring forth a new generation until we could create a semblance of a normal life for our women."

I look around at our audience. They are so quiet I wonder if they are still breathing. Clearly they are hanging on to every word.

I then say, "It's really no wonder we're down to a couple hundred of us." I choke, and then cough before going on. "My youngest son, Dancing Swan, was about seven years old when we started. I think he's the youngest of us now, which would make him about fourteen. It's a miracle he lived as so many other children his age or younger didn't make it. Or those who did were with families who decided to not continue and joined one of the settlements along the way."

After a long silence, Warm Stone asks, "I see The People are wearing animal skins. I remember all of you wore the most beautiful garments, exquisitely woven, made of soft materials, often intricately dyed and in patterns sometimes. I fondly remember all the pearls sewn on the shirts or dresses. I recall some of them had feathers sewn on and copper and so many other adornments." He pauses a moment then adds, "Oh, I realize that those who worked in the fields wore plainly woven garments. Just the same, it must have been hard to make the transition in clothing."

I frown before replying. I did not relish having to remember this aspect and say, "We obviously were all forced to learn how to tan hides and also how to make clothing out of the hides. Buffalo Cloud's people showed us how to make these buckskin clothes. This was one of the most challenging parts of the transition to this new way of life.

After another brief pause, Warm Stone says, "Say, do you still keep your traditional ceremonies, like the Solstice Ceremonies? I remember you stored great importance on those."

"Yes, we do," I answer, "fortunately for us, Shining Bird has kept us on track. I am so grateful to her, for many things, and that is just one. She has conducted those special ceremonies herself and made sure everyone remained aware of the importance of each."

Warm Stone nods and then says, "I remember the Summer Solstice Ceremony you held at your village when I was living with you. I could not believe how complete, how really opulent that ceremony turned out to be. I've never experienced one like it since."

His words brought a new sense of awareness to me as I pause and then say "We are from an advanced and ancient civilization with many specialties which provided an elegance, and a grace and sense of sophistication for the entire population. We are now a migratory clan living off the land in animal skins. Looking back, I see we took that elegance for granted."

Returning to the topic of survival, I continue, "Many of us already knew how to hunt for game. That was not a problem. The difference came when we realized that there was no one but us to dress the kill, to butcher the meat, and tan the hides. Fortunately, for us the people we met in the settlements and small villages were kind enough to show us how they did it. Then there was no one but us to prepare the meat, smoke it, or preserve it in some way, and to cook and serve it. And, again, The People we stayed with taught us how to survive, how to find the foods we needed and how to cook them."

Murmurings and sighs.

"Ah, cooking. That brings up an entirely different subject," I say. "Our mode of cooking had to change as well. I'm sure you know about that as you travel constantly." I see Warm Stone nod in affirmation, and I continue, "We learned to cook differently. We did not have Raven's Wing to bake for us the delicacies she was so expert at. We also learned to search for new edible plants and found ways to nourish our bodies from the new lands we encountered . . . as you can see by what we were able to serve you. We had to learn all of this from The People who we met along the way.

"All of them were part of our People who had settled there generations before we left Ohio. We were indeed grateful to them. I don't know why they chose to settle so far away from the main population with all of the support systems in place back home.

"Where we were in Ohio, so much of our food supplies came from the large farms worked by those living in and around Baum and Gartner. Oh, yes many of us had our little gardens and small fields close to home that gave us the very freshest in vegetables and so forth. For the most part, foodstuffs were provided for us.

We really didn't have to work hard for it, so physical survival never entered our consciousness. It was never an issue really."

Murmurings from the audience.

Warm Stone just sits and listens, sometimes nodding his head, sometimes lifting his eyebrows in acknowledgement. I poke the fire occasionally. I pause briefly to reflect before realizing that I need to put more wood on the fire. The crowd has grown and we need the heat as the night is getting colder. I get up and walk over to the woodpile, pick up several more sticks and logs, then turn to add them to the fire. All the while, my thoughts keep turning over in my mind as I contemplate what I had just said to Warm Stone. I don't think I had verbalized the contrasts in lifestyles to myself quite so clearly as during this conversation with Warm Stone.

"When we first started out on this journey," I say, "none of us could have imagined just how challenging it was going to be."

Nodding and murmurings.

Warm Stone looks up at me in surprise, and then says, "I don't find it too difficult myself. But then again, I travel either alone with my dogs, or I'm accompanied by several others who either are traders or just want to make the journey. I know the territory pretty well especially up and down the main north-south rivers and their systems. Sometimes I travel into the south and east from the Mississippi River. I've been to the big ocean on the east and all the way to the ocean on the west. Occasionally, I get down into Mexico too. I pretty much know how to survive in just about any of the different climates and landscapes.

"But I got to tell you, Gray Wolf," Warm Stone continues, "moving the thousands of people you did over those kinds of distances, now that's completely different. It should be no surprise that you have dwindled down to just the hundred or so you have here. Some might be surprised that you made it this far."

Many in the crowd sitting around us suck in their breath.

Warm Stone goes on without noticing. "I must tell you though, your little band here is definitely the true believers."

I blink and just look at him cocking my head to one side and say, "True believers. *True believers*? What's that?" As I ask I feel a stirring inside.

My old friend, Warm Stone, frowns then looks up. His eyes search the diamond studded night sky. Large clouds drift between us and the dark blanket of night. The stars fail to provide the answers he seeks. After taking in a deep breath, he finds his answers within.

Finally, he says, "Your People are The People I lived with for a season. You truly are a remarkable group."

I sit back to listen. I can tell this might take a little while, so I get comfortable.

Warm Stone continues, "You call yourselves The Children of the Law of One. I believe that to be true. I have personally experienced how you live. You live in the sense that all of you are part of the One. You, as The People, live in a unity of consciousness.

'Sometimes you call the One your Creator, or you say, Great Spirit. You all treat each other and strangers like they were all embraced in the sense of Oneness."

I nod realizing he was just beginning and is intending to say something important.

He goes on uninterrupted, "You treat Mother Earth as if you belonged to her, as though she is part of you. You honor Great Spirit. You honor each other. You honor Mother Earth and all creatures. You listen to Mother Earth. You honor her by how you talk to all creatures and how you commune with Mother Earth. You honor each other by what you say and how you talk to each other, and how you choose to live. You recognize the Divinity in yourselves, in each other individually and in every stranger. You see that Divinity in all others and claim that Divinity to be the same in them as within you."

"Shouldn't that go without saying?" I ask.

"No." Warm Stone responds. "When you lived in the Ohio Valley, your abundance overwhelmed me. Your People flourished in a way of living that accepted and allowed each one to work and do and contribute doing whatever they were good at or had an interest in. You shared openly without asking for anything in return.

"Your ceremonies were all about gratitude and recognition and affirmation, never asking for something more. Your ceremonies included Sister Moon, Father Sun, and Mother Earth. You communicated with all living things and enjoyed a level of civilization that was equal to none . . . at least none I've experienced. You and your shaman always connected with Spirit, with Mother Earth and took direction from those Sources. And, the outcome always seemed to be divinely right, serving The People in ways that continued your success."

I raise an eyebrow, unsure as to where he is going with this thought. The listeners shuffle some, shifting their positions as they sit. They must be wondering also.

Warm Stone breathes in, holds his breath a moment then exhales slowly before saying, "While you were living in the Ohio River Valley, life was easy. All your needs were met and more. You had so much surplus and abundance in every category of living."

I interrupt at this point, "So far you haven't said anything to explain yourself. You said we were true believers. Would you get to the point!"

"I am," Warm Stone smiles and says, "it was easy for all of you to share and warmly commune with each other. Life was easy for you there. Because life was rich, prosperous, overflowing with wealth, so to speak, it would be easy to remain in touch with your beliefs."

"Beliefs?" I challenge. "We live how we live. We know our relationship with everything. We are One."

"Yes, that's right." Warm Stone says. "My point is you are here in *this* place. Plains on one side, daunting, snowcapped mountains on the other. It's not the place you lived for thousands of years and created a lifestyle of ease and comfort. Your People have suffered much along the way. You've experienced hunger, sickness, loss of loved ones, deprivation and untold hardships. You've suffered much.

"My point is, you still live and treat each other and me and my little band of strangers the same. It's easy to maintain your beliefs when life is easy. But it's not always so easy to do when life gets hard. When confronted by unknown challenges and landscapes, when you must do without, when you must learn new ways of surviving the elements, it's not so easy to keep your faith." He finishes, tilting his head slightly while nodding, contemplating his last statement, then says. "But, you kept your faith. You did not change. You still are the same People you were when you left."

Murmurings among the listeners.

"Of course, we are," I assure him. "We are who we are. We are who we have always been."

"My point is," he says, "You are the *only* ones left of The People who still are the true believers, who haven't changed who you are to fit into ever changing circumstances."

Silence.

I'm stunned by what he just said. Then I ask, "What do you mean?"

"You are the only ones left who still are The People," Warm Stone says. "There is no one left who is like you, who believes like you, who treats each other and Mother Earth like you do."

"No, no," I say shaking my head. "We still have family back home. We still have . . . ."

Interrupting me, Warm Stone holds up his hand to stop me from continuing, and then he says, "A few individuals may be left there. I don't know. Everyone is scattered. Nothing is the same as when you left."

Gasps from the crowd of listeners.

I can hear my heart beat and can feel my stomach turn in rebellion to what I am hearing. I want to deny the images coming to mind as he speaks. I challenge what he said.

"No, you are wrong."

Warm Stone then says, "I've been through there. Many thousands of The People left there. Your group left first, and then many thousands followed in waves. Few are left and those who are must fend for themselves. Each little group lives in competition with each other for game. Each family must grow their own food. No more foodstuffs come from Baum or Gartner anymore."

Gasps and choking come from the listeners.

"What do you mean?" I challenge again feeling anger at his words. I know he would always tell me the truth. But the truth as he is telling it is not conceivable.

Warm Stone then says, "The furnaces at Spruce Hill have been abandoned. None of the other artisans are working their crafts. No one is weaving or making garments. The organization of a large complex society has simply disappeared. Everyone is pretty much on their own."

The audience members are startled too with this information, and they gasp and mummer among themselves.

My eyes tear up. I want to stand up and shout just how wrong he is. *No one left.* I finally say, "What do you mean no one is left?"

He replies, "That's right." He looks at me and straight into my eyes before saying, "I saw a few familiar faces as I passed through. Essentially no real villages exist." He stops to breathe in a painful breath and then says. "I found scattered settlements here and there as people do need each other, but they were not like the real villages of a thriving population like the ones all of you lived in."

"Wait a minute," I insist. "My family must still be there. My mother and father and grandmother for sure. Did you see them? What about Water Dog and Singing Hawk? What happened to everyone?"

"Let me see," he says rubbing his chin.

I can feel members of the crowd around us lean forward as if to energetically pull the information from Warm Stone.

Then after another moment, he says, "Singing Hawk left and took off north to Canada. She took with her a load of stuff. Floating Lily went with her. When I was there I looked around for your mother, Raven's Wing. I anticipated some great eats. But no, I had heard that she and your father left for Canada also. I think they headed for the same place as Singing Hawk, but I'm not sure.

"Your Grandmother Shining Moon is still there. She just was not up for long distance travel. She said that she traveled around enough just tending to those who were still there. She and Speaks With Plants were a great team and are still together.

"Of course, you must know that Bluebird Near the Lily died."

I choke at this news. I hear others in the crowd gasp.

Murmurings.

"I heard that she was sick or in a coma or something," Warm Stone says looking up trying to recall.

"What happened?" I ask. "How is Water Dog? I can't imagine him without her."

Warm Stone responds, "As I remember her, she always had a weak constitution. She never made it. Both Speaks With Plants and Shining Moon worked on her for weeks. She just died in her sleep."

Soft moans of grief come from the audience.

"Water Dog just would not be the same without her I imagine," I say.

"Right. I heard that when she died, he was inconsolable. He wasn't the same after her death. When he went to the Healing House and discovered that she had died, he staggered outside and fell on the ground moaning and groaning and yelling all the while rolling around in the dirt. He really suffered. I met up with him in St Louis after I returned there later. That's how I know," Warm Stone says.

"Tell me more. Is he on his way to us?" I ask hopefully.

"Uh, no," says Warm Stone. "He tried to catch up with you, but didn't make it. I directed him toward the way you went. As it happened, he met up with a small band of People traveling north along the Mississippi River. I heard they headed toward Minnesota. I think he ended up there. Most of the folks he met in this little group were giants, like him but with both red and blond hair. I don't think he could help himself . . . and I think he found a young woman among them and liked her a lot. That's all I know."

Murmurings.

I stand up, stretch and look over to the woodpile. I notice the night sky, as the stars seem to revolve on their never-ending journey around the heavens. Clouds continue to move across the skyscape. A chilling breeze picks up disturbing the silent stillness that had prevailed during the earlier part of the evening.

After a moment of contemplation, I walked over to the pile of firewood we had set up. I noticed a few of the listeners had left, but most stayed riveted to the conversation. They had pulled up their buffalo robes or blankets around their ears, not wanting to close off the sounds of our voices, but needing a little protection against the cold spring night. I selected the last of the large pieces and brought them over, setting them into the diminishing blaze.

Warm Stone and I sat looking at each other. My mind struggled with the news he brought. Before I could speak, I saw two men approach with arms of additional firewood. They set the wood down without speaking then returned to their spot in the huddled crowd of listeners.

"I need to get back to something you said earlier," I say renewing the conversation. I can hear shuffling noises from our listeners. "I'm still working at getting my arms around what you meant when you said no one of The People was left but us here in this camp." That thought pains me deeply.

My old friend senses my internal pain. Then he says, "The civilization that once was, the one you left, is gone. The few people who are left have settled into smaller groups. I heard that hostilities even broke out between several factions. Mostly the skirmishes occurred over food and supplies, and some for other reasons. Not at all the same culture that prevailed when I lived among you. Your great earthworks are all overgrown with weeds, trees, and brush. Some I saw had been damaged by flood waters." Warm Stone pauses momentarily recalling something more, and then says, "The Great White Road of Sister Moon has fallen into serious disrepair."

Struggling with shock, my voice comes out sounding like gravel while I try to keep my emotions in check as I say, "I can't believe it. I'm finding this all so foreign to me. It goes against everything that I know . . . against all my life experiences . . . against what I know to be true . . ." Choking I stop.

"The thing is," Warm Stone continues, "of all the thousands of The People who left the Ohio River Valley and scattered to the four directions, your People here are the only ones left who remain Children of the Law of One."

Gasps.

I look down and sideways, not wanting him to tell me more.

He continues despite my unspoken desire to have him stop the nightmare I am experiencing.

"Most of The People headed south down the Mississippi River. Some went as far as Mexico and settled there. Others stayed right there in the area where we met up. Months later many tried to follow your trail northwest along the Missouri River, but never made it all the way. As you had said, many of your people just couldn't go on. The journey was simply too grueling for them.

"I can hardly blame them. What you probably don't know is they did join up with others, creating new villages along the river and beyond," says Warm Stone and then pauses, and I look up at him.

"So they still are The People," I state.

"That's just it," he explains, "they are all living as fragments of a whole. Even those who chose to stay in the Ohio River Valley are fragments. I enjoy trading with the settlements along the Missouri River, because I feel like I can relate to them, but they do not live the Principle of Oneness. No one does. Each is a segment of what once was. Each segment has changed to suit their circumstances. Each changed slightly and in ways that differ from each other.

"I find it heartbreaking to see. I actually find it disappointing," he says and pauses a moment to reflect on his feelings before going on. Then he says sadly, "You are not on a migration. You and your People have created an exodus. I find it heart-wrenching to witness."

Murmurings and sounds of anguish come from the audience.

Silent tears run down the faces of many.

43

FLAMES SHOT SKYWARD

Flames shot skyward again as I added more wood to the fire. Warm Stone and I continued our conversation into the night.

Listeners in attendance felt reluctant to leave, not wanting to miss out on any information Warm Stone would or could provide. Starved for word about "back home" and the rest of the world we had encountered on our journey, they stayed glued to the conversation.

"Going west from here seems next to impossible," I say. "We've sent out small groups of men several times to scout out the best way west so we can get over those mountains," I say as I swung my arm out to point out the mountains that everyone knew were there. "But they have not found a way over them . . . yet, at least. One group ran into some grizzly bears and had to return before they could find anything. And one of those scouts who did make it to the top of one of the mountains said that all he could see was more mountains as far as the eye could see. I don't mind telling you, we sure felt disheartened at that news."

Nodding, Warm Stone contemplates his thought before speaking. After a few more moments, he says, "That's the problem." Then he pauses again.

I just sit and wait for my friend to speak.

"That's the problem," he repeats, "going over those mountains. You don't go *over* them."

"What do you mean you don't go over them?" I ask incredulously.

"You don't go over them, you go around them," Warm Stone says with a smile and a wink. "I've been this way several times. I know the route to take."

My jaw drops in surprise.

At that, Warm Stone stands and looks around for a stick he can use to draw in the dirt.

The listeners move and shuffle, their bodies now sitting in an alert position, leaning forward. They do not want to miss anything. All eyes are focused on Warm Stone standing by the fire. He begins to draw something on the ground with the long stick he found.

"See, we are here," he explains as he points to his diagram in the dirt. "Here is the river. You must leave the river and turn in this direction, south to southwest. Here is a mountain range and over here is another one. But through here is a pass. Then after you go through that pass, you will encounter another set of mountains that actually have a pass . . . here."

Still drawing, he points on the ground as if he could see the landscape in three-dimensional mental images. Then he comments further, "As you can see, first we go south to southwest, then west, then north, then over the Bitterroot Mountains and head west. I realize your goal is to go west to the ocean."

He pauses, scratches his forehead, frowns before speaking again, "I know it seems round about, but it will get you to where you want to go. You can't go *over* them, so you have to go *around* them . . . . That's the way to do it." Warm Stone nods his head again, takes a step back and looks at his map on the ground then at me.

Murmurings.

I look at Warm Stone, stunned, blink my eyes several times with my lower jaw open. Then I smile as I feel a warm tingling all over. With an even broader smile, I look at my friend with happy tears running down my cheeks. Warm Stone remains standing waiting for me to say something.

"Warm Stone," I finally say, "do you know what you just did for us? Do you?" Warm Stone takes another step back.

"You just made a map for us to follow," I exclaim exuberantly. "A map . . . a map.

"Now we can move forward on our journey. *Now* we can move off dead center and get on with it. It was one thing when you led us part way up the Missouri River, and then Buffalo Cloud led us to where the Missouri turned west. After that, we knew to follow the Missouri River. Now that we need to change direction, we have a map!" At that I jump up and began dancing by myself, and throwing my arms in the air, smiling and chanting in gratitude.

Putting my hand on my friend's shoulder, Warm Stone waits for me to stand still.

Then he says, "I'll do one more thing."

He pauses a moment to ensure the listeners can hear him and says, "I'll draw you a map on a deer hide so you can take it with you."

Long, happy gasps and murmurings.

I cannot stop smiling. I grab Warm Stone's left arm at the elbow and shake it once, then once again. Then several members sitting in the crowd of listeners stand up also. They stroll over to the two of us by the fire. Seeing that they want to thank Warm Stone, I graciously move aside for them.

With the fire having burned down, I threw some loose dirt on it. It acted like a signal that the conversation had ended for the night. With that everyone broke off into two's and three's and headed back to their respective shelters with hope in their steps and a song in their hearts.

Early the following morning, our settlement hummed in excitement. The food was ready and The People's spirits were high. The day was filled with happy anticipation.

In the night, we had surrendered our despair and began feeling the joy of knowing what we were about. We now had a sense of direction.

Shining Bird stepped out into the morning and sensed the shift of energy and smiled. Carrying a deerskin under her arm and several writing utensils in one hand, she walked over to a neighbor's shelter. Several women were busy with last minute preparations for the day's feasting.

Looking around for someone in particular, she asks, "Is Blue Cornflower here?"

"Oh, yes," replies one of the women, "She went to get some water. She should be back any minute."

While Shining Bird waits, she turns west to face the mountains that had so terrified the hearts of The People and now saw the mountains as powerful and majestic, as a work of art by

Mother Earth that added another form of beauty to Mother Earth's already marvelous splendor.

"Here I am, Shining Bird," Blue Cornflower says, "You are looking for me?"

Shining Bird turns around to see the beautiful young widow. Her long black hair had been pulled up but was partially hanging down in disarray. Shining Bird notices a slight line of dirt on her left cheek and dirt on her hands from fetching the water.

"I need some help," Shining Bird begins. "Would you help me bring some food to Warm Stone?" The young woman blushes then nods in agreement.

Shining Bird continues, "First, let's clean you up a bit. I'll comb your hair. While we're doing that, maybe someone here can put together several dishes for us to take over to him."

By the time Shining Bird and Blue Cornflower had finished, several of the other women had put together several dishes for Warm Stone. Blue Cornflower blushed again and picked up the food and left with Shining Bird.

Warm Stone had been busying himself with his camp, rearranging some of his packs of trading goods. While bending over, he looked up and saw two beautiful women seemingly walking in his direction. "Hmm," he thought to himself. Then he recognized Shining Bird. He appreciated her beauty and elegance that he had remembered when they had first met about seventeen years ago. Even though he had seen her at the St. Louis meeting and along the Missouri River, he was unable to visit with her much.

This time Shining Bird's demeanor seemed different, business like, but almost provocative, as she walked with a younger and very beautiful companion. Despite Shining Bird's slightly graying hair, he still found her to be an attractive woman.

Warm Stone stood where he was wiping his hands with a cloth. Clearly, he felt the need to make himself more presentable as he watched the two women approach him. Warm Stone smiled his most charming smile in greeting, tilting his head to the left slightly, he said to them when they came near enough, "To what do I owe this pleasure?"

Blue Cornflower blushed.

Shining Bird spoke, "We've brought you some food, Warm Stone. I hope you are well and have enough to eat. Of course more meat from the hunt will be ready soon and we'll be feasting." She looked at Blue Cornflower who never took her eyes off Warm Stone. Shining Bird paused to allow a moment to pass, and then introduced them.

"Blue Cornflower, I should like you to meet Warm Stone."

At the introduction, Blue Cornflower lowered her eyes as she presented the food to him. Warm Stone smiled again at Blue Cornflower as he reached for the bowls. Shyly she handed them to Warm Stone, looked him in the eye for a moment, lowered her eyes again and said, "I . . . I must return to finish helping with the rest . . . ." Turning to go before finishing her sentence, Blue Cornflower walked away in a rush to avoid what seemed like an uncomfortable encounter.

Warm Stone kept his eyes on her until she was out of sight. He noticed that her feminine form swayed ever so gently beneath her buckskin sheath. He was not sure if his imagination was playing tricks on him as he thought he saw Blue Cornflower pausing to turn a moment to look back at him.

Shining Bird waited patiently with a half-smile on her face. Holding the folded buckskin she had brought with her, she continued to wait for Warm Stone's attention to turn to the conversation she was hoping to have.

When Warm Stone finally turned toward Shining Bird, she said, "You mentioned to Gray Wolf, I believe, that you would be willing to make a map for us to get around the mountains." He nodded with another smile. She continued, "I brought this buckskin and some writing utensils for you. If you had planned on leaving us after tonight's feasting, I wanted to make sure to give you the opportunity to draw the map. And, if you would, please, explain it again to Gray Wolf, so we know what we are looking at."

"Sure, sure," he commented absently-mindedly. He took the bundle from Shining Bird then asked, "Who is she again?"

"Blue Cornflower? Oh, ah," Shining Bird, acted surprised at the question. "Her story is a sad one. When we began our journey she was the wife of Dancing Otter. They had one child and another on the way at the time we met up with you in St. Louis."

Warm Stone nodded.

Shining Bird continued, "Our journey was so arduous that her only child died. She miscarried the other one. She suffered the loss terribly. The only one she had left was Dancing Otter."

"So where is he?" Warm Stone interrupted.

Shining Bird paused and swallowed as she recalled what happened to Dancing Otter. Then she went on, "He went with a scouting party to seek a way over the mountains. The group met up with several grizzly bears. One bear chased him a long way after clawing him up some. The other men in the group were able to rescue him after the grizzly lost interest."

Warm Stone put one foot up on a pack and learned forward, intrigued at this story.

"They brought him back on a travois," Shining Bird noted the interest and told the rest of the story. "Gray Wolf attended him. We think he had a heart attack from the terror of it all."

"Heart attack?" interrupted Warm Stone.

"Yes," said Shining Bird, "a heart attack can happen when the body or the mind or the nerves become so stressed that the heart speeds up in response to the issue and cannot work fast enough to serve the body. It seizes up and stops functioning. Gray Wolf was able to attend to the wounds of his body. But Dancing Otter had been so terrified by his encounter with that grizzly, Gray Wolf could do little to ease his mind, his heart or his terror. He continued to relive the terror in his mind. It filled his dreams. Blue Cornflower told us he woke up nearly every night screaming. Then one night he clutched his heart and died in her arms. She grieved for a long time, poor thing. She lost every one of her family. Except for the young teenaged girls, we have no other single woman among us. She's had quite a hard time of it."

Stunned by this news, Warm Stone did not speak. Finally he said, "I'm so sorry." He paused another moment to reflect, then he asked, "Then she is . . . alone?"

Heaving a long sigh, Shining Bird nodded sadly.

Warm Stone furrowed his brows and looked off into the direction Blue Cornflower had gone. Moments passed.

"She's too young and too beautiful to be alone," he said at last.

"You will make the map?" Shining Bird interrupted Warm Stone's reverie.

"Oh, yes, yes, indeed," Warm Stone said in a way that appeared he had something else on his mind. "I'll be sure to do it this afternoon."

The celebratory mood began slowly and grew. That day, as it wore on, became one day of feasting, music, and dancing. The People ate, and then ate some more. The little band of traders ate with The People, mixing in with them. Music played most of the day when the music makers were not eating.

By mid-afternoon, Warm Stone, as good as his word, had finished his map for me. With the small bundle under his arm, he began wandering among The People as if looking for someone. Avoiding the dancers, Warm Stone noticed a shelter with several women still puttering around outside cleaning up, putting away food left over. Strolling over with a confidence, he asked one of them which way to my shelter. One of the women stopped what she was doing and began pointing the way out to Warm Stone who was not looking in the direction she was pointing.

He had fixed his eyes on Blue Cornflower who had just stepped out of the shelter with breads she was intending to put on the serving table. When she saw Warm Stone, she hesitated a brief moment, looked down, stepped forward then looked up again at him directly. The other women saw an energy field develop between them. Feeling they were intruding upon a personal moment, they felt compelled to honor the couple, and they disappeared without a word.

Neither Blue Cornflower nor Warm Stone spoke. They just stood there looking at each other frozen in time. Suddenly aware of the moment, Warm Stone spoke softly, "Blue Cornflower."

"Yes," she replied.

"Blue Cornflower, which way to Gray Wolf's? I need to give him his map. I finished it just as I promised Shining Bird. I need to take it to him," he said.

"Gray Wolf's," she began to point, ". . . is, uh, that way."

Warm Stone did not turn to see which way she was pointing.

Blushing, she put down her breads, looked down again, and then looked back up again at him, smiled and said, "I'll take you there."

As the couple walked across the compound, many noticed them but said nothing. They all noticed others noticing. But the couple noticed nothing. Neither spoke until they reached my shelter.

"Gray Wolf, Shining Bird," Warm Stone calls out. We both step out into the late afternoon sun.

Warm Stone says formally, "Gray Wolf, I have your map for you. I promised Shining Bird, I would have it finished by the end of today . . . just in case I left tomorrow. I guess she didn't want me to leave and not have it done. So here it is." He hands it to me. Shining Bird says nothing.

I look at Warm Stone, hesitate then I say, "Okay, well, why don't we go over it again, so I know the route. Let's step over here and you can show me." We step aside and lay the deerskin down on the ground. The two of us kneel down and begin going over the map, engrossed in our conversation.

Shining Bird reaches for Blue Cornflower's hand, and holds it tenderly between her two hands. Shining Bird looks straight into the young woman's eyes saying nothing and everything.

Into the evening more of The People participated in the dancing around the huge fire they had built for the occasion. After having feasted all day on the game so deliciously prepared, and on the other complementary dishes, The People remained joyous.

Warm Stone found himself wandering over to the crowd and just stood there in contemplation. Then, his eyes landed on Blue Cornflower standing on the edge of the circle across from him. Not being able to restrain himself, he made his way through the crowd toward her.

When she saw him approaching her, she blushed, making her that much more attractive to him. When he finally reached her, he stood next to her. Finally he looked at her. She pretended for a few moments that he was not there. Finally she looked at him. At that, he took her by the hand and twirled her, then led her out on to the dance area. She could not help smiling. She found herself unable to hold back her delight. She smiled into his eyes at the endless surge of joy and belonging.

The music continued on into the night, but the two slipped off into the darkness. Even though The People noticed, they looked the other way smiling and winking to each other. This day and night was indeed one of celebration.

Because the previous night had not ended until late, the little settlement of The People found themselves feeling lazy the next day. While the sun had been up for several hours that late spring morning, The People cleaned up after the festivities by mid-day moving slowly.

The celebration needed to have happened, because it inspired and invigorated The People's spirits. Knowing we had a map built confidence for us in our future. The mountains no longer intimidated us. We also began packing in anticipation of moving forward on our journey. Many had already begun preparing supplies and food weeks before in anticipation of moving in some direction, not knowing where. Now it was time to go, and now we knew in which direction.

The little band of traders began assembling their packs in anticipation of traveling south to the Yellowstone area and the Grand Tetons assuming that Warm Stone was anxious to get back on schedule.

At about mid-day, Warm Stone joined the other traders. He kicked the dirt then folded and unfolded his arms. They all stopped packing and looked at him as if asking him what he was doing.

"I'm staying," he announced to their shock. "I've decided to lead them to the Bitterroots. I'm not sure they can make it without a guide."

"Why do you feel you must help these people?" one asked. "You have no ties to them. Moving so many people to the Bitterroot Mountains will be a challenge. It will be hard, not to mention slow."

Another one chimed in, "You don't owe these People anything. You already led them part way up the Missouri River. How much can they ask of you?"

"I owe them plenty," Warm Stone said. "And, they have never asked me for anything. Maybe I didn't tell you the story of when I was an apprentice trader with Turning Rabbit many years ago." They stop what they were doing to listen.

Warm Stone continued telling a tale that he had never told anyone before. "I feel strange thinking about it. I don't believe I've ever mentioned to you or anyone that I lived among these People for a season."

He stopped speaking, looked down at the ground then up at the sky, then spoke again, "It was about seventeen years ago. I was traveling with Turning Rabbit through some treacherous terrain. I fell and broke my leg. The bone was sticking out of my leg. Turning Rabbit did not leave me there, but made a travois for me and dragged me into the next village."

Pausing to get his emotions into check, he looked down at the ground again then went on, "It happened to be the very village that Gray Wolf and Shining Bird lived in. By the time we reached the village I was delirious with fever, because my leg had become infected. Turning Rabbit had done all he could to help me and was expecting me to die any day.

"After several days I regained consciousness in their Healing House. Their best healers attended me. Speaks With Plants kept giving me a tea or something ugly to drink, I remember. I was in and out of consciousness a lot.

"It all seems so vague to me . . . those days of healing. One thing I do remember is Shining Moon, an old Grandmother, who repaired my leg, reset the bone and wrapped it in a parfleche so it would heal right.

"They were all so kind to me. Turning Rabbit could not stay, so he took off promising to swing by that village on his way back from Canada and the east ocean. I needed that time to heal anyway. I ended up staying with Gray Wolf and his family.

"We became the best of friends. I recall the many things we did together during that summer."

"You mean you stayed with them for months?" asked one of the other traders. "Did they make you serve them or work for them? What did they ask for in return?"

"Nothing," Warm Stone said. "They asked for nothing in return. I could have left anytime. I didn't have to wait for Turning Rabbit to come by and pick me up on his way south. Of course, I contributed by assisting them with whatever they were doing, but they never asked for anything from me. One time I almost drowned in the river, diving for mussels. I would have died then also, had it not been for Gray Wolf rescuing me. So they actually saved my life twice.

"They saved my life twice, fed me, took me in, took care of me, . . . and never once did they ask for anything in return, nor ever even talked about it."

"I find that hard to believe," said one trader with skepticism. "I mean, they gave you a lot. According to your story, they gave you everything . . . and they never asked you for anything? Come on."

Nodding, Warm Stone said, "Yes, I know. It does sound incredible. Yet it is true. It's my observation that these People align themselves with what they call Great Spirit. I won't go into it, but they truly behave and treat each other like everyone was part of this Great Spirit of theirs. What do I owe them? A lot. In fact . . . everything.

"It's their dream, their vision, to get to the west ocean. I don't know what they will do once they get there. I'm sure they will figure it out. I think if I can get them to the Bitterroot Valley, then I can show them the trail that goes up and over the last range before the lands and rivers slope down to the coast."

"How long will that take?" asked another. "We could do it in a month or so as we can move pretty fast. They are an entire village. I can't imagine moving that many people, plus all their stuff over those passes. Even though you know the territory, it's still pretty rough country."

Clearly, this little band of traders did not like it that Warm Stone would not be traveling with them. He knew the land better than any one of them.

"My guess is, it should take me several months or more to get them to the Bitterroot Valley, maybe more," Warm Stone said. "All of you can go south as planned. I'll catch up with you by fall."

"Are you sure you want to do this thing?" asked another.

Warm Stone did not respond. He simply began sorting out his packs and moving them aside. Before all the traders had finished bundling up their goods, Warm Stone stood up and looked at each of them.

"You know," he began, "why don't I give you some of my trade goods to take with you? If you can trade them for something, then do so and give me the trade when I see you again. If you don't make a trade before I catch up with you, then you can return them to me later."

"Hold on there, Warm Stone," objected one of them, "you're talking like we will be meeting settlements to trade with near Yellowstone. No one lives there or anywhere around there. What are you thinking?"

"I don't know," replied Warm Stone in surprise. "Maybe I'm fooling myself on how long this trip could take."

He looked up blinking his eyes struggling to think. After a few moments, he looked at them and said, "I'm thinking it may take longer than a few months. On top of that, I hadn't counted on the time it will take me to meet up with you guys again."

"Uh-huh," one commented before turning away and bending over to complete his packing. They were not happy with Warm Stone's decision to travel with The People. Warm Stone then turned and walked away, not wanting to continue the conversation.

As Warm Stone walked through the camp, he could see nearly everyone preparing to break camp and move on. When he finally reached my shelter, he found me just returning there also from another direction.

"Come to say good-bye?" I ask with a smile on my face. Then I add, "I can't thank you enough, Warm Stone, for everything you have done for us. Because of the news you brought about the rest of our People, and by giving us a map, you single-handedly brought unity once again to us. No dissension exists now among us. We are all going forward on our vision quest. Thank you for what you have done for us."

Nodding in affirmation, Warm Stone, starts to speak, then pauses. He steps closer to me before saying, "Yes, and I've one more thing I will offer to you . . . . He pauses for effect. I just stand there looking directly at Warm Stone.

Warm Stone then says, "I will go with you."

"I will be your guide through the passes to the Bitterroots. I will take you to the Bitterroot Valley. From there you can catch the trail through the final pass to the down slope side. I'll even give you another map to get you to the coast."

Shocked and stunned, my face went blank, and I took several steps backward to catch myself from falling. This was not expected . . . at least by me. Recovering myself, I grabbed Warm Stone and hugged him. When I finally released my friend, I began another little dance that I accompanied with a muffled chant. At just that moment Shining Bird approached.

"Hello, Shining Bird," Warm Stone says in greeting.

"I see something is happening here," she says with a smile, "my husband is dancing. Must be good news. What is going on?" Tilting her head slightly to the left, she waits for an answer.

Caught in a moment of joy, I stop my dancing, turned to Shining Bird and put both of my hands on each of her shoulders. With the broadest smile, I announce, "Warm Stone just said he will be our guide through the passes around these mountains and some others, I can't remember which ones, so we will survive! We will make it!"

With that exclamation, I begin my little dance again.

Shining Bird smiles at Warm Stone and mouths the words to him, "thank you." Then she says, "I guess I must get my husband into the mood of work now that we know where we are going and have a guide to help get us there."

Blue Cornflower busied herself with getting her shelter disassembled for the move forward. As she was reaching up to take part of it down, suddenly two masculine arms reached up also to help. When she turned her head to see whom this man was who was helping her and standing very close to her, she found herself nose to nose with Warm Stone. When she looked into his eyes and smiled, she found herself being kissed. After a few kisses, she blushed and turned away. To her sense of shyness, this was too much information for the neighbors. She did not notice, but the neighbors politely looked away to give the two lovers a space to be in, in unconventional circumstances.

Six months passed as The People, led by Warm Stone, made our way around several mountain ranges, through passes and up into the Bitterroot Valley. By the time we arrived and set up camp, late summer was in full glory. Warm Stone and Blue Cornflower had shared a shelter during this trek. By the time we reached the camp where we would stay throughout the winter,

Blue Cornflower stood one late afternoon alone, near a stream where the water circled. Watching the water swirl around, she put her hand on each side of her slightly plump belly and smiled.

44

THE BLESSING

Relieved that our summer's trek was finally over, The People began making our camp in preparation for a winter's stay. We found a satisfactory site at the base of the eastern slope of the Bitterroot Mountains. Immediately, many, mostly women, began scouring the countryside for edible plants. Some men and women packed up their hunting weapons and went off in search of game. The rest stayed in camp and helped each other set up their shelters. Placement of each shelter and meeting space, central campfire and cooking area, were given careful consideration. Several days passed as The People settled in with a village atmosphere building around us.

After Warm Stone had finished setting up Blue Cornflower's shelter and seeing to it that she had everything she needed, he walked over to see me. As he approached our shelter, he saw that Shining Bird was busying herself with arranging the inside. She looked up to see Warm Stone at the entrance just after Star Rising and Dancing Swan brushed past me going out to help some others .

"Gray Wolf," Shining Bird says to get my attention. "Gray Wolf, we've got company."

"Oh, yes, Warm Stone," I stand up with a smile. "Come on in."

"Thank you, Gray Wolf," Warm Stone replies with a resistance in his tone. "Can we talk?"

I turn to look at Shining Bird a moment, turn back toward my friend, Warm Stone, and say, puzzled by the sense of awkwardness I am detecting, "Yeah, sure."

The two of us left the shelter and walked out into the meadow past the compound of shelters where most of The People, who were left in camp, were actively involved with completing the new camp. Few noticed the two of us wander off.

"Don't tell me what I think you are going to tell me, Warm Stone," I begin the conversation after we have walked far enough as to not be overheard.

"Gray Wolf, you know that I am a trader and cannot stay in one place too long," Warm Stone says. "Long ago, I stayed a season with your People because you were helping me. Now I've stayed a season with your People because I was helping you."

I frown and look at my friend. After another moment, I say, "Yes. The cycle is complete. When are you planning on leaving?"

"I'd like to leave right away, maybe at first light tomorrow. I've a long way to go before the snows catch up with me. I've prepared a map for you to cross over the Bitterroot Mountains. They are formidable, but once you get through them, you know that the way is west to the ocean."

Warm Stone put the map on the ground as before. And, as before, the two of us knelt down to study the map. Warm Stone pointed out the Clearwater River and where to pick up the Columbia River.

"The most challenging part is getting over and down from this range of mountains," he says, pointing to the Bitterroot Range. "After that, it's all downhill, so to speak," he smiles then becomes serious as he continues. "They can be very rough and steep in spots. I recommend that you send a small scouting party to visually and physically experience the terrain, make notes, ah, and one more thing."

Warm Stone pauses a moment to reflect on what he wanted to say. He looked up and around then back at me. I simply sat there unmoving and not wanting to breathe until I could hear the next recommendation.

Warm Stone resumes, "Because there are so many of you, I would have the scouting parties build stone piles along their route as they go. That way, everyone following the marked trail would know they were on the correct path. With so many People, it might be advisable to ensure everyone stays together in groups and that the leader of each group knows what direction to go."

At that I swallow hard.

Warm Stone continues, "This mountain range is challenging, even for a trader. So do everything you can to make sure everyone knows what he or she is supposed to do, where everyone is

The Blessing

supposed to meet at day's end. It is too easy for individuals to get lost and never be heard from again."

I nod in comprehension, the wrinkles in my forehead relax a bit after hearing Warm Stone's instructions.

Warm Stone goes on uninterrupted, while pointing to the map, "Up about here, you should find a nice place to make camp if you need to settle in for a short while." Still pointing he says, "Also, at about here, you should find some hot springs. I think The People would so enjoy a soak. But remember that is just the beginning of this trek, and I wouldn't want you to get too relaxed about moving forward." I nod as I bend down and study the map even more.

Warm Stone let me contemplate the map for as long as I needed to while still in each other's company. Then he says, "At the rate your People can travel, I'd say it should take you about a year to a year and a half to make it to the ocean, maybe longer. There are mountains here also," he adds pointing to the map, "but you can still follow the rivers to where you want to go. The Columbia River empties into the western ocean." Frowning again, I continue to study the map, asking more questions of Warm Stone.

We stayed out much longer than Shining Bird had been expecting. Sensing a shift of energy in the air, Shining Bird left the shelter and began walking through the camp to Blue Cornflower's shelter. As she did, a movement near the stream where the meadow opened up caught her attention.

Stopping to see just what it was that shifted her focus away from her destination, she moved her head from side to side, peering through the distance and the summer bloom of bushes downstream. Eventually she caught a glimpse of two young people romping, laughing, and chasing one another in play. Finally, she saw who they were.

"Oh," she said to herself with eyebrows raised, smiling inside and out. Shining Bird stepped a little lighter as she floated toward Blue Cornflower's shelter.

"Come in, Shining Bird," Blue Cornflower said in welcoming her visitor, "I'm so glad to see you."

At the invitation, Shining Bird stepped inside the shelter of this lovely young woman, whose face shone with happiness, while sitting on the ground stirring a pot of soup. "Do you see how nicely Warm Stone set this house up for me? He has made sure I have everything I need to make a home here for our winter camp."

"So when is your baby due?" blurted out Shining Bird, unable to hold back her sense of things in the intimacy of a woman's private conversations. Shining Bird remained standing, looking at Blue Cornflower, with her lips pursed, head tilted forward and eyebrows raised as a cue to announce she did not want any denial or false modesty to impede a declaration of truth.

"Spring," said Blue Cornflower with a broad smile.

Breaking into an equally broad smile, Shining Bird knelt down on her knees facing her friend with eyes tearing up in joy and affirmed, "What wonderful news!"

She grabbed Blue Cornflower's free hand and pressed it between both of hers still smiling. "We have the winter to prepare to get you set up for the trek across these mountains. We will also make sure we have set up adequate provisions to get us as far as we need to get before the summer is over again. But we've got time." They both giggled in anticipation of the joyful event.

As the two women continued their conversation, their male counterparts continued theirs until it grew too dark to see.

While walking back into the camp, I suggest to Warm Stone, "Why don't we talk with several of the others who I think would be helpful in organizing the scouting parties just to make sure they don't have any questions I can't answer after you leave?" Warm Stone agrees, and we head off toward one of the campfires already blazing.

Back at Blue Cornflower's shelter, Shining Bird stood about ready to move through the door as she thanked her hostess for the dish of soup and the conversation. As she stepped out into the bright moonlight, she turned back toward her pregnant friend and said, "You should see this moon. Come on out here and take a look. Sister Moon must be celebrating the coming of the new member of The People."

Unable to resist the invitation, Blue Cornflower climbed up out of her spot she had been occupying that evening and stepped outside too.

The Blessing

"My goodness," she declared with eyes opened wide and that smile still on her face. Feeling in awe of the moment, Shining Bird grabbed Blue Cornflower's hand and stepped out further away from the shadow of the trees surrounding the little shelter.

Then she said, "Let's go over to the water over there and feel this moment." As they walked in silence, Shining Bird wanted to ask one more question of her friend. "Just one more thing I'd like to ask you, if you don't mind," she said.

"Oh, ah, he's leaving," Blue Cornflower answered in anticipation of the yet unasked question. Shining Bird gave a nod in acknowledgement. Blue Cornflower continued, "Don't know when, exactly, but I suspect it will be pretty soon." She smiled again and commented, "The way he has worked so diligently to set me up here with everything, it was like he was screaming it without saying a word." They both laughed.

"He doesn't know, does he?" Shining Bird asked.

Shaking her head slowly from side to side, Blue Cornflower added, "No, and I have no intention of telling him either. He needs to go. He feels the pull to resume his trader life-style. He's been so good to me, I wouldn't want him to think he had to stay for me, and then resent it later." She paused to reflect on her feelings then continued. "I don't want to create that scenario. Besides he is leaving me with something I couldn't have gotten any other way . . . the gift of new life." Shining Bird looked at her as they walked and nodded in affirmation. Blue Cornflower went on, "Besides, my son will be the first baby born to The People in a long time. This is a tremendous blessing Warm Stone has bestowed upon us, in addition to leading us through these mountains and bringing us to this point. I would not ask him to give up one more thing for us. I have loved him, and will always continue to love him. His gift to us is continued life. My gift to him is the continuance of his life as a trader, his journey in this world."

"And, so it is," smiled Shining Bird as she spoke softly.

They approached a shallow bank of the river. The full moon was just above the distant horizon shining like a spotlight, lighting up the entire valley. They stood at the river's edge absorbing the breath-taking view of the moon over the backdrop of the mountains. Their minds quieted to hear Sister Moon speaking to the water.

As the two women stood there beside the eddying pool at the water's edge, they knew they stood on the brink of the sacred. A large turtle emerged on to a rock and faced them with a prayer of connectedness to Mother Earth. As they focused on the turtle, small waves murmured around it bathed in the light of Sister Moon. Fed by the energy of the prayer, particles of brilliant pure white light danced on the tops of the waves echoing the sacred energy enveloping the two women and the quickening new life. The two women remained transfixed at the sight and attuned their energies into the experience of witnessing both wave and particle existing in the same location. The experience expanded into constant strobes of light shining angelic poems into their hearts.

Unable to move away and in complete harmony with what they were witnessing, neither could take their eyes off the sacred vision unfolding before them. At the blending of energies, this constellation of living, sparkling lights reached out to them and caressed them from the ground up to their heads in a total embrace of celestial light.

45

EYE OF THE HAWK OVER THE BITTERROOTS

Several days later, Shining Bird still enjoyed the afterglow of her experience in the moonlight by the water with Blue Cornflower. The camp had been busy settling in our new winter grounds, building, gathering wood, and hunting. I noticed her unusual dreaminess of late. Because both of us had been preoccupied by the preparations for our winter stay, we had not communicated much until now. Our three offspring had left for the day, each off on their own errands. We found ourselves alone. Finally, I broke the silence while I brushed her hair early one morning.

"Warm Stone left," I begin. After not receiving a response from my beloved, I say, "He made me a map on buckskin before he left. It's sketchy, but it should take us all the way to the western ocean." I stop brushing her hair and tilt my head sideways to see if she is listening to me.

Shining Bird smiles her most luscious smile at me from her sideways position, only slightly tilting her head toward my awkward position. Her smile endears her to me all the more, but it was a look in her eyes of a faraway dream twinkling with promise that catches me off guard.

At this moment I know something is up. So I move and land on my knees directly in front of her. Opening my soul before her, I ask the question without saying a word. Shining Bird smiles again while looking directly into my eyes. Then she takes my hand in both of hers before speaking.

"It's the best news," she finally says with an even bigger smile than before and eyes twinkling. "Blue Cornflower is pregnant!"

I freeze in place. I lower my head a little and peer into her face prying for a validation of this most precious and heartening news. Shining Bird gives one long nod with eyes lowering as she does so. I stand up as if lifted by my eyes that had grown into saucers. I lose my balance and begin falling backward, but catch myself before I fall all the way over backwards. At that antic, we both break into hysterical laughter.

I put my hands to my mouth before finally saying, "I am speechless. No wonder you've been acting funny. You've bottled up this great news for several days now. I'll bet you were waiting for just the right moment to tell me. I just don't know what to say," I say almost breathless but happy.

"Let me just tell you what Blue Cornflower and I experienced several days ago. It's so potent, I feel confident about our future." Shining Bird says and then tells me about the event by the water and how both of them saw the eventuality of Warm Stone leaving and more.

After she finishes, I sit a moment in silence. Then I say, "All that makes sense to me when I put that with the recommendations Warm Stone gave me on the strategy of moving The People over the Bitterroot Mountains. Because the mountains are so treacherous, he gave me several ideas on how to make it to the other side and down and across with the least amount of loss and greatest amount of success."

I tell her about building stone cairns as way points and managing people in groups with runners to maintain communication between the groups. I tell her about sending out scouting parties before too much snow falls before winter, and again in the spring when the snow melts to set up a trail and blaze it for all of the groups to follow.

"Yes. It sounds like we will really need to get organized. I would suggest that we talk about this during the winter months around community campfires and so forth, so that by spring, everyone will know what he or she needs to do," says Shining

Bird. "This way each one of us will be clear on what each needs to do and what our part will be." I nod in agreement.

After a comfortable silence, I point upwards with a finger and say, "Oh, by the way . . ."

"Spring," says Shining Bird with a smile. "Perfect, isn't it?"

"Yes, that's when the little turtles come up out of the sand after they have hatched," I say wistfully remembering my vision and the promise.

Still lying in bed and with me before her, Shining Bird reaches for both of my hands with both of hers. I look at her quizzically.

"Ah, one more thing, my dearest beloved," she offers with a sly smile on her radiant face.

"Yes, my beloved," I hesitate unable to imagine what the next piece of news could be.

With eyebrows raised and the sly smile still on her face, Shining Bird wiggles in bed to get really comfortable but unable to keep her enthusiasm under cover while still lying on her stomach. "The day I met with Blue Cornflower, I couldn't help but notice two young people playing a kind of a hide and seek game in the large bushes downstream from her shelter."

I raise one eyebrow and hold my breath.

"I saw our son, Stalking Bear romping with Whispering Dove."

I suck in my breath.

I cannot breathe.

Finally, to break the spell, Shining Bird says, "What was that vision you had? You know the one about the little turtles and the falling stars?"

Choking air back into my lungs finally, I nod while coughing.

"Well, it's best we plan for our success as The People," I say finally.

"Yes, dear," Shining Bird says, "and I've already begun."

Bewildered at my wife's comment I ask, "You have?"

"Yes, in my quiet hours, I traveled into Mother Earth. We sat and talked about how important our continuance as The People depends upon our physical survival, especially during the last segment of this journey. We acknowledged each other as mothers and what our commonalities are. I recognized her power and her beauty. She recognized The People as always honoring her throughout our physical lives and for past countless generations. I honored her for her relationship with our Creator and she did the same for us. I honored her for having intentions in cooperation with Creator and those of us living upon her and for her making manifest those intentions in the overall effort to provide the environment necessary for the continuance of all of life.

"After a long conversation, I asked her for a very light winter this year in this place. I had overheard Warm Stone say how deep the snows can get here and how long they can sometimes last. She acknowledged this. In the end, however, she agreed to not only give us a light wintering of snow, but relatively mild temperatures so as to not pose a threat to The People and especially the new life on its way to us.

"She further offered to make available plenty of game to ensure our survival. She even said there may be more she can do. In return, we must always acknowledge her presence and recognize her as a force in our lives as long as we live on her. She also asked that in return The People acknowledge our oneness with Mother Earth and our oneness with Spirit so that we can maintain and continue in the Ways of Oneness. She said Great Spirit is her Creator as well as ours, and that we were meant to live in partnership."

Stunned, I find myself speechless again that morning.

Those in the scouting party, both men and women, readied themselves for their trek up the mountainside. We packed items and food for camping, anticipating a venture lasting several days at least. This was our initial exploration as a group to begin to familiarize ourselves with the way over the top. These mountains, both threatening and enthralling, appeared forbidding in their presentation.

Several small parties of individuals, both men and women, finally worked their way to a top ridge. Each group explored surrounding areas to see what path could be found or made that would present the least in the way of barriers and obstacles.

Several of us marched north along the ridge avoiding the steep slopes and making our way through or around stands of trees and rock outcroppings.

I had joined the explorers from the beginning. I wanted firsthand experience at what the landscape offered in the way of challenges to The People crossing the stalwart beauty of this range of mountains.

Several men, along with me, wandered even farther along the ridge. As we stood and gazed out across the lands in front of us, we could see more mountains, mountain ridge after ridge. We could not see mountains sloping down toward the west from where we stood that day. Silently we viewed this formidable elegance. Without speaking, the group I was with turned to leave to meet up with the other groups.

I remained standing there looking up to the sky where I spotted a gray hawk circling gracefully up and back calling out with each pass. With each circle, the magnificent bird of prey drew closer, and ever closer to where I was standing.

When the main body of explorers grouped together to return back to camp, they noticed that I was not among them. Someone offered to go back to see what was taking me so long to join them. Meanwhile the group lost no time in discussing their ideas for which path would be best and where the rock cairns should be built.

"I think we should build as many as we can before the snows come. That will give us a head start," one man offered.

"Right, but I think we should continue exploring the other side and down as far as we can go before then. I think we should build just as many cairns and blaze the trail as much as possible before the snows," one woman commented. "That way we can make the most of late spring and summer traveling."

"It looks like it could take us months to cross, so I think we need to choose where we should camp and where we should make sure to meet. That way we might not feel so lost," suggested one of the women.

Another man added, "That sounds good if we can before too much snow falls."

"If we could then, we could make the most of the good weather and be on the other side of this mountain range . . . maybe by summer . . . or at least by the end of summer," another said scratching his chin.

Meanwhile, I never let the soaring gray hawk out of my sight while I remained standing in the spot where my group had left me. Then the bird flew in boldly close. It hovered over me, eyes connecting, man and bird of prey, so close I felt the splendid bird could count my nose hairs.

Suddenly with a *whoosh*, I felt myself soaring over the mountains too. I looked down and saw with a clear eye the mountains sloping ever westward covered with tall trees. Within the eye of the hawk, I could see the streams, mountain passes, rivers, which rivers joined other rivers and the direction each one flowed in a maze of puzzle pieces all fitting together.

"He's not there!" yelled the man who went to find on me. "I tell you he's not there!"

"Gray Wolf couldn't be lost," emphatically remarked a woman in the group.

The group members just stood in disbelief.

"Maybe he's fallen and needs help. I'm sure he's not lost," commented another. "I say several of us go back to where we last saw him, spread out, and see if we can find him or find which direction he went. If he fell, or is hurt in some way, I'm sure we can find him." Several nodded and joined the posse, turning from the main group to see about rescuing their beloved shaman.

The afternoon sun glinted off the water as I could see the ever-widening rivers as I sailed west in the eye of the hawk. Soaring high and low, I made mental notes as to the exact landscape I was viewing. I witnessed which rivers joined the Columbia River that headed straight west. When I glimpsed the vast ocean, past the last mountain range near the coast, my heart leaped inside me. From there I also noted the mountain peaks that I remembered Warm Stone said smoked from time to time.

"I can't believe this. He was right here when we left," breathed one man heavily as the search party returned to the place where they had last seen me.
"Well, all right," ordered one, "Let's begin here and split up to look for him.

Returning back to the Bitterroot Mountain range, I made more mental notes as to which areas would be best for my People to make camp and to find our way down from the top. The countryside appeared rugged and almost impassable. Yet, somehow, because I could see from this vantage point, I knew we would find our way without getting lost among the differing draws and ridges carving the western sloping side of this breathtaking range of mountains.
When we returned, landing at the place where we started, I touched down and said, "Thank you, Gray Hawk. You showed me the ways we need to go to get over the mountains, down to the rivers, then on to the ocean. I am so very grateful. You have greatly blessed The People." With that, the gray hawk shrieked a responsive acknowledgement and flew off.

"It's getting late in the afternoon, we need to stop and re-group. We can't stay here until dark. We won't be able to see our way back," grumbled one of the searchers.
"We just can't go and leave him here," another objected, "it gets too cold at night up here, I suspect, this time of year to leave a man exposed without shelter."

THE CAMP OF GOD'S TEARS

"Yes, but we need to look after ourselves. This is treacherous country to be out and about in the dark of the night," resolved one.

"Some of us can make a camp here and begin again in the morning," suggested a woman.

"I think that is what we will have to do," confirmed another.

They all had turned, heads hanging low, hearts dragging, and had begun heading back to the meeting place of all the groups when they heard me call out to them, "Hey, wait for me."

Upon hearing my voice, they turn in surprise to see me, their beloved shaman. Almost out of breath, I stumble toward them, glad to see everyone.

"What happened? Where were you? Where did you go?" several ask questions all at once. I point to the sky, and do not answer.

We all walk single file back to the original group meeting place where all the rest of the explorers had reluctantly begun making a camp. Surprised to see everyone returning so soon and with me among them, questions appear on all of their faces, but no one speaks.

After a while of getting comfortable, I tell my tale of what I had experienced and witnessed in the eye of the hawk.

"It was like," I say, "being part of the All Seeing Eye, like being part of the Knowing."

Awed silence.

Finally one woman says, "Well, that gives us confidence to continue. The way has been shown to us, and we can go forth with not just our raw courage, but with *faith*," she lowers her voice as she says the word, "faith." "Courage has taken us this far, and combined with faith gives us confidence that we can know where we are going and how to get there. What a relief!" she says as she looks at everyone assuming everyone else would agree with her.

Everyone nods, still stunned by the story I had just told them.

Finally, one says, "I propose that some of us return to the village, and some of us go forward to see over the ridge at the top here and what direction we should go in from there." He then turns to me and asks, "Are you able to give us direction as to where to go from here? I think we should make the most of our time here before winter sets in, don't you think?" He looks around at the others as if he asked a rhetorical question.

"Sounds like a great idea," I say. "In fact, I think we should spend the night here, so that I can spend the rest of the afternoon making maps for us to follow. Shining Bird put some buckskin in my pack before my journey today. She must have known I'd need them . . . "

Grunts and other sounds of affirmation are made by the group members.

With that, many of the group members make camp in earnest, while I and several others work out maps first in the dirt then onto the buckskin for the way west.

46

A PROMISE

True to her word, Mother Earth granted a light wintering of snow for The People camped in the Bitterroot Valley near the point of crossing. Despite the fact that it was winter and that we camped in such a treacherous part of the country, The People thrived during that season. True to her word, Mother Earth provided The People with much game, resources and other foods so that our survival was guaranteed.

The new life growing inside Blue Cornflower was assured, not only a happy welcoming, but also, a place among the members as a promise for the continuance of The People. During this winter, the camp fairly hummed with hope and gratitude in the expectation of flourishing. We knew the upcoming journey over this mountain range would be the most physically challenging endeavor we had experienced thus far.

Coming up the Mississippi River and then along the Missouri River had been exhausting spiritually and draining emotionally as The People endured all the different aspects of the environment. That part of our journey west drained us physically as well, due to the years it took us to where we now find ourselves. That part of our journey drained us in one way or another of family members and many of our children.

Yet this new challenge brought with it hope for our future. With the new life on its way to us, and with the confidence inspired by my vision and maps, The People felt re-energized spiritually.

Many found themselves smiling as they went through their day. Each day The People prepared and stored food, tanned hides, and otherwise planned for the daunting task of overcoming the Bitterroots. However, many still harbored a measure of fear.

Fear seldom found its way into the hearts of this spiritually driven People, a People who claimed and knew of our oneness with Spirit. On clear late winter nights, as the grip of the season lessened, the Elders and others spent some time outside, searching the unknown, star gazing.

As a People who read the stars from time immemorial, this activity was a part of our usual routine. Yet, it was at this time that many marveled at the promise they kept seeing spoken to them through the stars.

"My heart is filled with a joy," commented one with eyebrows furrowed, "I feel a little hesitant about speaking the message I am getting."

"Yes," admitted another, "I feel the same way. How can we dare to hope for the manifestation of this promise?" Many nodded in agreement.

Shining Bird, cloaked in heavy winter furs, found herself drawn to the group of Elders that evening as she took her own late night stroll in contemplation. She had heard them talking as she approached.

"I see it, too," she commented.

Surprised by the voice behind them, the group members looked up. Those with their back to her approach turned to greet a beloved member. Others nodded and looked up at her as she took a place among them.

"Yes," she began, "I see it too. It is a promise, no doubt about it."

Many nod.

Silence.

"In my mind's eye," one began, "I see a shower of stars, stars falling. What does that mean?"

"I'm not sure what it means, but I feel it portends a significant event that is a promise to us," announced Shining Bird. "Oh," Shining Bird emitted a sound that startled her as she then blinked through a message only she could hear. The circle of Elders remained silent but turned to look at her expecting an announcement.

Breathing.

Silence.

Breathing.

Blinking again, Shining Bird spoke softly, "Oh my, yes, indeed, a promise."

Still, more silence.

All eyes remained on Shining Bird. They witnessed her eyes tear up and her mouth move into a smile, then not a smile.

"Oh, my," she croaked out, "I see, yes, a promise." By this time everyone unfroze and began shifting their weight in their sitting positions, wanting to ask, wanting to hear, but not speaking, waiting politely for her to share with them her vision.

Nodding to each of them before she spoke, Shining Bird began, "Yes, indeed, a promise is given to us and to them."

Just who the "them" was that she referred to suddenly arose as a mystery to her listeners.

"The stars will announce it. They will also announce a fulfillment of a promise after we complete our trek over these mountains."

Murmurings.

"I was shown, that not only do we have a baby on the way to us, but I heard in the whispering of a dove, another is on its way to us . . . and they are promised to each other."

Gasps.

Smiles.

"By this time next year, we will be able to smell the nearness of our destination. It will be near the smoking mountain on a river near the great western ocean. Our destination will be where the ground can shake, but with cool breezes off the coast, with plenty of fish in the river, and game in the mountains. I see a winter camp and a summer camp with two small children at play. Those two children are our destiny. Our People will grow from them, and they will lead us into our future." Shining Bird finished with a smile.

With winter showing signs of passing, The People's hearts lifted gradually not unlike the new dawn as the sun warms the land slowly as it rises in the eastern horizon on cold mornings. Shining Bird, ever sensitive to the comings and goings of her People, could not ignore another shift as it etched it way towards her attention.

Blue Cornflower was by now only a month or more away from delivering her baby. The entire camp had over the winter ensured her comfort and health by ever vigilantly bringing her food and other items of necessity. Remembering the whispered promise of that one night outside with the Elders and the star-gazing they participated in, Shining Bird suddenly felt a specific thought, an unexpected knowing as she made her way down to Blue Cornflower's shelter.

"Hello, the house," called out Shining Bird as she came close to Blue Cornflower's abode.

"I'm over here, Shining Bird," responded Blue Cornflower near the grouping of trees standing between her home and the river. It was those same trees that the two women had walked by when they both experienced the blessing by the water's edge months ago. Through the snow, Blue Cornflower had created a well-worn path between her shelter and the stream created by her frequent trips to the water.

"I brought you some soup," said Shining Bird, initiating the conversation.

"Oh, thanks," Blue Cornflower responded. "Why don't you set it inside and come out with me. I feel the need for a walk and some fresh air." After doing so, Shining Bird quickly joined her friend. The two woman chatted enjoyably for a while before the conversation turned to giving birth and how several other women in the camp were preparing what they felt would be needed to assist the new member into the world.

Then suddenly Shining Bird grabbed Blue Cornflower's arm while looking off in the distance.

"What?" Blue Cornflower inquired looking around. She looked into the direction that Shining Bird was looking. "Oh, yeah, they've been keeping company. I've noticed Stalking Bear and Whispering Dove several times, walking, talking, kissing," Blue Cornflower smiled.

Taking in a deep breath and letting out a loud sigh, Shining Bird turned to her friend with a big smile on her face.

A Promise

"I suspected so," announced Shining Bird. "I suspected it last summer. Well, finally, the promise is coming to pass." Across the expanse of snow-covered meadow, she concentrated her focus on Whispering Dove's figure and the energy field around her.

Later, on an errand to somewhere else, Shining Bird encountered Whispering Dove on a narrow path away from the compound of shelters.

"Hello, my daughter," Shining Bird greeted the young woman who blushed at the surprise meeting. "I'm delighted to see you." Blushing again, Whispering Dove looked down, then up again, with a smile, not really knowing what to say.

"So, my daughter," Shining Bird pursued, "when are you due?"

With mouth dropping open and eyes opening wide by the unanticipated query, Whispering Dove, stammered and blushed again.

"I don't know what to say. I don't know how to answer," she replied feeling ever so awkward.

"Never mind, sweet daughter," assured Shining Bird. Then she circled her right arm around Whispering Dove's shoulders and whispered into her ear, "We are all one family. Our camp is small. It is hard to keep these kinds of secrets close especially when I am so very connected with the stars and Great Spirit."

Weeping in relief, Whispering Dove, wiped away tears from her cheek, looked up at Shining Bird and smiled broadly. Then she said, "I didn't know how to tell you, or when to tell you. Everyone is gearing up for the climb over these mountains, and I can feel the tension as we all prepare for it . . . I just didn't want to be one more burden to The People." Then she added shyly, "I didn't know what to do."

"Well, my daughter, your news is the best news we can possibly have," exclaimed Shining Bird. "Well, my dear, the child you are carrying is a fulfillment of a prophecy. Your daughter will direct The People to their destiny. You bring such a blessing to us. Your baby comes to The People with such significance that it is unimaginable. She comes with a promise." She paused before going on then asked again, "So, when are you due?"

"Fall, I think."

Lifting her head back a moment and looking up to the ethers, Shining Bird then looked down at her new relative and said, "Ah, good. We should be on the other side of these ranges by fall."

After another pause, Shining Bird said with a big smile, "I'm bursting with so much joy, I feel like I want to dance." At that last remark, both women laughed out loud.

The two women continued to talk on their way back to Shining Bird's shelter. As they walked, Shining Bird said, "You know, dear, we do owe it to everyone to let them know right away. It's not about making an announcement, but about allowing us time to make any special preparations for bringing a pregnant woman up and down the treacherous terrain that we expect to encounter . . . and more.

"We will all do everything we can to ensure you don't lose the baby on the way. Heaven knows just how many unborn babies we lost just getting here . . . despite our best efforts, that is." She stopped briefly for a thought and then added, "For those women who were even able to conceive. So many women, you know, stopped having menses due to the rigors of our journey. With this trek coming up, no telling how long it will be before our women will be able to conceive again." Looking at her new daughter, she smiled again, and finished, ". . . and that's another reason why your baby is so special! With two babies on the way, we know we will continue as The People. Between your daughter and Blue Cornflower's son, between the two, they will seal the fate of The People."

"What do you mean, mother?" Whispering Dove asked.

"When we left Ohio and the village near the Great Serpent, tens of thousands either went with us or followed us. We migrated from what had been our home for a thousand years or even longer . . . maybe even longer than that. Mother Earth promised us that as long as we stayed there, she would provide for us. Life was easy, and fun, and well, without worry or stress of any kind. No one wanted for anything. We were so prosperous that anything other than total prosperity was an unknown. Warm Stone told Gray Wolf that it wasn't a migration, but an exodus of The People."

"So what happened? I think I was too little to remember much," Whispering Dove prompted.

"No one certainly intended, or even imagined, for that matter, for our leaving to be quite the exodus it turned out to be." Whispering Dove turned her head to listen for more as Shining Bird continued, "Not everyone left. Some stayed. Yet, according to Warm Stone, those remaining there were not able to keep the culture . . . uh . . . to keep our ways, that is, our sense of being the Children of the Law of One.

"So, if true, then we took our sense of belonging in the Oneness of the One with us, and we are all that is left of The People," Shining Bird observed softly. Then she added, "The implication is, of course," she peers into Whispering Dove's eyes deeply to burn the message into the pregnant woman's soul, "that your baby and Blue Cornflower's baby represent The People continuing on for *future generations*. They represent the last of a culture, the last of our ways, and the last of The People . . . the last of the Children of the Law of One."

Whispering Dove gulped and said, "I see."

Spring came early that year. The People felt anxious to move on. Several scouting parties ventured up the mountain to see just how far they could get before the melting snow stopped them. While there, they searched for our stone cairns and other markings to affirm we would be able to see them and not lose our way when the entire camp traveled over these mountains. They made sure to mark sources of water and camping spots. Moving nearly two hundred people through these mon-strous mountains with one pregnant woman and one woman with an infant felt like a gargantuan undertaking, one of monumental proportions. Yet we as pioneers, as it were, felt up to the task.

Each time an exploring group returned, they brought with them an excitement that generated more enthusiasm among those who stayed in camp.

At one of the debriefings after everyone had a say, I suggest, "What we will need is for one small group of us to go straight through to the other side. When you get there, search for a place to camp suitable for our entire clan to settle for a little while. We will need to recoup and rest before moving beyond that. Besides, we don't know how much of summer we will have at the end when everyone comes together again. Since we will be moving in small groups, of about twenty or so each, we don't really know how long it will take for the last group to make it through."

Many nod in agreement.

"Also," I add, "we don't know if we will have to spend a winter there. I suspect so. If I'm correct in my judgment about this, then that group and the first to arrive will need to begin to prepare for the rest of us spending the winter there."

". . . And we should be having another baby about then," says one of the women explorers. Many nod in agreement and murmur among themselves.

Long after I left the session, those engaged in the exploring tasks gave and accepted assignments in the effort of organizing for success.

One misty, moist morn, when the newly arriving geese could be seen on the ponds and at river's edge, women working in silent support could be heard only through their whispered thoughts as several of them attended the first birthing of a new clan member in recent years.

The cry of a newborn echoed through the camp and sent its own announcement to the Heavens that the baby boy had arrived safely and in good health. For a number of days after, different women could be seen coming in and out of Blue Cornflower's home. One usually stayed the night to keep the hearth fires burning for mother and child as often cold temperatures still accompanied the spring nights.

After several weeks, Blue Cornflower, finally alone with her son, wrapped him up in furs to walk out into the warm spring sunshine.

A Promise

Stopping to deeply breathe in the delicious fresh mountain air with sunshine on her face, she heaved a great sigh. Feeling like her entire body was a smile, she looked at her son in her arms and just felt love passing between them.

". . . And what will I call you, my son?" she asked aloud. Carefully moving down her well-trodden path toward the river, Blue Cornflower felt herself connecting with Spirit as a wave of energy washed over her. She felt tears of joy running down her face interrupted only by her smile. She stood at the rim of the eddy where she and Shining Bird had stood only six months earlier. Unable to speak, no words could contain or express her powerful feelings of connectedness, so she just stood there silently holding her infant.

At first she did not notice them as they struggled for life, for air, for being. They wriggled out of the wet sand, waves beckoning them to the water. Crawling down the sanded beach they emerged full-fledged to, not just survive, but to take on the world on the world's terms. Dozens of little turtles engaged life alone and in numbers as they made their way into the water.

Finally pulling back into the here and now, Blue Cornflower looked down and admired the little turtles making their way into the world as was their custom every year at this time. Taken aback by the tenacity of these small creatures and their obvious courage to move in their own direction, she grinned at her son.

"Ah, I know what I will call you, my son," she murmured quietly. "I shall call you, Little Turtle."

Over six months of travail awarded The People with a successful crossing of a most formidable mountain range. Due to our planning, forethought, and organization, the entire clan renewed our community at our new winter camp on the western side of the Bitterroots. We experienced only mild mishaps with no one getting killed or receiving a major injury.

Fall definitely made its presence felt by the end of our sojourn. Preparations were underway, so we could see ourselves through our last winter before reaching the coast. New edible plants were discovered and harvested. Game meat filled our boiling pots and drying racks. We built some new shelters while waiting for everyone to reach our wintering destination.

With babe in arms, Blue Cornflower made it as well. The expectant mother, Whispering Dove, slowed the procession somewhat. But when she arrived at last, everyone in the new camp cheered. The new life was indeed welcomed heartily in this new land. The People felt shielded by the formidable mountain range now to the east, a barrier against the visions that prompted the journey in the first place.

We felt in this place that we were on the edge of our new beginning.

During the time of Little Turtle's infancy, and the settling in at our new camp site, all remained ever watchful in anticipation of the arrival of another promised child. During a particular night the Elders watched the night skies . . . waiting.

In the middle of the night, the sharp cry of a newborn baby girl echoed through the camp, signaling the sudden explosion of brilliant stars sweeping across the black canvas above them. The meteor shower streaked through the heavens like a brilliant explosion of lights with several dropping down to Earth just overhead, melting into the atmosphere as they fell. The Elders remembered the promise.

Falling stars on that night assured the perpetuity of our People, the continuance of our ancient knowledge, and our identity. The baby girl born that night came with a Promise. She would be known as *"The One for Whom the Stars Fell."*

47

FALLING STAR AND LITTLE TURTLE

The People had struggled to face the many challenges experienced on this long journey. Many of the older ones had walked on into Spirit even as they approached the western ocean. A new generation had grown up while on this journey. Those few who had left Ohio as children, and who had survived the trek, were now young adults. This generation, only a handful of individuals, could barely remember the material comforts and ease of living in the lands now abandoned.

Having reached our destination, the Pacific Ocean, the remnants of a now forgotten civilization set out to explore our new home. We found the Columbia River reassuring as it flowed westward into the ocean. Camping north of it, The People felt the presence of the river itself gave us a sense of nostalgia, reminiscent of the Ohio River that also flowed westward.

After several seasons we found that wintering close to the coast made survival easier to manage, especially taking into account the heavy snows that the higher elevations experienced. Yet, after years of travel and again nostalgic for forests and abundant game, we also found that summering in the treed slopes of the mountains much to our liking, especially within the vicinity of Mt. St. Helens.

As a result, we resigned ourselves to a pattern of spending winters nearer the waters, and making summer camp in the mountains. It took several years to settle in to a routine and a sense of balance, with no real threat to survival. Yet new babies still did not come to join The People as soon as we would have liked. For a long while Little Turtle and Falling Star were the only children. Later after a time, additional babies joined The People.

THE CAMP OF GOD'S TEARS

Falling Star and Little Turtle played together as children. The Elders watched them and nodded knowingly to each other, remembering the promise. As childhood faded with physical growth, they played while working at their group tasks inseparable from each other.

Each year the Elders watched the phases of the moon, seeking guidance from Spirit as to when to move to our summer quarters. We also watched for when the last spring frost would come and for when to plant our summer crops in the rich mountain soil. This was especially important living in the high country. The seasons dictated our movements toward rivers, beaches and surf during winter, and toward pined mountain meadows during summer, and the forest migrations between.

Only a generation before, The People had lived in the Ohio River Valley. Our villages had traded seeds with other villages, some from great distances. Over time each village shared seeds of the best strains of each crop, so prosperous village crops were assured, despite the vast storehouse of foodstuffs maintained at Baum and Gartner. Corn, may grass, pigweed, knotweed, goosefoot, sumpweed, sunflower, kidney bean, march elder, gourds and squash grew successfully. Some crops had their own field while others were planted together. Those experienced in raising each crop oversaw the care and tending as spring turned to summer and summer to harvest time in the fall.

In present time of the high mountain country, native plants of the meadowlands, especially near springs, competed with demands from The People for crop cultivation. Unfortunately, The People summering in the mountains discovered that not all of our favorite crops produced or survived at the high elevations and shorter growing season. As a result some of the cultivated areas were left to return to their natural state.

Summer in the high country afforded splendid varieties of wildflowers that were plentiful in the meadowed areas lavishly painting the landscape. A variety of naturally-occurring wild berry patches flourished on the edges of the abandoned disturbed soil near the forest's edge, delighting both man and beast.

Early one morning Falling Star and Little Turtle joined the younger children, their mothers and grandmothers to begin the day's task. They all came with baskets to bring back berries that grew past the fields near the creek at the edge of the tall pines. As the little band moved in their intended direction, many joked or gossiped in twos or threes along the way. Some children ran ahead laughing, while some straggled behind.

Little Turtle felt displaced being older than the pack of children he was grouped with. He stood at least a head above or more than even the next oldest. His sense of maturing masculinity in his adolescence had already alerted him to his physical development, sensitizing him to his need to not be classed with the other children. Falling behind the group, his attention riveted on Falling Star. He eyed the way she moved beneath her buckskin dress, the rounding of her hips, the protrusions growing on her chest. He loved watching her throw her head back with laughter as she stole a glance in his direction.

Compelled to pull away from the group, Little Turtle let them round the next bend without him so he could sneak away. Unnoticed he bounded up the hill utilizing his growing strength as if to shed childhood and breathe the air of adulthood. Of course no ceremony of The People had officially recognized him as a man yet. Feeling impatient with the betwixt and between stage, Little Turtle remained frustrated with his social status. His thoughts shifted to Falling Star as he hiked in the general direction of the berry patches.

On his way there the fragrance of the many wildflowers, the mix of colors and patterns, caught his attention. He was struck by their beauty and placement. Gathering many different wildflowers, Little Turtle compulsively began weaving them together. Unconsciously yet by design, he had fashioned them into a necklace. Finally catching up to the berry pickers, he approached Falling Star with the necklace behind his back.

"Little Turtle, what are you hiding behind your back? And why are you walking so funny with that big smile on your face?" said Falling Star. Little Turtle blushed.

"Falling Star, I have made something for you and I hope you like it." From behind his back he produced the flower necklace. Her face brightened as she accepted the intent and meaning behind the gift.

They had been close friends since they were babies together. He was a part of her soul. Her sense of self included him as part of who she was. The promise that they would be together forever vaguely whispered itself in the back reaches of her mind. And yes, stirrings in her body caught her attention when she was with him. However, this was the first time Little Turtle gifted her with a physical demonstration of his feelings toward her.

Gently he lifted the garland over her head placing it delicately around her neck. As he did so, Falling Star extended her arm toward him, laying her hand on his chest over his heart. Energy surged between them. Surprised by this reaction, his heart leaped up to grasp the hand that awakened it.

At the same time he felt his emerging manhood swell. It had taken weeks for him to build up enough courage to show his new feelings toward her, and now he was floating. After what seemed like eons of time, each stepped back and staggered to regain their balance. Her eyes focused on him. Nothing else in the universe existed beyond him. Little Turtle's sense of self expanded at the realization of the moment.

"This is the most wonderful gift. Thank you, Little Turtle. I have a gift for you too, but I was not sure how to give it to you, and . . . " From her pouch she selected a small effigy of a bear that she had carved from a piece of stone. Little Turtle's eyes widened as she placed it in his hand. "I had a dream about you, Little Turtle. The spirit of the bear is your spirit guide." His dream about a bear occurred frequently but the understanding, the meaning of the dream, eluded him. Little Turtle stood speechless.

"Are you alright Little Turtle?" Falling Star asked.

"Yes!!!" he announced emphatically. "This is very special to me. I will get a leather cord and wear it around my neck." Lost in the joy of the moment, they reached for each other hugging tightly.

"Hey, what are you kids doing over there? It's time to go to work," yelled one of the Grandmothers. She had been watching them and remembered the gift from her future husband when the two of them were at about the same age. He had recently walked on to Spirit. The Grandmother's heart endorsed the joy of the young ones.

At that comment from the Grandmother, Little Turtle backed away still facing Falling Star. He spun around on one foot heading off in the opposite direction like he knew where he was going. As he left, Falling Star touched the flower necklace lying over her heart all the while hoping he would turn around and look back at her before disappearing into the trees near the stream. He did. She knew at that moment that she was in love.

While some were working on one side of the berry patch, Falling Star followed a Grandmother and other children around to the opposite side of the berry patch where more blackberries were ready for harvesting. Although it was still early and cool, the day would be getting warm and there was much to do.

When she got there many baskets had already been filled and were lying in the shade. Falling Star picked up an empty basket and began to gather berries, but her heart was across the creek with Little Turtle.

Large and dense was the berry patch. She could hear the women talking, telling stories, and laughing as they picked, lifted, shuffled, arranged, organized baskets of berries, as well as generally sorting out children. Women socialized while they worked. With the many tasks mothers and Grandmothers were called on to do that demanded constant attention all day long, the women found little time to sit and visit. Events such as this one enabled them to move around, position themselves close to a friend to tell tales or share other vital information while still getting the job done. Berry picking was a happy time for the group, almost festive in nature.

Then, without warning from behind and between two thick stands of berry bushes a giant grizzly bear reared up on his hind legs roaring menacingly, berry dyed saliva dripping from huge fangs. Then like an instant blizzard freezing all who had once been playing and working in the warm summer sun, fear seized them. Only the roar of the monster was heard above the shrieking silence.

The bear dropped down on all fours and headed for several children just down the hill. Once again he stood on his hind legs now very close to the children who remained rigid in petrified panic as he continued his roaring threatening their survival.

Male grizzly bears were known for killing their own offspring.

Seeing and hearing the bear so close to the children, Little Turtle moved out from behind a promontory rock and then roared at the bear himself. This distraction shifted the grizzly's attention away from the children. Little Turtle grabbed a large rock and leaped across the stream and ran directly at the bear. He threw the rock at the bear as hard as he could. Everyone remained frozen in silence.

A baby's cry sliced the landscape like a bolt of lightning. The cry triggered Falling Star into action. Mother bear energy awakened in Falling Star and was now streaming through her veins. With deliberate speed she made her way around the others toward the monster grizzly. Smaller mother grizzly bears will attack a large male in defense of her cubs and win. The same energy coursed through Falling Star to protect her People in the same way as a mother grizzly . . . fearlessly.

Little Turtle's thrown rock hit the center of the bear's chest. The bear was stunned but quickly recovered. He became more aggressive and fell to all fours moving closer to the children and Little Turtle. Little Turtle placed himself between the children and the bear. Searching for another large rock, he stumbled and fell backward just yards from the approaching bear. The bear leaped forward.

Little Turtle, lying on the downhill slope, looked up at the bear coming at him. All he could do was roll to the right to try and get away.

The right paw of the bear slashed his upper left arm leaving three deep gashes. Little Turtle cried out in pain as blood spurted up in all directions. He looked up helplessly at the bear as if it would be the last thing he would see before he died.

Then . . . without warning the bear stopped cold and backed off.

Little Turtle suddenly was aware of Falling Star standing beside him. She had raised her right arm, her hand flattened in greeting. She spoke no words aloud but directed her thoughts to the bear, "Sorry we startled you Brother Bear. We honor you and your spirit. These are your berries too. We all wish to go in peace."

Brother Bear shook his head, snorted, slowly turned and walked back into the forest. All witnesses recalled what had happened, but later each interpreted the event differently.

The mothers and Grandmothers rushed over to sooth the children and to gather them up. Little Turtle's wounds were deep. He saw Falling Star standing at his side. She helped him up. He was shaky and weak as he began going into shock. No words were spoken between them. None were necessary.

Little Turtle became faint, and then lost consciousness. Several of the stronger women had approached and wrapped their arms around him and managed him back to the village.

In all the confusion, Falling Star was forgotten. She was last seen walking back into the forest.

48

FALLING STAR AND MARK OF THE BEAR

"So they call you Falling Star?" asked Great Bear.

"Yes," Falling Star replied.

Great Bear continued, "In our memories from a time long ago humans and animals spoke to one another."

Falling Star said, "Yes, Brother Bear, that is also in our legends of the First World. Thank you for what you said to me before you left. I am learning that I have many gifts. Spirit showed me what you saw through your eyes. I knew that you were startled. You had been sleeping after eating your berries. Our laughter and talking awoke you. When Little Turtle hit you with the rock, you felt attacked and reacted accordingly. All you said to me was – *'I understand.'* But no words were spoken between us, then or even now."

Great Bear answered, "This is the way it used to be. I did not know that you had heard me."

Responding, Falling Star went on, "The People honor the spirit of the bear. Our legends speak of your great power and medicine. We have special ceremonies honoring you as part of Mother Earth. We have carvings, drawings and stories that remind us of your strength and power.

"We celebrate the connectedness with all life forms. We are one with Mother Earth. We are one with Great Spirit. You and I are one. You know this and I know this. I'm not sure every one of The People remember the Oneness with all of Earth and all life existing as part of the Earth. Some, I think, feel disconnected, separate from all that is. Would you be willing to show our Oneness by honoring our village with a visit?"

Great Bear pondered this request, "If I walk into your village would all The People remember our Oneness? Would I not strike fear to the hearts and minds of those who do not feel the total connectedness with all of life?"

After a few moments of pondering the issue, Great Bear said, "I know The People are kind as I have watched your village for a long time. Perhaps if you rode on my back into the village, this would show the Oneness that we both feel now and know as the Way."

Moved with joy and gratitude, a tear ran down her shining face. Stretching out her hand to touch the side of his neck, and with a warm smile, she replied, "Our Elders would be honored to speak to you though me. Yes, I would be privileged to ride on your back." And so it was.

Falling Star climbed on his back gently rubbing his ears and neck. Not since the First World was anything like this known to have happened in the memory of The People.

Mother Earth rejoiced at the union of spirits and minds. Falling Star was aware only of the Oneness she was experiencing while with the bear. Hands nestled in his thick fur, she sat upright, body undulating in a oneness with his as he lumbered out of the forest toward the little valley where The People villaged in their summer camp.

As earthy of an experience as this was for her, Falling Star could barely feel her body as if in a total celestial state of being. The light projecting through her informed her of the journey in this lifetime she chose and was chosen by Heaven to fulfill. She willingly accepted with serenity and a clear sense of direction, but without seeing the steps or challenges that would present to her along the way.

As Brother Bear walked through the forest, they spoke without words of many things, all of life and how everything and everyone were all part of a larger scheme. They indulged themselves in affirmations that to hurt another means to hurt oneself, that to help others means to help ourselves. They spoke of Mother Earth, how intelligent she is and how she expresses life by producing the various landscapes and creatures, expressing life on life's terms. They each affirmed that the Great Mother and all her expressions must be honored as part of the Great All. They spoke of the continuity of all living things both on Earth and beyond.

Falling Star knew these things intuitively, yet the conversation reminded her of what she knew as well as the meaning behind all the stories I had, as her grandfather, told her by way of instruction.

When they came to the place where the events of the early morning had occurred, Brother Bear said, "I hope that Little Turtle is going to be all right. Fear is such a blinding emotion. He was afraid at my actions. Fear serves to separate us from the All. Since he and I were not able to communicate, fear dictated the actions. This day will be remembered." Falling Star shared the bear's vision.

They were now just outside the village. A handful of men posted themselves in view of the entrance to their encampment. Feeling somewhat unsure of the morning's event and a little shaky as to the meaning of it, they nervously paced, fondled their weapons without purpose, but held them close just the same.

Someone shouted, "It's the bear. The bear is coming." Bodies alerted, weapons poised, and bows drawn. Several hunters carrying deadly flint spears ran to vantage points where they could attack the bear in a crossfire if need be. Great Bear was now just outside the effective range of the arrows.

Two Feather's shouted, "Don't shoot. Falling Star is riding on the bear!"

Disbelief gripped them all.

Unable to hold their weapons in readiness and maintain an attack stance, they let their weapons drop. The guardians gradually shifted from their positions of defense to moving curiously closer yet within a safe distance, so they could absorb as much of this unbelievable event as possible.

As the grizzly passed through the invisible boundaries of the settlement, some of the men who were slightly more wary than the rest remained on guard in a defensive posture. Despite the fact that light projected from Falling Star, and she appeared comfortable and at one with the bear, they did not trust the experience they were witnessing.

Within the settlement, Tall Swan attended to Little Turtle's wounds. The Elders, family members and most of the village had gathered in a big circle around him. They saw him as a very brave and courageous young man, no longer a child. The Elders gave him special acknowledgement for being fearless in the face of the enormous icon of strength, the grizzly bear.

After all, Little Turtle had placed himself between the bear and the children, an intention of courage and protection for those who were vulnerable at the risk of injury to himself. His mother, Blue Cornflower, was very proud, unable to hold back a constant smile. She basked in the great honor that was bestowed on him and her.

An Elder spoke, "Little Turtle, you have shown yourself to be of great spirit. As your wounds heal, there will be three scars on your upper left arm. This is very powerful medicine. You are now seen as a man among The People. You will now be known as Mark of the Bear."

Little Turtle, now Mark of the Bear, was unable to hold back his pride. He celebrated the defining moment of his rite of passage into adulthood with a big grin on his face.

This had been quite a morning for Little Turtle. It was now close to noon. The medicines, teas and healing foods that he had been so lovingly provided had eased the pain. He was feeling stronger.

Memory of his dream about a bear stirred up from the back of his mind. Now the dream was starting to make sense. In one dream he was in the middle of the village and everyone was gathered around him listening to what he was saying and paying great attention to him. As Little Turtle this made no sense to him. But as Mark of the Bear it made all the sense in the world. Being a leader of his people now appeared destined.

Mark of the Bear's chest inflated with his new status as a result of all the recognition and praise. His sense of himself enlarged even more. He felt invincible. He was now a very important person. After all, his vision had come true. He was being admired, honored and clearly on a path to leadership of The People. His life had now changed by this one event.

"Bear . . . bear in camp!"

People on the outer edge of the village cried loudly, "Bear!" Bear!" to announce that a bear was entering their camp.

While Mark of the Bear could not see the bear, he knew that this was the same bear that attacked him this morning. He felt it was up to him to kill the bear. Despite his recent wounds and still a bit woozy, he jumped up, ran out of the shelter looking for a weapon. He spied a long spear propped up against a shelter. Grabbing the spear, he thought that since the rock had hit its target and had made the bear turn and leave, the spear would hit its mark and kill the bear. He was ready. His personal sense of destiny was coming true sooner than he anticipated.

As he moved toward the crowd with his spear, he failed to notice the shouts of alarm had shifted to murmurings of wonderment at the sight of Falling Star riding the Great Bear.

As Mark of the Bear marched into the crowd, with his own ferocious intent and spear ready to thrust, the crowd parted. People drew in their breaths, freezing their lungs to prevent exhaling, eyes widened, aghast at the opposition of forces clearly playing out before them.

Mark of the Bear felt he could easily run through the crowd and slay the bear single handedly *right in front of everyone*. His heart was pounding with pride. Twice in one day, he had been given the opportunity to show how brave, courageous and powerful he was. He felt now ready to launch the spear into the heart of the bear. He cleared the last group of people . . . and halted dead in his tracks.

He could not believe what he was seeing. His body went numb. His mind raced in confusion. His heart was split in two. For a few moments he wanted to turn back to "Little Turtle" again. His entire being asked silently, "How could she *do* this to me?"

Falling Star rode into the village on the back of the bear.

All that he had done that morning, all the pride and power that had surged through his body vanished in an instant. He asked himself repeatedly, "How dare she do something like this to me, especially in front of the entire village?"

After what seemed like an eternity, he reversed his direction, dropped his spear, turned on his heels and raced back through the crowd on and on nearly stumbling several times, until he reached the nearby forest. Unstoppable tears ran down his face. He experienced great anguish and unimaginable pain.

Falling Star had witnessed the faltered attack by Mark of the Bear on her grizzly companion. Still feeling the oneness within, she began to waver from feeling the celestial Oneness that had elevated her consciousness during mutual joy of their shared journey to the camp. She felt the need to address the physical now-ness of the moment.

She gracefully slipped down the side the enormous animal. As she did so, she let her hand linger on his side as a way of saying, "Thank you, thank you, thank you, Brother Bear. You have taught me much. Maybe now is not the time for a sharing with the Elders and The People."

Brother Bear winked an acknowledgment, "Perhaps it was meant for you alone."

As the crowd began to disperse, some curious friends and family moved in closer to Fallen Star wanting to affirm that this indeed was she and to ensure that she was all right. This allowed Brother Bear a moment to slip away unnoticed as he trotted off back into the environs he called home.

As the event subsided and everyone allowed themselves to exhale, some wanted to talk about it with Falling Star and each other. Most however felt that the incidents were portentous and they needed to contemplate what meaning it all had for The People. Confident that discussion would occur at the council fires later, most chose to keep their feelings and opinions low key despite their immense curiosity.

Imbued with the sense of the Oneness and overpowered by her sense of serenity, Falling Star desired not to be singled out for recognition of what was a most amazing experience.

She desired only for two things. One was to find the boy-turned-man, the one she was promised to be together with forever, and me, her grandfather, Gray Wolf. She especially needed the comfort of my assuring company, explanations and stories of old. They were beginning to make sense to her now. Now she felt ready to spend more time with me, knowing that the great knowledge I had access to might find its way to her. Craving that treasure, she longed to see me just as soon as she could make her way to me.

On her way to my abode, lost in thought, Falling Star became aware that she was walking the paths into the forest toward where she knew Little Turtle often went when he wanted to be alone. She spotted him by the creek, kneeling, sitting on his heels, arms wrapped around his knees, rocking back and forth. She overheard his sobs of pain that screamed out from the center of his soul. He had lost face. He was jealous. He had been upstaged by the very girl who had won his heart.

"How could she do this to me?" his heart cried out. "Doesn't she know how I feel about her? She had to know what would happen when word got back to the village. *I was a hero*. I had done great things this morning. I had fought the great grizzly and chased the bear away and saved the lives of the little children." He felt devastated and completely heart-broken.

Still in touch with the All of the day's events, Falling Star silently stole up to him. Absorbed in his ego-driven emotional pain and self-pity, he was unaware of her presence. As she approached, Falling Star began to realize what had happened. She felt great sorrow as it had not been her intent to hurt him or upstage his pride. After all Little Turtle was a hero in her eyes. She gently touched his shoulder. Startled as though awakened from a bad dream, he jumped up with his flint knife drawn ready to stab.

"Little Turtle, I did not mean to startle you."

"Don't touch me. I am now Mark of the Bear, not Little Turtle."

"You were so very brave to confront the grizzly like that. Had you not done what you did, I could not have been able to get there in time. We partnered in the event.

"I had no idea that I had the power to speak to the bear. A voice inside me told me what I needed to do, gave me strength and dismissed my fears. It was like I had become someone else. I became in touch with Great Spirit, Mother Earth, the Bear and everyone and everything there, all wrapped up in One.

"After the bear left, this same voice told me that you would be all right and to go into the forest and speak with the bear. I was so embraced by what had happened. The stories and legends that Grandfather has told us are true and have meaning in real life. I wanted to bring Great Bear back to the village so that we could learn from him and to experience the Oneness we say we believe in."

As she spoke, his body and emotions began to unwind themselves from the knot Mark of the Bear had twisted himself into sitting by the creek. As he listened, he wanted to resist her.

Thin shafts of afternoon sunlight cut through the coolness of the recess at his favorite creek spot. Soft breezes whispered by causing strands of her soft black hair to play in its movements scented with the summer's fragrances. He wanted to resist, stand up to her and yell out his humiliation that he suffered at her expense. He wanted to punish her for taking away his glory. He wanted to remain angry, wanted to scream to the Heavens at feeling cheated by the woman he loved, being cheated out of glory and worship.

To his amazement she just stood there looking into his eyes, not at all intimated by him. As he stopped yelling internally, he felt himself distracted by other desires. Her hand lifted up and stopped halfway between them, palm facing him. Resistance no longer available, his hand reached for her.

They found themselves falling to the ground involved passionately touching and loving, loving and touching endlessly. Exploring each other's bodies with both curiosity and engagement, they both experienced the feeling of a universe exploding in its initial big bang.

Indeed it had been a day to remember.

A time when a young man and a young woman chart their future and choose the path they will walk in this the Fourth World.

49

SUMMER CAMP AND WINTER CAMP

Life unfolded gently and consistently for The People now living in their permanent home near the Pacific Ocean. During the winters near the water, they discovered other tribes living in the same area. Their first encounter was witnessing seagoing canoes out on the water, with fisherman silhouetted against the ocean backdrop of a late sunny afternoon as they waved to us standing on the shore. Getting acquainted with our neighbors took a little effort at first, because The People's history and background included knowing only other villagers of the same culture, except for the traders passing through. Despite the differences in culture and language, we felt that at some level, these others were some distant relatives of ours.

Gradually over the years we established a comfort level with our neighbors. Trading began between us. The neighboring tribes introduced us to the delicacies of the ocean, including new foods, such as abalone, and whale oil for cooking and for lamps.

While in Ohio, our oil for lamps had been produced from nuts that so prolifically occurred in that part of the country. In return, we offered animal hides, tanned with fur and without fur, as well as some other foodstuffs grown in the rich soil of our summer camp. Beads and other decorations made from porcupine quills, dyes, and other trinkets, such as some pearls served to enrich each tribe as the trading continued.

We had successfully endured our exodus from Ohio. Despite the fact that many had died along the way, including babies, the unborn, and the very young, some children did live to see the promised land. Among those were Stalking Bear, Whispering

Dove, Dancing Swan, Star Rising and several others. It took us over nine years to complete our journey. During that time, we witnessed the growing of these children into adolescents and young adults. They provided the opportunity for The People to grow in numbers.

Occasionally, youthful members of neighboring tribes found their way into the hearts and hearths of our young adults, giving rise to an expanded new generation of The People.

On occasion, more matured adults filtered into our little band from other tribes as well. Our troupe of true-believers indeed began to re-establish ourselves, slowly, gradually. Falling Star and Mark of the Bear were the first and the oldest, and were followed by a wave of other children later after The People settled into our summer and winter camps.

Those who had left Ohio as adults, found themselves aged by the time we arrived at the Pacific Ocean. The trek and trepidations took their toll on The People, hastening the aging process. We became the Elders and beloved Grandmothers and beloved Grandfathers. By the time Falling Star and Mark of the Bear reached their age of maturity for pairing, they represented yet the next generation.

Falling Star vaulted high in the regard of The People, particularly due to the grizzly bear incident. The People acknowledged the uniqueness of both Mark of the Bear and Falling Star. Mark of the Bear measured himself to be special and therefore exalted. However, Falling Star endeared herself to The People at a deep level within each individual. Regardless of her youth, she was considered a shaman and an Elder, if not before the bear incident, then certainly because of it.

Falling Star and Mark of the Bear sometimes spent time sitting and talking at the beach near the close of a winter day watching the sun melt into the western horizon, dipping into the water. Falling Star would share stories and information with her beloved that she had learned from my tutelage. She would speak about the all of All, the total connectedness, reaching through to the realm of Spirit for guidance, direction and information, and seeing the perfection in all things. She saw it as a way to be as The People in these new lands.

"It's like this," she offered on one occasion, "events we experience are often interpreted through our past knowledge. And the way we interpret the event then becomes truth for us. What we might not realize is that truth to one might not be truth to another. Our truth then generates our thought about something that then colors our emotional response. We think we are subject to our emotions, and yet, that is not true at all."

Mark of the Bear only half listened as he shifted his attention to the beauty of the setting sun and then back again to his beloved. Just sitting quietly with her alone seemed enough for him, with little need for him to consider the depth and meaning of what insights she was sharing with him.

"Uh-huh," he mumbled in response.

"Our perspective can influence our thought about an event. Then what happens is that our sense of reality is influenced by how we experience an event." She paused for a few moments and looked out toward the ocean blazing with yellow and orange reflections of the glorious sun as it progressed toward the horizon.

Turning back to her beloved she continued, "But there is another way, a way that I have found to be so practical as to take my breath away." Mark of the Bear turned to look at her encouraging her to continue.

"Yes," she nodded, "Great Spirit presents Itself to us in many forms. One is that of a Knowing that we can tap into. When we access this knowing from Spirit, it impacts our consciousness, our awareness, so to speak. We can apply this knowing connection and influence our own knowledge that shades our truth, so that our thoughts can then align with the All, the One, or Spirit." As she spoke, she looked far off beyond the horizon, beyond the Earth, beyond the stars. With that faraway look in her eye and light radiating from her face, she continued, "Then that offers us ways of seeing that we might not otherwise have. Of course, when we see something in only one way, we must know that we are choosing to not see in all the many other ways to see that are available. Yet this is a challenge to our sense of awareness. It is very easy to just follow old and accepted ways of viewing and reacting to an event.

"The advantage of seeing something in multiple ways is that we then have a wider range of solutions or behaviors to choose from in resolving a conflict for example. Or, we can allow ourselves a choice of behaviors, so we can better select which behavior is best or which behavior that will produce the best result for the good of all concerned."

She tapped his knee with a fingertip as she finished, "The thing is, we are all one, and one in the One, sharing a unity of consciousness. But experiencing that sense of oneness, in the physical life we seem to be living, is the challenge. So remember, what happens to one, happens to all. What I am given to know is each of us, every individual, contributes to the All, and for all of us as a group to benefit, every one of us must benefit. And for each of us to benefit individually, then absolutely all of us benefits. The Whole is in every part and in every part of every part."

Unsure that he followed her reasoning, Mark of the Bear gave a half nod then turned to look at the sun kissing the horizon as layers of fog rolled in occluding the next stage in the closing of the day.

The evening breeze chilled the air, and he wanted to return back to camp and says, "While I hear what you are saying it seems so disconnected from our experiences here. These are stories from your Grandfather about how he lived in lands so very far away from here. We are in new lands, and I just don't see what this has to do with our ways here. Besides the tribes we have met so far don't follow these ways that your Grandfather talks about all the time." Mark of the Bear shook his head as he finished.

As they stand up and brush off sand and plant debris, Falling Star remarked, "Well, for example, the bear incident . . ." Mark of the Bear rolled his eyes revealing his reluctance at discussing that sensitive topic.

Not noticing she continued, ". . . the bear incident was interpreted differently by many of us. When I reach into the Knowing, for instance, I can see it from many perspectives. I can see how each person experienced that event. And, with the influence from that, I can see the entire event differently and that allows me to see the perfection in it." Mark of the Bear sighed to signal he really did not want to continue listening. ". . . See the perfection is all I'm saying," she finished. Falling Star wanted to go on sharing her insights but chose otherwise. They returned to their homes in silence.

As much as she wanted to continue sharing her truth, she found Mark of the Bear resistant to some of her thoughts, ideas, and ways of seeing. Little did she know that he closeted resentment from the bear incident and from her stealing from him his moment of glory. The kernel of jealousy he felt from her being elevated to shaman level, a position of high-esteem, without him remained buried deep in his heart concealed from Falling Star. Resolution of his inner conflict between his love and adoration for Falling Star, and his unfulfilled desire to be a hero and a leader in the minds of The People, never took place.

During their times at summer camp in the mountains, Mark of the Bear excelled in two areas of life that The People grew to depend on. One was his keen ability to hunt. He provided much game for The People and taught others how to coordinate a hunt for the best possible outcome.

The other was his innate ability to build shelters for us, complete with beds raised from the floor like we had in Ohio. Because we had found a neat meadowed valley snuggled in among the lower peaks amid the forested landscape, we claimed that spot as our summer camp, returning every spring.

THE CAMP OF GOD'S TEARS

The occasional earthquakes connected to the dormant volcano, Mt. St. Helens, would rattle loose parts of the shelters he built, or the heavy snows would sometimes collapse a part of one. So every spring he anticipated a need to set about repairing any damage occurring during our absence. Mark of the Bear enjoyed this activity. He felt rewarded when his work was done. He had figured out how to reinforce our shelters so as to prevent possible future damage from earthquakes or winter snows.

This summer camp offered much to us, contributing to our sense of well-being, offering a stable environment complete with land for crops, nearby streams, a plethora of game animals, as well as space for permanent shelters. It reminded the older folks of home in the Ohio River Valley. However this became a place we grew to know and love.

Mark of the Bear had deftly built permanent shelters from the trees from the surrounding forest. As a result, The People enjoyed a sweeter sense of stability being able to count on those homes being there every time we returned at the end of winter.

Winter was not a time to spend in our summer camp. Heavy snows blanketed this area in the winter. Climbing out of our little valley seemed tricky enough even in good weather as we had to climb up and over large rocky areas to access the trail that wound down steep slopes as the trail descended through the forest. During the winter months this trail would be impassable. Even though The People had attached themselves to their summer camp, it remained our summer camp. We left it for a more pleasant clime nearer the coastal waters during the harsh winter months. In a favorite winter locale, near the ocean's edge, Mark of the Bear, with the help of many others, engineered winter homes there as well.

Wintering near the coast provided us with opportunity for trading and for a change in diet that suited us. The now older folks particularly relished the seafood, as they fondly remembered days of old devouring the succulent mussels and fish so prevalent back in Ohio.

At the beginning of one winter, while fall still prevailed under cloudy skies, we had already set up for winter camp. We were happily engaged in our normal activities, children playing, adults talking and laughing, without real concern for survival, especially with plenty of dried meat in our stores and hides to trade for other items.

Emerging from the fog that hugged the coastline, three images appeared.

"Hey, we've got company," alerted one as he gazed north to watch three men outfitted to hunt approach our camp.

When the three strangers arrived, they just stood still not really knowing our language too well. After a few awkward moments, one woman, who had been stirring a pot of stew heavily loaded with meat, stepped forward with a bowl and a spoon and offered it to one of the strangers. He looked at the bowl steaming its inviting aroma into his face, and then he looked at Flying Cloud, then down at her offering. Suddenly he grabbed the bowl from her, then the spoon, and began eating standing up. At that, the other two shifted weight from one foot to the other indicating they wanted some too.

Another woman, Drifting Wood, watching this, suddenly realized what was happening and moved into action. She filled two other bowls, grabbed two spoons and moved toward the strangers with a smile. They both accepted the food with a nod of gratitude and acknowledgment.

After each of the three hungrily finished, they handed back their bowls with a hopeful expression on their faces. The rest of us could breathe again after watching what was going on. Flying Cloud and Drifting Wood took their bowls and filled them again. In the meantime, others of us offered places for the three men to sit. This time they ate sitting down with the entire number of those present watching. After one of them finished his second bowl, he looked up sheepishly appearing as though he was asking for a third helping. The other two evidently feeling a little less assertive still held on to their bowls and set them in their laps.

When Flying Cloud gladly grabbed the one bowl and filled it again, the other two men lifted up their bowls asking for another portion as well.

When the three were finally satisfied, they remained sitting for a while.

Awkward silence.

The silence was broken by murmurings, as Shining Bird brought out a much loved bread dripping with a sweet syrup. The strangers' eyes grew large as she handed each of them a small serving on a small wooden platter. Hesitating only for an instant, they each grabbed the luscious dessert and began eating despite the fact they had just eaten three bowls of stew.

After finishing, they could not hold back their smiles. Everyone breathed in the new friendship and alliance between us and the three strangers and their people.

After a while, the three strangers got up from their places and stood awkwardly, wanting to leave, but also wanting to give something in exchange. One offered his knife, another offered several arrows, and the third offered a leather pouch that hung from his belt. Just at that moment I made an appearance. Clearly, to the strangers, I was a shaman and possibly a chief. They bowed their heads in respect momentarily and stood still holding their items for exchange.

I stood there, with much gray hair and a presence that could not be denied, looking at them and into them. When I finally spoke to them, they felt my words in their hearts despite the difference in verbal language.

"Dear ones," I begin, "we are brothers of one family. We belong to each other. Go in peace, remembering our bond. We do not wish to be repaid for the food we gave you. We shared our food, because we are all one in the One. Go in peace."

Feeling my message in their hearts, they hesitated then turned and left.

Not too long after that incident, Shining Bird fell ill. She had never really been ill much of her life. Of our long and loving life together, I could not remember a time when she had been ill. She had always cared for me and our children and anyone else she could. She had always been a stalwart partner in our spiritual expression together as we sojourned through this life. Her hair now white, her body seemingly strong, belied the fact that now she laid in bed unable to get up.

After each of our now adult children, Star Rising, Dancing Swan, and Stalking Bear had spent time alone with their mother, they left her bedside to allow me time alone with my beloved. As I kneel beside her, she heaves a sigh.

"My time here with you is over, my dearest beloved," she says softly to me as I kneel at her bedside. She lifts a frail right arm and tenderly runs her fingers through my hair and down the side of my face. Tears run profusely as I gaze upon my lifetime companion.

"It's been a trip, in more ways than one," she softly says with a smile.

"No, no, no," I counter, "you can't go. You can't leave me. What will I do? What will I do without you, my love, my dearest, dearest beloved?" I say with rivers of tears streaming down my face devastated with sorrow.

"What you always do, my love," she offers with another smile. "Keep the faith. Pass on your knowledge and connectedness to our granddaughter, Falling Star. She is the shaman who will replace you. Teach her. Train her in the way we both know, in the way we learned from Singing Hawk and White Eagle. Teach her more than what she already knows. She represents the future of our People."

With that, I sob with my head in her hands resting on her solar plexus. I could not hold back. After gasping for breath, I lift my head to catch one more glimpse of my beloved Shining Bird. Our eyes meet in one final connected gaze.

"Keep the faith," she murmurs as she fades out of my life forever, but never out of my memory or my heart.

I had her body cremated as was her wish. I prepared a very large stack of wood on the beach down by the water's edge. Lovingly and carefully I laid her body to rest on the top of the wood stack and lit the funeral pyre at sunset. With the next tide her ashes blended with Mother Earth.

Feeling extreme grief in my bereavement, I went off to be alone for several days, taking no food or water with me. The rest of the camp watched me go, also feeling the loss of the ever beautiful, graceful Shining Bird, who always knew what to do in any given moment, one who remained in touch with Great Spirit endlessly for the benefit of all. She would be missed greatly.

Just after I left to be alone in my grief, a runner from the tribe of the three hunters arrived in our camp.

Despite the differences in languages, they got their message communicated with the help of Falling Star. Their message came in the form of an invitation for us to join the other tribe in a tribal hunt. They were anxious to offer an exchange that had been offered earlier by the three hungry hunters. Evidently they had not been successful in finding enough game to get them through the upcoming winter.

Inviting The People to join them would provide them with two solutions, one was a gesture of repayment for a debt, and the other was to increase the hunting party with obviously skilled hunters that would ensure greater success. So impressed were the three hunters while in our camp of The People, they instigated the invitation. And, it was a way or at least an opportunity to repay The People for the meal so gratefully accepted by the three hunters.

While many of the younger and more energetic members of The People, including the older children mature enough to join in, went off to join their neighbors for the hunt. The rest stayed behind in our winter quarters to keep the hearth fires burning.

Mark of the Bear certainly felt within his element as hunting was one of his two specialties. He and his close friend, Floating Hawk, always enjoyed hunting together. The two of them walked in to the other village side by side. When the entire group from our village arrived, they were warmly greeted by members of the other tribe. The People were received with gracious hospitality given the limited resources of the hosting tribe.

Falling Star enjoyed being a part of the festivities and anticipated joining in on the hunt as well. However, much to her dismay, she discovered that the other tribe did not permit women to join in on any hunt.

To them, there was women's work and men's work, and hunting was a man's prerogative, not a woman's. Women were not allowed to encroach upon the activities seen by men as their territory. Hunting was an activity that belonged solely to the men, which was satisfactory with Mark of the Bear. He preferred not to have to be in competition with Falling Star.

In The People's way, women's work and men's work did not exist. Some men cooked and some women hunted. No distinction between the genders existed as there was just work to be done. No taboos existed among us as each served the community according to the special gift of each individual regardless of gender. As a result, the taboo against women joining in on the hunt irritated Falling Star. She longed to be a part of the action. She felt challenged to overcome this taboo, because she desired to participate in everything.

During the several days that passed for the preparation of hunting and the ceremony up to the eve of the hunt, some of The People mingled with the tribe members they were visiting. Several of our men and woman who were pottery makers happened to wander over to those folks who were the pottery makers for this tribe.

Before the conversation got started, the People spotted several clay pots of their own style and making. Curious as to how these coastal people should obtain pots originating with The People in Ohio, the question was asked.

"We traded for them. Sometimes traders from very far away would bring these to us for trade for our obsidian and other items," was the answer.

"We made those pots," one of The People said in response, ". . . or at least our People made those pots. So it was the traders that brought us the obsidian that brought those pots to you?"

"Yes," was the response from one of the coastal pottery makers. She continued, "So you are *those* People! The People of the pots!" At that each of the coastal pottery makers stopped what they were doing to look at The People who had made such unusual pottery.

With nothing much else to do for those days leading up to the hunt, several pottery makers of The People offered to make pots for their hosts. With much deft and grace, we produced a style of pottery common in the Ohio River Valley that was familiar to them and which impressed our hosts.

As we worked, each worked at learning the language of each other. As the work progressed, The People showed our new friends several pottery-making techniques that later our friends adopted. Those of The People who were pottery makers felt the joy in sharing our skills with our new friends. And, of course, they happily produced results that pleased everyone.

The night came that preceded the day of the actual hunt. Much feasting and dancing took place that evening. A big bonfire centered itself in the middle of the celebratory spirit anticipating a successful hunt.

Falling Star was not to be constrained by any rules that said she could not participate in what she wanted to participate in, especially when it came to ceremony. After all, if she can ride a grizzly bear into camp, she could dance the dance of the hunt and join in on the total event. She felt she would not allow herself to miss out just because some rules said so.

She watched the dancers prepare for the dance. They each wore a costume of either a predatory animal or one of a prey. Behind the scenes, she talked someone into letting her don furs of a red fox and its head, masking her face. Because she was so slight of build, the costume fit her without compromise.

At the time of the actual dance, Falling Star, dressed as a red fox, joined in with the other dancers. She followed their lead and performed intuitively, with no one the wiser. Although Floating Hawk thought he recognized Falling Star, he quickly dismissed the thought. She danced eloquently and discovered that in the end she led the dance with all others following her. She could not help smiling to herself at this outcome. This ritual was one that belonged to the other people and their history. Yet, she was the one who in the end directed its performance.

In the hours before dawn, the dancers removed their costumes and donned their hunting outfits with the appropriate hunting gear. Realizing this, Falling Star carefully and silently stole off to a secluded spot to remove her costume and grab a hunting outfit that would disguise her gender. Trailing the hunting party so as not to give away her identity to those who might be particularly perceptive, she followed the hunting party into the dawn. Mark of the Bear and others from our village was among them.

Dawn came. The hunters moved silently into the forest, up and down the slopes, around thickets, over ridges, down draws, and back again, through meadows and back again. No game presented itself. By late in the day, the hunters felt discouraged. They had traversed many miles with much frustration. Still disguised as a man, Falling Star saw and felt the discouragement and spiritual fatigue of the hunting group. Unwilling to allow a failure of a venture of which she was a part, Falling Star stepped forward yet at a distance from them.

She stepped forward on a slight ridge overlooking another empty meadow that was filled with grasses and dried flowers awaiting their winter's rest.

Falling Star stepped forward not caring if anyone saw that she was a woman, not caring that anyone saw her, uncaring about anything but success of a people needing food. She stood there as a silhouette against the late afternoon setting sun with both arms outstretched, fingers taut pointing to nothing and everything.

Being in the moment, being in the spiritual energy of the All, being in the oneness, her entire body vibrated as she sang a song for calling in game.

All the hunters saw her step up to the ridge not knowing who it was.

With eyes believing what they saw, yet not wanting to believe what was happening, because it was beyond their comprehension for such a thing to happen, they witnessed herds of deer and a herd of elk step into the little meadow. The animals meandered there, some nibbling on tidbits of something here and there. The hunters had surrounded the meadow and unleashed their hungry bows.

Dozens of animals fell dead at the touch of an arrow. Some of them escaped to reproduce another day. Those lying on the meadow floor would serve to feed both villages through the winter. Before anyone was allowed to touch the now dead animals, Falling Star called out loudly in a sweet but powerful voice a song of prayer thanking Mother Earth for providing for the people, and then sending the souls of each animal back to her. Her song also thanked Great Spirit for allowing provisions for the people.

Stunned by her song, the hunters only then realized who she was, not only a young woman, but a shaman who called in the game for them. At that moment, Falling Star found herself accepted by the members of the hunting party and later the entire tribe as well. And, in the last rays of the sun the hunting party swarmed out onto the field with knives ready to gut, clean, and carve the exquisite animals lying before them. Sister Moon rose overhead and provided light by which to work, so the people could take care of the meat without spoilage.

Coming back home successfully meant everything to their neighbors. Back at the other tribe's camp, the hunters told the story over and over to all who had not been there and even to each other. Falling Star was able to take off her costume of a hunter and wear her everyday clothes as a member of The People. Our new friends insisted on dividing up the meat so hunters of The People took home meat as well. From that moment on, the alliance between the two groups stood and proved later to serve The People at a time of need. They recognized in Falling Star her connection to Great Spirit.

All during this time Mark of the Bear had not concerned himself with the night's dance prior to that day's hunt. Had he paid attention, he might have noticed the little red fox exquisitely leading the dance and possibly recognized his beloved. Because he knew that this neighboring tribe did not permit women to join in the dance or the hunt, he gave no thought to any possible exception.

He had made a kill that day, in fact several kills, standing on the edge of that now bloodied meadow. Pride in his performance, especially in front of the many other hunters, stoked his ego. He felt like a hero and that meant so much, even if it was just within himself. What he did not know was that the prayers and affirmations Falling Star made that day on behalf of her hungry neighbors reached Mother Earth. It was because of her connection to the Great Mother, that the hunters' arrows only had to come near the animals before each one fell over dead.

The group of The People who had joined the neighboring tribe returned home to their winter camp the next day, happy.

Not surprisingly, several members, including hunters, of the other tribe returned with them, and eventually melted into the welcoming arms of The People.

Those home waiting were glad to have everyone back and set to work preparing the meat for winter. Sitting around the evening's campfire, they told the story of Falling Star, how she danced, and covertly joined in on the hunt, how she called in the game, and how she sang out the blessing for the souls of the animals and gratitude for the winter's provisions. Mark of the Bear sat by, hearing but not listening.

His friend, Floating Hawk, noticed and mentioned something to him that evening, "Not that I want to rain on your parade, my friend," he began in a whisper over his friend's shoulder, "but it was, after all, Falling Star who called in the game in the first place. Don't let your ego get in your way of fully appreciating her and what she did. Remember, overuse of ego is fatal. What she did made all of this possible." Mark of the Bear grumbled to himself and said nothing.

Falling Star went off to bed not caring about the stories. Her People were well and happy and that was what she cared about.

Realizing that the debt they wanted to repay The People by inviting us to their hunt only served to deepen the debt they felt they owed. As a result, the neighboring tribe set about to prepare a gift to The People. One clear winter day, a small band of men from the neighboring tribe advanced toward our winter camp.

"We have company," announced Star Rising. All members of The People within hearing distance came to the edge of our camp to witness the entourage approach in silence. When the visitors finally arrived, they stood in the middle of our winter camp and presented gifts. We smiled as several of them came forward to offer the pots filled with whale oil, beads and other trinkets. One gift remained.

"We are looking for Falling Star," sputtered one awkwardly in our language, holding a large soft package in a neatly woven bag. Hearing her name pronounced even at a distance, Falling Star felt alerted to direct her attention to the center of camp. She moved out from beyond a shelter. Seeing her new friends, with a graceful stride, she walked over to them, touched the arm of the one who spoke her name and bowed her head in respect.

"Our clan is grateful to you, Falling Star, for what you did for us. We recognize your status as a shaman and a leader of your People. It is our wish to honor you in particular for your contribution to us as a people. We will always honor you and keep your memory in our hearts. This is our gift to you," he finished then extended the package to Falling Star.

Falling Star, obviously touched by this presentation of heartfelt gratitude, tilted her head back holding in her emotions. Then, in recognition of their gratitude, she silently tipped her head forward in a half-bow. Falling Star felt she was being recognized for something that was only a natural event of getting in touch with Great Spirit and Mother Earth, for accessing the knowing that exists beyond the physical experience of life. This was becoming a way of being for her and did not require any special acknowledgement. However, she did want to pay respects for the respect being paid to her.

"Thank you, dear ones," she began with a formal smile. "I accept." As she received the package from them, they all breathed easier. It was like a signal had sounded, and those working with food began to scramble to put food together for a small feast in celebration of the event. Yet, at that same silent signal, the visitors turned and left the camp without further ceremony.

Taking her package with her, Falling Star searched for her mother, Whispering Dove, to share with her the honor in opening the gift together.

"Oh, my," Whispering Dove commented as they held it up for all to see.

Breaths sucked in.

Murmurings.

As Falling Star held up the gift, everyone present recognized the exquisite beauty and craftsmanship. The gift was a long dress made of softly tanned white buckskin with matching boots. The dress was elaborately decorated with colored beads, dyed porcupine quills and fringed hems. Such a gift was fit for only a most honored person, and that person was The One For Whom The Stars Fell.

I, having spent significant time alone in the wilderness grieving my loss of my beloved, Shining Bird, finally returned to The People. The People relished telling me the stories of the several events that had transpired during my absence. When I asked to see the gift given to my granddaughter, she gladly brought it out for me to see. Instead of just holding it up for me to look at, Falling Star decided to put it on. Wearing the dress with the matching boots, she walked out to show me.

At the moment my eyes landed on my beloved granddaughter, I sucked in my breath and my eyes widened to the size of saucers. Without taking my eyes off her, and still holding my breath, I choked and sputtered as I attempted to regain my breath.

"Oh, my," was all I could say.

Sometime during the following summer, Mark of the Bear had completed several new houses in our summer camp. With each one, he found himself incorporating new techniques to constantly improve the quality of his product. Finally, especially proud of his most recent one, he brought Falling Star to it to show her and point out what he had accomplished.

Smiling broadly at her beloved, Falling Star found herself reaching for him with her hand. Caught in the moment of pride and passion, he surrendered to her, wholly and completely. The two found themselves on the floor in love's embrace, locked in the dance, yielding to their bodies and their bonding. The agreement of their souls, their promise to be together forever, never screamed more loudly in their consciousness than on this day.

After several weeks had passed, Whispering Dove suddenly found herself facing Mark of the Bear on a path not too far from camp. At this chance encounter, Whispering Dove boldly spoke to Mark of the Bear about one of his new houses.

"I understand you have built an especially grand one," she mentioned as a follow up to their conversation.

"Yes, indeed, mother," he responded.

With one eyebrow raised, Whispering Dove looked at him with a question on her face that was not spoken.

"Yes, mother," Mark of the Bear repeated, "that one I intend to move into myself with your daughter, Falling Star. When do you think would be a good time for the ceremony?"

"The sooner the better," she replied with a grin. "Your first child is on his way. It's a boy, and you will need the room, because he will be much like you, very energetic. He will become a hunter like you."

With that remark, Mark of the Bear puffed out his chest with pride. "A son," he said quietly with an even bigger grin on his face, and a great hunter. To himself, he said, "What more can I ask for?"

On the day of the marriage ceremony, I call Falling Star aside. I show her my bundle of sacred objects. I begin, "In this bundle are many sacred objects. I will teach you and your children the meaning of them and the meaning of much, much more."

The beautiful bride wearing her white buckskin dress and boots given to her by the neighboring tribe stood there listening to me. She tilts her head slightly trying to comprehend the meaning of my words, specifically the part about much, much more.

"What do you mean, Grandfather?" she finally asks.

"You already know Great Spirit," I say, "but there is more you can learn, more to the history of The People you should know. As your sense of motherhood grows, you will want to pass on your knowledge as well as information about our People, so that it can be carried on.

"You represent the future of our People. What you do will impact our People forever. Your access to the Knowing combined with knowing who your People are will impact many beyond The People and may possibly impact Mother Earth. You have already begun to do that, and there is more for you to do."

At this, I reach into my sacred bundle. My hand fumbles inside, and then stops for a moment as my hand touches the object of my search. Removing an item wrapped in a soft covering, I breathe hard and my eyes well up with warm tears. I open the covering to reveal a necklace.

Falling Star gasps at the sight of this sacred object. Flickers of light reflect as it hangs from my hand as it turns and moves.

She had never seen it before. It was the necklace that White Eagle had worn for so many years, one that had been worn for generations before her. It seemed to her that it was alive, breathing again, finally awakened from a long sleep.

When I put this necklace over her head and lay it on her shoulders, instantly, Falling Star feels a powerful surge of energy flow through her, overwhelming her with images from ancient times. So powerful was this wave, she falters a bit while still standing there and finds herself unable to speak.

Finally, she chokes out, "*I accept.*"

The marriage ceremony was a simple one. Falling Star wore her necklace laid against the background of her beautiful white dress. As she and Mark of the Bear walked hand in hand among The People, the abalone shell with the silver and copper insignia flashed in the light of everyone's eyes a message. This ancient message affirmed what they knew in the depths of their souls, "as above, so below."

50

THE CAMP OF GOD'S TEARS

Gingerly, tenderly, she lifted the rolled buckskin out from my bundle, the bundle that I had made from the wolf hide so very long ago. As she unrolled the precious buckskin and gazed upon it for perhaps the hundredth time or more, she still could not stop feeling amazed by the genius that went into the drawing of the Great Serpent drawn by Red Fox.

Falling Star, now with a few gray hairs hanging loose in the air from her normally tightly wrapped hair style, again felt the genius that went into the exquisite thought, engineering and construction of the actual Great Serpent. It was the Great Serpent that had been built, honored, danced around, and abandoned by her People in the heartland of Ohio. She would never travel to Ohio. She would never see the Great Serpent. She only knew Red Fox through the stories told to her by me and Shining Bird.

As her own three children grew, Running Deer, Yellow Lily and Painted Star, she felt compelled to ensure they and all the other children knew the stories I had passed down to her by way of the oral traditions. I had spent many an afternoon or evening, year after year, sitting with all the children and their parents telling and re-telling the stories of The People. While I was still performing this vital cultural sharing, I was letting Falling Star take over more of this function.

When she told the stories about Red Fox or the Great Serpent, she felt it necessary to show the beautifully tanned buckskin, so carefully drawn upon by Red Fox. The image of the Great Serpent on this buckskin was the one Red Fox used as a template to create his model. It served as a visual illustration that enhanced the stories to our children. The actual buckskin, however, showed signs of wear and tear. The leather was by now several generations old. It had torn in several places and the edges were deteriorating.

While neatly replacing other items in my bundle, her hand ran across a small leather pouch. Surprised by it, she felt it and pulled it out of the bundle. Just at that moment, I entered the shelter used for gatherings in our summer camp where she sat preparing for another such story-telling time.

Holding up the small pouch, she asks me, "What's this? I don't remember you showing me this before."

"Ah," I reply with one nod of my head covered with white hair hanging loosely around my shoulders. "That my dearest, granddaughter, is a talisman that Red Fox received near the end of his sacred journey when he was showing The People his model of the Great Serpent. It's a clay tablet, baked with those markings etched on it. Remember the stories I told you about how White Eagle and the other Elders asked him to build the model of the Great Serpent?" She nods showing she remembered.

"Well, because he had learned so much and was sharing what he had learned as he traveled from village to village, he grew in knowledge of Spirit. He became a shaman and a respected Elder, at a young age, because of how much he had learned of the mathematics, reasons for the sacred geometry of the earthworks and their meanings. He was able to remind his listeners of the meaning behind everything he knew. In that way he reinforced what everyone already knew. He simply reminded them to remember.

"In those days, some of The People were starting to feel separated from each other, which also implied they felt separated from Spirit. This sense of separation was seen by the Elders. If the People should lose their sense of Oneness with Mother Earth and Great Spirit, they would lose those principles derived from our heritage that provided unity of consciousness and our thousand years of peace. I've already told you this story, so if you remember, The People consider themselves the Children of the Law of One."

She remembers the story, and nods in acknowledgement, allowing me to tell the story again.

"Several incidents had happened that had been brought to White Eagle's attention that revealed a disharmony growing among us. In council, the Elders and White Eagle felt that a way to remind The People of who they are, among other things, would be to have someone travel around to as many villages as possible telling our story and showing a model of the Great Serpent as a way to enrich the stories. The precision of the Great Serpent with all of its inlaid meanings represents an entire encyclopedia of ancient knowledge. Red Fox built the model using this buckskin as a template," I tap my fingers on it as I speak. "It incorporates all the math and engineering principles necessary for the re-creation of the Great Serpent with all of its nuances of meaning."

"But how did he acquire this piece?" asks Falling Star, holding up the clay tablet with its markings etched upon it.

"Yes, well, Rising Wolf gave that piece to him in recognition of his efforts. Red Fox had demonstrated great personal advancement in his connection with Spirit through his investment in learning and comprehending the vast ancient knowledge as he journeyed sharing this information. He was the first of my generation, and indeed the last person, to be initiated into secrets left to us by our Ancient Ones and those from far away.

"That knowledge left to us included certain technologies, plus stellar, lunar, and solar movements, mathematics and engineering principles incorporated into our many earthen structures, including the Great Serpent.

"That knowledge also included why and how we are all one and one with the One. In recognition of his successful initiation, Rising Wolf awarded Red Fox this talisman. The recognition became a part of his journey. His journey was, not only a physical journey, but a metaphoric one as well. That journey was one of an apprentice becoming a master."

Satisfied with that explanation, Falling Star returns the piece back into its holding pouch and then back into the large, wolf skin bundle. As she did so, I say softly.

"This bundle will become your bundle at my death."

Stunned by the thought of my death, she sits upright.

She had not contemplated my death.

"Grandfather," she responds after a few moments with tears welling up. "That event is not something I care to look at. Nor do I care to think about it."

"Nevertheless," I say to comfort her and to prepare her for the inevitable, "that time is not too far off. We need not speak of it just now."

Of her three children, the oldest, Running Deer, seemed less inclined to sit for too long listening to her stories. Running Deer's attention and energy levels responded more to physical activities, such as hunting and fishing. Falling Star felt her oldest son resembled his father, Mark of the Bear, much more so than her other son, Painted Star, and her daughter, Yellow Lily. Often, during the story telling times, she would see her oldest son, Running Deer, drift off to sleep or have some faraway look in his eyes, showing just how little he wanted to pay attention.

One late morning during the early part of the summer, Falling Star sat with several of the camp's children talking about harvesting food from Mother Earth.

"When we hunt, we take only what we need. We take only what we need and leave the rest. It's not about taking as much as we can for sport or for ego, to show how grand we are. It's about harvesting enough to satisfy our human need for food. It is critical that we remain in balance with the ebb and flow, the flux and constancy of our life in partnership with Mother Earth. We are already grand just being who we are, breathing air, and having our being on Mother Earth."

She paused momentarily to let that thought float through their minds then continued, "We need the animals and the plants for food and clothes and for our other supplies. The animals and plants do not need us. Mother Earth does not need us. It is us who needs Mother Earth to provide for us. She would continue on without us if we were not here. But we could not continue as human beings without her."

"Is that why father says a prayer every morning outside the house with an offering to Mother Earth?" asked one little girl.

Smiling, Falling Star nodded then said, "Yes, many of us engage in that practice daily. We give gratitude for our sustenance and for our bounty. It's a way of giving recognition that we are all in this experience together. The ritual of giving gratitude is a way of recognizing the oneness."

"Well," spoke up Running Deer, "I think I'm going to go out and recognize my oneness with my bow and arrow and a rabbit." With that he got up and left the circle.

A few weeks later that summer, many of The People were sitting around sharing stories with a fire burning nicely in the center. Children were nestled snuggly near their parents.

Then one child asks, "Grandfather Gray Wolf, tell us a story. Tell us the story of the ancient ones."

"Yes," I respond, "my children. I will tell you one of the stories that my Great Grandfather told my father.

"We live on sacred ground. We do not own or possess that which Mother Earth has made for us. It is not ours. The animals and plants are not ours. These do not belong to us. We take only what we need, and when we do take, we must replenish. We say a prayer to the spirits of the animals and the plants and give gratitude for what they give us, so that we may live and in doing so, we honor Great Spirit. As I have shown you and told you in other stories we have shared, we must live in harmony with our Mother Earth and that which she provides.

"The Ancient Ones told us stories of when man lost his harmony with the world in which he lived. How he took and took and destroyed without gratitude, and not from need, but from greed and selfishness and for taking more than was needed. This became so great that many did not have enough to live. Anger . . . and distrust . . . and disharmony . . . swept through the land. Brother fought brother. Sister fought sister. Great harm came to all, and strife came to the lands. The rains stopped. The winds blew. The crops would not grow, and the animals that were left fled. Hunger and death and disease came to those who had abandoned the ways of Great Spirit.

"Time passed, and those aligned with Spirit fled to distant lands to escape the disease that had taken over the lands. The Ancient Ones told us of even more distant times when Great Spirit told Mother Earth to raise her waters and flood the lands to destroy those who had done such great harm. Yet, those of the people who honored the earth, the animals and the plants and Great Spirit were saved and were once again brought to new lands to begin again. Yet each time their survival became more difficult and their way upon the land was more challenging. It is for these reasons, children that I, the Elders, your mothers and fathers give gratitude and a prayer to the deer when it has brought us meat, the plants for their food, and to Mother Earth from which all is given.

"This is why I teach you these ways, so that you will know to take no more than you need, one fish instead of two, one deer instead of many and to give thanks to their spirit, so that they will return to us in the future to provide for us and your children. This is the way of harmony, this is the way of Oneness, and this is the Way of Great Spirit. In so doing there will be enough for all, and for our brothers and sisters who live apart from us.

"We have our great ceremonies to honor Father Sun, and Mother Earth, and all that she provides when we plant in the spring and when we harvest in the fall, so that when the cold winter comes, we will have enough and none will starve. These things do not belong to us, and we must treat the plants, animals and Mother Earth, herself, with respect and honor, and in so doing they honor us. This is why we do not destroy or kill these things just because we can. You must never forget that we live only because we live in harmony with that which has been given to us."

Our summer camp that had begun as a simple camp with make-do shelters had, by this time, developed into an entire village of homes. Falling Star and Mark of the Bear had been only babies when The People found this little valley that accommodated our needs. It was within the forest, but entertained a beautiful openness that allowed The People to feel comfortable with more than enough space for permanent shelters. It offered a wide, open area, and space for cooking ovens for village meals and ceremonies. It also included land for summer crops, and streams nearby for a sure supply of water. Because it was situated about halfway up the mountain, plenty of game was available as needed. It was a perfect spot.

From our camp we could sometimes see smoke rising from Mt. St. Helens that often accompanied tremors and minor earthquakes. We had experienced rare earthquakes in Ohio, and soon became accustomed to them here. Usually only minor damage occurred as a result. Of course to Falling Star and to all the others born after our arrival here, feeling the earth quake beneath their feet on occasion was typically noted only in passing.

One who complained about any damage from earthquakes was Mark of the Bear who took it upon himself to complete repairs to our shelters even if it was a mere crack in the clay covering a wall or a floor.

And, he had help. Even though his close friend, Floating Hawk, was much younger, he enjoyed helping Mark of the Bear building and repairing.

Our homes typically were curved but three sided, constructed from planks of pine or small logs from the nearby forest. The fourth side or curve usually boasted a blanket or elk hide for privacy, and protection against any summer storms coming through. Usually during the daytime, this one side remained open, so the delightful summer breezes could wander through the sunlight that filtered in.

One such structure, larger than most, was where the children and young adults gathered for storytelling. Falling Star attached Red Fox's buckskin hide boasting the Great Serpent to a straight piece of wood to hang on a wall, so she could point to it as she spoke.

Falling Star said to those who sat in on her story-telling, "As we have already talked about, The Serpent tells of the motions of the moon and of the sun . . . and we do acknowledge that it is Mother Earth who revolves around the sun and Sister Moon revolves around Mother Earth." She paused after that parenthetical remark and said, "The Serpent tells us the time of the Solstice, both the summer solstice and the winter solstice. The head of the snake, as we already know, faces the evening sunset on the day of the summer solstice, and there is a reason for that." Her listeners squirmed, mostly children, but included several older adolescents and adults.

She continued, "The mouth of the serpent looks like it is about to devour the circle. It is the circle of life protecting The People and humanity. However, due to the shifting of priorities from spiritual to material, the circle of life now succumbs to the pressures of that shift, and bends to allow the serpent to begin to swallow the people, no longer protected. This represents the destruction of The People and the rest of humanity, because at this point the energy of the serpent is not in alignment with Great Spirit. The snake is built lying in the wound of a scar. *The Great Serpent's prophecy warns that at the end of the Fourth World, destruction and darkness may come with great power, with great force that none, nothing would survive except Mother Earth. All life would be gone. Mother Earth could even be shattered."*

"So when will this happen, Grandmother?" one child asked.

"Good question. I'll get to that," replied Falling Star. "What makes this information important is for one reason, it comes from the ancient knowledge of our People. In ancient times, members of our People who built this Great Serpent knew all of this and more. They built it as a message from Mother Earth and Great Spirit that was meant for them and for all generations that followed.

"For a second reason, and just as important, that message was meant for me and for you, so that we are reminded of the ways of our People, and we are reminded we are one with each other and one with Mother Earth, and one with Great Spirit.

"Even more importantly, this message was designed for your children, and for your children's children, and their children, and on until humankind living in the Fourth World evolves and emerges into a higher state of being, or until this World ends and a Fifth World begins.

"Exactly when that will occur, I'm not sure, but we will see the signs." Her audience members look around with question marks on their faces.

After a long pause, Falling Star said, "The Great Serpent was built upon a scar on Mother Earth that was made by a part of a star falling into her, creating a large wound. *That star may return and in my visions, is scheduled to return.*

"The urgent message of the prophecy of the Great Serpent brings the message of choice and power for humanity, for our children's children to return to the way of Spirit, the Great Oneness.

"The Serpent speaks to how parts of The People and others come to feel separated from each other and from Mother Earth. In my visions, I have seen powerful separations occur. I also know that these separations have occurred before in prior worlds, times that have been long forgotten.

"We have stories about those times of great power being used among the great civilizations, and stories of misuse of that power. They were during times, of course, again now forgotten, of greed, lust and material things that forced Mother Earth to do the bidding of those not aligned with Great Spirit that harmed the balance that Mother Earth provides. *When these things happen again,* I suspect, it will be the time of the Fourth World ending.

"Mother Earth preserved those who were in alignment with the Great Oneness. However, she might not be capable of preserving us or the rest of humanity this time as she did at the end of the prior worlds.

Summer's breeze wafted through the space of deep consecration of thought and intent as her listeners pondered what they were hearing. For some reason, they felt particularly riveted to today's stories, even though they had heard much of this before as part of other stories. Today they were hearing all of this in a new way.

"The prophecy of the Serpent also shows how the jaws are closing as the Serpent prepares to swallow The People. Should that happen, Mother Earth will not be able to provide for us. Because of the separations occurring, because of the damage done to her by those in power, and because of neglect and dishonoring of her by humanity, she might easily have a heart attack."

"Heart attack?" asked one of the adult listeners, "what's that?"

"No one in our memory has suffered or died of a heart attack," replied Falling Star, "but Grandfather Gray Wolf has told his story of one man who did. Grandfather Gray Wolf was unable to save him. He was a friend to Blue Cornflower long before Mark of the Bear was born. That man had been scared by a big grizzly bear."

Murmurings.

"Yes," Falling Star went on, "several men had been exploring mountain country to try to find a way over the mountains on the way to where we are now. Then all of a sudden a big grizzly bear stood up in front of him and roared. He turned around in fright and ran as far and as fast as he could go. He had never encountered or even seen a grizzly before. Grandfather Gray Wolf said that the stress of the encounter caused that man's heart to beat so fast that it couldn't keep up with itself. Finally, that man died. He died of a heart attack that was caused by stress."

"So, are you saying that if we and our children and so on fail to honor Mother Earth, she might have a heart attack and die?" asked an adult listener.

"In essence, yes," Falling Star admitted reluctantly and added, ". . . and yet, there's more to it. If Mother Earth comes to a point at which she can no longer keep everything going, in what she provides for us, plus maintaining her beauty and balance, and taking the abuse from humanity, she just might have a heart attack."

"How could she have a heart attack?" challenged an older child.

"Do you remember the two twins? The ones who sit at each end of her pole or axis?" Some nodded.

"Well, that pole or axis runs right through her middle. She turns on that axis. Her turning and the way she turns gives us day and night. Father Sun provides us with light. He shines upon Mother Earth constantly. What happens is, Mother Earth turns or rotates from left to right in relation to Father Sun. As she turns, sun shines on that part of Mother Earth that is facing the light. The other part of her turns into darkness. That is what makes day and night.

"We as humans living upon her require both day and night. Plants and animals require day and night. We have grown to require both day and night as well. And, as we live, we need both day and night to survive. We cannot have all day all the time, or night all the time. This is part of the balance that Mother Earth provides.

"Yet, here is where the prophecy of the Serpent comes in to play. Mother Earth is stressed and may become even more stressed, so stressed in fact that her axis may vibrate so fast, she gets sick from the stress of it. If it vibrates too fast, so fast that it couldn't keep up with itself, it could stop vibrating, just like when a heart attack happens. That means that Mother Earth would stop spinning on her axis. However, she would be still in the heavens and still circling Father Sun."

Falling Star stopped momentarily to clear her throat.

"My visions tell me that *the star,* I mentioned earlier, *is still coming.* Whether or not that star collides with Mother Earth or simply brushes by, I can't tell. It might smash into Mother Earth to cause her destruction. Or, that star may come as a friend to her, I don't know.

Squirming.

Shifting of positions.

"What I do know is that change is on the way, and it is a change that no one will want to happen."

Silence.

"Another layer of meaning the Serpent offers us is that during this time where we would have three days of darkness, others would have three days of daylight. The three undulations of the Serpent going up signify three days of daylight, while the three going down signify three days of darkness, all the while the Serpent is devouring humanity."

Silence.

"Of course, you might imagine the destruction this might cause, the tremendous death and suffering of everyone. We would find great changes occurring. What was of great value before will no longer have value. Everything that was created by humanity will become as nothing. Things that stand that require power from the sun or from water or from something else will not work. Few will know how to survive.

"I'm not sure what all of this means, because all of us live in oneness with Mother Earth. But this is the legacy the Great Serpent leaves us."

Shifting of positions among listeners.

Silence.

"But, Grandmother, what about that star you said was coming? The star you see in your visions?" asked another child.

"Oh, yes, the star," answered Falling Star. "That could be a star that either adds to the destruction from Mother Earth's heart attack, or could be the cause of the total destruction of Mother Earth entirely . . . or it could be her friend."

"Her friend?" challenged another.

"Think of another alternative," offered Falling Star. "It could be that while Mother Earth would still revolve around Father Sun, she would sit in a stand still . . . in the heavens . . . not rotating . . . burning up on one side and cloaked in blinding darkness on the other.

"Remember Sister Moon?" Falling Star asked and looked around for nods of acknowledgement. "In my visions, Sister Moon tries very hard to get Mother Earth to rotate again. She tugs and pulls her hardest and actually starts Mother to turn a bit. As Mother Earth begins to turn slowly, that star traveling through the cosmos moves at such a speed we cannot even comprehend it. Well, that star speaks to Mother Earth. Just as that star comes close, Mother Earth hears the star and Great Spirit, and she moves herself slightly, just enough to get out of the way. Yet that star still brushes by very close.

"As she brushes by Mother Earth, it causes her to begin spinning again. So then, we would have day and night much as before. Her twins that keep her pole spinning may stop and switch places at just that moment, so that the North Pole will switch with the South Pole. The twins at each pole would be performing their tasks, again, keeping Mother's axis in line much as before, except for one thing . . ."

Falling Star paused for effect and then continued.

". . . *Mother Earth rotates in the opposite direction.*"

Silence.

Shuffling.

Shifting.

"The prophecy of the Great Serpent says that when this occurs, the sunrise of the Summer Solstice will occur in the *west,* the direction in which the head of the Serpent points."

THE CAMP OF GOD'S TEARS

Gasps.

Yes, my beloveds," Falling Star concluded, *"the sun will rise in the west for us and set in the east."*

Silence.

One by one, each of the listeners got up and left the meeting house. Many felt, especially the adults, the need to contemplate what had been spoken that day. Falling Star remained the only one left in the room. She quietly took down the deerskin showing the Great Serpent. In contemplation herself, she rolled it up, still admiring its genius as she did so. While putting it back into my bundle, she felt again the small pouch that held the clay tablet so cherished by Red Fox.

Throughout that summer, The People continued on as before living harmoniously in our little valley. Some tended their crops planted there year after year. Some fished. Some played. Some tanned the hides of animals brought in. Some decorated the hides with paint, or worked strips of skins and sinews into ropes or usable ties. Some worked on beadwork. Others worked clay. Others cooked. Some told stories. As small as our village at our summer camp was, it was a microcosm of the larger civilization that only the oldest could remember and that only dimly.

By this time I was the oldest living member of The People. As babies were born and children grew, the oldest generation rejoined Spirit in the natural order of things. I had lived in the Ohio River Valley, rich in natural resources and rich in friends and relations living in joy. I had grown into a healer for The People and a great shaman, all before leaving Ohio.

As a young father, I migrated with my friends and relatives along the banks of the Ohio River, and following the Mississippi River north to St. Louis. Then when leadership fell to me, I led my People up the Missouri River.

Despite the extreme hardships, toil, and emotional struggles, I was able to get my People, with the help of an old friend and trader, Warm Stone, from the great falls to the Bitterroot

Mountains. As a shaman I was then able to get my People over the daunting Bitterroots, through the maze of rivers and mountains westward to the Columbia River, and on to the Pacific coast.

Now I was experiencing the end of my personal journey on Mother Earth. I felt fortunate to get to know my grandchildren and great-grandchildren.

However, I still missed my beloved Shining Bird. I longed for her company. Recently she visited me in my dreams. As the summer eased into late summer edging toward autumn, I spent less and less time telling stories and more time in meditation alone somewhere.

This summer more than any other had seen many storms coming through the mountains. The People experienced an unusually cold summer, and our crops did not fare as well due to the reduced heat and light resulting from the cooler than normal summer and unusually frequent cloud covered days. Fresh snow covered the snow capped mountaintops as the late summer storms dropped snow prematurely.

"There you are, beloved Grandfather," scolds Falling Star, as she approaches me sitting on a rock ledge with my legs dangling over the cliff's edge. "I've been looking all over for you." I turn to acknowledge her presence. "I was feeling frightened that something had happened to you, Grandfather."

I sit silently.

I turn back to look out over the view. From my vantage point I could see Mt. St. Helens and the ridges that worked their way up her sides. Thick fog allowed for only the ridge tops to be seen poking their elegant lines above the eddying mists.

Holding my hand out pointing to the peaks, I say, "Look, granddaughter. See the snows there?" Falling Star looks in the direction in which I point. Then she nods looking puzzled. I continue, "It's too early for that much snow. I've been watching the weather this summer. I don't have a good feeling about it. Are you getting everyone in camp ready to migrate down to our winter camp?"

Surprised by this question, Falling Star shakes her head and says, "No, it's too early. We usually don't go down for about another month or so."

I nod silently, eyes half closed, and focus on something far away.

The two of us sat together for a long while in silence. Falling Star did not want to be the one to break the silence. Her heart pounded in anticipation of what I might have to say.

"It's time I return home," I begin softly. "It's time I return home wrapped enfolded into love's warm blanket of the Absolute. My journey in the world of the relative is now over."

Stunned, Falling Star sits motionless and speechless. Inside, her emotions want to scream, *Nooo, no, you can't leave me. You can't leave The People. We need you too much.* But she remains silent.

"In fact, my dearest, dearest Falling Star," I say after long moments with a chilled wind kicking up, I turn to look at my beloved granddaughter in the eye and softly say again, "in fact, my beloved Falling Star," I falter a moment then continue, "now is the end of my journey on Mother Earth. Take me to my house and prepare my robes so that I may lie down."

Struck by the impending finality of the existence of her beloved Grandfather, Falling Star's throat closed. She choked trying to speak. Her emotions held a firm grip on her body causing her to lose her balance. Clumsily she got up from her position, staggered backwards a few steps while still trying to reach for me. Tears flew from her eyes as she moved. Regaining her composure, she helped me up and put her arm around my now seemingly frail body.

It was a long walk back to the village. All the members of this little community who were in camp that afternoon witnessed the two of us slowly making our way to my shelter. They all knew without words the meaning of the scene playing before them. The day grew cold and dark and the chilled wind picked up even more. Children stopped playing and went inside their shelters. The People moved the blankets over the opening of their homes to keep out the cold. Inside chimneys lighted up and smoke curled up and out disappearing in the wind.

Once she got me inside, she arranged my buffalo robe in the center and had me lie down on it. She positioned several other hides with fur on the outside under my head. Then she got up and looked around and found my worn red trader's blanket with the two black stripes at each end and placed it over me, seeking to make me as comfortable as possible. That blanket had been the one my Grandmother Shining Moon used on her bed back in Ohio, and had given to me when I left Ohio. Feeling the cold herself, she built a little fire in the inside hearth.

"Can I get you something to eat? . . . Maybe some soup or stew, or something?" Falling Star asks knowing that someone would have something ready to eat and willing to share.

"No, dear," I reply in a hoarse whisper. "My journey in this physical life is over. Shining Bird is here now. She has come to take me home. I will no longer need food after tonight."

Falling Star releases an emotional gasp.

The two of us stayed in the shelter for most of the night. During this time I completed my telling of the Story of The People. No one disturbed us. After the evening turned into night, then into deep night, the wind calmed down, and silence pervaded the village. I did not stop speaking until the dark began turning into dawn.

As I finish, I look deeply into her eyes and affirm, "We are the last of The People. Because we are the last remaining remnant of a once grand civilization that felt, understood and lived the oneness with Great Spirit, we are the last of the true believers. It is up to you now, my dear granddaughter, to see that The People continue as The People living in the oneness as the Children of the Law of One."

She listened intently to everything I said to her.

THE CAMP OF GOD'S TEARS

Falling Star just sat and looked adoringly at me, unable to take her eyes off me. With tears running down her face, Falling Star put her hand on my torso as I lay there stretched out. Her hand opening and closing while still resting on my middle, trying to grasp on to my soul to keep it with her, yet unable to actually take hold of it as I breathed my last few breaths.

Falling Star saw me smile from time to time and nod to someone in the room she could not see. Shining Bird then appeared to me with her arm outstretched. We both smiled at each other as I lift up out of my body and together we journey into the Absolute.

Falling Star spent the next few hours silently weeping with her head resting on her beloved Grandfather's now empty body.

Winter had hit the summer camp early that year. It came sooner than expected. It had been their usual practice to begin their trek down to the coast long before the snows came. Yet this year storms dumped heavy snows at the higher elevations and a light dusting of snow to their little valley far earlier than normal.

By the time Mark of the Bear had returned with Floating Hawk and others from exploring the mountain to identify potential locations for game due to the early buildup of snows, they sense something had happened. Those in camp had already built a pit filled with wood for the funeral pyre for Gray Wolf's body, and the fire was already ablaze in its own ceremonial dance.

"What happened?" Mark of the Bear asked Falling Star. She told him what had happened as he put away his gear. As she spoke, she noticed that Mark of the Bear reacted with far less emotion than what she had expected.

After he had eaten, he turned to her with a smug look on his face and stated, "Finally. Finally with him gone, I will be seen as the leader of our People. Finally, I will get to take *my rightful place* among The People," he said loudly hitting a fist on something in the air.

"Hah! All the other tribes around will now know that I am the new leader of The People. They will know Mark of the Bear as the leader of

The People, fearless fighter of grizzly bears . . . and I will take my place among the great leaders of The People." He threw his head back as he spoke, taunting some unseen challenger he conjured up while speaking.

Falling Star could not believe what she was hearing and seeing. She knew that Mark of the Bear wrestled with his ego, but she had been blind to his hidden aspirations. Her eyes grew wide as she sat and heard what she did not want to hear.

"Yes, my dear, my beloved," he continued with a voice tinged with a sneer. "Yes, my dearest, for too long now I've lived in your shadow ever since the grizzly bear incident. Finally, I will be seen for who I am, and for what I can offer The People. Your Grandfather will no longer cloud everyone's mind as to who leads The People. It is now your husband, Mark of the Bear." His fist hit the center of his chest as he finished.

Falling Star turned away with head lowered. She wanted to argue with him about his sense of leadership and how that did not correspond with the sense of leadership traditionally experienced by The People, and how his sense of leadership was incongruent with the overarching custom of not really having leaders.

The overwhelming grief she felt for the loss of her Grandfather was now layered with shock at the words she was hearing. Her grief felt further compounded by another kind of grief. Her beloved husband, the one she was promised to be together with forever, had re-positioned himself in relationship to her and The People. This grieved her deeply. All of her feelings jumbled together, and she felt unable to articulate her thoughts and feelings at that moment.

Due to her painful grieving, Falling Star withdrew from her normal daily activities and found herself in need of solitude. She felt she needed to lose herself in meditation that she found to be soothing. Connecting with Great Spirit at a very deep level assisted her grieving process. She also felt in need of inner guidance and a more focused orientation. As a result, she paid little attention to much of what was going on around her for most of that day.

Her parents, having aged into grandparents, collected her children at their home to allow her emotional space to complete her grieving. Even though Stalking Bear, Star Rising and Dancing Swan also grieved the death of their great-grandfather also, they could see the incredibly strong tie Gray Wolf had with Falling Star. They could see how deeply affected Falling Star was at his death and understood the importance of the loss of his counsel to her as the leading shaman in their little village.

During the next several days while Falling Star spent time off alone in her meditation, Mark of the Bear got busy organizing himself and the rest of the village, not for returning to their winter camp, but for going on one last hunt.

He and several of his friends had spotted large herds migrating early from the higher elevations, and Mark of the Bear wanted to reach them before they moved farther down the mountain.

Ambition ruled his ego, as he imagined himself returning to the coast and offering other tribes plenty of meat, for a price of course. The planned hunt for game cloaked his hunt for power.

Snow flurries blowing through their summer camp caused much discomfort, because their summer shelters, while sturdy, were not designed to house The People during the cold winters in snow country. However, Mark of the Bear assured everyone that as soon as he and the hunters returned with their game, he would make sure The People would leave for winter camp.

He felt very good about organizing hunting parties, especially for this one last hunt. In the absence of Falling Star to give council or caution, Mark of the Bear persuaded all able-bodied villagers to join in. Nearly all the men, many of the women and nearly all of the older children agreed to make this one last hunt of the season a successful one, including his oldest son, Running Deer.

His reasoning made some sense. The more people engaged in this effort, not just to hunt, but also to clean and carry, the less time it would take to come back successful. Then they would all return to winter camp with an overstock of meat to see them and their neighbors through the winter.

By the end of the third day, Falling Star jolted back to reality. She awakened from her grief with a sense of impending doom. While in meditation, she had glimpsed a vision of snow-covered bodies with one feather sticking up out of the snow, Mark of the Bear's feather. She felt directed to change the flow of energy that was occurring. She jolted out of her dream-state anxious to find Mark of the Bear. She found Mark of the Bear visiting with several villagers just as his meeting was about finished.

"We need to leave camp immediately!" she exclaimed as she approached the small group.

"What are you talking about?" challenged Mark of the Bear. "We are just about ready to go on one last hunt. We know where large herds are, and we will be supremely successful if we hunt now."

"What are *you* talking about?" challenged Falling Star right back at him in front of the others. "We have to leave for winter camp, and we have to leave right *now!*"

The other hunters shifted weight feeling uncomfortable witnessing this confrontation.

"I have been in conversation with Mother Earth," said Falling Star as she escalated the challenge. "She told me that winter . . . solid winter, is coming early this year. That a gigantic storm is coming that will prevent us from leaving summer camp."

She paused briefly to catch her breath then continued, "If we leave now, we will be able to get out in time. Otherwise we will be trapped here for the winter." She looked directly at Mark of the Bear as she spoke. "We must get everything together to leave at dawn for winter camp. I just hope we can get down to the coast in time. I beg of you, please change your mind about this."

Turning to Floating Hawk and the others, she desperately warned, "We don't have time for this hunt. Don't you see that we must leave these mountains while we still can? You *don't* have to go on this hunt." She caught her breath then said accusingly, "You're going only because Mark of the Bear wants you to. Don't you know that blind obedience to a leader is fatal? . . . You know better, Floating Hawk."

"Now, now, dear," Mark of the Bear soothed, but with no intention of changing his plans. "Let's just go back to our place and talk about this." He put his arm around his beloved Falling Star, turning her around so they could walk back to their shelter together. As he did so, he turned his head back over his shoulder and gave a wink and a nod to those watching this unusual display of conflict between the two most revered in their village.

"Mark," Falling Star began when they had reached their shelter. "You can't go on this hunt. It would mean we will have to spend the winter here. Don't you realize that we are not equipped to winter here in the snow and cold?"

"Now that your precious Grandfather is dead, *I* am the leader. Don't you realize that? Don't you understand that *I* think we need this one last hunt to get just as much game for meat and other supplies as we can?" he countered.

"*What?* What are you saying?" she escalated the argument again. "We already have enough. We don't need any more than what we have right now. You know it is not part of the balance with Great Spirit and Mother Earth to take more than we need. The fish and other seafood supplement our winter's supply of meat. What are you talking about?"

"I'm talking about coming back to our neighbors down below with meat to swap with them for other items. We will have so much. We will impress them with our hunting skills. They will be much impressed with us and with me as the leader."

Falling Star felt shocked at hearing this.

"We are Children of the Law of One." Falling Star said. "Have you forgotten your . . . *our* . . . alignment with Spirit? Have you forgotten that we are Children of the Law of One . . . that we are one with each other and with Great Spirit? Have you forgotten that we descend from a long line of those who understood, practiced and lived their oneness . . . their alignment with the Great Oneness?"

"We have always lived in oneness with ourselves, oneness with others, and oneness with Great Spirit and Mother Earth. What you are talking about is not-oneness. What you are describing is power *over*, not power *with*. What you are talking about is separation. We, as The People, *cannot tolerate separation.*

"You are revealing your ambition, planning on committing acts that do not manifest oneness with Mother Earth, and that do not promote oneness with others. Your desire to be a hero and a worshipped leader also says you wish to elevate yourself over all of the rest of us. That is separation and that leads to a total breakdown of our society. If you do this, we will no longer be *The People*! That will be the end of us as The People."

Smirking, Mark of the Bear retorted, "You talk about oneness as though it really existed. I've never bought into that idea and don't believe in it . . . Yes, I felt you upstaged me from the beginning and that is not oneness."

Falling Star's eyes widened as she heard these devastating words.

He continued, "Yes, my beloved. I have loved you and still love you. I don't believe in the oneness doctrine you spout all the time. I knew my time would come eventually, and finally it has. I knew that if I just said all the right things, and comported myself in just the right ways, no one would know.

"Finally, my time to be a hero and the rightful leader has come, and you, my beloved, cannot stand in my way any longer. Your Grandfather is dead and that opens the door for me to be what I have desired to be my entire life . . . and, so, my lovely, I will go through with my intentions as planned. You are not robbing me of my glory this time, like after the bear incident and the hunting event with that other tribe."

"Your ego is running you, Mark of the Bear," Falling Star forcefully challenged again with a stern but quiet voice. "You're letting your ego drive this plan. You are not concerned with The People's needs. *You're a mess!* What's driving you is the desire to impress others with how great you think you are.

"Don't you see that you already are a leader in the eyes of The People? Don't you know that you always have been a leader and a hero among our People? You make yourself sound like a 'wanna be.' You also just admitted to being a fraud, not being genuine, or true to your divine self. Pretending to embrace the Oneness allows a sense of separation. No wonder you've been unhappy all these years. That tells me you do not value who you are and who you are to our village.

"By the way you're talking, clearly you do not see yourself as The People see you. You talk like you have nothing and are nothing until you accomplish some feat to show everyone your prowess. You already *are* a highly valued and honored member and have to do nothing to prove it or show it. *There is nothing you need to do to make you more of who you already are.*"

She paused briefly to collect her thoughts and went on. "My love, I have always felt you suffered from some kind of turmoil inside." As she spoke she moved closer to him and touched his arm to give her words greater impact. "We've had so many conversations about being one and being one with the One. I could see you struggle over the years with that concept. I knew you didn't feel it, and not everyone does . . . and if you don't feel it, then it's okay.

"It's just that when you can feel that oneness, your path opens up for you. It becomes easier to breathe your way through your life's journey. It becomes easier to know what the right thing to do is." Mark of the Bear turned slightly toward her, allowing her to continue.

"I can now see that it is your ego that craves satisfaction for something it can never get. I can see your appetite has moved from wanting hero-worship to power . . . power over others. By convincing the others to follow you on this one last hunt, you are exercising power where you have no responsibility.

"Since we already have adequate supplies to last a while until we can get what the ocean offers us, you are acting irresponsibly. We as a People do not need to offer meat in trade so as to impress the other tribes. We, as a People, do not *need* to influence others to honor us. We need only to honor ourselves. What you are attempting to seek is something that will cause an out-of-balance state among us and an increased sense of separation with other tribes."

After another brief pause, she swallowed hard and continued, "The People have never had a leader in all of its history, at least this kind of 'leader.' By you proclaiming yourself leader, you are disrupting the energy of a People with a thousand years of peaceful history without a leader and without a need for one. What you're attempting to do is a betrayal of our identity as a People. By doing this, you are showing that you have become a two-hearted person."

"I am betraying nothing!" her husband responded forcefully with a wave of his arm through the air and a sound of anger in his voice. "My destiny is to be with you forever, and to be the leader to our People. I intend to fulfill my destiny, my beloved. I intend to lead everyone on this one last hunt, and then our People and all other tribes will see how great I am and will see me as *their* leader."

Gulping in disbelief, she asked, "You mean you still intend to go? . . . After all that I have said?" He turned his back on her at that question.

"Don't you realize that Mother Earth told me this next storm, and another one that will follow right behind that one, will bring deep snow? Winter will come early and stay. If we remain here for the winter, we might not survive. Don't you understand that? . . . Or doesn't your ego want to accept the responsibility for that possible outcome?"

Turning back to her with his face congealed with determination, he spoke softly but decisively, "We are going on this hunt tomorrow. I've made the arrangements with everyone who is going . . . including Floating Hawk. And that my dear, is nearly all the adults and the older children. Our son, Running Deer, is coming along as well. I can't back out now. Don't you see? . . . I can't change plans now . . . what would that look like? . . . I can't let anyone think I would back down because my wife begged me not to go.

"Besides, I won't let you upstage me again! You did that when we were young with the grizzly bear. You stole my glory then, and I will not let you take away the glory that is due me now. You robbed me of my glory of fighting a grizzly bear. I was a hero until you walked into camp riding that bear, the very bear that was mine to kill!

"Then you did it again. You robbed me of my glory again when we first hunted with that other tribe. You had to play shaman by calling in the game. I would have been a hero then, except for you overshadowing me in front of everyone.

"*This* time I don't need you to call in the game for me. I know just where they are. They are there waiting for me, Mark of the Bear!"

A moment of shocked silence overwhelmed Falling Star.

"The bear incident? What do you mean? I thought you released your childhood anger and saw the perfection of that event. Don't you see that I took nothing from you that day? We both acted in the best interest of our People. We each performed according to how we were inner-directed. *Together, as a team,* we effected protection for everyone, and it resulted in a harmonious outcome.

"I can see that your ego wanted to wring hero-worship from everyone beyond what was already afforded you. When we allow our egos to run us, it develops an appetite that can never be satisfied, no matter what. You allowed your ego to create a self-centered focus that fragmented you in a sense of separation. I can see that by you clinging to that sense of 'not-having-enough,' and not enough hero-worship, you felt that this event thwarted your desire to be seen as a hero.

"Yet, you've been seen as a hero ever since then . . . by everyone. From what you have said just now, I can see that you never let that go. You allowed it to cling to you, and it festered creating a toxic space within you. And that goes for the hunting incident as well. You contributed to that event significantly. We each acted in our own capacity. We each contributed to the success of that hunt in our own way. It's just that your ego was not given the energy that it craved."

"No, my dear," he countered again, "you don't know what you are talking about. I intend to be a hero in the minds of The People and all the other peoples we know. You're not going to take that away from me *this time*."

Eyes still wide, Falling Star spit out again, "Your ego is running you. Don't you know that's fatal?

"Grandfather told me about greed and lust and ego. Now I can see what that looks like. You are lusting for power, power over others so that you can feed your ego with it. Don't you know that this energy throws you and everyone here out of balance?

"You want to take more than we need. We don't need more meat and supplies. We don't need to impress anyone down below. That is nothing more than greed and lust, empty appetites that can never be satisfied. It constantly drives to get more and take more and never to the point of satisfaction."

"Oh, what do you know?" Mark of the Bear slaps the air as he turned away from her.

"What I know is," she lightly strikes her forehead with her fingertips expressing a sudden insight, "if you do this . . . If you take everyone and go on this one last hunt, that will be the end of The People. You will end us with your ego-driven greed and lust for power. You don't want the meat for The People. You want to use it as a bargaining chip to influence the other tribes to bow to your whims."

THE CAMP OF GOD'S TEARS

With his back to her, he tossed his head over his shoulder with a grimace.

"And what's this about taking everyone with you? So, you've managed to persuade everyone to follow you blindly," she raises her voice tossing her head back. "Blind obedience to a leader is also fatal."

Turning while standing then beginning to fold down to the floor with tears streaming down her face and arms holding her stomach, she added, "You don't care about The People. Your plan will end The People. You and your ego will cause us to extinguish the last of a great civilization. Abuse of ego is fatal, and you will end us."

She began sobbing and choking and crumbled on the floor in an emotional heap.

She choked as she tried to speak one last thought and said, "Please, please, don't go." Choking, she folded completely down on the floor.

Realizing that his beloved felt so distraught as to be on her knees, sobbing with her entire body, he turned toward her and kneeled down and gently embraced her tenderly in his arms. With the children elsewhere, he realized they were alone. He laid her down on their sleeping robes, and then he stoked up the fire, adding more wood to take the chill off their home.

To comfort her, he laid down alongside her stroking her head gently. As the hours passed, the two of them dissolved into a space of oneness together, moving from their place in bed to another dimension, not looking back at the strands of invisible silver cord that held them bound to their physical bodies. Totally oblivious as to what was around them or where they were, they continued to embrace one another beyond their bodies, entwining themselves in and around each other. The two lovers felt the ecstasy that comes from experiencing wave after wave of climatic energy occurring between them. They both felt the unexplainable thrill of love, joy, and pleasure that comes from this kind of a union, a union not of the physical that cannot be described with words.

Falling Star slept soundly after their other-worldly love making. Her sleep ended, again with the mysterious dream-like vision of an eagle feather sticking up out of a bank of snow. Startled she awoke abruptly. She felt for Mark of the Bear. After reaching and finding the bed empty, she sat up alarmed by his absence and perplexed by her vision.

The sun was up and sent warming rays into their camp between threatening clouds overhead. She grabbed the red trader's blanket her Grandfather had left to her and threw it around her as she rushed outside.

Standing in the middle of the village open area, Falling Star looked around at each of the shelters to see who was up and out. At first she saw no one. Then she spied several children playing together beyond several shelters on the other side. She could see Blue Cornflower and several Grandmothers were watching them. Squinting her eyes to see farther, she could see her parents, Stalking Bear and Whispering Dove sitting outside as well, watching her two youngest children play. She saw no others.

It was then she comprehended that nearly everyone in their summer camp had gone with the hunting party, led by Mark of the Bear.

With the terrible realization that the existence of The People was in jeopardy, she crumbled to her knees with a loud desperate scream from the depths of her soul that reached everyone's ears. The desperation of her scream reached Great Spirit.

The choice was not Mark of the Bear's alone.

Those choosing to join in the one last hunt, and those choosing to ignore the warning to leave summer camp early, chose ultimately to blindly follow Mark of the Bear.

They had the power to choose to go or to stay.

The villagers chose to go without a sense of their responsibility.

Falling Star realized that most everyone had chosen to empty the village to follow an ego driven idea without a sense of responsibility to remain in alignment. With that realization, torrents of tears flooded her broken heart.

Their choice to go was a fatal one.

With that choice, the very last of The People was doomed.

With that choice, all of Heaven cried.

With that choice, it became the Camp of God's Tears.

51

THE TRANSITION

Snow fell.

Winter came to the mountain summer camp early as predicted.

One morning before the sun had had a chance to warm the camp between the storm clouds, the earth shook with a vengeance. The earthquake caught everyone off guard, especially the first shock. Rumbling and quaking continued for a while throughout the day before tapering off.

No one in the village was injured. Most had still been in their beds. Those up and about had either fallen or had grabbed onto something for support during that first jolt.

Those who had remained in camp spent the rest of that day seeing after each other and checking for any damage to their homes. Falling Star noted the homes that sustained damage, and that evening they discussed who could work the repairs. Several homes sustained more damage than others. For purposes of conserving heat and resources, she requested several families to combine living quarters, especially those whose homes could not be immediately repaired.

Days passed.

More snow fell.

The hunting party had still not returned.

They were long overdue.

Falling Star had now assumed the responsibility for organizing those who had remained in camp. This included the Grandmothers, Grandfathers, her parents, Stalking Bear, Whispering Dove, and Star Rising, her aunt, Dancing Swan, her uncle, Blue Cornflower, Mark of the Bear's mother, and few of the older children, all of the younger children and babies along with their mothers, and several other adults who had chosen not to go. Some of the hunters had left their children with relatives or friends. Falling Star dearly missed her oldest son, Running Deer who had insisted on going on that one last hunt with the others in the hunting party.

Walking through the summer camp with her red trader's blanket wrapped around her, the ground now covered with snow, Falling Star took inventory of her People, The People for whom she now felt solely responsible. She continually asked in her prayers and meditations as to the welfare of the hunting party, the hunting party that consisted of the rest of The People.

No answers came.

Standing in the snow with her red trader's blanket draped over her, she peered off into the mist-covered distance trying to see, hoping to see indications of her People returning to camp. Her heart told her they were not coming.

Her imagination wished them to return. Hope against hope she stood at the edge of camp for a very long time, peering, imagining movement through the mists and clouds, beyond the mists and clouds . . . and not seeing. Returning to the same spot day after day, she stood there at the edge of the camp and tried to see what was not to be seen.

No such image manifested.

Falling Star was not anxious to face the unwelcomed thought that the hunting party would not be returning. She was not anxious to face the unwelcomed thought that the few remaining in camp were the only survivors of a once magnificent People. She was not anxious to face the unwelcomed thought of maintaining the survival of those who remained throughout the winter in a camp so unprepared to face bitter cold and heavy snows.

"Someone's coming," she heard a voice call out. Falling Star's heart skipped a beat, her pulse raced. She rushed out into the

The Transition

center of the camp looking, reaching with her eyes and her heart for the return of those she loved.

Off in the misty distance, she finally spotted one lone hunter, staggering but still pushing forward by only his sheer will to reach home.

Several Elders and Falling Star scurried to greet him. His awkward balance caused him to wheel around and fall to the ground. Falling Star made a dash and reached him first just as he hit the ground. Kneeling down she moved his arm from over his face to see who it was.

"Floating Hawk," she said as she sucked in her breath. "Floating Hawk, you're hurt. We'll get you to my house so we can tend to you."

"No," he gasped. "Don't move me. I'm grateful I made it here at all." His eyes closed then opened as he suffered to breathe. "I won't live long enough to make it there or anywhere."

Wheezing, with a cough, he paused then spoke to Falling Star, "The earthquake . . . caused rocks . . . and trees . . . and snow . . . to . . . to . . . fall . . . . fall on where we . . . where we . . . camped."

As he labored to speak, several more Grandfathers and Grandmothers had approached the spot in the snow where Falling Star held Floating Hawk's head in her lap. Her knees and arm served to prop him up. They listened and wished he could speak louder or repeat himself. However, that was not to be.

Falling Star cocked her head to bring her ear closer to his words. He coughed again and spit up some blood. Several drops of blood stained her cheek and hand.

"Then . . . when . . . the snow fell . . . an avalanche . . . covered us . . . an avalanche from the rock overhang above us . . . Our entire . . . everyone . . . died . . . under that . . . under that mountain of snow and rocks . . . It . . . buried . . . everyone."

He coughed again, this time more blood came up. Saliva mixed with blood drooled from his mouth. Tears filled his eyes. Not wanting to interrupt him, yet wanting to pull more information from this dying man, Falling Star remained listening, not moving.

Then with another cough, he added, "I knew . . . I was badly . . . badly hurt . . . but managed . . . to crawl out. The last thing . . . I saw . . . before I was able to . . . crawl away from the . . . from the snow covered rubble . . . was . . . only of snow . . . only snow with part of Mark of the Bear's feather sticking up."

With that his body coughed internally. After a few more painful moments, he opened his eyes and looked into hers and added, "You were . . . right . . . blind obedience to a leader is fatal . . ." Floating Hawk's eyes then closed for the last time.

Pain shot through Falling Star's gut as she listened to the last of his words, remembering her vision showing her the scene as described by Floating Hawk.

Doubling over in emotional grief suffered at many levels, she slumped over his chilled body sobbing uncontrollably. Everyone there stood around in shock for a few moments. Then one by one, several reached for Falling Star to help her back to her home. The others picked up Floating Hawk's body and moved him to a more appropriate place to keep him until they could determine what they should do.

Several homes had been reconstructed to add wind breaks of wood angled from the frame to shield the doorway opening previously protected only by hides and blankets. Everyone worked together to take stock of food for the remaining survivors of this camp. Even though everyone received equal portions of whatever foodstuffs were available, some nursing mothers found extra shares appearing without mention or notice.

Homes that had been left empty by those in the hunting party were appropriated for any remaining clothes, furs, food or firewood. Some of these homes were moved into by combined families whose homes were not repairable. The severely damaged homes were torn down for firewood.

Now that the camp had been consolidated and reorganized, Falling Star began holding meetings. She found these meetings helpful by keeping everyone informed and as a source for ideas and solutions. These meetings also served to reinforce their sense of community, and their connectedness after a disaster that threatened their survival. There was no way out and they were isolated from their sense of connection to the coast where they had a winter village with occasional interactions with other tribes, and a sure source of food . . . the ocean.

"When we have the next break between storms, I'll take some of the older children out with me to see if we can find any game," Falling Star informed the group who met regularly to negotiate survival through the winter. The Elders nodded. "We still have a supply of smoked meat, but if we can get some fresh meat, then we know we still have the smoked meat for later should we need it . . . Besides that will get them out of camp for exercise and give them something else to think about."

Survival was Falling Star's only focus, survival of her People. She refused to allow herself to drift off to the past. The past would not help her and her People now. She was unsure of the future. So now was the only time she thought about, now, and getting her People to the next now to continue living. Getting everyone through the winter and then down to the coast as soon as winter permitted was her primary and only objective.

Then, one night, deep in the caverns of her dreams, she saw Mark of the Bear coming for her. She saw herself smiling broadly and reaching for him. He reached for her.

"Come with me," he invited as he smiled into her eyes. He smiled at her with a light that had shed all ego attachment to the physical world. As she heard his words and saw his smile, she felt happy and lighter and relieved of all deadening responsibility tying her to an earthbound experience.

Emotionally charged by her delight at seeing him again, she opened her eyes from the dream only to find that this was not a dream at all. He was standing beside her bed, smiling at her with his arm extended in invitation.

Surprised by the reality of what she thought had been a dream, she found herself tempted to lift up out of her body to join him . . . to frolic in the ethers, to dance among the stars.

"Oh, how I long to join you, my beloved," she murmured softly to him. "Life here is agony, too tortuous to go on . . . without you."

"Yes, my love," Mark of the Bear responded, "we were promised to be together forever. Come with me, now, my love."

Just at the moment Falling Star began to lift up out of her body, suddenly a sharp crack of a baby's cry sliced through the night. This desperate sound from one of the infants startled Falling Star into the realization of what it was she was doing.

"No," she suddenly announced to Mark of the Bear. "No, I cannot go with you. I love you and I love my People too. I cannot leave my People . . . your People."

"But," he countered, "we were promised to be together forever. Do you know what you are turning down?"

"Yes," was her answer. "There are many kinds of love, my dear. I love you . . . and I love our children . . . and I love our People. Right now, I am the only hope they have of surviving, and I intend to get them through this winter and then down to the coast. If I leave them now, they will all die. If any die despite my efforts, well, at least I tried to save them. I refuse to abandon them." She paused smiling sadly at her beloved, "And I guess I love them more than I want to be with you."

At that last remark, Mark of the Bear faded from her sight.

Throughout the remainder of the night, Falling Star slept soundly and awoke rested and with a renewed sense of determination.

For much of the cold bitterness of that winter, Falling Star had managed to ration food and kept most everyone busy with tasks designed to promote survival. Some worked at snow removal from the doorways and roofs, while others searched and collected wood, and more.

Due to the stress of the living conditions, nursing mothers found their supply of milk drying up, resulting in their babies suffering from dehydration and starvation. All the babies died before winter ended.

The Transition

Reminding everyone to keep hearth fires going throughout the night was a constant task. Letting the night's hearth fires go out worried Falling Star. Not everyone would or could keep at least one person awake during the night to keep those fires going.

As a result some folks died, having frozen to death in their sleep. On her usual rounds in the morning, she found both her parents having died in the night while still tenderly holding each other. Near them were the frozen bodies of her aunt, uncle and Blue Cornflower. A tear found its way down her cheek as she gazed upon them. She had experienced too much emotional agony and social trauma to afford her a greater expression of grief than that lonely tear.

With the ground frozen and covered with several feet of snow, neither burials nor cremations were conducted. Cremations required too much precious wood that was needed for keeping the living warm and still living. As a result, all the dead bodies were piled up outside away from the camp until such time as this treacherous season permitted a more passable treatment. The bodies would not thaw until the mountain thawed.

As part of her routine as the only shaman, Falling Star meditated to keep her connected with Great Spirit and Mother Earth. She felt grateful for the guidance she received in this way. She followed the direction she felt inside, and nearly every project or task proved successful for keeping a central core of her People alive, which included her two children, Painted Star and Yellow Lily.

When meat supplies dwindled to a frightening level, Mother Earth instructed her to show the older children how to use a slingshot. So, Falling Star tasked several adults to make slingshots. On their first sunny day despite the cold, just as the heart of winter was passing, the slingshots were finished.

"Is everyone ready?" she asked the children. She looked them over, the would-be hunters, the oldest about ten years old and the youngest about seven. If anyone but Mother Earth had given her these instructions, she might have doubted. As it was, she tried to appear not skeptical based on what these rag-tag dozen children dressed in make-do winter clothing appeared to be . . . on a hunt for quarry that might mean the difference between life and death of The People.

"Now show me how you make it work again, please," she asked them. Some showed more proficiency than others. Several children clumsily juggled the slingshot without getting much of the hang of it. Nevertheless, Falling Star encouraged everyone and gave each a pat on the head or shoulder with kind words of support.

Together they marched off through the deep snow in search of game . . . armed with slingshots.

After what seemed like a long distance in the cold, several of the children showed signs of fatigue. Slim rations had reduced their capacity to exert much in the way of extended activity, especially in the devastating cold.

The group had staggered itself along the way, the stronger children able to push farther ahead. Those weaker just stopped where they were when they found they could no longer move forward. Just then, someone spotted a rabbit.

"Hey, there's one," shouted one child.

"I see it," affirmed another.

With these announcements, suddenly their energy levels felt the rush of adrenaline, and several began running.

"Don't chase the rabbits," cautioned Falling Star, "they will run from you. When you see one, stalk it until you can get close enough to take a shot."

With that, the children, seeing the possibility of actually getting something, followed her advice. One child put a stone in his slingshot, pulled back the leather sling and let go.

Whhoooosh!

"I got one! I got one!" announced the proud hunter. That one success provided the rest of the children with the emotional fuel they needed to continue.

Falling Star went over to inspect the rabbit. Picking it up by its ears, she noticed that the stone had never hit the creature but lay off to one side in a snow bank, not even noticeably close. "Ah, Mother, you clever one," she spoke to herself, "you *gave* us your rabbit. Thank you . . . and thank you for letting the children think they did it."

By the end of the afternoon, every child had at least one rabbit to offer the hungry tribe. Not one had a mark on it from stones. Several Elders took the rabbits and showed the children how to clean and prepare the meat for cooking. Others involved the children in showing them how to cook the meat in several ways. It was a day to celebrate life and living and a day to give deep gratitude for the ability to continue life and living.

Falling Star retired without engaging in any of these activities following the hunt. When her children came in from enjoying a life-giving meal and the celebratory spirit of The People, she grabbed them tightly and hugged them closely to her without saying a word. Bending her head down, she wept in gratitude.

Subsequent hunting parties went out, each one led by Falling Star. On occasion several children went out by themselves believing themselves to be great hunters. Rarely did any come back with game. They began to accept Falling Star as a shaman who was able to call in game, even if it was only rabbits. Twice, when she had been with them they had been able to bring home a deer.

Winter began passing and patches of ground began to appear. Falling Star focused her thoughts on taking everyone down to the coast.

"It's still a little early yet," one of the Elders cautioned her in a group meeting. "Winter isn't yet over."

"Right, and the trek down to the coast will be a tricky one if we should run into snow banks," commented another.

"I believe the pass out of our little valley is blocked by fallen trees and rocks from the earthquake," added someone else.

"That might mean that the path down might be blocked also."

"What if we had to find a new way back down?" asked someone.

After everyone had finished speaking, Falling Star suggested, "I really don't want to wait another month, but maybe we should. Between now and then, why don't some of you begin exploring and seeing what we might be facing?"

"We could do that," remarked another, "but we are very nearly starving. I'm not sure how much strength we have to explore ahead like we did in the old days like the stories we've heard. I remember the stories told how we would send out parties of searchers to mark paths for The People to follow."

"Those days belong to the past," Falling Star reminded him. "We can't bring them back."

"To his point, though, Falling Star," interjected a Grandmother, "we need more food . . . and I just wish it could be something more than rabbit."

Murmurings in affirmation.

Falling Star returned home that evening. She found her children sleeping soundly. Drawn to them as a mother does sometimes, she gazed on each one with a deep love as they slept. As she did, she spoke to them softly, touching the cheek of each, "You, my beloved little ones, are the future of The People."

Feeling utterly alone in her responsibility for the survival of The People, she felt an emotional pain that had become a physical pain. Lines of anguish deepened into her face. While brushing her once long black hair in preparation for going to bed, she realized her hair had turned white in color. She pursed her lips and slowly shook her head from side to side as she contemplated the toll this experience was taking on everyone including her.

In the night Mother Earth presented another vision. The vision showed a very large elk stuck in a quagmire of some kind. Falling Star looked around to check out the terrain to enable her to identify just where this bog was. The bog had been created by the melting snows, collecting water in a place where the soil was particularly dark and loose, no longer frozen from the receding winter. In her vision, the large elk, trapped in the bog, fought to escape, but without success.

"So who is coming with me on an elk hunt?" asked Falling Star as she awoke the camp. "C'mon, I need some rope and . . . let's see, several adults, at least." She paused to see who showed interest in joining her. Hunger can be a great motivator. Most of the Grandfathers, strong enough, but still a bit sleepy, appeared wrapped in warm garments holding knives and other butchering tools.

"Hmm," she continued as the group of several children showed up with their slingshots, "yes, we'll need a weapon to put Brother Elk out of his misery." She looked around and saw several adults holding ropes. Then she said, "How will we get it back here?"

One Elder said, "If we field dress it, then part it out into sections, we can drag back the pieces in hides or blankets."

"Sounds good," Falling Star said. "Would someone go get some skins or blankets so we can get the parts back?"

When all were assembled, the would-be elk hunters followed Falling Star beyond the camp, but not too far away. Every time she thought she had found the spot, the elk was not there. Not wanting to doubt her vision, Falling Star continued looking for the landmarks she had identified in her dream.

A little unclear as to where exactly she was going, the group noticed their own tracks twice as they wandered in search of the elk. Nevertheless, their deep and implicit trust in her never wavered.

Suddenly, a sharp-eyed youngster yelled and pointed, "Hey, over there."

Indeed, there in the beyond was a bull elk struggling to escape the mud that had trapped him. Silently, breathing quietly, the hungry hunters approached the edge of the bog. Standing for what seemed like very long moments to everyone else, Falling Star stood saying nothing, then sang a song to the elk and to Mother Earth. To the listeners her song sounded soothing and sacred. To everyone's amazement, the elk stopped trying to free himself and stood still for the duration of her song. As the song finished, Falling Star raised her slingshot and aimed a stone at its throat.

Whiiizzzz. Thump.

The elk slumped over.

Working as a team intuitively, the group labored at retrieving the large game animal from the mud. Before the field dressing could begin, Falling Star ensured the animal's head faced east. She raised her arms in prayer to the heavens and sang a song of gratitude and to invite the spirit of the elk to return to his origins in Spirit. She sifted sunflower seeds from her hands as a token of returning the gift of life back to Mother Earth. Then she pulled out a small piece of cloth to close its eyes in reverence to the animal that had agreed to help continue the life of The People.

As they worked together to free the creature from its trap, they discovered that it took far less effort than what they had imagined initially. Falling Star silently gave thanks for Mother Earth's assistance in this endeavor.

"A ceremony is in order for our expression of gratitude for this wonderful meat," announced Falling Star when they returned back to camp. Nearly everyone pitched in to help in some way.

One of the Grandmothers instructed the group who would be preparing the meat for consumption, "As hungry as we all are, we had better not gobble up as much as we can at first. I believe it would be better for our systems if we made soup first, and ate only small bits of meat."

"Yes," affirmed another, "it's best that we plan how to prepare and when to prepare it. I think it would be best to make a plan. We still can start a meal, though, now as everyone is so hungry."

The butchers cut. The cooks cooked and planned. Several others gathered musical instruments long hidden away. After the first meal, a large bonfire blazed proudly in the ceremonial center. All those who could bundle up enough came out of their homes to dance and sing. As they joined voices, they felt an energy inside that they had forgotten was there. Falling Star grabbed the head of the elk and held it above her own head in a dance that had resembled a dance as a red fox she had once participated in with a neighboring tribe at a time ever so long ago. Throughout the evening, The People found themselves smiling. Tears of gratitude and hope ran from eyes, including Falling Star's.

As the weather turned from winter into early spring, The People knew they would be leaving never to return to the Camp of God's Tears. With hope in their hearts and a renewed sense of direction, The People had made it through a most dreadful winter and were organizing themselves for the trek down to the coast . . . and other peoples, other tribes, other families and friends.

The bodies of loved ones who had died that winter began to thaw with the increase in temperatures. Days before leaving camp, one by one, houses were taken down or taken apart. Those strong enough to move bodies carried them to a place where they could be all cremated together. They stacked wood under, around and between the bodies.

On the day of departure, the wood was lit. Then they left with heavy hearts at the sight of the bodies of their beloveds being kissed by the flames of the funeral pyre. Several stayed behind to tend to the fire and would catch up later. The main body of The People quickly left to avoid the odor of burning bodies affixing upon them as they began their new life.

The journey down proved indeed a challenging one as the well-worn path had changed considerably as a result of the earthquake. Everyone carried what they could, yet much was left behind. Because most of the adults were more aged the pace went slower than usual down the mountain. They found themselves camping along the way more days than normal, and everyone's spirits stayed buoyant despite the lack of conversation as they moved through the forest down toward the coast.

When finally reaching the ocean waters, some of the Elders immediately began fishing. Several others found shellfish to add to their first meals. For many, sitting down in the sun's warming rays with a gentled breeze kissing their faces and not hungry, felt like life could be lived again. At that point, winter seemed like a bad dream best forgotten.

As they approached their winter camp location, they discovered that the fierce winter storms left only remnants of their former homes.

What remained of The People stayed in their temporary encampment until Falling Star felt directed to take them to find another tribe. While staying there near the waters to regain their strength, several adults and some children had put together partial shelters made of driftwood, pine boughs and hides. These lean-tos provided a sense of protection from the elements.

In preparing for another sojourn in search of another people, Falling Star opened the wolf skin bundle left to her by her Grandfather Gray Wolf. Inspired to examine its contents one more time, she found her sacred necklace, the one her Grandfather had given her on the day of her marriage ceremony to Mark of the Bear. She lifted it up to the light and admired how it still glistened in the late afternoon sun. "As above, so below," she murmured to herself as it dangled from her hand. Then, without thinking, she slipped it on over her head and let the abalone shell with the sacred insignia shine forth as it warmed her heart beneath it.

Uplifted by the energy she felt now as a result of wearing this ancient symbol, Falling Star found her hand again fumbling inside the bundle, stopping only when the pouch holding the stone with its etched markings touched her hand. She pulled it out. Just as she had begun to open the pouch, her son, Painted Star approached.

"What's that," he asked his mother.

Emotionally, and with no tears, she answered, "It's the stone Red Fox was given after the completion of the first part of his initiation."

"What's initiation?" he questioned with heightened curiosity.

Falling Star thought for a moment and replied, "Initiation is the process of learning the ancient knowledge. It's actually a

The Transition

commencement or beginning of learning the details of ancient knowledge and the ancient ways of living that is so ancient no one can remember how long ago it was when humanity actually received it." He nodded in acknowledgement.

Falling Star continued softly, "The People have been living a certain level of these ancient ways for so long, no one left living among us can remember." She paused as her throat closed in tearless emotion.

After a brief pause, she kneeled down to look her son straight in the eye and spoke softly but intently, "Now, my son, this stone is yours. Keep it with you always. You can keep it in this pouch and tie it to your belt or hang it around your neck. It is the only thing I will be able to leave to you that will help you to remember to remember the way of oneness, the sacred way, the only way to live and walk upon Mother Earth."

Knitting his eyebrows in question, her son asked in a worried tone, "But, mother, where are you going?"

"Well, we are all going up the coast to find another tribe of people in the hopes we can join them. Before too long, our Elders who are with us now will be walking on into Spirit. That will leave the mothers and all the children to care for. We need another people to join if we are to survive at all."

"I'll keep it as my medicine pouch," he said as he smiled and turned, leaving her to engage in his own contemplation of changes in his life.

As the last remaining members of The People straggled up the coastline in their sojourn to find another tribe, they saw a small hunting party approach them. Falling Star thought she recognized one or two of the older ones. Remembering only a little of their speech, she asked if they would lead her People back to their camp.

One of the older hunters stepped forward to speak to Falling Star.

"Are you the People who winter here at the coast and migrate into the mountains in the summer?" he asked with a glint of recognition in his voice as he gazed upon Falling Star.

"Indeed," she replied, "we are. And, you, I believe are Fighting Badger."

Stepping back in surprise when she said his name, he smiled and asked, "How do you know me, Grandmother?"

"At the time I danced the hunting dance as a red fox and joined you in the hunt, calling in the game, I was a young woman with black hair," she said with a smile.

At that comment, each man relaxed with eyes opened wide in recognition of who she was. The younger hunters had heard the stories of this unusual event that had happened a long time ago. The two oldest hunters had participated in that event as very young men and finally remembered her.

"We are honored to know you, Grandmother," one of the younger hunters said as he bowed his head. "We will take you back to our village."

Fighting Badger then asked, "There should be more of you. Where is everyone else? Where is Mark of the Bear?"

As Falling Star began collecting her people and gathering them more into a group, she replied, "They are all gone. They were killed in an avalanche. The rest died during winter."

"We didn't see you down at the coast in your winter camp. Where did you spend winter? . . . not in the mountains, I hope."

As they began walking, Falling Star related only what she felt was necessary about the events that left them stranded in the mountains for the winter. Two of the younger hunters ran ahead to announce the arrival of The People.

As The People entered their new home and new village, they all felt grateful. The village members embraced them with warm hospitality, matching up family members, absorbing The People into their homes, hearths and hearts.

After several days passed of settling into the new surroundings, The People found they could smile again. Some

The Transition

wore new clothes supplied by their hosts as tattered garments became discarded. The children no longer felt pangs of hunger claw at their empty bellies.

For these several days Falling Star walked around the village looking in on her People as they settled into their new home. Although the languages differed this did not impede the progress that was being made. Her People were adapting and learning the basics of the tribe's language.

However, she could not help but notice that the tribal elders were gathering in the council house. Some of these meetings lasted for hours. Although she was curious about what was being discussed, she felt this had to do with the process of absorbing her People into the tribe. On occasion she noticed that the male tribal shaman and Elders were eyeing her strangely from a distance and neither approached her nor spoke to her.

Because of this, Falling Star found herself surprised at an invitation to join the tribal council. Chief Whale Talker and several Elders and a shaman of the hosting village invited Falling Star to join them one evening.

All of the council members were men. She was the only woman. As she sat down, her necklace jostled as she moved catching a striking reflection of the fire. They interpreted the insignia of her necklace as one of a chief and leader.

After sitting around the fire for a while, finally the Chief broke the silence. "Falling Star, as you know, in our village, only men can be leaders, hunters, and shaman."

Falling Star nodded in acknowledgment.

He continued, "We accept you as a leader and honored shaman among your People. However, that is a hard thing for us to do as our ways are different from yours." He paused before continuing, "We have taken in your People and adopted them as our own." He paused again briefly then went on, "The only reason we have done so, is because of you, Falling Star."

Falling Star remained quiet and motionless holding her breath.

Chief Whale Talker looked down for a while, and then looked up again fixing his gaze on her before speaking again. "When you were a young girl, you danced the dance of the hunt as a red fox. The dance of the hunt is a sacred one to our people. Women are not allowed to dance that dance. Yet, you danced our dance as if you already knew it. You performed it so well, that no one guessed you were a woman *and* a guest, at that. I was there. I remember it."

Falling Star not being able to guess what was coming only nodded humbly.

"Then after a very long effort in searching for game so we could get through the winter, you stepped forward, at risk to exposing your identity as a woman, and called in the game for us. You sang your song, and game came in.

"Because of that, our hunt that day was a supremely successful one. We owe you much, Falling Star. We are taking in your People as a way to repay our debt of gratitude to you. If it were not for that, we would not be able to accept your People into our homes. We would go on about our business and let your People go on about theirs."

A long silence prevailed.

As much as tears wanted to spring out of her eyes at this, Falling Star found that no tears were forthcoming. She had shed too many tears since the beginning of the end of her People. She felt tears welling up and spilling over, but none actually manifested.

"My heart is full of gratitude," Falling Star humbly responded.

Another long pause.

"Our question now to you, Falling Star, is . . . ," the Chief asked breaking an awkward silence, "our question is . . . what is your intention now?"

Falling Star cocked her head as she listened to the question, not really understanding its meaning.

Seeing that she appeared not to comprehend the question, he asked again, "What do you plan to do now?"

Not knowing how to answer this question, Falling Star remained quiet seeking inner guidance.

Then, one of the men dressed as a shaman as opposed to a leader, interjected, "We are comfortable with you as a shaman of your own tribe . . . when you lived with them.

"*Our* people have only men shaman. Now that you and your People live with us . . . well, we have only men shaman. What we are not comfortable with is that you are a woman *and* a leader *and* a shaman. We are not prepared to change our ways of having only men as leaders and shaman."

Then Chief Whale Talker asked again, "So, Falling Star, we must have your answer. We accept you on the personal level. It's at the tribal level where we are having problems. What can you say to us?"

Taking a moment, she looked down then back up again contemplating her answer. Looking around the circle, she made eye contact with each man in turn before speaking, "That thought had never occurred to me. Your question is completely foreign to our way of thinking. Our ways have served us for a thousand years.

"As you know, my People do not distinguish between men and women when it comes to tasks, assignments, food providing or preparation, leadership or giving spiritual direction. In fact, women are held in high esteem simply because they are carriers of wisdom from one generation to the next, especially the older women."

Shifting in position as she paused, she then said, "Would you be so kind as to allow me some time to ponder your question? Since I had not expected such a question, I have not contemplated an appropriate response. I realize I must consider a few things. I realize I must take into account my new home and my new family and friends. I must take into account your ways as I live among you. At the same time, I cannot deny my identity. I have lived as who I am for too long, as both a leader and a shaman . . . So if I may, with your permission, delay my answer for a day or two, I honor your concerns and will respond to your question."

Silence.

Chief Whale Talker nodded and then said, "We will be waiting for your answer in two days. Go in peace, Grandmother."

All the next day Falling Star contemplated the question looming on the horizon of her consciousness. She had been caught off guard by the challenge to her identity as a shaman. The emotional and physical exhaustion of getting her people through the last winter, down to the coast and to the host tribe had consumed her. She felt rewarded by the host tribe accepting her people. She felt a burden now lifted. With this she finally remembered who she was. However, who she was . . . was not welcome.

She interacted with her children absently-mindedly until she finally had to seek a spot to quiet her mind and meditate.

She did have some options. She could remain with her people. She considered if she did stay, her People would want to continue in the ways of The People and would see her as their shamanic leader. She saw this as setting up a potential conflict between The People and the host tribe. This conflict could end badly.

If she did not stay, then her People would blend easier into the ways of the host tribe, adopting their ways to more successfully participate as members of the host tribe, thereby creating more harmony. And that would perhaps be the best for all concerned.

On the other hand, she argued to herself, because of her abilities as a shaman, she saved her People from a cruel winter, and her People would support her efforts before the tribal council.

She could tell the tribal council the full story of their winter survival as a demonstration of her shamanic power and abilities. She could seek to convince them to change their ways. To do otherwise would be to deny her role and identity as a shaman for her People, denying the core of who she was.

She saw that in order to do this she would have to fight with the tribal council members into changing their ways and show them that they were wrong about her being a woman shaman. She would have to present her ways as being better than their ways. She might have to demonstrate her power again, like she had by calling in the game on that well-remembered hunt. Also, she could relate to them the story of the grizzly bear and how she communicated with it and how she rode it through the forest and into her village. Then she could relate about what she and the bear discussed and more.

If she did this, then she felt that could be interpreted as an act of ego rather than a demonstration of the oneness she experienced. So far they had not questioned how she called in the game or how the power came to her. They did not ask. Not one member of the others asked her how she called in the game or expressed a desire to learn what she knew.

They were aware of her power, and felt uncomfortable with that kind of power resting in a woman. She thought how they did not allow women to hold positions of power. That concept ran counter to what she knew to be true and what she knew of the Great Oneness.

Falling Star thought about her meeting with the Elders. The Elders expressed their discomfort with her being in their village as a permanent member. She saw that their discomfort caused them agitation and turmoil inside themselves, so much so that they felt they had to confront her about her intentions. Then she realized a truth spoken to her by her Grandfather Gray Wolf, *if you don't have peace within, you won't have peace without.* She asked herself what kind of relationship would her People have in this village if peace did not reign?

As she continued contemplating, she realized that their ways did not seem to embrace the sense of oneness and connectedness The People experienced all day long. The ways of The People did not seem to harmonize with some of the ways of this host tribe who had welcomed her People into their folds.

But their ways served them. What was right for them was not right for her. What served her, and what was right for her People, was not right for the tribe adopting her People. To ask for them to change their ways of doing things felt "wrong" to her. If she wrestled with the council members to gain the necessary power and acknowledgements to remain a shaman with this tribe, to change their ways to accommodate her ways, she knew a larger conflict would ensue.

The conflict could be men against a woman or those with imagined less power standing together against one person with imagined more power. Or it could be both. It seemed to become a question of *power over*, rather than *power with*. She felt her identity, as a shaman, as a powerful woman, threatened the status quo in this community. If she took a stand to remain in this new tribe and remain a shaman, she could see she would be picking a fight . . . quite possibly coming from ego, coming from the need to be right.

She knew she was right. She also knew that being right does not justify coming from the position of being right. And as her Grandfather had taught, *you become what you fight.*

She could come from the position of being right. Or, she could come from the *position of knowing*. It was then that she also remembered the story of the two wolves . . . *you become the one you feed*. She asked Great Spirit for her answer.

No answer came.

Rising the next morning before sunrise Falling Star made her way to the top of a hill overlooking the ocean and beach below . . . and remembered the place where she had spent much time with her Grandfather Gray Wolf. From a similar spot the two of them witnessed the soaring of the sea gulls and the breaching of the magnificent whales on their journeys along the coast.

She sat for hours on that hilltop, the words of the tribal council and shaman, although given with respect, did not bring her comfort. Their words echoed through her soul.

Falling Star asked herself over and over, should she stay or should she go. Grandfather Gray Wolf had spoken to her often on the anguish facing The People at Newark when White Eagle's vision manifested at the northernmost moonrise generations ago. She remembered her Grandfather Gray Wolf's words from White Eagle's prayer at the Newark moonrise ceremony,

We see death in staying.
We see death in leaving.
If what is coming means death to The People, then we surrender and go humbly into the All That Is.
We will return with dignity to our Creator, and we then look forward to our resurrection in whatever form that takes.

This was prayed generations ago in a different place in a different time, and remained true today. Grandfather Gray Wolf had told her that merely leaving Ohio had not answered the question as to the best way to deal with the coming of the foreigners.

The question of 'to go or to stay' arose again in St. Louis and then again at the great falls camp.

Grandfather had also told her of his vision at great falls and how both she and Mark of the Bear would become great leaders of The People in the new lands so very far from those of their ancestors and the Ancient Ones.

She remembered the "promise" Grandfather Gray Wolf spoke of as he reminisced about The People's journey, their hardships, their challenges, and their victories after finally reaching the coast. She remembered the serenity with which her People lived as they adapted to the new landscape and as the landscape adopted them.

The promise given to her Grandfather was just that, a promise.

. . . Two children will be born on the journey through the great mountains.
They are a sign that The People are on the right path in fulfillment of The Promise. One will be a boy . . . He will be a great leader of The People and will bring new ways, new ideas and guide them to a successful, full life in the new lands in which The

People will settle . . . The other will be a girl. She will be a great spiritual leader, one of vision, one who will bring great wisdom and knowledge to The People in fulfillment of The Promise. Together they will lead The People to a manifestation and realization of The Promise.

Feeling that the promise had been fulfilled Falling Star mentally acknowledged how her People had prospered. Yet something had gone very much out of alignment that resulted in the choices made by Mark of the Bear *and those who chose to blindly follow a leader.*

The wisdom of her Grandfather's words came to her again about *tapping into the space between knowing and not-knowing wherein all possibilities exist . . . which can become potentials available to manifest from an intention that creates experiences.*

Her Grandfather would remind her, "Always remember, my little one, that in this lifetime we cannot always predict how we will flesh out the divine framework with our intentions. Our intentions are breathlessly waiting to manifest. The divine framework provides a structure for us, much like a constancy. We flesh it out in a physical world as we walk through this life by setting our sights, intending our intentions, creating the flux or chaos we find ourselves experiencing. It is up to each of us to maintain our sense of harmony and oneness with each other, Mother Earth, and Great Spirit. When we lose that sense of connectedness with each other in the Great Oneness, then it becomes easy to fall out of alignment and create disturbing or harmful effects."

Falling Star's thoughts drifted to her heated arguments with her beloved, Mark of the Bear. She recalled how he had shifted his focus from the good of The People, to himself . . . to a place of self-centeredness, driven by ego. Because of that choice and because she found herself unable to persuade him to do otherwise, he created the experience of an end to a culture . . . to an end of The People as she had known them, and as far as she could see, that choice created an extinction to a way of living and being that defined that culture.

The Transition

At that thought, she heard her Grandfather's words whispered in her ear, "Sometimes our visions, expectations, and intentions, merely rearrange the Great Mystery. We can change outcomes by changing our focus, either for good or for not-good . . . and sometimes we can't know whether an outcome is good or not good until much later or until we see it from a different perspective.

"The Great Mystery remains mysterious because in our awareness of the Great Oneness, our perspectives can broaden and inform our thoughts to see more which then informs our beliefs and which then shapes our experience . . . or not. Our experience of our physical reality shifts depending on the depth and breadth of our awareness."

The People lived in a keen awareness of oneness, oneness with each other, with Mother Earth, and with Great Spirit. She wondered if that was just being rearranged and would re-emerge in another time and another place.

Now she was facing a choice . . . one destined for her alone. The People were so far away from their ancestral lands. The few surviving Elders were the only ones who knew of the Story of The People.

Grandfather Gray Wolf was the last of the Elders who had actually lived the life in Ohio so prosperous and so consciously connected to the Great Oneness. The remainder of The People knew of this only from the retold stories.

The People were so few now that another migration was simply not possible . . . and to where? If the remnants of her People did leave, she knew they could not survive without the security of the larger community which now embraced them.

She knew that she must resolve this matter in a way that would be best for the common good. The path to "home" was closed, and she remembered what Warm Stone had told Grandfather Gray Wolf at the great falls camp that The People with him were the last of the true believers and that the culture of the ancient lands no longer existed. So many things had changed.

Her People had been taken in by this coastal tribe and welcomed into its society. Their ways were established . . . as were hers.

She felt a warm calmness come over her. Falling Star felt that she would know what to do when it was time to do it. While she had asked for an answer, she now knew that it would be provided. She sang a song of gratitude for The People.

Late that afternoon, she took Painted Star and Yellow Lily to a secluded place in a nearby grove of trees. She longed to connect with them in a way that they would never forget.

"Do you remember all the stories that the Grandmothers and I have told you?" Falling Star began. They nodded, sensing a strangeness and unable to identify it. "Do you remember all the stories that Grandfather Gray Wolf told?" They both nodded. "What I am asking you to do . . . is *always* to remember them. I am asking you to always remember how we know Great Spirit, and our oneness with each other and our oneness with Great Spirit and Mother Earth. Never, ever, forget our stories," she admonished.

After she had spoken a long time to them, Painted Star asked, "Why are you telling us this mother? Why now? Why is it so important that you have to remind us like this?"

"Good question," she responded, "I don't know. I have been asked a very important question by the leaders of this village. I don't know the answer to their question. I have been meditating on it, and I still have no answer. The leaders are waiting for an answer from me tomorrow, and as yet, I have none. And, my dearest little ones, I have no answer for you either. I only know that I love you and will always love you. I know that I must ask you to remember to remember." At that she grabbed both of them in a huge bear hug, holding them tightly until they relaxed into her.

After seeing to it that her children were sleeping soundly that night, she laid down beside them on the floor, still dressed from the day, still wearing her necklace. As she slept, she drifted in her dreams trying to see through a mist that blocked her vision.

The Transition

Suddenly without any warning, a baby's piercing scream sliced into her dreams, causing her to bolt up wide-awake. Sitting up next to her slumbering children, she reached over and tenderly touched each one on the cheek with a silent prayer on her lips and one last tear in her eye.

Silently with great stealth, Falling Star got up and moved out of the shelter. At that moment she knew what she was going to do at such a high level in her consciousness, she had no word for it. She began walking. She walked all night and all the next day, climbing into the mountains.

She felt a bone-searing fatigue from the struggle to survive, the loss of her People, the loss of Mark of the Bear, and the need to rely on another tribe to take care of the last of The People and her children. She had been responsible for much and had completed everything within her power. Falling Star knew she had accomplished all that she could in this lifetime *and felt satisfied with what she did accomplish.*

She realized her death *as a shaman* to her People was required by the culture of this tribe and Chief Whale Talker. She saw death in staying. She saw death in leaving.

For her People to continue with this coastal tribe, which had taken them in, she would need to relinquish her position as a shaman, a leader, and a person with strong and unquestioned connection to the Great Oneness. This was her identity among The People. Clearly her identity appeared as a threat to this tribe. Giving up her identity would mean a death of who she is and what she represented to her People. Realizing this, she surrendered to that thought.

She considered how gently these new people had absorbed her People into their homes. She felt assured that her People would be well cared for without her. Realizing that the power to provide for her People had shifted from her to the others, she was no longer shouldered with that responsibility. Power and responsibility again equaled each other.

When she finally climbed to a spot high up on the mountainside, she saw a ledge. By the time she climbed up onto that ledge, Father Sun had begun to slip below the distant horizon and evening began folding over the land. Stars slowly emerged from the darkening blanket overhead.

Falling Star's heart was heavy with the reality that no one was left to tell the Story of the People in the same way and with the same richness and fullness, as Grandfather Gray Wolf had told her over so many years.

For now the story of their heritage, their history, their traditions, their knowledge, their elegance, serenity, and their conscious connection to the Great Oneness and the Story of the People was surrendered to preservation *within* the Great Oneness.

Twilight prevailed.

After squatting down to move a few rocks out of her way, she lifted her necklace from around her neck and set it down on the rock ledge next to her. Looking up, she witnessed even more stars twinkling and shining with an intensity she had not noticed before. At that moment, Falling Star laid down on that ledge next to her sacred necklace.

While she had taught her children well, the complete telling of The Story of The People was for later as they grew. That later was now, and her children had already begun to learn the stories of the coastal tribe, mixing with the stories of The People.

Falling Star suffered the anguish of feeling . . . *no one left to tell The Story . . . no one left to tell The Story . . . no one left to tell The Story* . . . it was lost for now . . . her thoughts faded. Closing her eyes she surrendered to the Great Oneness and resurrection within.

Death, surrender, resurrection.

Stars twinkled.

From the shadows surrounding the white haired, wrinkled, tired, yet now fulfilled Falling Star, came a warmth and a presence that Falling Star recognized. She opened her eyes to witness her beloved, Mark of the Bear, smiling down on her. The light in his eyes embraced her with the unconditional love of the Absolute.

Smiling radiantly back at him, she reached for him in response as he extended his hand out to her in invitation as before. She rose up out of her body in full greeting as a young beautiful, black-haired girl wearing her elaborately decorated white buckskin dress and matching boots.

Just then, Mark of the Bear bent down and reached for her necklace, flashing starlight reflections, and slipped it over his beloved's head, allowing the abalone shell with the sacred symbol of "as above, so below" to rest on her heart.

As the faint glow in the west transitioned into night, the two of them disappeared from the realm of the physical and blended into the Absolute.

52

NOT THE END

Clouds.
Mists.
Clouds.
Swirling mists.

Tom Perkins stood speechless overcome by his sudden awareness that this was the woman he had been searching for all of his life . . . the woman of his dream.

Silently he watched the young beautiful woman take off her fascinating necklace without saying a word. She offered it to him.

Still totally captivated, he automatically reached for her. Before their fingers touched, she faded from his sight into the mists swirling around them.

His mind was deluged with images, his body engrossed in feelings and emotions that deeply touched his soul. As his body quivered with a sense of returning from a distant past, the words of the song softly echoed, *something you left behind to remind me of you.*

As the voices of the Story echoed through his mind the mental images faded. A tear escaped and etched its way down his face. Tom choked with emotion.

The echoed voices repeated to him as he continued to contemplate this experience . . . *we are one . . . we are one with the One . . . the Whole is in each part and in each part of each part . . . if we hurt someone else, we hurt ourselves . . . if we help someone, we help ourselves . . . overuse or abuse of ego is fatal . . . power and responsibility must be equal . . . blind obedience to a leader is fatal . . . you become what you fight . . . if you do not have peace within, you will not have peace without . . . make choices through your heart . . . come from the position of knowing rather than from the position of being right . . . honor Mother Earth and all living things . . . your intentions create your experiences and are waiting to manifest . . . Great Spirit breathes through our heart . . . stay in alignment with the Great Oneness . . . .*

What was once a lost memory now filled his sense of destiny. A deep feeling of responsibility overwhelmed him. He softly spoke . . . "I accept."

The next thing he knew, his left hand held the necklace with the abalone shell dangling. The mesmerizing symbol shimmered in the rays of bright sunlight as they pierced through the clouds overhead. These clouds had transformed into the faces of Gray Wolf, Shining Bird, White Eagle, Rising Wolf, and Singing Hawk, faces he might have recognized had he looked up.

At just that moment, Hal steps out onto the patio. The mists clear away.

As Tom looked at the sacred necklace hanging from his hand still extended, he said, "Oh my God!" As Tom turns to see Hall, he lifts the necklace up for Hal to see. Tom says with great feeling, "Oh, my God, Hal. It is true . . . all true. They lived the Oneness Principle. I must tell someone."

Hal just smiles, relieved that his friend was all right, even if he was in a state of shock.

Then Tom repeats softly, "I must tell someone."

Faces in the clouds smiled with the new beginning.

THE WISDOM OF CRAZY HORSE

"Upon suffering beyond suffering: the Red Nation shall rise again and it shall be a blessing for a sick world. A world filled with broken promises, selfishness and separations. A world longing for light again. I see a time of Seven Generations when all the colors of mankind will gather under the Sacred Tree of Life and the whole Earth will become one circle again. In that day, there will be those among the Lakota who will carry knowledge and understanding of unity among all living things and the young white ones will come to those of my people and ask for this wisdom. I salute the light within your eyes where the whole Universe dwells. For when you are at that center within you and I am that place within me, we shall be one."

Chief Crazy Horse, *Tȟašúŋke Witkó*, **Oglala Sioux**

AFTERWORD

Many researchers believe that the Native Americans, known as the Mound Builders, living in North America prior to the arrival of Columbus were an ancient race (Silverberg 1986; Little 2001). Their culture came to an end *circa* 325 A.D. The only information we have about this highly developed culture comes from physical evidence left behind.

Nearly ten centuries elapsed from the end of this civilization before the first Spanish explorers reached these lands. Tens of thousands of mounds were plundered for supposed riches, destroyed by subsequent settlers, the growth of cities, and the farming of these rich lands.

The remaining treasures we have today are the result of the internment of these priceless artifacts with their honored dead under tons of dirt, clay, gravel and sand, which has provided evidence of elaborate burial ceremonies. These tantalizing artifacts may in fact represent only a brief glimpse of the true magnificence and sophistication of this civilization. So much of their true legacy was destroyed.

We know it was magnificent by virtue of what it left behind. We know it fell, because it ended just as mysteriously as it had thrived. Exactly who these people were remains another mystery. American archeologists have dubbed them, variously, as the Mound Builders, the Adena Culture and the Hopewell Culture. The Hopewell life and culture were quite different ". . . from those of the later Indians" (Moorehead 1922:176).

The names or labels used to identify or refer to this civilization come from our contemporary culture, typically taken from specific locations existing in the present day. What the people of this civilization left behind speaks to their material culture and products of human manufacturing, their social culture and their ideological culture as demonstrated in their architecture and artifacts

> Hopewell artifacts, including textiles, can be used to understand the lifeways of the people who produced and used them including their craftsmanship, technological knowledge and their interaction with the physical and social environment (Baldia 2008: 197).

From What They Left Behind

Much can be derived about a civilization by examining evidence of their material culture, such as clothing, art, and architecture.

From what they left behind, we know some things about their civilization. We know they used higher mathematics, geometry, and engineering, engaged in home construction, as well as participated in building large ceremonial wooden structures. They engaged in textile production, and extensive farming, in some areas, often with irrigation (Hubbard 1878; Shetrone 1930; Fowler 1969).

It is likely that the buffalo was important to their culture as archaeologists have found a complete buffalo skeleton at an archeological site. Buffalo roamed the Ohio area well into the late 1700's (Shriver 1987; OHS – Bison). Moreover, it is probable that they had domesticated the turkey for food and used their feathers for ornamentation and other uses (OHS – Turkey).

The quantities produced by their agriculture allowed much of their population to engage in non-subsistence and productive activities. In addition they enjoyed many types of foods and practiced large scale food storage (Silverberg 1986).

Material culture: clothing, art and artifacts, and architecture
Clothing and art

As part of their agricultural practices they produced a variety of plants used in the manufacturing of cloth. They utilized plant fibers for the weaving of textiles for clothing described as: some very sheer, "very fine reticulated weaving" and "delicately woven fabrics," "remarkably fine textile fabric" (Mills 1907; Moorehead 1922). Plant fibers utilized included milkweed, swamp milkweed, slender nettle, wood nettle, Indian hemp, dogbane, elm and basswood (Moorehead 1922; Church 1984).

They also used plant fiber to delicately weave footwear, such as this sandal (Holmes 1886).

Holmes-1886

What we know of their fabrics comes from what they left behind, as much fabric was preserved because it was attached to copper.

> Recent analysis of these copper-preserved fabrics reveal that some were portions of tunics manufactured of an extremely fine, white fiber that would have required hundreds, if not thousands of hours to construct (Church 1984:11). Multicolored stamped designs were found on some. Like the Chilkat blanket of the Northwest Coast, the Hopewell tunics represent labor intensive investments that were not meant to be worn on a daily basis. Shining copper plates on the chest or back of the head and waist simply added to the overall visual impact of the robes and ultimately, the physical appearance of their owners. (Cowan 1996:142)

Fabrics have been found that showed the use of various textures of weaving, plus use of dyeing in exquisite patterns, such as pieces of fabric dyed maroon with tan designs outlined in black. Other colors employed included yellow/brown, turquoise/white, red-brown, yellow-brown, green, dark brown, dark red, dark yellow and beige brown (Shetrone 1931; Baldia 2008).

> These textiles reflect multifaceted textile construction methods with elaborate decoration techniques as well as the use of complex dye technology . . . the complexity of these textiles, including the colored patterning and design motifs, is indicative of sophisticated artisanship . . . The construction of their textiles was intricate, their design was complicated, the colors were dyed and not painted. . . . Hopewell textiles were elaborately decorated with detail such as fringe and multiple colors on a single fiber, yarn or textile. (Baldia 2008:197, 199, 214, 217)

> The [Mound Builders] were great weavers, surpassing the plain plaiting or basket weaving of their predecessors to excel in complex twining: techniques including twill; chevron; lattice or complicated bird cages; and over two and under, with a zigzag direction of the warp members in fine strands and the weft members crossing obliquely. Although no more than rare and fragmentary patches have survived the passage of time, enough original fabric still exists to prove that the Mound Builders arrayed themselves in magnificent attire. (Joseph 2010:68)

It is likely that they also created designs cut from thin sheets of native copper to use as stencils for painting their finely woven cloth (Griffin 1967, 1978; Baldia 2008). Additionally, they engraved intriguing designs on the smoothed surfaces of a variety of stone tablets to imprint textiles and leather with a variety of pigments (Penny 1980; Romain 1991a). They also crafted fine soft leather works (Mills 1907).

These textiles, combined with the attachment of adornments, such as their extensive use of pearls, revealed a sense of style and elegance.

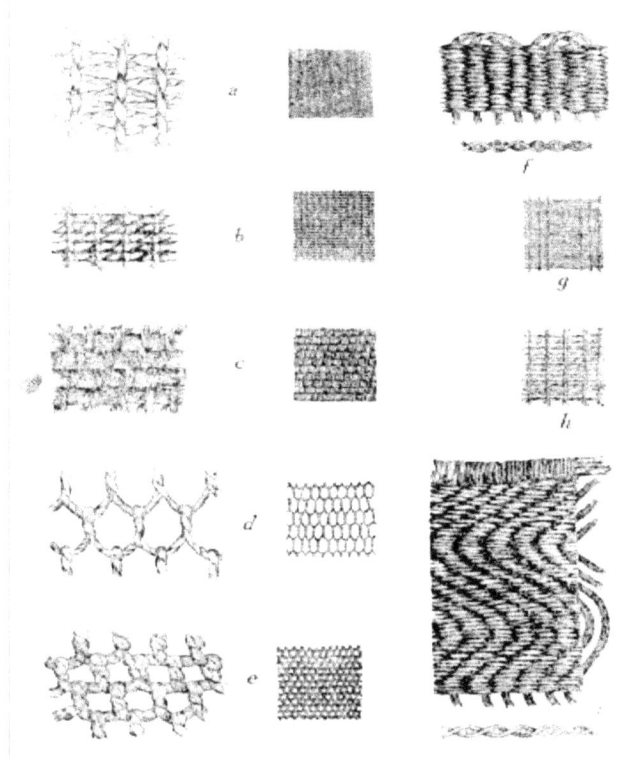

Moorehead-1922

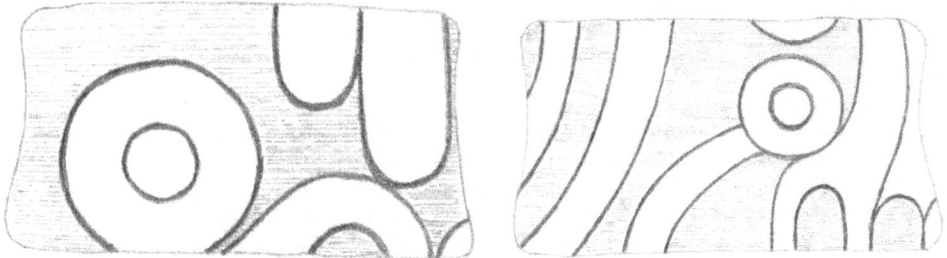

Fragments of a mantle in close twined weaving preserved by contact with copper plates. The background is a dark maroon with designs in clear yellow, outlined in black. Seip Mound, Ross County, Ohio. Redrawn and adapted from Shetrone 1931.

Fresh water pearls were highly prized by this culture and formed "a leading industry" that collected and processed them (Shetrone 1926).

Fresh water pearls were found sewn on to clothing, complete with holes drilled and sides flattened for invisible attachment to the garments. It can be surmised that pearls attached to clothing implies

THE CAMP OF GOD'S TEARS

a sense of style and/or meaning. Pearl necklaces, still beautiful, with over 300 pearls were discovered (Shetrone 1926).

While an irregular shape is characteristic of this form of pearl, many spherical and iridescent specimens were found (Moorehead 1922; Shetrone 1926).

The following illustrations are cross-sectional views of fresh water pearls and bear's teeth which have been intricately drilled. The pearls, greatly enlarged in the illustration, range in size from seed pearl to marble size. When one considers the hardness and varying shape of these pearls and teeth, great skill was required to perform this task.

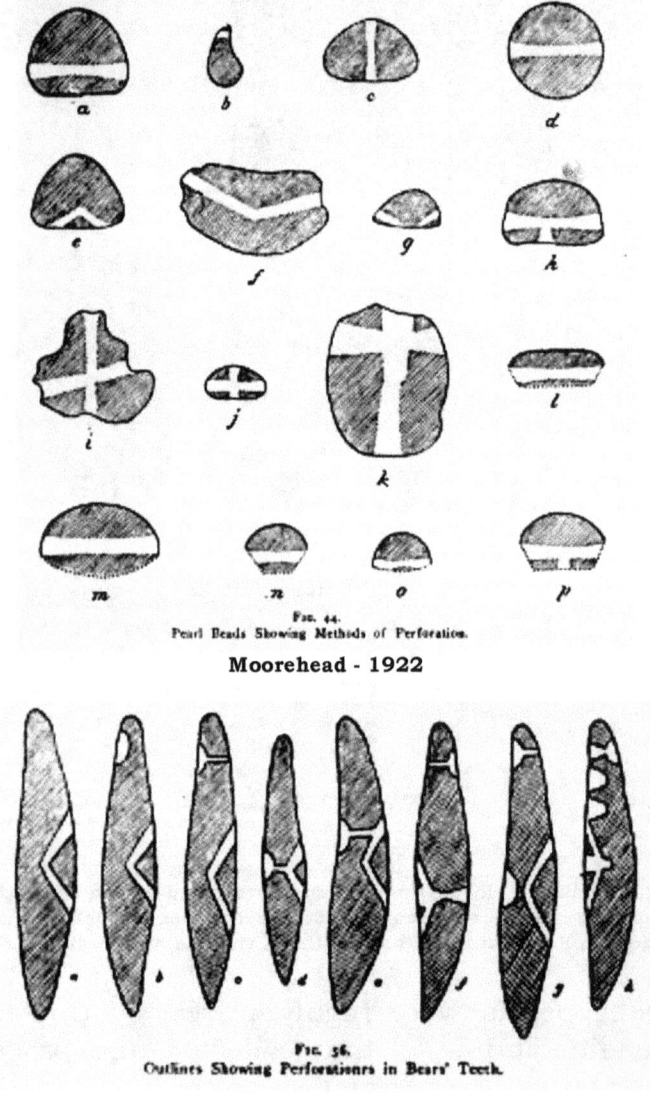

Fig. 44.
Pearl Beads Showing Methods of Perforation.
Moorehead - 1922

Fig. 36.
Outlines Showing Perforations in Bears' Teeth.
Moorehead - 1922

Afterword

Pearls, flattened on one side, were also attached to stone tobacco pipes becoming the eyes of the animals depicted in the sculptures.

Moorehead 1922

Pearls were also placed in sockets drilled in bear canine teeth and other objects for jewelry or other ornaments. In many instances, tens of thousands of pearls were placed in burial mounds throughout Ohio (Willoughby 1922; Shetrone 1926, 1931).

Obviously they prized their personal adornments, not only their earrings, necklaces, but also breastplates, pendants, hair ornaments and beaded bags (Kavasch 2004). They also employed buttons for their clothing. Buttons were made from wood, pottery clay or stone (Church 1983, 1984). Some were covered in silver or copper (Moorehead 1922).

Moorehead 1922

Moorehead 1922

Tools

They crafted refined tools and utensils for common living, as well as for artistic endeavors such as iron drills (Grogan 1948; Prufer 1961; Moorehead 1922; Shetrone 1931; McGuire 1900). Quartz crystals were found perforated with holes one millimeter in diameter (Moorehead 1922). Additionally, they used rivets, copper plugs and dowel rods to make and repair ceremonial objects (Mills 1916, 1922; Shetrone 1926). They also employed the use of saws (Donnelly 1821; Moorehead 1922).

This culture developed an extraordinary lithics technology, i.e., items shaped or carved from rock (Kavasch 2004; Cowan 2006). They crafted distinctive bifacial projectile points and unifacial blades many of which were heat-treated. The most notable natural resource for lithic tools such as arrowheads, spear points, knives, scrapers and others was the Flint Ridge flint.

The flint from Flint Ridge is known for its distinctive bright coloration. While the most common variety is white with light gray streaks, the most prized include various combinations and shades of blue, green, red and yellow (Lepper 2001, 2005; Yerkes 1995). Flint is the official gemstone of Ohio.

In 1921, Williams Corliss Mills, a noted Ohio archaeologist, while conducting his definitive study of Flint Ridge, discovered a unique stone structure while excavating a large earthen mound. This structure proved to be a house that had been constructed of flint bearing stone placed together without mortar. Its outside measurements were 35 by 35 feet. It had a fireplace and a post supported roof with a six-foot ceiling. At one time the house had been freestanding. At some point an internment had been conducted, the interior was filled with earth and then the entire structure was covered by an earthen mound.

Prehistoric quarries in Licking and Muskingum counties in Ohio were mined for over 12,000 years. Flint Ridge flint is from

Afterword

the Vanport Formation of sedimentary rock that formed under tropical shallow seas during the Pennsylvania Geologic period. While ancient quarries are found throughout the nearly eight mile length of Flint Ridge, the highest concentration is located within the 525 acre Flint Ridge State Memorial Park about four miles north of Brownsville, Ohio and approximately nine miles east southeast of Newark, Ohio.

Artifacts made from this flint have been found to the east as far as the Atlantic coast, west to Kansas City, and south to Louisiana and north to the Lake Superior region (Lepper 2001, 2005; Yerkes 1995).

Unique to this culture were flint bladelets. These multipurpose tools were about 1 ½ inches to four inches long and as small as a half inch wide and a tenth of an inch thick (Genheimer 1996; Greber 1981; Cowan 2006; Jefferies 2006).

Mills-1922

These small highly standardized flint tools required high quality flint and advanced technical skill to produce. Edge-wear analysis indicates these prismatic blades were used as light duty knives, gravers, perforators, shaving, engraving and scraping tasks for both plant and animal materials (Genheimer 1996; Dancy 1991; Byers, 2006; Charles and Buikstra 2006; Snyder 2008). "Hopewellian bladelets remain not only a highly "enigmatic" artifact class but one that continues to spark interest and debate in the archaeological literature" (Snyder 2008: 42).

Bannerstones were carefully crafted counterweights which were used in conjunction with the atlatl. Most of the bannerstones that have been found were made from slate. Their shape varied from simple hollow tubes to elaborately carved and polished wing forms.

The atlatl was a flexible wooden shaft with a hook at one end into which the back of the spear was fitted. At the other end was a handle of some sort. The effective distance and striking power of a spear was increased several fold with the counterweight of the bannerstone attached to the shaft of the atlatl (Converse 2003; Lepper 2005).

Art and artifacts

This culture's art expression was highly developed in both geometric and naturalistic representation (Griffin 1978). Their works of art rival that found among other ancient civilizations. Part of their art included elaborate ceremonial headdresses which were formed of copper, mica, feathers, and pearls.

> The worldview and rituals of the Scioto Hopewell inspired their artistic exploration of the principles of three-dimensional perspective a thousand years before Renaissance artists discovered them in the Old World and unlike the artistic norms of any other Native American people. (Carr and Case 2008:5)

Elegantly carved stone effigy pipes, copper and silver jacketed panpipes, molded copper jewelry, pearl and shell necklaces and metallic artifacts were found in abundance. Distinctive and technically complex ear spool earrings made from copper and silver were fashioned by the artisans of this culture. Hundreds and up to a thousand earspools were found in individual burial mounds.

Copper Earspools

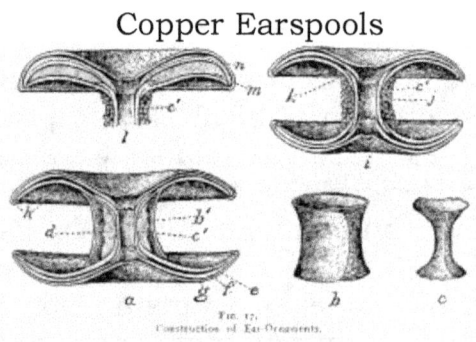

Moorehead-1922

Fine tempered pottery and ceramics, precision crafted and highly polished stone rings and bowls, beautiful banner stones, celts and decorated leather pieces graced the people of this culture (Mills 1916; Shetrone 1926; Converse 2003).

Of particular note are the stone rings. They are most remarkable. Technically, they are perfectly fashioned and finely made symmetrical circles up to 2 ½ inches in diameter. Such precision and polish would not have been possible without some mechanical device based on the principle of the lathe (Donnelly 1821; Willoughby 1922; Shetrone 1926).

Stone Rings

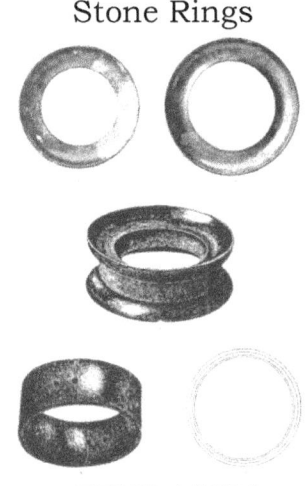

Moorehead-1922

Vast amounts of mica were acquired by this civilization from the southern Appalachians. Highly skilled artisans fashioned it into a dazzling variety of zoomorphic and geometric cutouts some of which were painted with white, black and red pigment (Milner 2004).They subjected mica to fire rendering it as flexible as tin foil for their artistic renderings (Mills 1916).

 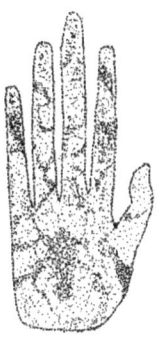

Hundreds of pounds of obsidian gathered from Wyoming and Idaho had been crafted into large ceremonial spear-heads and arrowheads some of which were eighteen inches in length (Hughes 2006).

THE CAMP OF GOD'S TEARS

Moorehead-1922

"There is hardly room for doubt that the Hopewell peoples had arrived at a stage of human culture where they conceived of "art for art's sake" (Shetrone 1926:199).

Copper

They left evidence of, not only copper artifacts, but of their furnaces in which to process the metal into molds. The thought that pre-contact Native Americans utilized the skills of smelting copper and iron remains controversial. Nevertheless several modern researchers have brought this information to light. At Spruce Hill, near Bourneville, Ohio, remnants of limestone rock furnaces with clay-lined pits were discovered (Hempstead 1878; Connor 2009, 1997-2007; Mallery 1979; Neiburger 1991; Mertz 1986).

> As early-nineteenth-century pioneers began developing the Ohio Valley, the obliterated most . . . mounds they encountered during the process of clearing new farmlands. But some of these old earthworks revealed a surprise. When the venerable monuments gave way to shovel and plow, settlers occasionally left standing a primitive kind of furnace. On inspection, they found nodules of smelted iron inside, amid heaps of white ash, the result of very high temperatures. (Joseph 2010:56)

What is certain, however, is the fact that the surface of many of these rocks had been fused or glazed which can only occur at temperatures above 2012°F (Squire and Davis 1848; Peat 1892; Ruby 1997). This temperature far exceeds that of a campfire or bonfire and represents evidence of a smelting process (Neiburger 1991).

Ancient copper mines found in Michigan and Wisconsin have been dated back as long ago as 5,000-6,000 B.C. (May 2006). Additionally, in the Keweenaw area of the Michigan Upper Peninsula and on Isle Royale in Lake Superior, archeologists found over 5,000 ancient copper mines. These mines contained some of the purest copper ever found in the world. Vast amounts of pure copper metal with particles of silver embedded in it, in addition to copper ore, were extracted. Estimates of the amount of copper removed from these mines go as high as a million tons (Whittlesey 1863; Fox 1911; Smith 1915; Drier 1961; Little 2001; Joseph 2009; Rydholm 2009; Joseph 2010). On the other hand, only about five tons of copper artifacts have been documented in all of the Native American burials and caches (Whittlesey 1863; Hagar 1865; Wright and Spaulding).

> Little known to the general public is America's greatest archaeological enigma: namely, the excavation of at least half a billion pounds of copper ore in a stupendous mining enterprise that began suddenly in the Upper Great Lakes Region of the Michigan Peninsula about 5,000 years ago. Although the identity of these prehistoric miners is unknown, Menomonie Indian tradition remembers them as "the Marine Men," white-skinned, bearded foreigners who sailed out of the east. (Joseph 2001:108)

With relatively small amounts of this exceptional form of copper found among the Mound Builder treasures, it becomes clear that the vast amount of mined copper did not stay with them. Interestingly, it is during the pre-historic time period in which the Mound Builders thrived, that copper was being utilized extensively and prolifically in the Middle Eastern and Mediterranean cultures (Donnelly 1821; Fox 1911; Mertz 1986; Corliss 1999). Coincidently, it appears that the copper mining ceased about the time nearing the end of the Mound Builder civilization.

Trading

This gives rise to the suggestion of global trade and trade routes. Shell beads (*Cyproea moneta*) originating in Africa are included among the artifacts left behind by the Mound Builders (Greenman 1932).

It is generally accepted by archeologists that trade routes existed throughout North America. Also accepted is the idea that traders traveled these long distances, despite the lack of horses. Even though evidence shows the Mound Builders had large rings, disc-shaped stones with center holes, and pulley shaped stone rings, they did not use the wheel for traveling overland. Considering more evidence, it is suggested by scholars that these trade routes extended, not only throughout North America, but through Central and South American, as well (Jennings 1993).

We further suggest that it is possible the Mound Builders or their predecessors participated in global trading as evidenced by the amount of copper mined from their territory in the Lake Superior region. It stands to reason that global transoceanic trading occurred, considering the abundance of physical evidence left behind. Since copper artifacts were found in relatively small quantities throughout the culture, and used in large quantities elsewhere in the world, logic implies global transoceanic trading occurred (Joseph and May 2006; Joseph 2009; Rydholm 2009; Schrag 2011).

This idea becomes especially salient when considering the comparatively limited quantity of mined copper produced in other parts of the ancient world where it was used in significantly greater quantities. The Sinai, Cyprus, and other parts of the Middle East produced some copper. The Alps produced additional tonnage.

Yet the use of copper in the Middle East and the Mediterranean areas during the Bronze Age time period occurred in larger quantities than what can be explained by the amount of copper mined in those parts of the world.[3]

As noted by Vine Deloria, Jr.,

> A note of passing interest in this respect concerns Chief Joseph. After his surrender in 1877, he gave a pendant to General Miles, and this object eventually found its way to West Point. A few years ago it was examined and turned out to be a Mesopotamian tablet recording the sale of livestock, a disturbing

---

[3] The History Channel program "*Who Really Discovered America*", which aired in June 2010, reported that copper of a purity only found in the Lake Superior region was used in Mediterranean boats around 1400 B.C.

anomaly and an undeniable fact . . . . How this tablet got into Joseph's family and became an heirloom is a matter of some speculation, telling us that our view of Western Hemisphere prehistory is not as complete as we might think. (Deloria, Jr. 1997:48)

4000 year old Mesopotamian tablet - West Point Museum [4]

Trans-oceanic global navigation by ancient mariners was well established before the Bronze Age and flourished during that time (Gordon 1971; Joseph 2009; Rydholm 2009; Schrag 2011). Transporting copper to market during the Bronze Age occurred precisely at the same time period as the Nipissing phase of the Great Lakes, a time when the Great Lakes formed one enormous lake.

> Throughout this period, the entire region could have been navigated without portages, thus, copper might be mined and transported without resorting to any burdensome overland routes. If we couple this fact with the purity of the copper itself, virtually free of the need for smelting, we may understand how the Michigan trade network was economically viable . . . . Traders could follow the North Bay outlet through Ontario or take the Chicago outlet to the Mississippi. Evidence exists that both routes were used. Large copper storage pits, for example, line both probable water routes. (Wood 2006:118-119)

At that time it was possible to travel east directly to the oceans via North Bay and the Ottawa River, and thence out the St. Lawrence to the sea or south via Chicago, Des Plaines and the Mississippi River. The route over Niagara Falls was also open (Drier 1961:17).

---

[4] Drawing based on original photograph by Helen Schreider appearing in *Smithsonian* February, 1979:36.

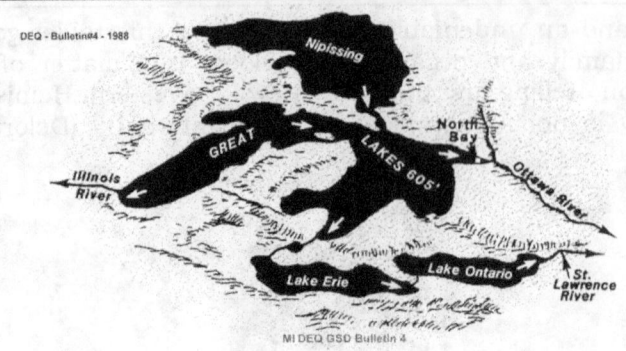

Figure 11: With the ice burden gone, the earth's crust in the northern part of the region began to rise. When the North Bay outlet rose to the same level as the Port Huron and Chicago outlets, the Nipissing Great Lakes were born. (about 6,000 to 4,000 years ago)

Architecture

The scientific and archeological community within the United States has taken several hundred years to appreciate the incredible sophistication of the design and construction of the Mound Builder earthworks, such as Newark, High Bank, and Serpent Mound, among others cited. These are the names that the dominant culture and the scientific community have given them. Their true names remain a mystery.

What is not a mystery is the precision with which the earthworks were constructed. Their alignments with celestial events are not debatable (Hively and Horn 2006). However, no written records have, thus far, been found that reveals their intended purpose.

Why they constructed these immense complexes remains the subject of much speculation. Additionally, the purpose of such accurate alignments of the gigantic earthworks to celestial events continues to remain a mystery.

Several stone walled enclosures, located on hilltops, exceeded 100 acres and led to the mistaken belief that they represented fortifications.

Clearly, these people celebrated their position in the known universe as evidenced by their magnificent earthworks aligned so precisely with solar, lunar, and stellar events. This would imply a sense of participation amid a gigantic cosmic tapestry. They knew they belonged as part of the patterns of creation. If this were not so, they would not have constructed such earthen structures that enclosed from a few hundred square feet to well over one hundred acres. A worldview as expressed in such a fashion sets them apart from all other so-called primitive cultures.

"The predominant European view of the Native American as a barbaric and stupid savage obstructed the European's ability to understand the intellectual accomplishments of the New World natives" (Williamson 1984:16).

From what we now know of these people, it becomes a challenge to think of them as primitive. In many ways their level of technology appears equal to or higher than their counterparts in Europe during the same time period. Conceivably, opinions regarding their civilization should be elevated to a considerably higher level of appraisal.

Earthworks and Recent Mound History

When early European settlers first came into the regions of these earthen mounds, the American Indians living near the mounds were unable to provide answers to questions of their origin or meaning. Some reported hearing stories that they were built by an ancient culture (Silverberg 1986; Kavasch 2004). It is estimated that over 10,000 such mounds existed in the State of Ohio *alone* (Joseph 2006). Earthen and stone mounds have been found in over 20 states. Thousands of mounds were destroyed by the expansion of the dominant culture. What had survived for thousands of years almost completely disappeared in less than two hundred years.

Fortunately, there were those who appreciated the need to preserve the few remaining structures. Various historical societies and private individuals assumed this challenge. Were it not for their vision and sense of historical importance, the few remaining earthen mounds would have also vanished.

Today, the High Bank Circle and Octagon complex, near Chillicothe, Ohio, is barely discernable having been subjected to years of farming.

THE CAMP OF GOD'S TEARS

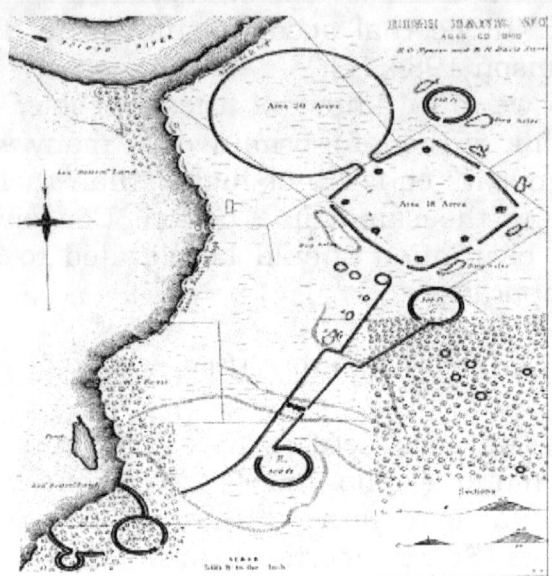

Diagram of the High Bank Earthworks, Chillicothe, Ohio. Squier and Davis, 1848.

The Newark circle and octagon complex, located in the City of Newark, Ohio, fairs better.

Originally it occupied over four square miles with many additional structures constructed on, what was then, open prairie lands. In the center of the Complex was a natural lake which occupied over 100 acres when first seen by the European settlers. While most of these structures were destroyed, the main complex was preserved by being incorporated into the Mound Builders Country Club as part of its golf course. However, access to it by Native Americans and others for ceremonial purposes has been problematic and limited.

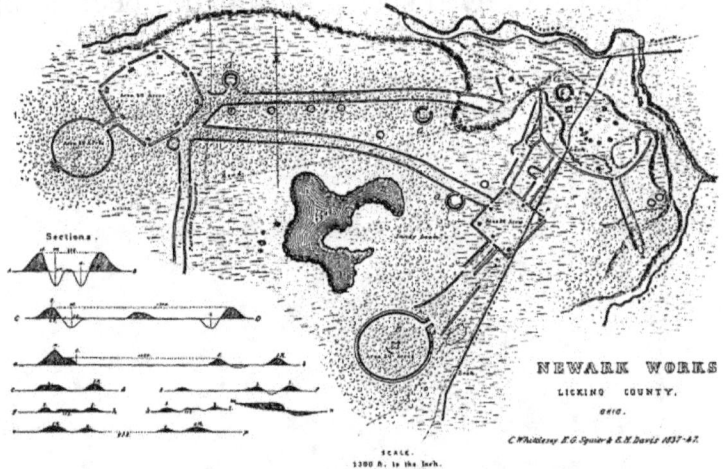

Diagram of the Newark Earthworks complex. Squier and Davis, 1848.

Afterword

The Newark Circle and Octagon complex also bears an interesting connection to the Great Pyramid of Cheops at Giza. It was discovered that the Great Pyramid would fit perfectly if placed within the Circle (Hamilton 1999; Doutre).

Clearly, Newark and High Bank were demarked as major ceremonial sites as they were connected by a remarkably straight sixty mile road, nearly 200 feet wide lined with brick walls three feet high (Salisbury 1862; Knapp 1998a, Lepper 1995, 1996, 1998, 2006, Romain 2008a). This quasi-paved road was a significant monument in itself. Very little of it remains today. The fact that it begins as an avenue off the Newark octagon, passes just east of Geller Hill and ends on the east bank of the Scioto River about six miles north of High Bank, with their respective cluster of earthworks, speaks to the significance of the two sites it links. Its exact placement and angle proffers additional meaning at the time of the Summer Solstice as it aligns parallel to the Milky Way and perpendicular to the Summer Solstice sunset (Romain 2005c, 2005d; Magli 2007). It also aligns with the rising sun at the Winter Solstice (Magli 2007).

Serpent Mound

In southern Ohio, Serpent Mound was built on a plateau overlooking Brush Creek in southwestern Ohio's Adams County.

The Great Serpent Mound
Serpent Mound State Memorial Peebles, Ohio.[5]

---

[5] Drawing by Nick Drakides

It lies on the outer southwestern edge of an asteroid impact crater five miles in diameter encompassing 12 square miles. Such impact craters are now called astroblemes - *star wounds* (Dietz 1961). Some 300 million years ago this asteroid impacted with the force of 34.18 gigatons of TNT (Hanson 1994; Carlton 1998; Povenmire 2000). One gigaton equals one billion tons of TNT.

Serpent Mound is unique. The undulating body of this sacred serpent is over a quarter of a mile long, up to twenty feet wide and was as much as five feet high. Serpent Mound also marks the travels of the sun, charting both equinoxes and solstices and portions of the moon's Metonic cycle (Hamilton 2001; Romain 2000). No other effigy with all of its unique characteristics has been discovered.

Hopi legends tell us that it was built in the ancient times by the Hopi Snake Clan after they had entered the Fourth World. They were heading West on their migrations searching for the place where they would finally settle. The head of the Serpent is aligned with the Summer Solstice sunset. To them it is known as *To'kchi'i*, the Guardian of the East (Waters 1977; Joseph 2009a).

Serpent Mound was nearly lost due to farming operations. In 1848 E.G. Squier and E.H. Davis published the first map of Serpent Mound based on their 1846 survey. Shortly thereafter the area was cleared for cultivation, crops were planted and cattle grazed on the site.

Restoration of the Serpent Mound began in 1883 by Frederick Ward Putnam of the Peabody Museum, Harvard University. Were it not for the visionary efforts of these three gentlemen, and ultimately the Ohio Historical Society, its message to our post-modern era would have been lost for all time.

With the advances in present day archeology, computer assisted design programs, advanced surveying techniques, aerial photography, and most importantly, Archaeoastronomy, a few of today's scientists and researchers have begun to unravel the mysteries of the High Bank, Newark and Serpent Mound sites. Their verified findings stunned the scientific community.

"Until a few years ago, archaeologists abruptly dismissed even the suggestion that the ancestors of present-day Native Americans were deeply interested in the intricate movements of the heavens" (Williamson 1984:2).

It was inconceivable that such complex and precisely accurate calculators of movements in the heavens could have been built by primitives with no known written language. Additionally, according to mainstream archaeologists, their only known tools were believed to be simple stone hatchets, sharpened sticks,

Afterword

antler picks, shovels and hoes made from animal shoulder bones, mussel shells, clam shells or flint, hafted on to strong hickory shafts. Moving millions of tons of stone, sand, dirt and clays to build these intricate and expansive earthen mounds, was most likely done, it is presently believed, by woven baskets, one basket load at a time.

For example, it has been estimated that the amount of earth moved to construct the square enclosure at Baum equaled 34,450 m^3 (45,059 cubic yards) and the square enclosure at Seip 33,000 m^3 (43,162 cubic yards) which are located between Bourneville and Bainbridge, Ohio (Bernardini 2004).

More remarkably, the dirt, clays and other materials used in the construction of the earthworks mentioned in this book had, in many instances, been transported considerable distances (Squier and Davis 1848; Marshall 1978; Greber 2006). This phenomenon, known as allogentic transport, was noted by the early archaeological examinations of mound structure. However, the extent to which entire mounds were comprised of allogentic materials is only now becoming apparent (Van Nest 2006).

Social culture: social organization

All of the physical evidence speaks to their prosperity and organization. For such artifacts to come into being, farmers, artisans and others would not have had to concern themselves with survival or subsistence. This implies division of labor and social organization.

> The data . . . indicates that Hopewellian agriculture practiced a sophisticated system of agriculture based upon a wide variety of crops and most likely utilizing some form of swidden or garden plot rotation system. (Wymer 1996:47)

It is also likely that many native plants were domesticated (Smith 1992).

The very geometric earthworks and burial mounds themselves speak to the organization of a sizeable and organized work force so necessary in the construction of earthworks of such monumental size and complexity (Carr and Case 2006).

Evidence of their social organization also reveals their social structure as having little or no social hierarchy. While they may have had some leadership and leaders, distinctions for individuals of a higher ranking were not clearly demonstrated. However, some burials showed distinction by having more artifacts and richer grave ornaments than others, indicating perhaps some special honoring. Moreover, no distinction has been found between the genders, implying little or no difference in status between men and women. From this, it is accepted that Western Civilization concepts like prestige, political position or social ranking to be minimal or non-existent (Tooker 1979). Having noted that, construction of the massive earthworks appears even more impressive due to the organization that the building of such monuments would have required.

> One large picture that emerges from . . . the grandeur of the archeological record of the Scioto Hopewell, and the labor organization implied by it, was accomplished with only a moderate degree of social hierarchy among individuals and groups, only the barest of centralized leadership at the end of the era, and only moderately formal and institutionalized social positions. Scioto Hopewell society was comprised of complementary groups and positions that had complementary roles and that were tied together largely horizontally as approximate equals. (Carr and Case 2008:39)

While American archaeologists and anthropologists have classified this civilization under various names, these are not the names of any Native American Tribes or ethnic groups. Rather these names describe an archaeologically defined culture on the basis of similarities in artifacts and architecture. The actual meaning and use of their earthworks also remain a mystery, which has led to an on-going debate among those interested in these monumental works and the civilization that created them.

Genetic Analysis

Other mystery surrounds the repeated discovery of "unusually large" "massive" "unusual size" "exceptionally tall" male and female skeletons as they were described by the early archaeologists in Ohio (Shetrone 1926, 1931; Buikstra 1979; Silverberg 1986).

Additionally, beginning as early as 1783 and continuing for well over a hundred years, numerous Ohio newspaper and other accounts document the finding, by average citizens, of skeletons measuring nearly 9 feet in length some with skulls that would easily accommodate the head of an ordinary person (Hempstead 1878; Hamilton 2001; Wright and Spaulding). Elsewhere in Ohio such skulls were found that contained double rows of teeth (Ohio Valley Bones).

Afterword

Near Conneaut, Ohio, in 1844 an ancient burial ground was found which contained the "Conneaut Giants" – human remains of very large stature (Wright and Spaulding). Advancements in dental anthropology and morphology sciences have made teeth a valuable source of information of population histories, relationships and origins (Greenberg 1986).

It is well accepted by the scientific community that mitochondrial DNA (mtDNA) can be extracted from ancient teeth and that this information can reveal a wealth of genetic information (Schwarz 1991; Ginther 1992; Potsch 1992; Smith 1993; Alvarez 1996; Pfeiffer 1998; Mornstad 1999).

Although many of these finds were sent to various museums, including the Smithsonian Institute, little has been published, and the subject is not discussed in the scientific literature, including the DNA research.

In the 1980's DNA analysis on Native Americans began and intensified in the early 1990's. The initial research on present day Native American tribes demonstrated four distinct mtDNA haplogroups: A, B, C, and D which indicate four distinct lineages. A, C, and D are found primarily in Siberian Asia. However, the B haplogroup is found only in aboriginal peoples in Southeast Asia, Tibet, China, Japan, Melanesia and Polynesia (Brown 1998; Little 2001).

This research took an unexpected turn in 1997 with the discovery of an unusual type of DNA - mtDNA haplogroup "X". The X haplogroup is of ancient origin (Brown 1998). While not all present day Native American tribes have been tested by mtDNA analysis, the X haplogroup is present in greater percentages in the Ojibway, Oneota, Nuu-Chah-Nulth tribes, and lower percentages in Yakima, Sioux, and Navajo tribes. While relatively few ancient remains have been tested, ancient remains in Illinois and a few other areas near the Great Lakes have demonstrated the X haplogroup. The actual source of the X haplogroup is unknown and first showed up in America as far back as 36,000 years ago with a major influx occurring in 10,000 B.C. The X-type is also found in Spain (Basque), Morocco (Berbers), Italy, and an isolated tribe (Altasians) in the Gobi Desert, and parts of the Middle East (Little, 2001).

Among the original founders of Native American populations were those harboring the X haplogroup (Brown 1998; Little 2001).The geographic source of the specific variant of the Native American X haplogroup remains unknown (Brown 1998; Reidela 2003).

This data implies or suggests that the source of the people we call the Native Americans came from two primary global directions, from the far west of North America shores and from the east of North America shores a very long time ago. Ultimately, however, the research remains on-going and incomplete (Buikstra 1979).

With respect to the Hopewell cultures genetic markers, one study did discover the X haplogroup in an Illinois Hopewell burial site. This study's data also suggests that the direction of gene migration and hence population movement was from Ohio to Illinois (Bolnick 2007).

Another detailed examination of the Hopewell DNA and mtDNA markers revealed that their genetic markers were found in the Cahokia earthworks burial sites located near Collinsville, Illinois just east of St. Louis and near the confluence of the Illinois, Mississippi and Missouri Rivers. Additionally, these same unusual markers appeared in indigenous cultures in the Northwestern United States, Central and South America (Mills 2003).

Ideological Culture

Architecture and the Cosmos

Knowledge of the earth in relation to the heavens is required to accurately chart the movements of the sun, moon, planets and stars. In order to construct the earthworks, in correct astronomical alignment, extensive knowledge of mathematics, engineering, trigonometry, Euclidean geometry, *pi, phi*, mathematical calculations, and the Pythagorean Theorem was required (Marshall 1980, 1987, 1996, 1997; Doutre; Hively and Horn 1982, 1984, 2006; Lepper 2005; Romain 1991d, 1992c, 1995, 1996a, 2000, 2005a, 2005b, 2005c, 2005d). Further, the Mound Builders had knowledge of the Fibonacci mathematical series (Marshall 1987).

These earthen structures reflect the same level of knowledge and sophistication possessed by those who built the Pyramids, Stonehenge, Mayan and Inca temples, to name a few.

> The real problem with a paradigm or worldview is when it is held by a society that wields considerable economic and political power; for then a particular way of seeing begins to dominate other cultures and forces on them a single, uniform way of seeing where formerly there had been flexibility and diversity.

Afterword

> During the first contact, Europeans were confident that they were the bearers of truth, truth about religion and government, truth about science and law . . . .
>
> When Western science claims to be speaking the truth then, by implication, other peoples' truth becomes myths, legends, superstitions, and fairy stories. A dominant society denies the authenticity of other peoples' system of knowledge and in this way strikes at the very heart of their cultures. (Peat 2002:42)

Because it has been commonly accepted that the native people living in ancient North America were primitives, and in some cases, considered savages, it is no wonder many modern scientists have had some difficulty in accepting these indisputable facts.

It took our present day computer software to unravel the secrets of and reveal the sophistication of these ancient earthworks that track the celestial/stellar travels in the day and night sky. As the research continues, more earthworks are found to possess precise astronomical alignments (Hively and Horn 2010; DeBoer 2010).

> [These] . . . ruins are now interpreted by archaeoastronomers as primitive but sophisticated computers which can scan the horizon if properly used, and they are seen as providing proof of a complicated Indian star knowledge . . . . But even labeling a site as astronomical is an improvement, since it partially sidesteps the old stereotype of Indians being primitive and ignorant savages. (Deloria, Jr.1997:43)

Without question, the Native Americans who constructed the High Bank, Newark, Serpent Mound and many other earthworks possessed this knowledge, and more. This revelation led to a complete reversal of scientific thought and a growing recognition of the very advanced state of knowledge possessed by the Native American Mound Builders.

Most recently the University of Cincinnati's Center for the Electronic Reconstruction of Historical and Archaeological Sites (CERHAS) has created a state of the art exhibition which utilizes advanced multi-media and digital 3-D imaging to reconstruct, in vivid detail, the incredible sophistication of these sacred structures which lie on sacred ground. They must be sacred to hold their mysteries so close.[6]

---

[6] See, http://www.uc.edu/News/NR.aspx?ID=3757 See also, http://www.earthworks.uc.edu/

The Newark and High Bank Complexes

Dr. John A. Eddy, an American astronomer, first proposed that the Newark Circle/Octagon complex was aligned to and marked the northernmost moonrise directly along the Octagon axis:

> I have found by simple map examination that a line through the axis of symmetry of the octagon, the center line of the causeway, and the center of the connected circle coincides very nearly with the direction of the northernmost rise of the moon at the latitude of Newark. (Eddy 1977:150)

Five years later Hively and Horn confirmed Dr. Eddy's theory (Hively and Horn 1982).[7]

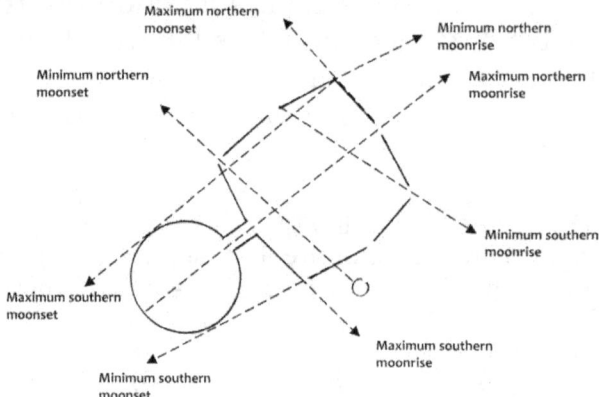

Redrawn and adapted from Lepper 2004

Scientific research indicates that the High Bank and Newark Circle/Octagon complexes precisely chart the travels of the moon on her 18.6 year cyclical journey, her metonic cycle, on both the eastern and western horizons. The moon has eight phases and an octagon eight sides (Hively and Horn 1982, 1984).[8] Additionally, the eight standstills of the moon are integrated into the specific design of these two Octagons over 60 miles apart.

> Of the infinity of possible octagons which could have been constructed . . . the one we find is precisely the one which matches the lunar extrema most closely. In fact we have been unable to design an equilateral polygon with eight or fewer sides which incorporates the extreme lunar points more efficiently and accurately . . . When this fact is combined with the apparently

---

[7] See, http://articles.adsabs.harvard.edu/full/1982JHAS...13....1H.

[8] http://adsabs.harvard.edu/full/1984JHAS...15...85H; see also http://www.octagonmoonrise.org/OnlineLINKS.HTML; http://www.copperas.com/octagon/; http://www.copperas.com/octagon/oindex.html

intentional distortion of the Octagon in the direction of more accurate lunar alignments, the hypothesis of deliberate alignment must be taken seriously. (Hively and Horn 1982:S12; 1984)

The Octagons track the eight standstills of the intricate cycle of the moon which are encompassed by four points on the eastern horizon marking a maximum northern moonrise, a minimum northern moonrise, maximum and minimum southern moonrises, and four points on the western horizon marking the corresponding moonsets.

> The rising point of the Moon as marked along the horizon oscillates between a northerly and southerly extreme during each sidereal month (27 1/3 days). Due to a slow precession of the Moon's orbit, these extreme northerly and southerly rising points oscillate between two fixed azimuths with a period of 18.61 years. A similar variation occurs in the setting point of the Moon. . . . A careful observer of the 18.6 year cycle would therefore notice eight significant directions along the horizon (four moonrise and four moonset points) where the Moon periodically reaches a maximum or minimum extreme. (Hively and Horn 1982:S11- S12)

Equally impressive is the finding that:

> The average accuracy associated with the alignments we have proposed is sufficient to allow the prediction of the year when lunar eclipses occur near the equinoxes or solstices. (Hively and Horn 1982:S17)

The Hopewell builders encoded all of these astronomical landmarks into the architecture of these octagons. These enclosures probably also served other unknown ceremonial purposes.

However, one mystery still has not been addressed in the literature by mainstream archeologists and archaeoastronomers.

While it is readily accepted that the Newark Circle/Octagon earthwork's central axis points to the northernmost moonrise, no recognized authority has been willing to state publically what the central axis of the High Bank Circle/Octagon complex is aligned with.

This central axis points to a location of 143° 67' on the southeastern horizon. It does not point to the southernmost moonrise (maximum southern standstill). This lunar standstill is at an off angle alignment to the central axis.

THE CAMP OF GOD'S TEARS

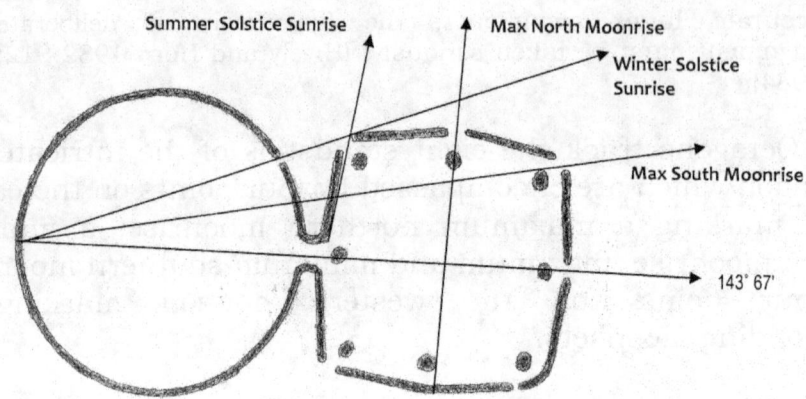

Redrawn and adapted from High Bank Earthwork, Hively and Horn 1984

The silence on this obvious conundrum is deafening.

In essence, we are being asked to assume that the Mound Builders moved tons of dirt to carefully craft gigantic earthworks, with acknowledged skill and acumen, to accurately track the movements of the sun and the 18.6 year metonic cycle of the moon at two locations over sixty miles apart. Yet when it comes to the central axis at High Bank, the Mound Builders somehow failed to align it to a significant astronomical event on the southeastern horizon.

It defies logic to assume that, at some distant time, the High Bank central axis did not *in fact* align perfectly with rising of a significant celestial event on the southeastern horizon. Hively and Horn recently proposed that this alignment is terrestrial and not celestial (Hively and Horn 2010:139-140).[9]

The primary focus of Archaeoastronomy is to provide us with additional data as to how humankind, in the past, understood the phenomena in the sky, how this information was utilized and what role this information played in past civilizations.

It is implausible that this calculation has not been performed by knowledgeable archaeoastronomers. However, the true alignment of the central axis at High Bank remains undisclosed in the scientific literature. Perhaps it is not mentioned because the results would call into question mainstream views regarding the pre-contact history of America.

A comment by Hively and Horn illustrates the fact that this information can be determined.

---

[9] See Appendix for Chapter 15.

> When considering possible alignments of the High Bank structure to rise and set points on the horizon, the uncertainty of the date of High Bank makes it necessary to restrict our attention to the Sun, Moon, and planets. The motion of the Earth's axis significantly alters the rise and set points of stars over the time span of a few hundred years. (Hively and Horn 1984:S94)

In other words, the phenomenon of the precession of the equinoxes will change the rising point of a star or constellation on the eastern horizon about one degree, on a compass bearing, every 72 years. So over a period of several thousand years a rise point would change considerably. The earth goes through one complete precessional cycle approximately every 26,000 years (25,771.5).[10]

The Newark Complex of geometric earthworks is the largest and the northernmost ceremonial center (Lepper, 1998). Detailed surveys and analysis of the various geometric earthworks that comprise the Newark complex revealed even more startling information. They were not arbitrarily placed on the landscape (Romain 1992b, 1992c, 2005a, 2005b, 2005c; Doutre).

Hively and Horn defined a standard unit of measurement supported by their analysis of the Newark Complex based upon what they termed the Observation Circle component of the Circle/Octagon earthwork - the *Observation Circle Diameter* (OCD) = 1054 feet (321.3m) which they utilized for their surveying measurements in relation to other features of the Newark complex (Hively and Horn 1982:S8; See also, Romain 1991d, 2005c).

Subsequently it was discovered that:

> Perhaps the most remarkable feature of the Newark Octagon is the fact that . . . this dual geometric and astronomical significance is only possible in a very narrow range of latitudes . . . from 40°.0 to 40°.4 N. This involves a north-south band of distances of some 44.5km (28mi) wide . . . which includes the Newark site.[11] (Hively and Horn 2006: 306-307)

> The data yield a factual picture of Hopewell people and their historical descendants, the American Indians, that is far different from that expressed in almost any book, television show or motion picture and is at odds with our understanding of our American history. (Marshall 1987:36)

---

[10] See, http://fuliginouspalaver.tripod.com/comingtolight/id16.html
[11] The Newark Circle and Octagon complex is located at 40°.05, whereas the High Bank Work is at 39°.3.

Marshall concluded that the Mound Builders planned their earthworks by some form of detailed drawings, "Nothing less than this explanation can account for the facts of the regularity and precision of these earthworks . . ." (Marshall 1987:37; see also, Silverberg 1986). After examining and surveying over 220 earthworks in accordance with standard engineering and land surveying procedures Marshall stated, "In general, Hopewell prehistoric surveying was a little more accurate than the average of such historic measuring in the eastern United States" (Marshall 1987:37). Further, he determined that both in design and mathematics a 'single school of thought' existed and that this knowledge was transmitted through the many generations of time required constructing these earthworks over vast regions of eastern North America (Marshall 1996).

Marshall carefully examined the Newark earthwork complex. He determined that a complex geometric pattern was defined by the center points of the Octagon, Great Circle and Wright Square. From these three center points a rectangle is described. The vertical sides are 4995 feet in length and the horizontal sides are 5819 feet in length.

As shown below, true north-south and east-west orientations are defined. Additionally, four triangles are defined: a 3-4-5 triangle, base 1 altitude 2 triangles, a 45°- 45°- 90° triangle and a 5-12-13 triangle (Marshall 1987, 1996, 1997).

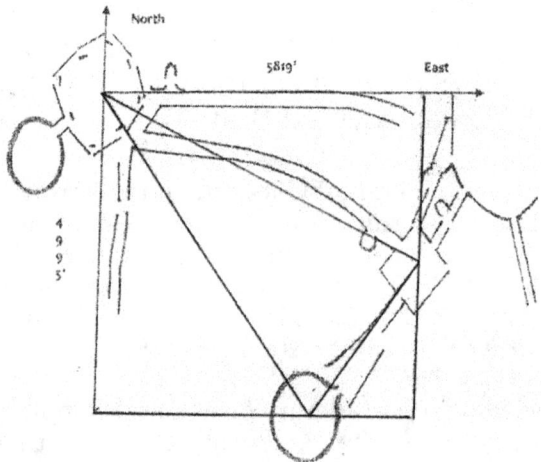

Redrawn and adapted from Marshall 1996 [12]

---

[12] Marshall defined a different standard unit of measure which utilized a grid system, 57 meters on each side which equals 187 feet per side. He further discovered that the same grid system was used in prehistoric Mexico to design the Teotihuacan complex near Mexico City. "If you take this grid and place it over any of the Ohio geometric earthworks, it is obvious that key points on the earthwork coincide with the grid, showing that the same unit of measure was used in Ohio as in Teotihuacan. Thus some small group of American Indians geometers must have made the trip from Mexico to Ohio as early as 400 B.C." (Marshall 1978:31; 1980)

Afterword

Romain conducted an exhaustive examination of the Newark earthwork complex based upon the OCD unit of measurement (1054 feet) proposed by Hively and Horn.[13] He discovered that, in fact, there existed a complicated mathematical and geometric relationship between the various earthworks that comprised the Newark Complex along with additional solar, lunar and stellar alignments.

While Romain acknowledged that other design scenarios were possible the critical point is:

> . . . that the complex was laid out according to an internally consistent logic based on the use of regular geometric shapes, astronomic alignments, and a basic unit of length." (Romain 11-21-2005c:7)

He further determined that seven OCD's (7,378 feet) southwest of the center of the Great Circle earthwork and seven OCD's southeast from the center of the Octagon is Geller Hill, a prominent hilltop, which rises over 35 feet above the landscape.

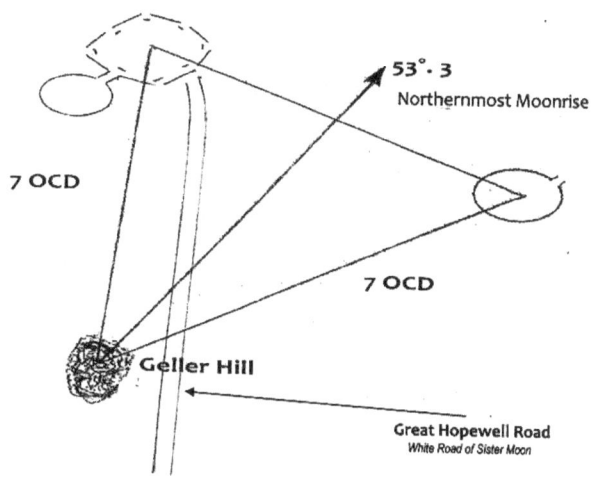

Redrawn and adapted from Romain 2005c

From the vantage point of Geller Hill the geometrical and astronomical relationships of the Circle/Octagon and the Great Circle become apparent. The other axis of this isosceles triangle between the center of the Great Circle and the Octagon is six OCD's. If a line is drawn from the highest point on Geller Hill to the middle of this

---

[13] Romain's survey measurement data at other earthworks indicated that indeed the OCD and its subunits had been utilized in their design and construction even though they were widely separated (Romain 2000: 68; 11-21-2005c). This, of course, clearly suggests integrated engineering and design concepts. Further, an interesting phenomenon arises when one considers the commonality of design, the distances separating earthwork complexes, their mathematical and astronomical interrelationships and the hundreds of years required for their construction (Romain 1996a). This phenomenon strongly argues for the diffusion of complex knowledge over hundreds of years.

axis a compass bearing is derived at 53°.3' which corresponds to the northernmost moonrise point at this latitude.

The totality of the measurement data, geometric relationships, archaeological findings and astronomical data suggests that Geller Hill was a part of the design and probable rituals functions held at the Newark Complex as it would have been visible from the features of the complex (See, Romain 2005a, 2005b, 2005c for detailed discussion).

Additionally, the tracking of the solar and lunar cycles on such a grand scale denote a calendric system in this culture.

On a much smaller scale, this celestial tracking is also reflected in calendric stone tablets. The most famous of which is the Cincinnati Tablet which was discovered in 1841 in a burial mound in downtown Cincinnati, Ohio.

Squier and Davis 1848

Romain concluded that the Cincinnati Tablet incorporated both solar and lunar information by references to the phases of the moon both on a monthly and annual basis. The notational system engraved into the tablet could be used to determine the summer and winter solstices, the thirteen lunar month year and the sun's solstice rising and setting points on the horizon at central Ohio's latitude (Romain 1991a, 1992d, 1996a; Caldwell 1996).

Language and worldview

Linguists and communication researchers have long held that the language of a people reflect their worldview (Whorf 1956).

> Although there was considerable linguistic diversity among the historic tribes, there were only four major linguistic stocks. The four stocks probably had a common source in North America in the far distant past. (Griffin 1967:175)

While a common source for all North American languages cannot be ruled out, at present it is not possible to identify a common source for the remarkable diversity amongst the hundreds of languages spoken at the time the Europeans arrived (Tooker 1979; Greenberg 1986; 1987; Lewin 1988; Diamond 1990; Wallace 1992; Sherzer 1993). Nevertheless, several studies have established that some linguistic groupings define meaningful genetic histories and relationships (Torroni 1993; Lorenz 1996; Malhi 2001; Bolnick 2003).

The grammatical features of Native American languages are anything but primitive:

> Quite the contrary, they exhibited an incredible complexity, albeit, of types sometimes strikingly different from those of European languages. Like all languages, they mirrored the speakers' view of universe and especially the world around them. Among the Indians, this view included fine attention to details of position, direction, motion, form, shape, and texture, all frequently encoded in and expressed through highly wrought words imaginative and poetic in form. (Sherzer 1993:255)

Additionally, there exist renewal ceremonial similarities among most North American tribes. Further, genetic research demonstrates many tribes are not only closely related, but quite likely have a common source or sources (Schurr 1990; Wallace 1992; Torroni 1993; Lorenz 1996; 1997; Brown 1998; Smith 1999; O'Rourke 2000; Kaestle 2001; Bolnick 2003; Reidla 2003; Malhi 2001; 2002; 2004; Eshleman 2004).

Because their linguistic structures are similar in the sense that they are verb based and embedded with motion, process, vibration and relationships within a dynamic, conscious and multidimensional universe, [14] it can be argued that the overarching worldview of most Native Americans remains too similar to dismiss the likelihood of ancient roots. It is postulated that Native American worldview exists and can be studied (Ferguson 2005).

The oral histories of several existing North American tribes relate that they are descendants of the people referred to here as the Mound Builders. The archeological, genetic and cultural evidence supports this oral history (Kavasch 2004).

We suggest that the present day Native American worldview also resembles the worldview of the Mound Builders and may even have been derived from a common source.

---

[14] This is in contrast to the Western languages dominant use of nouns.

Worldview

Western thought has accepted and continues to maintain a view of the world that has been handed down to us from Isaac Newton, René Descartes, and Charles Darwin and the like. It is a worldview of separateness. Everything is separate from everything else, and the most separate is the human being.

> Up until the present, biology and physics have been handmaidens of views espoused by Isaac Newton, the father of modern physics. Everything we believe about our world and our place within it takes its lead from ideas that were formulated in the seventeenth century, but still form the backbone of modern science -- theories that present all the elements of the universe as isolated from each other, divisible and wholly self-contained. (McTaggart 2008: xxv)

> We remain reluctant apostles of these views of the world as mechanized and separate, even if this isn't part of our ordinary experience. Many of us seek refuge from what we see as the harsh and nihilistic fact of our existence in religion, which many offer some succour in its ideals of unity, community, and purpose, but through a view of the world that contradicts the view espoused by science. Anyone seeking a spiritual life has had to wrestle with these opposing world views and fruitlessly try to reconcile the two. (McTaggart, 2008:xxv)

Quantum physics prescribes a "unified theory of mind and matter" as in David Bohm's words, "an unbroken wholeness." This research provides undeniably "evidence that all of us connect with each other and the world at the very undercoat of our being" (McTaggart 2008:xxvii). Results of exhaustive experiments demonstrate:

> . . . that there may be such a thing as a life force flowing through the universe – what has variously been called collective consciousness or, as theologians have termed it, the Holy Spirit. They provided a plausible explanation of all those areas that over the centuries mankind has had faith in but no solid evidence of as adequate accounting for, from the effectiveness of alternative medicine and even prayer to life after death. They offered us in a sense, a science of religion. (McTaggart, 2008:xxviii)

Archeologists and other researchers inform us that the Mound Builders celebrated renewal and rebirth. Basic tenets of the Native American worldview celebrate renewal, typically about the relationship between humanity and the cosmos, the cosmos being alive, breathing and conscious. Everything in creation, including the inanimate, is imbued with an essence of life or spirit, hence everything is alive. The essence of life or spirit that resides in everything remains connected to itself, making everything interconnected, or part of a whole. Should any aspect or attribute tip out of balance, the entire whole is impacted (Ferguson 2005).

In an environment that does not remain constant, change is inevitable. Constancy in our lives lends us confidence, stability, and faith in the future. Change is also a constant. **Often an unpredictable altering of the known into an unknown introduces chaos.**

> According to the laws of classical physics, particularly the law of entropy, the movement of the inanimate world is always toward chaos and disorder. (McTaggart 2008:122)

Chaos brings flux or instability, creating a need in humanity to negotiate order from the chaos.

> . . . Flux is cosmic breath, expanding and contracting---an invisible dancing energy of shape-shifting probabilities. Constant flux is a continual, non-stop wave of movement that encompasses all that is and all that is not. It is a symphony of change that is ever present and elusive to the eye, yet it influences every aspect of humanity. (Ferguson 2005:56)

> However, the coherence of consciousness represents the greatest form of order known to nature, and the . . . studies suggest that this order may help shape and create in the world. When we wish for something or intend something, an act which requires a great deal of unity of thought, our own coherence may be, infectious.
> On the most profound level, the . . . studies also suggest that reality is created by each of us only by our attention. At the lowest level of mind and matter, each of us creates the world. (McTaggart 2008:122)

In the Native American worldview this negotiation for order is accomplished through renewal ceremony. "Renewal refers to sacred intention, manifested in the form of ritual for the sole purpose of honoring the spiritual resilience of life. Renewal revives, respects, resurrects and reveres" (Ferguson 2005:77).

> For Indigenous cultures, chaos is reality; and out of that chaos comes order, influenced by the subtle process of renewal ceremonies that honour the cyclical waves and patterns of the flux as manifested in the cycle of the seasons, sunrises and

sunsets, the phases of the moon and in animal migrations. (Fergusson 2005:60)

Based on the construction of the earthworks, with their alignments to the solstice sunrises and sunsets, the phases of the moon, as well as some star/constellation alignments, we suggest that the ancient civilization of the Mound Builders practiced such renewal ceremonies for the purpose of intending to maintain order and balance within their known world. "Order is created out of the chaos/flux, through ceremony and renewal. Renewal ceremony keeps order in the cosmos and this concept complements notions of observer-created reality" (Ferguson 2005:80).

The ancient Native American's understanding of the universe and the inner-connectedness of the universe, in the way we now describe as quantum physics, eclipsed Western concepts of science until only recently.

Given the close relationship between language and worldview, a deeper examination of Native American language and worldview has been explored by well-known physicists, such as David Bohm,[15] linguists and others. Beginning in 1992, David Bohm explored the Native American worldview in relationship to quantum physics. The results proved astonishing.

> Quantum theory validates concepts of Native American paradigm. The elements of quantum physics have been in application for thousands of years in Native American paradigm . . . The allegiance between quantum theory and Native science is manifest in constant flux, trickster, chaos theory, animate, interrelationship or interconnectedness and observer created reality . . . Native America has always believed in energy waves. Out of this wave energy, patterns develop. In Native American paradigm, and consequently science, these patterns manifest as sacred astronomy; cycles of the seasons; birth, death and rebirth; growing seasons; bird migrations; sunrise and sunset. Patterns are identified through sacred mathematics. The number four encompasses the four directions, the four chambers of the heart, the mental, physical, spiritual and emotional, the four elements and so on. (Ferguson 2005:99-100)

David Bohm's concept of *"unbroken Wholeness"*[16] viewed the universe as:

---

[15] David Bohm, physicist and intellectual successor to Albert Einstein, with contributions in the fields of theoretical physics, philosophy and neuropsychology, and to the Manhattan Project, also major contributions to physics, particularly in the area of quantum mechanics and relativity theory, and had a series of meetings with the Dalai Lama.
[16] Bohm, David. 1980.

Afterword

> . . . a vast dynamic cobweb of energy exchange, with a basic substructure containing all possible versions of all possible forms of matter. Nature was not blind and mechanistic, but open-ended, intelligent and purposeful, making use of a cohesive learning feedback process of information being fed back and forth between organisms and their environment. Its unifying mechanism was not a fortunate mistake but information which had been encoded and transmitted everywhere at once. (McTaggart 2008:94-95)

Simply explained, quantum physics describes the universe as being comprised of energy, which remains in constant motion or vibration. This means everything, all seen and unseen in the universe remains in motion or vibration and can be experienced or seen as either waves or particles at a sub-atomic level. These waves can be most easily comprehended when we look at waves at a shoreline, for example, or an EKG monitor display. These sine waves move in a rhythm according to their rate of movement or frequency. Everything in the universe moves at its own frequency, when combined becomes a collective frequency or an energy field. This energy can also be viewed as particles as well. Energy then can be seen or studied as either wave or particle, moving or not (McTaggart 2008). "Particles point and wave at the same time, dependent upon observation. Particles communicate instantaneously" (Ferguson 2005:99).

How one experiences energy or the energy of an experience is dependent upon the intent of the observer or experiencer. ". . . Directed thoughts have a central participatory role in creating reality . . ." (McTaggart 2008:xxi).

How this works in our everyday lives is that our intentions influence how we experience our experiences. Our thoughts, being energy, impact or influence the outcome of our experiences. This concept relates to Native American worldview as observer-created reality. When engaged in the renewal ceremonies, Native America does so with great responsibility because it is accomplished with intention (Ferguson 2005).

Quantum physics further teaches that everything in the universe, both seen and unseen is connected and interconnected. The universe is a whole, and each individual frequency, each collective frequency, and each energy field is embraced in one tapestry of consciousness. This consciousness can manifest into the seen, visible, physical world through the use of intention, much like the ideas articulated in *The Secret* or *The Law of Attraction*, or *Happier than God*. Our words and thoughts send out intention that manifest into our experience and reality.

Physicists use the term "potential" when describing this phenomenon. Native Americans use the term "spirit" in a nearly identical way (Alford 1993).

> These were also discoveries which scientifically verified the ancient wisdom and folklore of traditional cultures. Their theories offered scientific validation of many of the myths and religions humans have believed in since the beginning of time, but have hitherto only had faith to rely on. All they'd done was to provide a scientific framework for what the wisest among us already know. (McTaggart 2008:226)

> By using rigorous scientific methods and theoretical constructs, scientists have recently arrived at the same truths- or, should we say, have made similar assumptions. It is now safe to say that quantum physics actually demonstrates the truth of what the mystics have known for centuries. How exciting it is to see a joining of these two distinct ways of approaching and arriving at truth. Science and spirituality have come together at last, with scientists becoming modern day mystics! (Tipping 2009:188)

Our hand-me-down Newtonian beliefs describe the distance between stars and the distance between individuals as dead space. Quantum physics informs us otherwise, that the distance between stars, as well as the distance between individuals, is a living, breathing, conscious fabric of the universe connecting each to all.

Newton described a world of separateness and the laws of motion, and Descartes postulated we are represented by our minds, separate from our bodies as another machine. This paradigm insisted on a world as a collection of discrete objects behaving predictably, much like a gearbox. "With a few deft moves, Newton and Descartes had plucked God and life from the world of matter, and us and our consciousness from the center of our world. They ripped the heart and soul out of the universe, leaving in its wake a lifeless collection of interlocking parts . . ." (McTaggart 2008:xxiv).

In both quantum physics and in Native America worldview, no parts stand alone in fragmentation or segmentation, but live and breathe as part of a whole. It is not that the whole is greater than the sum of its parts; the part enfolds the Whole; everything and everyone become the Whole (Alford 1993).

> Another important characteristic appeared to be an altered view of the world. People were more likely to succeed if, instead of believing in a distinction between themselves and the world, and seeing individual people and things as isolated and divisible, they viewed everything as a connected continuum of interrelations – and also if they understood that there were other ways to communicate than through the usual channels. (McTaggart 2008:134)

Because of the insights and efforts of Leroy Little Bear,[17] Amethyst First Rider,[18] David Bohm, F. David Peat,[19] and Sam Kounosu,[20] and others, we see that Native American language and beliefs expressed the basic principles of quantum physics. The basic principles of quantum physics were central to the Native American worldview (Cajete 2000).

So once again modern science is only now discovering what Native America knew and tacitly utilized for thousands of years: that humankind's responsibility is to maintain a harmonic balance with the rhythm of creation in both the manifested and unmanifested universe.

Spiritual values and worldview

While mystery still surrounds the Mound Builder's earthworks, we do know this, whoever built these mounds enjoyed a peaceful and harmonious existence for over a thousand years. Archeological investigations of Mound Builder gravesites revealed very few indications of hostile actions as the cause of death.

It is acknowledged that only a few skeletons were found with imbedded arrow or spear points or other evidence of violent death in the whole Eastern United States and none in Ohio (Carr and Case, 2008). Violent conflicts and warfare is considered fairly

---

[17] Leroy Little Bear is a former Director of Native Studies at Harvard University, moderator of the SEED (Source for Educational Empowerment and community Development - Albuquerque, New Mexico), *Language of Spirit* Dialogue which is an on-going annual interdisciplinary and international conference conducted to bridge Indigenous wisdom and modern knowledge and features quantum physicists, Native American Elders and linguists. Leroy Little Bear worked with David Bohm to initiate conferences creating dialogues among physicists, Indigenous elders, linguists and others, such as the Fetzer Conferences that began in 1992. http://www.seedopenu.org/.
See also: http://www.seedgraduateinstitute.org/index.htm and
http://www.seedgraduateinstitute.org/Conferences/language/index.html
[18] Amethyst First Rider is a consultant to the Centre for Particle Astrophysics, Lawrence Hall of Science at the University of California, Berkeley. Scholar of traditional knowledge of Blackfeet traditional stories, producer and director of Native theatre, lecturer in Native Literature and Native Drama in the Native American Studies Dept at University of Lethbridge.
[19] David Peat as a physicist authored books on quantum theory and chaos theory, as well as a study of Synchronicity. In 2002, he also authored *Blackfoot Physics A Journey into the Native American Universe*.
[20] Sam Kounosu is a theoretical physicist, Professor Emeritus, University of Lethbridge.

non-existent within this pre-contact culture whereas other co-extensive civilizations revealed evidence of conflict. This characteristic of the Mound Builder civilization distinguishes this civilization from virtually all other cultures in the New World.

> At this time, there is little sound reason for us to continue laying our own Western views of self-interested individuals and competitive social life upon Scioto Hopewell peoples, when the available data speak so loudly against this psychology and social form. To do so disrespectfully diminishes a major accomplishment of Scioto Hopewell people equal to their monumental earthworks and beautiful art. The Scioto Hopewell appear to have mastered to a considerable degree the art of cooperation in social relations, and to have created a well-orchestrated social and ritual life. (Carr and Case 2008:655)

Because the evidence indicates the Mound Builder culture sustained itself through a thousand years of peace that peace did not come from just the physical life they created. While a benevolent and rich environment offered them the opportunity to thrive without much struggle, peace among neighbors implies peace within the hearts of those sharing the environment. From this we derive a sense of deep spirituality expressed within this culture as a way of life.

Then suddenly, sometime between 325 and 500 A.D., the Mound Builders, as a people, disappeared. "There are old Indian prophecies that forecast the coming of the white man, and some of them predict the disappearance of tribes because of the actions of these invaders" (Deloria, Jr. 1993:443).

What brought their disappearance about and what happened to them is simply unknown.

> The end of the Scioto Hopewellian social and ceremonial life is documented to have resulted from the breakdown of an intercommunity spiritual-social alliance (a socio-political cause) that was most likely precipitated by a perceived spiritual event or problem of fundamental proportion (spiritual belief). . . . the end was likely caused by some critical, perceived spiritual event or problem - one concerned with a fundamental aspect of Scioto Hopewellian world view. (Carr and Case 2008:40, 317)

However, with their disappearance, there occurred a significant increase in competition, conflict, and warfare among those who did not disappear.

Afterword

Implications for the Future

The paradigm we inherited from Newton has dominated our worldview and still remains with us. We insist it is true, *a priori*. Or, we believe it to be true to the exclusion of all other competing truths, because we have always believed it to be so. In other words, it must be so because we believe it to be so.

Quantum physics was embraced by the Mound Builders and the succeeding generations of Native America. Despite Newton's, Descartes' or Darwin's influence on western thought creating a sense of separateness and fragmentation, quantum physics studies reveal a vision that is life-enhancing. Results of these studies are

> . . . ideas that could empower us, with their implications of order and control. We were not simply accidents of nature. There was a purpose and unity to our world and our place within it, and we had an important say in it. What we did and thought mattered – indeed, was critical in creating our world. Human beings were no longer separate from each other. It was no longer us and them. We were no longer at the periphery of our universe – on the outside looking in. We could take our rightful place, back in the center of our world. (McTaggart 2008:xxviii)

> This revolution in scientific thinking also promised to give us back a sense of optimism, something that has been stripped out of our sense of ourselves with the arid vision of twentieth-century philosophy, largely derived from the views espoused by science. We are not isolated beings living our desperate lives on a lonely planet in an indifferent universe. We never were alone. We were always part of a larger whole. We were and always had been at the center of things. Things did not fall apart. (McTaggart 2008:226)

The Serpent Mound has a story to tell. Its story comes in several layers. One layer holds a prophecy. The prophecy of Serpent Mound speaks to all generations, and speaks to us in this generation. Its prophecy is not what will come, but what *may* come, even to us as we live our lives here and now. "Bohm felt that for a genuine transformation of humankind to take place, the tacit knowledge of this society would need to change" (Parry 2007:3).

> Bohm frequently spoke of "tacit knowledge" as the knowledge of what we unconsciously do, riding a bicycle or driving a car is a form of tacit knowledge, but Bohm meant something deeper than this by tacit knowledge; he was referring to all the unexamined assumptions that govern our lives that create the particular lens

in which we individually and collectively see the world -- what he called "our tacit infrastructure"— but might also be called our paradigm. (Parry 2007:3)

Of all our stories, it is the scientific ones that most define us. Those stories create our perception of the universe and how it operates, and from this, we shape all our societal structures, our relationships with each other and our environment, our methods of doing business and educating our young, of organizing ourselves into towns and cities, of defining the borders of our countries and our planet. (McTaggart 2008:xix)

Our current scientific story is more than three hundred years old, a construction largely based on the discoveries of Isaac Newton – a universe in which all matter moves within a three-dimensional space and time according to certain fixed laws. The Newtonian vision describes a reliable place inhabited by well-behaved and easily identifiable matter. The world view arising from these discoveries is also bolstered by the philosophical implications of Charles Darwin's theory of evolution, with its suggestion that survival is available only to the genetically rugged individual. These, in their essence, are stories that idealize separateness. From the moment we are born, we are told that for every winner there must be a loser. From that constricted vision we have fashioned our world.

The Field tells a radically new scientific story. The latest chapter of that story, written by a group of largely unknown frontier scientific explorers, suggests that at our essence we exist as a unity, a relationship – utterly interdependent, the parts affecting the whole at every moment.

The implications of this new story to our understanding of life and the design of our society are extraordinary. If a quantum field holds us all together in its invisible web, we will have to rethink our definitions of ourselves and what exactly it is to be human. If we are in constant and instantaneous dialog with our environment, if all the information from the cosmos flows through our pores at every moment, then our current notion of our human potential is only a glimmer of what it should be.

If we're not separate, we can no longer think in terms of "winning" and "losing." We need to redefine what we designate as "me" and "not-me," and reform the way that we interact with other human beings, practice business, and view time and space. We have to reconsider how we choose and carry out our work, structure our communities, and bring up our children. We have to imagine another way to live, an entirely new way to "be." We have to blow up all of our societal creations and begin again, building over scorched ground. (McTaggart 2008:xx)

If we are able to awaken and attend to the message, and apply its meaning to our present day lives, then our so-called modern

Afterword

civilization stands a better chance of continuing life on Earth as we know it.

> We now have a planet in crisis. Our Mother suffers the indignities of a world gone mad with unbridled desire. The Western world has created a reality of "more is better," and "my better must be better than yours." Such thinking has led to inequity, fuelled by greed and a lust for power, which has bred fear and hatred among those who do not "have." *Imbalance*. Let's call it observer-created reality---Western style. The scientific sanctions of control and fragmentation have created a global mentality that is out of control and taking the sacred Mother with her. Great minds are challenging old methods and crying out in the darkness, warning humanity to change it ways. (Ferguson 2005:82)

We have reached a crossroad in history where it is time:

> . . . to relegate Newton and Descartes to their proper places, as prophets of a historical view that has now been surpassed. Science can only be a process of understanding our world and ourselves, rather than a fixed set of rules for all time, and with the ushering in of the new, the old must often be discarded. (McTaggart 2008:xxix)

> Scientific revolutions are forced upon us by the discovery of phenomena that are not comprehensible in terms of the old theories. Old theories die hard. Much more is at stake than the theories themselves. To give up our privileged position at the center of the universe, as Copernicus asked, was an enormous psychological task. To accept that nature is fundamentally irrational (governed by chance), which is the essential statement of quantum mechanics, is a powerful blow to the intellect. Nonetheless, as new theories demonstrate superior utility, their adversaries, however reluctantly, have little choice but to accept them. In so doing, they also must grant a measure of recognition to the world views that accompany them.
> Today, particle accelerators, bubble chambers, and computer printouts are giving birth to another world view. This world view is as different from the world view at the beginning of this century as the Copernican world view was from its predecessors. It calls upon us to relinquish many of our closely clutched ideas. (Zukav 2001:214 -215)

Someday we may discover more about the Mound Builders which could bring even a greater understanding to the times in which we now live. They lived for over 1,000 years in peace. Among their other mysteries, maybe we will discover, and we may be in the process of discovering, their secret to a peaceful and prosperous civilization.

Perhaps they have already shown us a new way to live our lives with a new realization and a new awareness of our unity of consciousness within a field of a collective frequency.

The Camp of God's Tears is a story of a people with a powerful and significant sense of spiritual connectedness that directed their everyday lives. Considering all that has been said here, they have much to teach us. It would behoove us to learn from them. By shifting our paradigm or worldview, by shifting the way we think and see and behave, we can change the direction in which we, as inhabitants on Mother Earth, are going. A change is required, a revolution, in fact.

A place to begin is to consistently think and see with new eyes that we are connected to each other and to the universe. To start, we can treat each other as if the other were us.

Perhaps you might say the task is daunting and how can I as one individual effect change in a world so troubled and so unbalanced?

Remember always that our thoughts have mass within the collective frequency and that profound change comes – one mind at a time.

APPENDIX FOR CHAPTER 6
RED FOX BUILDS THE MODEL

The dialogue between Singing Hawk and Red Fox in *"Red Fox Builds the Model"* introduces the reader to some rather remarkable data discovered by Romain, Hamilton, the Hardmans'[21] and others.

Some might question the validity of the information presented in the dialogue as fanciful imagination. However, the factual basis for this chapter has been documented by these researchers.

Based on the findings of Romain, Mitchell, Hively and Horn, the Mound Builders, not only possessed knowledge of geometry, mathematics and astronomy, they applied this knowledge in the design and construction of their remarkable earthworks.

Math is a universal language. Geometry is ". . . the universal means by which the intrinsic oneness of the universe may be comprehended" (Pennick, 1979:10). [22]

With the advent of advanced computer software and modern surveying techniques, these researchers and others have begun the process of deciphering the mathematical, geometric and engineering concepts that the Mound Builders relied upon in the placement and construction the Serpent Mound and so many other massive earthworks.

Many earthworks display a commonalty of design and were constructed over a time span of hundreds of years. This strongly suggests that the Mound Builders had an effective way of passing down this complex knowledge to subsequent generations.

> The remarkable precision in the design and layout of the great geometric earthworks of Ohio has been long recognized. Many of these earthworks are thousands of feet in length and breadth and describe geometric shapes including circles, squares, and octagons. (Romain 1991d:28)
>
> [T]here is little doubt that the Mound Builders possessed detailed observational knowledge of astronomical phenomena, a method of counting and manipulating fairly large numbers, an accurate means of measuring both angles and distance, and a basic unit of measure. (Romain 1991d:28)
>
> Hopewell [*Mound Builders*] surveying techniques were sufficiently advanced that they could lay out what are essentially perfect right angles . . . understood the idea of perpendicular lines . . . designed congruent obtuse angles . . . and understood the concept of parallel lines . . . and transversal lines . . . and the properties of equilateral triangles ... thousands of feet in length and breadth . . . . (Romain

---

[21] Clark and Marjorie Hardman discovered the Summer Solstice setting sun alignment with the oval and the Serpent's head.
[22] Nigel Rennick, 1979. *The Ancient Science of Geomancy: Living in Harmony with the Earth.*

1992c:35, 39-41) Obviously, the Hopewell were remarkably skilled at laying out very long sightlines, to rather precise limits." (Romain 1992a:4)

> In general, Hopewell [*Mound Builders*] prehistoric surveying was a little more accurate than the average of such historical measuring in the eastern United States. (Marshall 1987:37)

Serpent Mound represents graphic testimony to the acumen of its designers, engineers and those responsible for translating a concept into a physical expression.

With respect to Serpent Mound, Hamilton noted:

> The earthwork is aligned exactingly to the north. Numerous other features show that its builders oriented it to astronomical phenomena in a startling rich and detailed fashion and built it in accord with precise principles of geometry and arithmetic. Many other prehistoric earthworks and stoneworks also show astronomical and mathematical connections, but . . . the Great Serpent Mound is unique in the sheer number and complexity of these connections. In this regard it exceeds even the Great Pyramid of ancient Egypt or the Parthenon of Greece . . . . Truly it is a wonder of the prehistoric world archaeological researches, independent of one another. (Hamilton 2001:xiii, xix)

Hamilton also discovered that the layout of Serpent Mound replicated the star pattern in the Draco constellation:

> For the Serpent Mound, through an earthwork, through its exact correlation with the astronomical constellation Draco . . . nicely aligning with the most accurate map of the earthwork. Over thirty points of light were translated precisely as seen in the sky to the earth. (Hamilton 2001:xv, xvii, xix)

In other words, Serpent Mound captures the mirror image of Draco onto the landscape, *as above so below*. The earthwork's size and length ". . . is determined by the spread of the solar and lunar alignments, while the shape is figured to a greater or lesser degree by the star correspondence . . . ." with the Draco constellation. (Hamilton, 2001: 11, 29)

Marshall in his 1978, 1980 and 1987 articles determined that the Mound Builders intentionally utilized the 3:4:5 right triangle, the 30:60:90 degree and the 45:45:90 degree triangles in designing their earthworks. (Romain 1991d:28)

In his Book "*Mysteries of the Hopewell*" Romain provides a detailed discussion of his decade long research of the Serpent Mound (Romain 2000:233-253; See also, Romain 1987a, 1987b, 1988a, 1988b, 1988c, 1988d, 1991c).

APPENDIX FOR CHAPTER 6

In a series of six drawings he documents the presence of numerous triangular relationships between various key reference points on the body of Serpent Mound. He found 18 instances wherein triangles were composed of the lesser multiples of the 1,053-foot unit of length, utilized by its builders, to an accuracy of plus or minus 5 inches (Romain 2000:246).

In Chapter 6, *Red Fox Builds the Model*, a modified version of Romain's Figure A.5 is presented. What Romain discovered was astounding. By defining a variety of triangles based upon central points on the Serpent Mound, he determined that the lesser multiples of the 1053 foot unit of measure defined the lengths of the sides of the triangles. For example, as shown by Figure A 5, the length of a line drawn from the center of the oval to the tip of the tail comes very close to equaling the lesser multiples of 263.3 + 131.6 + 65.8 feet. Next, the line from the center of the oval to the bottom center of the first curve is very close to the lesser multiples of 131.6 + 65.8 + 32.9 + 16.5 + 8.2 feet (Romain 2000:239-240, Figure A.5).

Another drawing is presented below as another example of the incorporation of the lesser multiples of the 1053 foot unit of measure in the design of this remarkable earthwork.

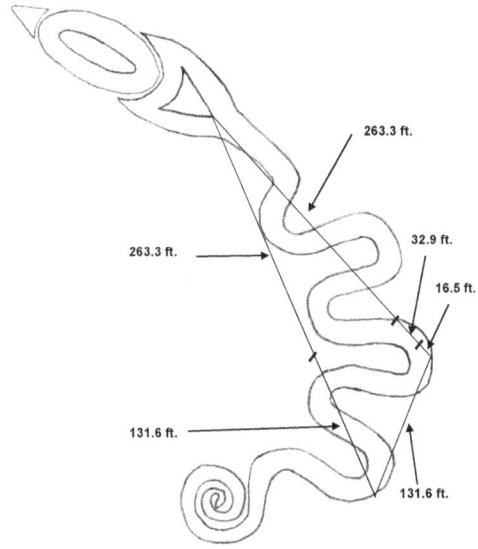

Redrawn and modified from Romain 2000, Fig. A.7

Ross Hamilton, in *"The Mystery of the Serpent Mound"* stated:

> After the efforts of the Hardmans and Romain to make known the possible solar and lunar alignments to the serpentine design, Robert Fletcher and Terry Cameron published an informal map demonstrating four possible solar alignments. Roughly corresponding to Romain's maximum south rising position of the moon, the second coil from the tail also serves as a comfortable area from which the

winter solstice sunrise may have been viewed. Similarly, the fourth coil from the tail likely hosts the spring and autumnal equinox sunrise; and the second coil from the head may have established a *coin of vantage* from which the summer solstice sunrise was seen. How ingenious to use the same coils for completely different celestial body alignments!

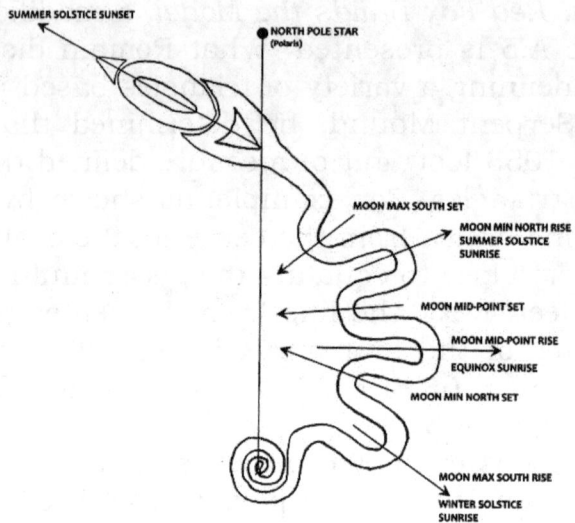

Redrawn and modified from Romain 2000, Fig. A.10; Hamilton 2001, Fig. 3

All told, there are at least twelve verifiable, geo-astronomical alignments contributed by competent archaeological researchers, independent of one another. . . . [W]e are now able to extrapolate the age of the Serpent at around 5,000 years. (Hamilton 2001:xix, xxiv, 7, 15-16)

In their article, "*Serpent Mound a New Look At An Old Snake-In-The Grass*," Fletcher and Cameron observed:

> . . . [T]he classic proportions of the Serpent Mound are obvious and undeniable, and the conviction grows that this effect was intentional, carefully planned and executed. The elegance of the design is even more remarkable considering the size of the mound .
> Again, this leads one toward the idea that the overall shape of the effigy was predetermined and then laid out on the ground. (Fletcher 1988:56)

In the center of the oval was a pile of fire-cracked rocks when Squier and Davis surveyed Serpent Mound in 1846:

> This oval is formed by an embankment of earth without any perceptible opening, four feet in height, and is perfectly regular in outline, its transverse and conjugate diameters being one hundred and sixty and eighty feet respectively. The ground within the oval is

slightly elevated: a small circular elevation of large stones much burned once existed in its centre; but they have been thrown down and scattered by some ignorant visitor, under the prevailing impression probably that gold was hidden beneath them. (Squier and Davis 1847:97)

Hamilton discovered the significance of the location of this pile of fire-cracked rocks:

. . . .[T]he American Society of Dowsers Great Serpent Mound Chapter has performed extensive examination of the earthwork and its vicinity. They have unanimously discovered six energetic lines of subtle magnetism converging in the oval bowl at the head of the earthwork. They are concentric and equidistant lines. (Hamilton 2001:67)

To the west and perpendicular to the oval, is a small cave located just below the crest of Serpent Mound ridge which rises up from Brush Creek (Romain 1988b:16).

Romain also determined:

. . . [T]he Serpent Mound is located almost directly on top of the most intense residual magnetic anomalies in the entire state . . . In summary, it seems clear that the Serpent Mound Builders located their effigy in a rather unique environmental setting. (Romain 1988b:15-16)

One might ask why these independent researchers would spend so much effort, time and money to conduct all of this intense research. The late James A. Marshall observed:

As to why one should do this research, an important reason is the very different impression of American history and the prehistoric and historic American Indian that emerges from these facts.(Marshall 1987:40)

APPENDIX FOR CHAPTER 11
RED FOX AT SEIP

Intricately drilled fresh water pearls, bear, wolf, fox and other mammal teeth along with quartz crystals perforated with holes, some one millimeter in diameter have been found by archeologists. These artifacts demonstrate the fact that the Mound Builders possessed a remarkable drilling methodology.

Many surviving specimens were drilled very carefully by drilling from both sides by countersunk holes that meet in the middle. The holes in many objects are so small and regular that they could not have been made with a flint drill. In fact, a shell bead and a pearl were found with a broken iron drill head lodged in the perforation. Moorehead 1922: 140, 146, 176.

> These perforations are executed with such accuracy and skill as to cause remark [as to] the means employed . . . declared [by many] to be inexplicable. Numerous theories have been advanced to account by which the work was accomplished. (McGuire 1894:627)

Experimental efforts to re-create the means by which these artifacts were drilled lead to the creation of working models of drilling apparatus similar to that witnessed by Red Fox in this chapter (McGuire 1894:656, 754-756; Fowke 1902:657-666).

SEIP MOUND [23]

Between 1925 and 1928 archaeologists Henry C. Shetrone and Emerson F. Greenman excavated the Seip Group of earthworks located in Ross County near Bainbridge, Ohio.

In the center of the large circular earthwork enclosure was a loaf shaped mound that become known as Seip Mound Number 1, which still exists today in a state park. This mound is 250 feet long and is positioned with about 6 degrees form a true east-west direction. The width of at is center is 150 feet and 32 feet high. It gently slopes on all four sides.

Shetrone and Greenman completely excavated this mound then re-constructed it. They discovered that this large mound was

---

[23] The complete reports of Shetrone, Greenman and Mills are available on-line at: http://publications.ohiohistory.org/ohstemplate.cfm?action=intro
Mills, William C. 1907. "Explorations of the Seip Mound," *Journal of the Ohio Historical Society, Vol 18*, 1907. pp 269-321.
Shetrone, Henry C., Greenman, Emerson F., 1931. "Explorations of the Seip Group of Prehistoric Earthworks." *Journal of the Ohio Historical Society, Vol. 40, 1931,* pp. 343-509.

actually composed of three separate earthen mounds which were individually constructed over many years. Once the three separate burial mounds were completed they were then covered forming the single large mound.

During the course of their excavations they discovered that a unique hardened oval-shaped clay floor had been constructed before any burial mounds were built. The original soil within this oval was dug out to a depth of between six and twelve inches and then refilled with six layers of various clays, sand and gravel. After re-filling, the surface was leveled and a top layer of clay was smoothed over its entire surface. This clay was then hardened by fire which turned the clay into various colors of red, yellow and brown.

In the center of this amazing concrete-like oval floor, five rectangular receptacles had been dug into the hardened clay to a depth of about between four and five inches. Each receptacle was lined with about three inches of smooth fire hardened pottery clay. The sides of each sloped down to a flat bottom.

Additionally, three other circular basins approximately a yard in diameter and six to ten inches in depth located south of the oval's center. The receptacles and circular basins had pieces of flint, obsidian, mollusk and marine shells, pottery, pearls and beads, and bear canine teeth, some with pearls set in them, mixed in with the charcoal, charred grasses, and ash from fires built in these basins. It is likely that these basins were ceremonial in nature.

When the three smaller individual mounds were excavated the archaeologists discovered a log burial chamber containing the remains of four adults and two infants. Logs were staked to create the walls and logs laid across the top of the walls to form a roof. This chamber also had slabs of rock both inside and outside the chamber to support its walls from the weight of the soil, clay, sand and gravels that were placed over it.

A variety of burial ceremony gifts accompanied the remains of the estimated 128 individuals buried within Seip Mound Number 1. These included thousands of fresh water pearls, tools made from bone and copper, and ornaments made from copper, mica and tortoise shell.

> The burials were accompanied by a rich array of artifacts, some of which were unique. There were thousands of pearls . . . Implements and ornaments of copper, mica, tortoise shell, and silver were found in profusion . . . [including] a huge ceremonial copper axe weighing 28 pounds . . . the richness and abundance of artifacts which were placed with the burials points to the conclusion that the individuals here

represented were of extraordinary importance in the lives of those who built the mound. (Shetrone 1930: 217; 1931:370)

Well-preserved but fragmentary patches of woven fabric and leather specimens were also discovered.

> The builders of the Seip Mound had learned well the art of textile making, for we know that the true textile art began with the spinning or making of the yarn . . . a very fine reticulated weaving was frequently met with . . . The great variety of woven fabrics secured indicate that weaving was assiduously practiced, and formed one of their most important industries. . . .
> Skins made into leather were found in a numbers of graves. The leather was very fine and soft, resembling the chamois skins of the present time. A piece of the leather was soaked in water and thoroughly washed. . . . The piece was found to be flexible and pliable, and retained some of its original strength. (Mills 1907:316-321)

When all three conjoined burial mounds were completed, the entire area was covered with layers of brown and black dirt, yellow clays, gravel and sand. Once the final loaf-shaped mound was finished, its sides were covered in heavy gravel, as much as ten feet thick, to protect the mound from the effects of erosion from rain and flooding.

APPENDIX FOR CHAPTER 12
RED FOX AT BAUM [24]
SPRUCE HILL FURNACES

The subject of smelting furnaces at Spruce Hill is mentioned in the *Afterward* under the topic of "*Copper.*"

The enigmatic archaeological site at Spruce Hill, and other locations in Ohio, has attracted the interest of researchers for decades. However, the discovery of heat vitrified stones and other evidence of pre-contact metal smelting has been questioned and dismissed by mainstream archaeologists.

Spruce Hill is an essentially flat-top hill which rises about 300-400 feet above Paint Creek near Bourneville, Ohio. In 1811, James Foster, a newspaper editor in nearby Chillicothe, Ohio, is credited as the first person to write an article about them. He was lead to the site by local residents who were curious about what they had discovered.

Foster reported seeing about thirty furnaces built into the stone wall which encloses 140 acres of the hilltop. The age of the trees growing in and around the wall suggested to him that the furnaces were at least several hundred years old and perhaps a thousand. He noted that the ashes in these furnaces resembled those found in a blacksmith's forge.

The archaeological team of Squire and Davis mapped Spruce Hill in 1847. Many of the furnaces were located on the west-side wall in the narrow neck of the plateau. They also found casting molds in these locations. They described seeing "strong traces of fire" and intense heat which vitrified the surfaces of the stones lining the furnaces. These celadon glazes are proof that temperatures of 2,300 degrees Fahrenheit (1,200 C) were reached which implies the use of both charcoal fuel and a powerful air flow.

Unfortunately no fully intact furnaces remain at Spruce Hill as a result of both natural forces and souvenir collectors.

For further discussion see, Mallery, Arlington, Harrison, Mary Roberts, 1979. *The Rediscovery of Lost America*, E.P. Dutton, New York, New York; Connor, William D. 2009. Iron Age America Before Columbus. Coachwhip Publications. Landisville, Pennsylvania; Connor, William D. *Neiburger's Evidence: Native Americans Melted, Cast Copper at 1,000 BC Site.* www.iwaynet.net/~wde/copper; Connor, William D. *Ohio Archaeo-Pyrogenic Sites Database.*

---

[24] Mills, William C. 1906. *Baum Prehistoric Village.* Journal of the Ohio Historical Society, *Vol.15*, 1906. pp. 45-136. Available on-line at: http://www.ohiohistory.org/portal/historyjournal-p.html

www.iwaynet.net/~wde/sites; Connor, William D. *Ohio's Prehistoric Furnaces; Spruce Hill Investigations April, 1992.* www.iwaynet.net/~wde/prehist; Connor, William D. *Ohio's Prehistoric Pit Iron Furnaces.* www.iwaynet.net/~wde/piofurn; http://www.perceptivetravel.com/issues/0907/olsen.html; Neiburger, E.J.1991. "Melted Copper from the Archaic Midwest." *North American Archaeologist* *Vol. 12, No. 4.* pp. 351-360.

APPENDIX FOR CHAPTER 13
RED FOX AT MOUND CITY

The scroll that Morning Star and Red Fox were discussing regarding the locations and inter-relationships between the earthworks on the scroll is based on Dr. William F. Romain's 1992 article *"Hopewell Inter-Site Relationships and Astronomical Aligments"* in which he reported on his analysis of the correlation of fourteen Hopewell earthworks and significant lunar events.

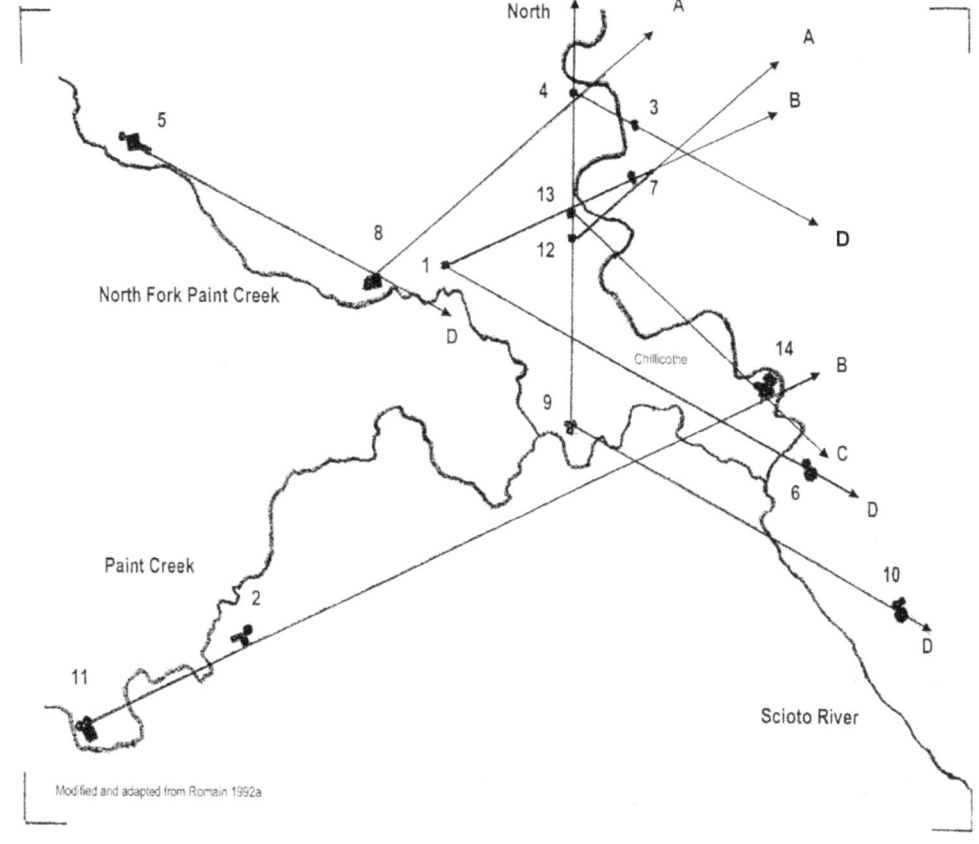

Lunar alignments between 14 earthworks
1. Anderson 2. Baum 3. Cedar Bank 4. Dunlap 5. Frankfort 6. High Bank 7. Hopeton 8. Hopewell 9. Junction Group 10. Liberty 11. Seip 12. Shriver 13. Mound City 14. Works East

A. Moon max north rise 53°.2 B. Moon min north rise 67°.3 C. Moon max south rise 130°.5 D. Moon min south rise 115°.9

Dr. Romain established that these fourteen earthworks separated by miles of hilly terrain aligned with each other on sightlines which intersected with minimum and maximum northern and southern moonrises. For example, the distance between the Seip Earthwork (11) and the Works East (14)

Earthwork is more than sixteen miles with intervening hills and forests.

> Obviously, the Hopewell were remarkably skilled at laying out very long sightlines, to rather precise limits . . . . Clearly, moonrise and/or the general direction of the east held special significance for the Hopewell . . . My thought here is that the Hopewell were well-aware of the above correspondences between local geomorphology site orientation, and observed lunar phenomena. Indeed, the synergistic effect of these correspondences may have been seen as further sanctifying, or making sacred, the innermost heartland of the Hopewell. [25]

In 1846 Squier and Davis performed a partial examination of the so-called Mound city group of earthworks near Chillicothe, Ohio. Their discovery of the rich and varied "finds" reverberated throughout archaeological circles around the world.

By the time archaeologists William C. Mills and H.C. Shetrone conducted their excavations, beginning in 1920, more than half of the original twenty-fours mounds had been destroyed by the Camp Sherman military encampment that had been constructed within the 13 acre enclosure during World War I.[26]

THE GREAT MICA GRAVE

As Mills excavated Mound Number 13 he discovered a large and important basin fashioned into the floor of the mound. The shallow rectangular basin measured 7 feet long and 6 ½ feet wide, its entire surface including its sides were covered by individual sheets of mica between 6 by 6 inches to 16 by 14 inches in size.

The cremated remains of four individuals had been placed on top of the mica lining. A copper headdress and a 12 inch mica mirror were found among the numerous burial artifacts which included over 100 platform pipes, countless pearls and shell beads, perforated animal canine teeth, more than 25 pounds of galena crystals, shark's teeth, bone and copper awls and quartz and obsidian spear points. This burial basin was capped by a layer of sand and more sheets of mica.

This elaborate burial with its extensive and culturally significant burial offerings suggests that the four individuals interred here were highly revered members of the Mound Builder civilization.

---

[25] Romain, William F. 1992a. "Hopewell Inter-Site Relationships and Astronomical Aligments" *Ohio Archaeologist, Vol. 42*, No. 1: 4-5.
[26] Mills, William C. 1922. "Exploration of the Mound City Group," *Journal of the Ohio Historical Society, Vol. 31*:423-584.

MOUND NUMBER 7
GREAT MICA CRESCENT MOON AND BASEMENT

On the floor of Mound Number 7 was a large crescent moon made from mica disks 10 to 12 inches in diameter which overlapped each other like the scales on a fish. It measured 20 feet long and 5 feet wide at its center. As Mills noted ". . . we might conclude that the mound-builders worshipped the moon, and that this mound was dedicated with unknown rites and ceremonies, to that luminary." (Squier and Davis 1848:155).

Beneath this mica crescent moon was an oblong subterranean basement carefully dug out of the gravelly ground. The basement had a harden clay floor and the harden clay extended up the walls securing the loose soil from collapse. The construction of the basement was substantial. Its southwest-northeast length was 40 feet and a width of about 30 feet. The northeast entryway consisted of a ramp with supporting perimeter wooden posts. Additional wooden posts, placed at regular intervals, lined the walls and formed the roof. A well used ceremonial pit 6 feet by 4 feet was located beneath the mica crescent moon which rested on the floor of the mound above.

MOUND CITY ARTIFACTS

> Probably no other American prehistoric earthwork has excited so great a degree of historic interest as the so-called Mound City Group of Ross County, Ohio. Certainly, from the prehistoric viewpoint, it stands unsurpassed. (Mills 1922: 423)

Mills' entire report on his excavations at Mound City is titled: "*Exploration of the Mound City Group*," Journal of the Ohio Historical Society, Vol. 31, 1922. pp. 423-584.

http://www.ohiohistory.org/portal/historyjournal-p.html

The reader is also encouraged to review the art work and other photographic displays regarding the various earthworks mentioned in the Story and others which is provided by the Ohio Historical Society.

http://ohsweb.ohiohistory.org/archaeology/index.cfm

The Mound Builders understood the principle of the hinge and rivet as demonstrated by the unusual and elaborate headdress discovered by Mills.

> The copper head-dress, representing the bear, is a unique specimen, in that the ears are ingeniously hinged to permit movement

> ... with every motion of the wearer ... while the legs are attached to the body by means of rivets. (Mills 1922:452, 544)

A cache of over 5000 exceptionally well formed and finely finished beads were discovered.

> The beads are barrel-shaped, somewhat less than one-half inch in length, and are made from the columella of marine shells. The material used, in many instances, was of extreme hardness, almost enamel-like in character; and in view of the difficulties it would present to primitive methods of workmanship, the unusually large number of beads, and the great care and exactness with which they were fashioned, it is apparent that they represent an exceptionally great amount of labor, skill and patience. (Mills 1922:453)

An ingeniously constructed leather belt embellished with 18 copper effigy turtles sown on to it was also discovered. The hollow copper turtles measured 2 inches in length and 1½ inches wide. Inside each turtle were a number of small beads or quartz pebbles, thus forming a rattle when the wearer of the belt was in motion. (Mills 1922:550)

During their excavation of Mound Number 8, Squier and Davis discovered over two hundred carved stone platform pipes:

> The bowls of most of the pipes are carved in miniature figures of animals. Birds, reptiles ect. All of them are executed with strict fidelity to nature, and with exquisite skill. Not only are the features of the various objects represented faithfully, but their peculiarities and habits are in some degree exhibited . . . . The otter is shown in a characteristic attitude, holding a fish in his mouth; the heron also holds a fish; and the hawk grasps a small bird in its talons, which it tears with its beak. The panther, the bear, the wolf, the beaver, the otter, the squirrel, the raccoon, the hawk, the heron, crow, swallow, buzzard, *paroquet, toucan*. And other indigenous and southern birds – the turtle, the frog, toad rattlesnake, etc. are recognized at first glance. (Squier and Davis 1848:152-153)[27]

---

[27] The pipes found by Squier and Davis are now exhibited in the Blackstone Museum, Salisbury, England.

APPENDIX FOR CHAPTER 13

APPENDIX FOR CHAPTER 15
RED FOX AT HIGH BANK

The Afterword also has a discussion of the High Bank circle octagon earthwork under the topic of *Ideological Culture: Architecture and the Cosmos*. Unfortunately due to centuries of plowing and other factors the High Bank circle/octagon earthwork is barely discernable today.

The reader is also encouraged to see the full text of the journal article "*Hopewellian Geometry and astronomy at High Bank*"[28] by Ray Hively and Robert Horn at this website: http://adsabs.harvard.edu/full/1984JHAS...15...85H

They noted that the circle-avenue axis at High Bank was rotated eastward by about 90° with respect to the corresponding axis at Newark, "Nevertheless, the striking structural similarity between the two sites at least suggests that the motivation for their construction could have been similar. The distance between the two sites is approximately 113 km." [70 miles]. They also determined that the circle component of the circle/octagon earthworks at Newark and High Bank shared essentially identical diameters (Hively and Horn 1984:S86, 91-92).

The walls of the circle were about five feet high and fifty feet wide at the base. The diameter of the circle was approximately 1054 feet. The eight walls that make up the Octagon were about 12 feet high and 50 feet wide at the base. The vertices to vertices distances within the octagon were about 1052 feet. The entire length of the earthwork was about 2147 feet.

The interior surfaces of the Circle and Octagon walls were covered with bright yellow clay and silt mixture and the exterior with a red clay and silt mixture (Greber 2006:89-90).[29] Most of these special soils were brought from distant sources for this earthwork.

They also reported an interesting feature:

> Just inside the wall of the circle, and north of the intersection of the circle and avenue, the trench dug by the excavating team cut across an apparent "pavement" of cobble-like, varying in size from 8 to 15 cm in diameter, the "pavement" appears to be concentric with the circumference of the wall. The "pavement" appears to be concentric with the circumference of the wall, and to be continuous for the 21m distance which was explored at 3m intervals. (Hively and Horn 1984:S88)

---

[28] Hively, Ray, and Horn, Robert 1984. "Hopewellian Geometry and Astronomy at High Banks," *Archaeoastronomy* Vol. 7: S85-S100

[29] See also, http://www.cr.nps.gov/mwac/hopewell/v6n2/three.htm

Hively and Horn noted that High Bank marked both solar and lunar events and commented:

> If these concepts were consciously applied by the builders in the construction of the earthworks, this would have significant implications for American archaeology. (Hively and Horn 1984:S86)
>
> If one assumes that the only two octagons constructed by the Hopewell were randomly oriented, the possibility of their both having a comparable symmetry axis aligned within 0°.3 to the same lunar event is 1 in 700. (Hively and Horn 1984:S95)

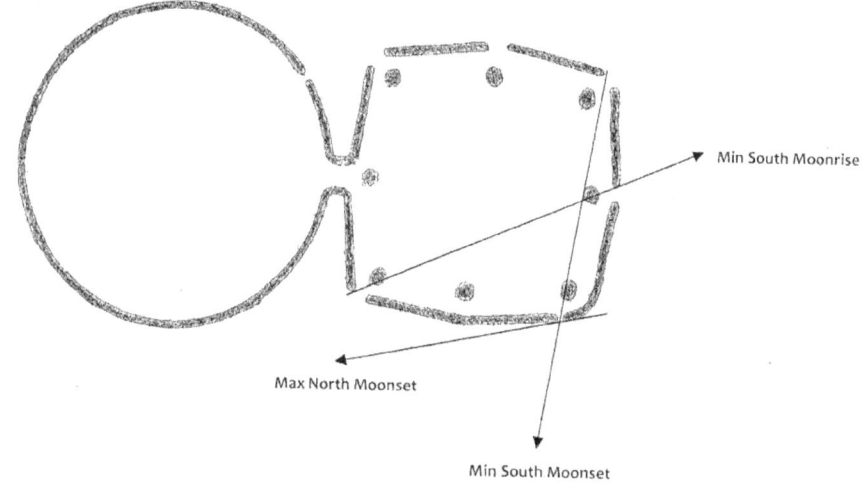

Redrawn and adapted from Hively and Horn 1984 fig. 8.

In Figure 8 one might notice that the lower right corner of the octagon wall (southwest corner) has been modified in that it is rounded and the corner gap has been moved. Hively and Horn also determined that additional modifications were made to the west wall. Their analysis revealed that these modifications from the "ideal symmetrical" octagon shape were made to establish sightlines for the minimum southern extreme moonrise, the minimum southern extreme moonset and the maximum northern extreme moonset.

THE CAMP OF GOD'S TEARS

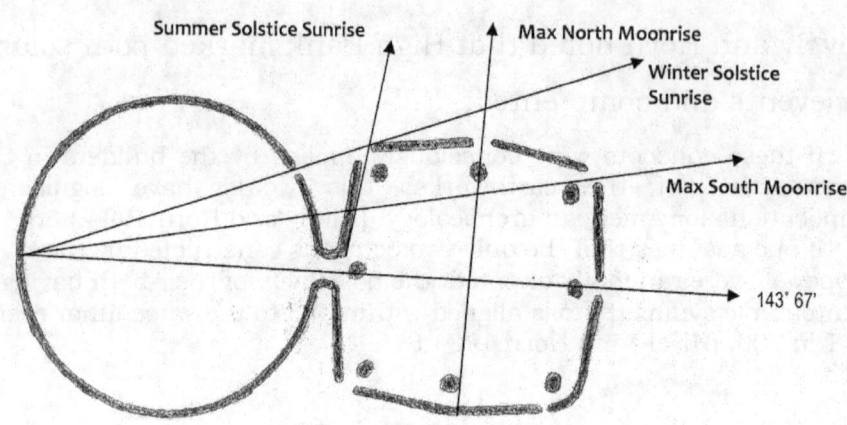

Redrawn and adapted from Hively and Horn 1984 fig. 7.

Figure 7 displays the sightlines for the Summer and Winter Solstice sunrises. High Bank also marks the maximum northern moonrise.

Here is where things get interesting. As the reader might recall the circle-avenue axis at the Newark circle/octagon earthwork marks the maximum north moonrise at 52° and while High Bank does mark the maximum southern moonrise it does not do so by its circle-avenue axis. As noted above the High Bank circle-avenue axis is rotated about 90° eastward from the Newark circle-avenue axis

Therefore, one might assume that High Bank was constructed to recognize the southernmost moonrise in the same manner as Newark marks the northernmost moonrise. In the literature High Bank is often referred to as marking the southernmost moonrise.

However, the High Bank central-avenue axis has a bearing of 143° 67' which does not point to any moonrise point. This seems to be an inconvenient truth which has not been reconciled in the archeoastronomy literature. However, recently Hively and Horn have postulated that the High Bank central axis does not orient to celestial events, merely other earthworks and the Scioto River:

> What is the focus of the long axis of the High Bank design? . . . [S]outh of High Bank, the Scioto abandons its meandering course to hug the west wall of the Teays Valley on a straight bearing of 143°.4 for more than 10 km; the 143°.4 bearing . . . on the High Bank Circle bisects the large circle of the Liberty Works [earthwork] 6.3 km to the south . . . the opposite 323°.4 bearing . . . on the High Bank Circle bisects the large Circle of Works East [earthwork] 3.5 km to the north, and . . . the north lunar maximum rise (53°.4 tangent to the local horizon) occurs at a 90 – degree angle to the major axis of the Circle – Octagon. (Hively and Horn 2010:139-140)

In a sense we are being asked to assume that the Mound Builders constructed the impressive High Bank circle/octagon complex and simply 'aimed' it at nothing celestial despite their obvious mathematical, engineering and astronomical sophistication as builders of massive earthworks.

Hively and Horn discuss this situation:

> When considering possible alignments of the High Bank structure to rise and set points on the horizon, the uncertainty of the date of High Bank makes it necessary to restrict our attention to the Sun, Moon, and planets. The motion of the earth's axis significantly alters the rise and set points of stars over the time span of a few hundred years. The rise and set points of objects near the ecliptic are not affected significantly over this time scale. We have not uncovered any convincing evidence for alignment with the planets. (1984:S94) . . . Radiocarbon dates for these sites would also be extremely useful as it would allow the possibility of testing for stellar alignments as well. (Hively and Horn 1984:S99)[30]

Of course this begs the question of what does the 143° 67' High Bank central-avenue axis align with on the southeastern horizon?[31] Archaeoastronomy applies modern technology to 'dial-back' the heavens to ferret out possible celestial events marked by man-made structures in an effort to "date" the structures devised by earlier civilizations.

Without question qualified archaeoastronomers have 'dialed back' the heavens and have discovered Native American culturally significant star and/or constellation risings that correspond to the High Bank "rifle sight" of 143° 67'. Their findings have not been made public.

As Morning Star explained to Red Fox the central-avenue axis at High Bank was designed by the Ancient Ones to mark the autumnal rise of the constellations of the Pleiades, Orion and the star Sirius about 5000 years ago. The cultural significance of these celestial objects to pre-contact Native Americans is well recognized.[32] Perhaps the true "answer" to this pending question would seriously challenge main-stream archeological dogma.

Nevertheless, the singular research of Hively and Horn does establish that this complex was originally designed with modifications from an ideal or perfect octagon shape to permit the

---

[30] Hively and Horn offer several explanations as to why the central-axis sightline is astronomically superfluous.
[31] High Bank Earthworks lie at lat. 39° 30', long. 82°92'.
[32] *Ancient Astronomers: Prehistoric North American Astronomy* http://paganastronomy.net/nahist.htm

marking of at least twelve Native American culturally important rises and settings of the sun and moon. The modifications were made in such a way as not to interfere with the overall astronomical function of the complex:

> [W]hen one considers the precision and the extravagant expenditure of energy in labour and planning evident in this and other earthworks, we believe it is more reasonable to assume that these deviations may well have been deliberate. (Hively and Horn 1984:S 92)

Figure 9 sets forth the remaining sightlines discovered by Hively and Horn.

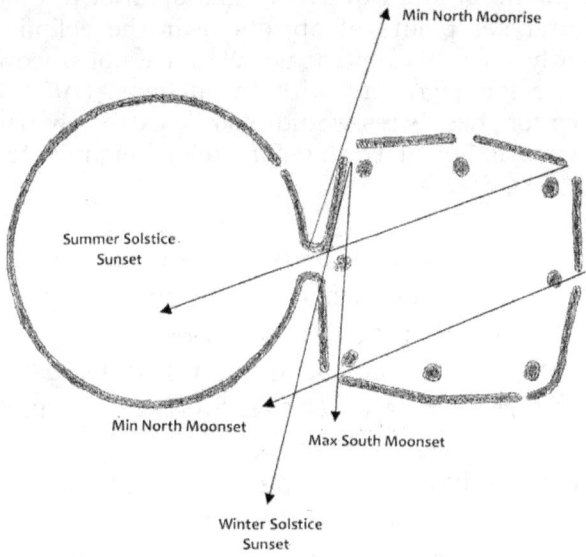

Redrawn and adapted from Hively and Horn 1984 fig. 9.

APPENDIX FOR CHAPTER 17
RED FOX AT NEWARK [33]

When Squier and Davis conducted their extensive and exhaustive survey of the earthworks in Ohio they came upon the Newark Earthwork Complex. These earthworks occupied nearly four square miles in what is now Newark, Ohio:

> The very extensive and complicated series of works here presented occur at the junction of the South and Raccoon forks of the Licking River, one mile west of the town of Newark, Licking County Ohio . . . .
> These works are so complicated, that it is impossible to give anything like a comprehensible description of them. (Squier and Davis 1848:67)
>
> Yet, in spite of their magnificence, many of the earthworks were obliterated by the plow and the unrestrained growth of the city of Newark. All that remains of the wondrously labyrinthine geometry are the Great Circle, the Octagon attached to its somewhat less great circle, a small fragment of the principle square, and a few additional shreds and patches of earthwork in front yards and scattered wood lots. (Lepper 2004:76)

Squier and Davis's observation of complexity of the Newark complex proved to be very accurate. It was not until 1982, nearly a century and a half later, that the complexity of these earthworks began to reveal themselves.[34]

> The Newark Earthworks are a remarkable testament to the architectural and mathematical genius of the Hopewell culture, but astronomers recently have come to realize that the Hopewell builders also aligned these earthworks to the cyclical dance of the earth and moon. (Lepper 2004:77)
>
> The highest levels of ability in the use of geometry are indicated at the Newark Earthworks and those at and near High Bank in the Scioto River Valley in Ohio. (Marshall 1987:40)
>
> The Newark Earthworks in central Ohio comprise the largest complex of monumental geometric earthen enclosures ever built by the Hopewell culture. The site originally encompassed more than four square miles and included two gigantic circles, an even bigger ellipse, a square, and an octagon — all connected by a network of parallel walls. (Lepper 2004:73)
>
> The Newark Earthworks are extraordinary. This complex of geometric earthen structures is the largest in the Hopewell world. The

---

[33] Please see the section titled Ideological Culture in the *Afterword* for more information about the Newark Complex.
[34] See, "*Geometry and Astronomy in Prehistoric Ohio*" Hively and Horn 1982.

Scioto River and Paint Creek valleys around Chillicothe hold a greater number of earthworks of more diverse form, but these are dispersed widely up and down valleys. In addition to being the largest complex of geometric enclosures, the Newark Works also are the northernmost of the great Hopewellian ceremonial centers. (Lepper 1996:226)

Our data and analysis show that the Newark Earthworks were carefully conceived and constructed to exhibit a remarkable degree of symmetry, precision and geometrical harmony, apparently based on a single length [of measurement].[35] Further, we have shown that the structure of the Newark Earthworks could be used for a relatively precise monitoring of the monthly and 18.6-year lunar cycles . . . . The intellectual power, tenacity of purpose, continuity, and desire for precision that would be implied by conscious lunar alignment is certainly no greater than that required in the construction of the earthworks themselves, a feat which is not in dispute. The geometrical regularity of the works shows clearly that the Hopewell had a strong concern for geometrical harmony, and it is not surprising that they might record celestial harmonies (perhaps essential to their calendar) in the same structure. (Hively and Horn 1982:S18-19)

However, as Hively and Horn discovered, the Newark Octagon held additional evidence of careful and purposeful astronomically based design:

Hively and Horn . . . explored the possible astronomical rising and setting turning points that might be embedded in the Octagon as horizon alignments and noted that the Octagon effectively incorporates all eight of the turning points of the 18.6 year lunar cycle. In fact, without "mispositioning". . . two out of the eight alignments would not have been marked. To confirm that deviance from 'ideal' geometry was deliberately motivated by lunar alignments concerns, they point out that but for several other deviations in the lengths of the embankments and the placement of some of the "gate mounds", several other alignments marking important lunar turning points would have been absent. In short, they conclude that these deviations from the ideal were deliberate and that this patterned irregularity was most reasonably accounted for as the builder's ensuring that all eight turning points of the lunar cycle were embodied in the Octagon primarily through alignments embedded in the placement of key features. They go on to examine other possible anomalies, focusing in the case on the High Bank Octagon, and again demonstrate certain anomalies and asymmetries that could be explained in the same terms. They conclude that the Octagon was constructed as part of a strategy to ensure that its formal properties would be aligned with the eight minimal and maximal rising and setting turning points of the moon defining its 18.6 year cycle. (Byers 2004:93) [36]

---

[35] The **OCD** – This unit of length represents the diameter of the Circle in the Circle/Octagon earthwork at Newark. One OCD equals 1,054 feet. Hively and Horn also determined that the linear dimensions of the Newark Octagon were also based on the OCD.

[36] Byers and Malhi also postulate that the Newark Circle and Octagon Complex was constructed after the High Bank Complex. (Byers 2004: 97; Magli 2007)

More significant are the intentional deviations from the geometric ideal, in order to bring various features into alignment with celestial events. Certain of the Octagon's walls, for example, appear to have been deviated from their geometric ideal in order to bring them into closer alignment to significant lunar events. (Romain 2005c:9)

THE GREAT CIRCLE

In describing the Great Circle Squier and Davis determined that it was more of an ellipse than a true circle:

> This work is not, as has been generally represented, a true circle; its form is that of an ellipse, its diameters being twelve hundred and fifty feet, and eleven hundred and fifty feet respectively. (Squier and Davis 1847:68)

As the Mound Builders were adroit at building perfect circular earthworks, perhaps the elliptical shape bore a symbolic and ceremonial significance.

With the coming of the dominate culture, the survival of this gigantic circular enclosure was in jeopardy as it rested on newly defined private farmland. However, as time went on some community members and community organizations recognized the need to preserve it by purchasing it and making it a municipal fairground in 1853. After 1853 it was used as a county fairground, horseracing track, and the site for one of Buffalo Bill's Wild West Shows. Subsequently it was used for motorcycle and automobile racing, an amusement park and a military training camp. Ultimately, in 1933 it was acquired by the Ohio Historical Society (OHS Site Plan 2003:A52-53).

> The walls enclose an area of about thirty acres. The circular wall varies in height from five to 14 feet with a ditch at the base of the wall inside the enclosure. The ditch varies in depth from eight to thirteen feet and is deepest at the entrance to the circle. The walls are at their highest here as well making this a dramatic gateway to the Great Circle. According to Atwater, who observed the site in the early 1800's, the ditch held water . . . perhaps the circle of water had a ritual or symbolic significance . . . . The finished enclosure [was] dark brown on the outside but yellow brown on the inside reflecting the different soils used in the construction of the embankment . . . .
>
> At the center of the Great Circle is a large mound – or set of conjoined mounds. Although it has been called "Eagle Mound" and many people seem to think it represents a bird in flight, it does not actually bear much resemblance to a bird or any other animal for that matter. Its three lobes have been compared to a bird's footprint, a bear paw print, or an arrow pointing toward the gateway. Whatever the Hopewell may have intended it to represent, the mound covers the site

of a similarly-shaped wooden frame structure . . . . This wooden structure must have been a special place. It was the focus of ritual activities performed at the Great Circle until the Hopewell occupants decided that it had served its function. They then dismantled it and erected a mound over its remains. (OHS Site Plan 2003:A.44).

A sightline drawn from the central mound through the middle of the entrance aligns to the vernal rise of the Pleiades star cluster which is followed by Orion and then Sirius. A similar sightline aligns with the minimum north moonrise (Romain 2006:3A-5; Romain 2000:144-146).

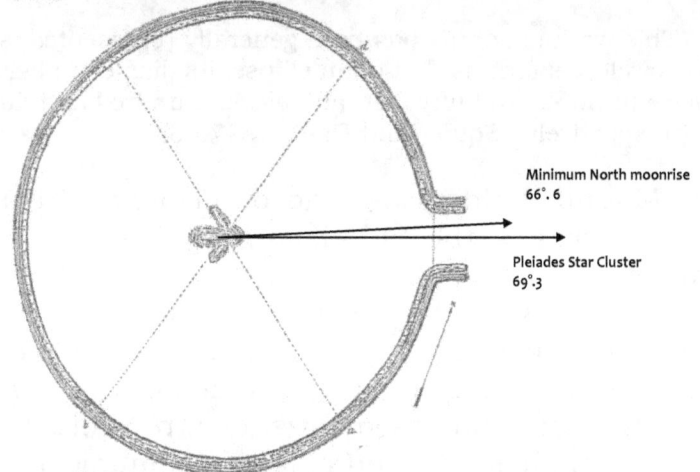

Adapted from Thomas 1889; Romain 2000, 2006

THE GREAT HOPEWELL ROAD [37]

The oral traditions of eastern Ohio Native Americans tell of long, straight roads through the wilderness strewn with white sand so that they could easily travel from one great ocean to the other safe from attack. The "White Path" also represented the Milky Way (Lepper 2006:126-131; Lepper 1998: 30-133).

An ample supply of white sand was available to those that built this magnificent Road:

> The Glenford hilltop enclosure, within a few miles of the Newark Earthworks, is situated on a hill bearing outcrops of rare white sandstone that today is sought out commercially for its abnormally high silica content. (Carr 2006b:589)

The Road was well constructed:

---

[37] Dr. Bradley T. Lepper is credited with naming the Road. In the Story we chose to call it the White Road of Sister Moon.

The walls form the boundaries of a meticulously graded road, crowned in the middle and constructed of clay differing from the neighboring sod. (Knapp 1998a:1)

By the time the first map makers began to record the Newark Earthworks many features had been destroyed but some features of this Road remained.

[L]ooking to 19th Century maps of the Newark earthworks, especially the one drawn by James and Charles Salisbury in 1862, it can be noted that an ancient road, composed of two parallel earthen walls, runs to the southwest. The Salisbury brothers traced this road for some kilometers, and proposed that it likely went all the way down to Chillicothe. During the course of the years, various attempts have been made to trace this road; finally, archaeologist Brad Lepper succeeded in recovering (either on the ground, or in aerial photographs) various parts of it. In particular, a well documented segment is located 26 km south of Newark, and another one runs near the terminus at Chillicothe. Lepper was thus led to the conclusion that a straight road, composed of two parallel earthen walls as least one meter high and separated by 60 meters oriented 31° 25' west of south if seen from Newark, once connected the two sites, a conclusion further strengthened by a recent LIDAR analysis.[38] The road is very likely to be interpreted as a ceremonial pathway – perhaps a pilgrimage route – which Lepper calls the Great Hopewell Road . . . . Indeed, inspecting the direction of the road (and thus the azimuth 31°25' from High Bank to Newark, and 211° 25' from Newark to High Bank) it turns out that the road aligns with impressive precision to the direction *orthogonal* to the direction of the setting sun at the summer solstice (or to the opposite one, to the rising sun a winter solstice). (Magli 2007)

Perhaps this Great Hopewell Road was a pilgrim's path like similarly long and straight roads built by the Mayan culture in Mesoamerica or the Anasazi of Chaco Canyon. Hopewell people may have followed this road, and perhaps others like it, to the great earthwork centers bringing offerings of copper or mica as gifts to the supernatural powers invoked by the monumental geometry of these sacred places . . . . (Lepper 2004:79)

Finally, the Great Hopewell Road was the unifying "white road" of 'rectitude and virtue' upon which pilgrims might travel to and from these centers "safe from attack." . . . Historic Algonquian [and Delaware] traditions of long, straight "white roads" equated with the Milky Way and with belts of sacred wampum may reflect cultural reconfigurations of actual, but abandoned, sacred roads functionally equivalent to Mayan long, straight "white roads" also equated with the Milky Way . . . the "Beautiful White Path." (Lepper 2006:126-131)

---

[38] LiDAR – Laser Detection and Ranging. See, Romain, William F., Burks, Jarrod, 2008a. "LiDAR Imaging of the Great Hopewell Road." Current Research in Ohio Archaeology 2008.

Dr. Romain has made several other startling discoveries:

> Of considerable interest is that the Great Hopewell Road is not only perpendicular to the summer solstice sunset, it is also parallel to the Milky Way. As indicated, the Great Hopewell Road extends along an azimuth of 30°–210°. During Hopewell times, as twilight turned to darkness on the date of the summer solstice, the Milky Way would have become visible – as a band of stars, roughly 10° wide, extending from the northeast horizon at an azimuth of 30° at the constellation Cassiopeia, upward and across the sky through Cepheus, Cygnus, and Aquila, down through Scorpius, Lupus, and Centaurus on the southwestern horizon, to an azimuth of about 210°. On the date of the summer solstice therefore, the Great Hopewell Road would mirror on the earth the direction of the celestial Milky Way. Moreover, as they crossed, the Milky Way and the summer solstice sunset azimuth would have effectively divided the Hopewell cosmos into quarters. These celestial azimuths would have crossed each other within 500 feet of Geller Hill. (Romain 2005c:11)

GELLER HILL

Further, Dr. Romain's research uncovered additional aspects of the complexity of the Newark earthwork complex:

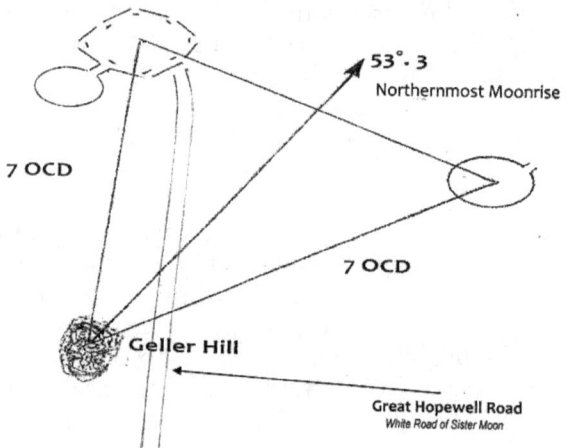

Redrawn and adapted from Romain 2005c

Several lines of evidence suggest that Geller Hill was included in the design and layout of the Newark Earthworks . . . . The statistical likelihood that the centers of two geometrically shaped Hopewell earthworks would be situated about the same distance from Geller Hill strictly due to chance is slim. The likelihood that both distances would also be near multiples of the OCD strongly suggests that the linear relationship between Geller Hill and the two geometric earthworks was intentional . . . . Like the Newark Octagon, the symmetry axis of Geller Hill triangle is closely aligned to the moon's maximum north rise point. From Geller Hill, the moon would have been observed to rise at a point on the horizon about equal-distant between the Octagon and

Great Circle and balanced between the two . . . . Geller Hill would have been the highest feature on the flat Newark plain where the geometric earthworks were built . . . . In summary, geometric relationships, measurement data, and archaeological evidence all strengthen the hypothesis that Geller Hill was included in the design, layout and possibly, ritual functioning of the Newark earthwork complex. (Romain 2005a:1, 3)

One of the most immediately obvious features of the Newark Earthworks, apparent in almost any map of the site is the close association of the enclosures with water. The entire complex of earthworks appears to have been built around a large pond, and streams formed the northern, eastern, and southern boundaries of the site: Raccoon Creek to the north, the South Fork of the Licking River to the east, and Ramp Creek to the south. (Lepper 2004:76; See also, Romain 2005a:6)

In this view, consistent with Native American understanding of the cosmos, the Newark Complex was balanced between cosmic realms. As such, the Newark Complex was a cosmic center, and it was in this center that the mound builders performed the most sacred of their rituals – i.e., rituals, intended to maintain cosmic balance, ensure plant and animal abundance, maintain health, and facilitate in death, the transition of the soul from the land of the living to the land of the dead. In this view, the Newark complex was a functional microcosm of the Hopewell universe. (Romain 2005a:6-7)

The location of each earthwork is geometrically and astronomically related and depends upon the other earthwork components. Each earthwork is an integral part of a larger design . . . . The Newark earthworks complex is the largest and most complicated geometric complex of its kind in the world. (Romain 2005b:1, 6)

APPENDIX TO CHAPTER 18
ON THE WAY HOME

CINCINNATI CALENDRIC TABLET

In 1991, Dr. William F. Romain published his analysis of the Cincinnati Tablet entitled *"Calendric Information Evident in the Adena Tablets."*[39]

This tablet was discovered in 1841 within a burial mound located in downtown Cincinnati, Ohio:

> Specifically, the thesis presented here is that three related units of time are referenced in the Cincinnati Tablet. First, it is proposed that the sun's summer and winter solstice risings and setting positions are represented in the tablet. Next, successive repetitions of the four monthly phases of the moon are depicted in such a way as to add up to one year. Finally, a series of 13 lunations which is equal to one year is represented in the tablet. (Romain 1991a:41)

In Ohio on the date of the summer solstice, the sun will rise at 59° 59' east of north and set at 300° 41'. On the date of the winter solstice the sun will rise at 121° 94' and set at 238° 05'. These angular relationships are marked by the four corner edges of the tablet (Romain 1991a:42).

The specific proportions of this tablet are important. It is five inches in length, three inches wide at each end and it narrows to 2 and 6 tenths inches at the middle. This particular size and shape is necessary to correctly establish the Solstice events. Additionally, the middle of the top of the tablet must be oriented towards the pole star:

> Importantly, the only way these azimuths angular relationships could possibly be expressed in tablet form is if the tablet were to have precisely the proportions found in the Cincinnati Tablet. . . . [H]ad the proportions of the Cincinnati Tablet been any different, the solstice's angular relationships would not be reflected. (Romain1991a:41-42)

Both the right and left edges of the Tablet display small engraved lines. Starting at the upper right corner of the Tablet which corresponds to the summer solstice sunrise:

> . . . if one counts the spaces between the engraved lines as a lunar phase, starting with the new moon closest to the summer solstice, it so happens that the number of spaces as counted

---

[39] *Ohio Archaeologist* Volume 41, No. 1, 1991:41-48.

APPENDIX FOR CHAPTER 18

around both sides of the tablet correspond to the total number of lunar phases in a solar year comprised of 12 months.

Further, . . . the number of complete lunar cycles separating the summer solstice sunrise from the winter solstice sunrise is equal to six months. Similarly, on the left side of the tablet, the number of complete lunar cycles separating the winter solstice sunset from the summer solstice sunset is again, equal to six months. Hence, the spaces between the small engraved lines which are equal to lunar phases are read in a clockwise (or sunwise) direction. (Romain 1991a:42)

Also read in a clockwise direction are the larger spaces – 13 in number which are formed by the diagonal lines adjacent to the smaller engraved lines:

. . . [T]here are six spaces between these large lines on the right side of the tablet, and seven such spaces on the left side of the tablet – for a total of 13 spaces.

As the reader will recall, the solar year of 365 ¼ days is not exactly equivalent to an even multiple of months, or lunar cycles. Thus we have 12 months in a year – but we have 13 new moons in a year. What I propose here is that the 13 large spaces on the Cincinnati Tablet reflect an effort to coordinate, or reconcile the moon's phases with the solar year. In other words, each of the 13 new moons or lunations, that make up one solar year. (Romain 1991a:42)

Romain also determined that the Tablet not only reckoned time by lunar phases, but that it also divided a year into two halves:

This conclusion seems indicated by the bipartite notational system evident in the Cincinnati Tablet – i.e., the right side of the tablet counts the six months from summer solstice to winter solstice; while the left side of the tablet counts the six months from winter solstice to summer solstice. (Romain 1991a: 42)

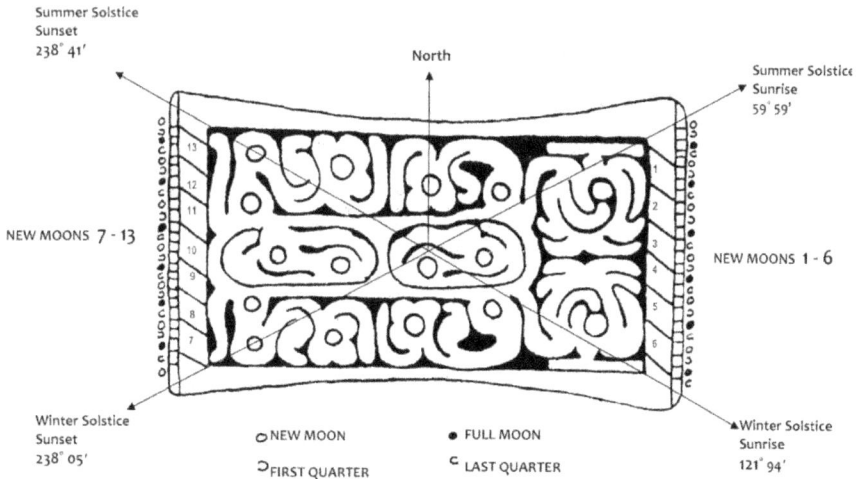

Redrawn and adapted from Romain 1991a Fig. 3; Squier and Davis 1848

Thirteen engraved stone tablets from this civilization have been discovered. As many as ten may demonstrate solstice and/or lunar information:

> That other tablets also incorporate astronomical data argues against any suggestion that the Cincinnati Tablet's proportions are simply due to chance. (Romain 1991a:42)

Romain concludes:

> In any event, the Cincinnati Tablet is certainly one of the oldest calendar devises yet discovered north of Mexico. . . .
> In fact, the emerging picture of the Ohio Mound Builders, is that they had a calendar system based on the movements of the sun and moon; a standard or basic unit of measurement . . . and . . . they aligned their sacred sites to significant celestial events. (Romain 1991a:44)

PORTSMOUTH EARTHWORK DIAGRAMS

In addition to the Squier and Davis diagrams, two other diagrams of the Portsmouth Earthworks have surfaced.

R. Gilbraith Map

The R. Gilbraith map is curated at the Cincinnati Museum Center, Cincinnati, Ohio. The date of the map is unknown. The original is 20 x 26 inches. Some notations are faded and difficult to read. Water colors may have also been used in the drawing. It is believed that R. Galbraith was a minister in the Portsmouth, Ohio area. The original map was discovered on a wall of an office within the Belfonte Furnace Building of the Ashland Iron and Mining Company, Belfonte, Kentucky.[40]

---

[40] Edwards, J.H. 1956. "Ancient Fortifications." *Ohio Archaeologist, Vol. 6, No. 3.* pp. 102-104.

APPENDIX FOR CHAPTER 18

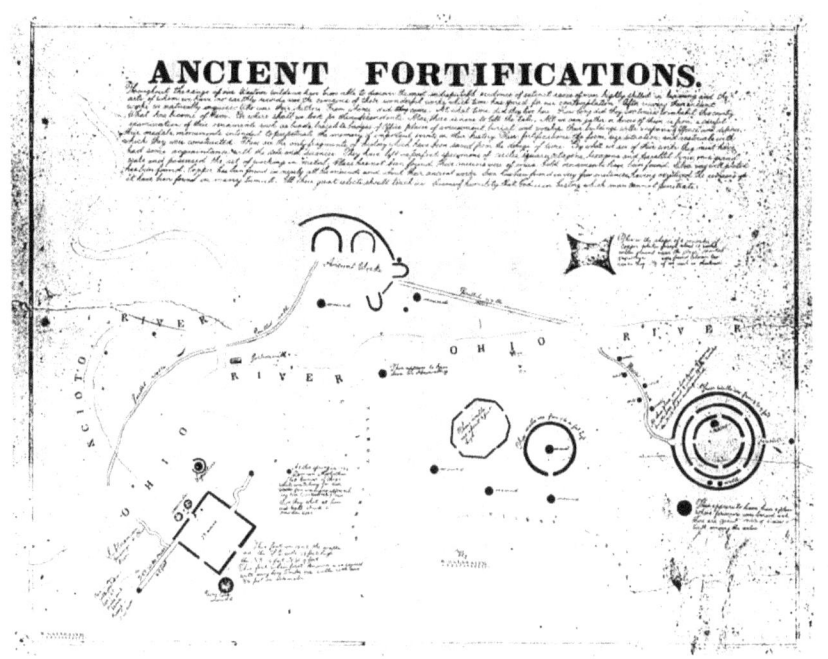

Courtesy of the Cincinnati Museum Center

G.S.B. Hempstead Map

This map appears in an 1878 article entitled "*The Earthworks at Portsmouth, Ohio, U.S.*" published in The Journal of the Anthropological Institute of Great Britain and Ireland.[41]

---

[41] *Vol. VII.* pp. 132-137.

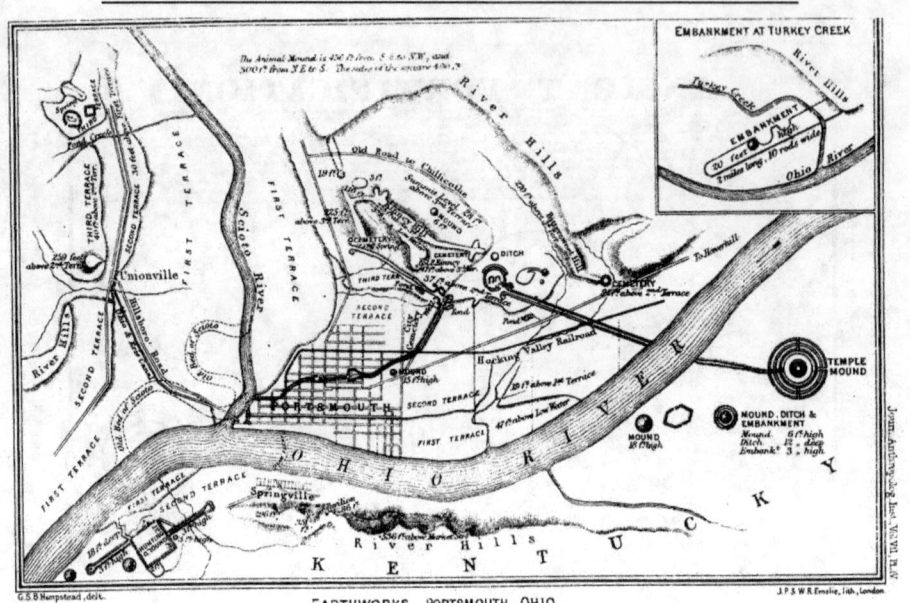

APPENDIX TO CHAPTER 25
THE DIALOGUE

The following quotes are from *Gathering Hopewell, Society, Ritual, and Ritual Interaction* 2006 edited by Christopher Carr and D. Troy Case with citations omitted:

> In the modern Western world, the self is defined as an individual separable from society, material in nature, and vitalized by ego. The problem with assuming this one view of the self uniformly in sociological theory and analysis is made evident by looking cross-culturally. Modern Western individualism lies at the extreme of a cross-cultural spectrum in which notions of the self, or "person," range from the largely individual to the largely social . . . . Creek Native Americans have a continuous concept of the self: a human being is connected through his or her heart to a pervasive energy continuum (*boea fikcha/puyvfekcv*) of which all beings and things are a part and, together, comprise the sacred All (*Ibofanga*). (Carr and Case 2006:38)

> The Creek entities - 'all my relations' - male, female, human and non-human, known and unknown, are all part of a continuum of energy [*boea fikcha/puyvfekcv*] that is at the heart of the universe. *Ibofanga* is above us all and is the unifying principle in the entire energy field which is existence. The field includes links between various entities . . . . Very traditional Creeks will talk about *figi/feke*, the heart, which provided the terminal for exchange of *boea fikcha/puyvfekcv* energy in the field of energy that belongs to *thakko boea fikcha*, the grand energy or spirit, which is ultimately *Ibofanga*, which is the sacred name and not even mentioned. It is all-pervasive and invincible. (Carr and Case 2006:49)

BIBLIOGRAPHY

"Appendix I: A brief History of the Newark Earthworks." In *Historic Site Management Plan for Newark Earthworks State Memorial, June 27, 2003*. Ohio Historical Society, 1982 Velma Avenue, Columbus, OH.

"American Indian Symbolism,"
http://www.sacred-exts.com/eso/sta/sta48.htm

A Short History of Copper Mining 2001.
http://www.exploringthenorth.com/cophistory/cophist.html

A View From The Core: A Synthesis of Ohio Hopewell Archaeology. 1996. Edited by Paul J. Pacheco. The Ohio Archaeological Council, Columbus, OH.

Aerotecture International Inc. Chicago, Illinois. www.aerotecture.com

Alford, Dan Moonhawk 1993. Dialog Between Western and Indigenous Scientists. A Presentation for the 1993 Annual Spring Meeting of the Society for the Anthropology of Consciousness.
www.enformy.com/dma-b.htm

Alvarez G, Munoz I, Pestoni C, Laurea M, Rodriguez-Calvo A, and Carracedo A. 1996. "Effect of Environmental Factors on PCR-DNA Analysis from Dental Pulp." *Int. J of Legal Medicine Vol. 109*. pp.125-129.

America in 1492. 1993. Edited by M. Josephy, Jr. Vintage Books, New York, NY.

Ancient Astronomers: Prehistoric North American Astronomy
http://paganastronomy.net/nahist.htm

Ancient Earthen Enclosures of the Eastern Woodlands. 1998. Edited by Robert C. Mainfort and Lynne Sullivan. University Press of Florida. Gainesville, FL.

Ancient Egypt: Mining.
www.nefertiti.iwebland.com/timelines/topics/mining

Ancient Hopi Indian Predictions.
http://www.dreamscape.com/morgana/pan.htm

"Ancient Inscribed Stones Found in Tennessee," Stone Artifact Archaeology of North America.
http://www.stoneartifact.com/tennessee/inscribedstones.html

BIBLIOGRAPHY

Ancient Objects and Sacred Realms. 2007. Edited by F. Kent Reilly III and James F. Garber. University of Texas Press, Austin, TX.

Archie Fire Lame Deer, Erdoes, Richard 1992. *Gift of Power: The Life and Teachings of a Lakota Medicine Man.* Bear & Company Publishing, Santa Fe, NM.

Atlantis: The Ante-Diluvian World 1821. Edited by Edgerton Sykes, 1950. Sidgwick and Jackson, Ltd. London, England.

Atwater, Caleb 1820. "Descriptions of the Antiquities Discovered in the State of Ohio and other Western States." *Transactions and Collections of the American Antiquarian Society, Vol. 1.* pp. 109-251.

Aveni, Anthony F. 2003. "Archaeoastronomy in the Ancient Americas," Journal *of Archaeological Research, Vol. 11, No. 2.* pp.149-191.

Aveni, Anthony F. 1972. "Astronomical Tables Intended for Use in Astro-Archaeological Studies," *American Antiquity, Vol. 37, No. 4.* p.531.

Baby, Raymond S. 1971. "Prehistoric Architecture: A Study of House Types in the Ohio Valley." *The Ohio Journal of Science, Vol. 71, No. 4.* pp.193-198.

Baker, Stanley 2007. "LiDar or Light Detection and Ranging Systems: A New Mapping and Survey Tool Useful in Archaeological Field Research." *Ohio Archaeologist, Vol. 57, No. 4.* pp. 18-19.

Baldia, Christel M., Kathryn A. Jakes, Maximilian O. Baldia 2008. "Coloration and Fabric Structure of Selected Polychrome Textiles from the Seip Mound Group." *Midcontinental Journal of Archaeology Vol.33, No. 2.* pp. 197-222.

Baldia, Christel M., Kathryn A. Jakes 2007. "Photographic Methods to Detect Colourants in Archaeological Textiles." *Journal of Archaeological Science Vol. 34*. pp. 519-525.

Banyacya, Thomas. http://www.crystalinks.com/hopi4.html

Bernardini, Wesley 2004. "Hopewell Geometric Earthworks: a Case Study in the Referential and Experimental Meaning of Monuments." *Journal of Anthropological Archaeology Vol. 23.* pp. 331-356.

Binns, Corey, "CSI Technology Unlocks Secrets of Ancient Fabric." www.livescience.com/history/070223_foresic_textiles

BioPowerSystems Pty. Ltd., Eveleigh, Australia. www.biopowersystems.com

Birch bark scrolls, http://en.wikipedia.org/wiki/Birch_bark_scrolls

Blanchard, Mark L. "Simulating North American Impact Craters with ArcView & Excel." http://proceedings.esri.com/library/userconf/educ05/papers/pap2012.pdf See also, gis2.esri.com/library/userconf/educ05/papers/pap2012.pdf

Bodley, John H. 2009. *"Culture."* http://ca.encarta.msn.com/text_761561730___61/culture.html

Bohm, David 1980. *Wholeness and the Implicate Order.* Routledge & Kegan Paul. London, England.

Bolnick, Deborah A., David Glenn Smith 2003. "Unexpected Patterns of Mitochondrial DNA Variation Among Native Americans From the Southeastern United States." *American Journal of Physical Anthropology, Vol. 122.* pp. 336-354.

Bolnick, Deborah A., Smith, David Glenn 2007. "Migration and Social Structure Among the Hopewell: Evidence from Ancient Data." *American Antiquity, Vol. 72, No. 4.* pp. 627-644.

Boszhardt, Robert F., Gundersen, James 2003. "X-ray Powder Diffraction Analysis of Early and Middle Woodland Red Pipes from Wisconsin." *Midcontinental Journal of Archaeology*, Spring.

Braden, Gregg 1997. *Awakening to Zero Point.* Radio Books Store Press, Bellevue, WA.

Briggs, Fran. Conversation Notes October 2006.

Brown, James A. 1997. "The Archaeology of Ancient Religion in the Eastern Woodlands." *Annual Review of Anthropology, Vol. 26.* pp. 465-485.

Brown, Joseph Epes 1989. *The Ceremonial pipe, Black Elk's of the Seven Rites of the Oglala Sioux.* University of Oklahoma Press, Norman OK.

Brown, Michael D., *et.al.* 1998. "mtDNA HaplogroupX: An Ancient Link between Europe/Western Asia and North America?" *American Journal of Human Genetics. Vol. 63.* pp.1852-1862

Buikstra, Jane 1979. "Contributions of Physical Anthropologist to the Concept of Hopewell: A Historical Perspective." *Hopewell Archaeology: The Chillicothe Conference.* Edited by David S. Brose and N'omi B. Greber. pp. 220-233. Kent State University Press, Kent, OH.

Bull, C., C. E. Corbato, and J. C. Zahn 1967. "Gravity Survey of the Serpent Mound Area, Southern Ohio," *The Ohio Journal of Science Vol. 67, No. 6*, November. p. 359.

Byers, A. Martin 2004. *The Ohio Hopewell Episode.* University of Akron Press, Akron, OH.

Byers, A. Martin 2006. "The Earthwork/Habitation Dichotomy: A Central Problem of Ohio Hopewell." In *Recreating Hopewell.* 2006. Edited by Douglas K. Charles and Jane E. Buikstra. University Press of Florida.

Cajete, Gregory 2000. *Native Science Natural Laws of Interdependence.* Foreword by Leroy Little Bear, J.D. Clear Light Publishers, Santa Fe, NM.

Caldwell, Duncan 1997. "Two Undescribed Adena Tablets and Some Speculations as to their Significance." *Ohio Archaeologist, Vol. 47, No. 3.* pp. 4-10.

Capps, Benjamin 1979. *The Old West: The Indians.* Time-Life Books, Alexandria, VA.

Carlson, John B. 1979. "Hopewell Prehistoric America's Golden Age," reprinted from *Early Man*, Winter. Northwestern Archeological Program. Craftsman Printing Inc. Chillicothe, OH.

Carlton, Richard W., Christian Koeberl, Mark T Baranoski, Gregory A Schumacher 1998. "Discovery of Microscopic Evidence for Shock Metaporphism at the Serpent Mount Structure, South-Central Ohio: Confirmation of an Origin by Impact." *Earth and Planetary Science Letters, 162.* pp. 177-185.

Carr, Christopher 2006a. "Salient Issues in the Social and Political Organizations of Northern Hopewellian Peoples: Conceptualizing, Personalizing, and Generating Hopewell." In *Gathering Hopewell Society, Ritual, and Ritual Interaction.* Edited by Christopher Carr, and D. Troy Case. pp. 73-118. Springer, NY.

Carr, Christopher 2006b. "Rethinking Interregional Hopewellian "Interaction." In *Gathering Hopewell Society, Ritual, and Ritual*

Interaction. Edited by Christopher Carr, and D. Troy Case. pp. 575-623. Springer, NY.

Carr, Christopher and Komorowski, Jean-Christophe 1995. "Identifying the Mineralogy of Rock Temper in Ceramics Using X-Radiography." *American Antiquity, Vol. 60, No.4.* pp. 723-749.

Carr, Christopher 1990. "Advances in Ceramic Radiography and Analysis: Applications and Potentials." *Journal of Archaeological Science, Vol. 17.* pp. 13-34.

Carr, Christopher, Sears, Derek, W.G. 1985. "Toward an Analysis of the Exchange of Meteoritic Iron in the Middle Woodland." *Southeastern Archaeology, Vol. 4, No. 2,* Winter. pp.79-92.

Chaney, Earlyne 1987. *Initiation in the Great Pyramid.* Astara, Upland, CA

Chief Dan Evehema's Message to Humankind.
http://dreamscape.com/morgana/telesto.htm

Church, Flora 1983. "An Analysis of Textile Fragments from Three Ohio Hopewell Sites." *Ohio Archaeologist. Vol. 33, No. 1.*

Church, Flora 1984. "Textiles as Markers of Ohio Hopewell Social Identities." *Midcontinental Journal of Archaeology, Vol. 9, No. 1.* pp. 1-25.

Clay, Berle R. 1987. "Circle and Ovals Two Types of Adena Space." *Southeastern Archaeology, Vol. 6, No. 1, Summer.* pp. 46-56.

Cochran, Donald R. and McCord, Beth K. 2001. *"The Archaeology of Anderson Mounds, Mounds State Park, Anderson, Indiana."* Reports of Investigations 61, June. Archaeological Resources Management Service, Ball State University, Muncie, IN.

Collins, Karen. Conversation August 2007.

Commanda, William, and Frank Decontie. "Sacred Instructions".
http://www.geocities.com/witchology/sacredinstr.html

Connor, William D. 2009. *Iron Age America Before Columbus.* Coachwhip Publications. Landisville, PA.

Connor, William D. 1997-2007. *America's Mysterious Furnaces.*
www.iwaynet.net/~wde/

Connor, William D. *Neiburger's Evidence: Native Americans Melted, Cast Copper at 1,000 BC Site.* www.iwaynet.net/~wde/copper

Connor, William D. *Ohio Archaeo-Pyrogenic Sites Database.* www.iwaynet.net/~wde/sites

Connor, William D. *Ohio's Prehistoric Furnaces; Spruce Hill Investigations April, 1992.* www.iwaynet.net/~wde/prehist

Connor, William D. *Ohio's Prehistoric Pit Iron Furnaces.* www.iwaynet.net/~wde/piofurn

Converse, Robert N. 2003. *The Archaeology of Ohio.* Archaeological Society of Ohio, Columbus, OH.

Coppens, Philip, "*Copper: a world trade in 3000 BC?*" www.philipcoppens.com/copper.html

Corliss, William R. 1999. *Ancient Infrastructure: Remarkable Roads, Mines, Walls, Mounds, Stone Circles.* The Sourcebook Project. Glen Arm, MD.

Cowan, Frank, L. 2006. "A Mobile Hopewell? Questioning Assumptions of Ohio Sedentism." In *Recreating Hopewell.* Edited by Douglas K. Charles and Jane E. Buikstra. University Press of Florida. Gainesville, FL.

Cowan, Wesley C. 1996. "Social Implications of Ohio Hopewell Art." In *A View From The Core: A Synthesis of Ohio Hopewell Archaeology.* Edited by Paul J. Pacheco. pp.130-148. The Ohio Archaeological Council, Columbus, OH.

Dancy, William S. 1991. "A Middle Woodland Settlement in Central Ohio: A preliminary Report on the Murphy Site (33LI212)." *Pennsylvania Archaeologist, Vol. 61, No. 2.* pp.37-72.

DeBoer, Warren 2010. "Strange Sightings on the Scioto." In *Hopewell Settlement Patterns, Subsistence, and Symbolic Landscapes.* 2011. Edited by A. Martin Byers and DeeAnne Wymer. University of Florida Press. Gainesville, FL. pp. 165-198.

DeBoer, Warren 2004. "Little Bighorn on the Scioto: The Rocky Mountain Connection to Ohio Hopewell." *American Antiquity, Vol. 69, No. 1.* pp. 85-107.

Deloria, Jr., Vine 1993. "Afterword." In *America in 1492.* Edited by M. Josephy, Jr. pp. 429-443. Vintage Books, New York, NY.

Deloria, Jr., Vine 1997. *Red Earth White Lies*. Fulcrum Publishing. Golden, CO.

Denver, John. *"Sunshine on My Shoulders" "Sweet Surrender" "Wild Montana Skies"*

Dexter, Ralph W. 1989. "F.W. Putnam at the Serpent Mound in Adams County, Ohio: A Historical Review." *Ohio Archaeologist, Vol. 39, No. 4*. pp. 24-26.

Diamond, Jared M. 1990. "The Talk of the Americas." *Nature, Vol. 344*. pp. 589-590.

Dietz, R. S. 1961. "Astroblemes." Scientific American, *Vol. 205*, August. pp. 51-58.

Discovering the Mysteries of Ancient America. 2006. Edited by Frank Joseph. New Page Books, a Division of The Career Press, Inc. Franklin Lakes, N.J.

Donnelly, Ignatius 1821. *Atlantis: The Antediluvian World*. Billing and Sons, Ltd., Great Britain.

Doutre, Martin, "**The Octagon:** an analysis of The Octagon earthworks complex, Newark, Ohio USA." Part 1 THE OCTAGON EARTHWORKS OF NEWARK OHIO, THE STONEHENGE OF NORTH AMERICA. Part 2 THE OCTAGON PROVIDES GEOMETRIC EVIDENCE IN SUPPORT OF A "FLAT TOPPED" GREAT PYRAMID. Part 3 THE CODED DISTANCES & ANGLES OF THE HORSESHOE'S HUB POSITION, TO OTHER STATIONS WITHIN THE OCTAGON COMPLEX. Part 4 THE FEW SET ASIDE TO BLESS THE MANY. Part 5 THE ACROSS SITE PHI RELATIONSHIPS. www.celticnz.co.nz/articles.html

Drier, Roy Ward, Octave J. Du Temple 1961. *Prehistoric Copper Mining in the Lake Superior Region*. Published Privately.

Dunn, Waldo H. 1904. *The Vanished Empire, A Tale of the Mound Builders*. 1904. The Robert Clarke Company. Cincinnati, OH.

Eddy, John A. 1977. "Archaeoastronomy of North America: Cliffs, Mounds, and Medicine Wheels." In *In Search of Ancient Astronomies*. Edited by Krupp, E.C. pp. 133-163. Doubleday & Co, Inc. Garden City, NY.

Edwards, J.H. 1956. "Ancient Fortifications." *Ohio Archaeologist, Vol 6, No. 3*. pp.102-104.

Eshleman, Jason A., Malhi, Ripan S., Johnson, John R., Kaestle, Frederika A., Lorenz, Joseph, Smith, David Glenn 2004. "Mitochondrial DNA and Prehistoric Settlements: Native Migrations on the Western Edge of North America." *Human Biology, Vol. 76, No. 1*. pp. 55-75.

Fagan, Brian M. 1991. *Ancient North America: The Archaeology of a Continent*. Thames and Hudson, Ltd. London, England.

Ferguson, Elizabeth 2005. *Einstein, Sacred Science, and Quantum Leaps - A Comparative Analysis of Western Science, Native Science and Quantum Physics Paradigm*. Thesis, Masters of Art, Native American Studies, University of Lethbridge, Alberta, Canada. www.uleth.ca/dspace/bitstream/10133/253/3/MR17392.pdf

Ferguson, Marilyn 1980. *The Aquarian Conspiracy*. J. P. Tarcher, Inc. Los Angeles, CA.

Fletcher, Robert V. Cameron, Terry L. Lepper, Bradley T. Wymer, Dee Anne and Pickard, William 1996. "Serpent Mound: A Fort Ancient Icon?" *Midcontinental Journal of Archaeology. Vol. 21, No. 1*. pp. 105-143.

Fletcher, Robert, Cameron, Terry 1988. "Serpent Mound A New Look At An Old Snake-In-The-Grass." *Ohio Archaeologist, Vol. 38, No. 1*. pp. 55-62.

Following the Star.
http://www.iamamerica.com/Media/following_the_star.pdf

Fowke, Gerard 1902. *Archaeological History of Ohio: The Mound Builders and Later Indians*. Press of Fred J. Heer. Columbus, OH.

Fowler, Melvin L. 1969. "Middle Mississippian Agricultural Fields." *American Antiquity, Vol. 34, No. 4*. pp. 365-374.

Fox, George R. 1911. "The Ancient Copper Workings on Isle Royale." *The Wisconsin Archaeologist, Vol.10, No. 2*. pp. 73-100.

Fox, George R. 1922. "Stoneworks and Garden Beds in Winnebago County." *The Wisconsin Archaeologist, Vol.1, No. 2*. pp. 47-55.

Fraikor, Arlene L., James J. Hester, Frederick J. Fraikor 1971. "Metallurgical Analysis of a Hopewell Copper Earspool." *American Antiquity, Vol. 36, No. 3*. pp. 358-361.

Freitag, Mark. "Phi: That Golden Number."
http://jwilson.coe.uga.edu/EMT669/Student.Folders/Frietag.Mark/Homepage/Goldenratio/goldenratio.html

Gardiner, Philip March 2006. "The Serpent Code."
www.gardinersworld.com/content/view/28/2/

Gathering Hopewell Society, Ritual, and Ritual Interaction. 2006. Edited by Christopher Carr, and D. Troy Case. Springer. New York, NY.

Genheimer, Robert A. 1996. "Bladelets are Tools too: The Predominance of Bladelets Among Formal Tools at Ohio Hopewell Sites." In *A View from the Core: A Synthesis of Ohio Hopewell Archaeology.* Edited by Paul J. Pacheco, pp. 92-107. **The Ohio Archaeological Council. Columbus, OH.**

Gibbon, Guy 2003. *"The Sioux: The Dakota and Lakota Nations"* Blackwell Publishing. Malden, MA.

Ginter, Charles, Laurie-Issel-Tarver, Mary-Claire King 1992. "Identifying Individuals by Sequencing Mitochondrial DNA from Teeth." *Nature Genetics, Vol. 2, No. 2.* pp. 135-138.

Gordon, Cyrus H. 1971. *Before Columbus Links Between the Old World and Ancient America.* Crown Publishers, Inc. New York, NY.

Greber, N'omi B. 2006. "Enclosures and Communities in Ohio Hopewell: An Essay." In *Recreating Hopewell.* 2006. Edited by Douglas K. Charles and Jane E. Buikstra. pp. 74-105. University Press of Florida. Gainesville, FL.

Greber, N'omi B. 2005. The 2004 Field Season at High Bank Works, Ross County Ohio. *Hopewell Archeology: The Newsletter of Hopewell Archeology in the Ohio River Valley. Vol. 6, No. 2,* March.

Greber, N'omi B., Davis, Richard S., DuFresne Ann S. 1981. "The Micro Component of the Ohio Hopewell Lithic Technology: Bladelets." *Annuals of the New York Academy of Sciences, Vol. 376.* pp. 489-528.

Greenberg, J.H. 1987. *Language in the Americas.* Stanford University Press. Stanford, CA.

Greenberg, J.H., C.G. Turner II, S.L. Zegura 1986. "The Settlement of the Americas: A Comparison of the Linguistic, Dental and Genetic Evidence." *Current Anthropology, Vol. 4.* pp. 477-497.

Greenman, E. F. 1932. "Excavation of the Coon Mound and an Analysis of the Adena Culture." *Journal of the Ohio Historical Society, Vol. 41.* p. 469-473.

Griffin, James B. 1978. "The Midlands and Northeastern United States." In *Ancient Native Americans.* Edited by Jesse D. Jennings. pp. 221-279. W.H. Freeman and Company. San Francisco, CA.

Griffin, James B., A.A. Gordus, G.A. Wright 1969. "Identification of the Sources of Hopewellian Obsidian in the Middle West." *American Antiquity, Vol. 34, No. 1.* pp. 1-14.

Griffin, James B. 1967. "Eastern North American Archaeology: A Summary." *Science Vol. 156, No. 3772.* pp. 175-181.

Grogan, Robert M. 1948. "Beads of Meteoric Iron From an Indian Mound Near Havana, Illinois." *American Antiquity, Vol. XIII, No. 4.* p. 302.

Guthrie, James L., *Epigraphy: The Study of Ancient Inscriptions.* www.neara.org/topics/epigraph.

Hagar, Albert D. 1865. "Ancient Mining on the Shores of Lake Superior." *Atlantic Monthly Vol. 15*, March. pp. 308-315.

Hagar, Stansbury 1933. "The Portsmouth Works." *Popular Astronomy, Vol. 41.* pp. 2-22.

Haich, Elisabeth 2000. *Initiation.* Aurora Press. Santa Fe, NM

Hamilton, Ross 2001. *The Mystery of the Serpent Mound.* Frog Ltd. Berkeley, CA.

Hamilton, Ross 2001. "*The Holocaust of Giants and The Great Smithsonian Cover-Up.*" http://web.archive.org/web/20040201205157/greatserpentmound.org/articles/giants3.html

Hamilton, Ross 11-12-1999. "The Great Highway Mystery," http://www.rense.com/ufo5/highwaymysty.htm

Hamilton, Ross. "Giants of the Ancient Ohio Valley." *Ancient American, Vol. 12, No. 76.*

Hamilton, Ross. "Ancient Ohio's Great Hopewell Highway." *Ancient American, Vol. 4, No. 29.* pp. 4-5.

Hamilton, Ross. "Holocaust of Giants: The Great Smithsonian Cover-up." *Ancient American, Vol. 4, Issue 40.*

Hansen, Michael C. 1994. "Return to Sunken Mountain: The Serpent Mound Cryptoexplosion Structure." *Ohio Geology,* Winter. pp. 1, 3-7.

Hardman, Jr. Clark, Hardman, Marjorie H. 1988. "More On Great Serpent Maps." *Ohio Archaeologist Vol. 38, No.* 4. p. 37.

Hardman, Jr. Clark, Hardman, Marjorie H. 1988. "On Romain's 1987 "Serpent Mound Revisited" Paper." *Ohio Archaeologist Vol. 38, No. 3.* p. 50.

Hardman, Jr. Clark, Hardman, Marjorie H. 1987."The Great Serpent and the Sun." *Ohio Archaeologist Vol. 37, No. 3.* pp. 34-40.

Hardman, Jr. Clark, Hardman, Marjorie H. 1987. "An Analysis of the Maps of the Great Serpent Mound." *Ohio Archaeologist Vol. 37, No.* 2. p. 18.

Hardman, Jr. Clark, Hardman, Marjorie H. 1987 "A Map of the Great Serpent Effigy Mound," *Ohio Archaeologist Vol. 37, No. 1.* p. 35.

Hatch, James W., Michels, J.W., Stevenson, C.M., Scheetz, B.E., Geidel, R.A. 1990. "Hopewell Obsidian Studies: Behavioral Implications of Recent Sourcing and Dating Research." *American Antiquity, Vol. 55, No. 3.* pp. 461-479.

Hawkins, David R. 2002. *Power vs. Force The Hidden Determinants of Human Behavior.* Hay House, Inc. Carlsbad, CA.

Hayward, Justin. Moody Blues. *"I Know You're Out There Somewhere."*

Hempstead, G.S.B.; Holt, R.B. 1878. "The Earthworks at Portsmouth Ohio, U.S." *The Journal of the Anthropological Institute of Great Britain and Ireland, Vol. VII.* pp. 132-137.

Hero, Hawk and Open Hand 2004. Edited by Richard F. Townsend, Robert V. Sharp, Lisa Meyerowitz. The Art Institute of Chicago. Chicago, IL.

Hertzog, Keith P. "Hopewell Meteoric Iron Artifacts." *Ohio Archaeologist, Vol. 15,* p. 8.

Hicks, Esther and Jerry 2009. *The Vortex.* Hay House. New York, NY.

BIBLIOGRAPHY

Hively, Ray and Robert Horn 2010. "Hopewell Cosmology at Newark and Chillicothe, Ohio." In *Hopewell Settlement Patterns, Subsistence, and Symbolic Landscapes*. 2011. Edited by A. Martin Byers and DeeAnne Wymer. pp. 128-164. University of Florida Press. Gainesville, FL.

Hively, Ray, and Robert Horn 2006. "A Statistical Study of Lunar Alignments at the Newark Earthworks." *Midcontinental Journal of Archaeology, Vol. 31, No. 2 Fall.* pp. 281-321.

Hively, Ray, and Robert Horn 1984. "Hopewellian Geometry and Astronomy at High Banks." *Archaeoastronomy Vol. 7.* pp. S85-S100. http://adsabs.harvard.edu/full/1984JHAS...15...85H

Hively, Ray, and Robert Horn 1982. "Geometry and Astronomy in Prehistoric Ohio." *Archaeoastronomy Vol. 4.* pp. S1-S20. http://articles.adsabs.harvard.edu/full/1982JHAS...13....1H

Holmes, William Henry 1886. "Prehistoric Textile Art of Eastern United States." Thirteenth Annual Report of the Bureau of American Ethnology to the Secretary of the Smithsonian Institution, 1891-1892. pp. 3-46. Government Printing Office, Washington, D.C.

Holmes, William Henry 1901. "Aboriginal Copper Mines of Isle Royale, Lake Superior." *American Anthropologist, Vol. 3, No. 4.* pp. 684-696.

Hopewell Archaeology: The Chillicothe Conference. 1979. Edited by David S. Brose and N'omi B. Greber. Kent State University Press. Kent, OH.

Hopewell Settlement Patterns, Subsistence, and Symbolic Landscapes. 2011. Edited by A. Martin Byers and DeeAnne Wymer. University of Florida Press. Gainesville, FL.

Hopi Prophecies. http://www.crystalinks.com/hopi2.html

Hosier, Sara. Conversations April and May, 2008

http://greatserpentmound.info/Ancient_Ohio_s_Tradition_of_Giants.pdf

http://www.fdavidpeat.com/bibliography/essays/black.htm.

Hubbard, Bela. 1878. "Ancient Garden Beds of Michigan." *American Antiquity, Vol. 1, No. 1.* pp. 1- 17.

Hughes, Richard E. 1992. "Another Look at Hopewell Obsidian Studies." *American Antiquity, Vol. 57, No. 3.* pp. 515-523.

Hughes, Richard E. 2006. "The Sources of Hopewell Obsidian: Forty Years after Griffin." In *Recreating Hopewell.*2006. Edited by Douglas K. Charles and Jane E. Buikstra. pp. 361- 375. University Press of Florida. Gainesville, FL.

Jefferies, Richard W. 2006. "Death Rituals at the Tunacunnhee Site: Middle Woodland Mortuary Practices in Northwestern Georgia." In *Recreating Hopewell.* 2006. Edited by Douglas K. Charles and Jane E. Buikstra. University Press of Florida. Gainesville, FL.

Jennings, J.D. 1978. "Origins" In *Ancient Native Americans.*1978. Edited by Jesse D. Jennings, pp. 1-41. W.H. Freeman and Company. San Francisco, CA.

Joseph, Frank. 2010. *Advanced Civilizations of Prehistoric America.* 2010. Bear & Company. Rochester, VT.

Joseph, Frank 2009. "Medallion Puts Buddhists in Michigan a Thousand Years Ago." In *Unearthing Ancient America The Lost Sagas of Conquerors, Castaways, and Scoundrels.* 2009. Compiled and Edited by Frank Joseph. pp. 24-30. New Page Books, A Division of The Career Press, Inc. Franklin Lakes, NJ.

Joseph, Frank 2009a. "The Serpent and the Meteor." In *Unearthing Ancient America The Lost Sagas of Conquerors, Castaways, and Scoundrels*. 2009. Complied and Edited by Frank Joseph. pp. 183-191. New Page Books, A Division of The Career Press, Inc. Franklin Lakes, NJ

Joseph, Frank and May, Wayne 2006. "Maine Minoans." In *Discovering the Mysteries of Ancient America.* 2006. Edited by Frank Joseph. pp. 258-262. New Page Books, a Division of The Career Press, Inc. Franklin Lakes, N.J.

Joseph, Frank 2001. *Edgar Cayce's Atlantis and Lemuria.* A.R.E. Press. Virginia Beach, VA.

Kaestle, Frederika A., David Glenn Smith 2001. "Ancient Mitochondrial DNA Evidence for Prehistoric Population Movement: The Numic Expansion." *American Journal of Physical Anthropology Vol. 115.* pp. 1-12.

Kavasch, E. Barrie 2004. *The Mound Builders of Ancient North America.* iUniverse, Inc. Lincoln, NE.

Kennedy, Ilyhana Kate, 2002. "Sacred Geometry."
   http://earthsouscience.com/Sacred%20Geometry.htm

BIBLIOGRAPHY

Knapp, Joseph M 2005. "The Octagon Earthworks: A Neolithic Lunar Observatory." http://coolohio.com/octagon/

Knapp, Joseph M. August 21, 1998a. "On the Great Hopewell Road," http://coolohio.com/octagon/onroad.htm

Knapp, Joseph M. July 19, 1998b. "Hopewell Lunar Astronomy: The Octagon Earthworks." http://copperas.com/octagon/lunar.htm

Koch, John "The Symbolism of Pi and Phi," http://www.labyrinth.net.au/~jkoch/sacred.html

Koeberl, Christian, Paul C Buchanan, and Richard W. Carlton 1998. "Petrography and Geochemistry of Drill Core Samples from the Serpent Mound Structure, Ohio: Confirmation of Impact Origin." *Lunar and Planetary Science. Vol. XXIX.* 29th Annual Lunar and Planetary Science Conference, March 16-20, 1998, abstract no.1392. Houston, TX.

Lake Superior Copper and the Indians: Miscellaneous Studies of Great Lakes Prehistory. 1961. Edited by James B. Griffin. Anthropological Papers Museum of Anthropology, No.17. The University of Michigan. Ann Arbor, MI.

Lepper, Bradley T. 2006. "The Great Hopewell Road and the Role of the Pilgrimage in the Hopewell Interaction Sphere." In *Recreating Hopewell.* 2006. Edited by Douglas K. Charles and Jane E. Buikstra. pp.122-133. University Press of Florida. Gainesville, FL.

Lepper, Bradley T. 2005. *Ohio Archaeology.* Orange Frazer Press. Wilmington, OH.

Lepper, Bradley T. 2004. "The Newark Earthworks Monumental Geometry and Astronomy at a Hopewellian Pilgrimage Center." In *Hero, Hawk and Open Hand: Ancient Indian Art of the Woodlands.* 2004. Townsend, Richard F. (Editor), The Art Institute of Chicago. Yale University Press.

Lepper, Bradley T.; Yerkes, Richard W.; Pickard, William H. 2001. "Prehistoric Flint Procurement Strategies at Flint Ridge, Licking County Ohio." *Midcontinental Journal of Archaeology, Vol. 26, No. 1.* pp. 53-78.

Lepper, Bradley T. 1998. "The Archaeology of the Newark Earthworks." in *Ancient Earthen Enclosures of the Eastern Woodlands.* 1998. Edited by Robert C. Mainfort and Lynne Sullivan. . pp. 114-134.University Press of Florida. Gainesville, FL

Lepper, Bradley T. 1996. "The Newark Earthworks and the Geometric Enclosures of the Scioto Valley: Connections and Conjecture." In *A View from the Core: A Synthesis of Ohio Hopewell Archaeology*, 1996. Edited by Paul J. Pacheco. pp. 224-241. The Ohio Archaeological Council. Columbus, OH.

Lepper, Bradley T. 1995. "Tracking Ohio's Great Hopewell Road." *Archaeology Vol. 48, No. 6.* pp. 52- 56.

Lepper, Bradley, "Searching for the Great Hopewell Road, The Search Continues..." http://www.ohiojunction.net/hopewell/research.html

Lewin, Roger 1988. "American Indian Language Dispute." *Science, Vol. 242.* pp.1632-1633.

Lipton, Bruce H. 2008. *The Biology of Belief.* Hay House Inc., Carlsbad, CA.

Little, Greg, John Van Auken, and Lora Little 2001. *Mound Builders, Edgar Cayce's Forgotten Record of Ancient America.* Eagle Wing Books, Inc. Memphis, TN.

Lorenz, Joseph G., Smith, David Glenn 1996. "Distribution of Four Founding mtDNA Haplogroups Among Native North Americans." *American Journal of Physical Anthropology, Vol. 101.* pp. 307-323.

Lorenz, Joseph G., Smith, David Glenn 1997. "Distribution of Sequence Variation in the mtDNA Control Region of native North Americans." *Human Biology, Vol. 69, No. 6.* pp. 749-776.

MacLean, J.P. 1879. *The Mound Builders.* Robert Clarke & Co., Cincinnati, OH. Reprinted 2005, Ancient American Archaeology Foundation Hayriver Press, Colfax, WI.

Magli, Giulio 2007. "Possible Astronomical References in the Planning of the Great Hopewell Road." http://arxiv.org/ftp/arxiv/papers/0706/0706.1325.pdf

Malhi, Ripan S., Beth A. Schultz, David G. Smith 2001. "Distribution of Mitochondrial DNA Lineages Among Native American Tribes of Northeastern North America." *Human Biology, Vol. 73, No. 1.* pp.17-55.

Malhi, Ripan S., Breece, Katherine E., Schultz Shook, Beth A., Kaestle, Frederika A., Chatters, James C., Hackenberger, Steven, Smith, David Glenn 2004. "Patterns of mtDNA Diversity in Northwestern North America." *Human Biology, Vol. 76, No. 1.* pp. 33-54.

Malhi, Ripan S., Jason A. Eshleman, Jonathan A. Greenberg, Deborah A. Weiss, Beth A. Schultz Shook, Frederika A. Kaestle, Joseph G. Lorenz, Brian M. Kemp, John R. Johnson, David Glenn Smith 2002. "The Structure of Diversity within New World Mitochondrial DNA Haplogroups: Implications for the Prehistory of North America." *American Journal of Human Genetics, Vol. 70.* pp. 905-919.

Mallery, Arlington, Harrison, Mary Roberts 1979.*The Rediscovery of Lost America.* E.P. Dutton. New York, NY.

Mann, Charles C. 2006. *1491. New Revelations of the Americas Before Columbus.* Vintage Books. New York, NY.

Margolin, Peter R. 2000. "The Sink Hole at Bandana: An Historic Blue Ridge Mica Mine Reveals Its Past." *North Carolina Archaeology Vol. 49*, October. p. 43

Marshall III, Joseph M. 2005. *The Journey of Crazy Horse: A Lakota History.* Penguin Books. New York, NY.

Marshall, James A. 1997. "Defining the Bounds of the Hopewell Core and Periphery Utilizing the Geometric Earthworks." *Ohio Archaeologist, Vol. 47 No. 4.* p. 24.

Marshall, James A. 1996. "Towards a Definition of the Ohio Hopewell Core and Periphery Utilizing the Geometric Earthworks." In *A View from the Core: A Synthesis of Ohio Hopewell Archaeology. 1996.* Edited by Paul J. Pacheco, pp. 210-220. **The Ohio Archaeological Council, Columbus, OH.**

Marshall, James A. 1995. "Astronomical Alignments Claimed to Exist on the Eastern North American Prehistoric Earthworks and the Evidence and Arguments Against Them." *Ohio Archaeologist, Vol. 45, No. 1,* Spring. pp. 4-16.

Marshall, James. A. 1987. "An Atlas of American Indian Geometry." *Ohio Archaeologist, Vol. 37, No. 2,* Spring. p 36.

Marshall, James A. 1982. "Discovering the Lost Race of Mound Builders." *Professional Surveyor Vol. 2, No. 2.* pp.20-21, 24-26, 37.

Marshall, James A.1980. "Geometry of the Hopewell Earthworks." *Ohio Archaeologist Vol. 30, No. 2.* p. 8.

Marshall, James A. 1978. "American Indian Geometry." *Ohio Archaeologist, Vol. 28, No. 1.* p. 29.

Marshall, James A. 1969. "Engineering Principles and the Study of Prehistoric Structures: A Substantive Example." *American Antiquity, Vol. 34, No. 2.* p.166.

Martin, Susan R. 1995. "Michigan Prehistory Facts: The State of our Knowledge About Ancient Copper Mining in Michigan." *The Michigan Archaeologist, Vol. 41, Nos. 2-3.* pp. 119-138.

May, Wayne. 2006. "Americas Oldest Cemetery: The Copper Miner's Graveyard." In *Discovering the Mysteries of Ancient America,* 2006. Edited by Frank Joseph, pp. 98-102. New Page Books, a Division of The Career Press, Inc. Franklin Lakes, NJ.

Mayfield, John R. *"Something Left Behind."* © 2004.

McCulloch, J. Huston 1996. "Ohio's Hanukkiah Mound." *Ancient American, Vol. 3, No. 14,* Sept/Oct. pp. 28-37.

McGuire, J.D. 1900. *A Study Of The Primitive Methods Of Drilling.* The Government Printing Office. Washington, D.C.

McKee, Arlo 2005. "Geophysical Investigations of the Hopewell Earthworks (33RO27), Ross County, Ohio." *Hopewell Archeology: The Newsletter of Hopewell Archeology in the Ohio River Valley, Vol. 6, No. 2,* March.

McTaggart, Lynne 2008. The *Field: The Quest for the Secret Force of the Universe.* Harper Collins Publishers. New York, NY.

Meisner, Gary. "The Golden Number."
http://goldennumber.net/classic/index.html

Meissner, Mary. Personal notes August 2007.

Mertz, Henriette 1986. *The Mystic Symbol - Mark of the Michigan Mound Builders.* Originally published posthumously by Herbert Mertz, Global Books, Gaithersburg, Maryland. Reprinted 2004. Ancient American Magazine. Hayriver Press. Colfax, WI.

Mills, Lisa A. 2003. *"Mitochondrial DNA Analysis of the Ohio Hopewell of the Hopewell Mound Group."* Dissertation. Graduate School of the Ohio State University. http://etd.ohiolink.edu/send-pdf.cgi/Mills%20Lisa%20Ann.pdf?osu1054605467

Mills, William C. 1922. "Exploration of the Mound City Group." *Journal of the Ohio Historical Society, Vol. 31.* pp. 423-584.

Mills, William C. 1921. "Flint Ridge." *Vol. XXX*. Ohio Archaeological and Historical Publications.

Mills, William C. 1917a. "The Feurt Mounds and Village Site." *Journal of the Ohio Historical Society, Vol. 26*. pp. 305-449.

Mills, William C. 1917b. "Explorations of the Westenhaver Mound." *Journal of the Ohio Historical Society, Vol. 26*. pp. 227-266.

Mills, William C. 1916. "The Exploration of the Tremper Mound." *Journal of the Ohio Historical Society, Vol. 25*. pp. 263-398.

Mills, William C. 1912. "Archeological Remains of Jackson County." *Journal of the Ohio Historical Society, Vol. 21*. pp. 175-214.

Mills, William C. 1907. *Ohio Archaeological Exhibit at the Jamestown Exposition.* 1907. Press of Fred J. Heer. Columbus, OH.

Mills, William C. 1907a. "Explorations of the Seip Mound." *Journal of the Ohio Historical Society, Vol. 18*. pp 269-321.

Mills, William, C.1907b. "The Explorations of the Edwin Harness Mound." *Journal of the Ohio Historical Society, Vol. 16*. pp 113-193.

Mills, William C. 1906. *Exploration of the Baum Prehistoric Village Site*. Press of Fred J. Heer. Columbus, OH.

Mills, William C. 1906. "Baum Prehistoric Village." *Journal of the Ohio Historical Society, Vol. 15*. pp. 45-136.

Mills, William C. 1904. "Explorations of the Gartner Mound and Village Site." *Journal of the Ohio Historical Society, Vol. 13*. pp. 129-189.

Mills, William C. 1902. "Painted Skeletons." *Journal the Ohio Historical Society, Vol. 11*. pp 246-248.

Mills, William, C. 1900. "Fish-hooks Found at the Baum Village Site." *Journal of the Ohio Historical Society, Vol. 9*. pp 520-524.

Mills, William C. 1900. "The Baum Prehistoric Village Site." *O.S.U. Naturalist*, November.

Milner, George R. 2004. *The Moundbuilders, Ancient Peoples of Eastern North America*. Thames & Hudson Ltd. London, England.

Montroy, Eileen. Email notes August 2007.

MOON MAZE The Newark Mounds: Native American Earthworks Sculpt Lunar Odyssey," *The Historical Times, Vol. IX, No. 2, Spring* 1995, reprinted from Richard Holden, *The Earlhamite. Vol. 105, No. 1, Autumn* 1984.

Moorehead, Warren K. "Report of Field Work in Various Portions of Ohio." *Journal of the Ohio Historical Society, Vol. 7*. pp.110-203.

Moorehead, Warren K. 1922. "The Hopewell Mound Group of Ohio." *Field Museum of Natural History Anthropological Series Vol. 6, No. 5.*

Mornstad H, Pfeiffer H, Youn C, and Teivens A. 1999. "Demonstration and Semiquantification of MtDNA from Human Dentine and its Relation to Age." *Int. J of Legal Medicine Vol. 112, No. 2*. pp. 98-100.

"Mounds of North America" www.crystalinks.com/pyrnorthamerica

Murphy, James, L.; Morton, James F. "Dodson 1984. "Village"; A Flint Ridge Habitation Site." *Ohio Archaeologist, Vol. 34, No. 3*. p. 23.

Native North American Spirituality of the Eastern Woodlands. 1979. Edited by Tooker, Elisabeth. Paulist Press. Mahwah, NJ.

Neiburger, E.J. 1991. "Melted Copper from the Archaic Midwest." *North American Archaeologist Vol. 12, No. 4*. pp. 351-360.

Nolan, Kevin C. and Deppen, Jacob E. 2006. "Experiments in Hopewell Blade Production: Lessons for Archaeological Interpretation." *Ohio Archaeological Council.*
http://www.ohioarchaeology.org/joomla/index.php?option=com_content&task=view&id=176&Itemid=32

Ohio's East Fork or "Hanukkiah" Earthworks. J. Huston McCulloch.
http://www.econ.ohio-state.edu/jhm/arch/efw.html See also:
http://www.econ.ohio-state.edu/jhm/arch/efw.pdf

Ohio Valley Bones: Reality? Or Imagination?
www.geocities.com/saqatchr/page46.html

OHS 2003. *Historic Site Management Plan for Newark Earthworks State Memorial.* Ohio Historical Society, 1982 Velma Avenue, Columbus Ohio. http://ohsweb.ohiohistory.org/places/c08/hsmp.shtml

OHS – Bison. Ohio History Central.
http://www.ohiohistorycentral.org/entry.php?rec=1125

OHS – Turkey. Ohio History Central. http://www.ohiohistorycentral.org/entry.php?rec=1053

Ojibwa Scrolls, http://www.crystalinks.com/ojibwa.html

O'Rourke, D.H., Hayes, M.G., Carlyle, S.W. 2000. "Spatial and Temporal Stability of mtDNA Haplogroup Frequencies in Native North America." *Human Biology, Vol. 72, No. 1.* pp. 15-34.

Osburn, Mary Hubbell 1946. "Prehistoric Musical Instruments in Ohio." *Journal of the Ohio Historical Society, Vol. 55.* pp. 12-20.

Overman, H. W. 1887. "Fort Hill, Ohio." *Journal of the Ohio Historical Society, Vol. 1.* pp. 260-264.

Pacheco, Paul J.; Pickard, William H.1992. "A Laterally Hafted Ohio Hopewell Bladelet from Dow Chemical #2 (33Li302)." *Ohio Archaeologist, Vol. 42, No. 2.* p. 12.

Page, Jake 2000. "*In the Hands of the Great Spirit.*" Free Press. New York, NY.

Parry, Glenn Aparicio 2007. Chapter Four: Dialogue. www.seedgraduateinstitute.org/conferences/language/ChapterFour-Dialogue.pdf

Patterson, Clair C. 1971. "Native Copper, Silver, and Gold Accessible to Early Metallurgists." *American Antiquity, Vol. 36, No. 3.* pp.286-321.

Peat, David F. "Blackfoot Physics and European Minds." http://www.fdavidpeat.com/bibliography/essays/black.htm

Peat, F. David 2002. *Blackfoot Physics.* Weiser Books. Boston, MA.

Peet, Stephen D., Ph. D. 1892. *The Mound Builders: their Works and Relics. Vol. 1.* Office of the American Antiquarian. Chicago, IL.

Penney, David W. 1980. "The Adena Engraved Tablets a Study of Art Prehistory." *Midcontinental Journal of Archaeology, Vol. 5, No. 1.* pp. 3-38.

Pfeiffer H, Huhne J and Seitz B. 1999. "Influence of Soil Storage and Exposure Period on DNA Recovery from Teeth." *Int. J of Legal Medicine, Vol. 112, No. 2.* pp. 142-144.

Pidgeon, William 1858. Traditions *of D-Coo-Dah and Antiquarian Researches.* Horace Thayer. New York, NY.

Pink Floyd 1972. *"Partially Obscured by Clouds"*

Potsch L, Meyer V, Rothschild S, Schneided P, and Rittner C. 1992. "Application of DNA Techniques for Identification using Human Dental Pulp as a Source of DNA." *Int. J of Legal Medicine, Vol. 105.* pp.139-143.

Povenmire, H. 2000. "The Serpent Mound, Ohio Astrobleme-New Access-Refined Data." 63rd Annual Meteoritical Society Meeting. *Meteoritics & Planetary Science, Vol. 35, No. 5, Supplement.* p. A130. pp.979-990.

Price, Timothy A. 2006. "The Great Hopewell Road: GIS Solutions Towards Pathway Discovery." *Hopewell Archeology: The Newsletter of Hopewell Archeology in the Ohio River Valley, Vol. 7, No. 1,* December.

Price, Timothy A. 2004. *The Great Hopewell Road: GIS Solutions Towards Pathway Discovery.* Thesis, Masters of Art, Department of Geography and College of Arts and Sciences, Ohio University.

Priest, Josiah. 1834. *American Antiquities and Discoveries in the West.* Hoffman and White. Albany, NY.

Prufer, Olaf H. 1961. "Prehistoric Hopewell Meteorite Collecting: Context and Implications." *The Ohio Journal of Science, Vol. 61, No. 6,* November. p. 341.

Prufer, Olaf H. 1962. "Prehistoric Hopewell Meteorite Collecting: Further Evidence." *The Ohio Journal of Science, Vol. 62, No. 6,* November. p.314.

Putnam, F.W., "The Serpent Mound of Ohio." *Century Magazine,* Vol. XXXIX, 1889/1890. pp. 871-888.

Putnam, F. W.1887. "The Serpent Mound Saved." *Journal of the Ohio Historical Society, Vol. 1.* pp. 187-190.

Putnam, F. W., Willoughby, Charles, C. 1886. "Symbolism in Ancient American Art." *Proceedings of the American Association for the Advancement of Science, Vol. XLIV.*

Putnam, Charles E. 1885. *Elephant Pipes and Inscribed Tablets: in the Museum of the Academy of Natural Sciences, Davenport, Iowa.* Glass & Hoover. Davenport, IA.

Putnam, F.W. 1883. "Iron from the Ohio Mounds." *Proceedings American Antiquarian Society, Vol. II. New Series, Part 3, April*. pp. 349.

Quayle, Steve. "Accounts of Giants in North America." http://www.stevequayle.com/index1.html

Quayle, Steve. "Hidden Proofs Of A Giant Race" http://www.stevequayle.com/index1.html

Randall, E.O. 1907 (2nd Edition). *The Serpent Mound*. The Ohio State Archaeological and Historical Society. Columbus, OH.

Rapp Jr., George, Henrickson, Eiler, Allert, James 1990. "Chapter 27: Native Copper Sources of Artifact Copper in Pre-Columbian North America." In *Lasca, N.P. and Donahue, J. eds. Archaeological Geology of North America: Boulder, Colorado, Geological Society of America, Centennial Special Volume 4*. pp. 479- 498.

Read 1879. *Archaeology of Ohio*. The Western Reserve Historical Society, Cleveland, Ohio. Reprinted 2005, Ancient American Archaeology Foundation. Hayriver Press. Colfax, WI.

Recreating Hopewell. 2006. Edited by Douglas K. Charles and Jane E. Buikstra. University Press of Florida. Gainesville, FL.

Reeves, Dache. M. 1936. "A Newly Discovered Extension of the Newark Works." *Ohio State Archaeological and Historical Quarterly, Vol. 45*. pp. 187-193.

Reidla, Maere, Toomas Kivisild, Ene Metspalu, Katrin Kaldma *et. al.* 2003. "Origin and Diffusion of mtDNA Haplogroup X." *American Journal of Human Genetics, Vol. 73*. pp. 1178-1190.

Romain, William F.; Burks, Jarrod 2008a. "LiDAR Imaging of the Great Hopewell Road." *Current Research in Ohio Archaeology*. http://www.ohioarchaeology.org/joomla/index.php?option=com_content&task=view&id=231&Itemid=32

Romain, William F.; Burks, Jarrod 2008b. "LiDAR Assessment of the Newark Earthworks." *Current Research in Ohio Archaeology*. http://www.ohioarchaeology.org/joomla/index.php?option=com_content&task=view&id=232&Itemid=32

Romain, William F.; Burks, Jarrod 2008c. "LiDAR Analysis of Prehistoric Earthworks in Ross County, Ohio." *Current Research in Ohio Archaeology*.

http://www.ohioarchaeology.org/joomla/index.php?option=com_content&task=view&id=233&Itemid=32

Romain, William F. 2006. "Appendix 3.1, Summary Report on the Orientation and Alignments of the Ohio Hopewell Geometric Enclosures." In *Gathering Hopewell Society, Ritual, and Ritual Interaction.* 2006. Edited by Christopher Carr, and D. Troy Case, CD-Rom. Springer. NY.

Romain, William F. 2005a. "1. Newark Earthwork Cosmology: This Island Earth." *Hopewell Archeology: The Newsletter of Hopewell Archeology in the Ohio River Valley. Vol. 6, No. 2,* March.

Romain, William F. 2005b. "2. Design and Layout of the Newark Earthwork Complex." *Hopewell Archeology: The Newsletter of Hopewell Archeology in the Ohio River Valley. Vol. 6, No. 2,* March.

Romain, William F. 11-21-2005c. "*Newark Earthwork Design Iteration II.*" http://www.octagonmoonrise.org/pdfs/NEWARK%20EARTHWORK%20DESIGN%20ITERATION%20II%2011-21-2005.pdf

Romain, William F. 11-10-2005d. "*Newark Earthwork Design Iteration II.*" http://www.octagonmoonrise.org/pdfs/NEWARK%20EARTHWORK%20DESIGN%20ITERATION%20II%2011-10-05.pdf

Romain, William F. 2000. *Mysteries of the Hopewell: Astronomers, Geometers, and Magicians of the Eastern Woodlands.* University of Akron Press. Akron, OH.

Romain, William F. 1996a. "Hopewellian Geometry: Forms at the Interface of Time and Eternity." In *A View from the Core: A Synthesis of Ohio Hopewell Archaeology.* 1996. Edited by Paul J. Pacheco, pp. 210-20. The Ohio Archaeological Council. Columbus, OH.

Romain, William F. 1996b. "Hilltop Enclosures: Were They the Dwelling Places of Underworld Monsters?" *Ohio Archaeologist Vol. 46, No. 2.* p.36.

Romain, William, F. 1995. "In Search of Hopewell Archaeoastronomy." *Ohio Archaeologist, Vol. 45, No. 1,* Spring. pp. 35-41.

Romain, William, F. 1994. "Hopewell Geometric Enclosures: Symbols of an Ancient World View." *Ohio Archaeologist, Vol. 44, No. 2.* pp. 37-43.

Romain, William F. 1993a. "Hopewell Ceremonial Centers and Geomantic Influences." *Ohio Archaeologist Vol. 43, No. 1*. pp. 35-44.

Romain, William F. 1993b. "Further Notes on Hopewellian Astronomy and Geometry." *Ohio Archaeologist Vol. 43, No. 3*. pp. 48-52.

Romain, William F. 1993c. "Early Aerial Photographs of the Ross County Hopewell Enclosures." *Ohio Archaeologist Vol.43, No.4*. pp. 44-49.

Romain, William F. 1992a. "Hopewell Inter-Site Relationships and Astronomical Alignments." *Ohio Archaeologist Vol. 42, No. 1*. pp. 4-5.

Romain, William F. 1992b. "More Astronomical Alignments at Hopewell Sites in Ohio." *Ohio Archaeologist Vol. 42, No.1*. pp. 38-47.

Romain, William F. **1992c**. "Hopewellian Concepts in Geometry." *Ohio Archaeologist Vol. 42, No. 2*. pp. 35-50.

Romain, William F. **1992d**. "Further Evidence for a Calendar System Expressed in the Adena Tablets." *Ohio Archaeologist Vol. 42, No. 3*. pp. 31-36.

Romain, William F. 1992e. "Azimuths to the Otherworld: Astronomical Alignments of Hopewell Charnel Houses." *Ohio Archaeologist Vol. 42, No. 4*. pp.42-48.

Romain, William F. 1991a. "Calendric Information Evident in the Adena Tablets." *Ohio Archaeologist Vol. 41, No. 1*. pp. 41- 48.

Romain, William F. 1991b. "Possible Astronomical Alignments at Hopewell Sites in Ohio." *Ohio Archaeologist Vol. 41, No. 3*. p. 4.

Romain, William F. **1991c**. "Symbolic Associations at the Serpent Mound." *Ohio Archaeologist Vol. 41, No. 3*. pp. 29-38.

Romain, William F. 1991d. "Evidence for a Basic Hopewell Unit of Measure." *Ohio Archaeologist Vol. 41, No. 4*. pp. 28-37.

Romain, William F. 1988a. "Geometry at the Serpent Mound." *Ohio Archaeologist Vol. 38, No. 1*. pp. 50-54.

Romain, William F. 1988b. "Terrestrial Observations at the Serpent Mound." *Ohio Archaeologist, Vol. 38, No 2, Spring* . pp.15-19.

Romain, William F. 1988c. "The Serpent Mound Solar Eclipse Hypothesis: Ethnohistoric Considerations." *Ohio Archaeologist, Vol. 38, No. 3* Summer. pp. 32-37.

Romain, William F. 1988d. "Ancient Eclipse Paths at the Serpent Mound." *Ohio Archaeologist, Vol. 39, No. 4.* Fall. pp. 24-28.

Romain, William F. 1987a. "Serpent Mound Revisited." *Ohio Archaeologist Vol.37, No. 4.* pp. 5-10.

Romain, William F. 1987b. "The Serpent Mound Map." *Ohio Archaeologist Vol. 37, No. 4.* pp. 38-39.

Ruby, Bret J. 1997. "Current Research at Hopewell Cultural National Historical Park." *Hopewell Archaeology: The Newsletter of Hopewell Archaeology in the Ohio River Valley. Vol. 2, No. 2.* pp.1-6.

Ruhl, Katharine C. 1992. "Copper Earspools From Ohio Hopewell Sites." *Midcontinental Journal of Archaeology, Vol. 17, No. 1.* pp. 46-79.

Rydholm, Fred C. 2009. "An Achievement to Rival the Pyramids." In *Unearthing Ancient America The Lost Sagas of Conquerors, Castaways, and Scoundrels.* 2009. Complied and Edited by Frank Joseph, pp. 114-123. New Page Books, A Division of The Career Press, Inc. Franklin Lakes, NJ

Salisbury, James A. and Charles B. Salisbury 1862. *Accurate Surveys and Descriptions of the Ancient Earthworks at Newark, Ohio.* Manuscript on file, American Antiquarian Society. Worcester, MA.

Samsel, William. "What is the Law of One?" The Ascension Network. http://www.ascension.net/libraryarticles.asp?article=14

Schrag, Paul, Haze Xaviant 2011. *The Suppressed History of America.* Bear & Company. Rochester, VT.

Schoolcraft, Henry R., Eastman S. 1855. *Information Respecting the History, Conditions and Prospects of the Indian Tribes of the United States. Part V.* J.B. Lippincott & Company. Philadelphia, PA.

Schroeder, David L., Katharine C. Ruhl 1968. "Metallurgical Characteristics of North American Prehistoric Copper Work." *American Antiquity, Vol. 33, No. 2.* pp. 162-169.

Schurr, Theodore G., Ballinger, Scott W., Yik-Yuen Gan, Hodge, Judith A., Merriwether, D. Andrew, Lawrence, Dale, N., Knowler, William

C., Weiss, Kenneth M., Wallace, Douglas C. 1990. "Amerindian Mitochonodrial DNAs Have Rare Asian Mutations at High Frequencies, Suggesting They Derived from Four Primary Maternal Lineages." *American Journal of Human Genetics, Vol. 46.* pp. 613-623.

Schwarz T, Schwartz E, Mieszerski L, Mc Nall L, and Kobilinsky L., 1991. "Characterization of Deoxyribonucleic Acid (DNA) Obtained from Teeth Subjected to Various Environmental Conditions." *J For Sci. Vol. 36.* pp. 979-990.

Science Frontiers Online. "*Missing; 500,000 tons of Copper.*" http://www.science-frontiers.com/sf090/sf090a01.htm

Searching for the Great Hopewell Road. PBS Video 1998. Pangea Productions Ltd. In collaboration with Algonquin Archaeological Consultants Inc. DVD.

Seed Graduate Institute 2003. Transcript: *The Language of Spirituality Conference.* August 1-3, 2003. Albuquerque, NM.

Serpent Mound, Part I: Great Serpent. 2003. www.mysteriousworld.com/Journal/2003/Spring/SerpentMound

Sherzer, Joel 1993. "A Richness of Voices." In *America in 1492.* Edited by M. Josephy, Jr. pp. 251-303.Vintage Books, New York, New York.

Shetrone, Henry C., Greenman, Emerson F. 1931. "Explorations of the Seip Group of Prehistoric Earthworks." *Journal of the Ohio Historical Society, Vol. 40.* pp. 343-509.

Shetrone, Henry C. 1930. *The Mound-Builders: a reconstruction of the life of a prehistoric American race through exploration and interpretation of their earth mounds, their burials, and their cultural remains.* The University of Alabama Press, reprint 2004, Tuscaloosa, AL. Originally published by D. Appleton and Company, 1930.

Shetrone, Henry C. 1928. "Some Ohio Caves and Rock Shelters Bearing Evidences of Human Occupancy." *Journal of the Ohio Historical Society, Vol. 37.* pp. 1-34

Shetrone, Henry C. 1926. "Exploration of the Hopewell Group of Prehistoric Earthworks." *Journal of the Ohio Historical Society, Vol. 35.* pp. 5-227.

Shriver, Phillip R. 1992. "Sacred Enclosures and Platform Mounds of the Ohio Hopewell." *Ohio Archaeologist, Vol.42, No. 3.* pp. 42-46.

Shriver, Phillip R. 1991. "Shadow from the Past: The Gray (or Timber) Wolf." *Ohio Archaeologist, Vol. 41, No. 2.* p. 4.

Shriver, Phillip R. 1987. "The Buffalo or American Bison in the Ohio Valley at the Time of Euro-Indian Contact." *Ohio Archaeologist, Vol. 37, No. 2.* pp. 53-55.

Silverberg, Robert 1986. *The Mound Builders.* Ohio University Press. Athens, OH.

Skinner, Shaune M.1992. "The Howard Baum Site a Baum Phase Fort Ancient Village Ross County, Ohio." *Ohio Archaeologist Vol. 42, No. 1.* p. 48.

Smith B, Fischer D, Weedn V, Warnock G, and Holland M. 1993. "A Systematic Approach to the Sampling of Dental DNA." *J For Sci Vol. 38.* pp. 1194-1209.

Smith, Bruce D. 1992. *The Rivers of Change: Essays on Early Agriculture in Eastern North America.* Smithsonian Press. Washington, D.C.

Smith, David Glenn, Ripan S. Malhi, Jason Eshleman, Joseph G. Lorenz, Frederika A. Kaestle 1999. "Distribution of mtDNA Haplogroup X Among Native North Americans." *American Journal of Physical Anthropology. Vol. 110.* pp. 271-284.

Smith, Ethan 1825. *View of the Hebrews or The Tribes of Israel in America.* Smith & Shute, Poultney, Vt. Reprinted 2002, Ancient American Archaeology Foundation Hayriver Press. Colfax, WI.

Snyder, Daniel; Powers, Michael; Pacheco, Paul J.; Burks, Jarrod 2008. "Brown's Bottom #1 (33RO1104) Bladelet Assemblage: An Experiment in Use-Wear Analysis." *Pennsylvania Archaeologist Vol. 78, No. 1.* p. 41- 60.

Song, Cheunsoon A., Jakes, K.A., Yerkes, R.W 1996. "Seip Hopewell Textile Analysis and Cultural Implications." *Midcontinental Journal of Archaeology, Vol. 21, No. 2.* pp. 247- 265.

Squier, Ephraim G., and Edwin H. Davis 1848. "*Ancient Monuments of the Mississippi Valley.*" Smithsonian Contributions to Knowledge Vol. I. Reprinted 1998. Edited and with an introduction by David J. Meltzer. Smithsonian Institution Press. Washington, D.C.

BIBLIOGRAPHY

Startech Environmental Corp., Wilton, Connecticut. Plasma Converter. www.startech.net. See also: http://www.popsci.com/scitech/article/2007-03/prophet-garbage

Stoltman, James B., Hughes, Richard E. 2004. "Obsidian in Early Woodland Contexts in the Upper Mississippi Valley." *American Antiquity, Vol. 69, No. 4.* pp. 751-759.

Stone, Ann C., Mark Stoneking 1993. "Ancient DNA From a Pre-Columbian Amerindian Population." *American Journal of Physical Anthropology, Vol. 92.* pp. 463-471.

Stone, Ann C., Mark Stoneking 1998. "mtDNA Analysis of a Prehistoric Oneota Population: Implications for the Peopling of the New World." *American Journal of Human Genetics, Vol. 62.* pp. 1153-1170.

Swartz, Jr., B. K. 2001. "A Survey of Adena-Hopewell (Scioto) Anthropomorphic Portraiture." *The New World Figurine Project, Vol. 2.* pp 225-252. Edited by Terry Stocker and Cynthia L Otis Charlton.

Swauger, James, L. 1984. *Petroglyphs of Ohio.* Ohio University Press. Athens. OH.

Swinford, E. Mac 1985. "Geology of the Peebles Quadrangle, Adams County, Ohio." *Ohio Journal of Science, Vol. 85, No. 5.* pp. 218-230.

Tankersley, Kenneth B., Tench, Patricia A. 2009. "Riker-Todd: A Salvaged Ohio Hopewell Mound." *North American Archaeologist, Vol. 30, No. 2.* pp. 195-217.

Tankersley, Kenneth B. 2007. "Archaeological Geology of the Turner Site Complex, Hamilton County, Ohio." *North American Archaeologist, Vol. 28(4).* pp. 271-294.

Tedlock, Barbara 2005. *The Woman in the Shaman's Body, Reclaiming the Feminine in Religion and Medicine.* Bantam Books. New York, NY.

The Grave Creek Stone. http://www.econ.ohio-state.edu/jhm/arch/grvcrk.html

The Scioto Hopewell and their Neighbors: Bioarchaeological Documentation and Cultural Understanding. 2008. Edited by D. Troy Case and Christopher Carr. Springer Publishers. New York, NY.

Thomas, Cyrus 1894. "Report on the Mound Explorations of the Bureau of Ethnology for the Years 1890-1891." In *Twelfth Annual Report* of the Bureau of American Ethnology for the Years 1890-1891. Smithsonian Institute. Washington, D.C.

Thomas, Cyrus 1889. *The Circular, Square and Octagonal Earthworks of Ohio.* Smithsonian Institution, Government Printing Office. Washington, D.C.

Thomas, Cyrus 1887. "*Work In Mound Exploration of the Bureau of Ethnology.*" Smithsonian Institution. Government Printing Office. Washington, D.C.

Thompson, Amanda J., Jakes, Kathryn A. 2005. "Textile Evidence for Ohio Hopewell Burial Practices." *Southeastern Archaeology, Vol. 24, No. 2,* Winter. pp. 137- 141.

Thompson, Amanda J. 2003. "Textiles as Indicators of Hopewellian Culture Burial Practices" Dissertation, Graduate School of the Ohio State University. http://etd.ohiolink.edu/view.cgi?osu1054507830

Tipping, Colin 2009. *Radical Forgiveness: A Revolutionary Five-Stage Process to Heal Relationships, Let Go of Anger & Blame, Find Peace in Any Situation.* Sounds True, Inc. Boulder, CO.

Torroni, Antonio, Theodore G. Shurr, Margret F. Cabell, Michael D. Brown, James V. Neel, Merethe Larsen, David G. Smith, Carlos M. Vullo, Douglas C. Wallace 1993. "Asian Affinities and Continental Radiation of the Four Founding Native American mtDNAs." *American Journal of Human Genetics, Vol. 53.* pp. 563-590.

Unearthing Ancient America The Lost Sagas of Conquerors, Castaways, and Scoundrels. 2009. Complied and Edited by Frank Joseph. New Page Books, A Division of The Career Press, Inc. Franklin Lakes, NJ

Van Nest, Julieann 2006. "Rediscovering This Earth: Some Ethnogeological Aspects of the Illinois Valley Hopewell Mounds." In *Recreating Hopewell.* 2006. Edited by Douglas K. Charles and Jane E. Buikstra. Pp. 402-426. University Press of Florida. Gainesville, FL.

Vernon, William W. 1990. "Chapter 28: New Archaeometallurical Perspectives on the Old Copper Industry of North America." In *Archaeological Geology of North America: Boulder, Colorado, Geological Society of America, Centennial Special Volume 4.* Lasca, N.P. and Donahue, J. editors. pp. 499-512.

Wallace, Douglas C., Antonio Torroni 1992. "American Indian Prehistory as Written in the Mitochondrial DNA: A Review." *Human Biology, Vol. 64, No. 3.* pp. 403-416.

Walsch, Neale Donald 2009. *When Everything Changes Change Everything.* EmNim Books. Ashland, OR.

Walsch, Neale Donald 2008. *Happier than God.* Hampton Roads Publishing Company, Inc. Charlottesville, VA.

Walsch, Neale Donald 1998. *Conversations with God, an Uncommon Dialogue, Book 3.* Hampton Roads Publishing Company, Inc. Charlotte, VA.

Walsch, Neale Donald 1997. *Conversations with God, an Uncommon Dialogue, Book 2.* Hampton Roads Publishing Company, Inc. Charlotte, VA.

Walsch, Neale Donald 1995. *Conversations with God, an Uncommon Dialogue, Book 1.* Hampton Roads Publishing Company, Inc. Charlotte, VA.

Walthall, John A., Stow, Stephen H. Karson, Marvin J. 1980. "Copena Galena: Source Identification and Analysis." *American Antiquity, Vol. 45, No. 1.* p. 21.

Waters, Frank 1977. *Book of the Hopi.* Penguin Books. New York, NY.

Waters, Rodgers; Gilmore, David 1972. *Partially Obscured by Clouds.* Pink Floyd

West, George. A. 1929. "*Copper: its mining and use by the aborigines of the Lake Superior region; report of the McDonald-Massee Isle Royale Expedition, 1928.*" Bulletin of the Public Museum of the City of Milwaukee, *Vol. 10, No.1.* pp. 1-182. Board of Trustees. Milwaukee, WI.

What are the Newark Earthworks?
http://www.octagonmoonrise.org/WhatAREne.html

Whittlesey, Charles 1863. *Ancient Mining on the Shores of Lake Superior.* Smithsonian Institution, D. Appleton & Co. New York, NY.

Whittlesey, Charles 1863. "Ancient Mining on the Shores of Lake Superior." *Smithsonian Institution Contributions to Knowledge, Vol. 12, Article 4.*

Whorf, Benjamin 1956. (Carroll, J.B. (Ed.) *Language, thought, and reality: Selected writings of Benjamin Whorf*. MIT Press. Cambridge, MA.

Williamson, Ray A. 1984. *Living the Sky, The Cosmos of the American Indian*. University of Oklahoma Press. Norman, OK.

Willoughby, Charles C. 1938. "Textile Fabrics From the Burial Mounds of the Great Earth Work Builders of Ohio." *Journal of the Ohio Historical Society, Vol. 47*. pp 273-287.

Willoughby, Charles C. 1936. "The Cincinnati Tablet: An Interpretation." *Journal of the Ohio Historical Society, Vol. 45*. pp. 257-264.

Willoughby, Charles C. 1922. *The Turner Mound Group of Earthworks Hamilton County, Ohio*. Peabody Museum of American Archaeology and Ethnology, Harvard University. Cambridge, MA.

Winkler, Louis 1992. "The Serpent Mound and Serpentine Meteors." *Ohio Archaeologist Vol. 42, No. 1*. pp. 56-59.

Wolfe, Mark E. 2005. "The Geology of Ohio Pipestone." *Ohio Geology, No.1*. pp. 5- 6.

Wood, Daniel 2006. "The Vanished Builders of Bronze Age Michigan." In *Discovering the Mysteries of Ancient America*. 2006. Edited by Frank Joseph, pp. 113-123. New Page Books, a Division of The Career Press, Inc. Franklin Lakes, N.J.

Wright, Aaron; Spalding, Solomon. *The GIANTS of Conneaut, Part 1.* http://solomonspalding.com/SRP/saga2/sagawt0a.htm

www.barefootsworld.net/chanunpa.html

www.geocities.com/ravnwolff2001/pipe.html?200726

www.nefertiti.iwebland.com/timelines/topics/mining

Wymer, Dee Anne 1996. "The Ohio Hopewell Econiche: Human-Land Interaction in the Core Area." In *A View From The Core: A Synthesis of Ohio Hopewell Archaeology*. 1996. Edited by Paul J. Pacheco. pp. 38-52. The Ohio Archaeological Council. Columbus, OH.

Yerkes, Richard W. 1995. "11. Investigations at the Flint Ridge State Memorial, Ohio, 1987-1988." *Hopewell Archeology: The Newsletter of Hopewell Archeology in the Ohio River Valley, Vol. 1, No. 1,* May.

Zukav, Gary 2001. *The Dancing Wu Li Masters.* Perennial Classics, HarperCollins Publishers. New York, NY.

Marilyn Lee

My last name comes from my family name, Lee. Many of my ancestors are the Virginia Lees who participated in the War of Independence, as well as the Civil War. Richard Henry Lee and Francis Lightfoot Lee both signed the Declaration of Independence. These men were statesman and passionate about what they stood for. The same can be said about Robert E Lee of the Civil War fame.

Two of my ancestors signed a contract that was intended to bring peace into the hearts of the people. This peace was intended to focus the energies in the realization that we all are valuable and needed in creating a way of life that engenders more peace within the heart as well as a part of the civilization.

Ages ago I signed a contract. I signed a contract that brought me to this moment in time. With my civilization crumbling around me, I pledged to help prevent the same thing from happening again. Writing *The Camp of God's Tears* is part of that pledge.

The Native woman on the cover, Falling Star, came to me in a dream and explained her culture as having lived and thrived for thousands of years in North America long before the Europeans arrived. As supported by empirical evidence and archeological findings, this civilization lived the last thousand years in peace. If true, then I figured they knew how to live in peace with prosperity. They knew something we don't know. Considering western history alone, we have not lived even ten years in peace, must less a thousand years. I was asked to write their story as a way to bring back to the people living in this time a template for living in peace. "If you don't have peace within, you won't have peace without."

I managed to earn a Bachelor's Degree in Communication from Boise State University. Later as a single mother raising two daughters, I achieved a Master's Degree in Communication from Arizona State University. From the time my children were old enough to attend elementary school, I worked at least one job. Over the years I typically worked a second job and on occasion, I worked a third. Both of my daughters graduated from a University and have successful careers and wonderful families.

My career history includes working in the insurance/banking/investment industries for thirty years. I hold insurance licenses and am registered with a Series 7 and Series 66 licenses.

The term Collective Frequency is federally trade-marked as its purpose is to create additional products, such as audio books, e-books, and a movie script.

In addition, I became an educator, teaching college classes at night at local colleges. As an educator, I funneled my passion for improving relationships through communication, so they enrich us as we go about our lives. After completing fifteen years of teaching, I reworked my notes and wrote another book, *Speaking Through Your Heart*.

After fifteen years of teaching, and working full-time day jobs, my back had grown worse that I could no longer stand without support. It stemmed from an early childhood injury. I was in constant pain, destined for a wheelchair and dependency upon pain-killers as a way of life.

Courage eluded me when I should have stood up for myself and spoken through my heart while in abusive relationships. Choosing to have back surgery was one of those courageous moments. I elected to have my entire spine re-aligned.

Off to Houston, Texas, to the Baylor Clinic I flew, alone, to undergo incredible surgery on my spinal column. The surgery took twelve hours to complete with three top surgeons working on me. They re-positioned every vertebra from the top of my shoulders to the very end of my spinal column. They inserted wire cages between each vertebra to hold the discs in place. Then they attached screws to most of the vertebra, and they added titanium rods the length of my back to hold the screws in place. I became a bionic woman in more than one way.

While I was on the surgeon's table, I died and found myself on the other side of life and death.

This proved to be a life-altering experience. I tell people I had my own 'conversation with God'. We communed. When our conversation concluded, I knew several things. One of those things was I knew I was to speak my through my heart every chance I got. So while I got a new backbone physically, I also got a new backbone metaphorically.

Now I can stand and speak.

For a period of about eighteen years on a part-time basis, I conducted a therapeutic practice of past-life regression. The purpose was healing issues manifested in this life that originated in a past life. Relief occurred as my clients experienced insights, and acknowledged their responsibility in the dance, and most importantly, experienced forgiveness, both giving it and receiving it.

Presently, I still work in investments and am writing more books. One is a work of fiction, *Peacekeepers,* and one is non-fiction, *Soul,* a collection of inspirations breathed through my heart. Another non-fiction is *Woman of Steel.* I support several charities, such as Aunt Rita's Foundation for help to Aid's victims, and to an orphanage in Guatemala, as well as others. I am an incest/sexual abuse survivor and believe that many of us as adults with this in our background often suffer from not fully actualizing ourselves until we address that issue.

In the meantime my star is rising. I smile as I look up at the next rung on the ladder of life, only too happy and focused on continuing to fulfill my contract to the point of overflowing. That gives me peace.

John R. Mayfield

John R. Mayfield, J.D., EMT, 64 years old, was born in Kansas City, Missouri and grew up in the Chicago, Illinois area. He graduated from The American University in Washington, D.C. with a B.A. in Political Science and a minor in International Relations. He returned to Chicago to obtain his law degree from The John Marshall Law School. After his admission to the Illinois Bar he moved to Phoenix, Arizona where he now lives. After his admission to the Arizona Bar he was employed by the Maricopa County Attorney's Office, Civil Division.

Subsequently, he was appointed as an Assistant U.S. Attorney in the Civil Division, United States Attorney's Office in Phoenix and served for over 26 years before he retired. Throughout his career at the U.S. Attorney's Office he worked closely with the Indian Health Service (IHS) regarding Native American health issues. Of particular note was his representation of the IHS in a lawsuit that attained worldwide attention regarding the protection of Hopi traditional beliefs and practices. He was instrumental in reaching a solution that was acceptable to the traditional Hopi Elders.

He was involved in the initial phases of developing a procedure to permit traditional healers' access to patients in IHS medical facilities in Arizona. These efforts ultimately led to a nationwide program which allows such access for all IHS facilities.

John successfully defended the Bureau of Land Management in a complex mining rights lawsuit. An international mining company claimed the right to mine uranium within the Grand Canyon National Game Preserve. This case established a legal precedent which excluded the Preserve and similar lands from the General Mining Laws of 1872.

He was awarded the second highest national award by the Department of Justice and several years later a second national Departmental award. Both of these awards acknowledged his superior performance and researching skills which he has now applied to researching the background materials for *The Camp of God's Tears*.

Mr. Mayfield was also instrumental in the successful effort to preserve the historic Sheep Bridge which spans the Verde River north of Phoenix. Basque sheepherders who had settled in Arizona completed construction of the 691 foot long wooden suspension bridge in 1944. He was also involved in a successful effort to preserve a sensitive ecological area threatened by a state highway reconstruction project.

He is currently a certified Emergency Medical Technician and a Board member of Phoenix Emergency Rescue, a volunteer Emergency Medical Services non-profit organization based in Phoenix.

www.ingramcontent.com/pod-product-compliance
Lightning Source LLC
Chambersburg PA
CBHW080918180426

43192CB00040B/2441